SPORTSCAPE

THE EVOLUTION OF SPORTS PHOTOGRAPHY

Acknowledgements:

I am especially grateful to those individuals who assisted and gave guidance in the selection of photographs for this book. In particular Darrell Ingham and Rob Harborne at Allsport, Philip Burnam-Richards at Hulton/Archive, Chris Boot and Neil Baber at Phaidon Press and my wife, Tricia, whose valuable advice and encouragement kept me focused on the project.
Paul Wombell 2000

The publishers would also like to express their gratitude to Lee Martin, Adrian Murrell, James Nicholls and all the staff at Allsport and Hulton/Archive without whom this book would not have been possible.

All photographers (if known) are credited in the picture captions.

Cover image: Start of 1500m race, Lausanne, 1992. Photographer: Mike Powell.

Phaidon Press Limited
Regent's Wharf
All Saints Street
London N1 9PA

First published 2000

ISBN 0 7148 3954 X

A CIP catalogue record for this book is available from the British Library.

Designed by Lippa Pearce

Printed in Hong Kong

SPORTSCAPE

THE EVOLUTION OF SPORTS PHOTOGRAPHY

Photographs from Allsport and Hulton/Archive, selected and presented by Paul Wombell, with an introduction by Simon Barnes

START INTRODUCTION BY SIMON BARNES

There are people who fear the camera, because they believe it takes away a portion of your soul. They have a good point: the camera, clicked at the famous 'decisive moment', does rather tend to take from the subject more than he or she – or, for that matter, it – is prepared to yield.

Sport supposedly builds character. But over the course of the twentieth century, as sport gradually established itself as an ineluctable part of mainstream global culture, it became quite clear that its fascinations do not come from its participants' moral rectitude. No, sport does not build character. Sport reveals character.

Thus, with the soul-stealing aspect of all photography and the like-it-or-not character-revealing nature of sport, sports photography gives us a double nakedness, a two-layer depth of revelation. In the stresses of the life of conflict, the athlete, caught at the decisive moment, is capable of giving up images of extraordinary vividness and power.

And they are images to which we can turn again and again without fear, because– despite the anguish, the humiliation, the cock-certain triumphalism – sport is something set apart from the real world. Sport is not, in the end, war, it is something that people walk away from.

Sport is a petri dish for the emotions, but the experiment is safe, confined in a laboratory, and we, like the camera itself, watch it from a vantage point of safety. Sport's ultimate triviality is a crucial aspect of its hold over the imagination: famine, death and disaster are more powerful, but we cannot gaze on them for long, because they are too much for us. Human kind, after all, cannot bear very much reality.

Sport provides us with myths, with heroes and villains, with situations of delight and horror, and all of it packed in the form of an enthralling narrative. The love of stories is a part of the human condition: we are a species of fabulists and that is why for so many, sport is a fabulous thing.

Thus the sports photographer has everything possible on his side when he seeks to create a memorable image. And sports photography not only illustrates the unwinding mythologies and soap operas of sport, it also defines them.

Narrative is the most beguiling aspect of sport: every race, every match, every season, every career is a self-contained story, and also part of many other interlocking tales. Sport is driven by its narrative power, and sports photography is an essential part of the way we understand and respond to the narrative.

The selection of pictures in this book is also a narrative, and a series of interlocking narratives. But the pictures are permitted to set their own agenda: they make their own history, rather than acting as slaves, as mere illustrations to the accepted narrative of sport's pattern of triumphs and disasters.

Rather than seeking to include a photograph of every colossus that strutted and fretted his decade upon the stage, every significant match, every memorable race, the selection here allows the image itself to be the star. This is not a trophy cabinet of big names, of big faces, but an image-led narration about the recording of sport in still pictures.

Because of this philosophy of selection – unique in the anthologizing of sporting images – we have, more or less incidentally, a uniquely vivid history of sport, and a powerful, spotty, chance-driven history of the twentieth century.

Sport has been a commentator on social upheavals of the passing hundred years, and as time went on and sport grew accustomed to its central place in our culture, it became more than an illustration of change: because of the power of its images and its narratives, it became a driving force for change.

No history of the twentieth century that ignores sport tells a complete story. Sport tells us, as we see here again and again, stories of change, some of them quite inadvertent, some of them stridently claimed and deliberately instigated. C L R James, the Trinidadian historian, said of the two seminal histories of the nineteenth century: 'I can no longer accept the system of values which could find in these books no place for W G Grace.' Grace being the cricketer and – in James's view – the defining figure of Victorian England.

Grace prepared the way for the sport of the twentieth century. He established new possibilities: for his own sport, but most importantly, for the way a sportsman is perceived. Grace became sport's first star, inventing the concept of stardom that we find later in the book, neatly summed up in an image of Michael Jordan, nothing in the frame but a pair of well-filled and over-priced shoes.

Thus Grace changed the possibilities for sport itself, and as the book opens we are presented with a collection of images that express a stolid sense of wonderment that

01
Photographer at a college rugby match, London, 1938
A Hudson

sport should become such a thing: a place where large numbers of people gather on a formal basis in order to watch people run, kick a bladder through a pair of sticks, hit a ball with a stick.

It was a new thing, and even then, a fairly immense one. The spectators watched their narratives unwind, not in places seized upon by chance for sporting convenience, but in places dedicated to this passing triviality, and in buildings specially designed for the purpose of watching bladder-kicking and ball-hitting.

It was rather more than a revolution in the use of space, it was a revolution in the use of time. Leisure had been invented. Previous and better-documented revolutions in agriculture and industry made survival for the unmoneyed a matter of endless toil, but as the century turned, so time off – on a day that was something more than a day of rest – became a right. Saturday afternoons became a time for active pleasures, rather than rest and contemplation.

Sport rushed in like a typhoon to fill this vacuum. A fair amount of the history of the subsequent hundred years has been a story of increasing leisure and the consequent increasing power of sport over the imaginations of those who had leisure as a regular luxury.

And thus the book begins with a celebration of space: of architectural studies of White City, built for the London Olympic Games of 1908, and of Aintree, venue for the Grand National, the world's most famous and dramatic horse race. These architectural studies recapitulate those of the photographic pioneers sixty years before, when buildings were a favourite choice of subject matter because buildings obligingly declined to move, a helpful trait when your exposure time is measured in seconds.

There was a sense of wonder that such things could come to be, that an audience for a sporting event could be listed in tens of thousands.

01

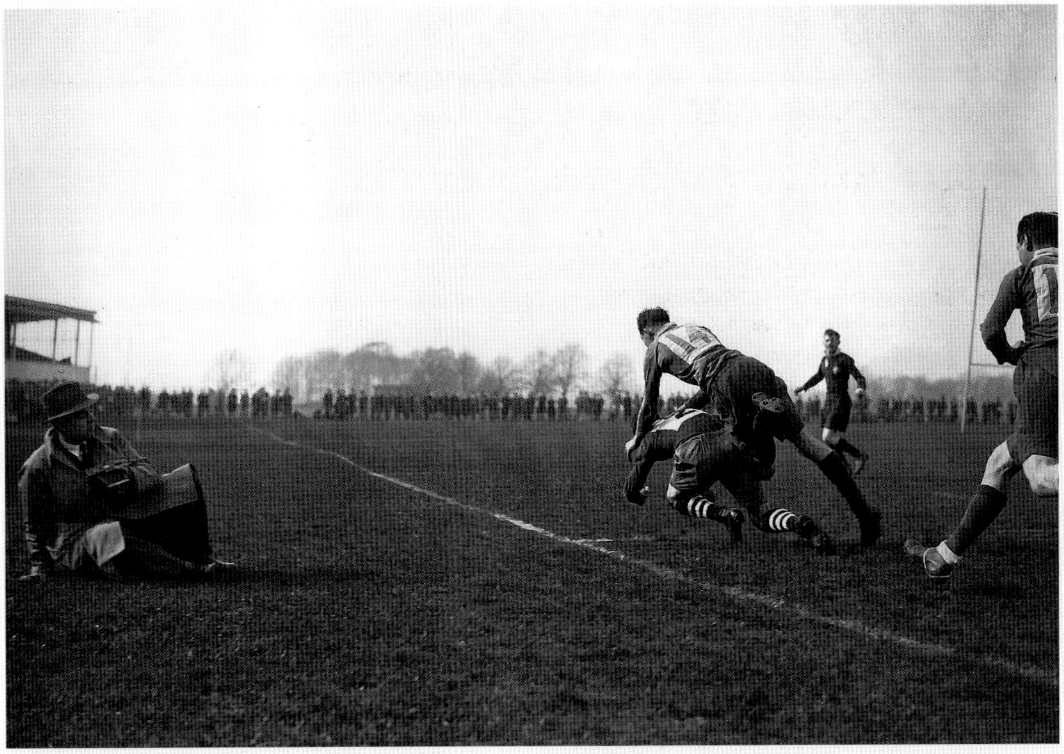

Before the century was out, audiences would reach the billion mark.

The images of these new-fangled things, sports arenas, are presented baldly, with little pretension to anything so fancy as art. Sport has seldom attracted the self-conscious art photographer. It was always the domain of the journeyman, the journalist: the man whose task is to supply a required image by a certain time.

The establishment of stadiums made that inevitable: right of access, right to a position, was granted only to accredited photographers, working for a legitimate publication or an agency. Pleasing posterity was not among the priorities of these photographers, sufficient unto the day was their aim.

Sports pictures are taken, in the main, as the fulfilment of an assignment. Majestic images are often taken, and many of them are never published: for reasons of space, or because they don't tell the story. A picture of a famous footballer scoring a great goal will not be used if his team subsequently lose, the story, and therefore the required image, is of the other side's victory, or perhaps of the famous footballer with tears in his eyes.

And thus many of the images in this book have never been seen before. Images once discarded acquire new meaning: the story they were taken for has, perhaps, been forgotten, but they become part of a new story, that of the century in sporting photographs.

This book is a record of a particular history. All the photographs have been selected from the Allsport and Hulton/Archive collections and reflect the specific circumstances of their development. Edward Hulton began his collection in 1947, as a logical step from his founding of the legendary *Picture Post* magazine in London. The collection was bought and added to by the BBC, becoming Britain's key historical photographic archive, and subsequently aquired by Getty Communications. Allsport was founded in 1968, and is both a photographic agency and a library. Operating from New York, Los Angeles, London, Sydney and Melbourne, it is the leading international source for sports images today, and now also part of the Getty group.

Collections such as these have a primary commercial function, but as time goes on, they become repositories of the history and culture of the twentieth century. This is borne not only by photographs as images, but also as objects. Photographs are physical things; created for particular purposes, using particular technologies, they become scarred by the notes of editors and the markings of re-touchers. Rather than treat these blemishes as an annoyance to be cleaned up, this book treats them as a revealing part of the story of sports photography and of sport generally.

So this book celebrates not one brilliant artist, nor even an artistic brotherhood, but the legion of sharp-eyed journeymen, the masters of technique and ever-changing technology who understood the limitations of their trade, of their equipment and of their assignments, and had the nous to make the limitations work for them. It is a book that praises, by implication, the serried ranks of snappers and smudgers, journalism's version of Kipling's famous men: 'Let us now praise famous men, men of little showing.'

Their pictures have been used and discarded, more merely discarded. There is a mystery about photographs in collections: the anonymous photographer, his work surviving his memory, though in no glorious fashion; a print, dog-eared, stained with coffee, telling a forgotten story of prizes sought and prizes lost.

Pictures were there to serve a purpose: to meet the requirements of publications. The imperfect and developing technology of photography had to serve the imperfect and developing technology of magazine and newspaper printing. Clarity was everything: an unfussy image was required, and created sometimes by cropping the original print, sometimes by painting out the background.

All these unknown photographers were aware of the crushing limitations of their manner of working, and all aware of the extraordinary possibilities of their subject. The raw power of sport is shown in two extended sections covering two races, eighty years apart.

Both races saw the winner break the tape in a storm of emotion, providing a vivid for-all-time sporting image: images that say everything about the time they were taken and of the timeless nature of sport. And in both cases, the winner so triumphantly caught in his moment of glory was disqualified, the second finisher given the victory. But the actual winners are bit-part players in the drama of the victory that never was: one disqualified runner walking away as one of sport's unforgotten heroes, the other walking away as one of its never-to-be-forgotten villains.

And the pictures tell the story: the non-victory of Dorando Pietri at the 1908 Olympic Games in London remains a sporting archetype today because of the photographs. The tiny man with the big moustache, attended lovingly by boatered and cloth-capped helpers – one crouching like a slip-catcher to seize the man should he fall again – is an emblem of frailty and courage, of humanity pushed to its limits, desperately needing and gratefully finding help.

Of course, the help was illegal. Pietri took a huge and apparently decisive lead, in a race that, at 26 miles and 385 yards, was believed to be on the far limit of human possibilities. But alas, he turned right instead of left on entering the stadium, and then collapsed. He was helped to his feet and staggered on. He fell another four times before finishing in 2 hours 54 minutes 46.4 seconds. (It is worth recalling that these days, modern marathon runners have the two-hour barrier seriously threatened – not to demean Pietri's achievement but to place it in context. Sport has changed massively, the times reflect this as much as the pictures do – but less vividly, on the whole.)

Johnny Hayes of the United States finished 32 seconds later and was the *de facto* winner. But it was Pietri's race: he was given a replica of the cup and Irving Berlin wrote a song about him. He was the hero of the Games, and it was a watershed in the history of the Olympics too. The first three Olympics had all been shambolic and obscure, the previous two taking place as sideshows to the World Fairs in Paris and St Louis.

This was the first Olympics to stand alone as a major sporting event and to attract the world's attention, and Pietri's run captured the world's imagination. It was the event that set up the Olympics for the giant it was to become, an event that could routinely enthral the entire planet. And it happened because of the story told here, and above all, because the photographs made the story vivid.

The second race took place in Seoul in 1988, not inappropriately at high noon, a blazing Asian day of hard, merciless light. I was there for that one, and it remains the one most vivid memory of twenty years of watching high class sporting action.

And the recollection is confused: the breath-taking power of the actuality, when Ben Johnson exploded off the start and seemed to run at a speed beyond that which the human body was capable, the endless re-runs I have seen on television, and perhaps, the abiding memory,

02
Sergei Popov photographing his wife Gallina Vinogradova, 1954

that of the swan-off moment of victory, the decisive moment, the final floating stride – what time would he have set had he not celebrated over those final two yards? – the index finger rammed skywards in ultimate exaltation. My defining memory is in fact the photograph that Said It All.

In the end, the photograph defines the moment, and there, in second place, head turned towards Johnson – who turned, quite extraordinarily, three times during the brief seconds of the race itself – is Carl Lewis, face twisted with disbelief and resentment. 'Those yellow eyes,' Lewis was to write later in his autobiography. 'I couldn't stop thinking about those yellow eyes. That bastard did it again, I said to myself.'

Johnson then failed a drugs test and, like Pietri, was disqualified, becoming in defeat, as much a villain as ever Pietri was a hero. That panther-strut as he walked away from the track at the finish, the golden collar around the neck: the photographed moment of quiet triumph is, like the finger-thrusting moment of victory, undershot with historical irony. We know, as Johnson does not, what will happen next.

02

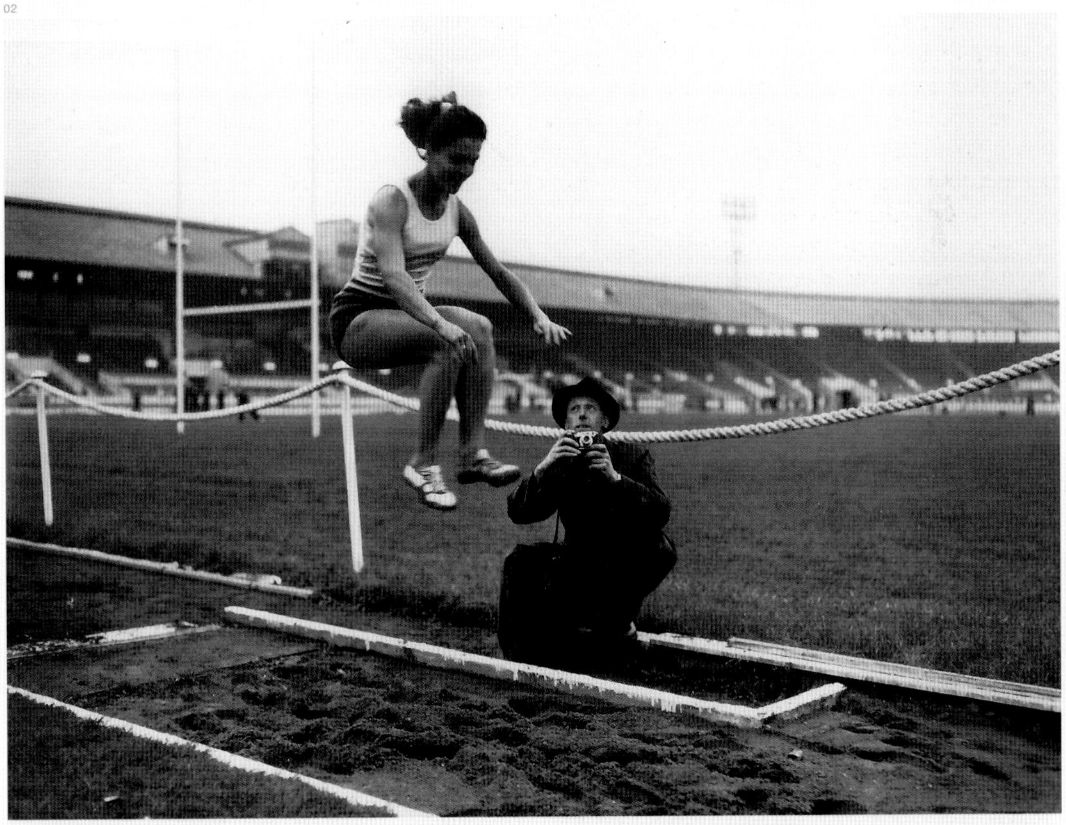

These are two examples of sport's classic double-nakedness: the psychological nakedness of the athlete in competition is further exposed by the soul-stealing nature of the camera. No other subject can provide such drama, such intensity, such self-revelation – and do so on a more or less daily basis.

Photography played its part in the way we see and understand sport. At the start of the century, sport was weighed down with moral baggage. The prevailing notion was that sport was there to improve a person's character. It was something that went back to Victorian education, the healthy pursuit of outdoor team sports was supposed to encourage all the things necessary to provide men with the manly virtues that were required to run an empire: self-reliance, toughness, willingness to sink all into the common cause, never shirking one's duty, never backing away from trouble, and, of course, not masturbating.

This concept began as a British thing, but it spread around the world: across Europe and to the United States. Sport was a moral matter, an essential part of education, in building a manly nation. Sport was preparation for life, it was something you did on the side, as part of the pursuit of the whole man. But in a divided and stratified society like Britain's, it happened that gentlemen could be beaten by people of the lower orders. This was clearly not on.

And so the notion of amateurism came about. Professional sport was seen as something degraded, low, grasping, lacking in the right spirit; amateurs were, by contrast, toffee-nosed poseurs. Again, this was something invented in Britain and taken up enthusiastically by the rest of the world. Sport had a moral purpose, therefore doing it for money was wrong. It was a debate, to use the term loosely, that continued for most of the century, the last bastions of amateurism finally yielding in the last decade.

And photography had a part to play here, and it did so by simply recording impartially, in the classic role of the camera. The fact is that the camera could not tell whether an athlete was being paid or not: it is capable of capturing nobility and grace, or for that matter, fear and defeat, in the face of every athlete who performs in public.

03

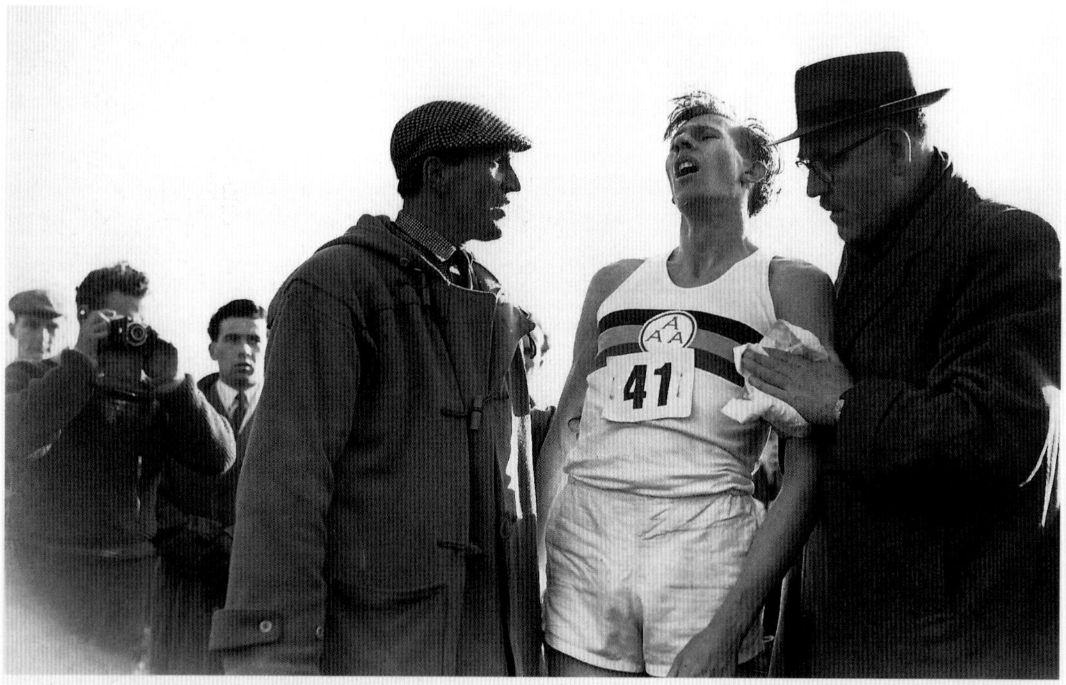

The revelation of inadvertent grace in sport was something the camera was increasingly able to do as the technologies advanced. Fleeting impressions of perfection could be converted into solid, unmoving images. The conversion of rapid and eye-baffling movement into icons of human perfection changed the way we saw sport: sport was always about struggle, but photography made us aware of its beauties.

Photography is always a slave to its technologies. The invention of the lightweight camera was a revolution of endless possibilities. Constantly improving lens technology reduced exposure times, the better to freeze the action, and made it possible to use the camera in sub-optimal light – increasing the number of opportunities for a photographer.

Lenses that could reach out and take photographs from a distance away were developed and then refined with the telephoto principle, which made lenses much shorter and easier to handle – in other words, better for sports photography. Faster lenses, faster film, lighter cameras all made it less difficult to reach out and capture that decisive moment. The development of flash technologies – bringing your own light – made the photographer still more versatile.

Colour, however, was the most obvious revolution. The development of colour film in a way mimicked the development of photography: limitations of early colour film required still, posed shots with copious artificial lighting, a matter for studios rather than stadiums. The development of high-speed colour film changed the way photographers thought about their images, and ultimately changed our own perception of sport, its intensities and its beauties.

Few sports try to be beautiful, their beauty is incidental, a by-product of strife. The camera captures it without prejudice, but it is very difficult, even with the modern cameras. The capturing of the defining moments of action, the decisive moments of self-revelation, is not easy to do technically. In some sports, with the equipment of earlier times, it was more or less impossible.

And so it often happened that sporting heroes were photographed in static set-up poses, often looking stiff and unconvincing to modern eyes that are accustomed to seeing moments sliced off in fragments of one thousandth of a second. Our eyes are educated by what we are used to seeing – back-projection in films was utterly convincing in the 1950s; to a modern eye the device is instantly hilarious, the artifice glaringly obvious.

These still, impassive sporting faces have a patient, sculptural dignity about them: the round face of Colin Cowdrey, the cricketer, eyes focused on a distant point as he waits for the photographer to tell him to relax. The white-out poses, which produced an isolated, posed figure, often a boxer gently proposing padded fists to the observer, have an appeal that is both dated and timeless: any boxer, at any time, aware of his own menace, and of the menace that must inevitably be visited on him when he fights again.

Some of the most unexpected images come from the touchlines of the territorial ball games. Modern cameras can reach out and pluck moments, close, intimate and intense, from swirling and distant action, but limitations of technology kept early sports photographers out on the rim of things, helplessly waiting until action came their way, then taking what they could get. They captured a passage of the continuing struggle, rather than the decisive moments that modern sports editors scream for. And so we get that beguiling image of the

03
Roger Bannister caught by a photographer after completing his historic sub-four-minute mile, Oxford, 1954

04
Ron Barton almost falls into a ringside photographer, London, 1956
Monty Fresco

04

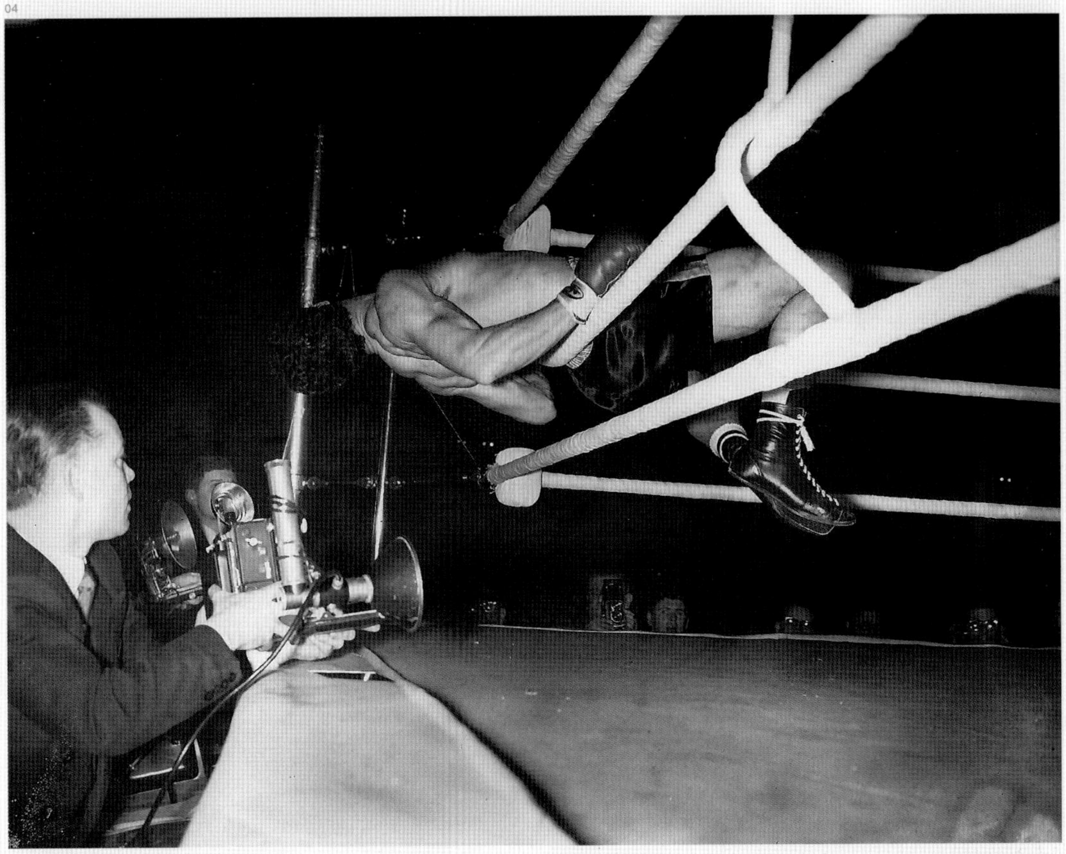

goalkeeper's punt-out, keeper hanging in the air in his follow-through, distant figures tracking the path of the ball which is suspended, motionless, like a planet above the pitch.

Further technical advances added yet more vividness to our understanding of sport: flash and strobe lighting bringing more revelations of grace and of beauty, the more compelling for their accidental nature.

Which brings us to women: one of the two major stories of liberation in the sporting century. The camera may not be able to tell the difference between amateur and professional, but it has no difficulty at all in distinguishing between men and women.

'Women have but one task,' said Baron de Coubertin, founder of the modern Olympic Games, 'that of crowning the victor with garlands.' Women were there on sufferance, to decorate an occasion rather than to take part in it. This is the philosophy that brings us what is perhaps my favourite set of pictures in the book, that of the young women performing mildly vigorous exercises intended to show off all kinds of feminine qualities.

In the vigour of the poses, the muscularity of the action, is there a yearning to do more, a discontent with the role of victor-crowners? Certainly it looks that way now. The emergence of women has been one of the most dramatic social changes of the twentieth century, and the story is told with the greatest possible vividness in sport. Sport was also the leader in this process: setting agendas, making public examples of strength and power and determination and, for that matter, victory. And the camera could not fail to rejoice in this.

The camera also faithfully recorded the second great liberation of the century. The rise of the black athlete was not just a symptom of the slow (and still continuing) switch in global attitudes to the question of race, sport was right at the forefront of the struggle, there on the front line, visible, and for all to see.

Jesse Owens won four gold medals at the 1936 Olympic Games, the Games that were supposed to be a showcase for Hitler's Germany and the all-conquering might of the Aryan race. The cameras caught not only Owens's sleek muscularity, but also his fragility, and the air of a man not quite certain of himself – or perhaps it was the world he was not quite certain about.

The story of Hitler's failure to shake hands with Owens has been much embellished and has become part of sporting legend, but Owens said himself: 'I came back to my native country after winning in Berlin to all those stories about Hitler and his snub. But I couldn't ride in front of the bus. I couldn't live where I wanted. I wasn't invited to shake hands with Hitler – but I wasn't invited to the White House to shake hands with the president either.'

Sport gave black people something that real life constantly denied them: a visible opportunity to excel. Which brought the world the most photogenic and perhaps the most photographed individual in sport, and perhaps anywhere: Muhammad Ali.

Ali's story alone is a history of sport in the twentieth century: the emergence of black people, the mingling of politics and sport, the notion of the sportsman as global superstar.

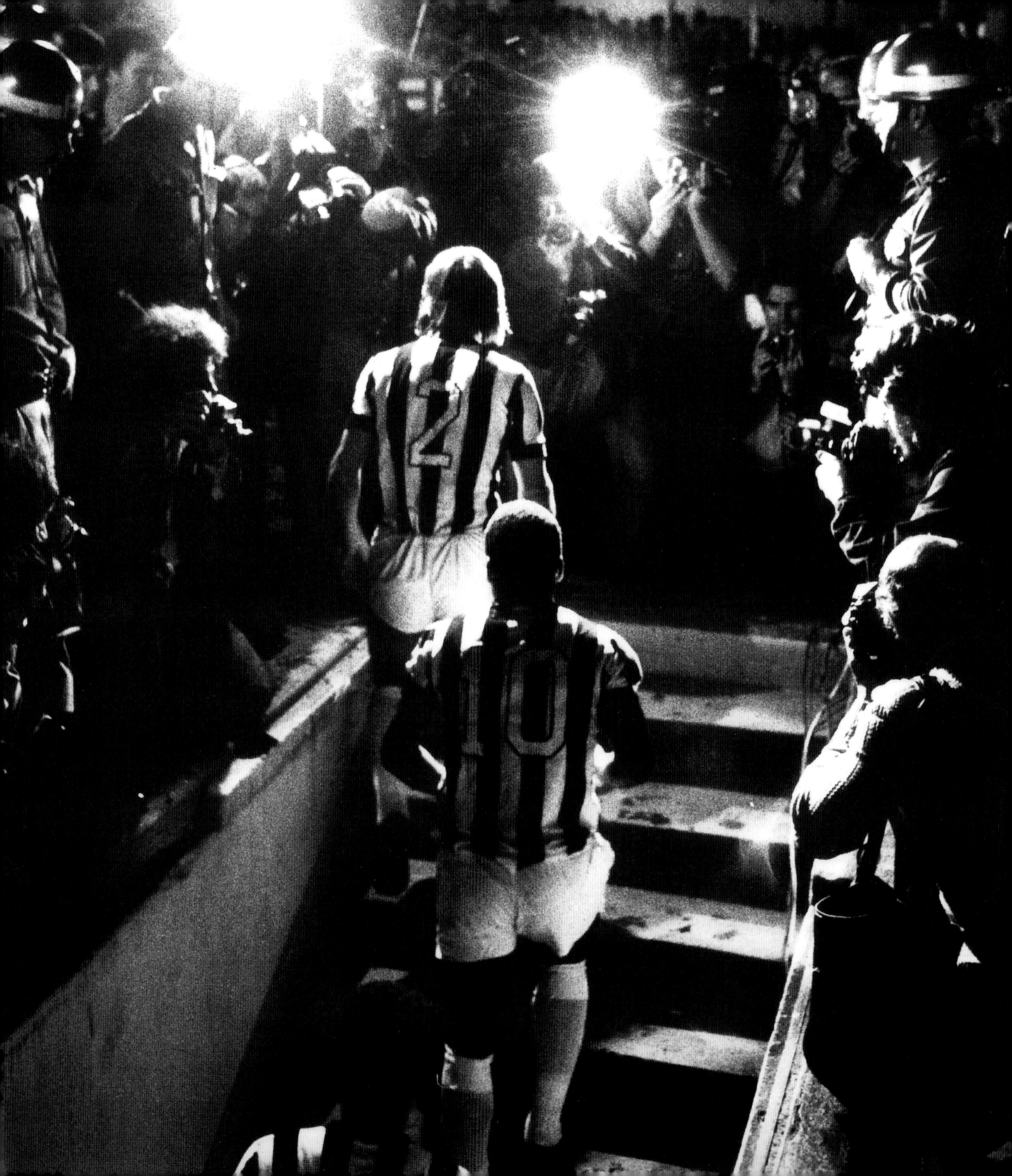

05
Pelé is greeted by a bank of photographers at his last game for Santos, Brazil, 1974

06
Jean-Claude Killy and Guy Perillat give the photographers their shot after winning gold and silver medals at the Winter Olympics, Grenoble, France, 1968

With a face and nature that loved all cameras, he became the one single perfect icon of sport, or for that matter, of the twentieth century. Ali consciously politicized sport, though he did so with wit and humour. Sport became more and more important, partly because of Ali.

The increasing reach of television was a revolution: live action is the most vivid experience television can offer, and sport offers that on a daily basis. The biggest global events – the soccer World Cups and especially the Olympic Games – became television-led events. As such, they became more powerful than ever before. Never in the history of the world had anything attracted as much simultaneous attention.

With every passing great event, an ever-greater proportion of the ever-greater population of the earth turns to sport. Sport, it was readily perceived, was too good to waste as mere entertainment. Sport became, inevitably, a flaunting of nationalism, of political ideologies. War, it was said, is a continuation of politics by other means. In the Cold War era, when these other means were too frightful to bring to actuality, sport emerged to play the same part: sport, the continuation of politics by other means. Again, the pictures tell the story, most especially in the vast numbers of people drilled and disciplined to perform in self-aggrandizing opening ceremonies.

Sport could make a point, make it vividly, and make it to the largest possible audience. The size of an audience is a kind of power, and politicians will seize on any device that gives its user power.

The secret of sport's power lies in the fact that people are interested in it. Sport offers stories that people want to hear, pictures that people want to see. No one wants to watch a party political broadcast, but the pleasures of sports are irresistible to people in their millions. Thus the pleasant trivialities of sport became a medium for the wrangling of superpowers. Great sporting events were seen as a stage on which you can make your mark on the world.

The Moscow Olympic Games of 1980, boycotted by the United States and other Western powers in varying degrees, were a celebration of the might of the Soviet Empire. Four years later, the Games came to Los Angeles, and were naturally met with a tit-for-tat boycott by the nations of the Eastern bloc.

But in these Games were a precursor to the triumph of Western capitalism, and the falling of Soviet power. This was the triumph of free enterprise, a triumph of the multinationals, a triumph not of military might but of corporate America. These are, indeed, weighty and portentous things to be associated with activities that began as children's games: who can run the fastest, who can jump the highest.

And the photographers were there to catch the political aggrandizing, the flag-draped look-at-me patriotism of the winners: obscure nations trumpeting the thrilling fact of their existence to the world, the larger nations parading their inevitable triumphs.

There was one Olympic Games that tried very hard to dispel all notions of militarism and triumphalism: the Munich Games of 1972. The Games were conceived with the benign, visionary nature more usually associated with the 1960s. The Games of 1972 were to be – in deliberate contrast to Hitler's Games of 1936 – a West German celebration of action, peace and laid-back friendliness. A new Germany (not to be confused with the Eastern country with the similar name), was there to offer a new world order, a new set of priorities.

The Munich Games were not to be so remembered. The reason for this is summed up in what is perhaps the most significant sporting photograph of all time. Not, perhaps, the greatest shot in artistic terms, but it is an image that is as mind-searing now as it ever

06
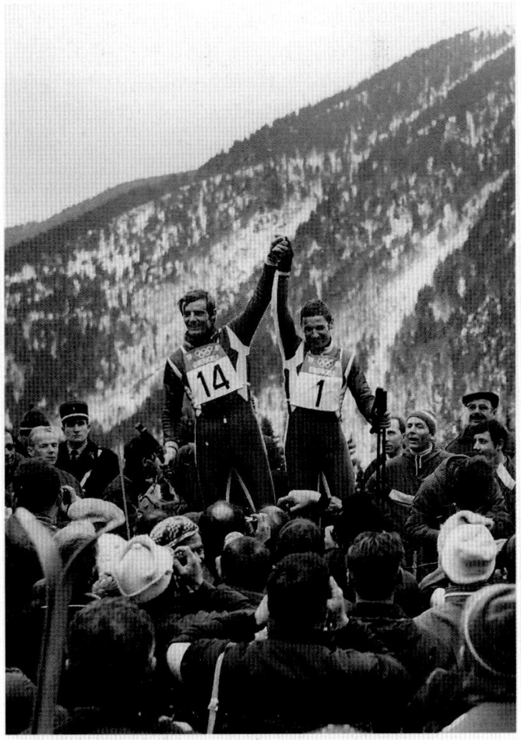

was: the masked figure on the balcony, the stooping, faceless threat.

The Palestinian Black September organization broke into the Olympic Village – as they did so, they bumped into a party of athletes who were climbing back into the compound after a night on the town, and exchanged friendly words – and killed two Israeli coaches, taking another nine members of the team hostage.

After protracted negotiation, during which the photographers trained their long lenses – carried to Germany to catch close-up images of distant athletes straining for distant laurels – on the Israeli quarters. The terrorists and the hostages were taken to the airport where there was a gun-battle. All nine hostages, five terrorists and a policeman were killed. It was

07
Photographers at the Olympic Games, Atlanta, 1996
Gary M Prior

08
Michael Johnson, Gothenburg, 1995
Gary M Prior

07

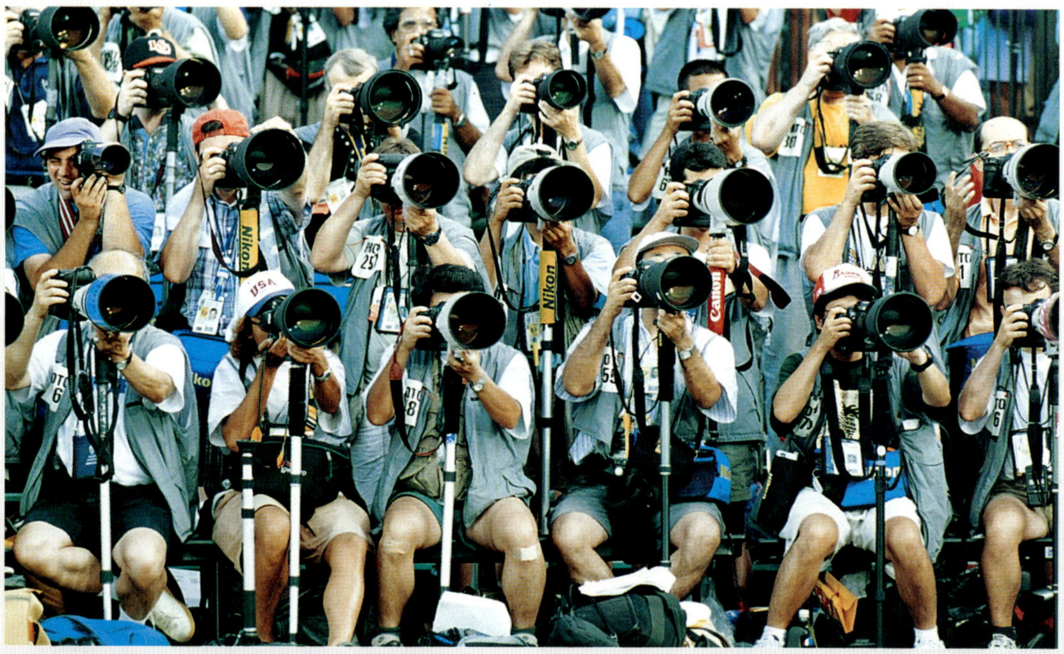

perhaps the blackest day in sporting history, and it increased the trend of the politicization of sport, rather than ending it.

Sport now pays the price for the events of 1972, and does so in the currency of vigilance. The price of peace is perpetual vigilance. We are in the middle of learning about the price of perpetual vigilance. It is no longer possible to stroll in and out of the Olympic Village, the Villages of the modern Games are surrounded by high fences, multiple layers of checkpoints, and there are armed guards everywhere.

And since that time, the great athletes have become less and less accessible to ordinary people, to journalists, to photographers. The trend these days is to control the story, to control access in staged press conferences, to control, as far as possible, the image.

Vast amounts of money and pan-global recognition have changed the nature of sporting fame. The collection of shoe-pictures sums that up: the adoring public is there as a tool for commercial power. Sport became less obviously an arena for political power after the decline of the Soviet empire – only China plays that game with the same vigour – but more and more obviously it has become a vector for the power of the money. The power of the market place increasingly dominates sport. This has reached its most extreme expression in motor sports, as the montage of helmet photographs makes clear, everything that can be a billboard is a billboard.

Following from this, the megalomaniac dimensions of the modern sporting stadiums provide a contrast with the architectural studies to be found at the beginning of the book. A modern sporting stadium is more than a place for watching sport, it is also a backdrop for the cameras, those of television and those of the photographer. And it is also an insolent expression of wealth and power: intended as symbol of the wealth of a nation or city or club, but in fact, a symbol of the power of modern sport.

Gaudy, greedy, slick and rather superficial, that is how much of sport looks as we enter the second century of big-time professional sport – at least, it looks that way if we take a relatively superficial view. But to be blinded by the amount of commercial interest that sport excites is to blind oneself to the reason that commerce got interested in sport in the first place.

Commerce does not lead us into sport, it follows us, snapping at our heels and demanding our attention. But we are drawn to modern sport for the same reasons that people were drawn to sport and to sporting heroes during the period shown at the beginning of the book: for the thrill of conflict, the compelling beauty of its action, the un-put-down-ability of the ever-changing storylines, and for the performers themselves.

The truth of sport is to be found in the same place that photographers looked for it when sports photography began: at the peak of the action, in the eyes of the contestants, in the thrill of victory and the equal thrill of defeat. Sports photography has always revealed the human being behind the superman: the vulnerability of the conqueror. It cannot help but do so, any more than the athlete can help giving himself away.

Sports photography has changed every bit as much as sport itself, and yet the essential truths, both of sports photography and of sport, are identical. They are to be found in the disbelieving stagger of the little moustached man, in the arrogant floating stride of the shaven-headed human bullet. No sports photographer's subject is sport, it is always humanity. And sport gives the best possible opportunity to pursue this subject in a vivid, safe, and ultimately revealing fashion.

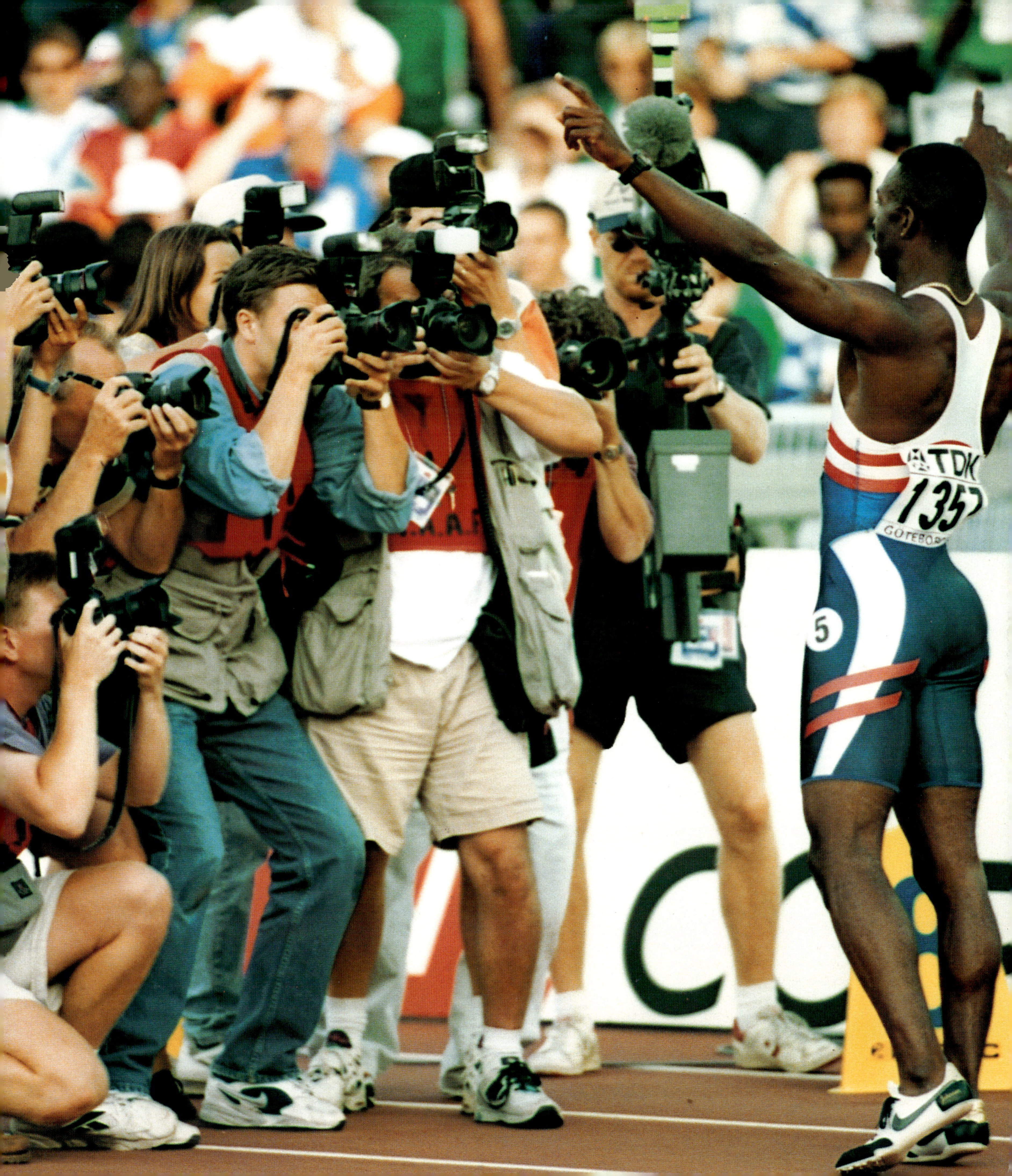
TDK

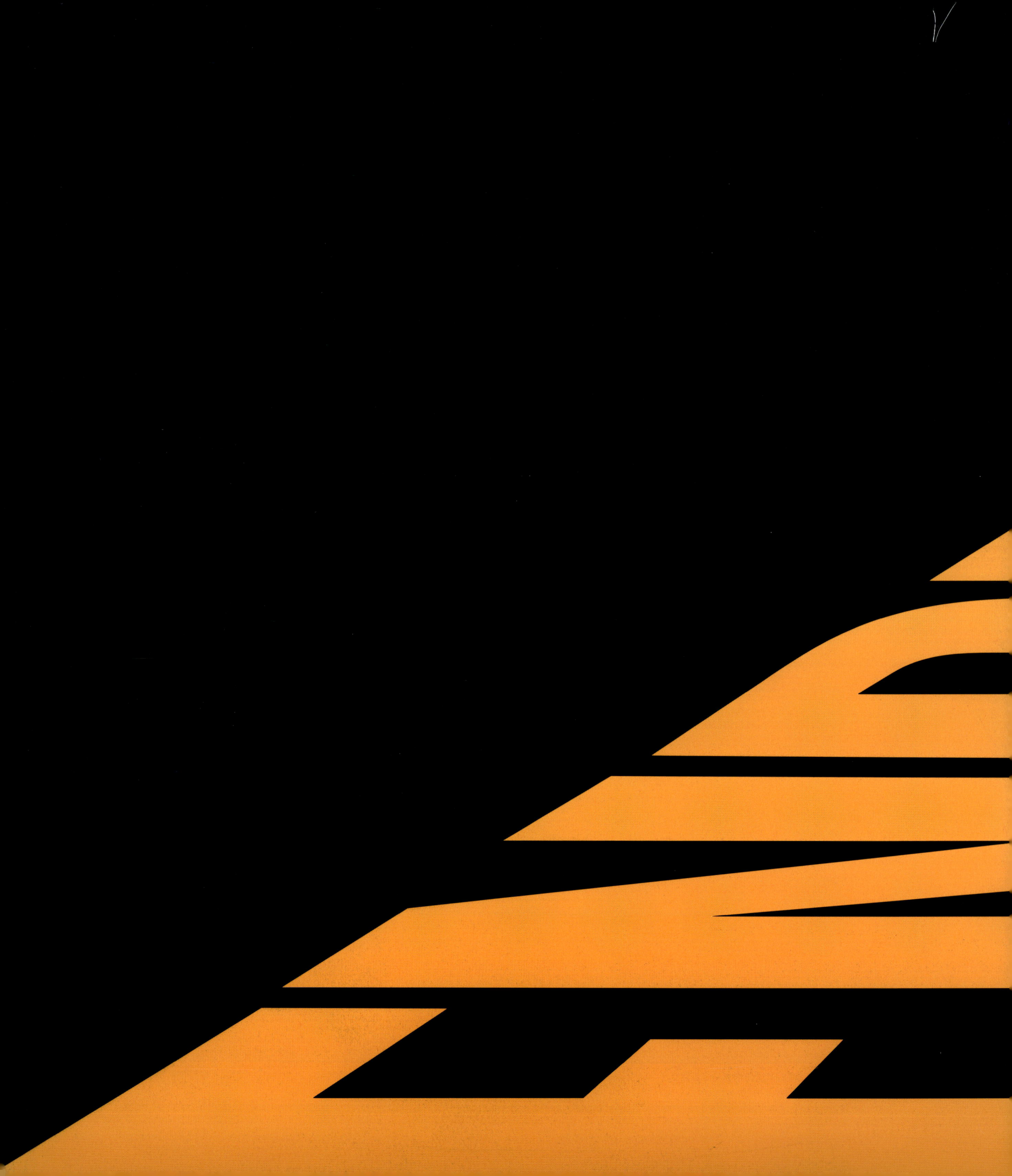

ENDURANCE

02

1900–1920

At the beginning of the twentieth century few of what we would now consider the mainstream sports had truly established themselves. The sports that would grow into multi-million dollar worldwide spectacles were still much closer to the unregulated field recreations from which they had emerged. And if the sports themselves had not developed a settled set of rules, neither had photographers developed a language for recording them. Borrowing from existing pictorial styles, the conventions of studio portraiture and the landscape tradition were the mainstays of this early sports photography. Static, full-figure portraits and long-distance views of fields and early stadiums were the standard images of sport. There was no such thing as a 'sports photographer' in the first twenty years of the century, sport was just one of many subjects that photographers would cover. It is therefore not surprising that we can see the influence of these established compositional styles in their treatment of sporting subjects. It would not be until towards the end of the century that photographers were able to specialize in sport.

The early photographers' equipment did little to encourage them to attempt to show the excitement and dynamism of sport. The speed of film available meant that very short exposure times were out of the question and, wherever speed was an essential element of the subject, images were difficult to capture. Action photos of sport were therefore rare. Coverage in newspapers and magazines was scant compared to what we have become used to today; sport itself was still only just emerging as a matter of significant public interest – the different games organizing themselves, standardizing rules, arranging regular matches and leagues, and attracting spectators. Although photographs were therefore not extensively used in the press, sport's growing popularity was forcing the media to carry images as events and personalities became big enough to be newsworthy. Top athletes were becoming well-known figures and a currency of sports photography was beginning to emerge as picture libraries serving the media gathered together photographs of the new heroes from every source possible.

The most significant international events of the period were the relatively new Olympic Games. The ancient Greek Games had been resurrected in 1896, and would steadily grow in importance throughout the century to become the single most important world sporting event. The 1908 Olympic marathon was one of the first great sporting moments of the century, and the dramatic finish made Dorando Pietri one of the first sporting stars. At the following Games, in 1912, Jim Thorpe of the United States staked an early claim to be one of the century's top athletes by winning both pentathlon and decathlon and then going on to play professional football in the USA. Team sports were establishing a loyal spectator following, making stars out of the most successful players such as Ty Cobb in baseball. In England cricket legend W G Grace had done much to establish the popularity of the game in the previous century and was one of the most famous men in England when the new century opened. The public also took great interest in sporting tests of endurance like the new cycle race, the Tour de France, the Grand Prix motor races and perhaps the one event that epitomized the period and caught the imagination of the public most: the marathon.

THE FIELD

The design and construction of purpose-built sporting venues was still in its infancy at the beginning of the century. The field games that had once been played on open land were undergoing a transformation as public interest in watching sport steadily grew and facilities were provided to accommodate them. The popularity of baseball in the United States was growing at such a rate that thirteen major league teams moved into new stadiums between 1909 and 1915. Spectators were catered for by only limited facilities, and in many cases the sporting arena was no more than a field with a few buildings on one side, providing changing rooms and perhaps a covered stand for spectators.

Though the facilities were rudimentary, some major sporting occasions were attended by enormous crowds. It was still a novelty to see so many people together in one place at the same time and photographers responded by making panoramic views of these events. Providing urban dwellers with sporting entertainment, a new landscape of sport was emerging at the edge of the city.

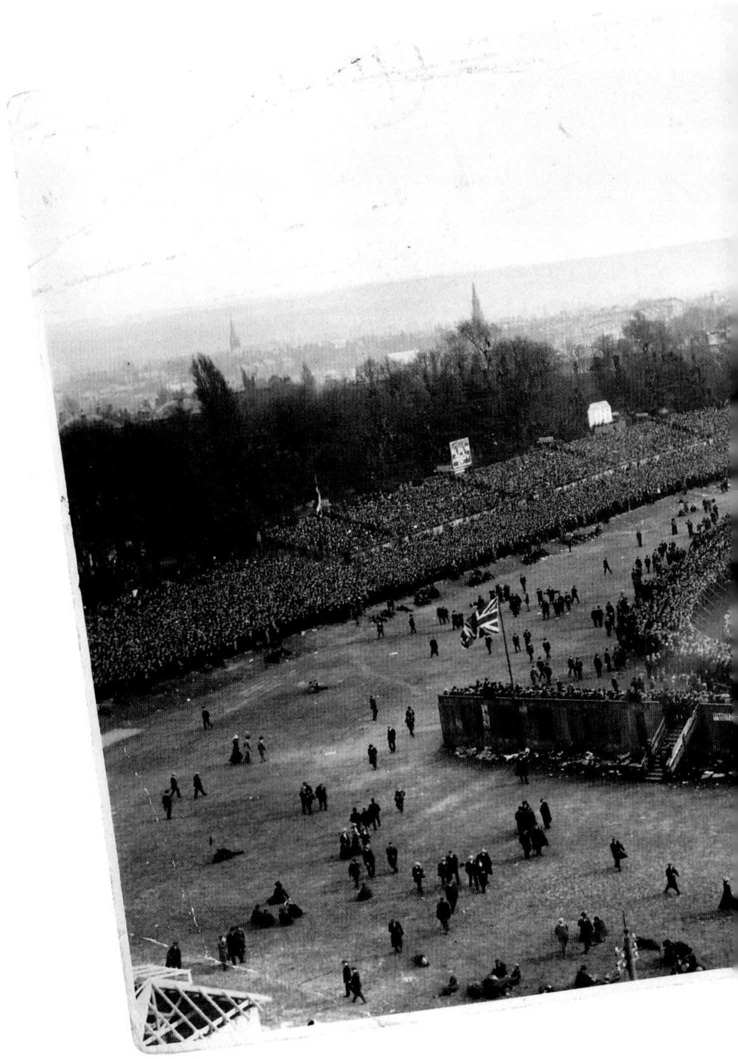

01
FA Cup Final between Bradford City and Newcastle United at Crystal Palace, London, 1911

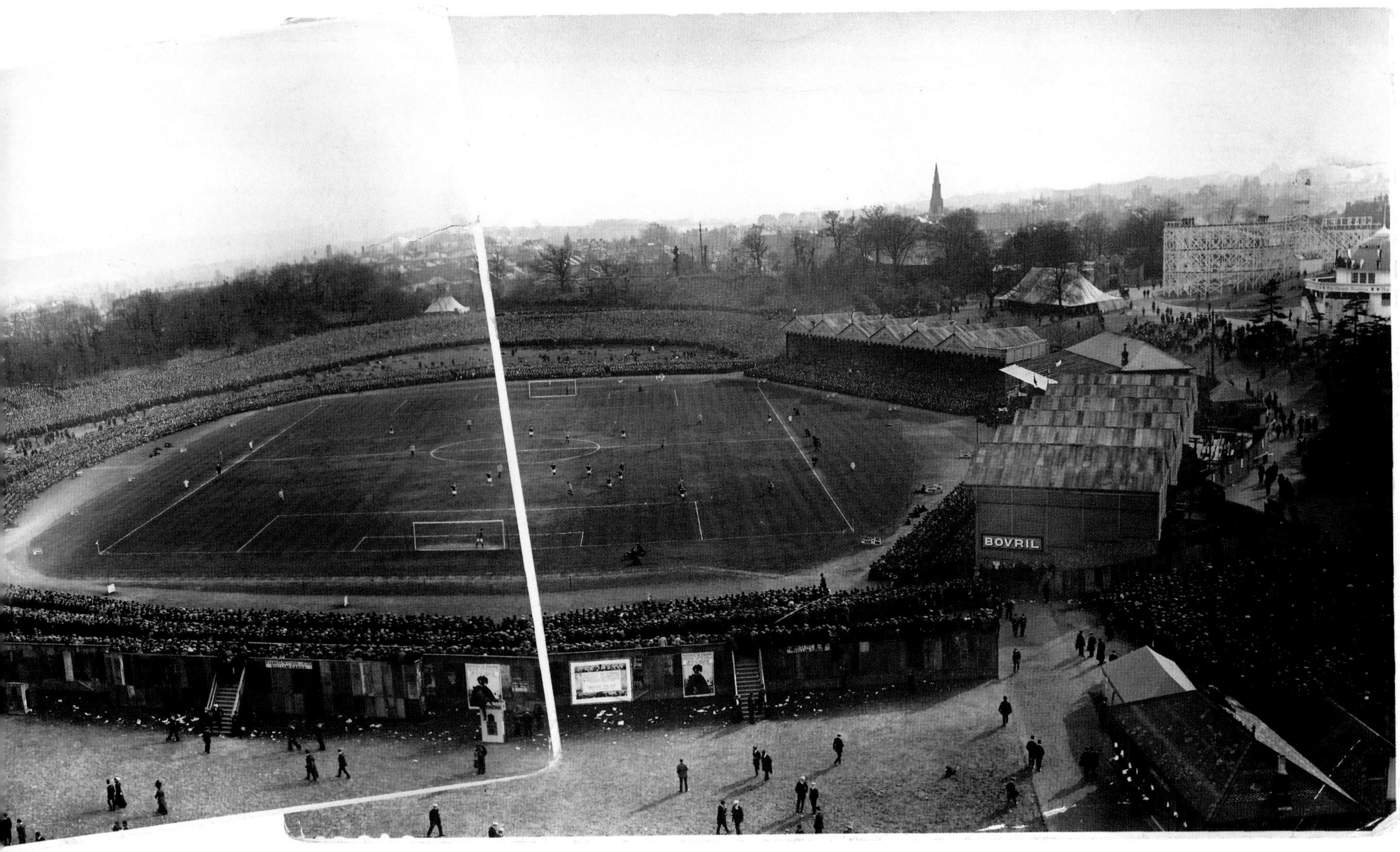

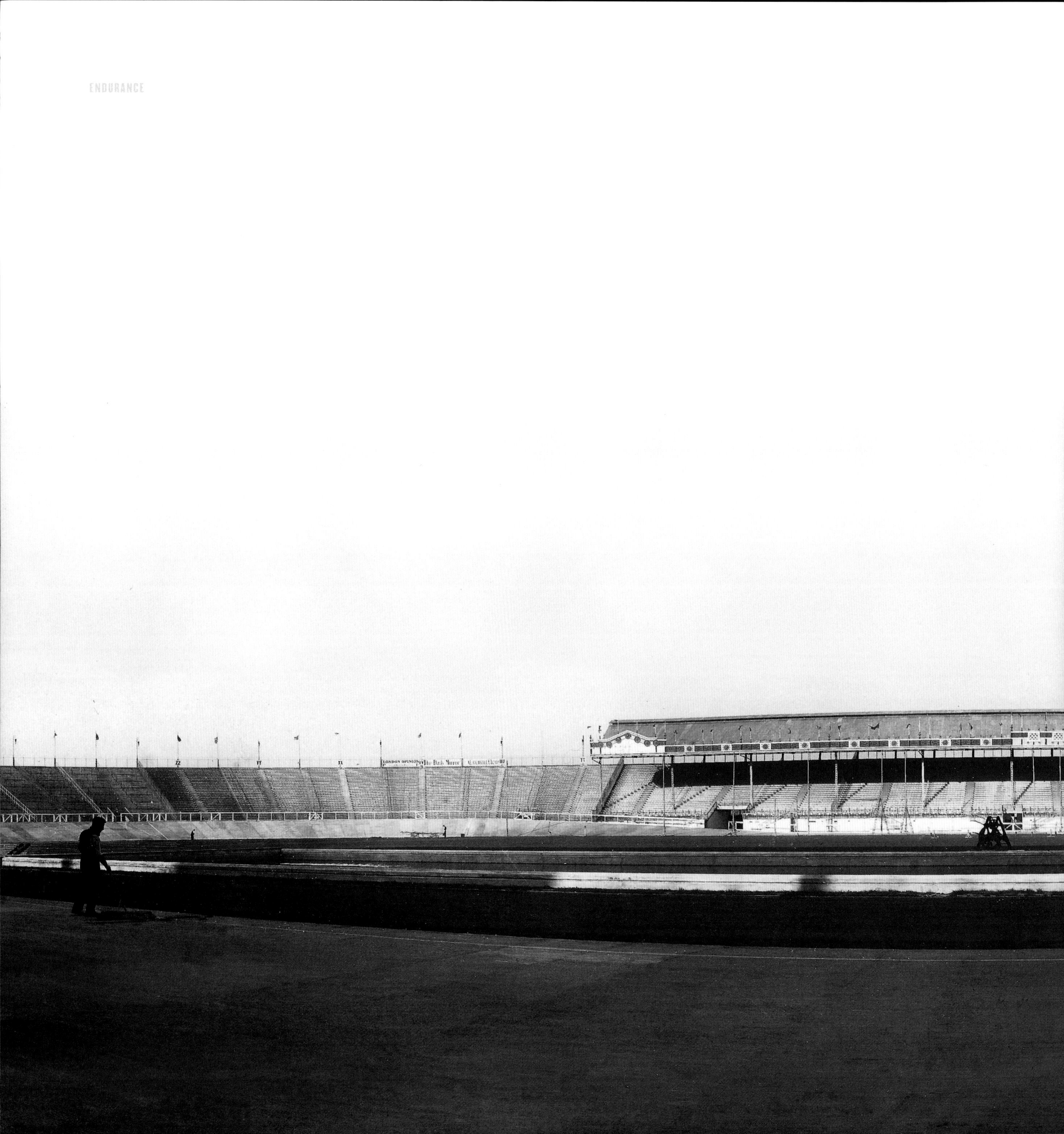
LONDON OPINION

02
White City Stadium, London, 1908

03 (OVERLEAF)
Spectators at the Olympic Games, White City Stadium, London, 1908

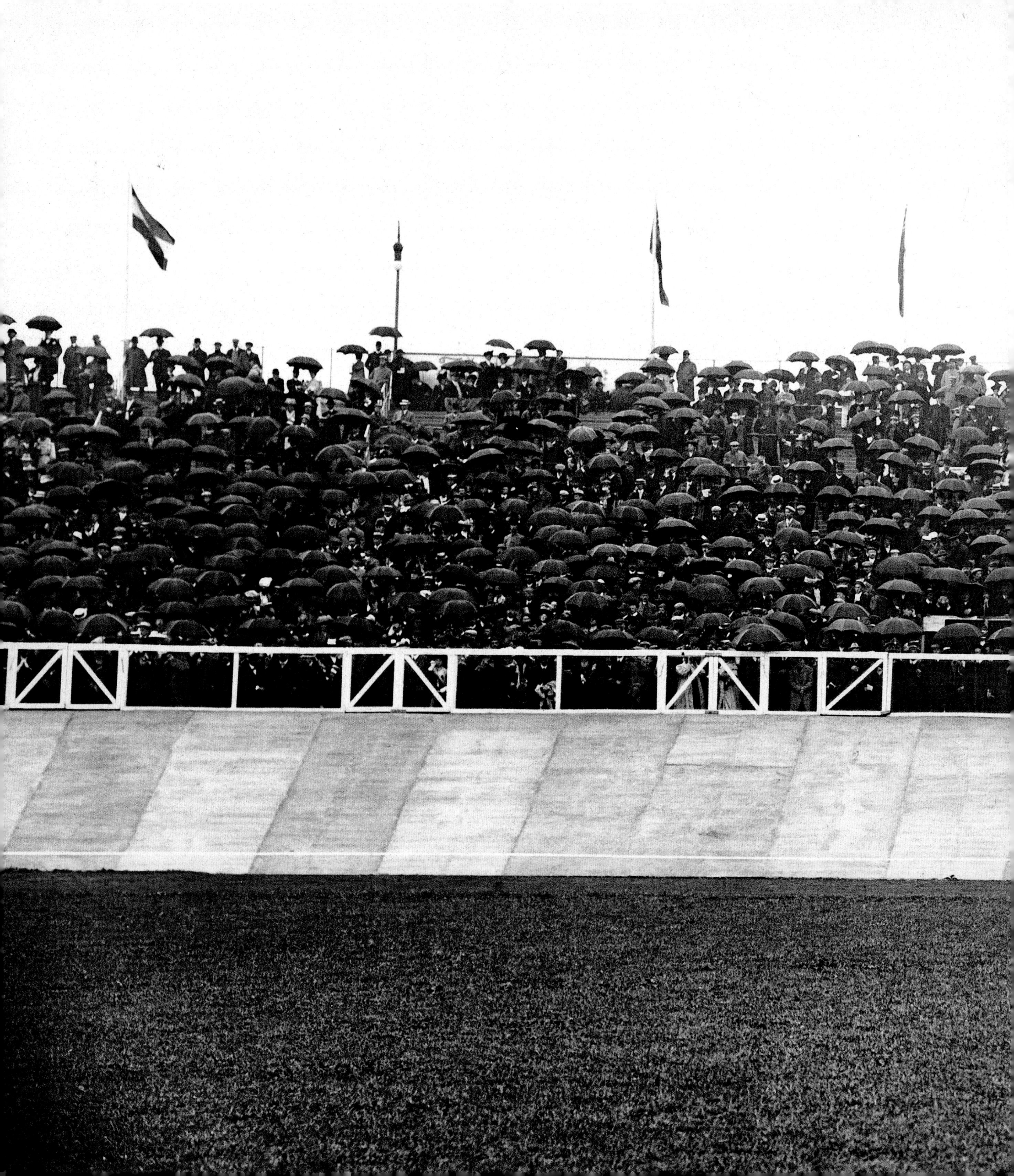

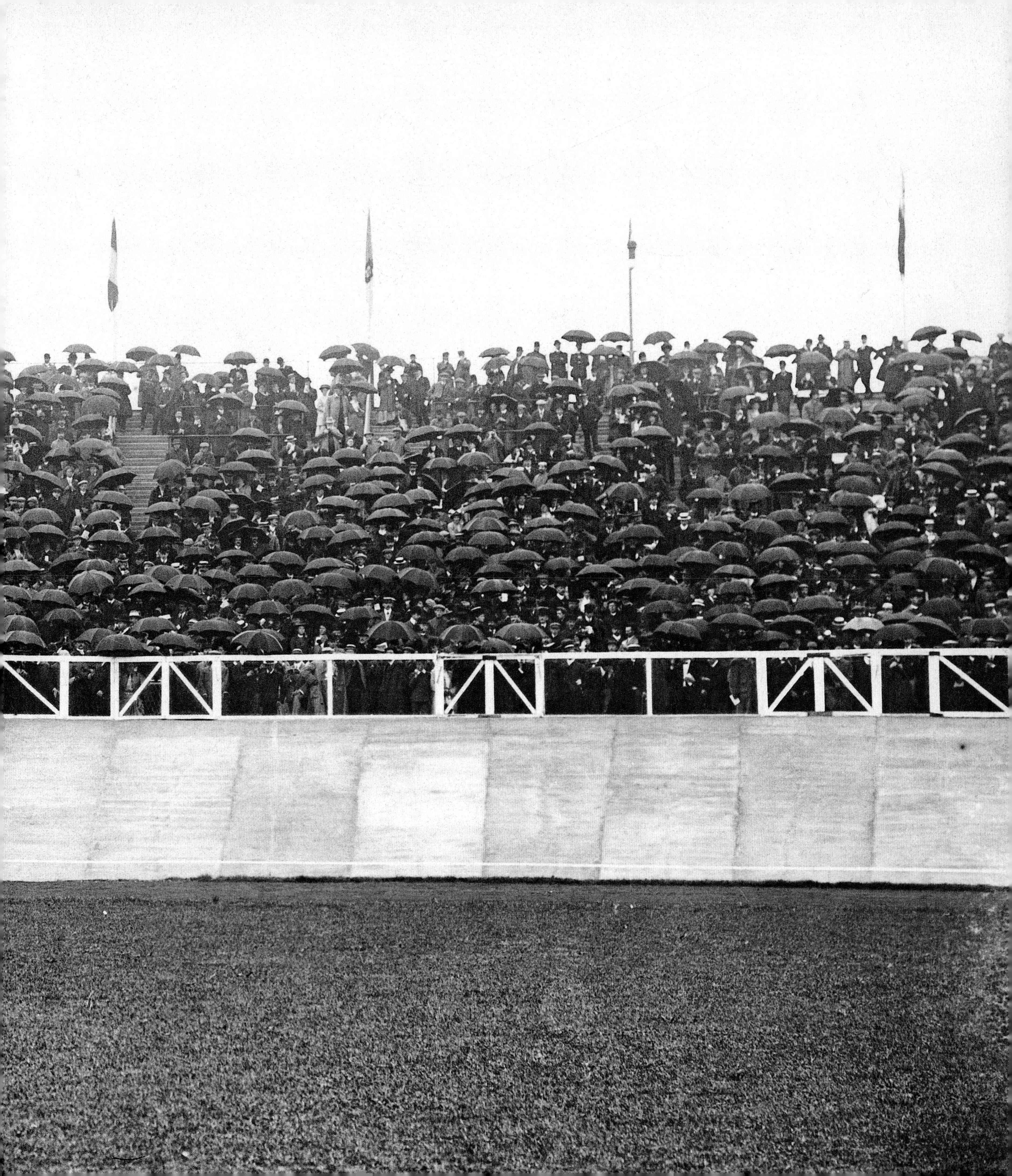

04
FA Cup Final between Aston Villa and Huddersfield Town at Stamford Bridge, London, 1920
A.H Robinson

05
Yankee Stadium, New York, c.1920

06
World Series between Cincinnati Reds and Chicago White Sox at Comiskey Park, Chicago, 1919

07 (OVERLEAF)
Boxing match at Bodmin, England, c.1920

04
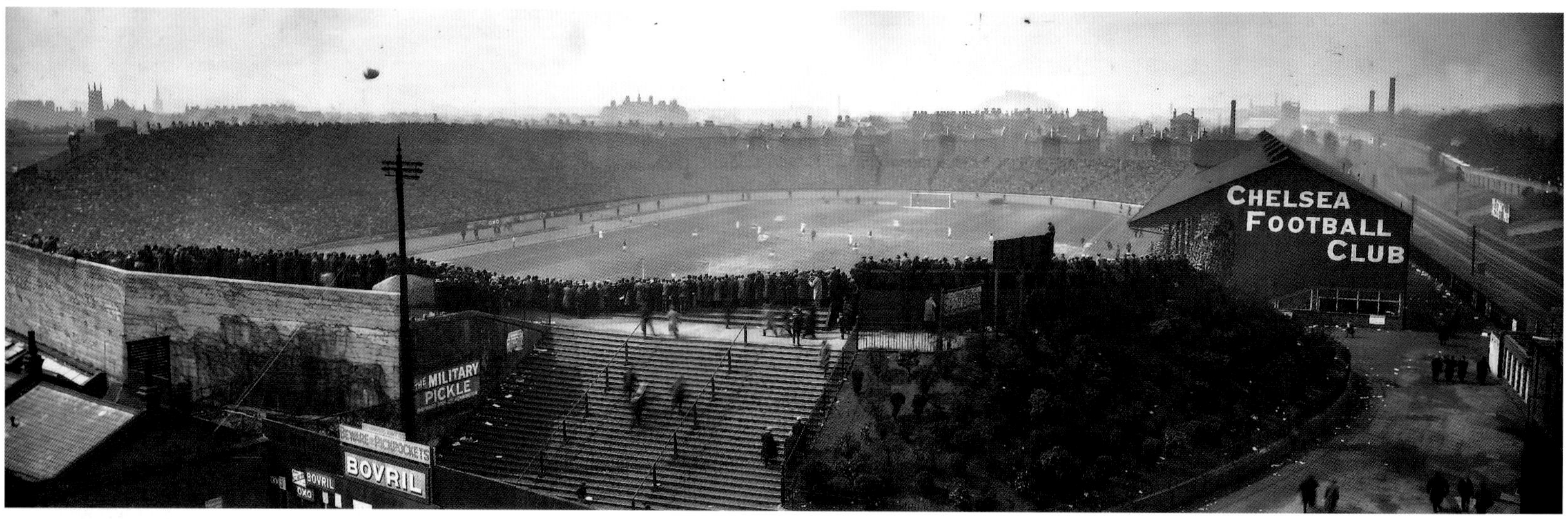

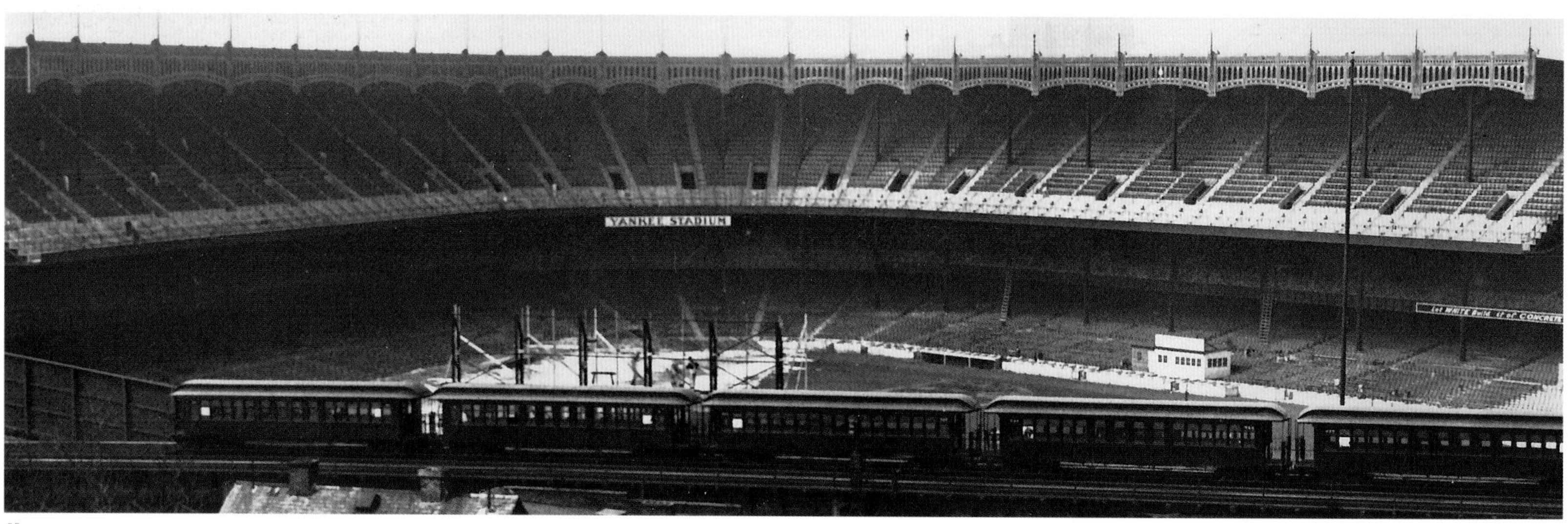

05

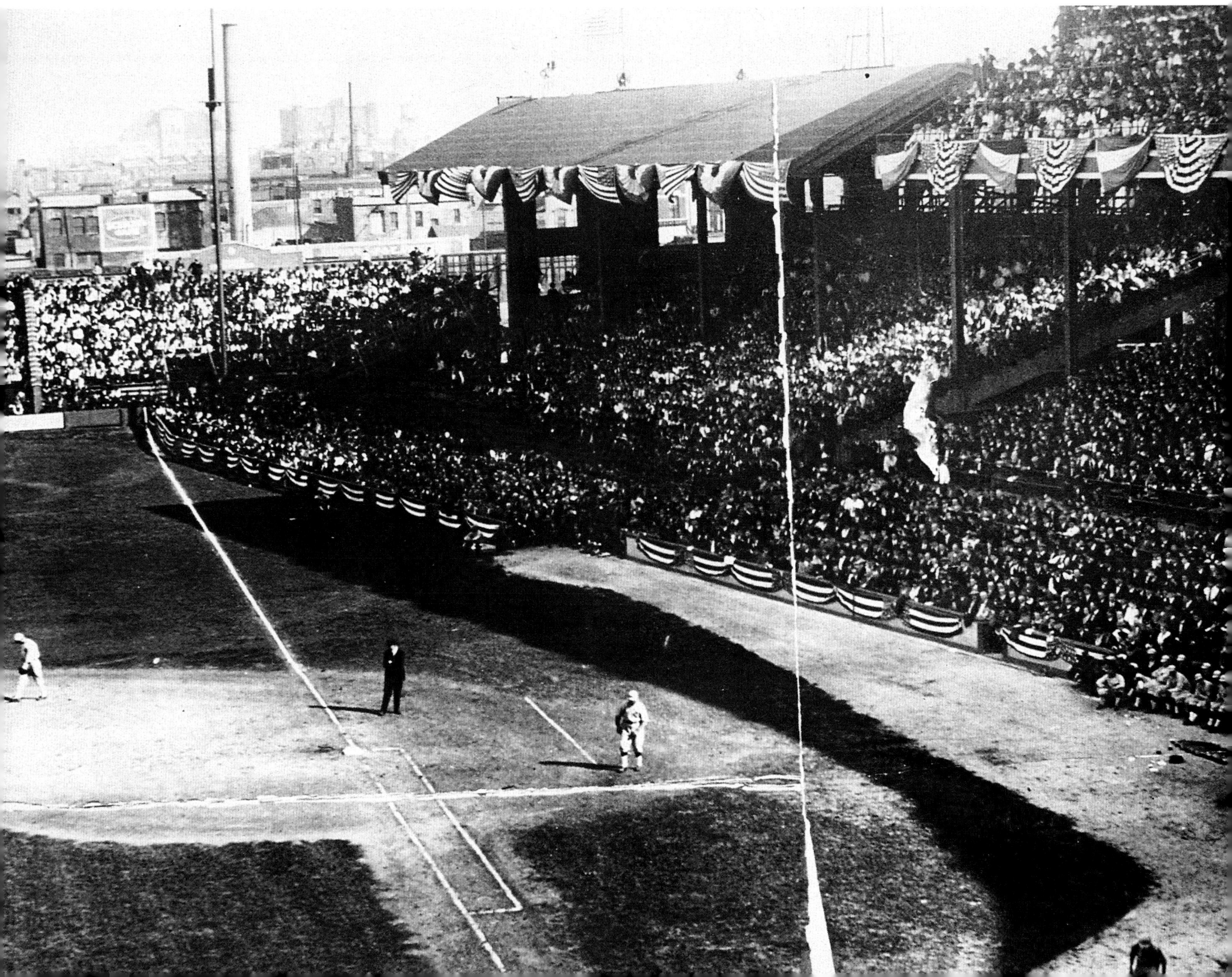

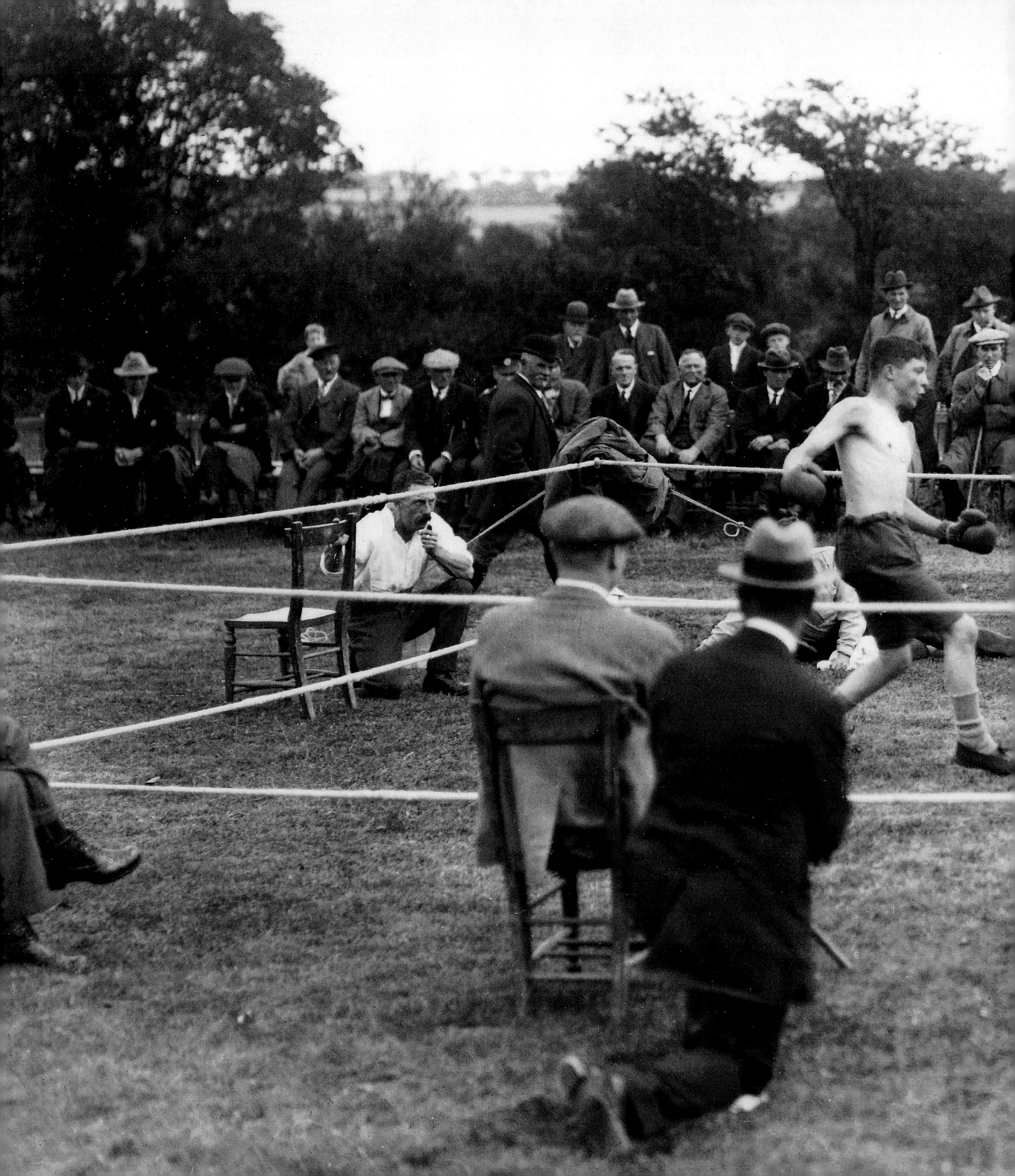

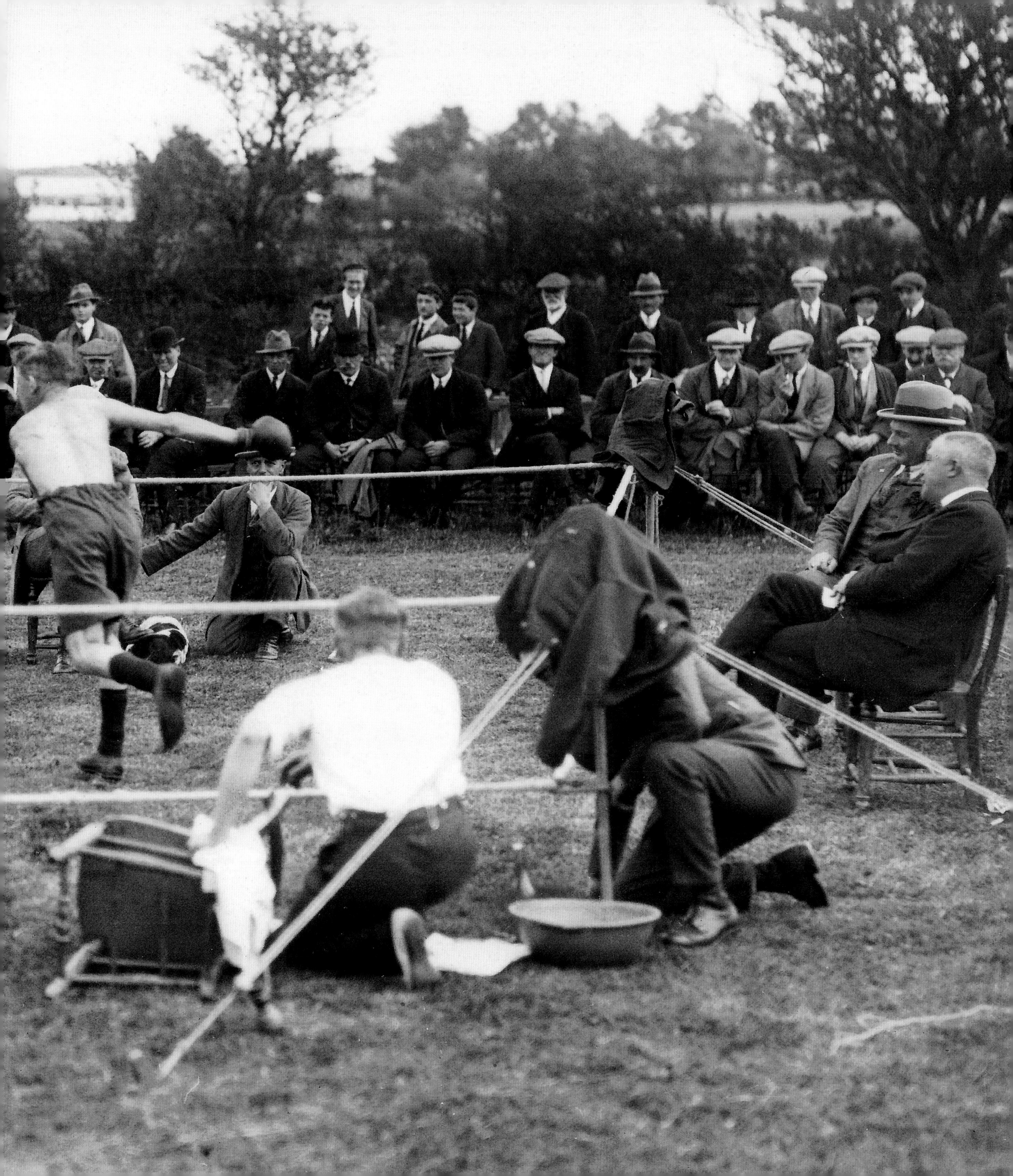

08

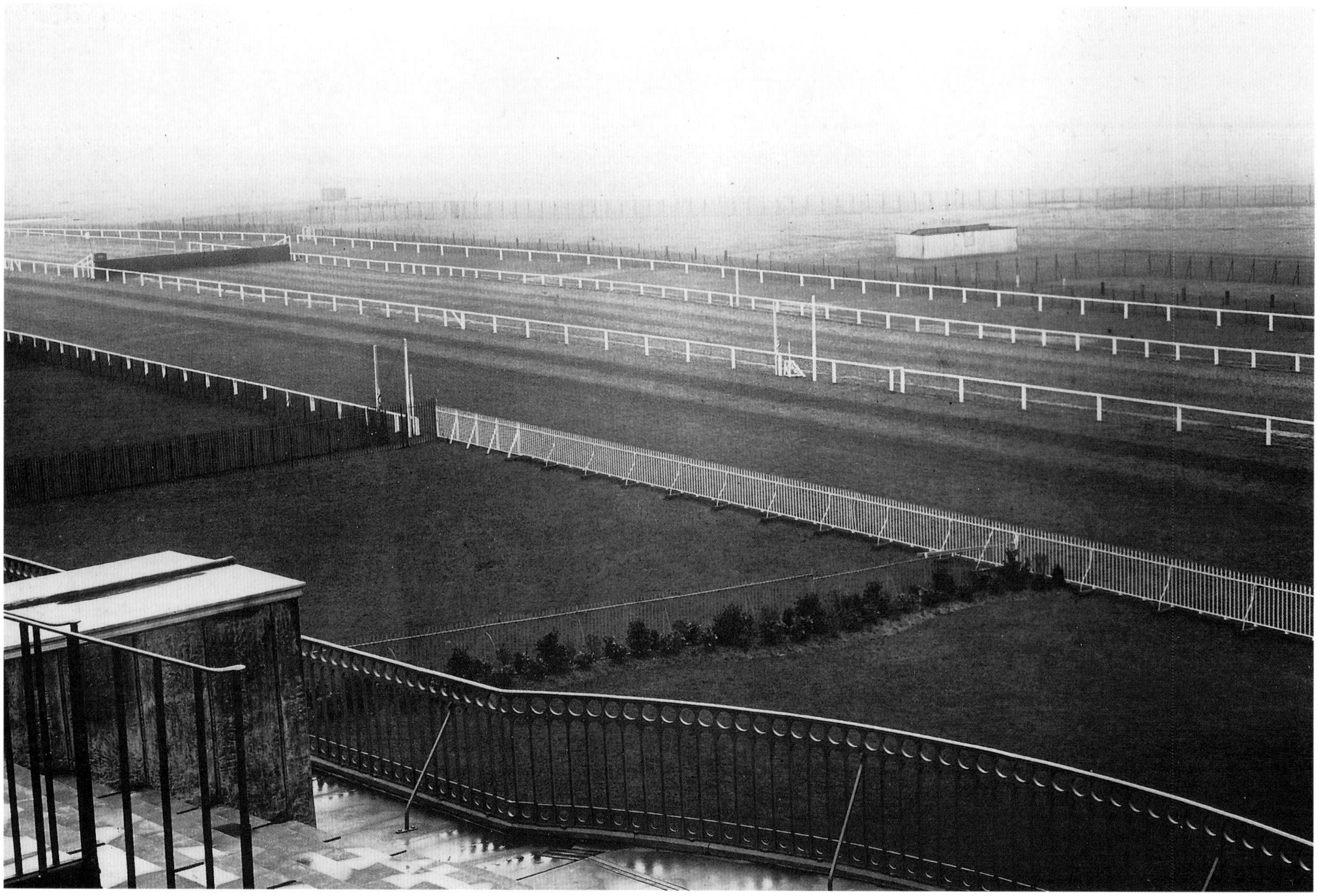

08/09
Aintree racecourse, Liverpool, 1907

10 (OVERLEAF)
Golf at Bamburgh Castle, England, 1901
A H Robinson

09

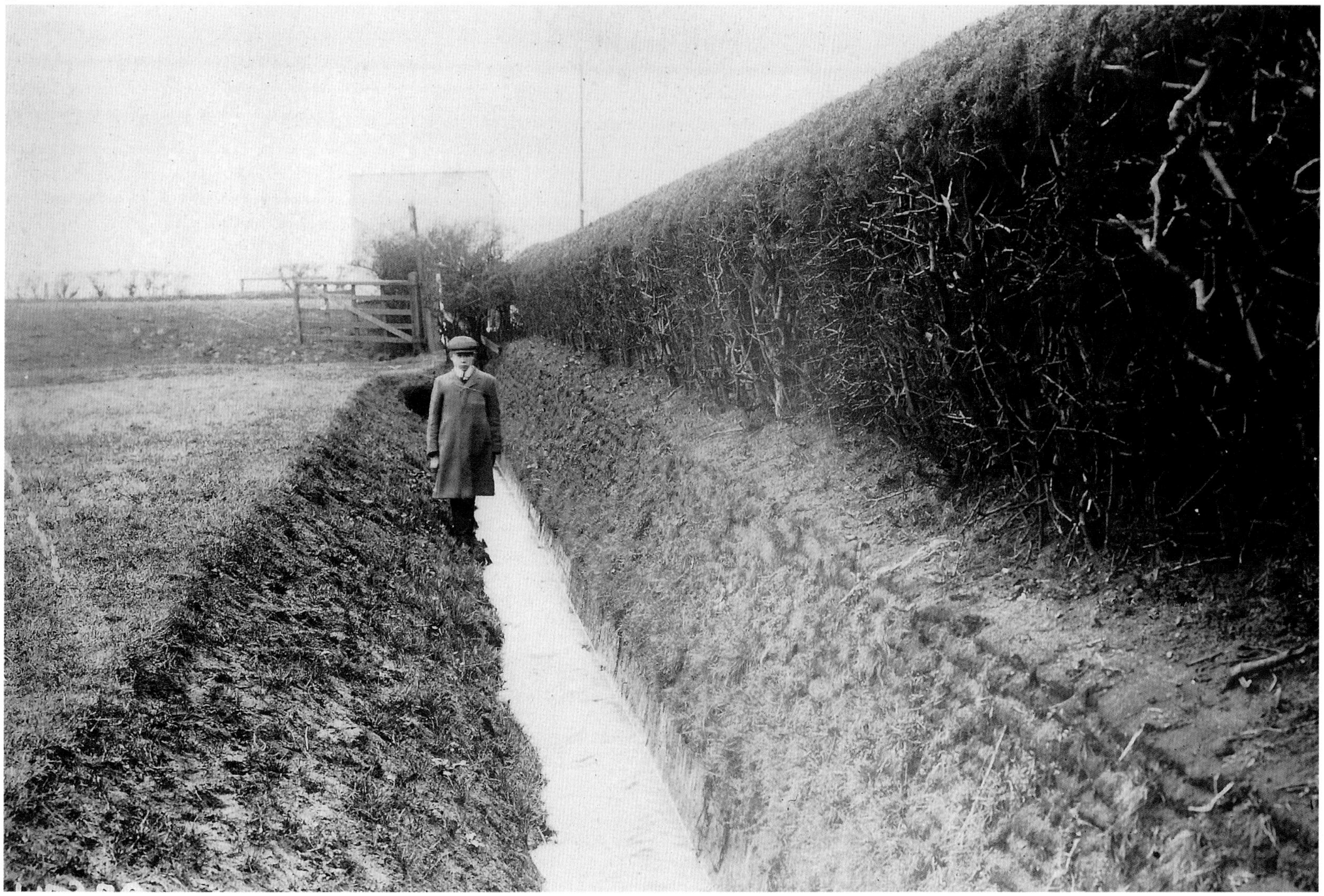

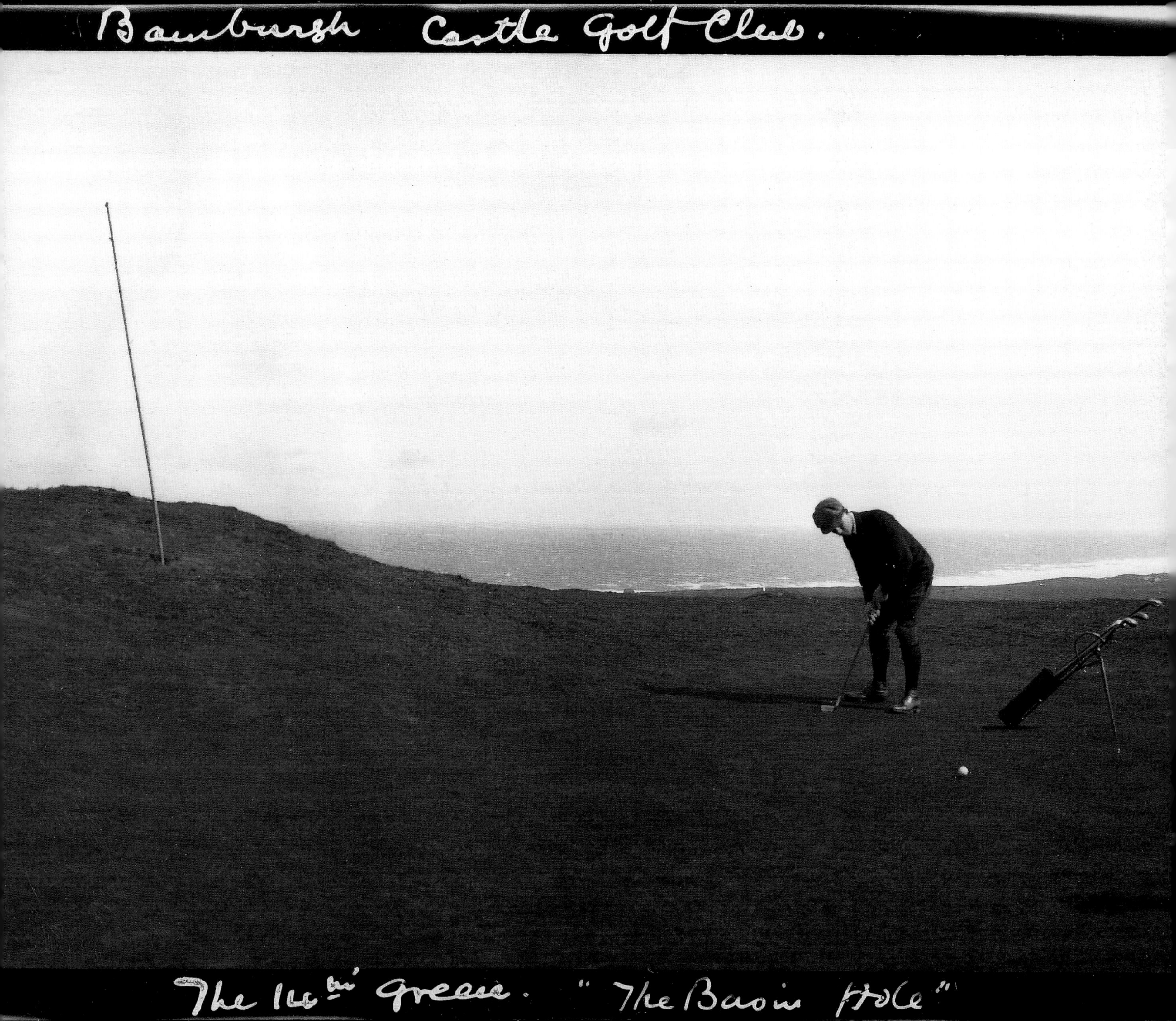
Bamburgh Castle Golf Club.
The 16th Green. "The Basin Hole"

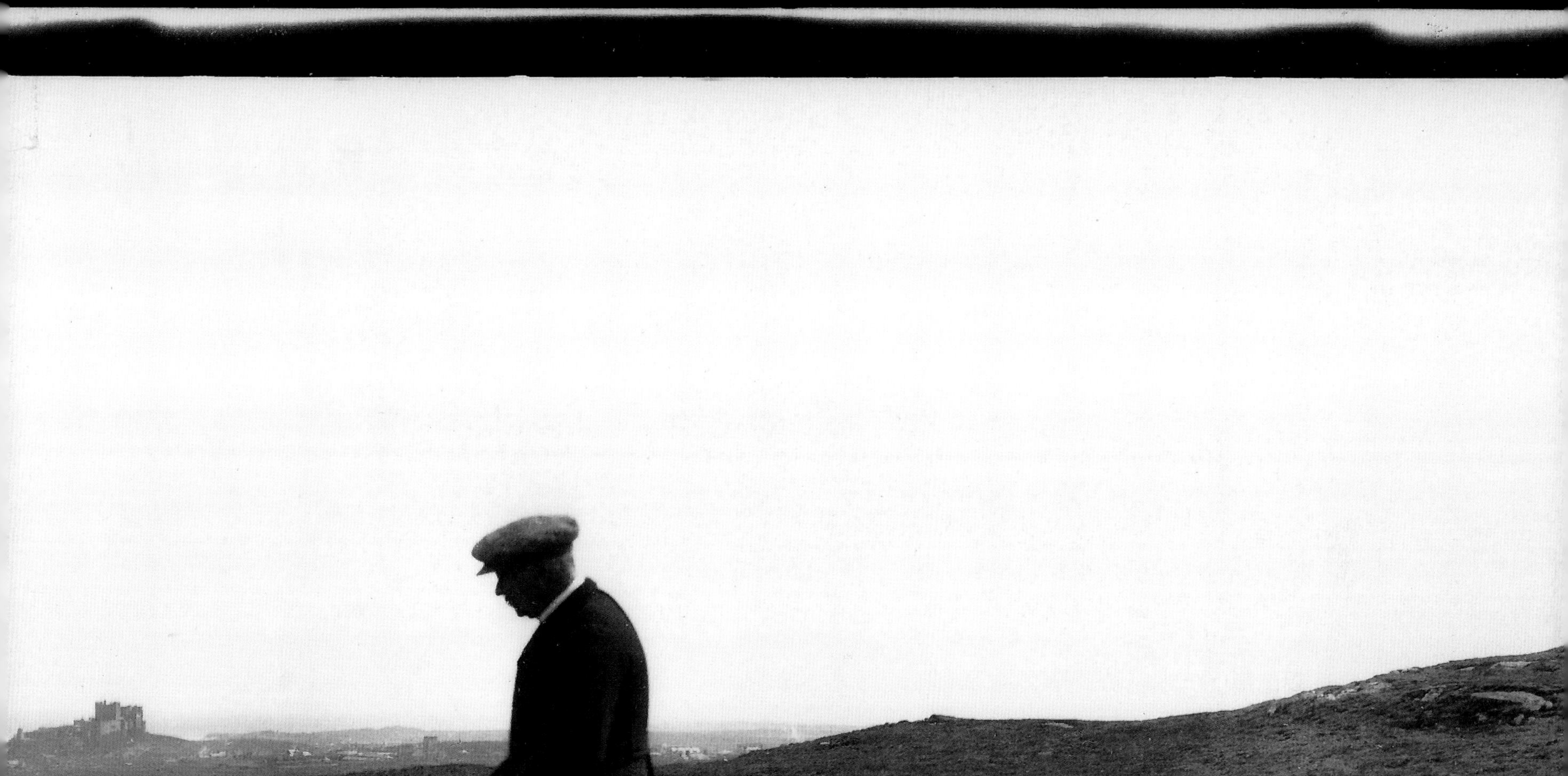
14
A.H. Robinson.
N.E.R. No1.

01/03
Jim Driscoll, *c.* 1910

02
Bob Fitzimmons, *c.* 1900

BACKDROP

During the early part of the twentieth century, portraits from traditional sports like boxing and horse racing followed the visual conventions of previous centuries: the fighter in classic pose with fists up, looking to one side, or the equestrian portrait of horse with jockey up. Photographers inherited these conventions, but soon started to develop a more relaxed style, creating increasingly dynamic portrayals of sporting personalities.

01

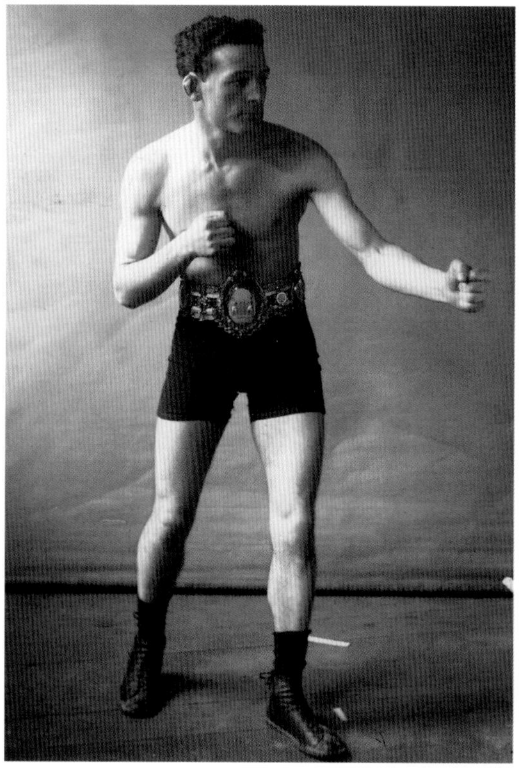

02

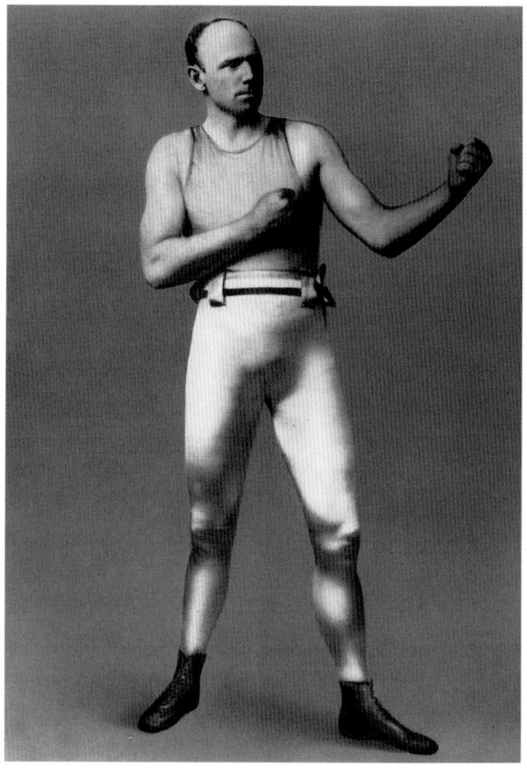

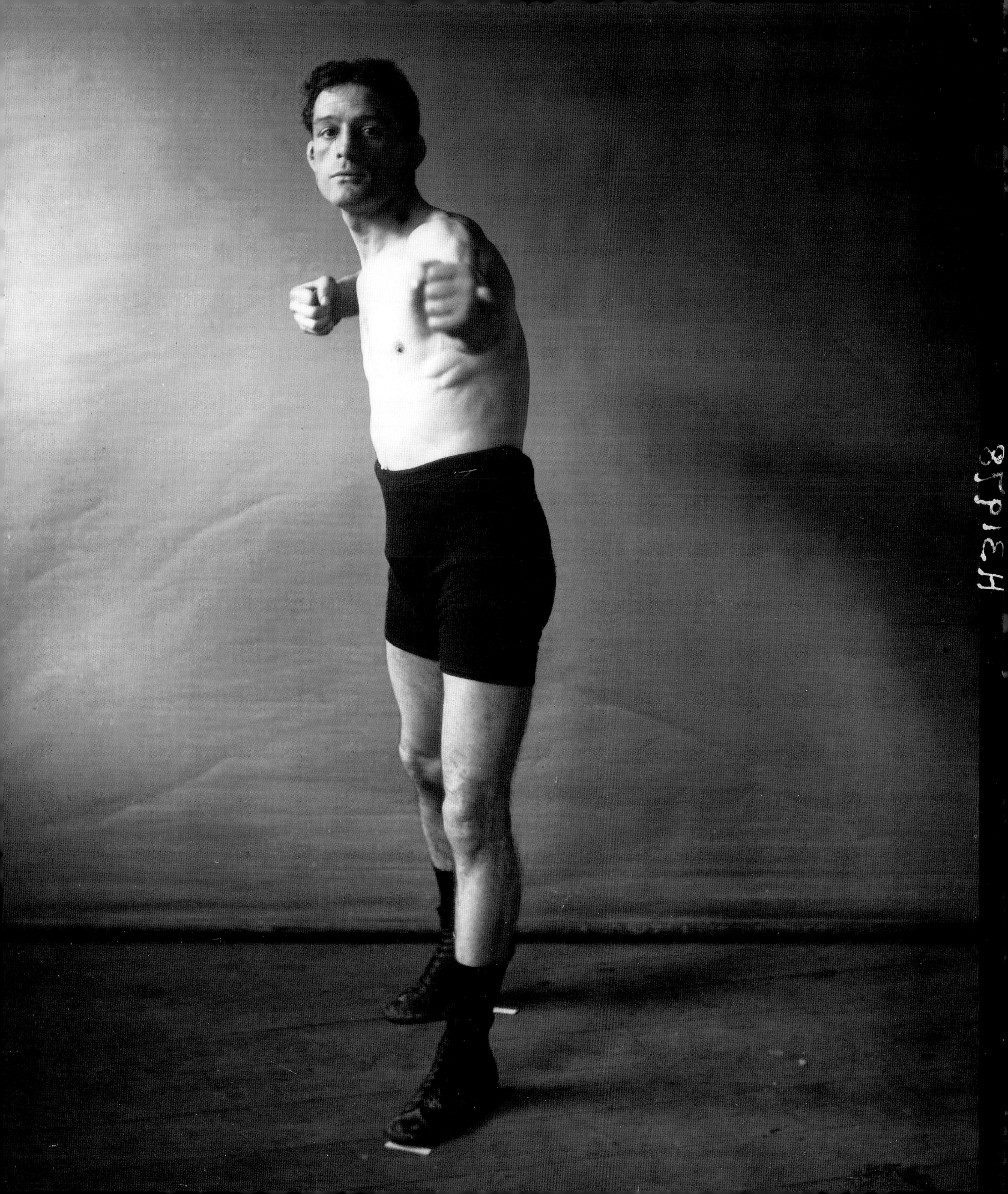

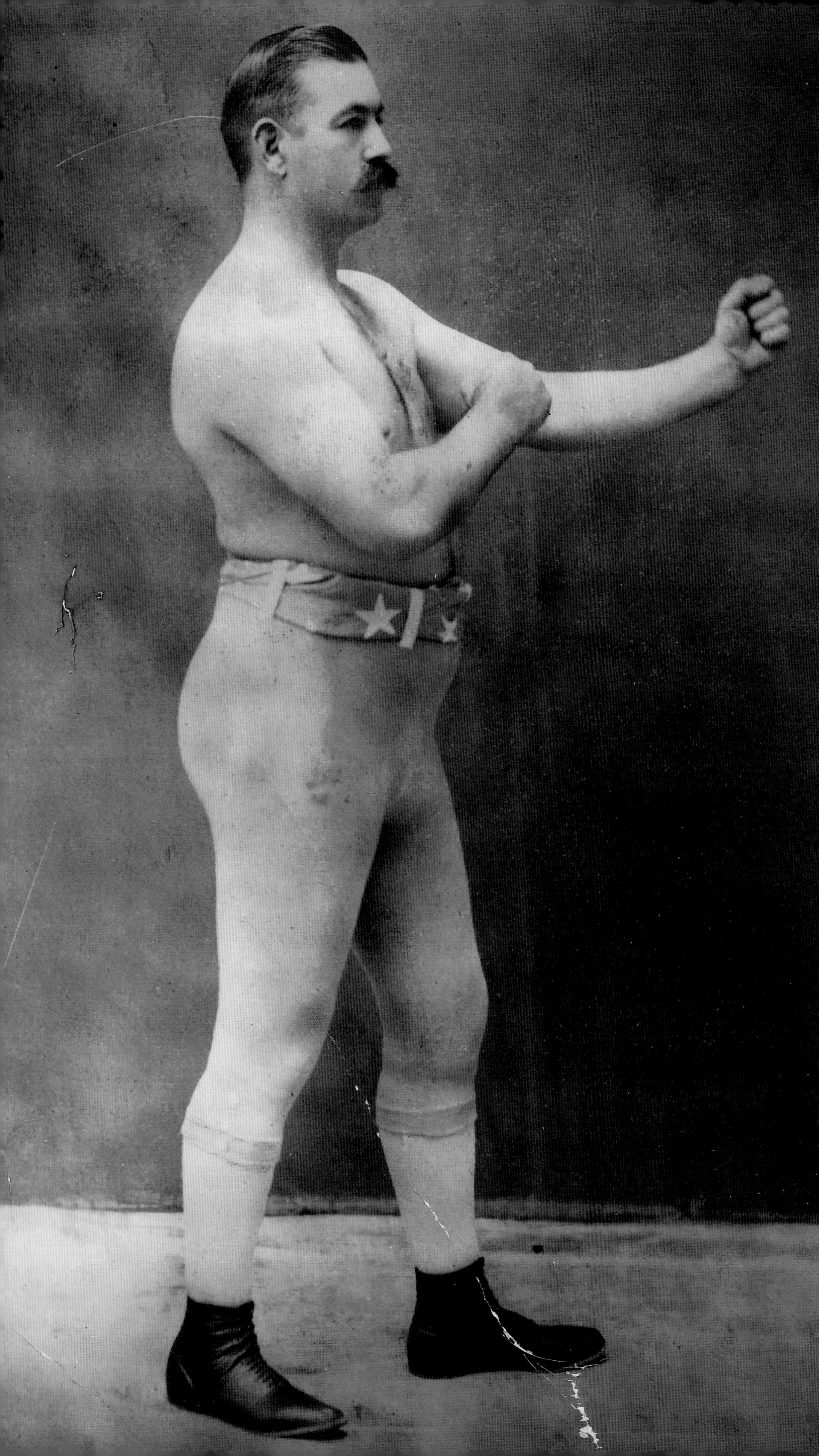

04
John L Sullivan, *c.*1905

05
Alfred Shrubb *c.*1910

06 (OVERLEAF)
Ally Sloper with jockey, Jack Anthony
and trainer, Aubrey Hastings, 1915

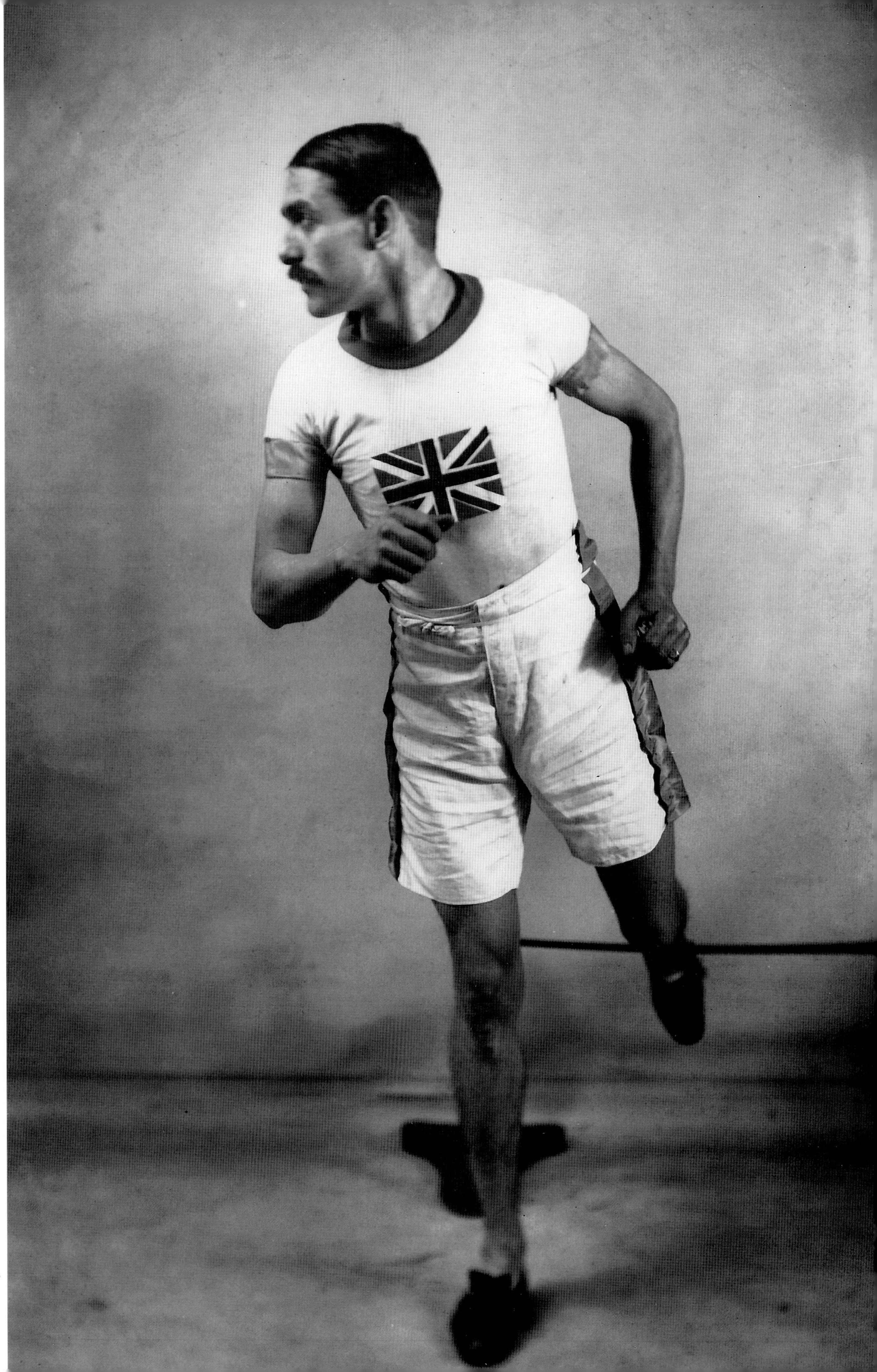

05

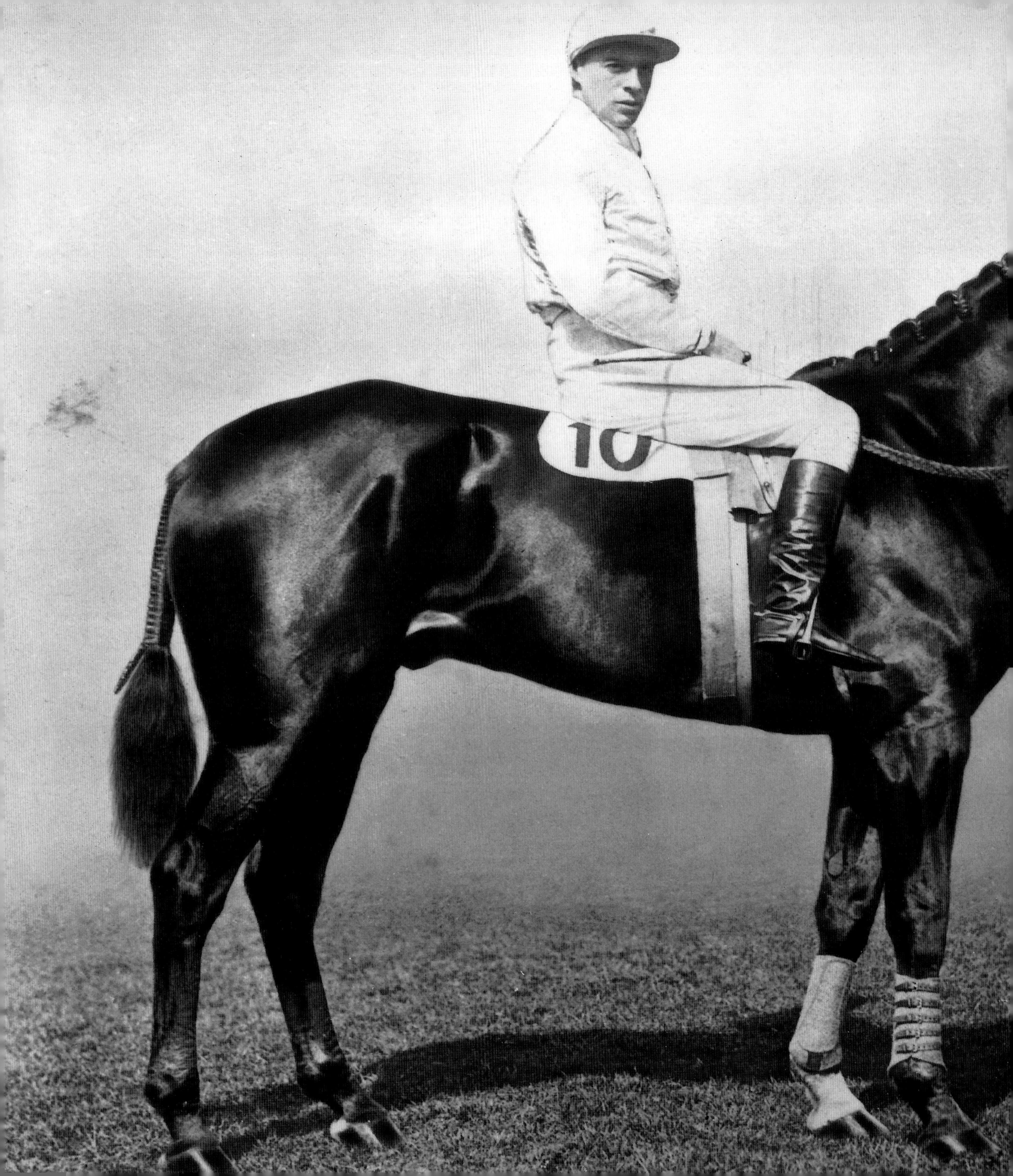
10

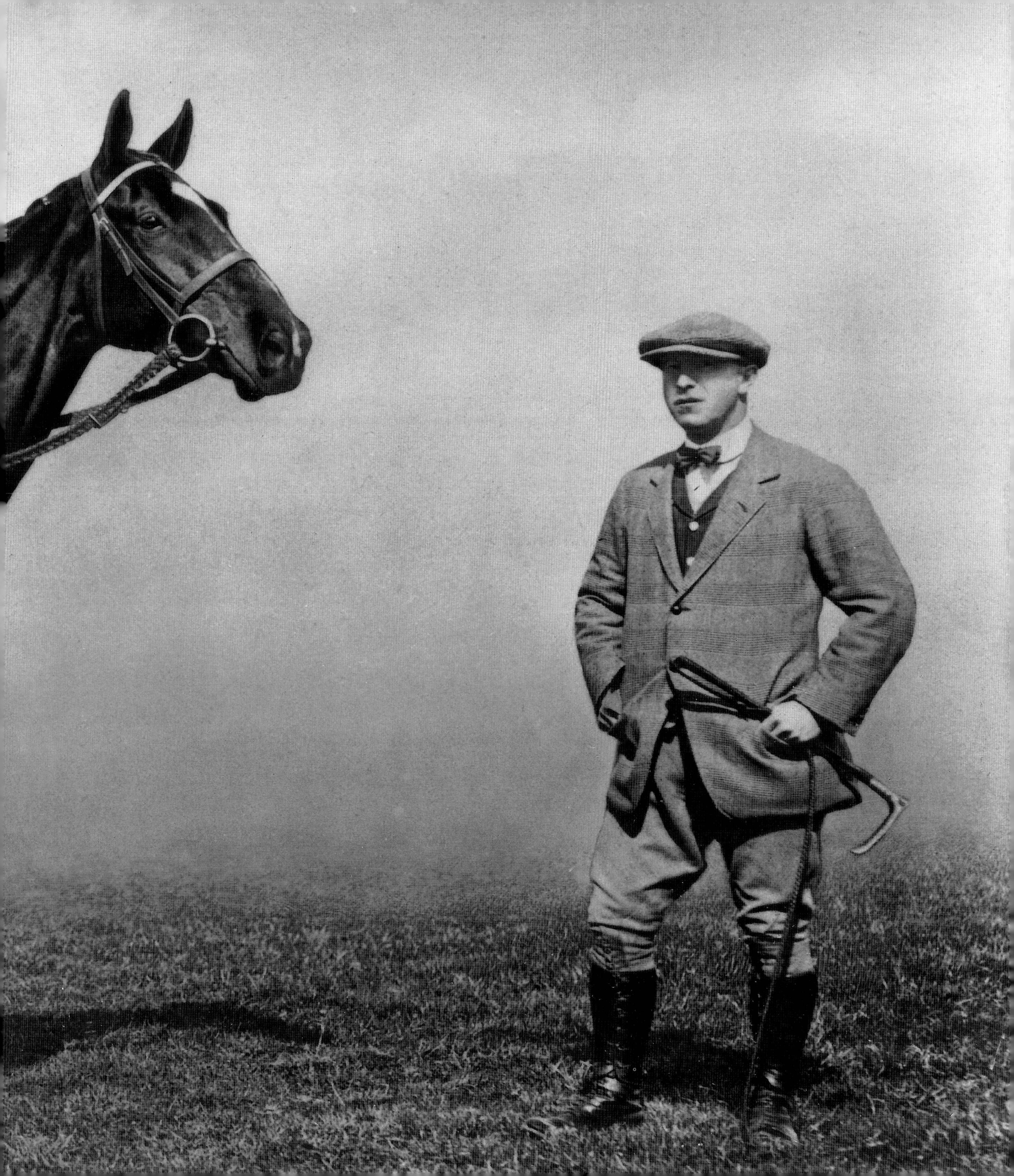

01/02
Jim Jeffries before the heavyweight title fight against Jack Johnson: the photograph as it appeared in a German newspaper and an 'improved' print made from it, Nevada, 1910

COLLECTING

In order to build up their collections and include international sporting events without incurring the cost of sending photographers on foreign trips, picture libraries collected images that had already been reproduced in newspapers and magazines by re-photographing them in the studio. In some cases the images would be 'improved' for better reproduction on the printed page, or to disguise their origin.

Some of the earliest examples of photographs of sports personalities appeared on postcards and collectors' cards. The tobacco industry had introduced cards as 'stiffeners' for paper packets, but once they started printing on them they became a useful way of advertising products while at the same time encouraging brand loyalty. Such a popular and widely distributed use of these photographs promoted personalities to the public and consequently enhanced the growing popularity of sport itself.

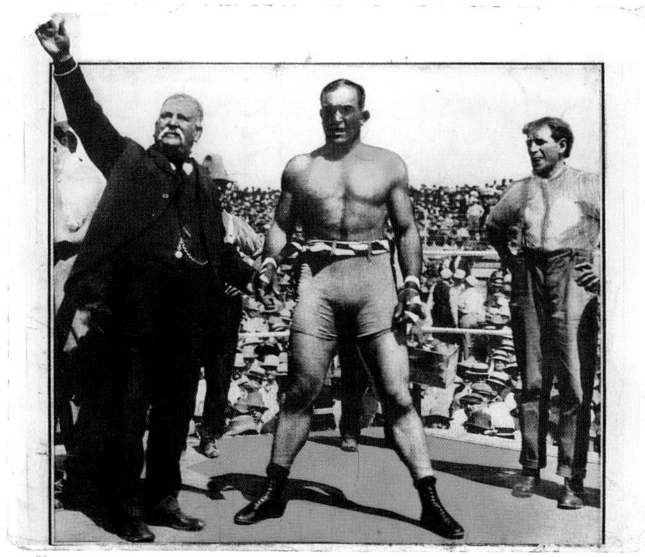

01

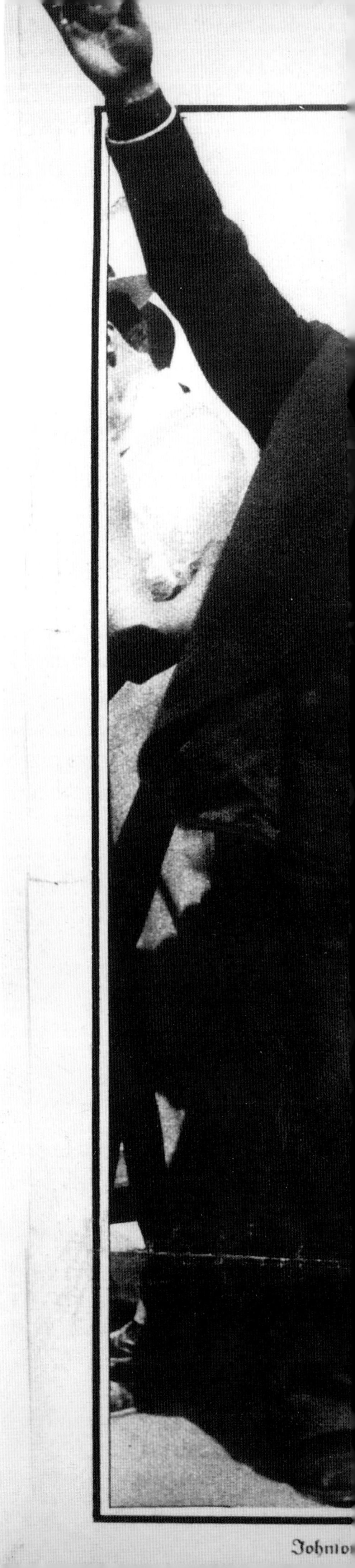

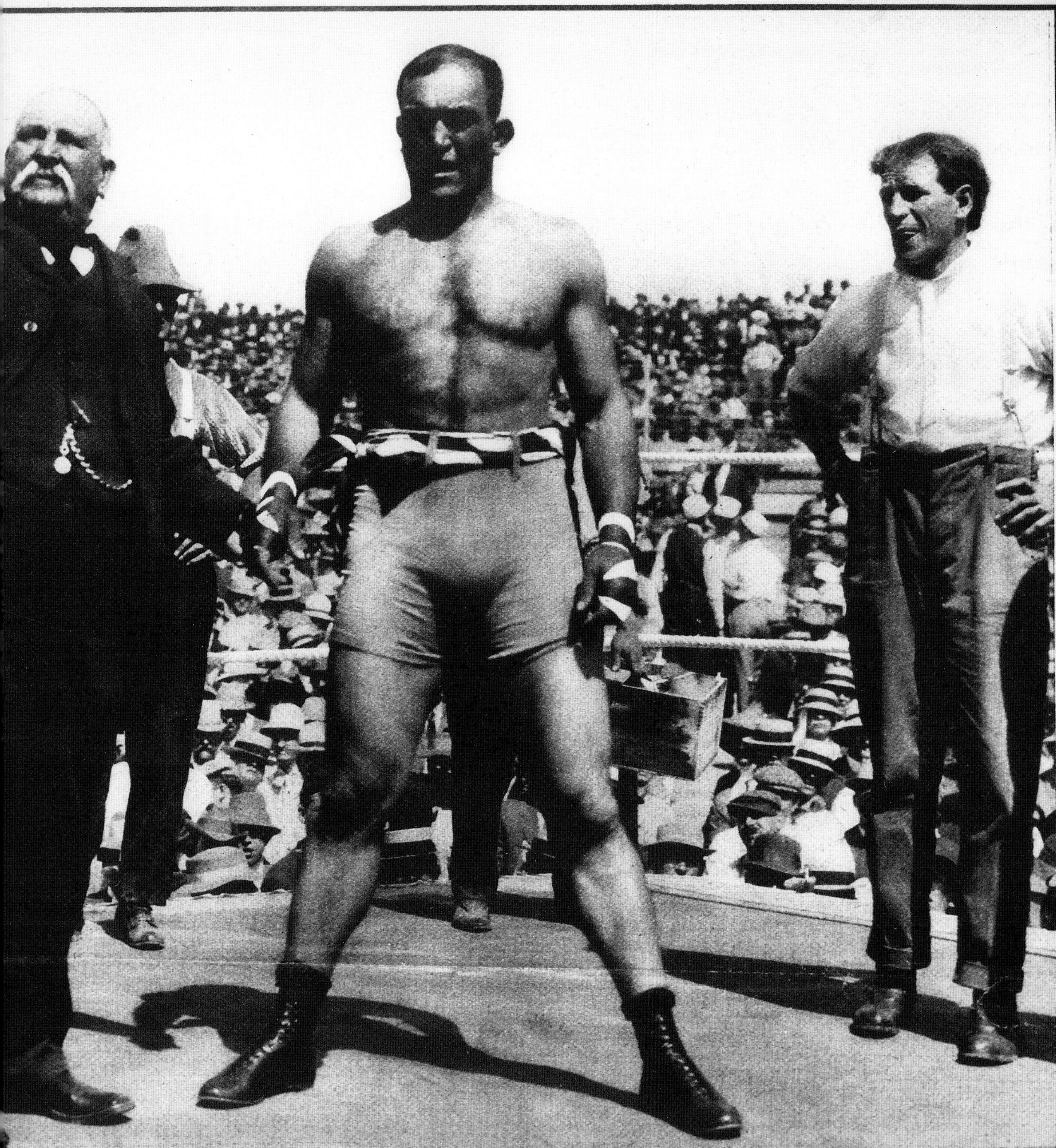

en Jeffries in Reno: Der bisher ungeschlagene Jeffries tritt nach sechsjähriger Pause wieder an

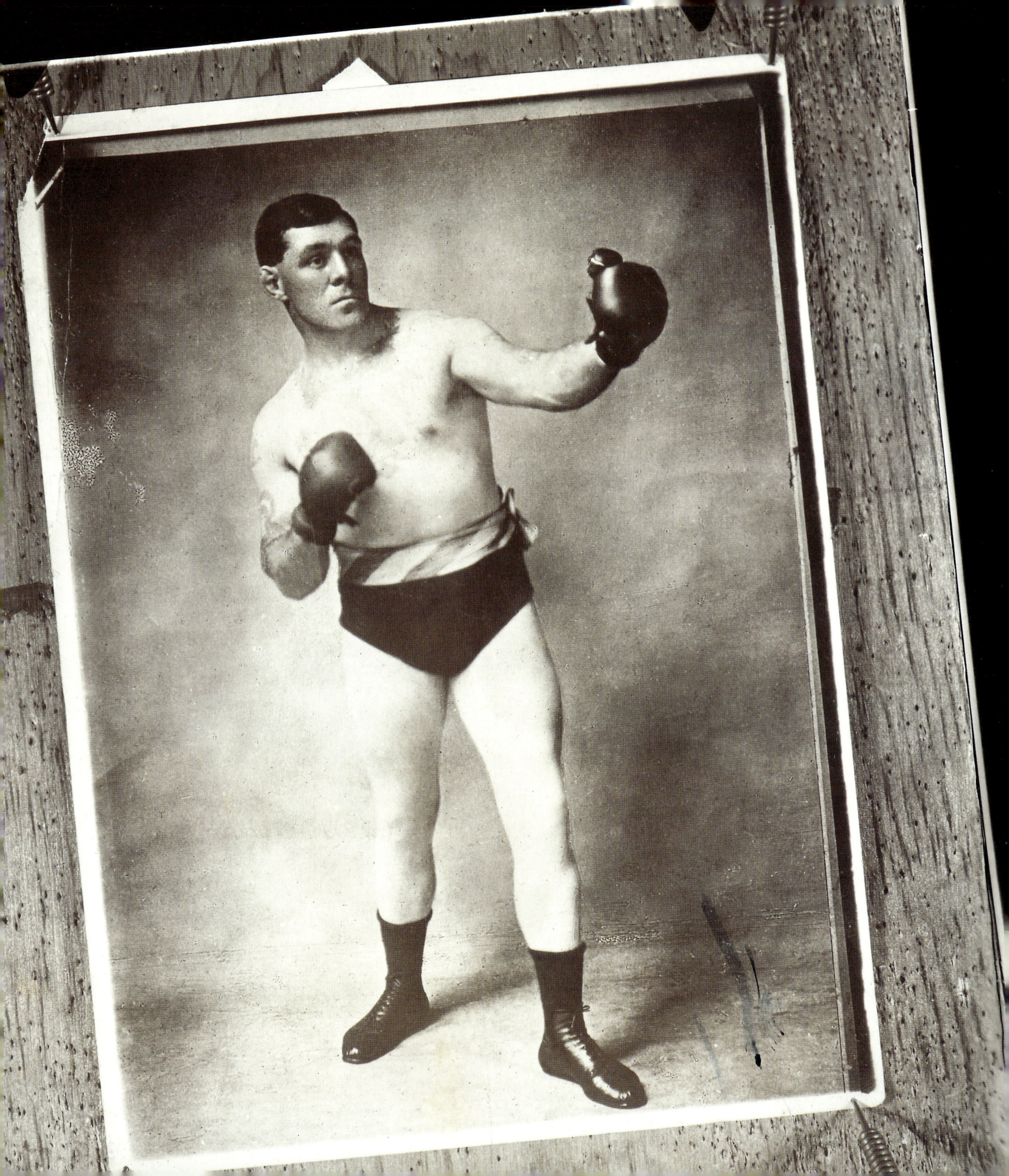

03
'Gunner' Moir, *c.*1907

04
Collectors' card of American cyclist Major Taylor from a set produced by the French chain of grocery shops, Felix Potin, *c.*1900

05 (OVERLEAF)
A page from the Felix Potin collectors' set of famous people, showing international cyclists, *c.*1900

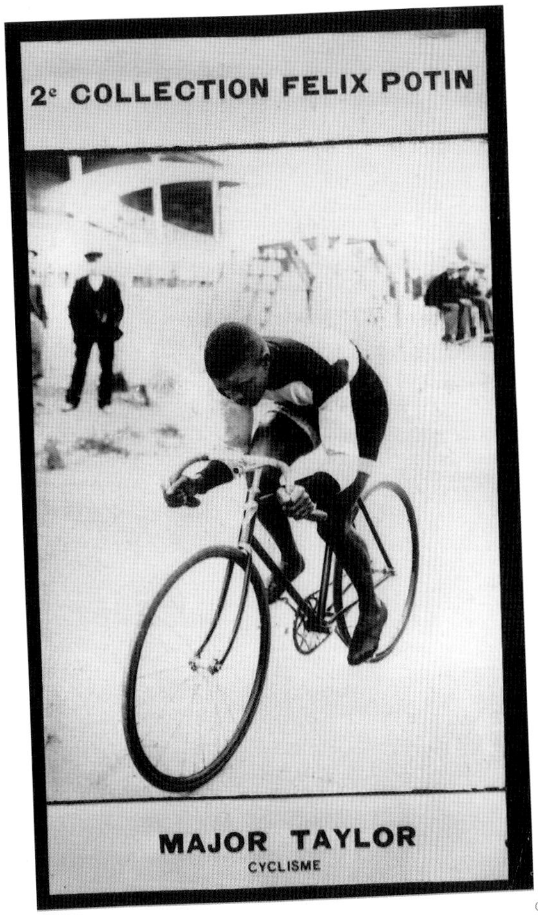

04

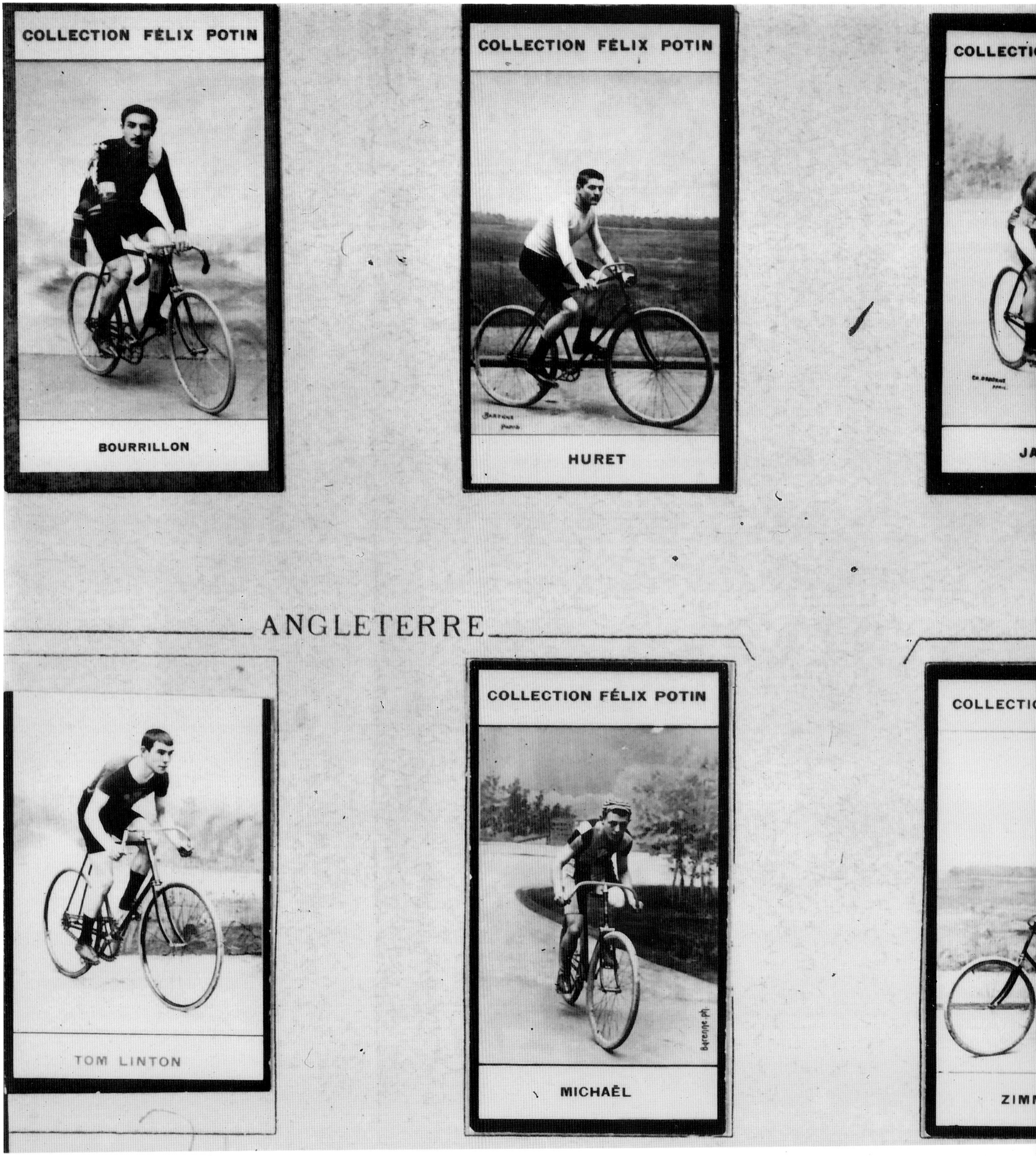
COLLECTION FÉLIX POTIN
BOURRILLON
COLLECTION FÉLIX POTIN
HURET
ANGLETERRE
TOM LINTON
COLLECTION FÉLIX POTIN
MICHAËL

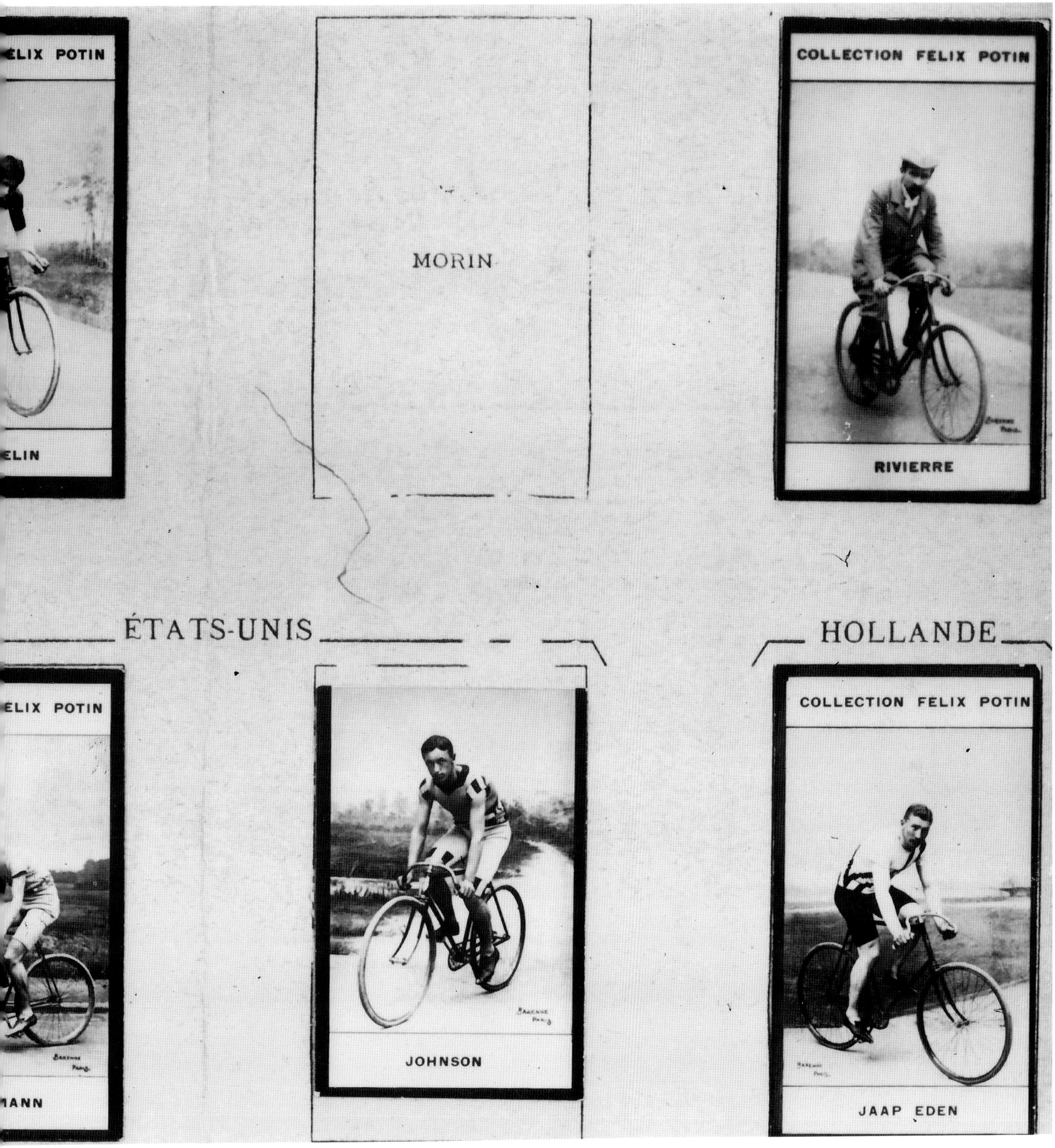
MORIN
COLLECTION FELIX POTIN
RIVIERRE
ÉTATS-UNIS
HOLLANDE
JOHNSON
COLLECTION FELIX POTIN
JAAP EDEN

01–07
Danish gymnasts warming up in the White City Stadium for the London Olympic Games, 1908

GRACE

Sport was predominantly a male activity. Only 36 women participated in the 1908 Olympics out of a total of 2,035 competitors. Their involvement was limited to the events considered to be more refined, like gymnastics. The skills of balance and posture were seen as feminine qualities while strength and stamina were the province of men. In this sequence, the photographer has concentrated on capturing the balletic posture of the gymnasts rather than the competitive side of the sport. Women were expected to grace the Olympics, not to win races. That was left to the men.

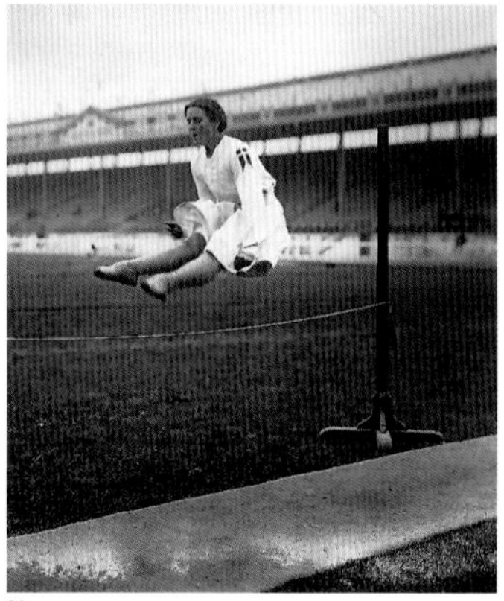
01

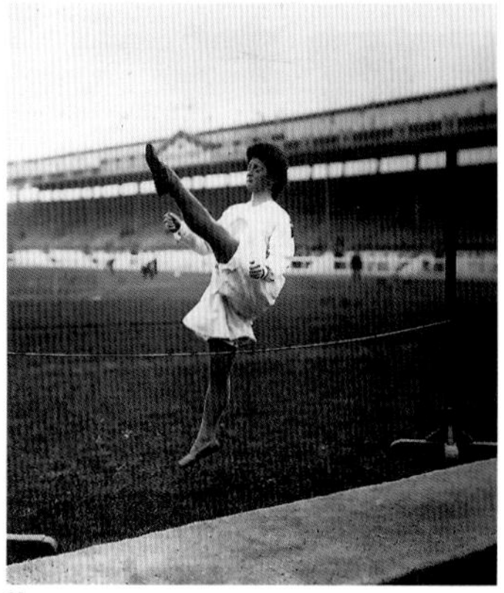
02

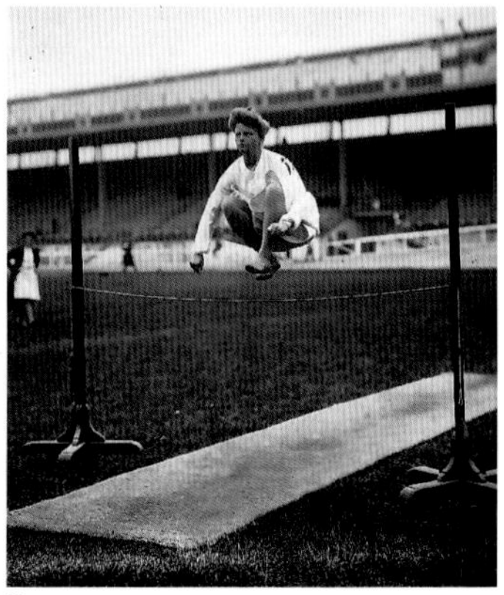
03

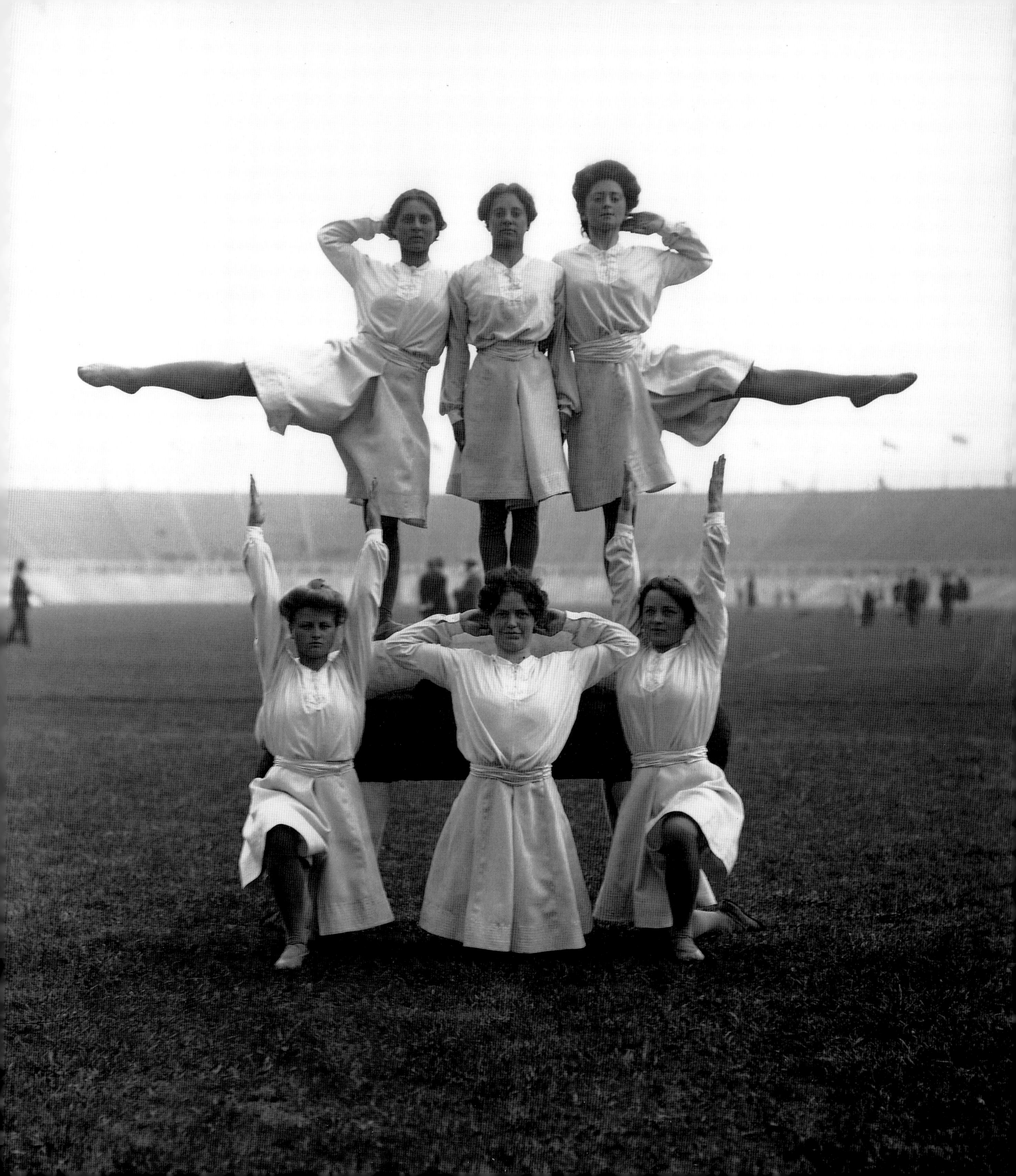

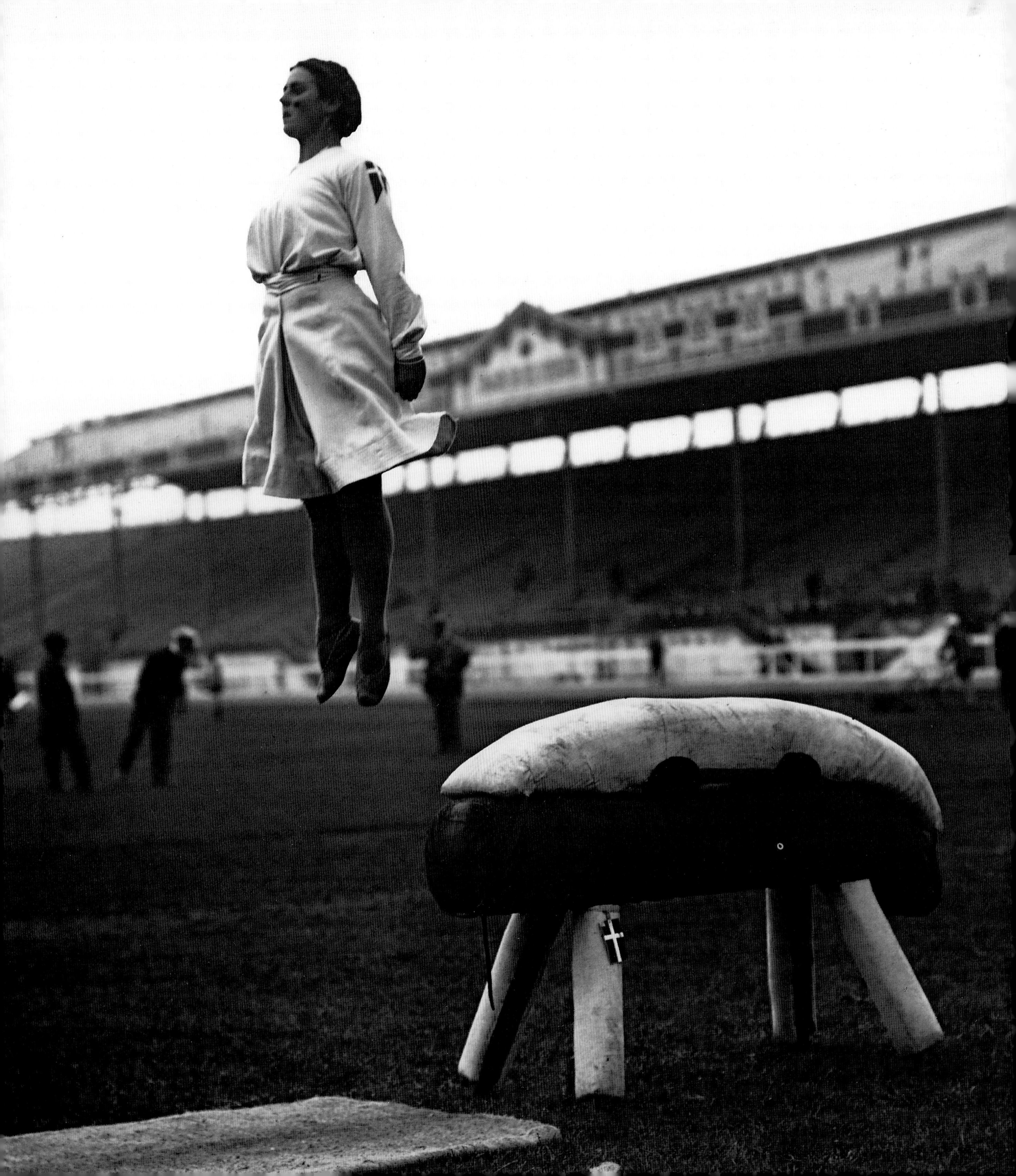

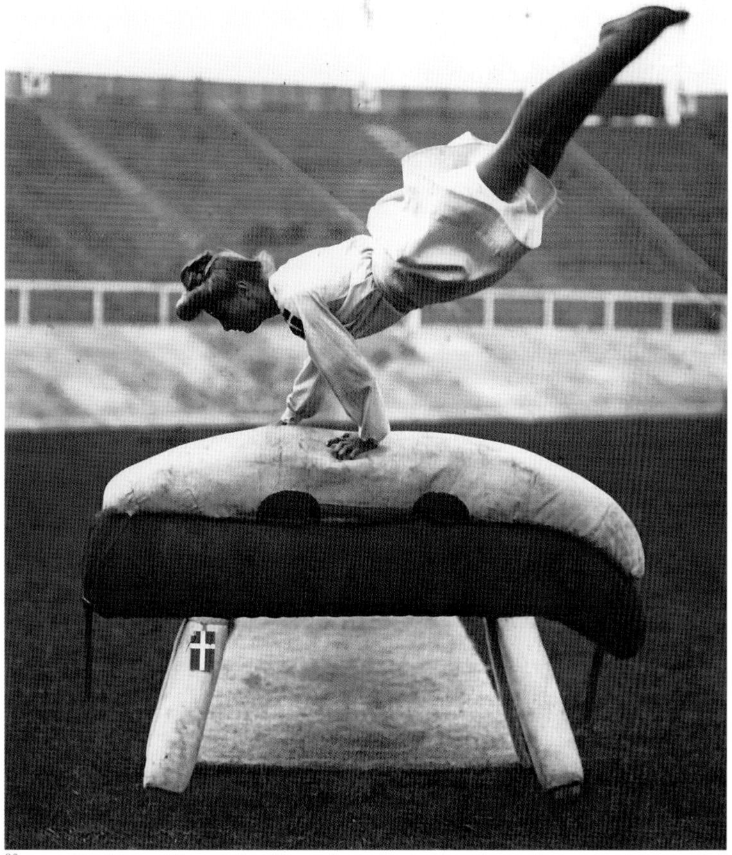

06

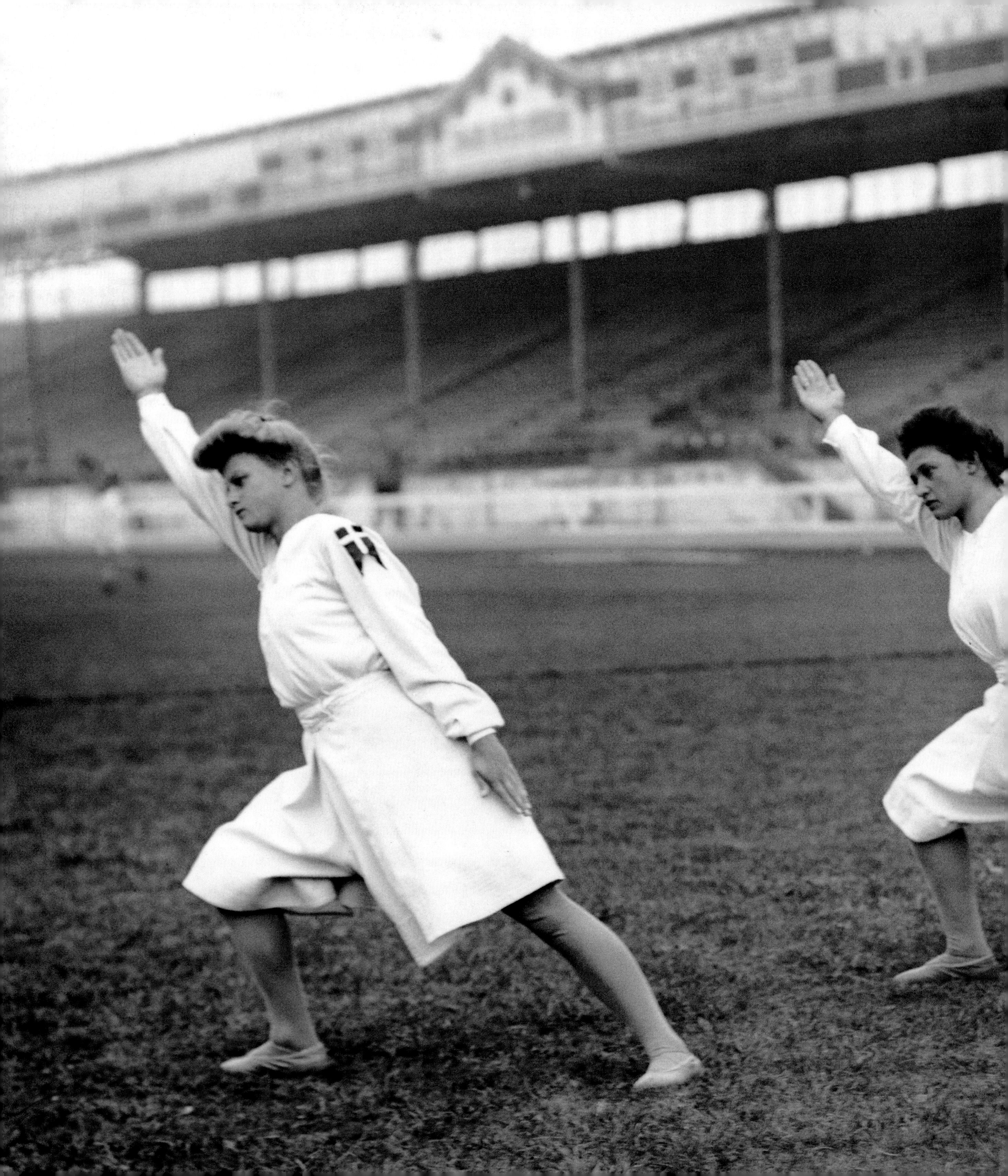

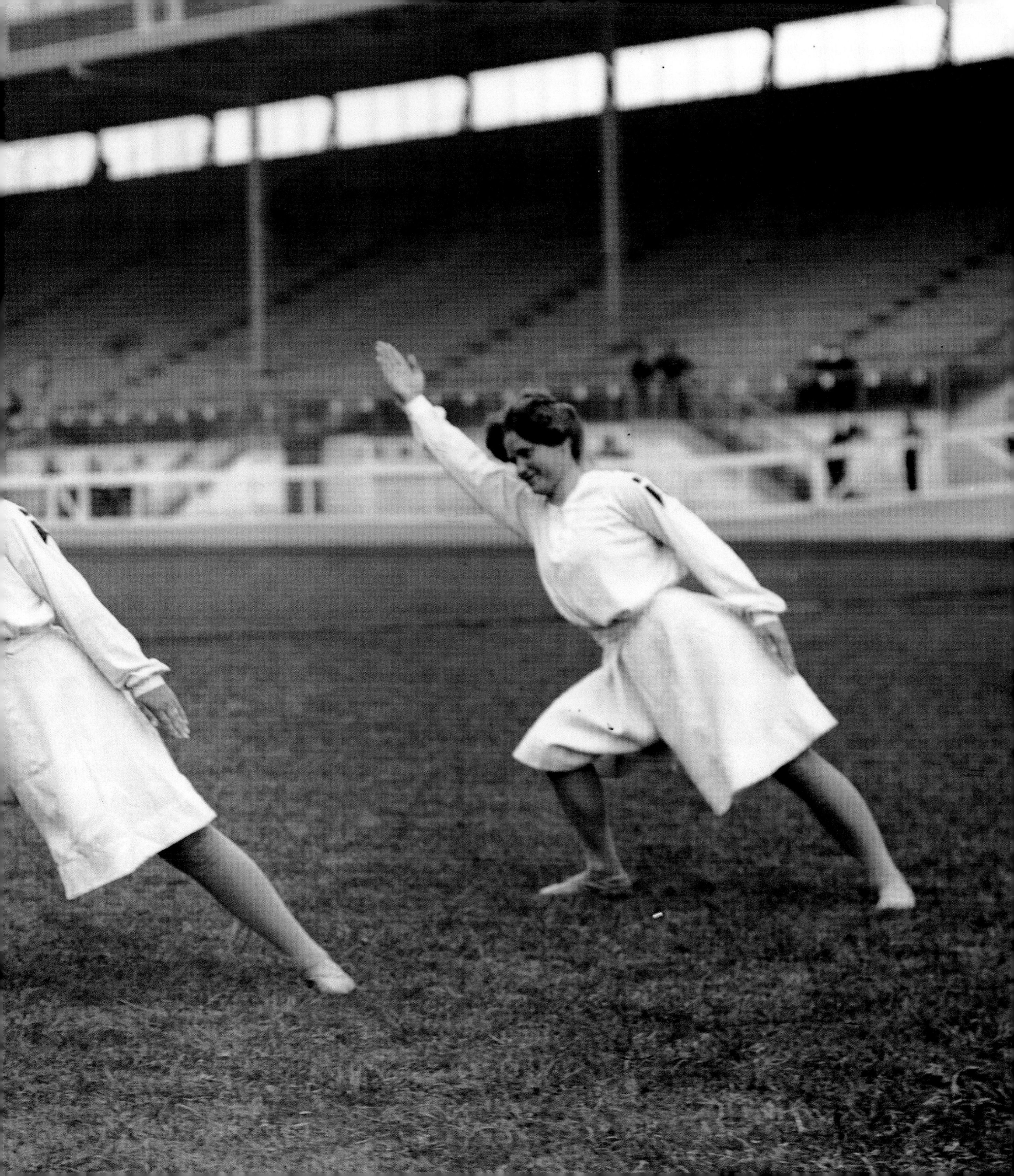

01
The inaugural meeting at Brooklands, 1907

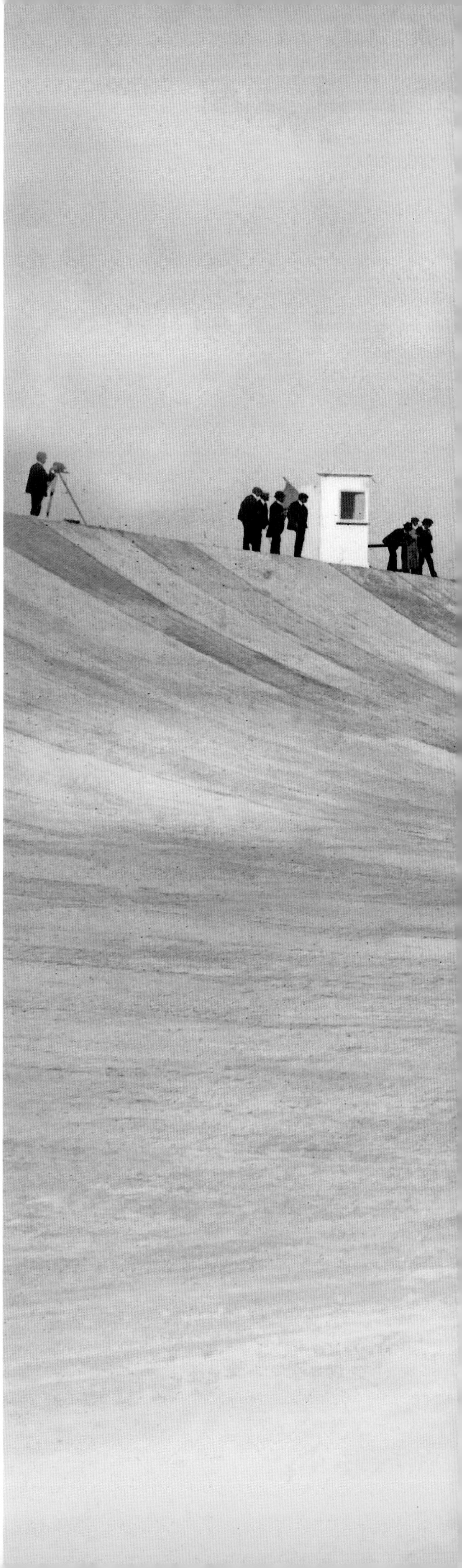

CIRCUIT

As the popularity of motor sport grew, the speed of racing cars increased and the danger of accidents became ever greater, motor racing moved from public roads onto purpose-built circuits where the danger to drivers and spectators was reduced, although by today's standards, safety measures were extremely rudimentary. Circuits like Brooklands in England and Daytona and Indianapolis in the United States, became the testing grounds of motor car design and the venues for record-breaking attempts. The ultimate test for car and driver was the new Grand Prix races, the first taking place in 1908 in France – a marathon event lasting two days.

The speed of motor racing was difficult for photographers during the first few decades of the twentieth century to deal with because of the limitations of the equipment they had at their disposal. The resulting images were static and did not convey the increased speeds in motor racing due to the improvements in design and engine technology. The repetitive nature of racing round a circuit, however, gave photographers the opportunity to pick their vantage point and to plan and control their pictures in advance more than was possible in other sports. This allowed them to take best advantage of advancing technology as the speed of film improved.

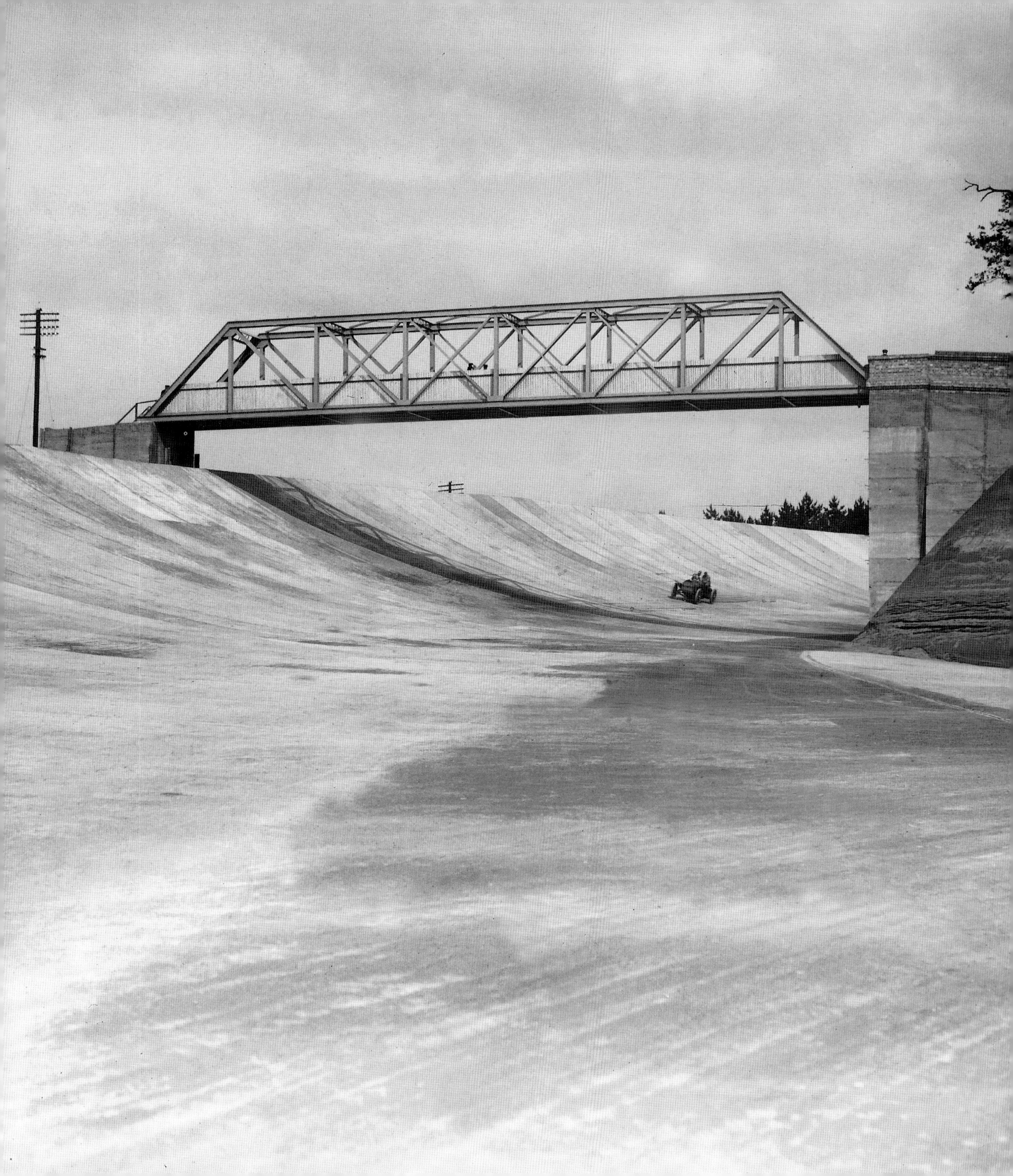

02
Jules Goux in his Peugeot at Brooklands, 1913

03
Chas Jarrot at Brooklands with his De Dietrich, 1908

04
Frank Newton in a Napier at Brooklands, 1907

05
A J Hancock in his Vauxhall at Brooklands, 1909

06
J Cocker on a Singer motorcycle at Brooklands, 1913

07
W O Bentley in his DFP car, 1914

08
A race in progress at Brooklands, 1908

09 (OVERLEAF)
Cars line up for the 100 mile race at Indianapolis, c.1910
Paul Thompson

02
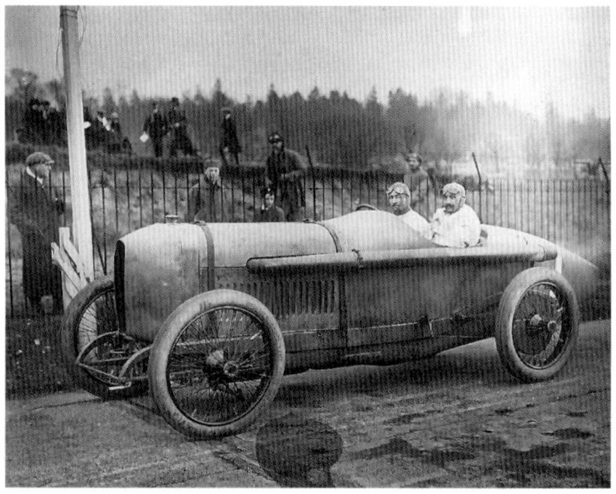

03
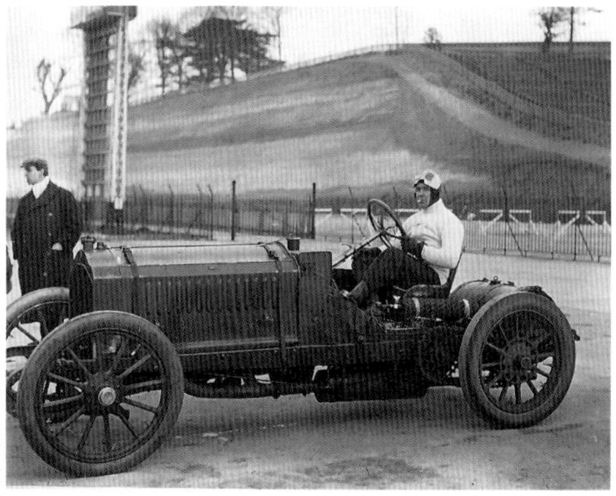

04
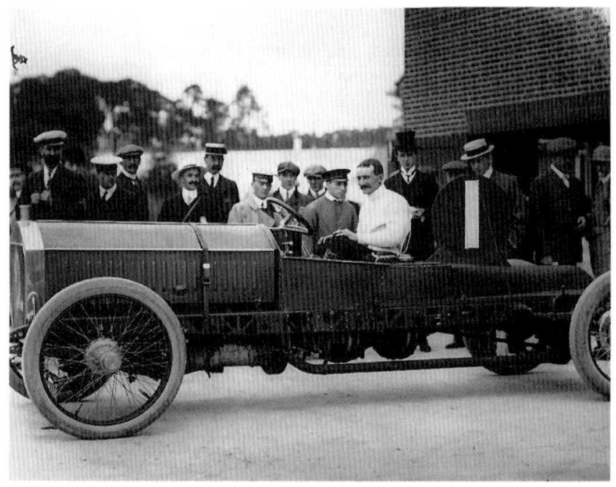

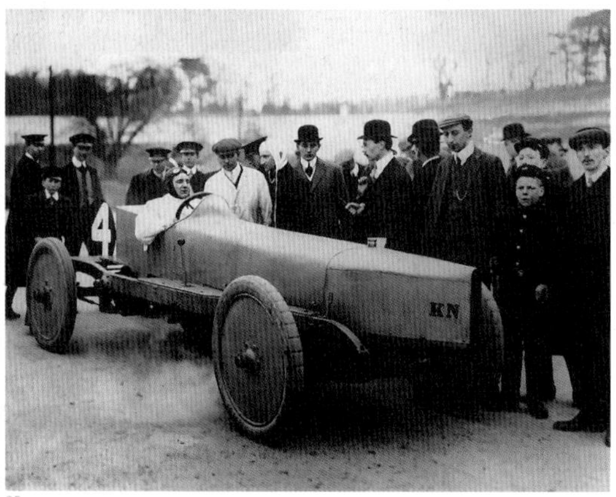

05

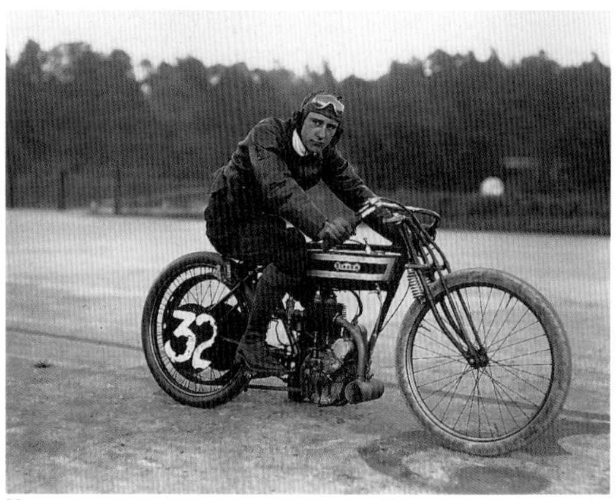

06

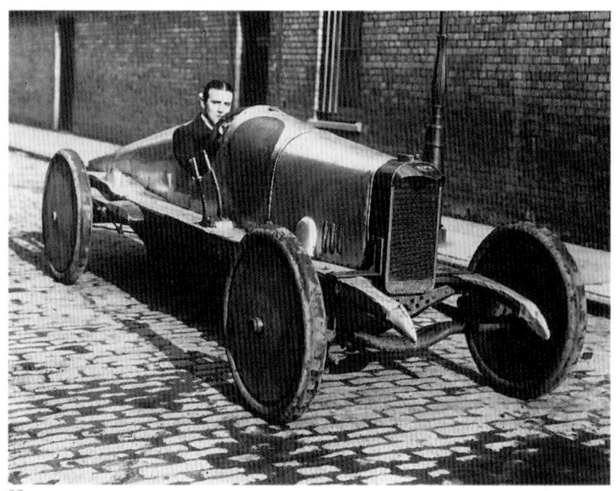
07

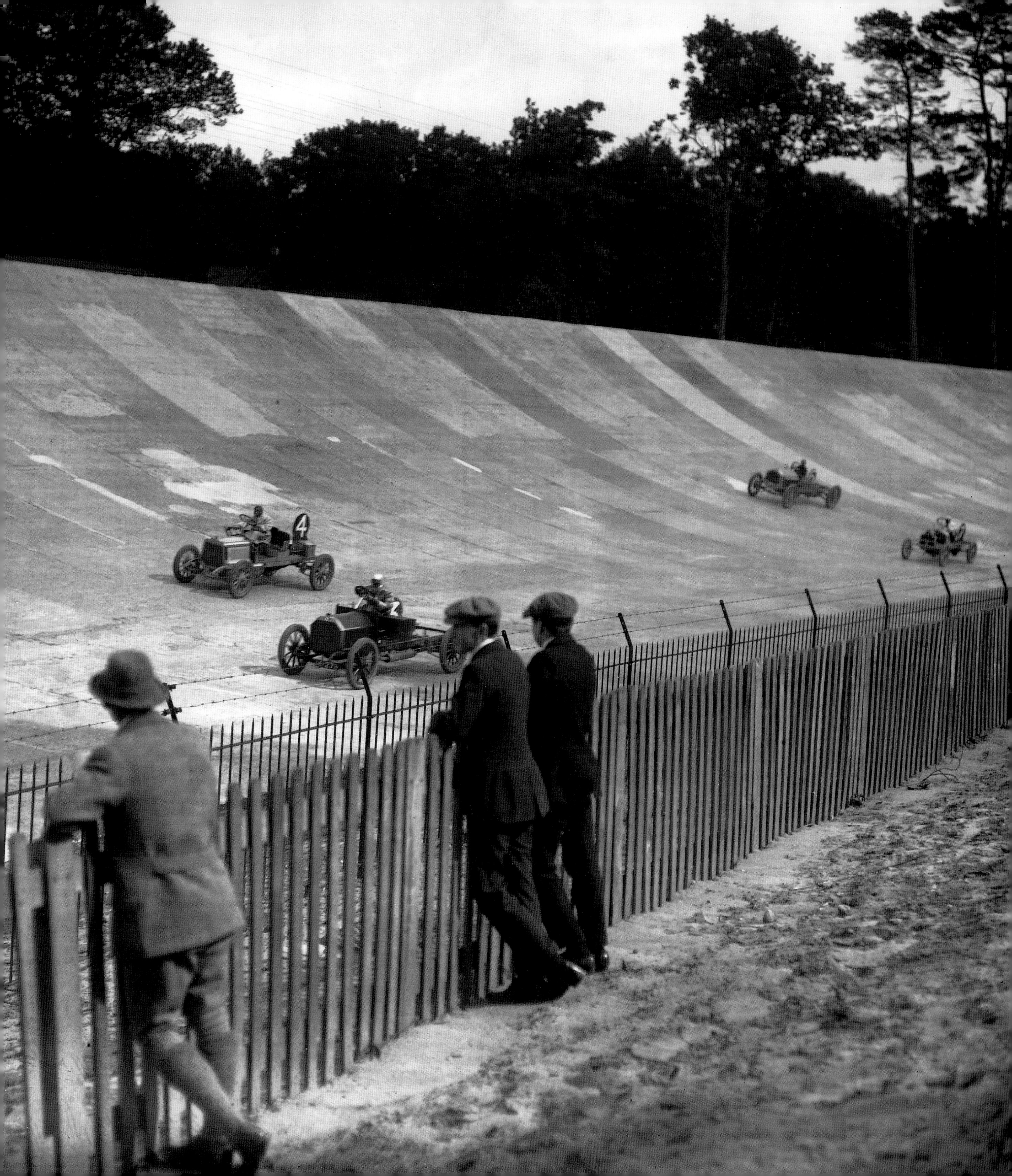
4

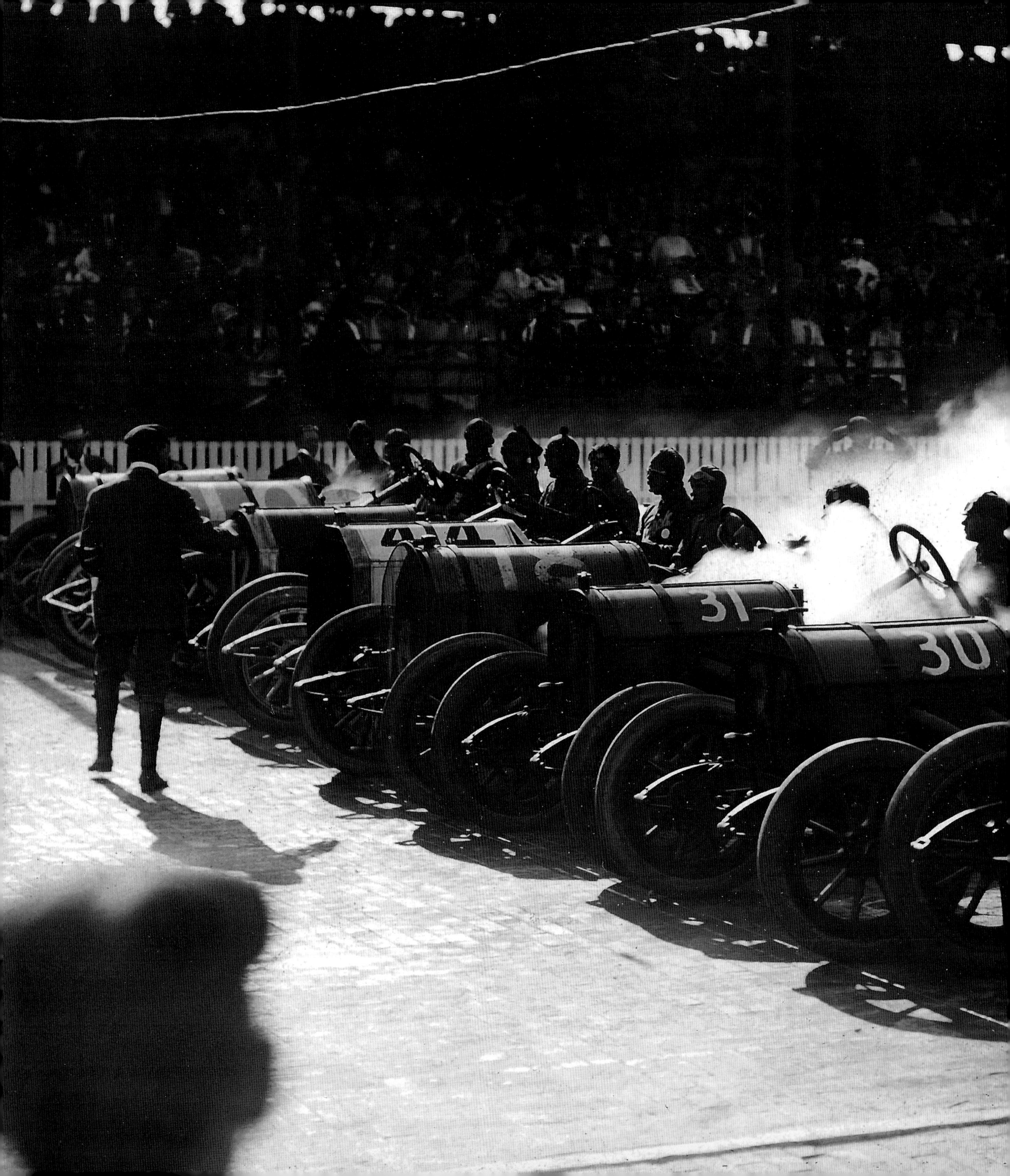

31
30

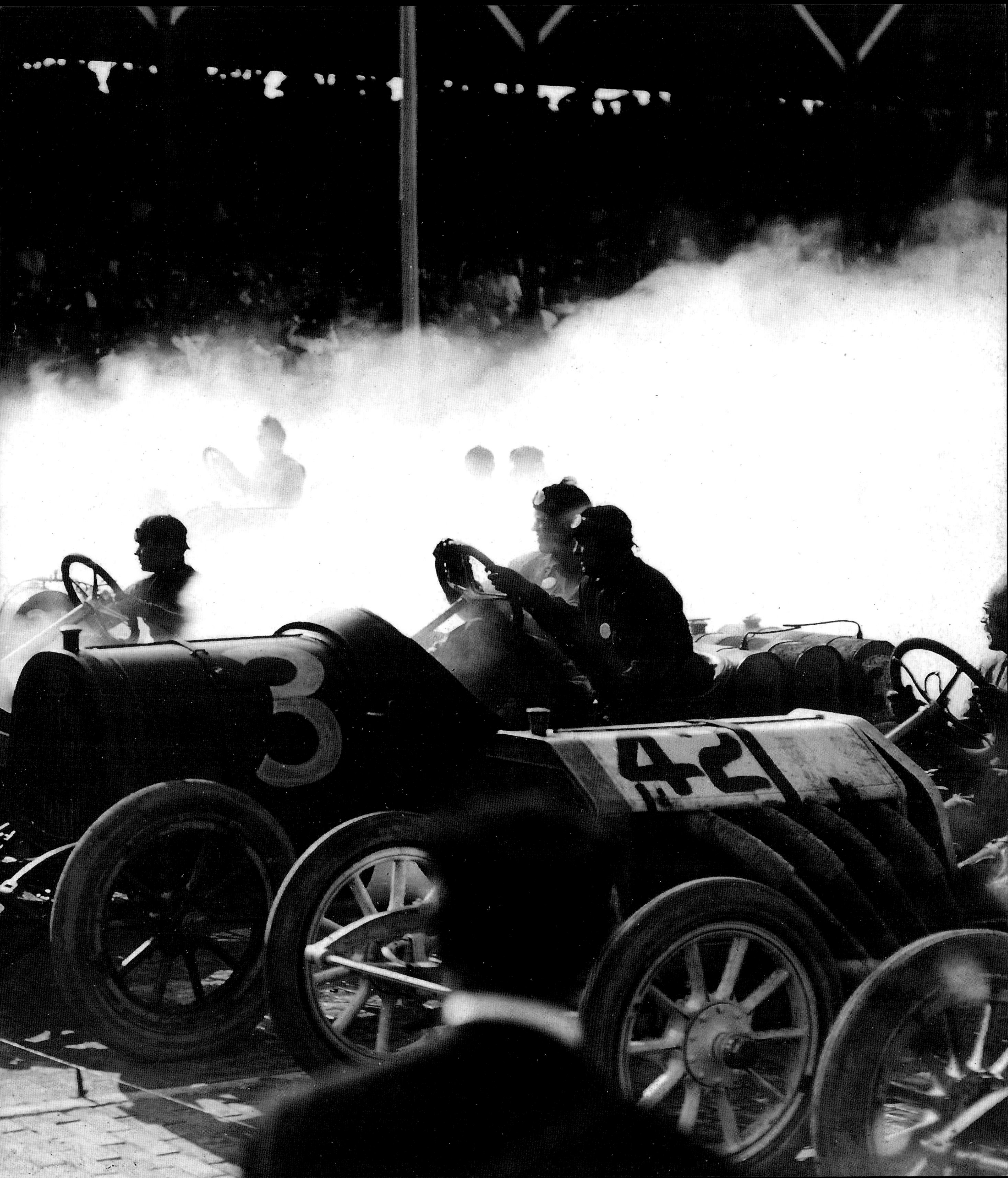
3
42

10/11
Georges Boillot on his way to victory in the French Grand Prix, Amiens, 1913

12 (OVERLEAF)
Moore-Brabazon's wrecked Minerva at Brooklands, 1907

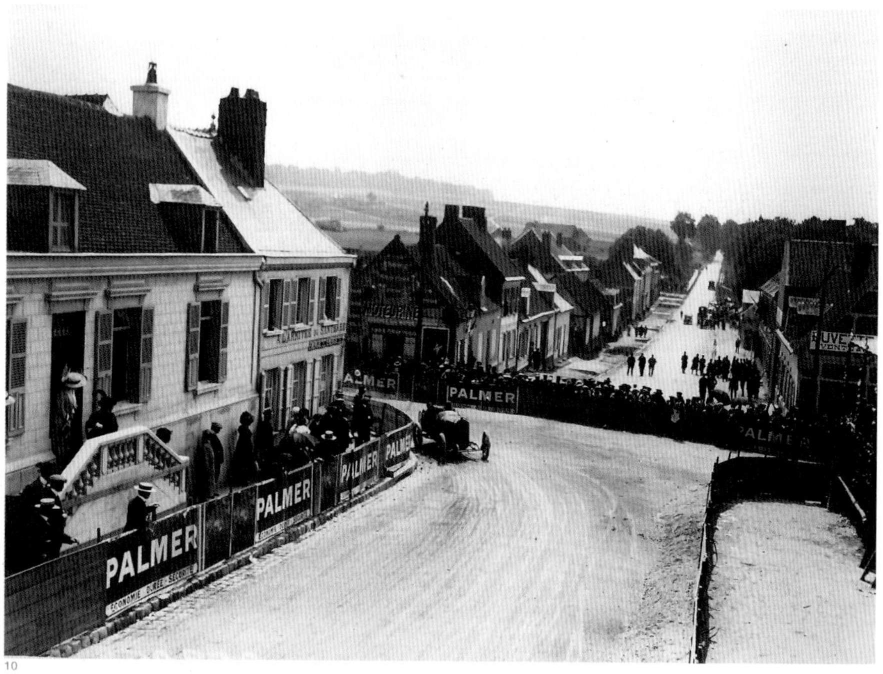

10

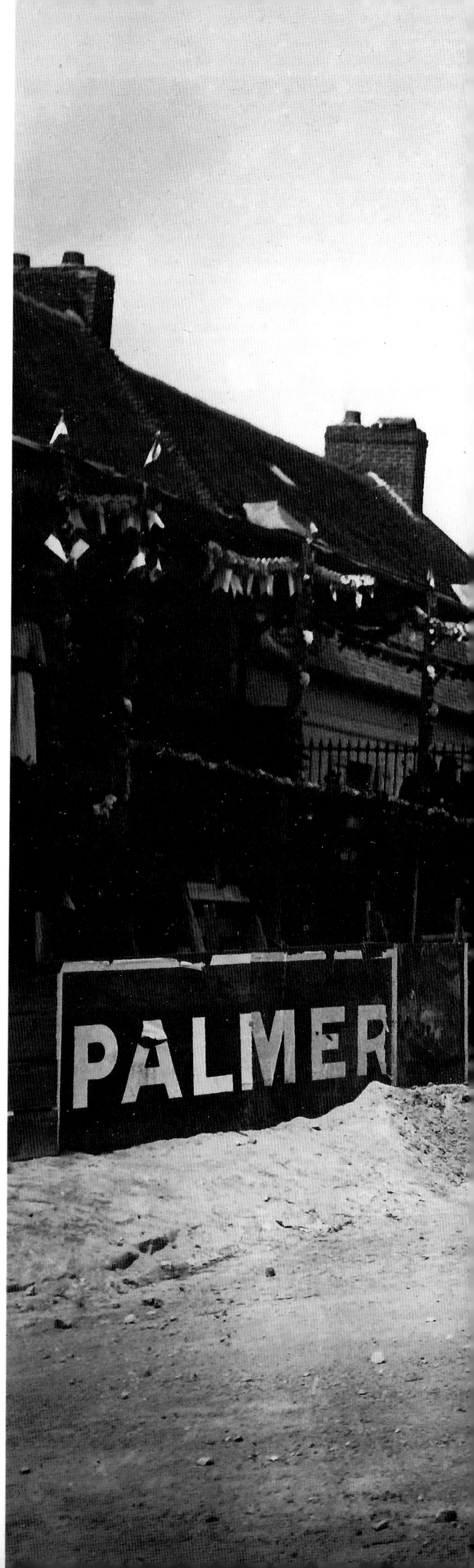

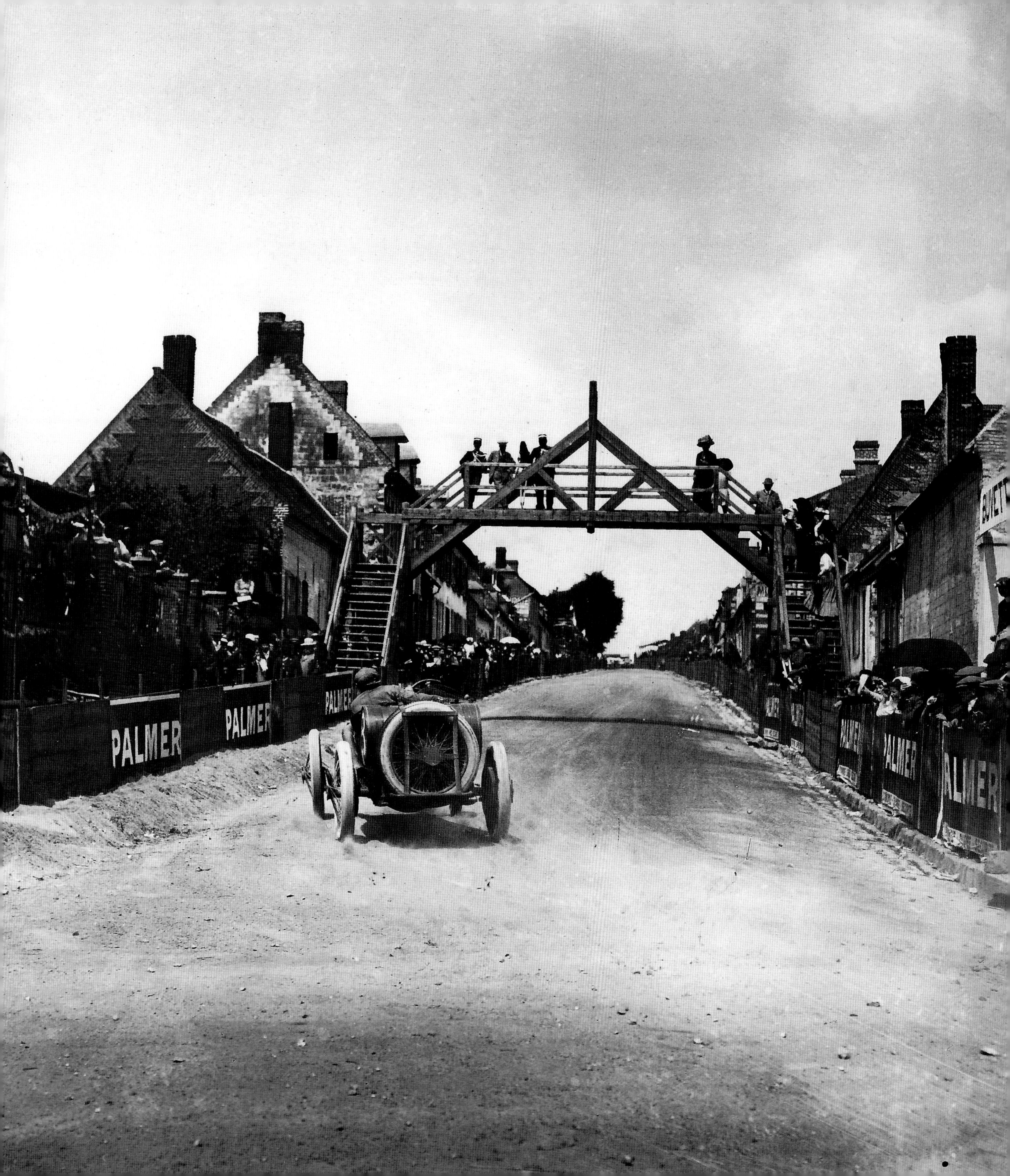
PALMER
PALMER
PALMER
PALMER

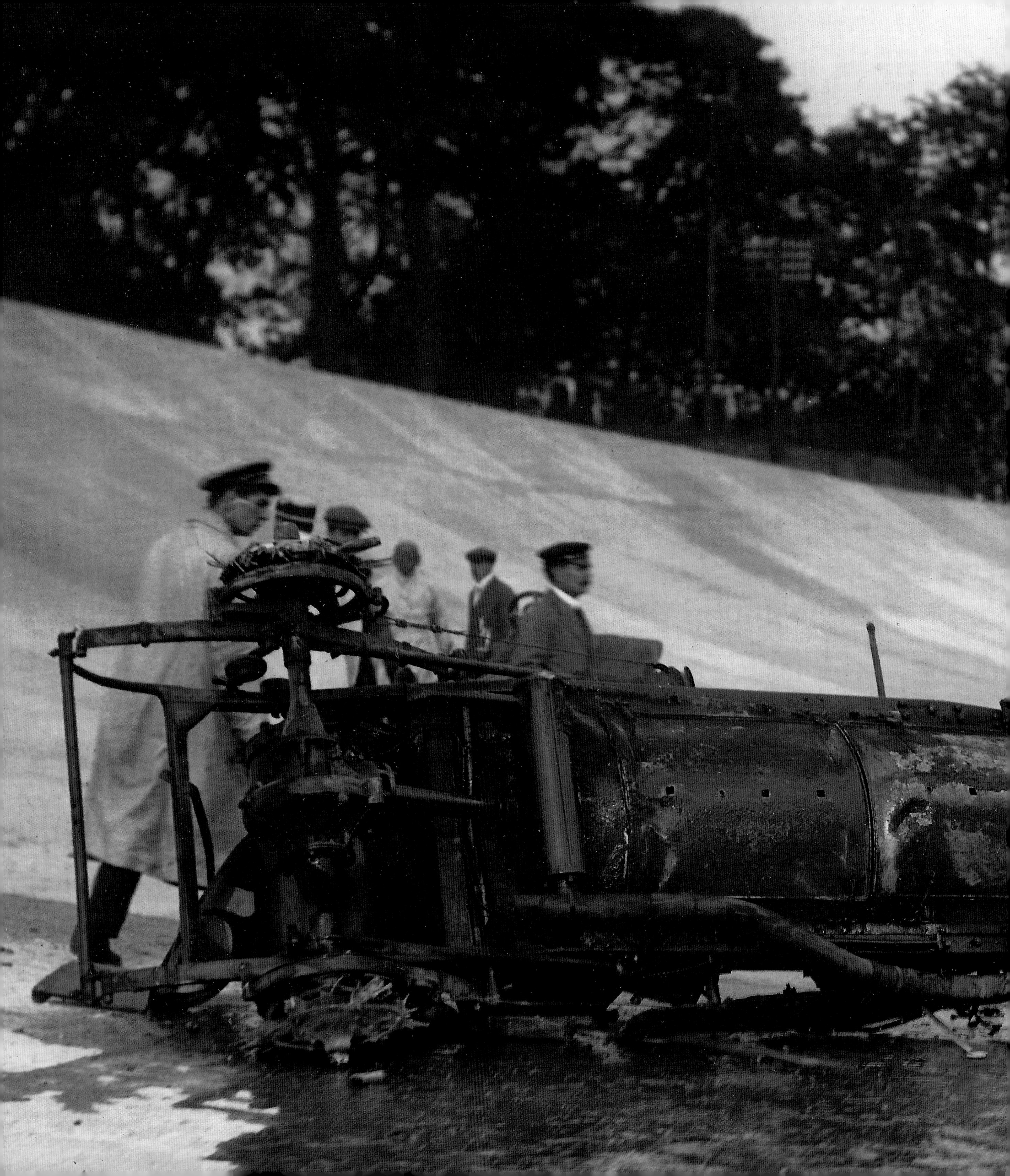

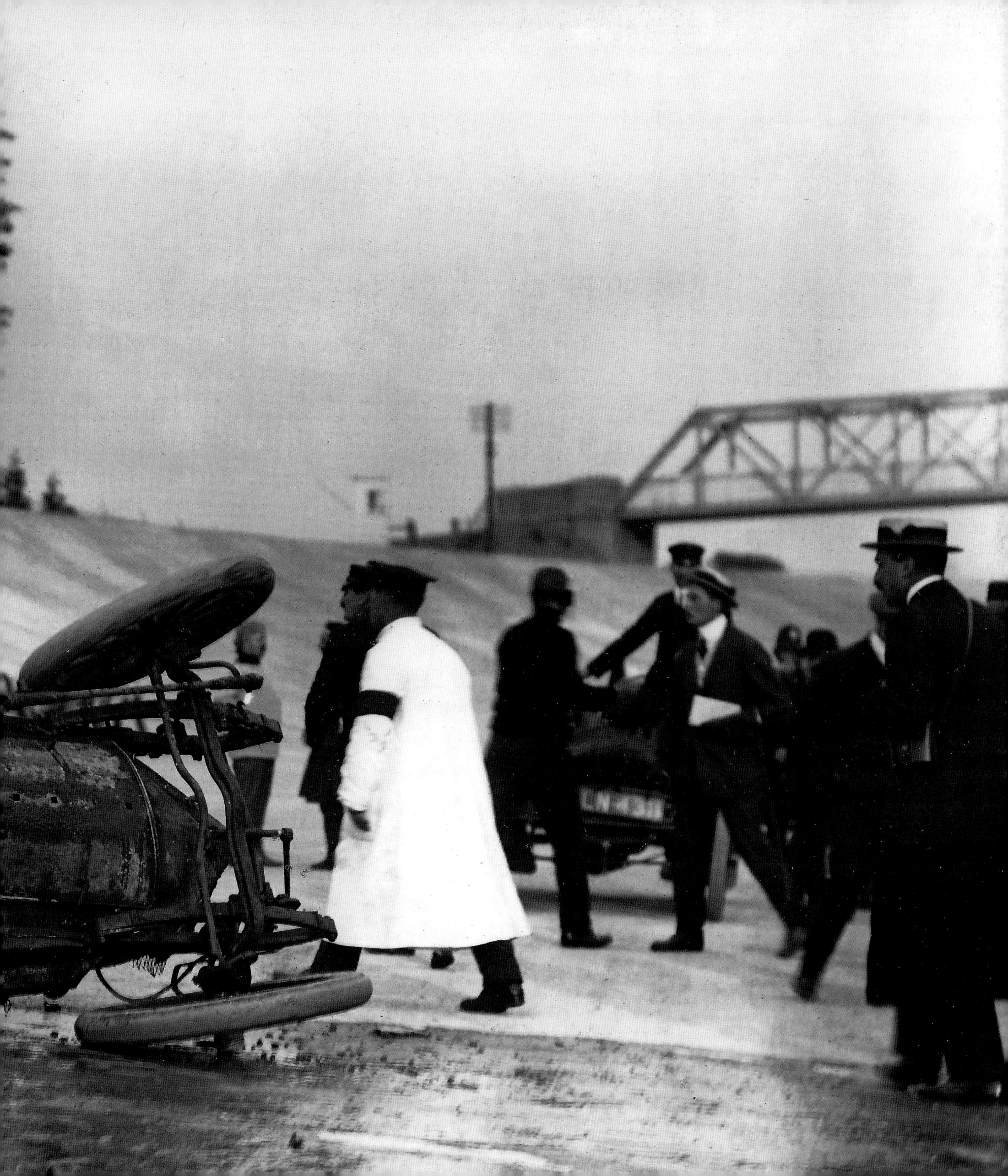

01–04
The marathon route running across open fields and into the stadium

MARATHON

The 1908 Olympics held in London at the White City Stadium, unlike the previous two Games, which had been part of World Fairs, was held as a sporting event in its own right. This was to prove successful, with crowds of 100,000 watching the proceedings. The Games produced both excitement and controversy with one race in particular catching the imagination of the public – the marathon. Starting at Windsor Castle and finishing in the stadium, the route can be traced by following the black line inscribed on these photographs. The Italian Dorando Pietri was the first to cross the finishing line, but was disqualified. On his last lap of the stadium he collapsed several times and was helped to his feet by race officials. Assistance being illegal, the gold medal was awarded to the American John Hayes who had come in second. For the majority of the crowd, however, Pietri was the true winner, and this was acknowledged the following day when he was awarded a special gold trophy. The photograph of Pietri crossing the finishing line is perhaps the first image of a sporting event to achieve the status of great sports photography.

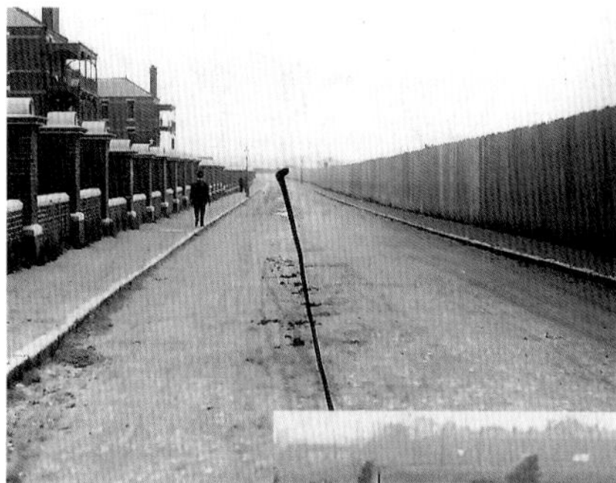
01

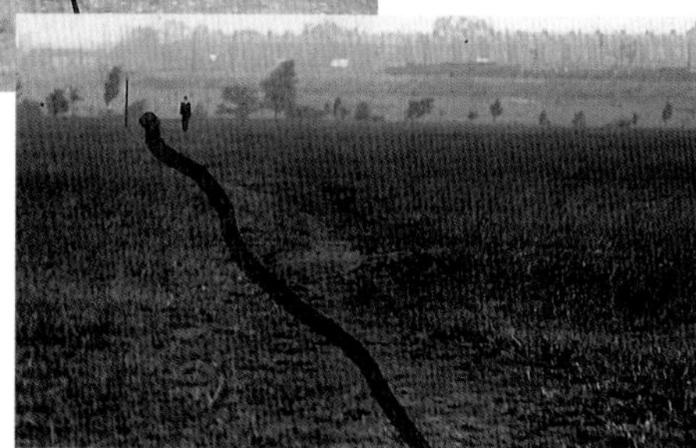
02

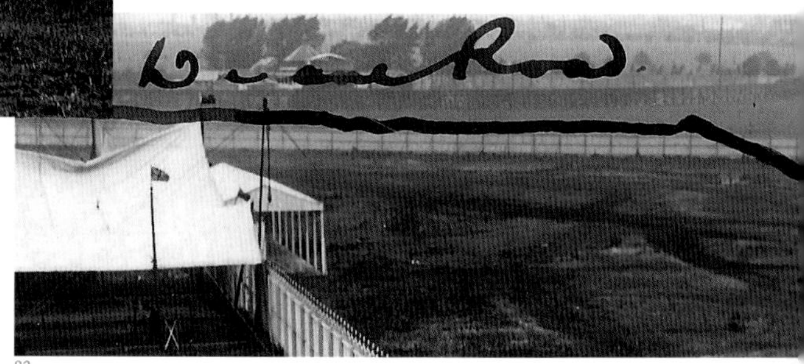
03

04

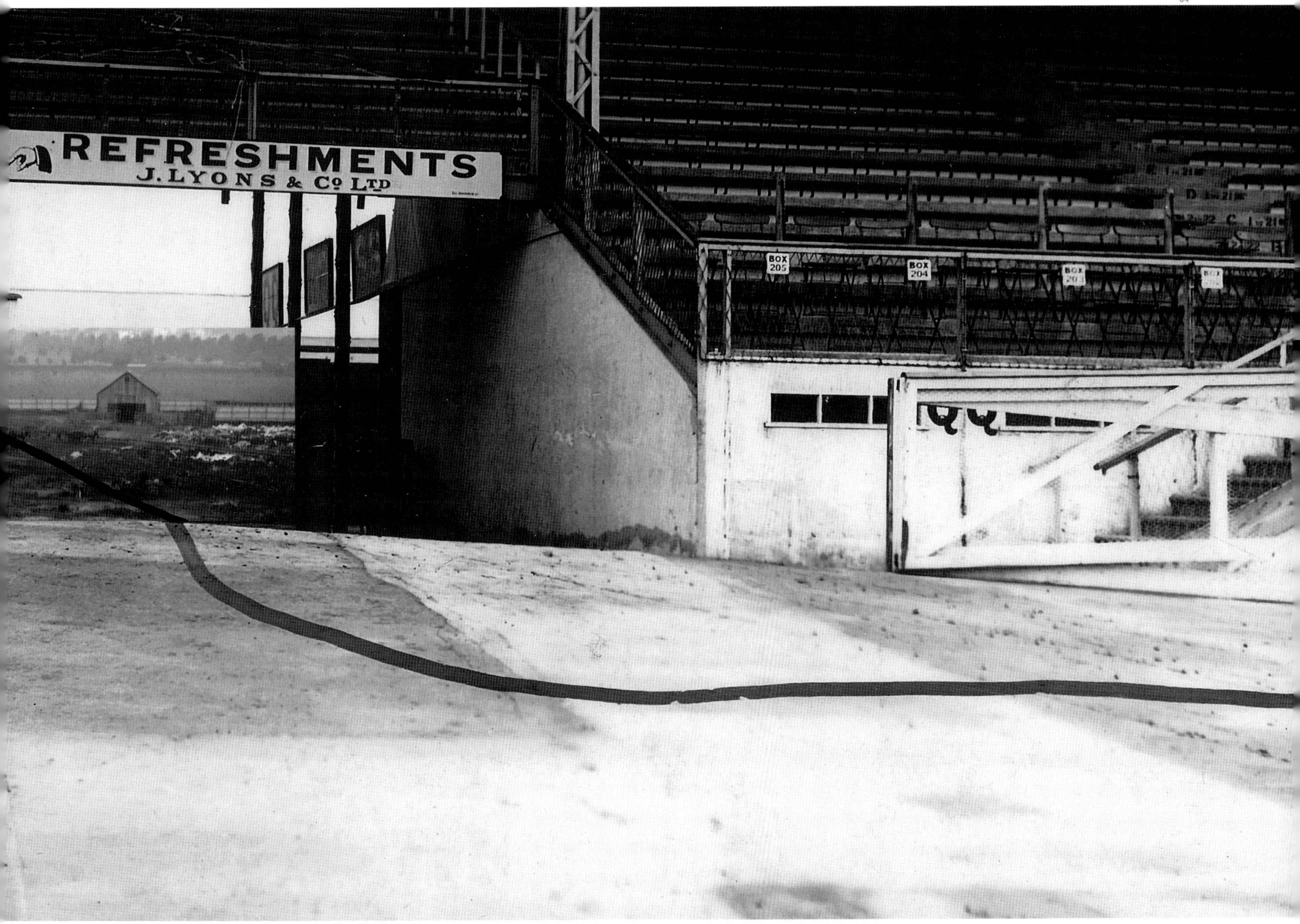

05
Pietri out in front towards the end of the race

06
Approaching the stadium

07 (OVERLEAF)
Pietri is helped across the line

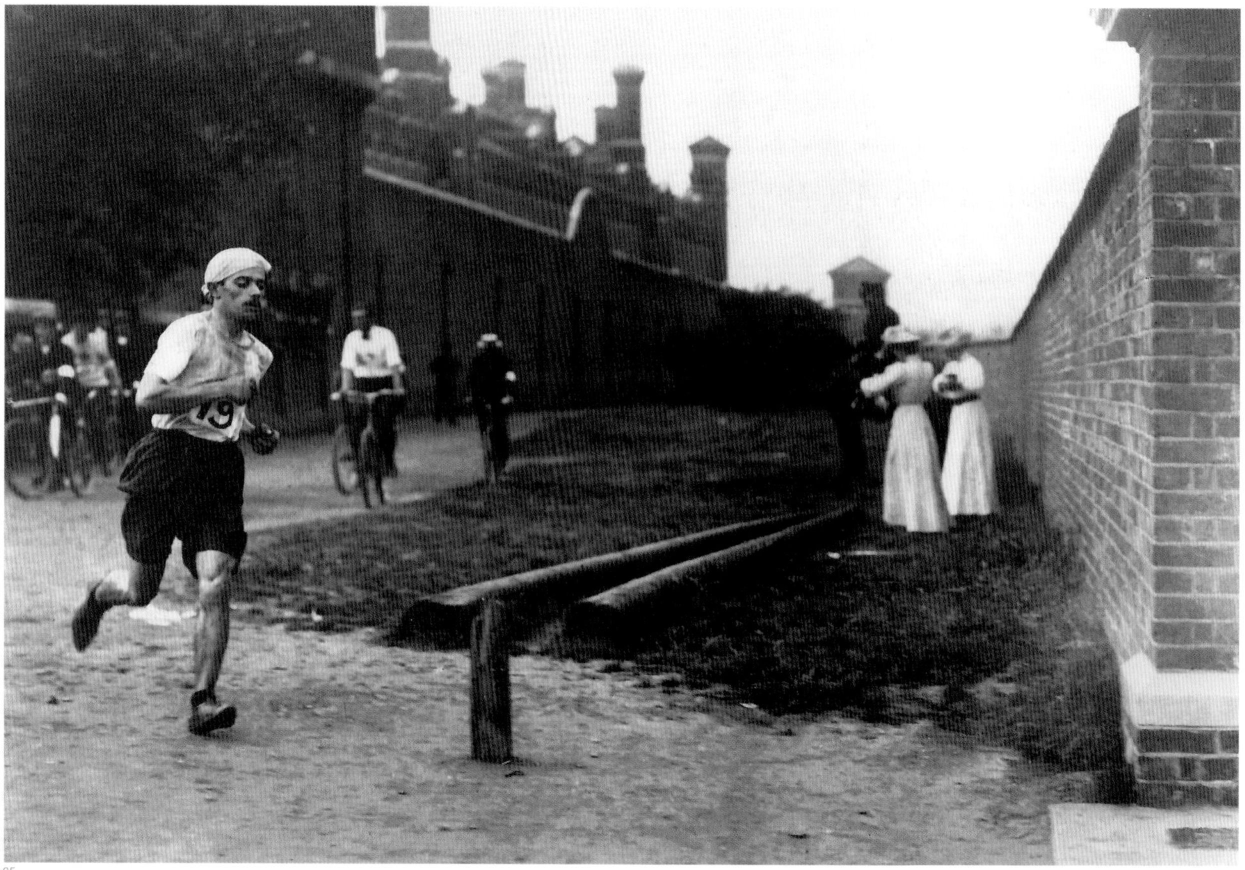

05

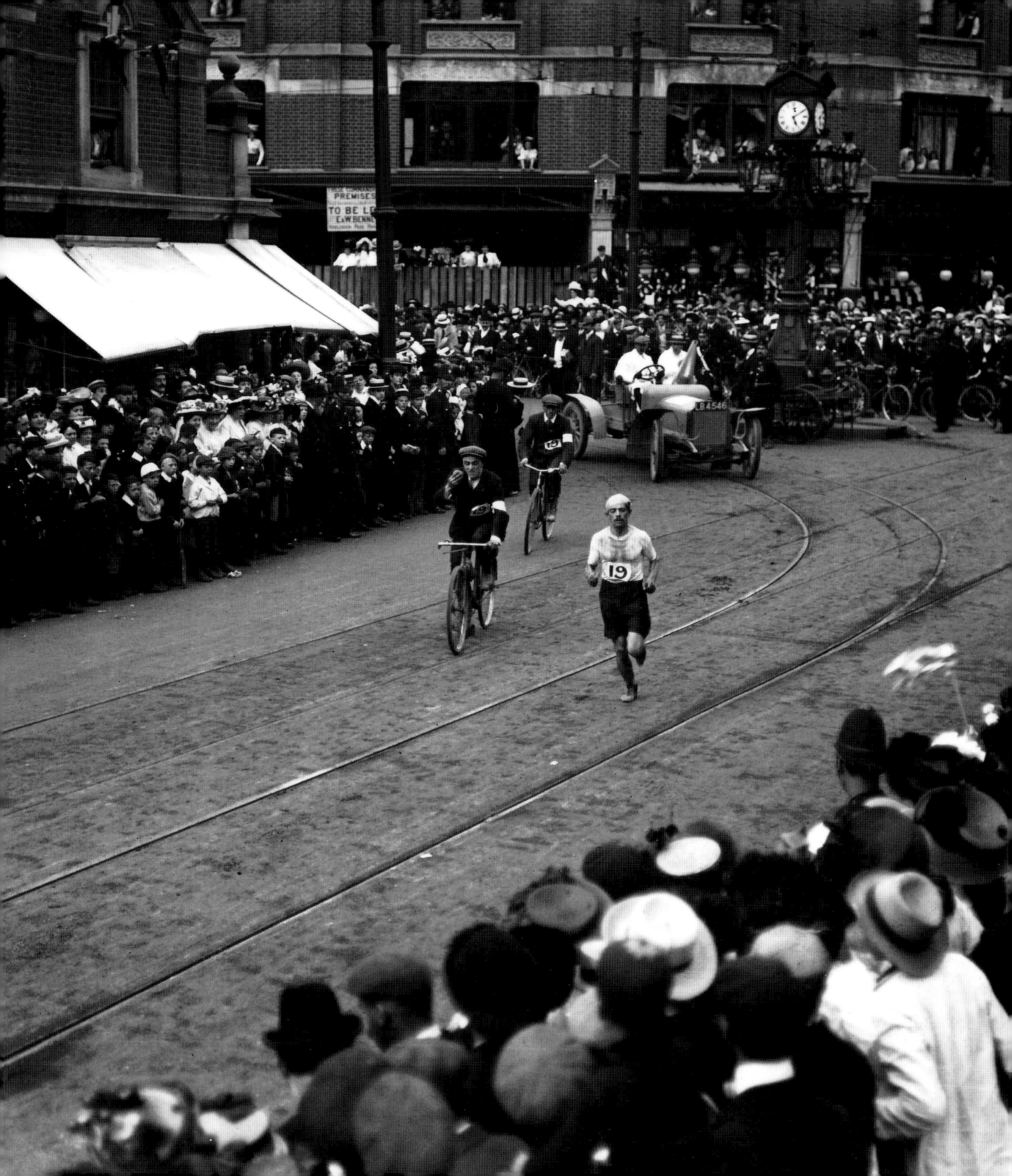
PREMISES
TO BE LE
E&W BENN
LB 4546
19

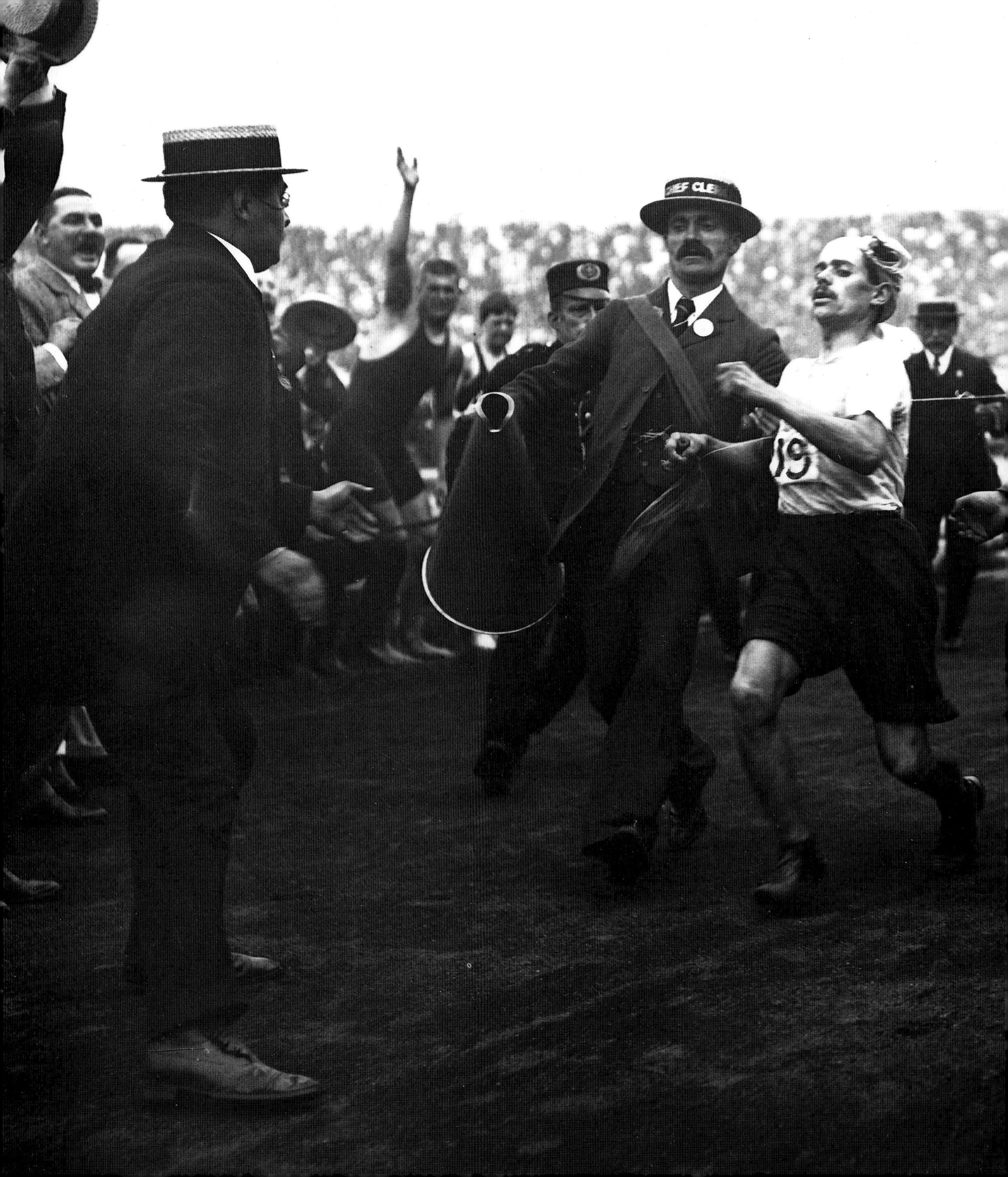
19

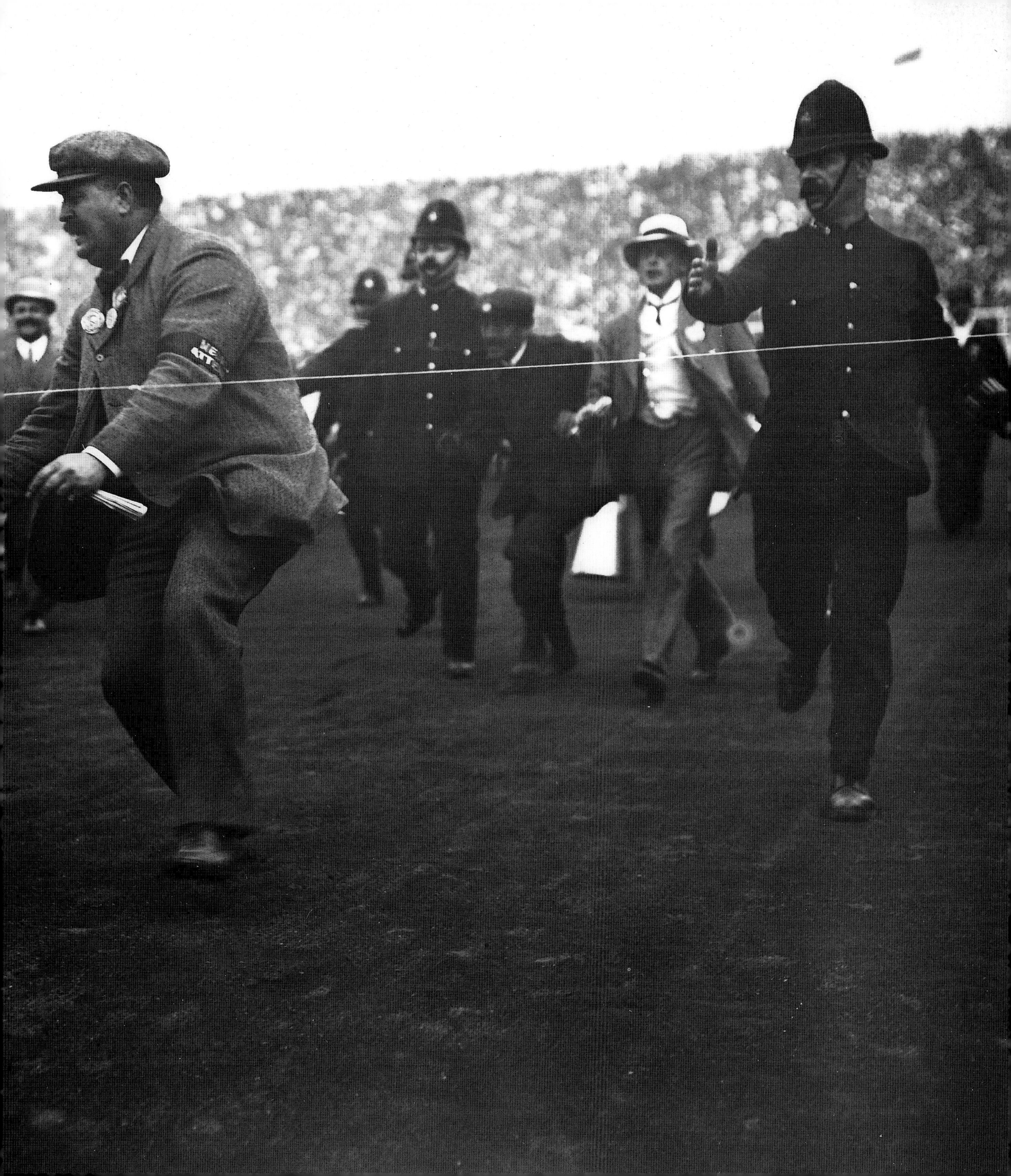

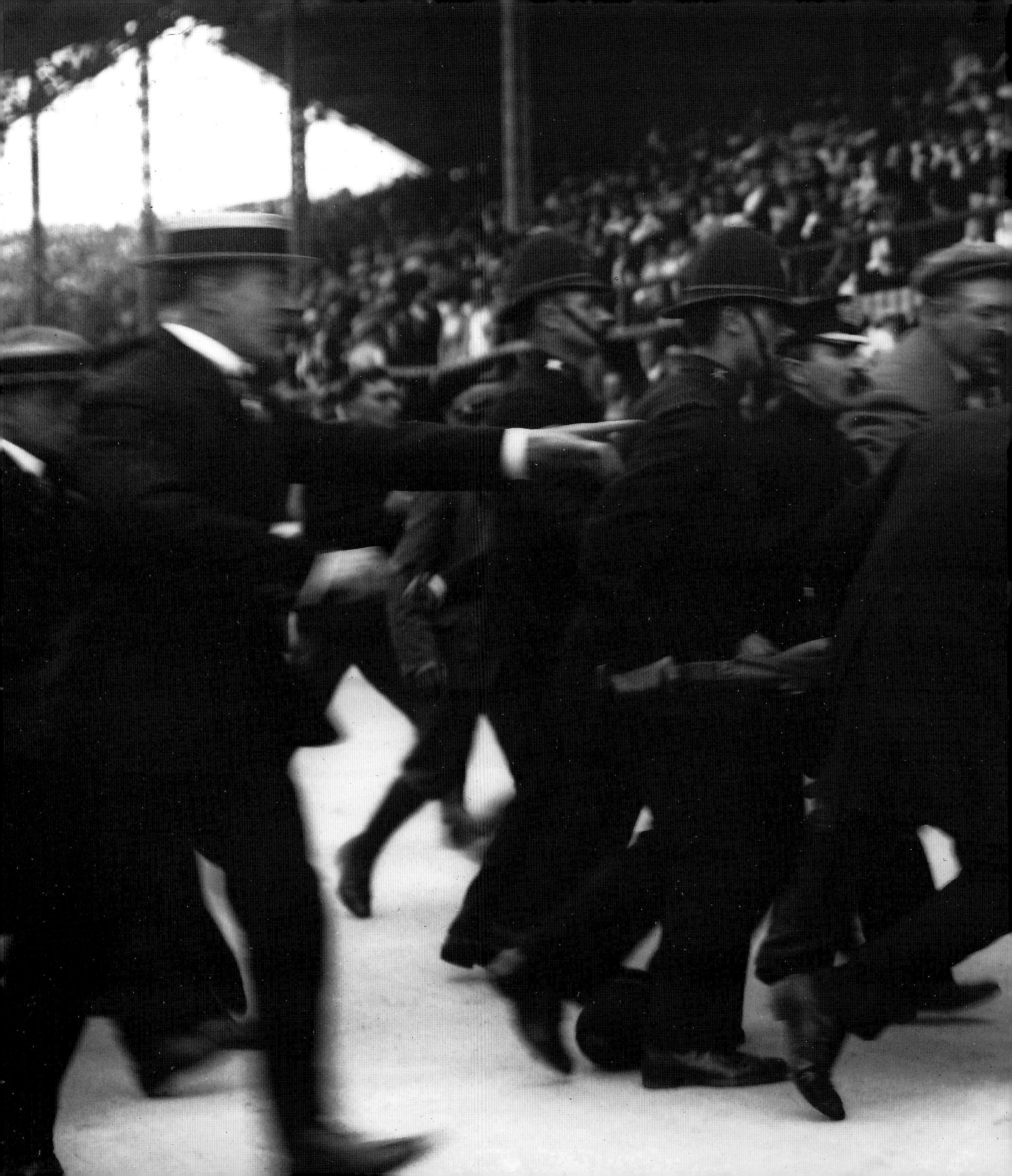

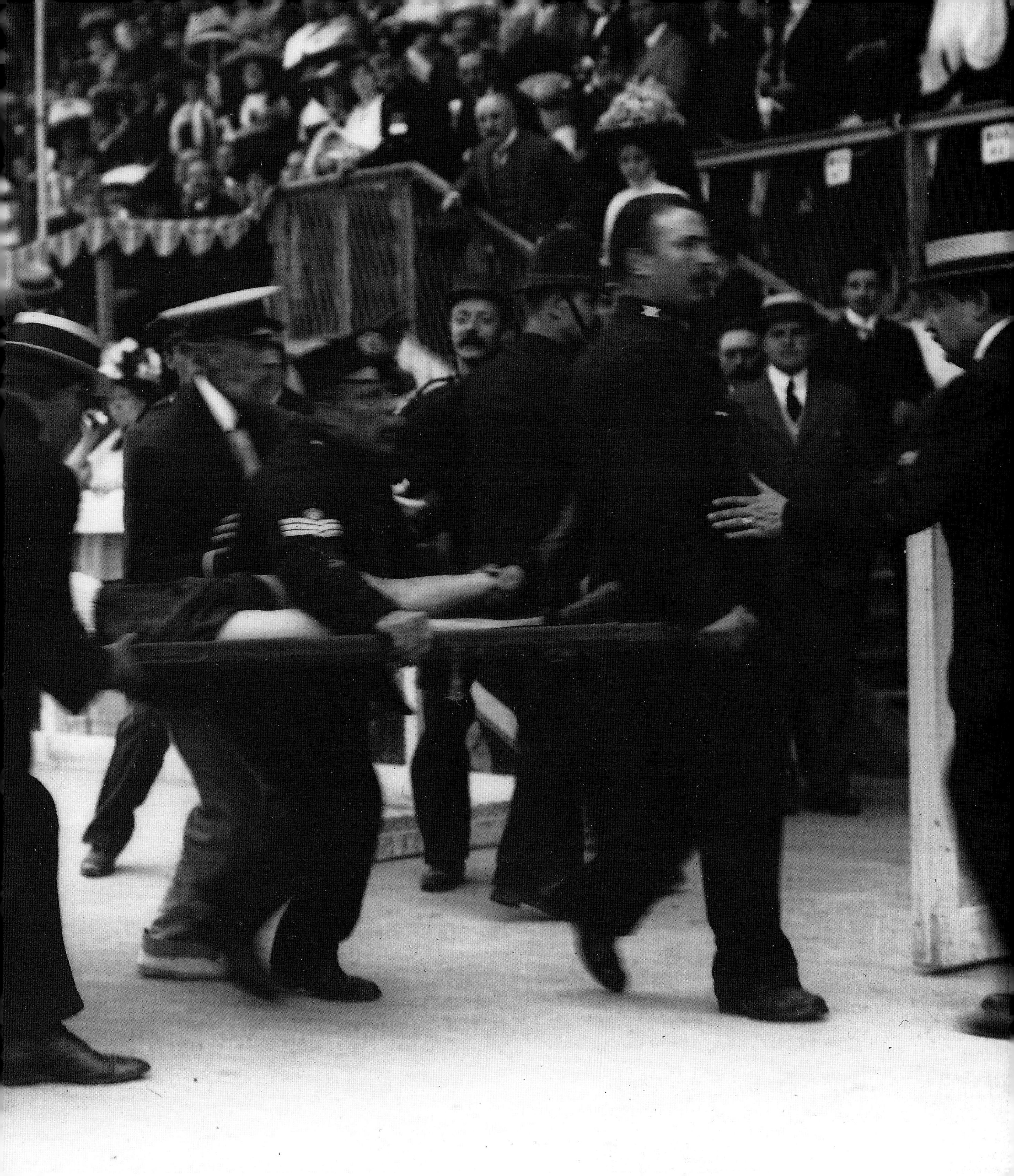

08 (PREVIOUS PAGE)
Pietri is stretchered away after the race

09
An official runs alongside John Hayes as he comes in second

10
John Hayes is carried on a lap of honour after being awarded victory as a result of Pietri's disqualification

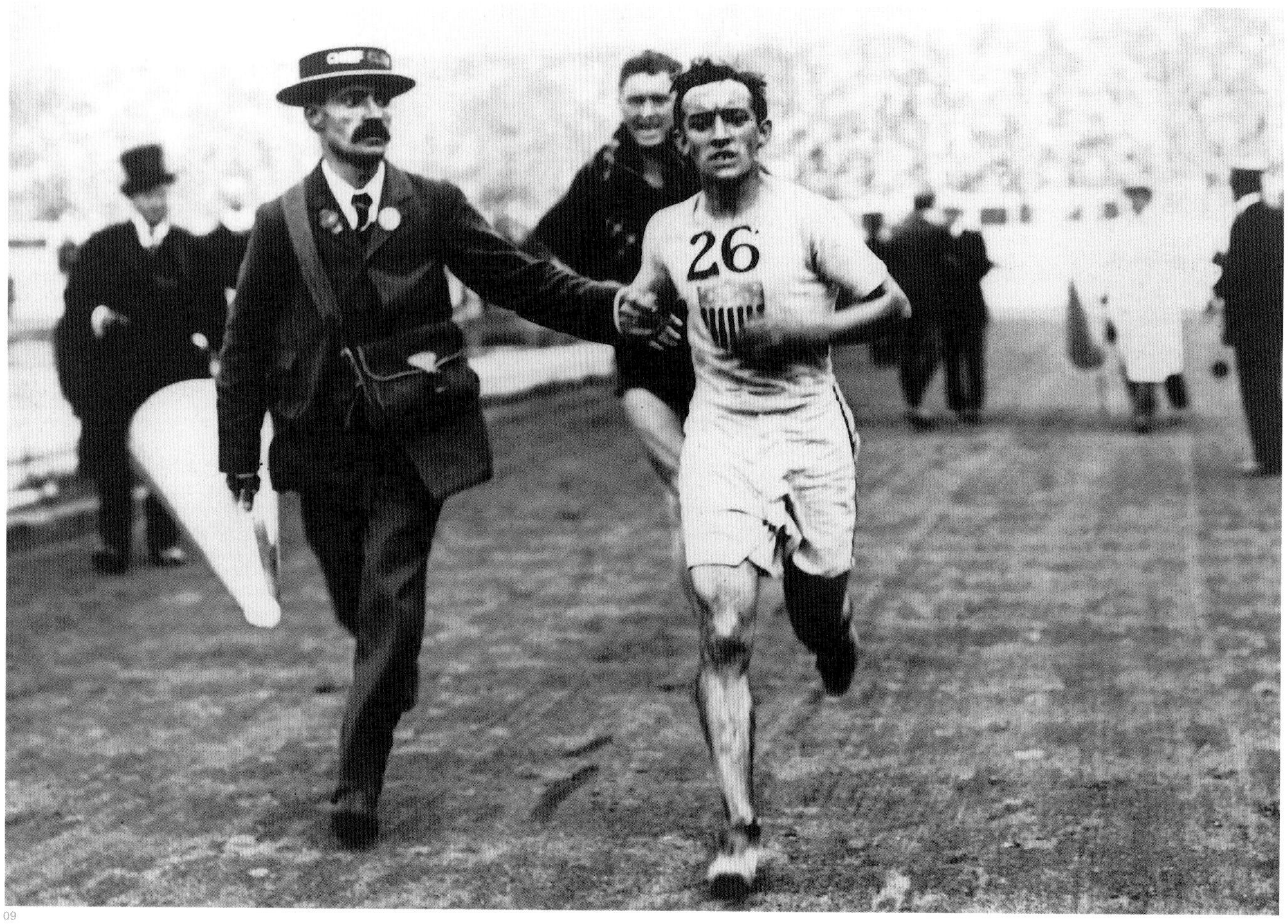

09

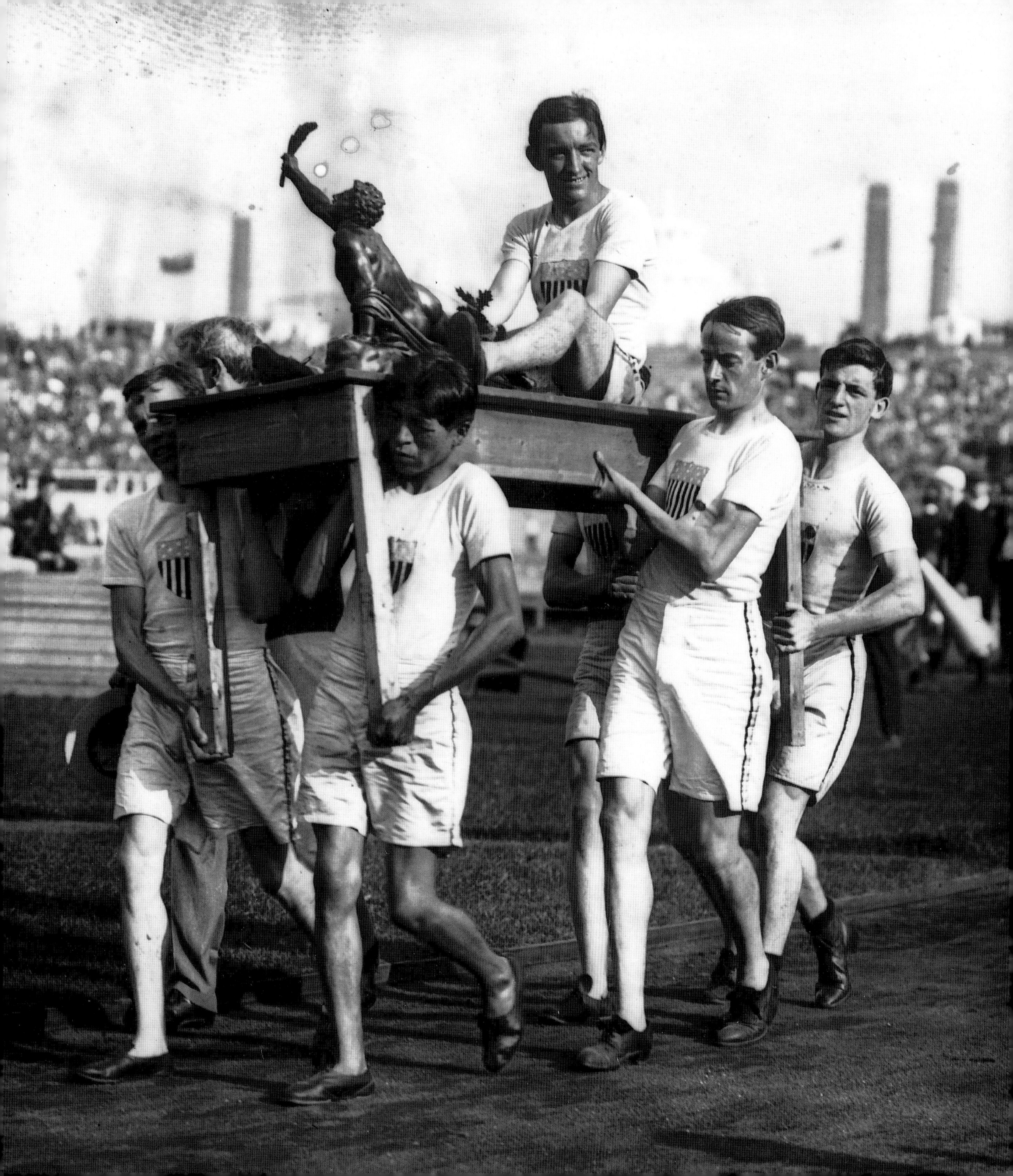

ENTHU

SIASM

03

1920–1940

During World War I most participating countries suspended professional sporting activity. When it resumed it was in an altered social climate. The war had encouraged an atmosphere of co-operation and togetherness, everyone pulling together for the greater good, regardless of class and sex, and this climate lasted for some years after 1918. People were willing to get involved in all types of sport and try new forms of games outside the rigid pre-war social structures – experimentation was rife, with new and unusual sports initiated. In the 1930s, faced with widespread poverty and consequently poor nutrition, governments encouraged their citizens to exercise and take part in sport, keen to improve their general wellbeing, or in Germany's case to promote the strength and fitness of its people. Health and fitness clubs encouraged people to take part in all sorts of gymnastics and synchronized exercises – everyone was enjoying themselves in the pursuit of achieving a healthy body.

Competing only for the glory of taking part was the abiding ethos of the amateur and the philosophy which encouraged mass participation in sport. The ideal of amateurism was already coming under pressure, however, as the public were keen to see the top international performers, who, unless they had substantial private means, could not afford to be full-time athletes. The struggle between amateurism and professionalism was to continue in some sports until the end of the century, but in the 1920s and 1930s it was still the amateurs who enjoyed the senior status, and some of the greatest sporting figures of the period proudly managed to maintain it.

Photographers in the 1920s and 1930s had to be generalists, sport being only one of the subjects that it was their job to cover. The sports photographs in this chapter therefore reflect the concerns of the photographers to record their subject in a clear way. In many respects these are simple and direct photographs, and our enjoyment in looking at the images today comes from what we see as the lack of contrivance by the photographer. Efforts were made to inject more dynamism into the sporting image, involving setting up unusual and original angles from which to make pictures, creating an apparently 'impossible' viewpoint. Photographers also took their cameras out onto the field and tried to create images of players close up, 'in action'. There was work to be done in the darkroom as well, doctoring the raw material of the photograph to create exciting graphic sporting images.

The greatest sporting achievements of the era included the remarkable success of Babe Ruth in baseball in the United States, attaining an unprecedented level of fame and popularity for a sportsman. American golfer Bobby Jones and Australian cricketer Don Bradman built reputations that few if any in their respective sports have challenged since, and the darkening political situation of the pre-war era was brought into sharp focus in sport when black American Jesse Owens upset Hitler's well-choreographed Olympics in Berlin in 1936, by winning four gold medals and making a mockery of the theory of an Aryan master race. Although only contested by thirteen countries, the inaugural soccer World Cup in Uruguay in 1930 established the way forward for the 'world game' and the tournament would, by the end of the century, challenge the Olympics as the world's premier sporting occasion.

INSTRUCTION

Through the medium of popular magazines photography took on the role of a visual aid, allowing 'correct' technique to be demonstrated to a wide audience. Sports like golf and tennis whose execution depends on some knowledge of technique, benefited from such instructional photo-stories, revealing the precious secrets of the experts to an eager audience of keen amateurs. Theories on how to hold a tennis racket or swing a golf club have changed over the years, but through the use of photography the special skills of sports became more accessible, increasing wider participation in sporting activities.

02

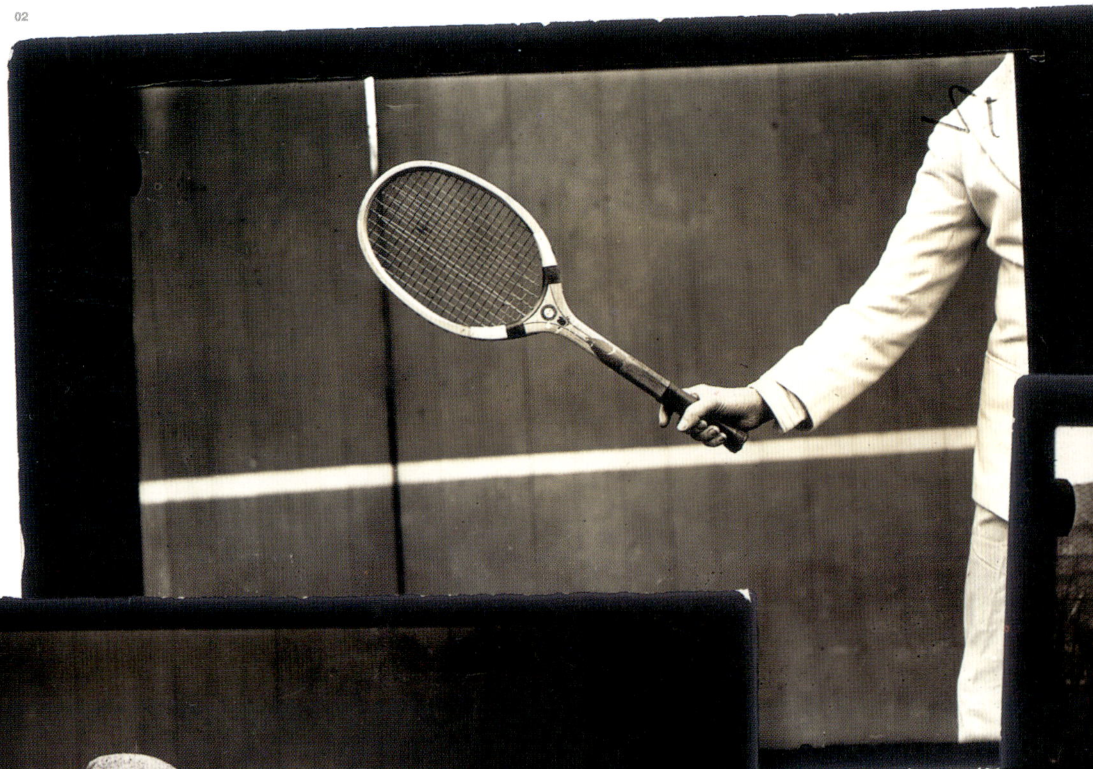

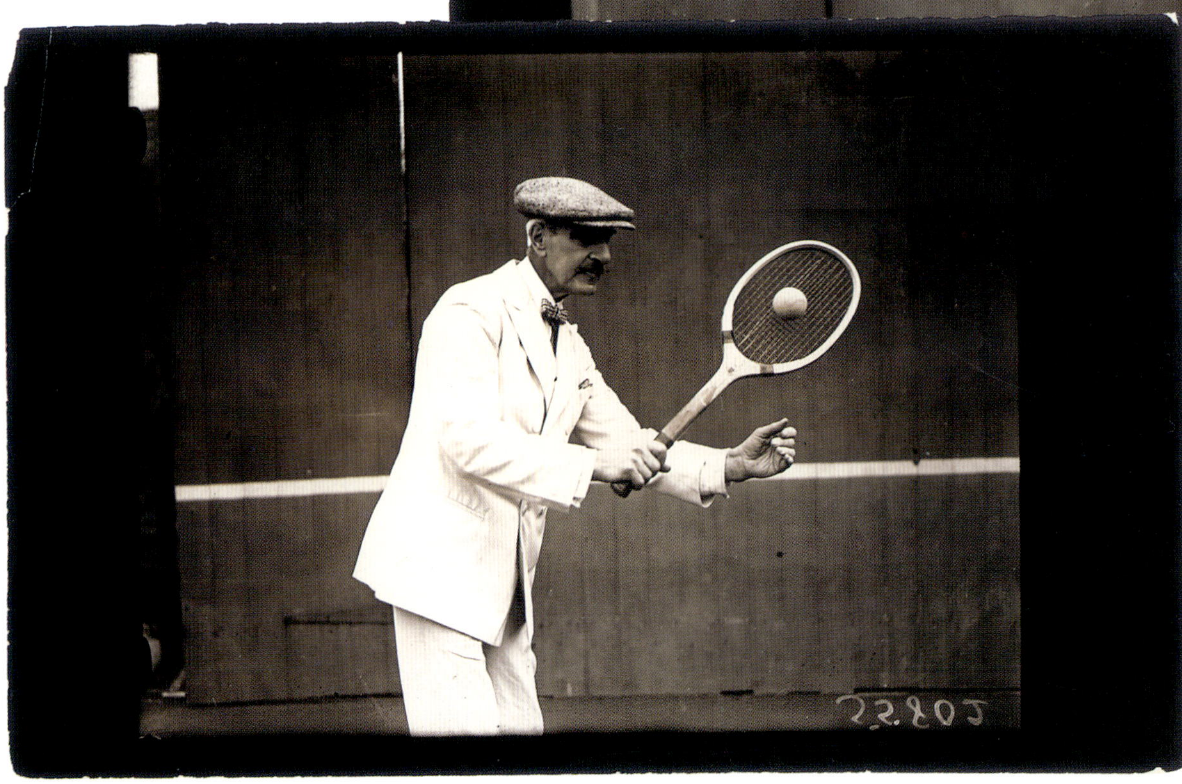

01

01–04
Demonstrating tennis technique, 1923

05 (OVERLEAF)
'Position for receiving service in doubles', 1920s

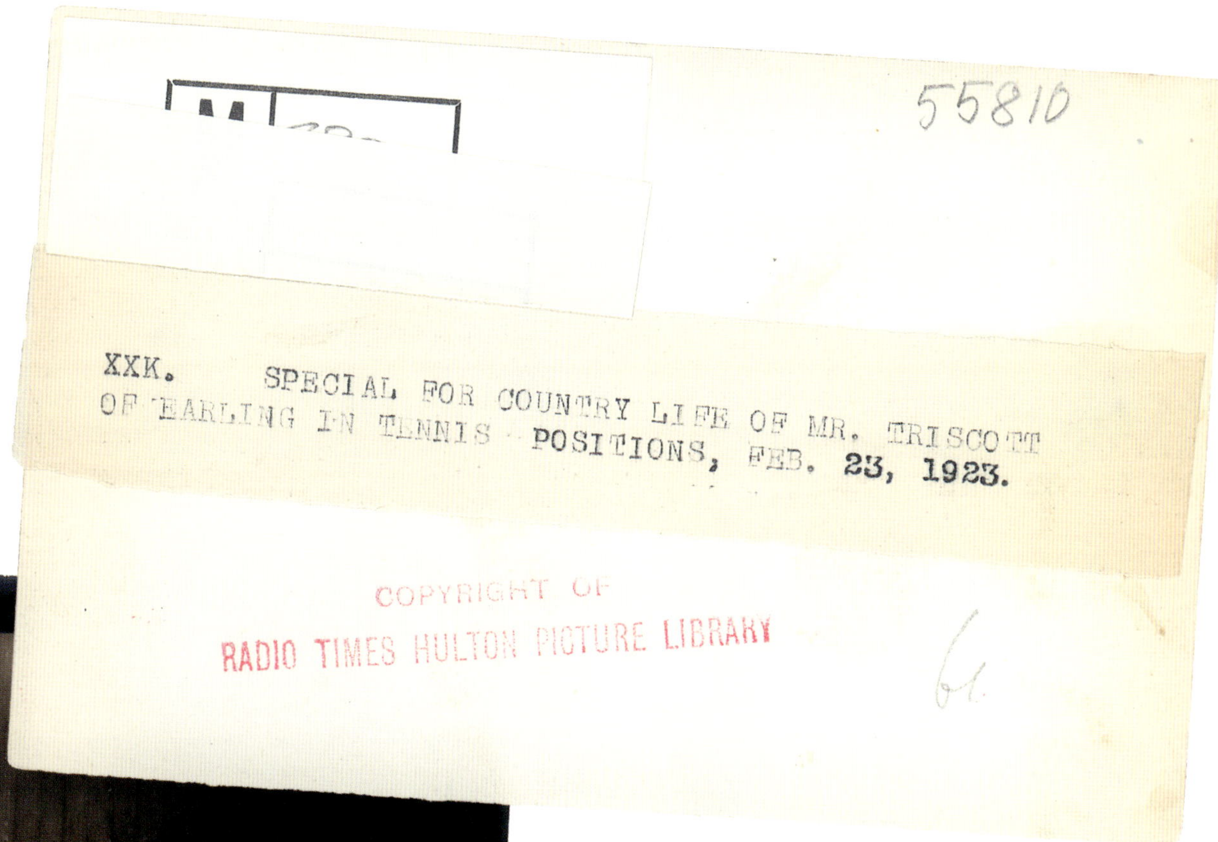

04

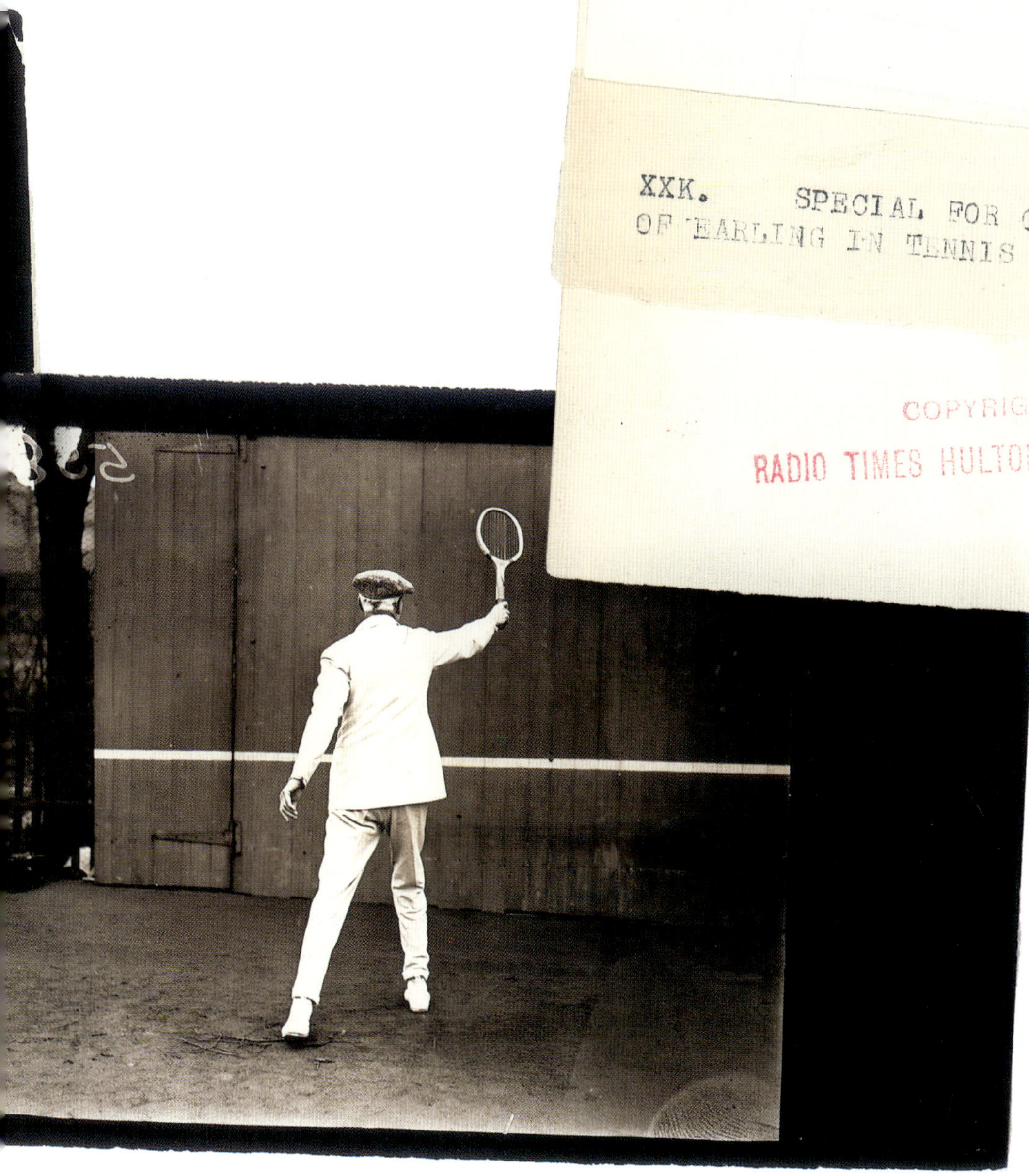

03

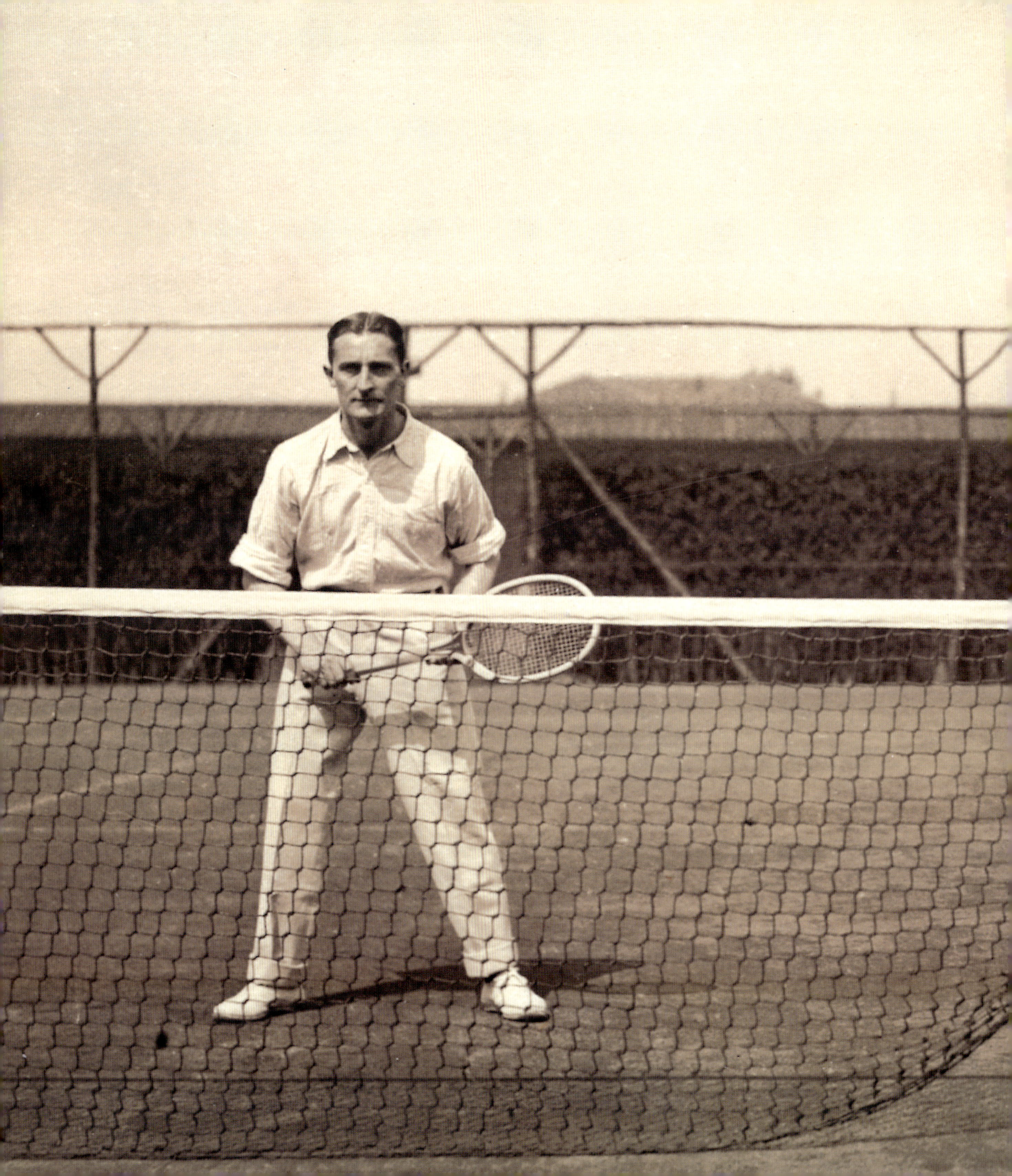

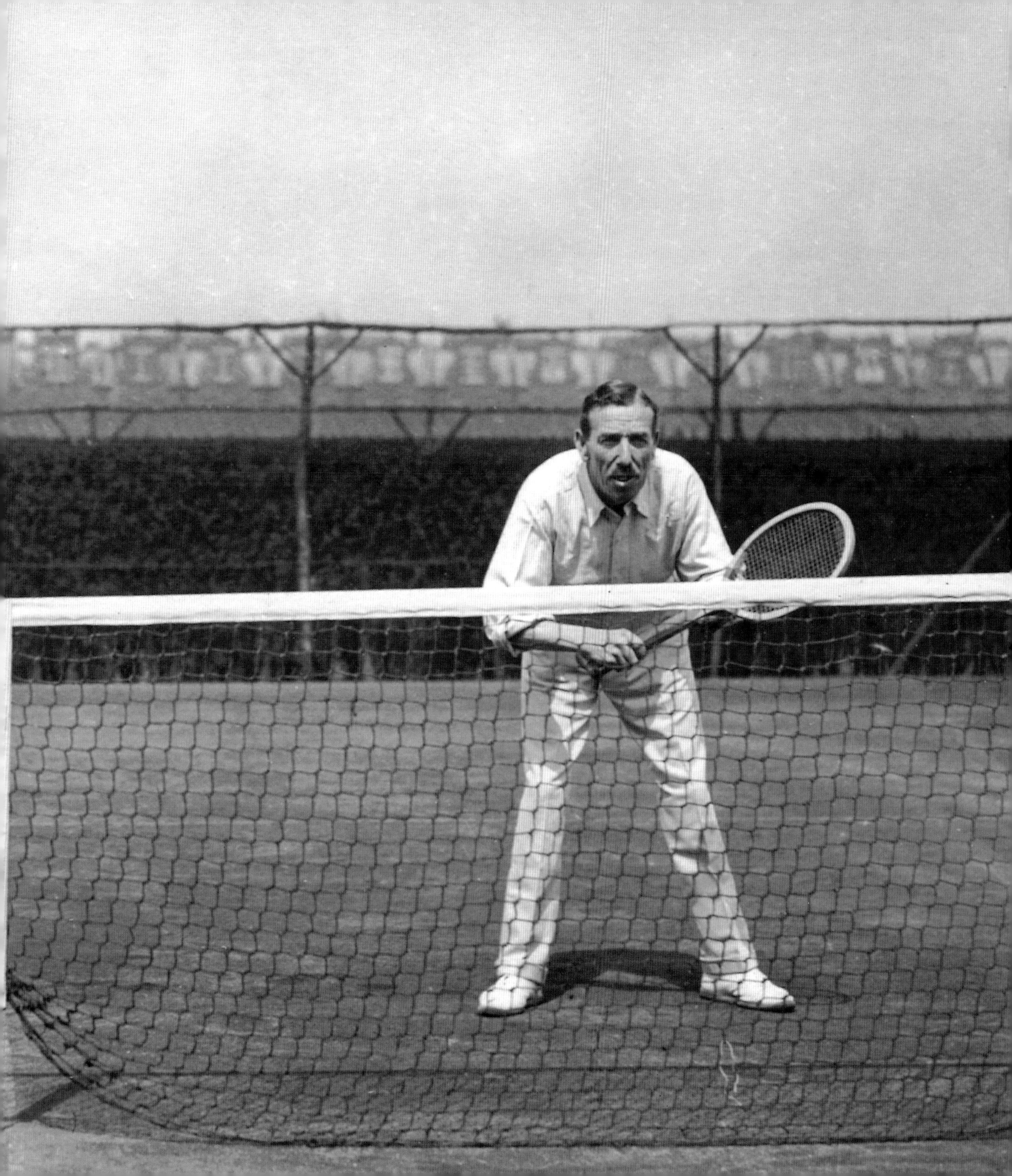

06–09
James Braid demonstrating golf technique, 1922

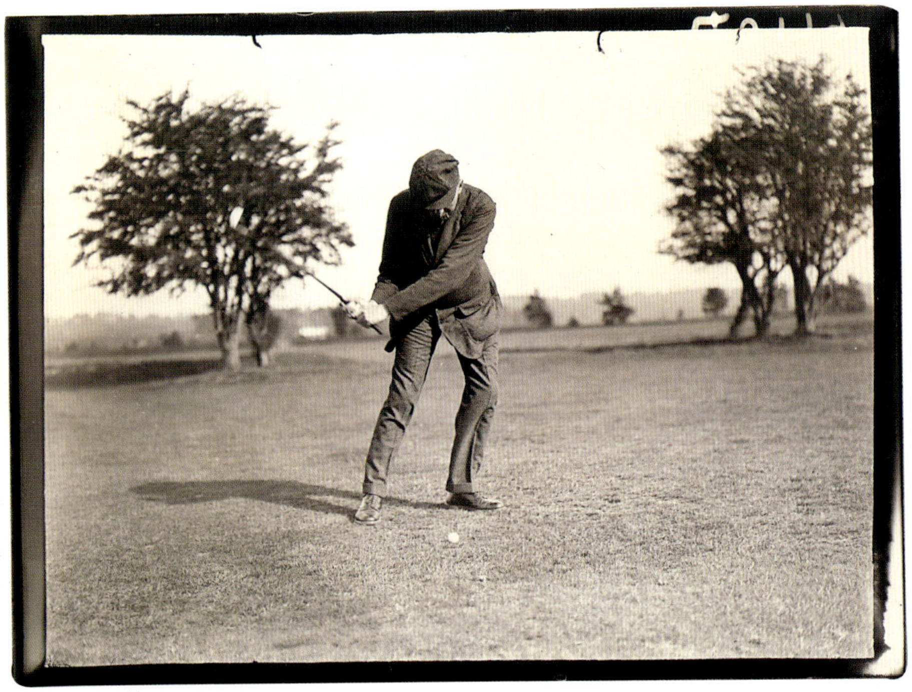
06

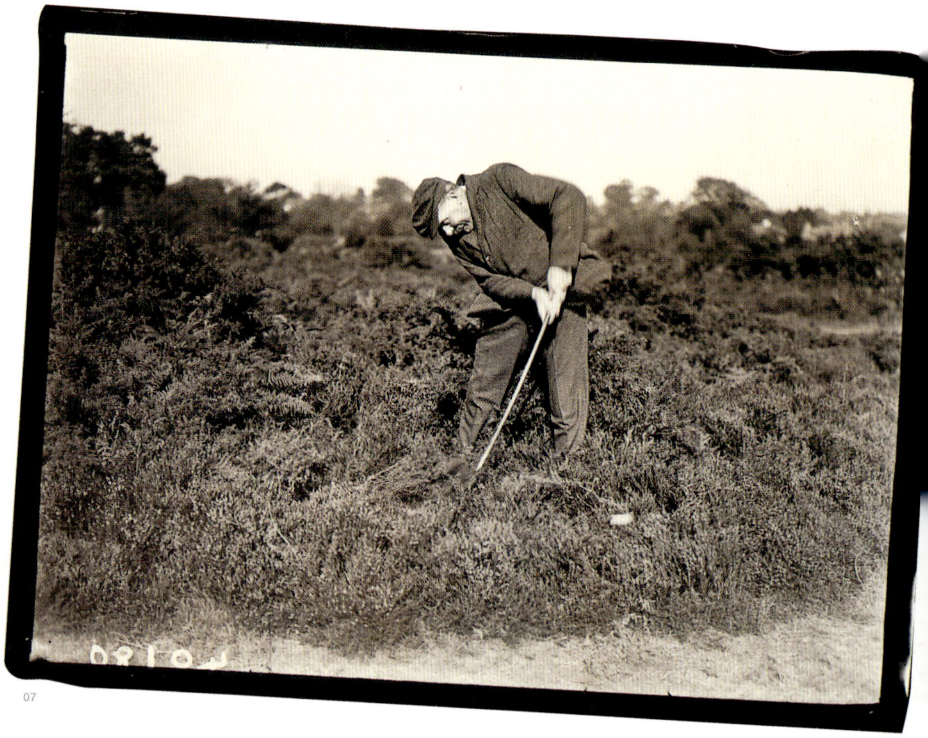
07

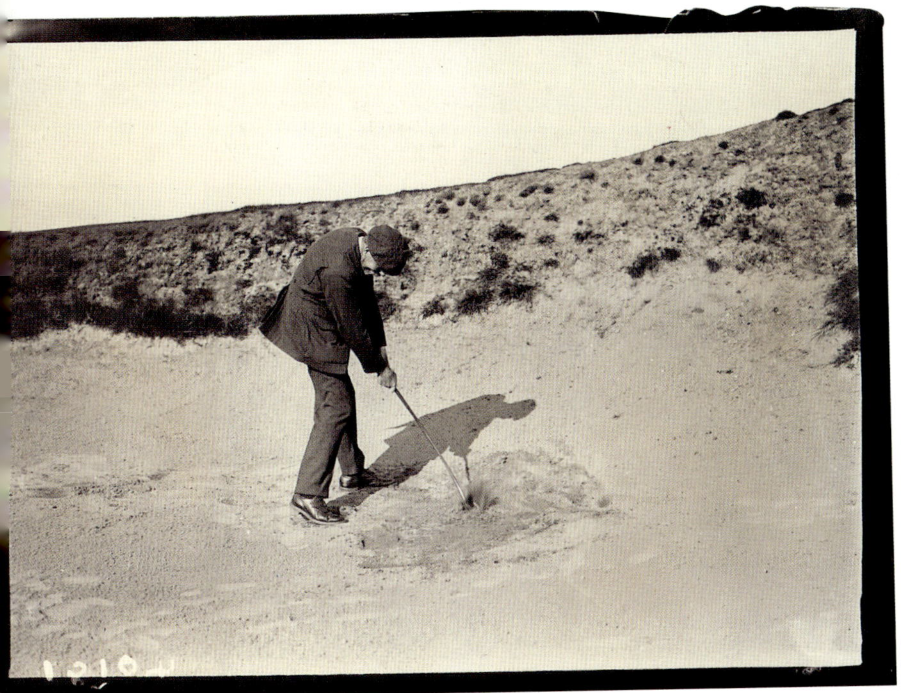

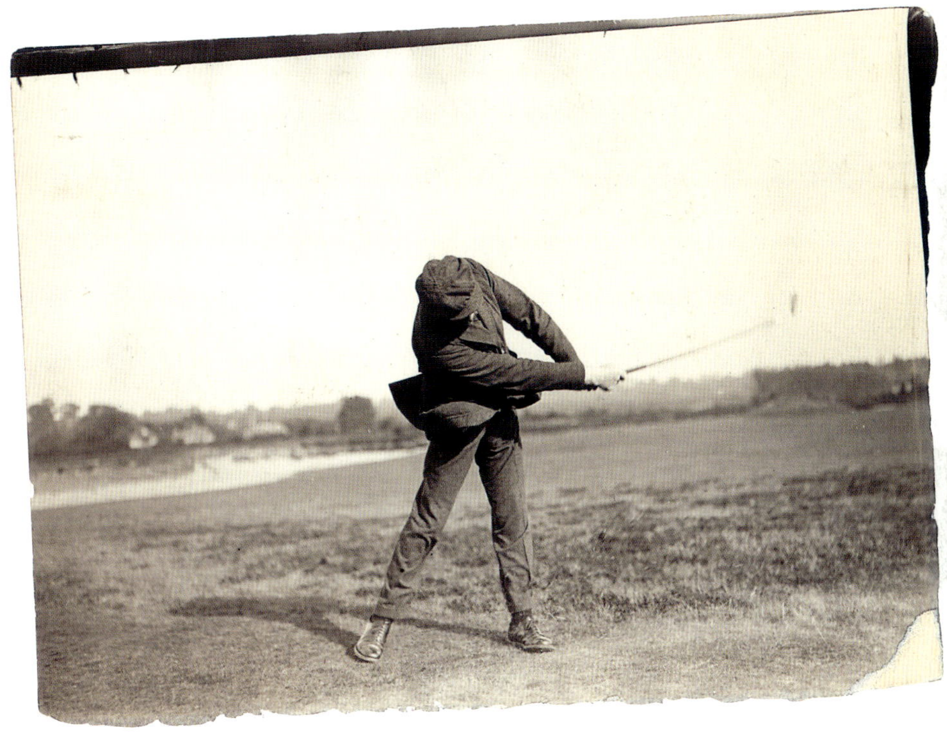

09

01
T C Tooks winning a university cross-country race, England, 1923

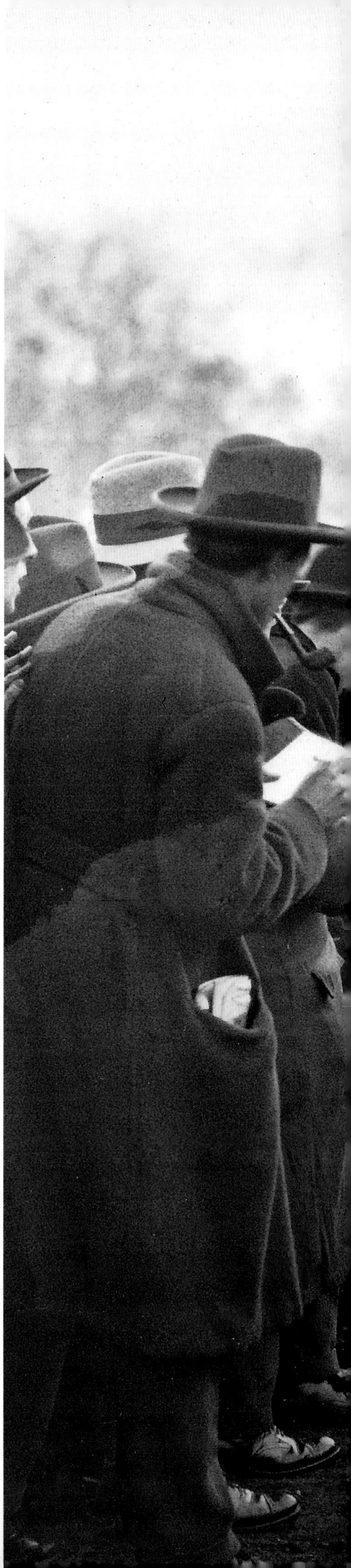

AMATEUR

The status of the amateur was highly regarded in sport, gentleman against gentleman playing for the pleasure and enjoyment of participating in the game. In Britain, the athletic clubs in particular, originally formed by universities, would perpetuate the idea of the gentleman amateur for decades to come. Amateur athletics meetings and company sports days typify the ethos of competition for nothing more than the honour and enjoyment of sport. In most sports, even at the highest level, amateurs enjoyed a senior status, and their professional counterparts were excluded from many of the games' most important events (a situation that in tennis would not change until the 1960s).

Some amateurs proved themselves to be world-beaters on the international stage while maintaining the integrity of their 'gentleman' amateur status. That sport was two different cultures did not seem to concern the photographers, they eagerly photographed both amateur and professional sporting events without making judgements on the social status of the participants.

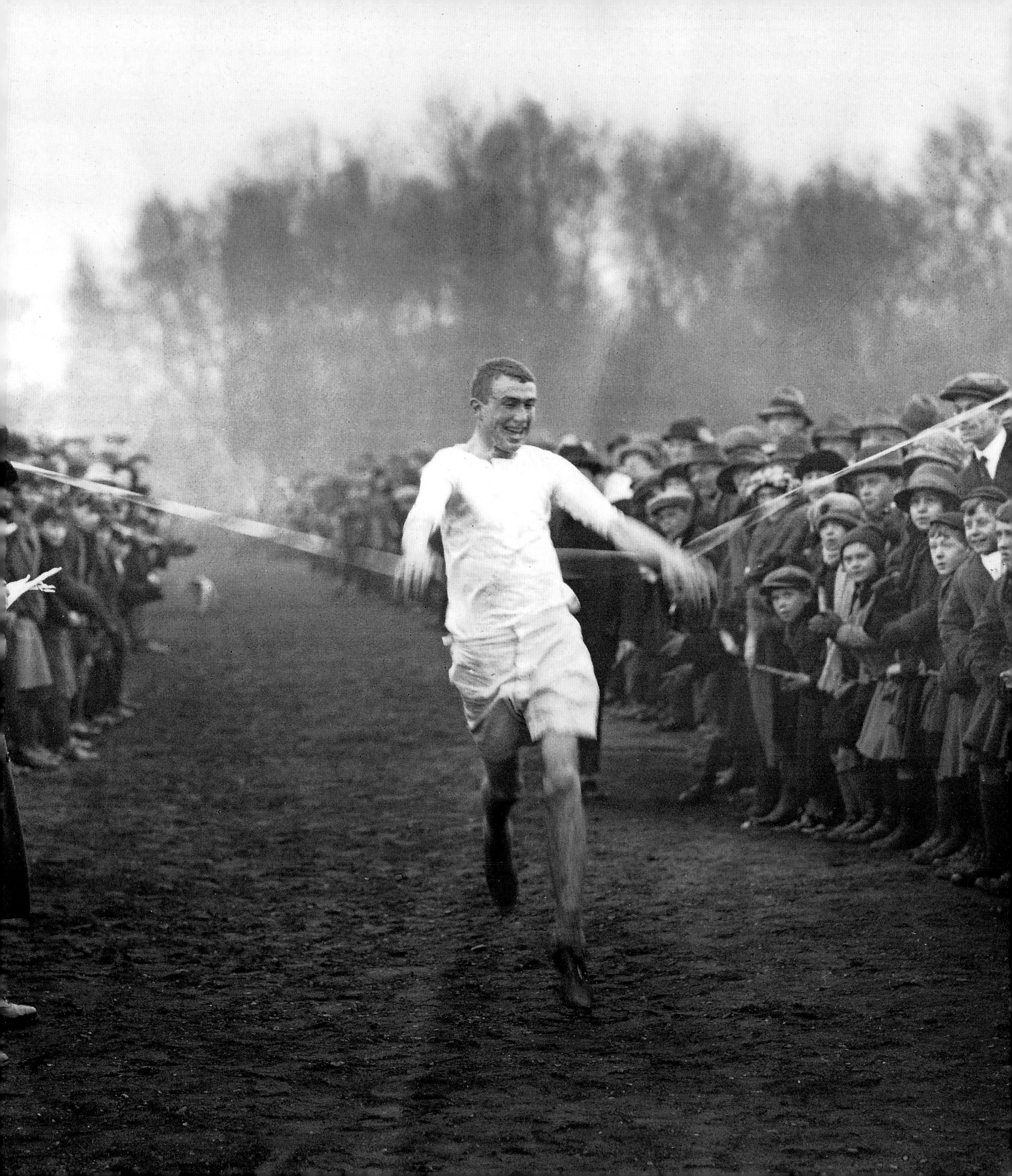

02
Miss Hurren shot-putting at a ladies' athletic meeting, London, 1923

03
A C Tickner winning a veteran's race at the London Fire Brigade sports day, London, 1922

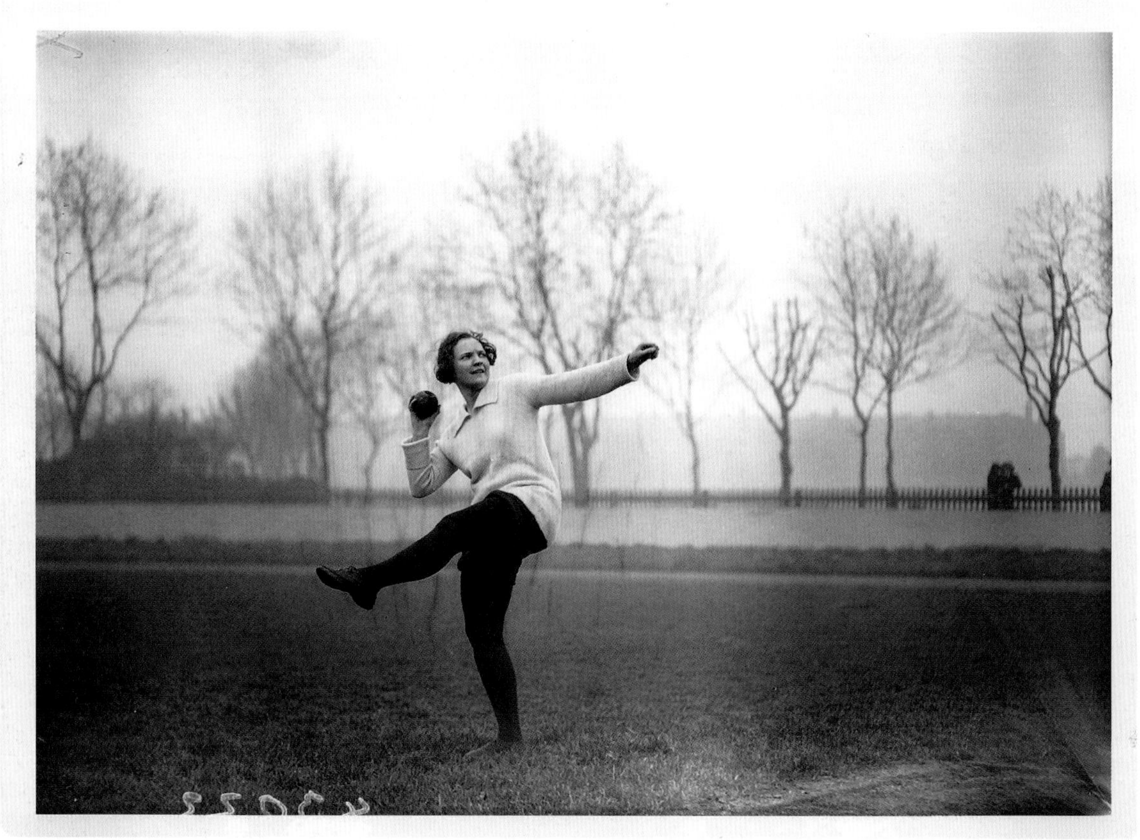

02

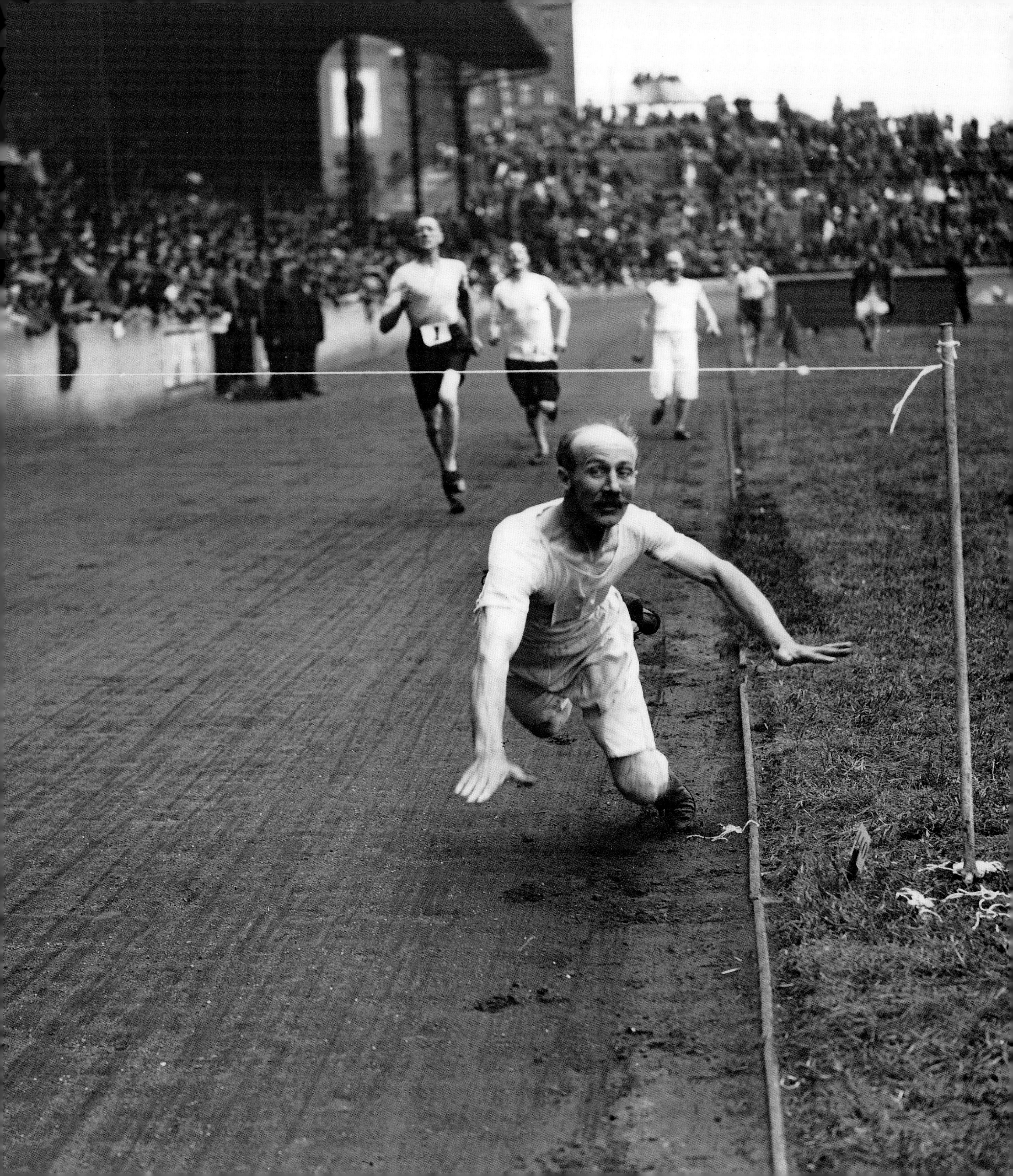

04
A R le Fleming at a university meeting, Cambridge, 1926
Macgregor

05
L Stanley at the Amateur Athletics Association Championships, London, 1924
A R Coster

06
Student athlete F Gordon practising pole vault, 1934
J A Hampton

07
F R Webster at the University Athletics Championships, London, 1936
A Hudson

08
K Kirtz at a university meeting, London, 1933
H F Davis

09 (OVERLEAF LEFT)
The Marquis of Clydesdale and his trainer at an amateur boxing championship, London, 1924
Kirby

10 (OVERLEAF RIGHT)
Sergeant F P Crawley of the Royal Tank Corps being examined before a fight at the Amateur Boxing Association Championships, London, 1928
Brooke

04

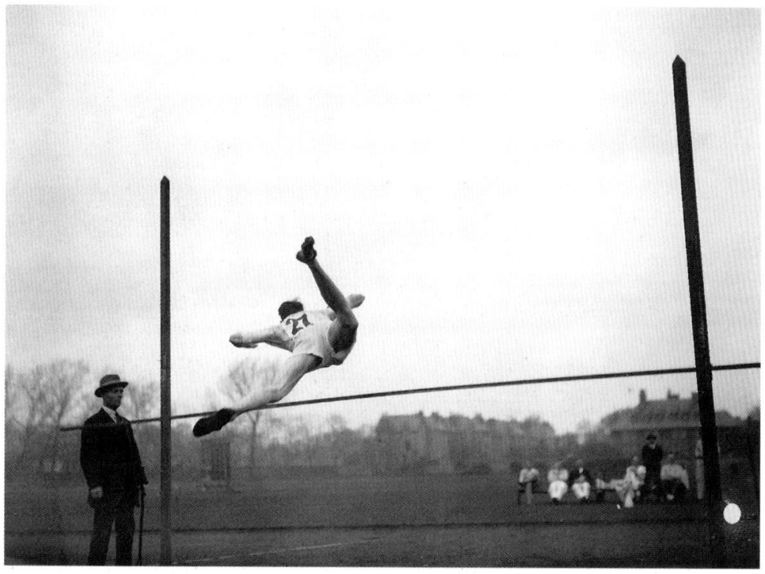

05

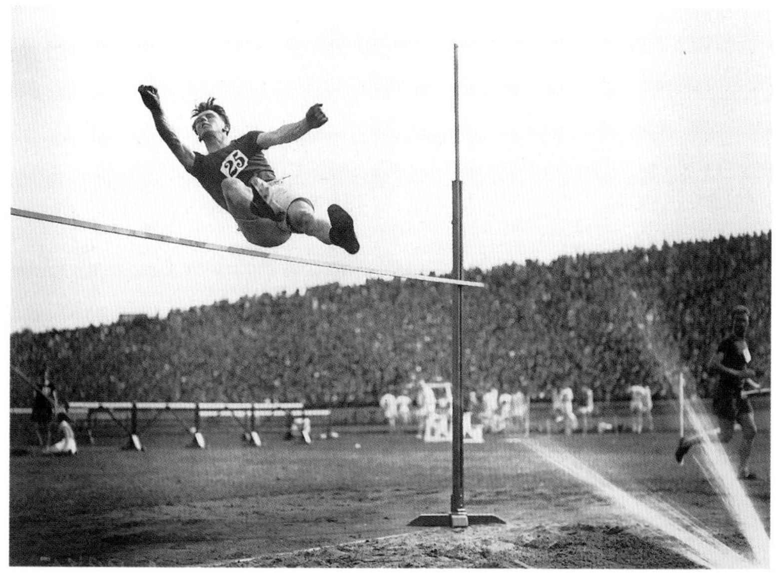

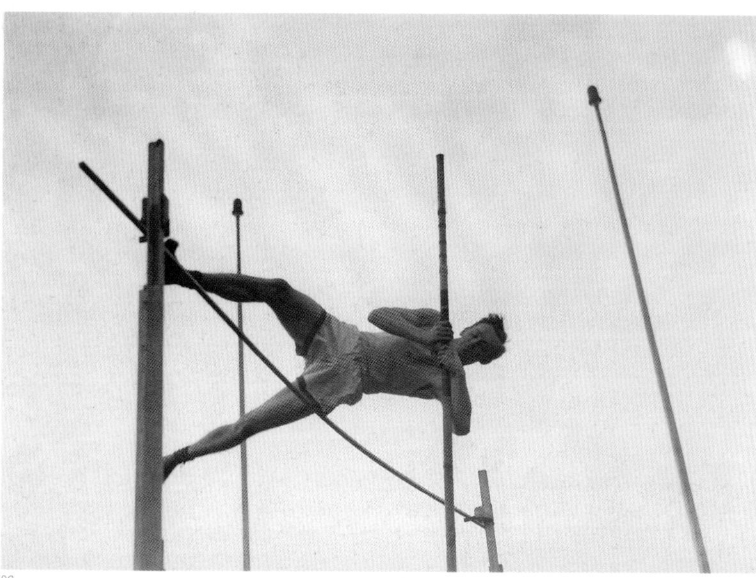

06

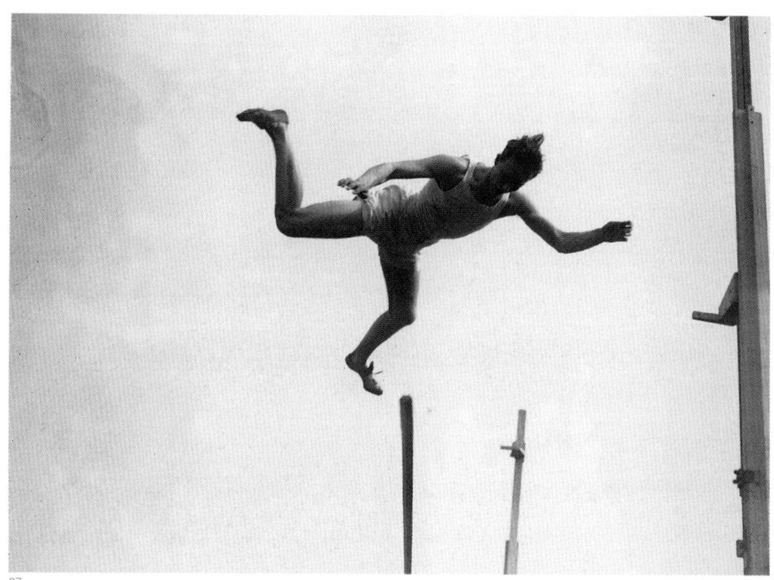

07

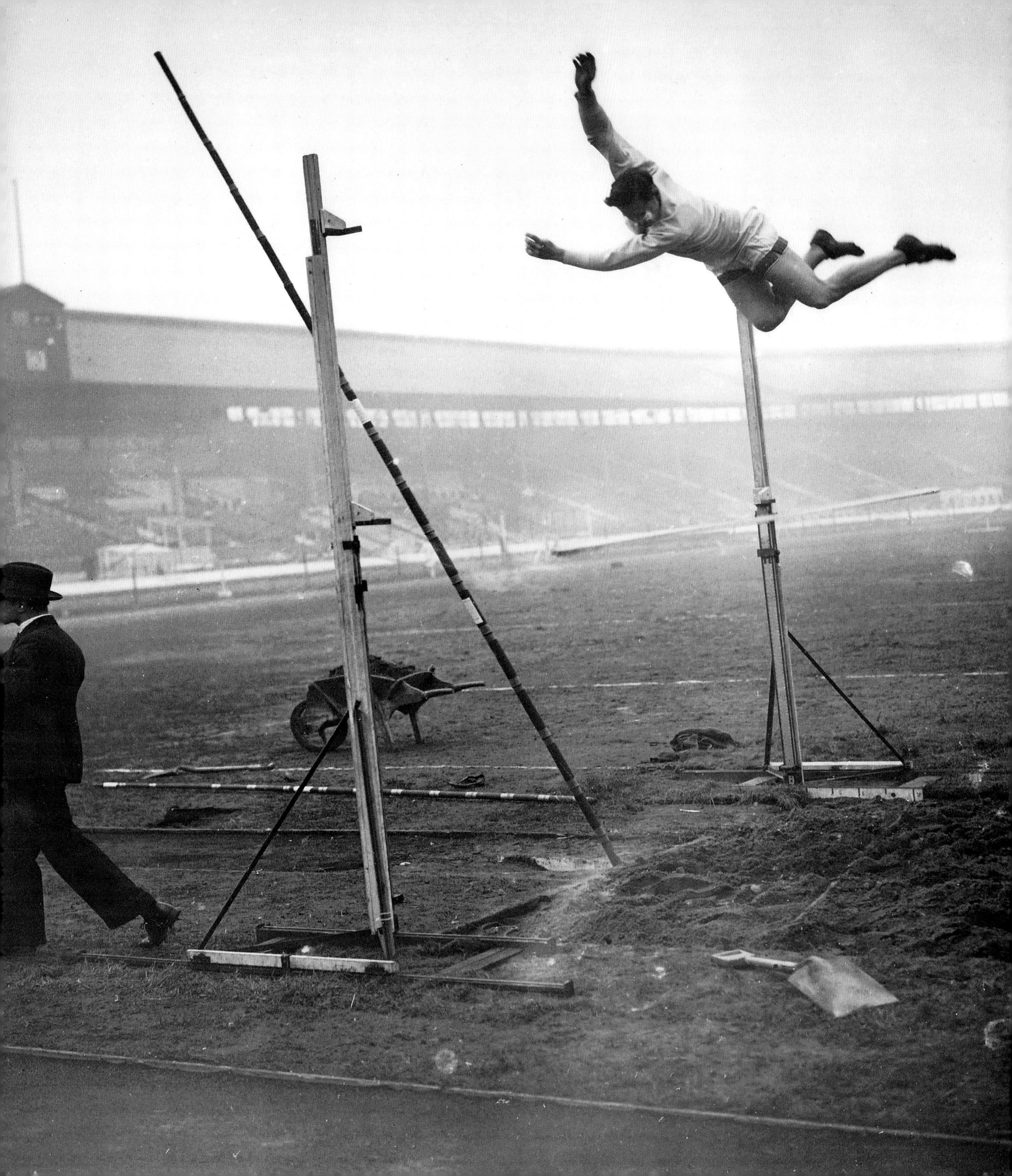

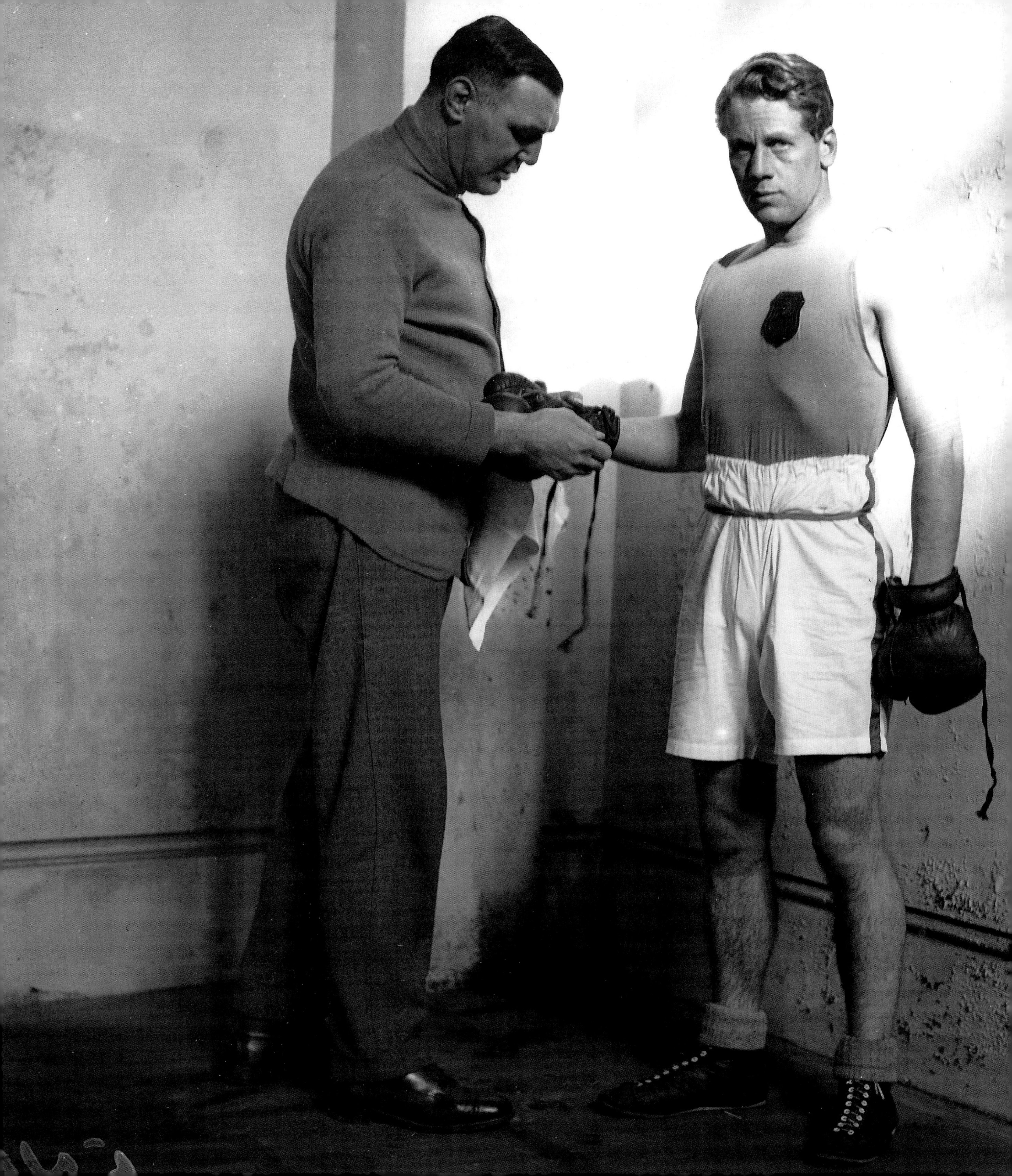

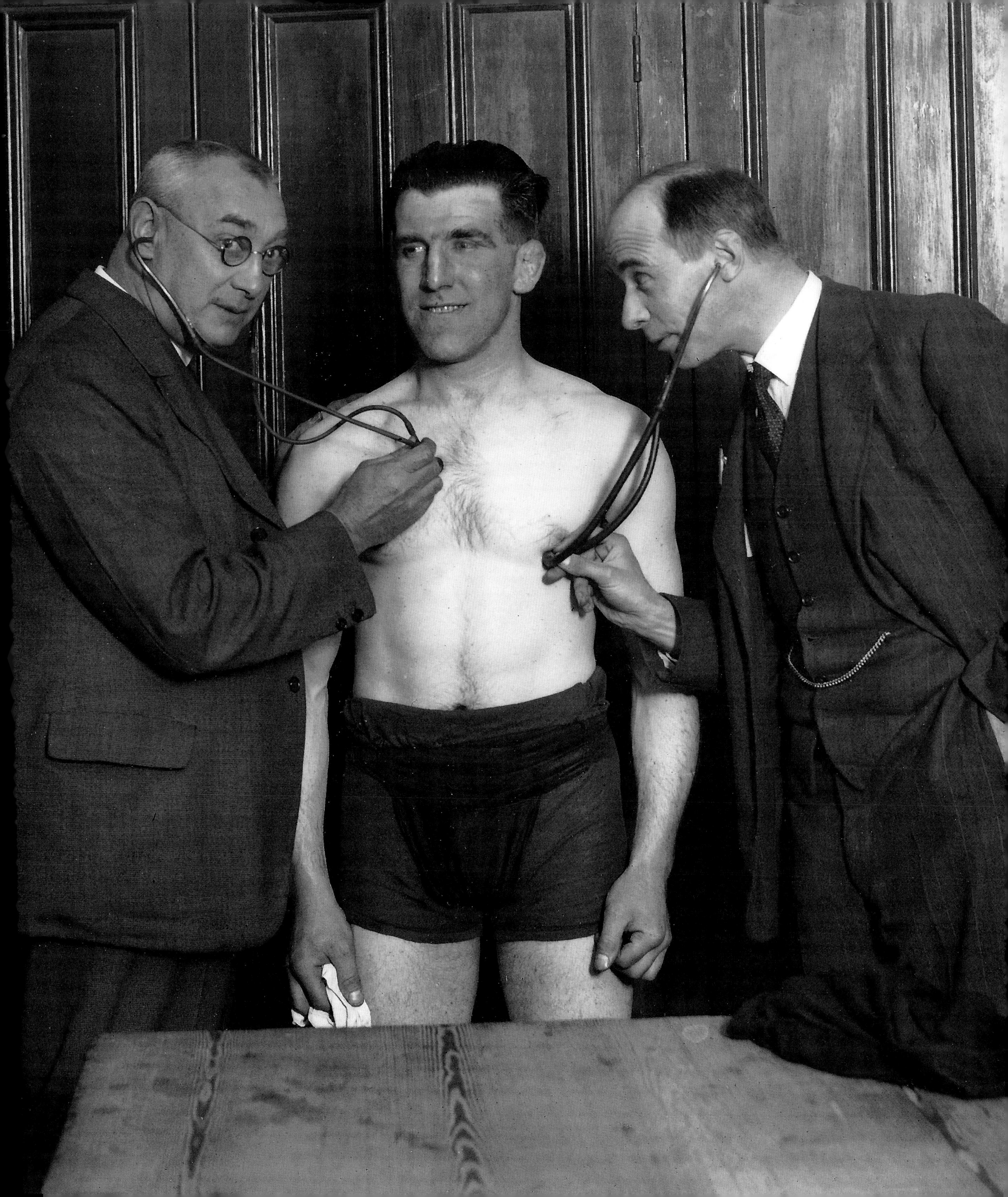

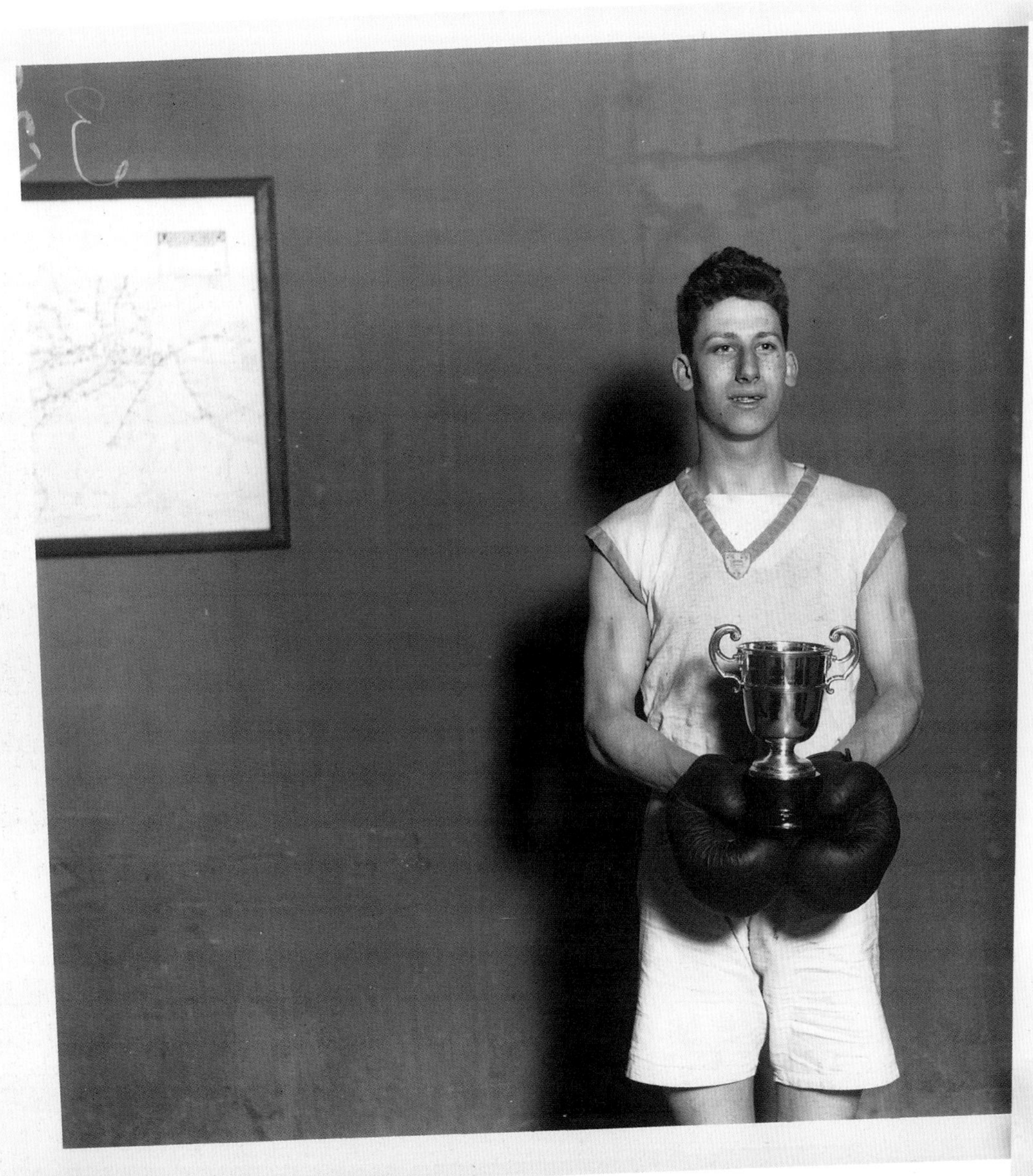

11

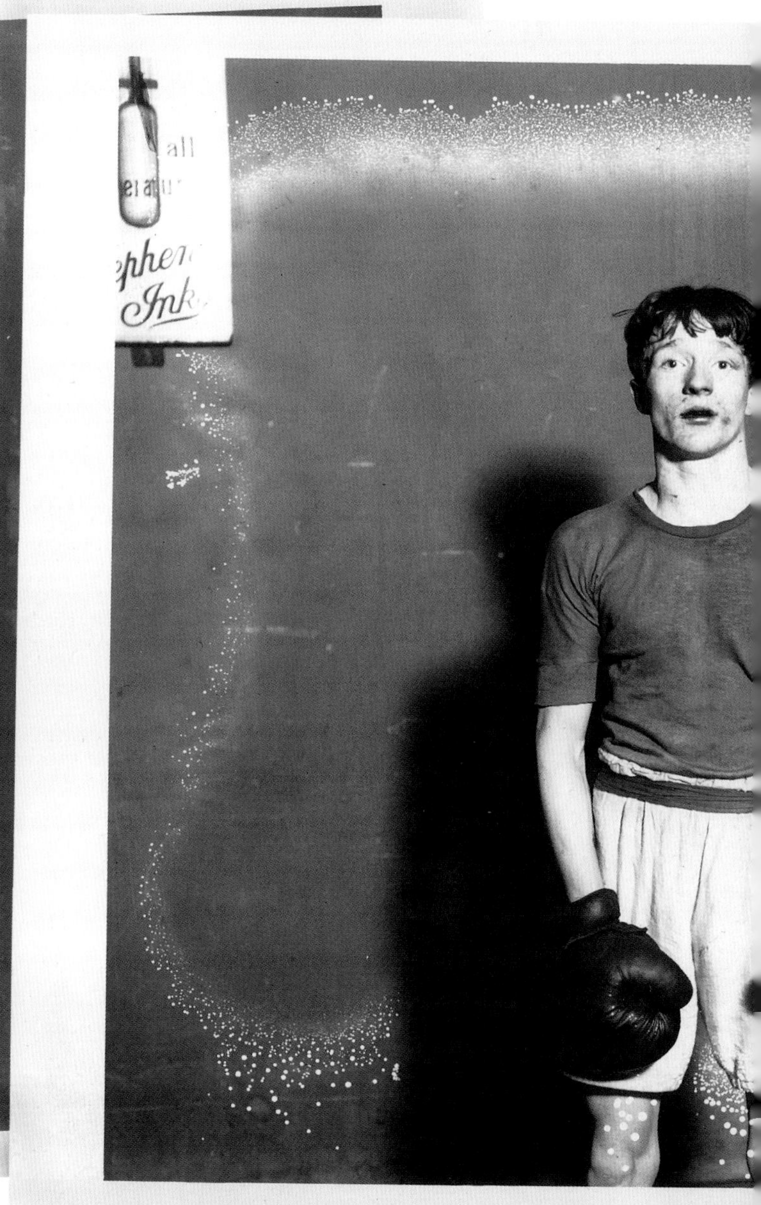

12

11–13
From left, D Hanlan, W Cuthbertson and
A Ireland at the Amateur Boxing Championships,
London, 1921
Morey

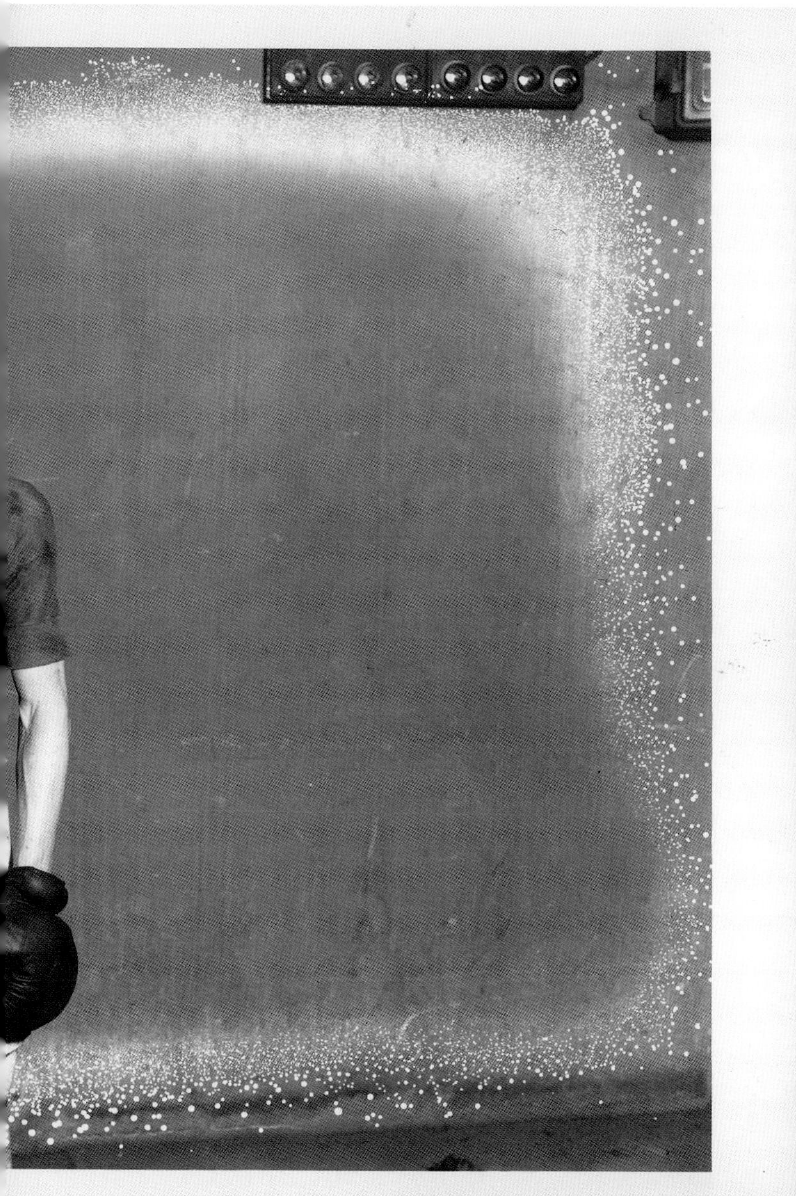

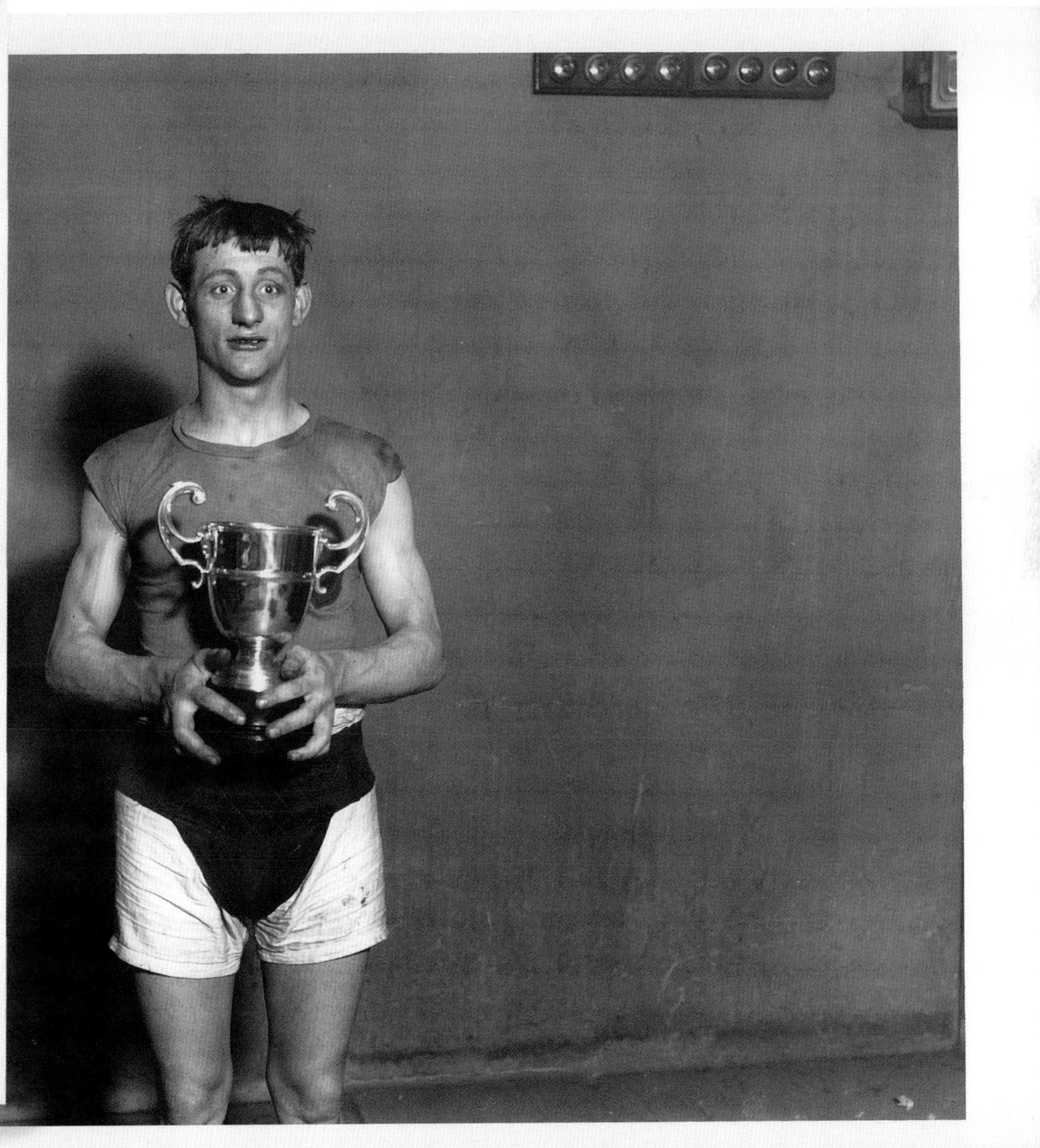

13

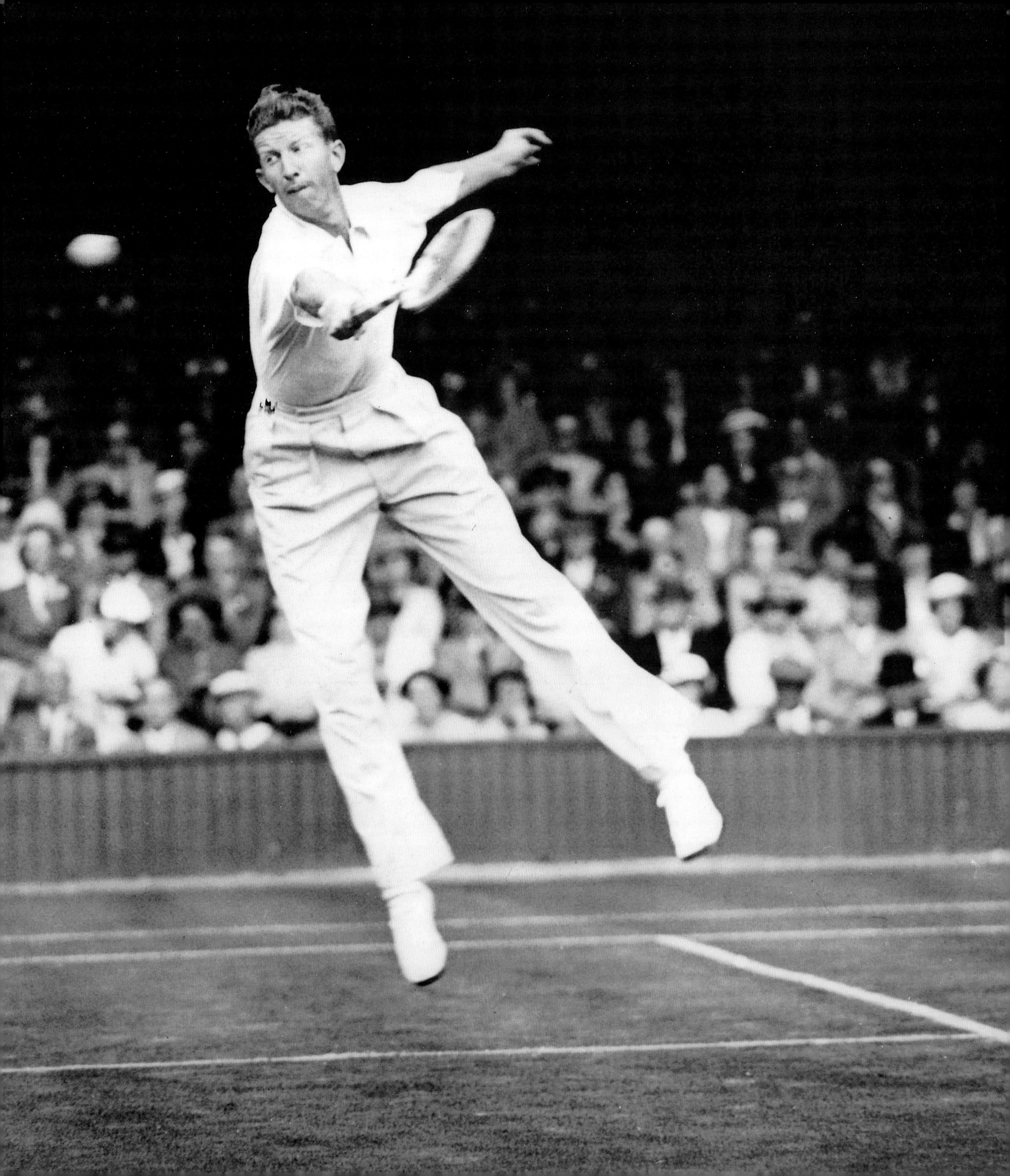

14
Don Budge, winner of tennis' four major championships, which were only open to amateurs, Wimbledon, 1937
J A Hampton

15
Winner of the Amateur and Open Championships of both Britain and the US in the same year, Bobby Jones, St Andrews, 1927
Kirby

16 (OVERLEAF)
Doris Soames taking part in an amateur tennis tournament, Croydon, England, 1926

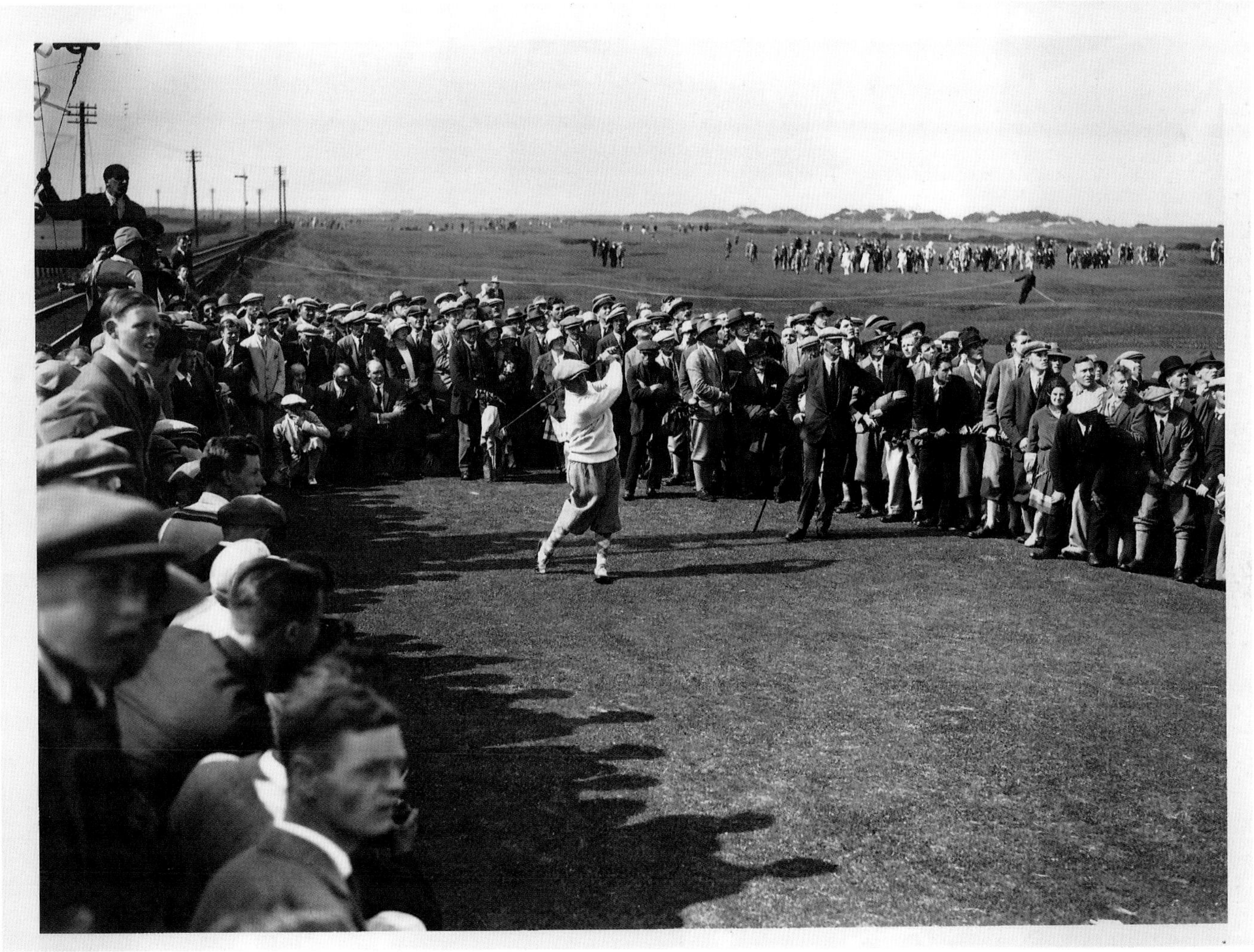

15

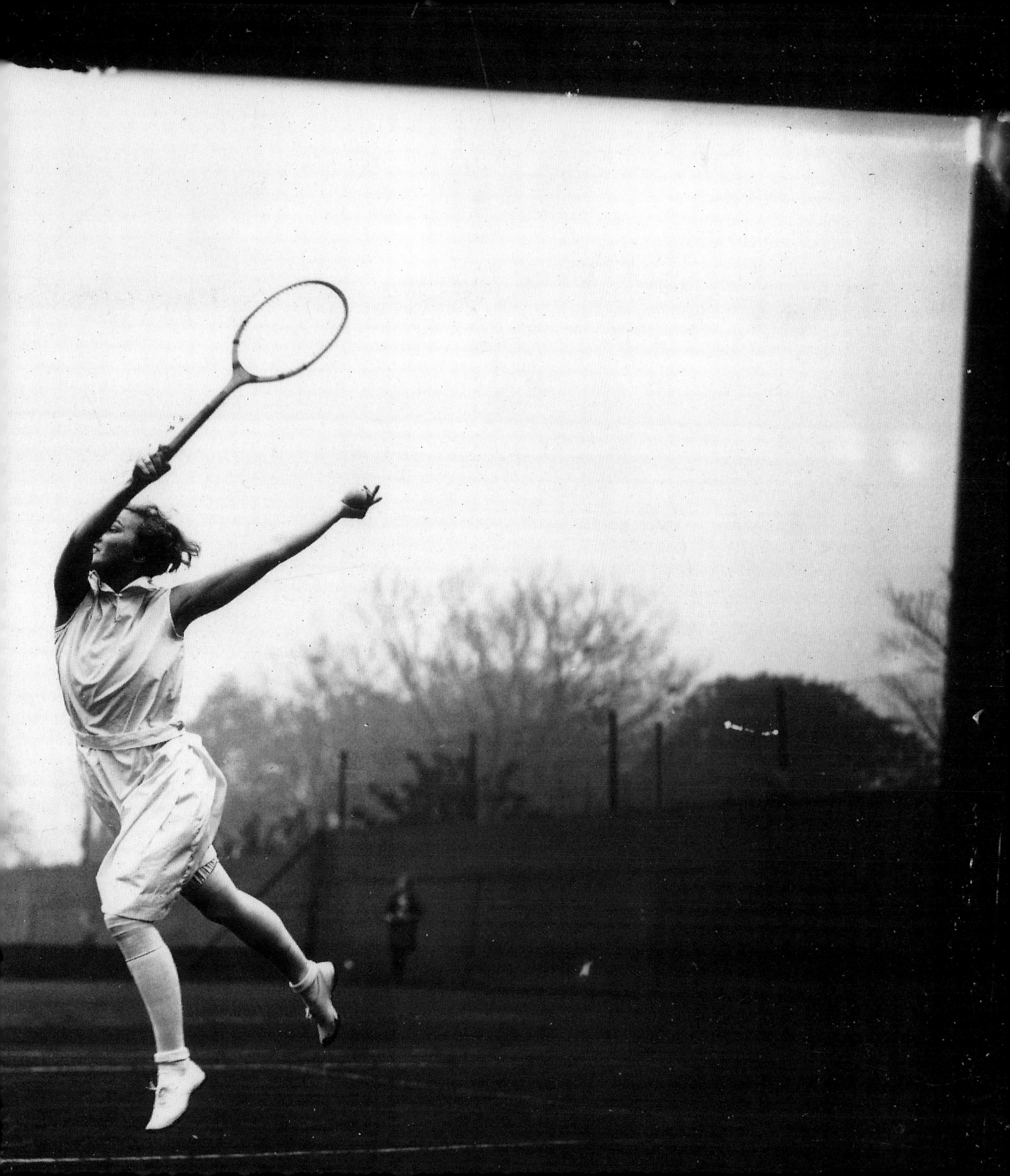

01
Greyhounds with stuffed and sprung monkeys as riders, 1928
E Bacon

02 (OVERLEAF)
Gymnasts demonstrating 'aero wheels', 1928
E Bacon

STRANGE GAMES

After the end of World War I the boundaries between different sports became less rigid. Many of the sports that we would consider traditional today had not been established for many decades before the war, and new hybrids were tried. Why not play basketball on roller skates, or let a boxer fight a wrestler? This was more than just amusement or novelty; the war had questioned fundamentally the old social structures of class and sex, and anything seemed possible. Photographers eagerly recorded the fun, giving their picture agencies just the sort of amusing and saleable images they sought. Although order would soon re-establish itself, for a period, social norms were questioned, experimentation was rife and strange games took place.

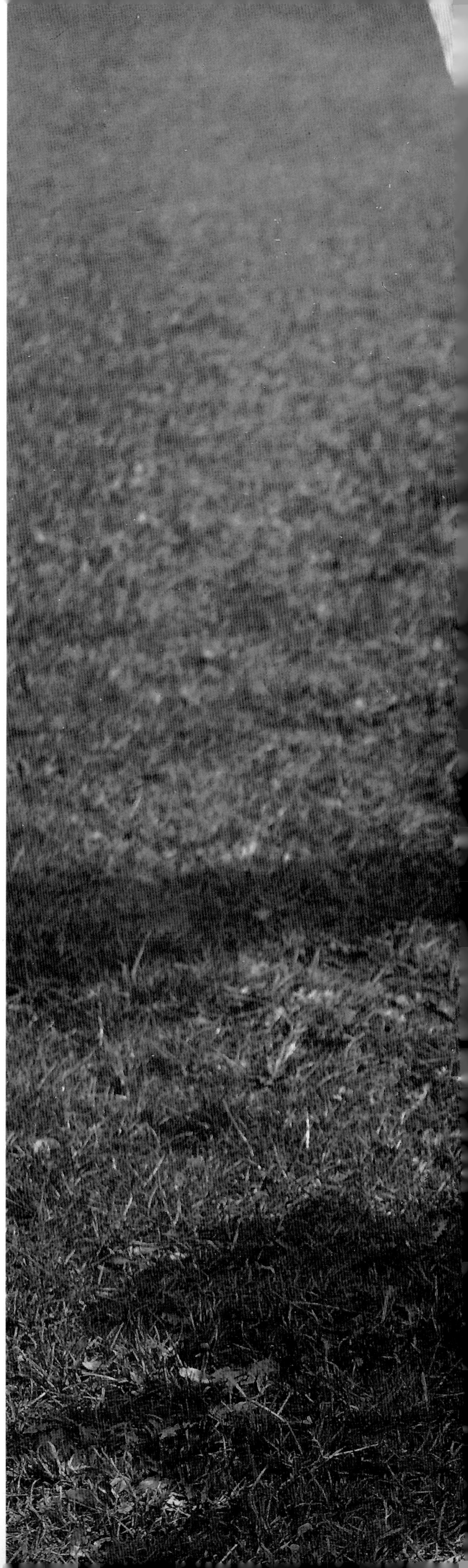

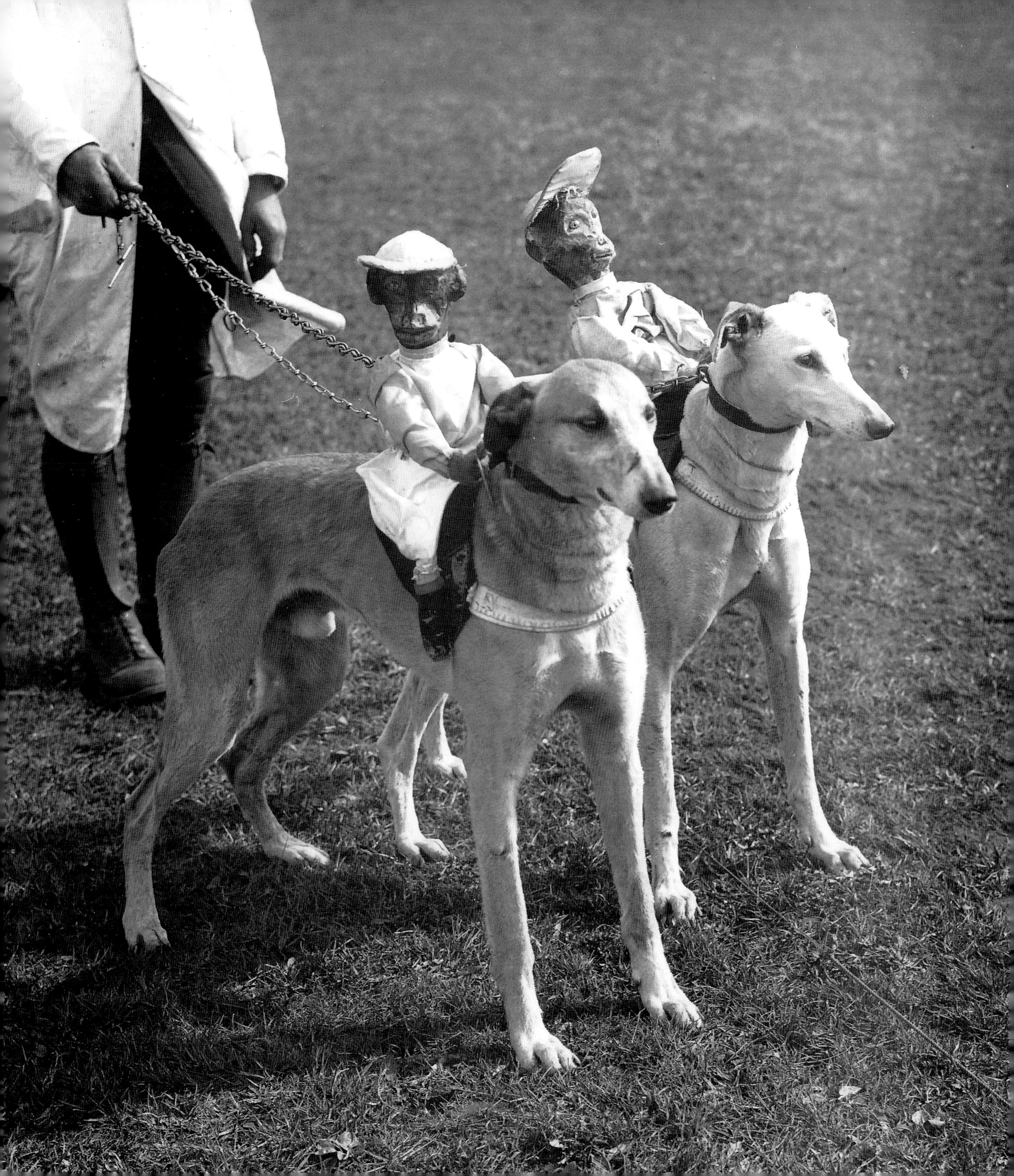

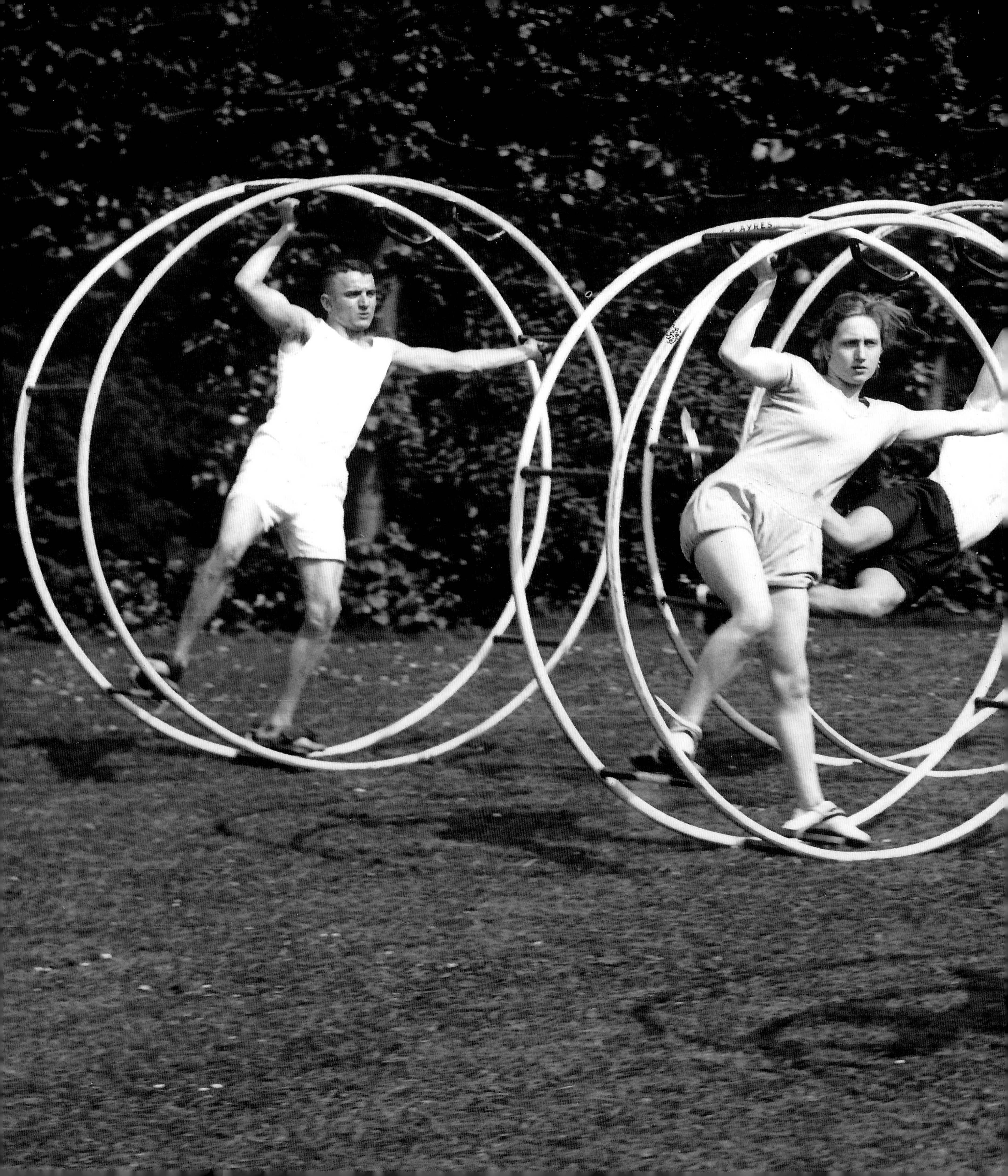
AYRES

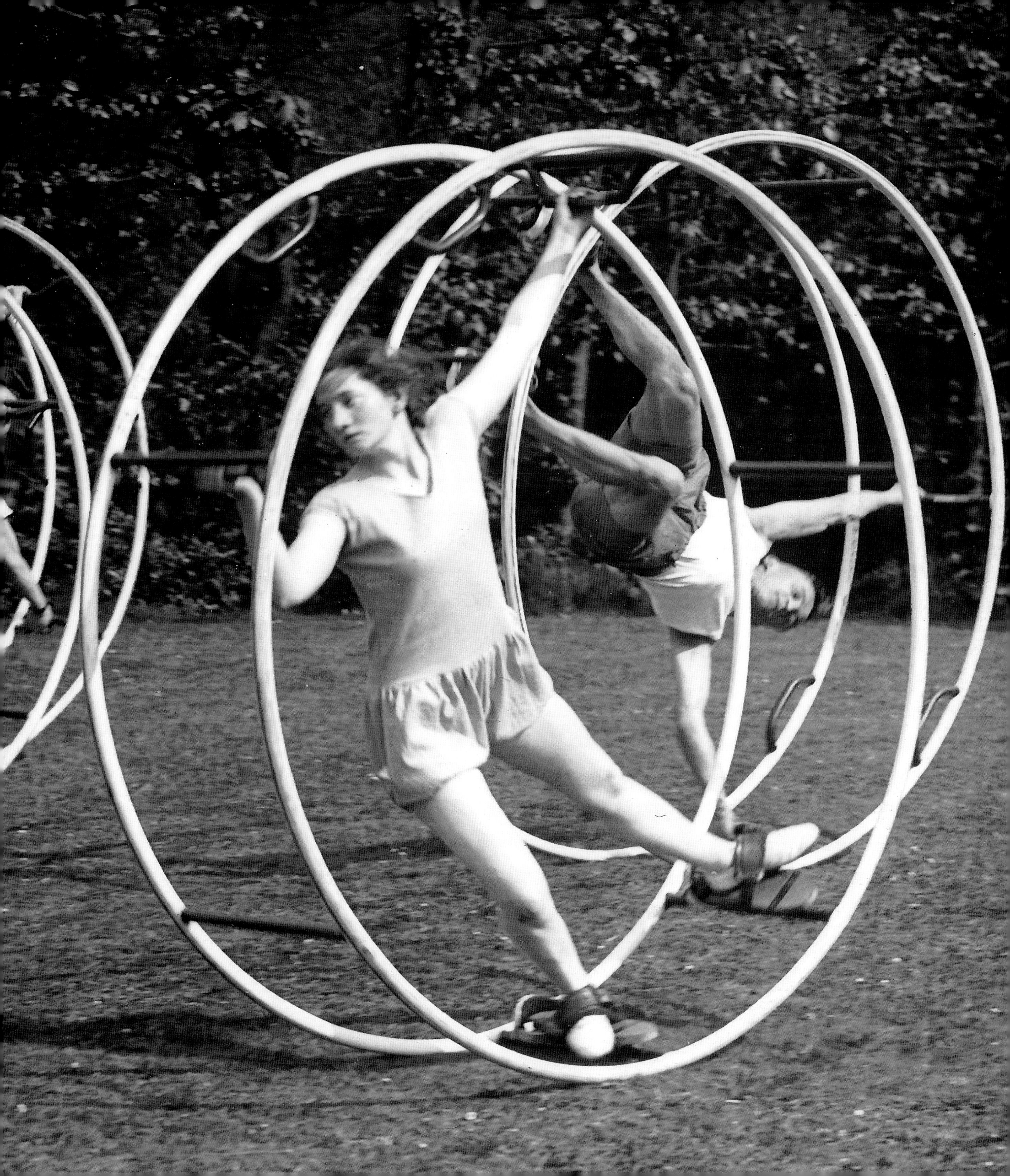

03
Archery experts shooting from a speed boat, 1923
H.F. Davis

04
A match between archers and golfers (the ball of straw has the same diameter as a golf hole), Cambridge, 1926
Brook

05 (OVERLEAF)
Basketball on roller skates, 1925
E. Bacon

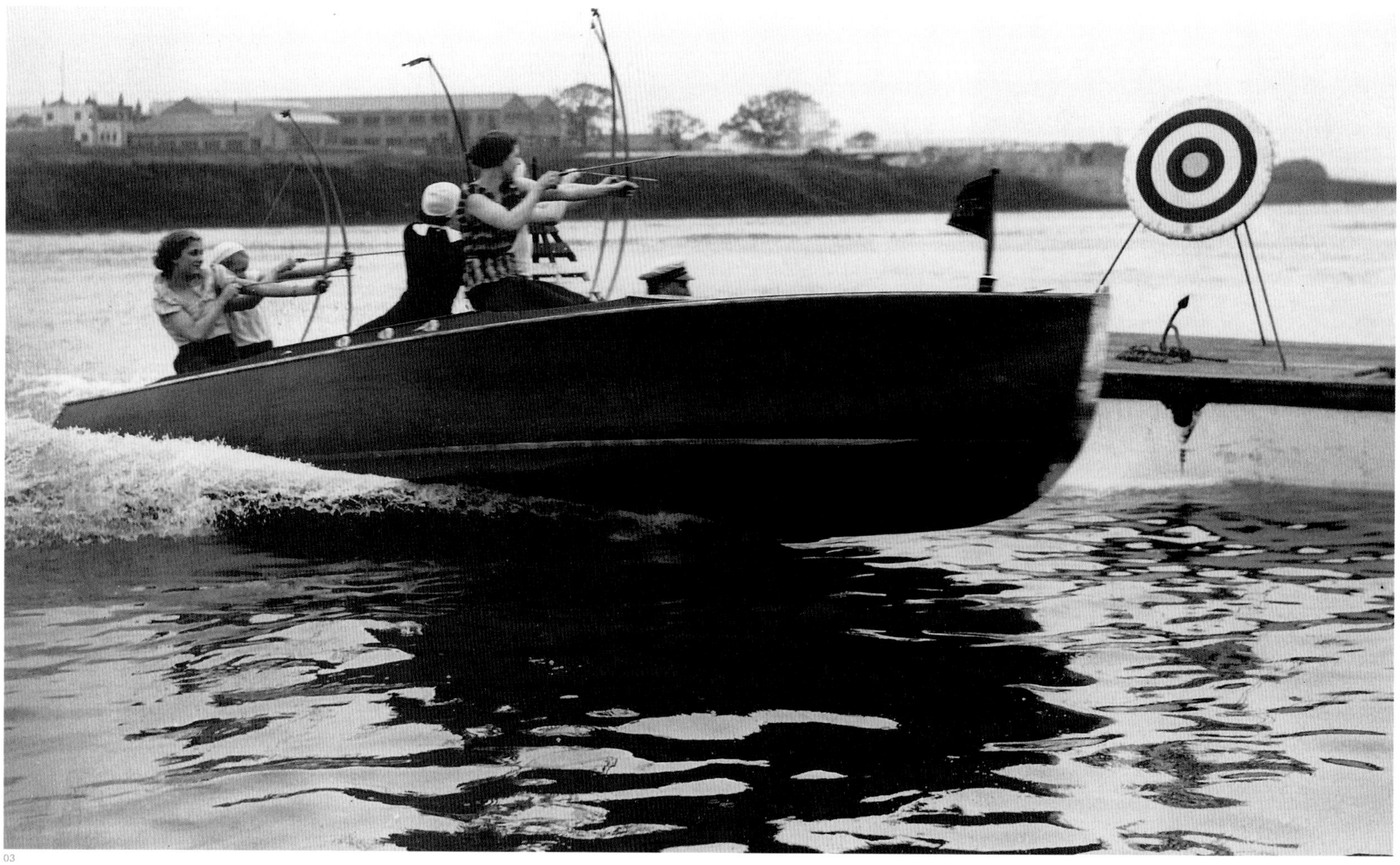

03

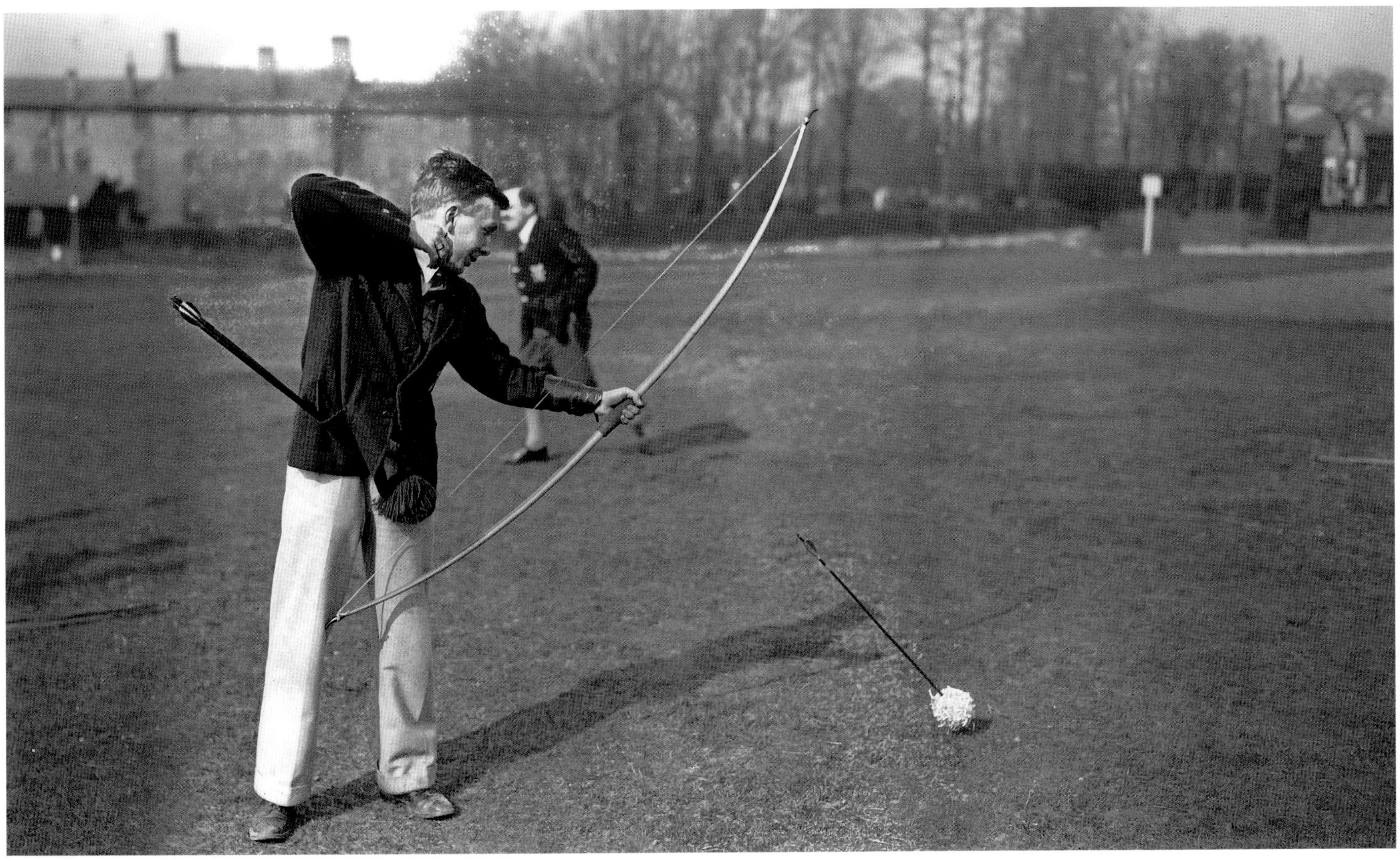

04

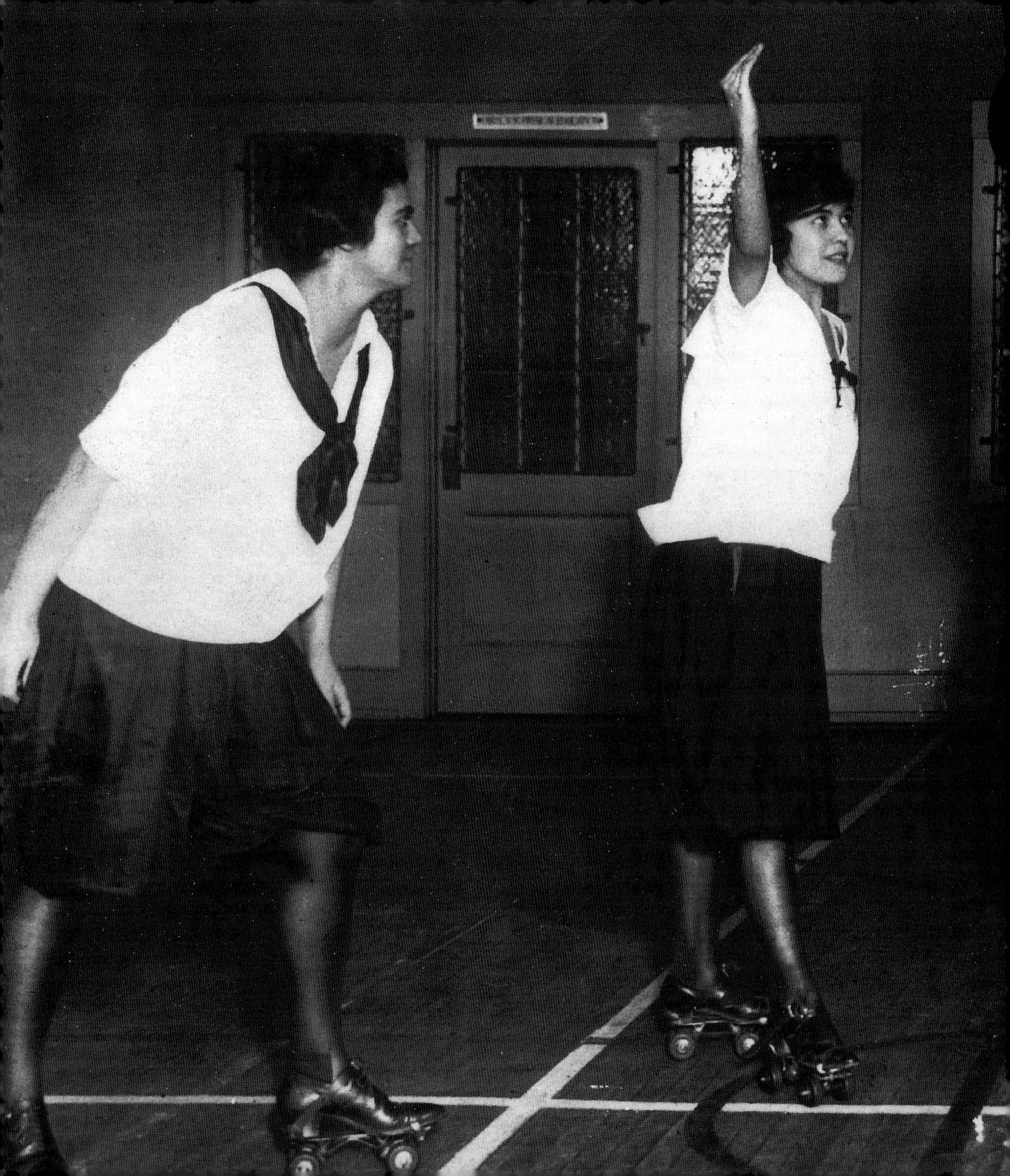

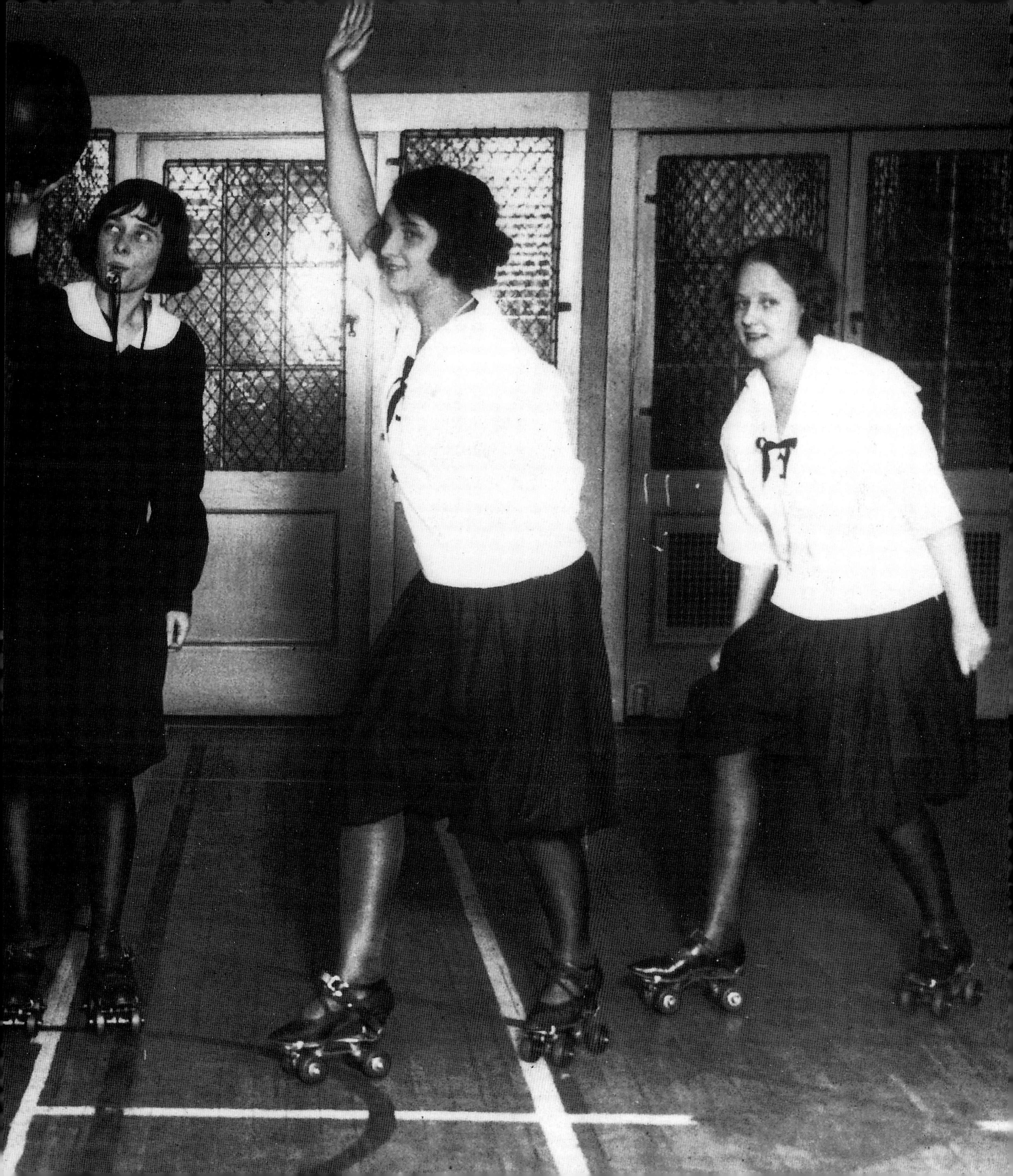

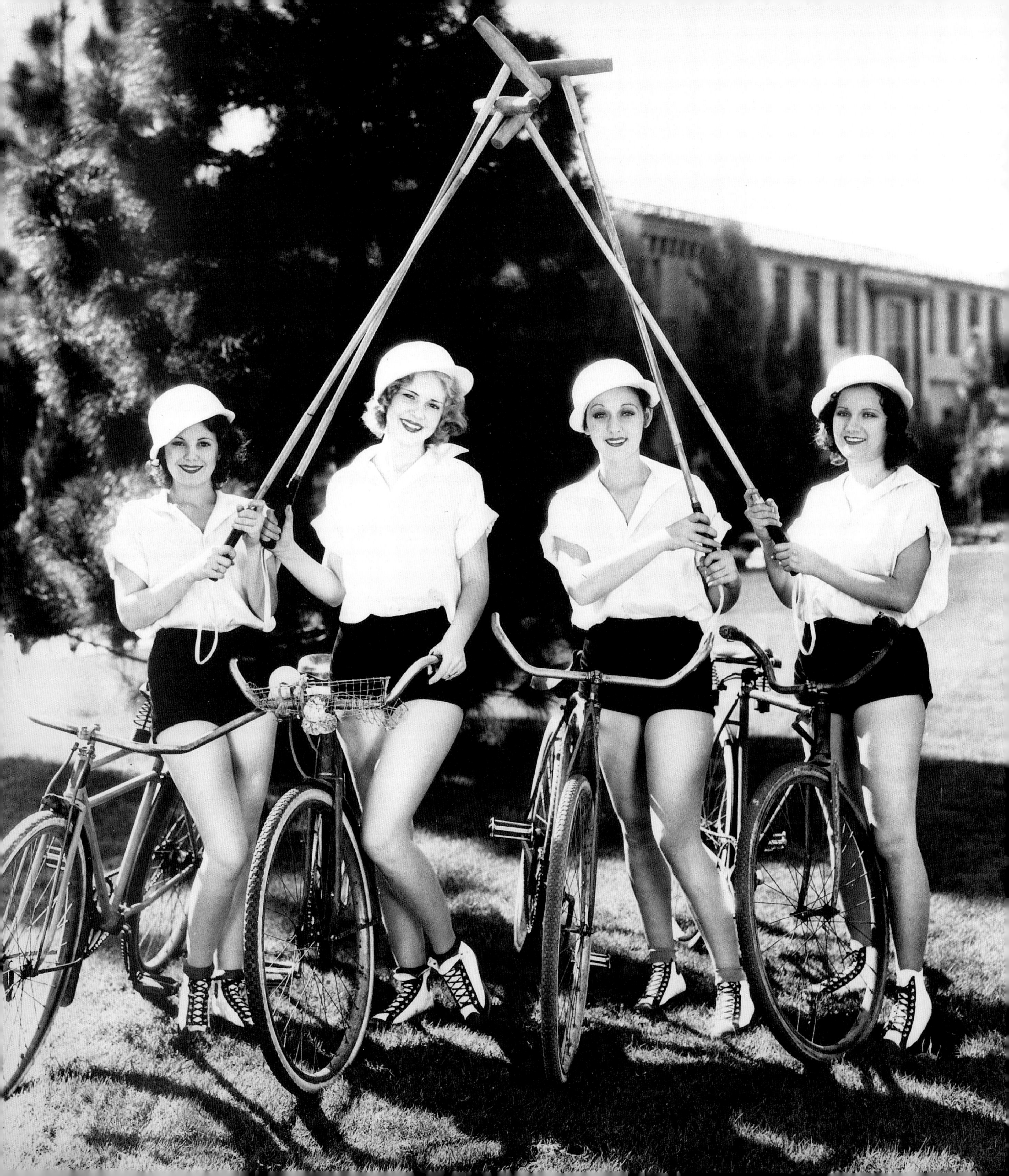

06
A team ready for 'Hollywood's latest sport' – polo cycliing, 1932

07
A 'hand skiff' race at an international cycle meeting, London, 1930
E F Corcoran

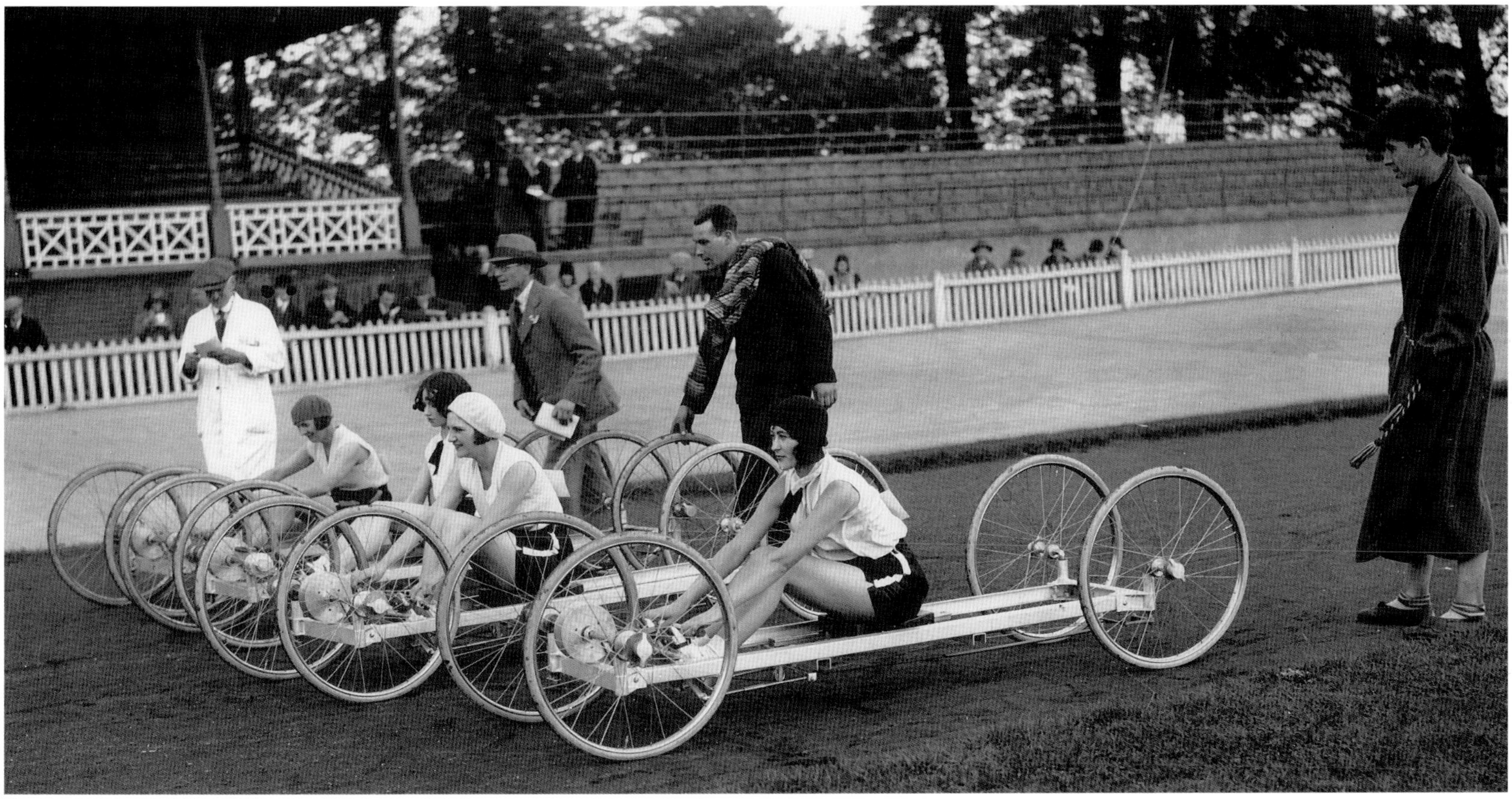

07

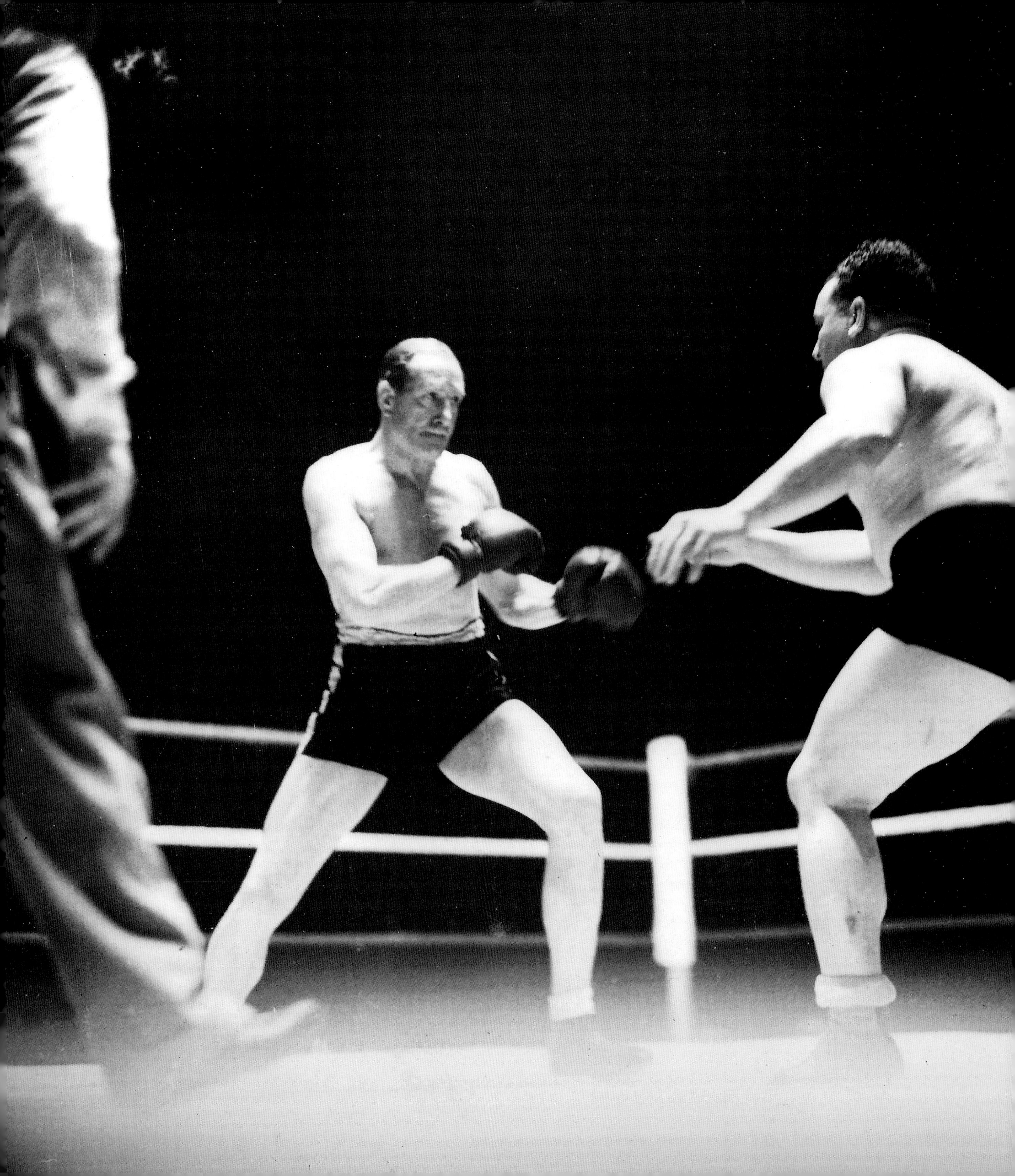

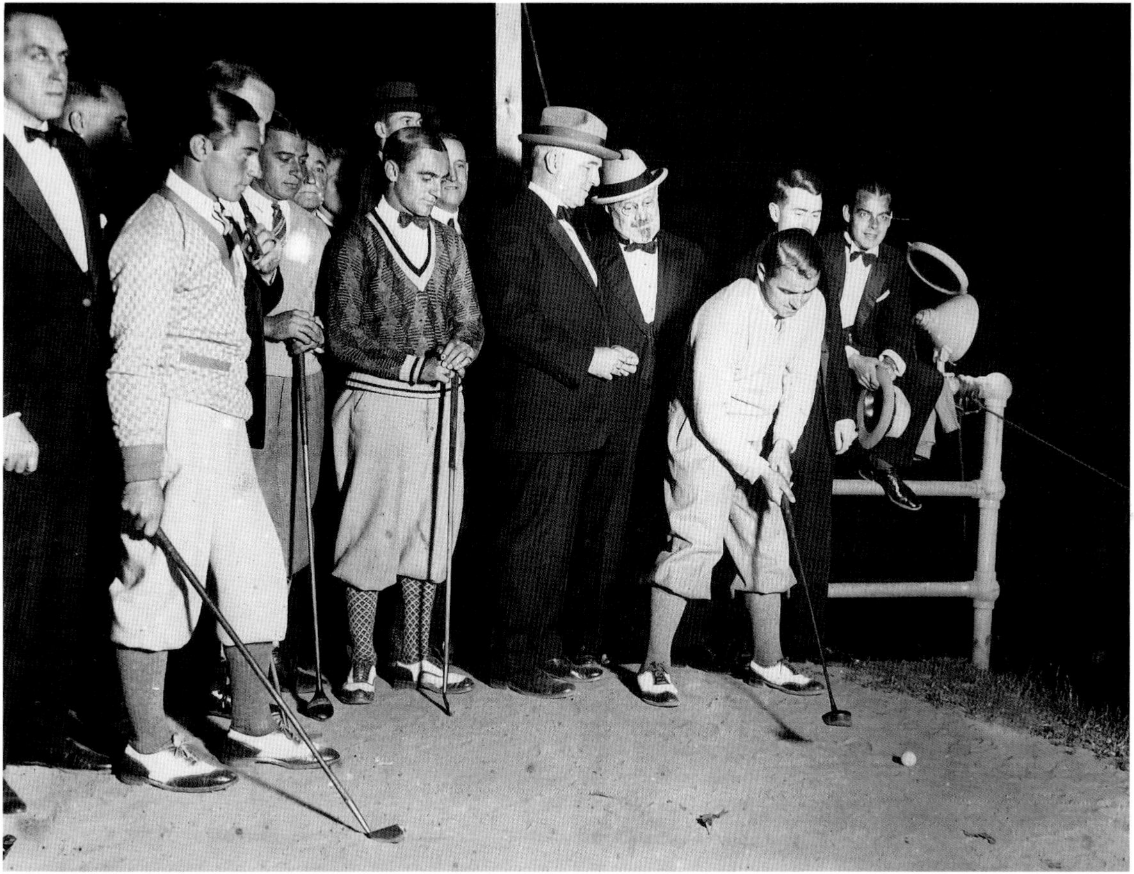

01
Practising tug-of-war technique against a tree, 1932

TRAINING

During the 1930s, the British government was so concerned about the poor physical condition of its citizens that a National Fitness Campaign was launched. Photography was used to illustrate the involvement of families, clubs and schools in physical education as a positive way of improving the wellbeing of the population. Encouraging outdoor activity for its citizens as an expression of the health of the nation, the phenomenon was echoed in other countries through the activities of fitness and health clubs. Everyone from the young to the old, men and women, seemed to be in training for some future event when their physical strength would be called upon.

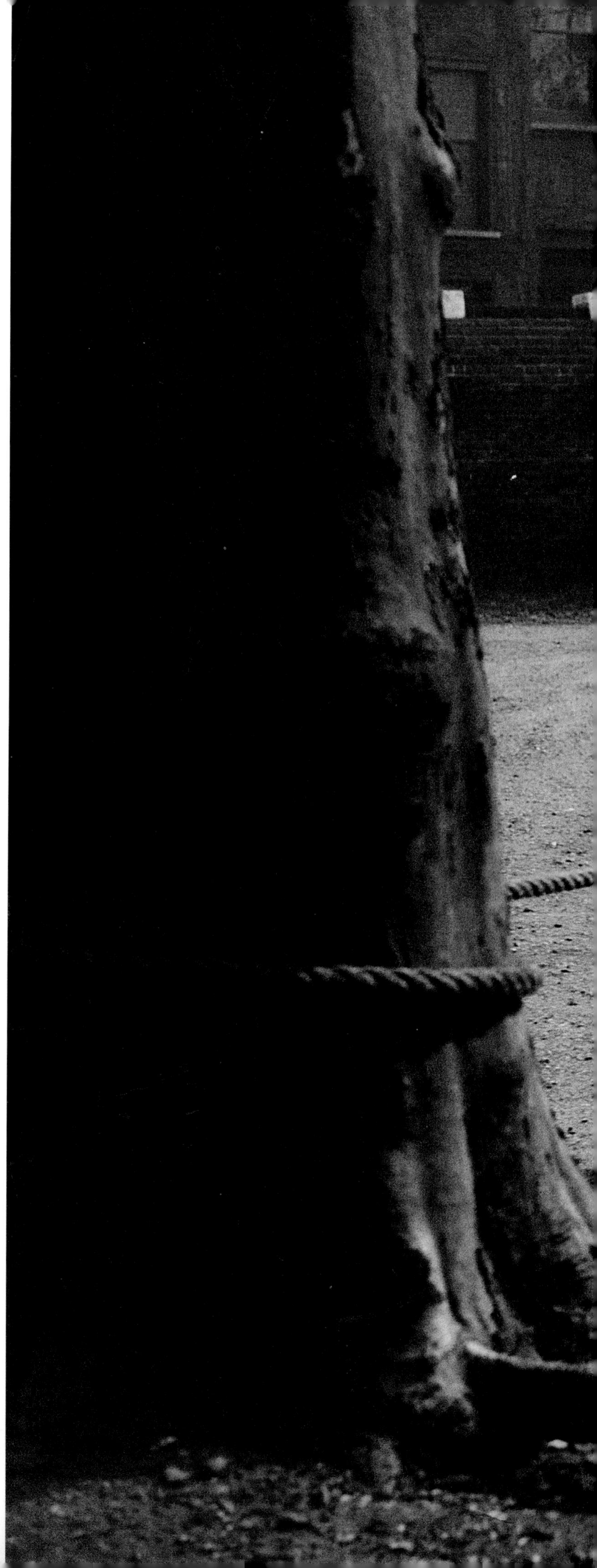

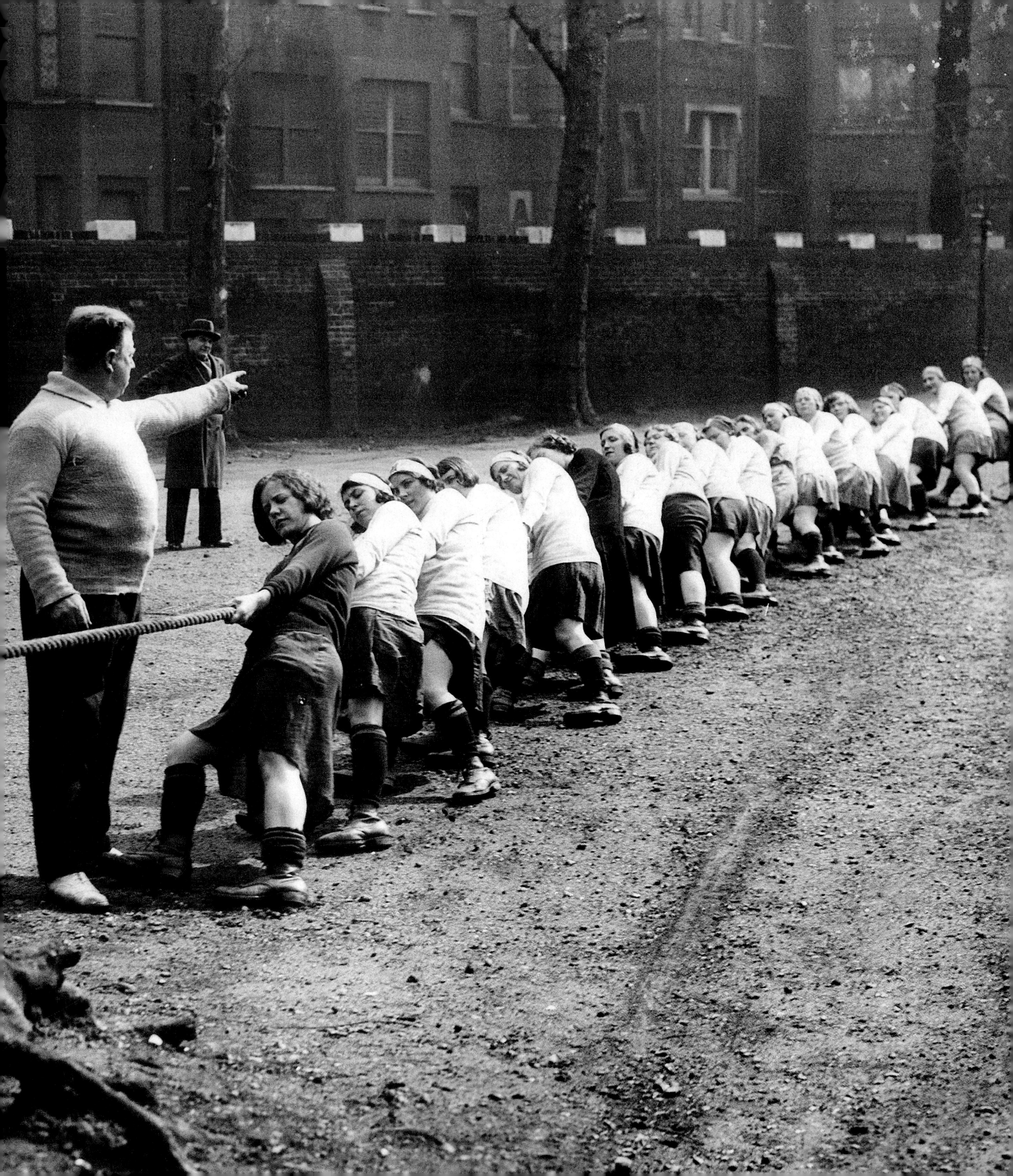

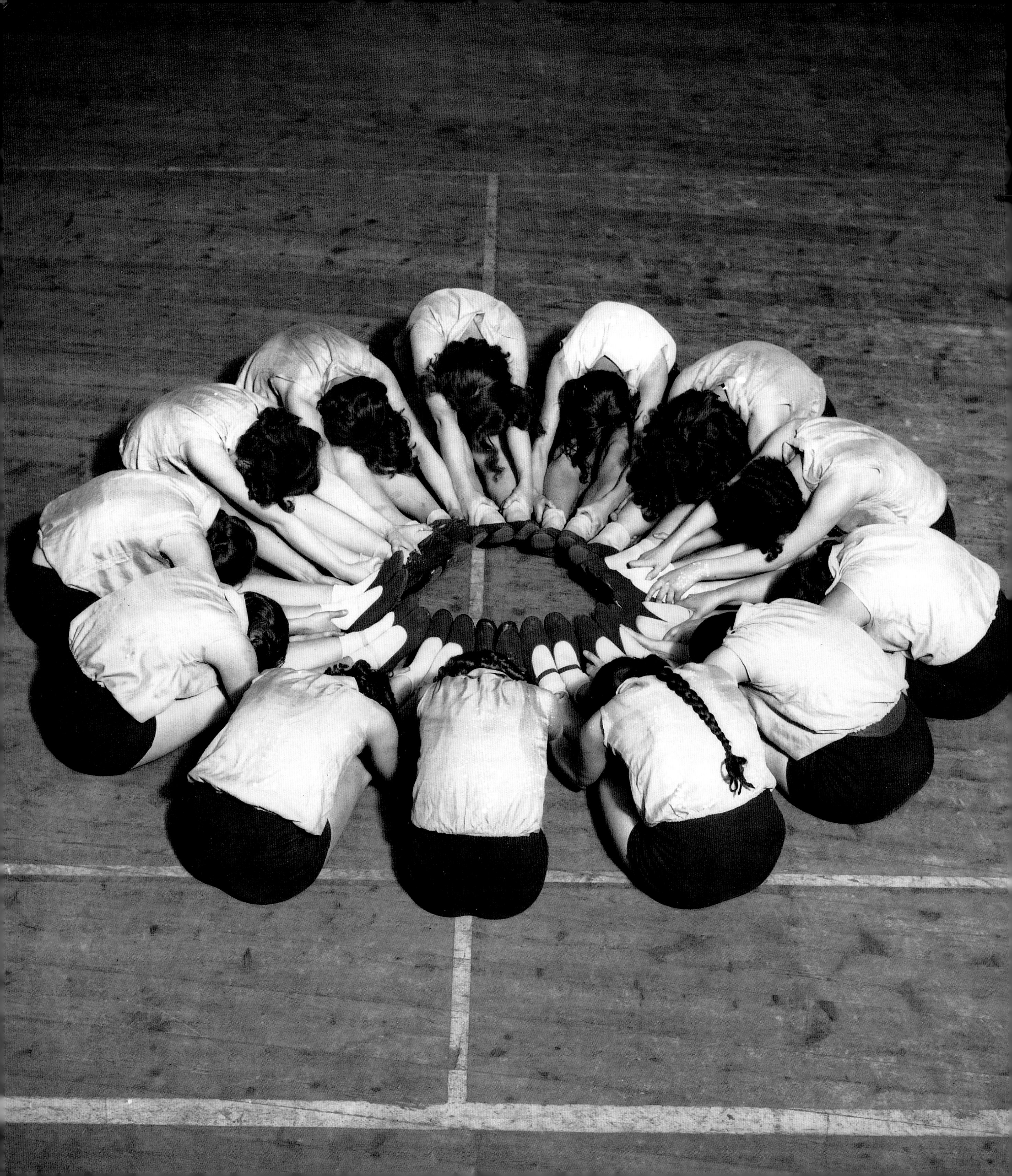

02/03
The Liverpool Street Ladies of London giving a gymnastic display, 1934
Hudson

04 (OVERLEAF)
The Hitler Youth give a display of physical exercises, *c.* 1935

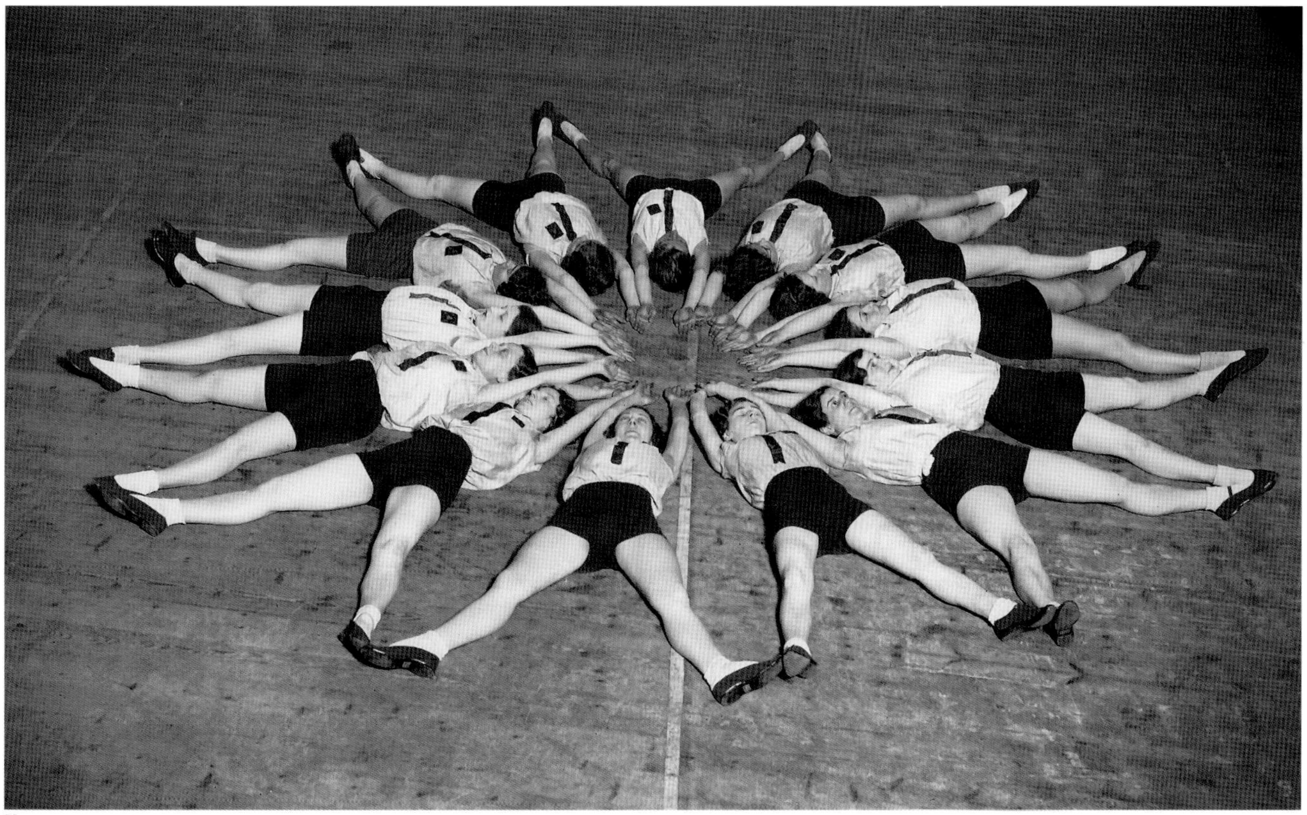
03

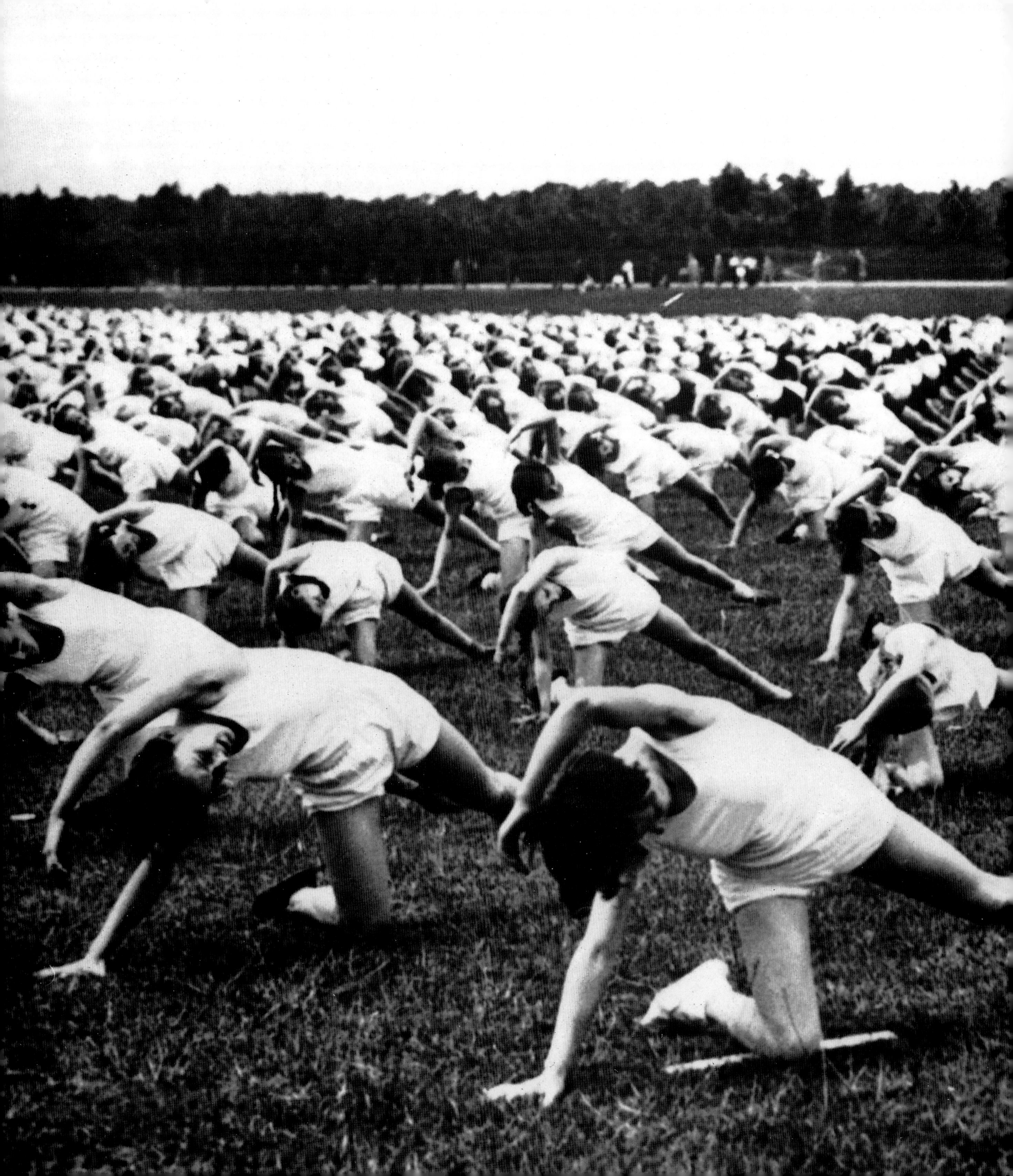

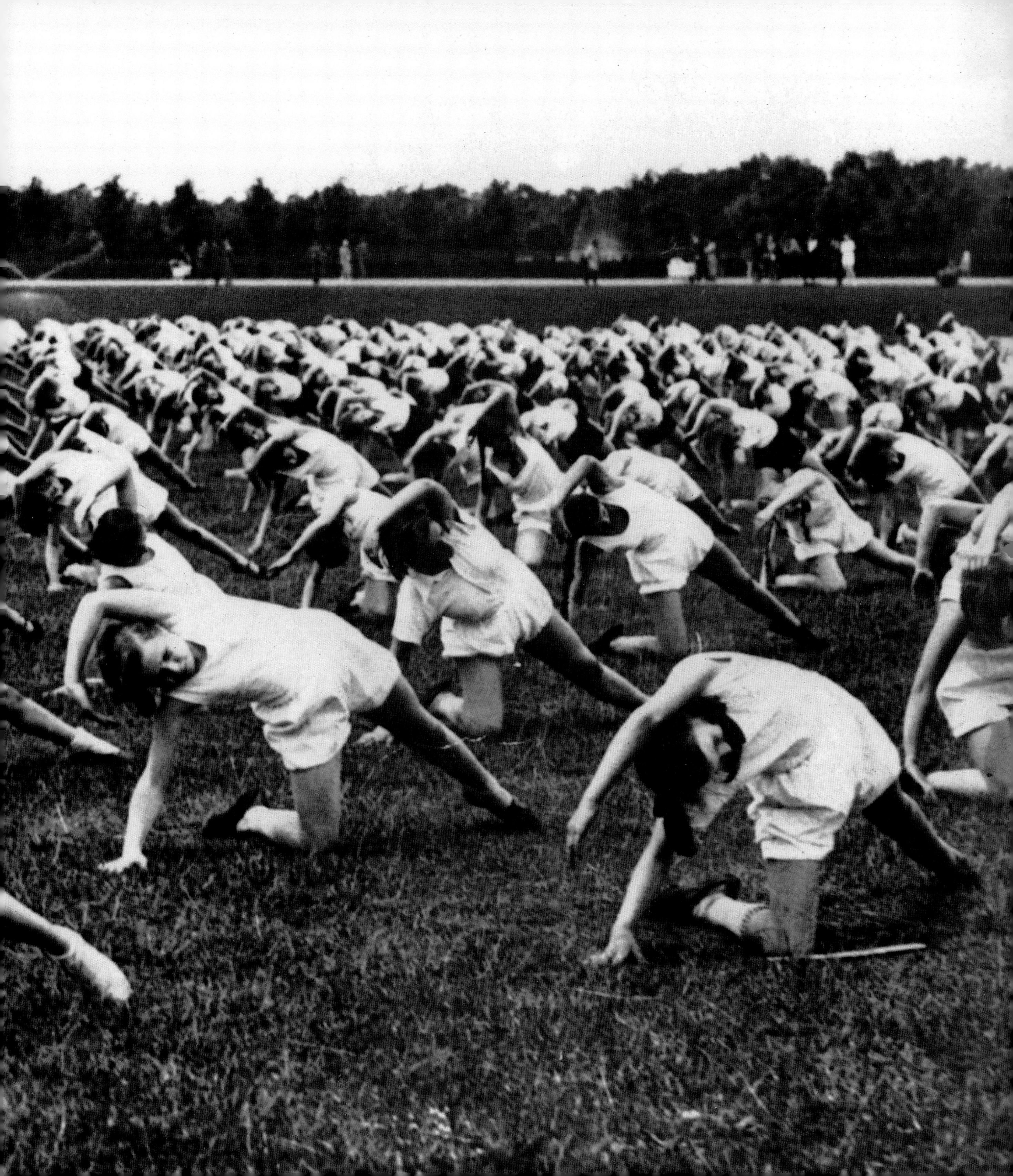

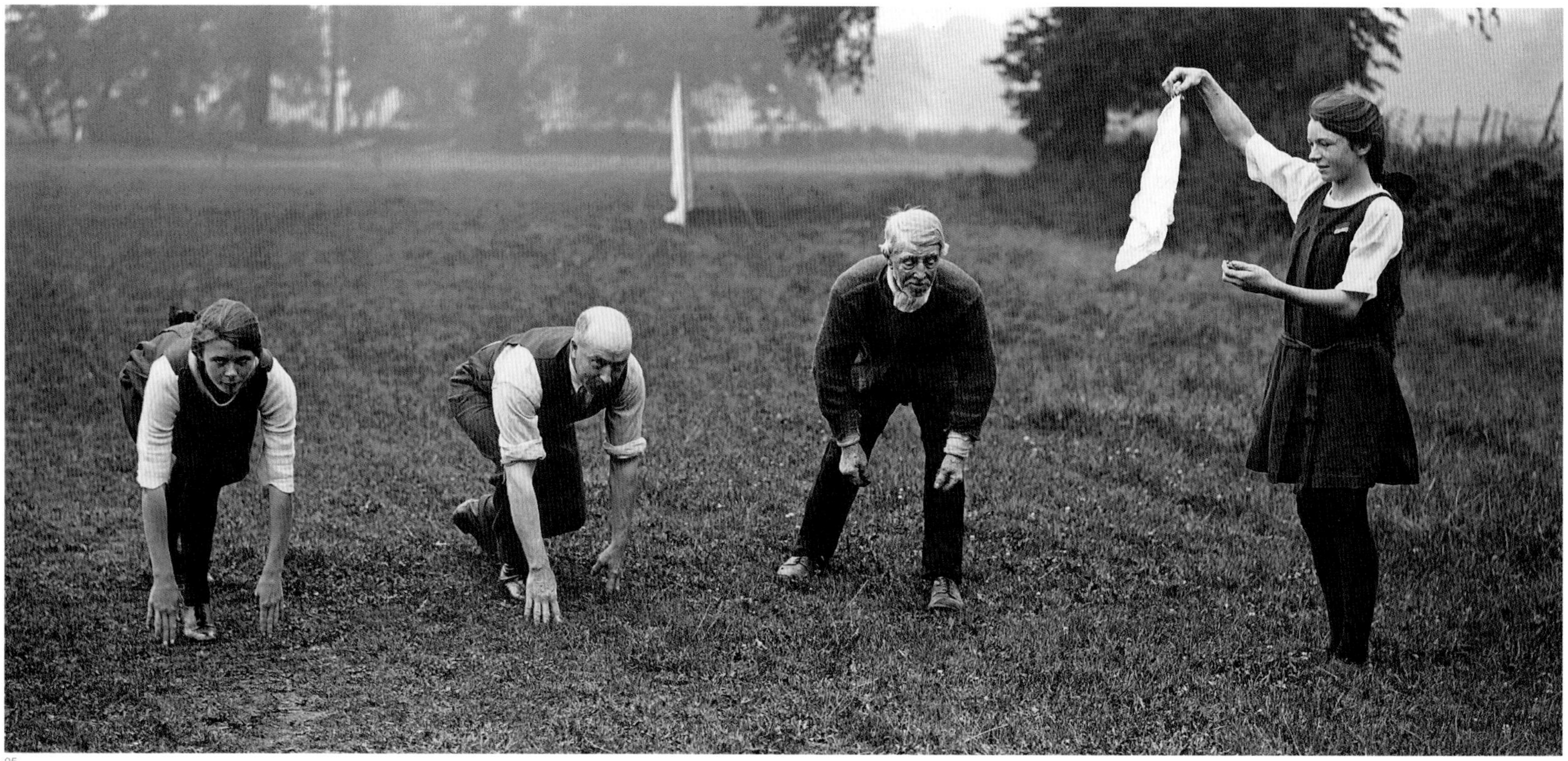

05

05
George Davey, 84, practising a race start with his son and granddaughter, 1922
McGregor

06
International runner Ruth Christmas coaching the sprint start, 1933
A Hudson

07 (OVERLEAF)
R G T Harper (centre) demonstrating 'a new style of exercise for general health and preparation for events', 1936
A Hudson

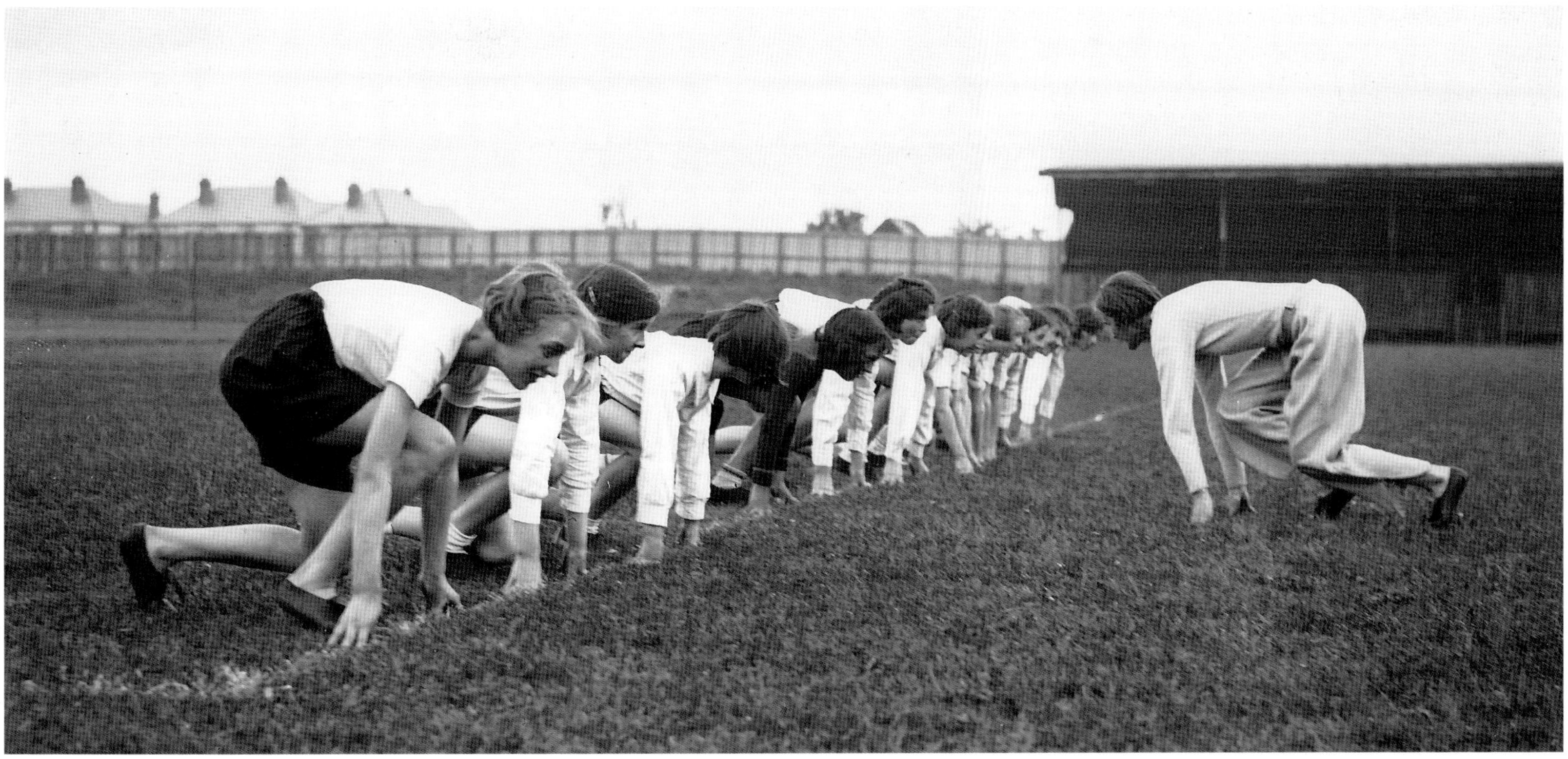
06

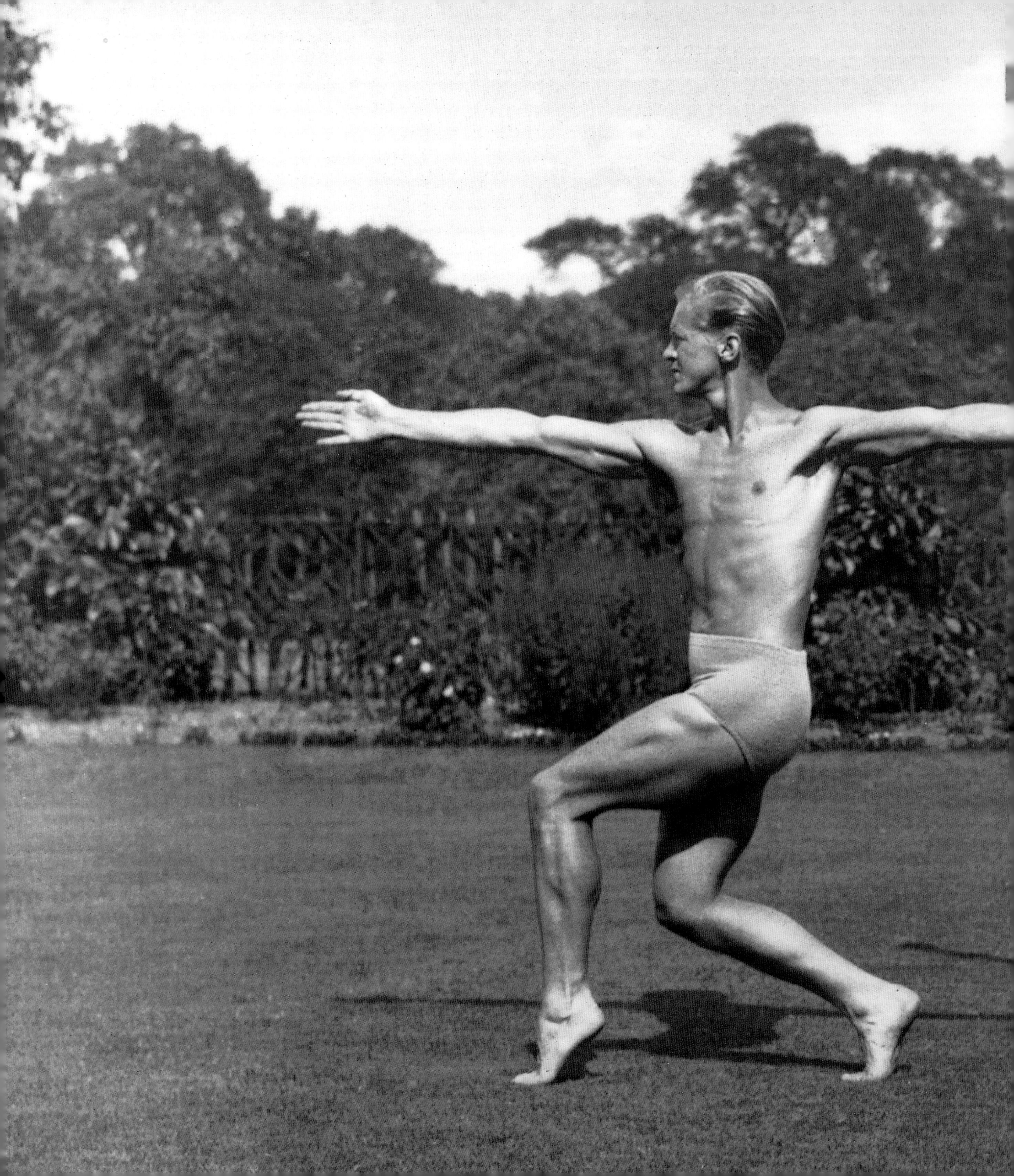

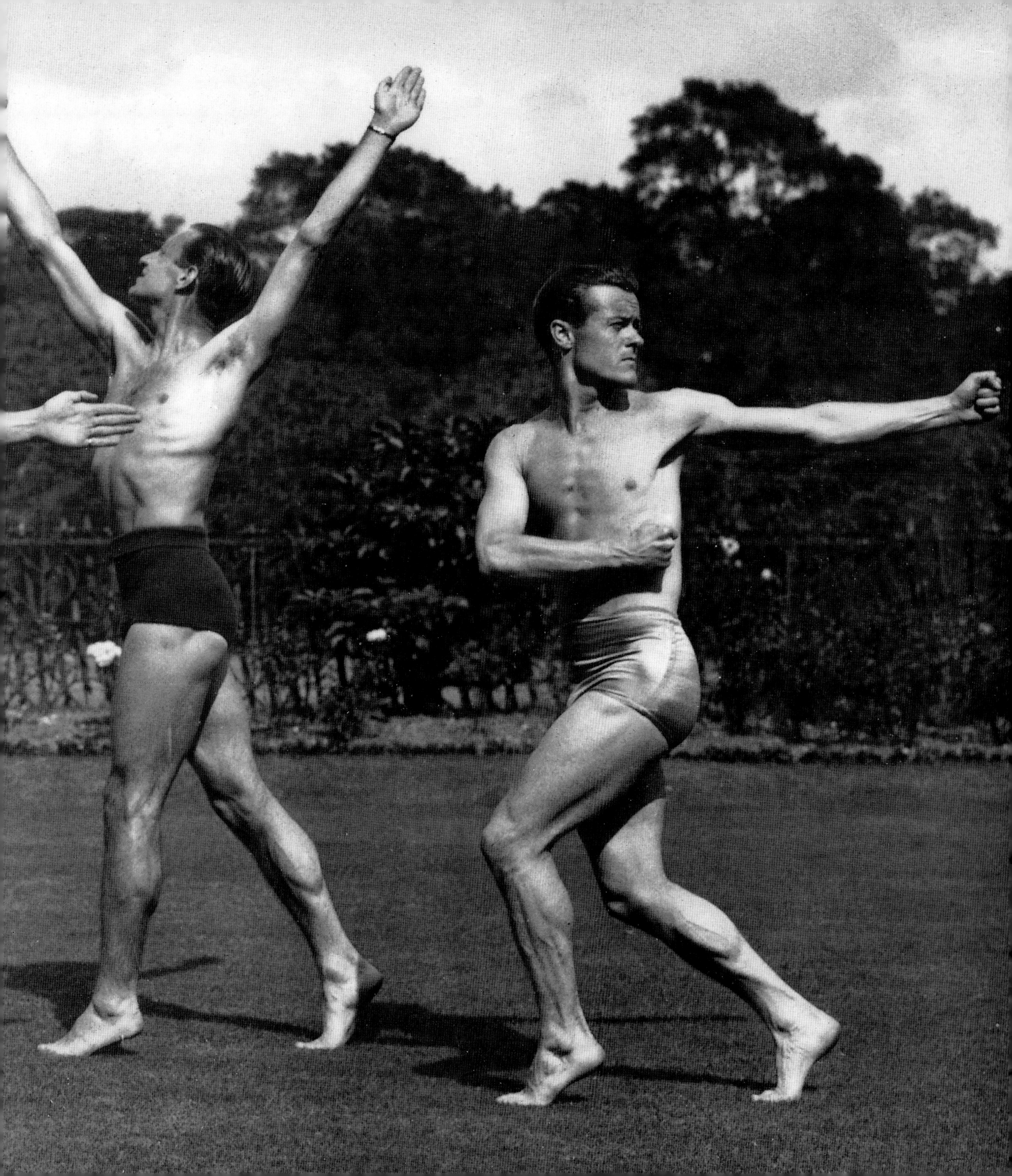

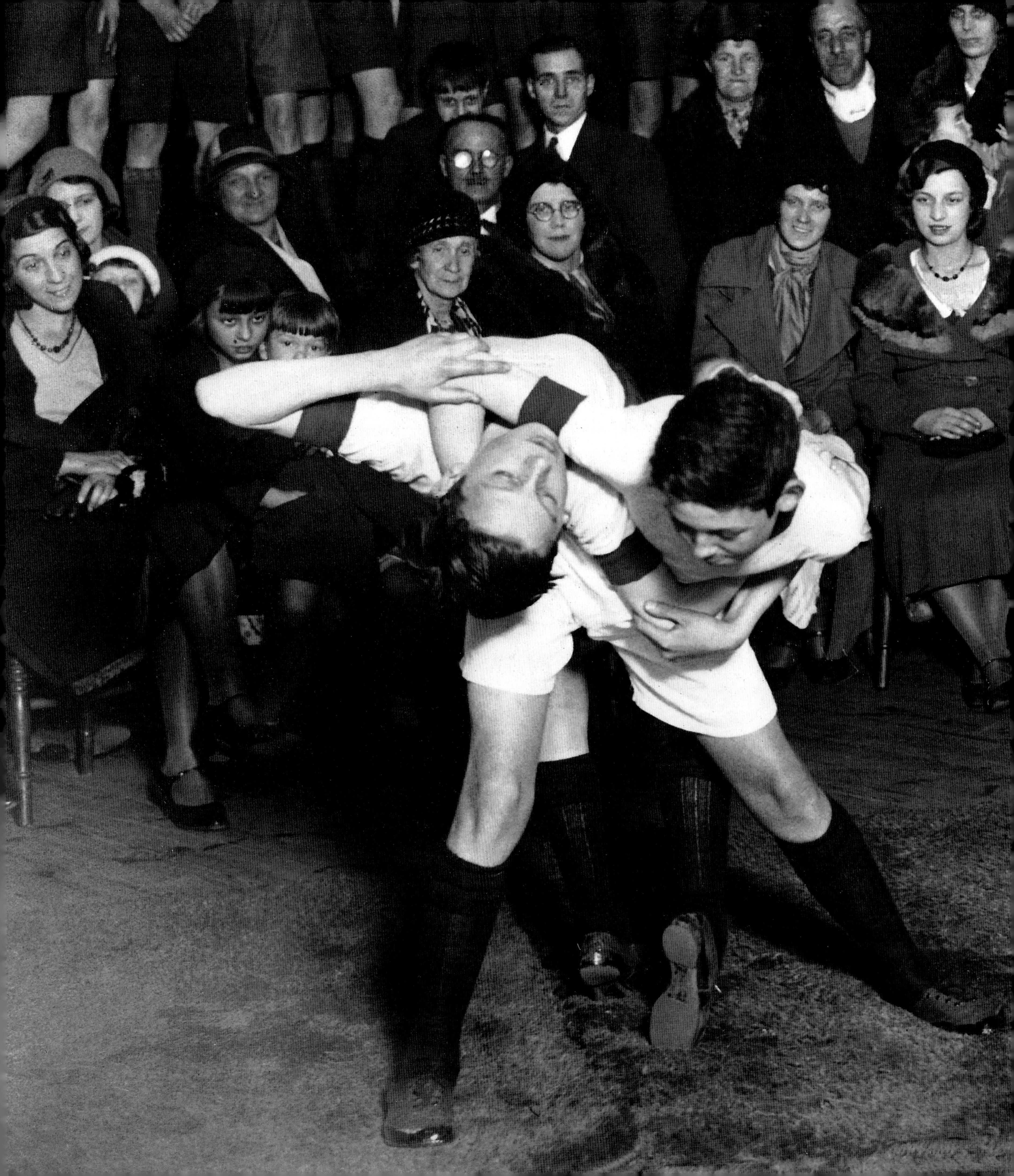

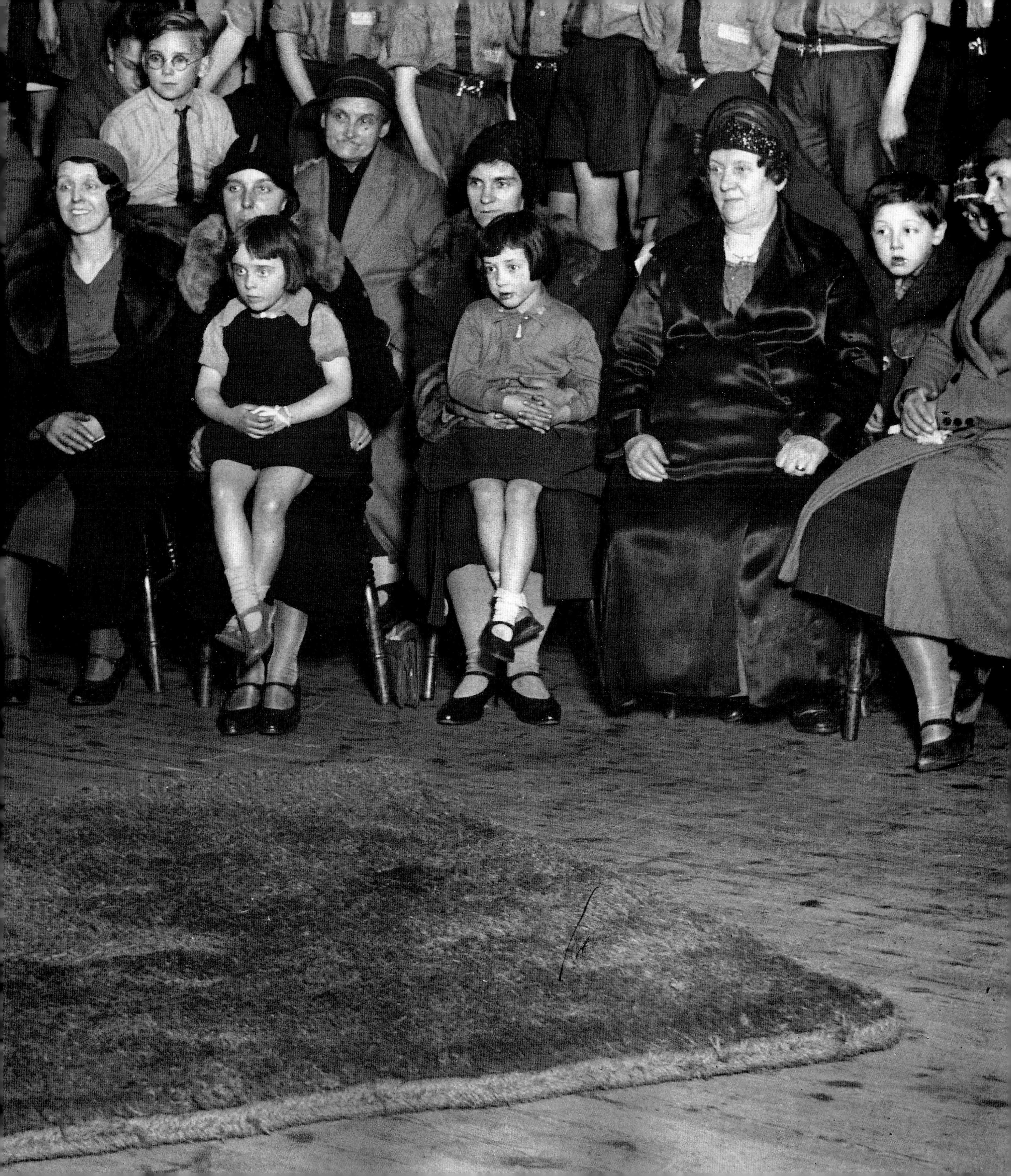

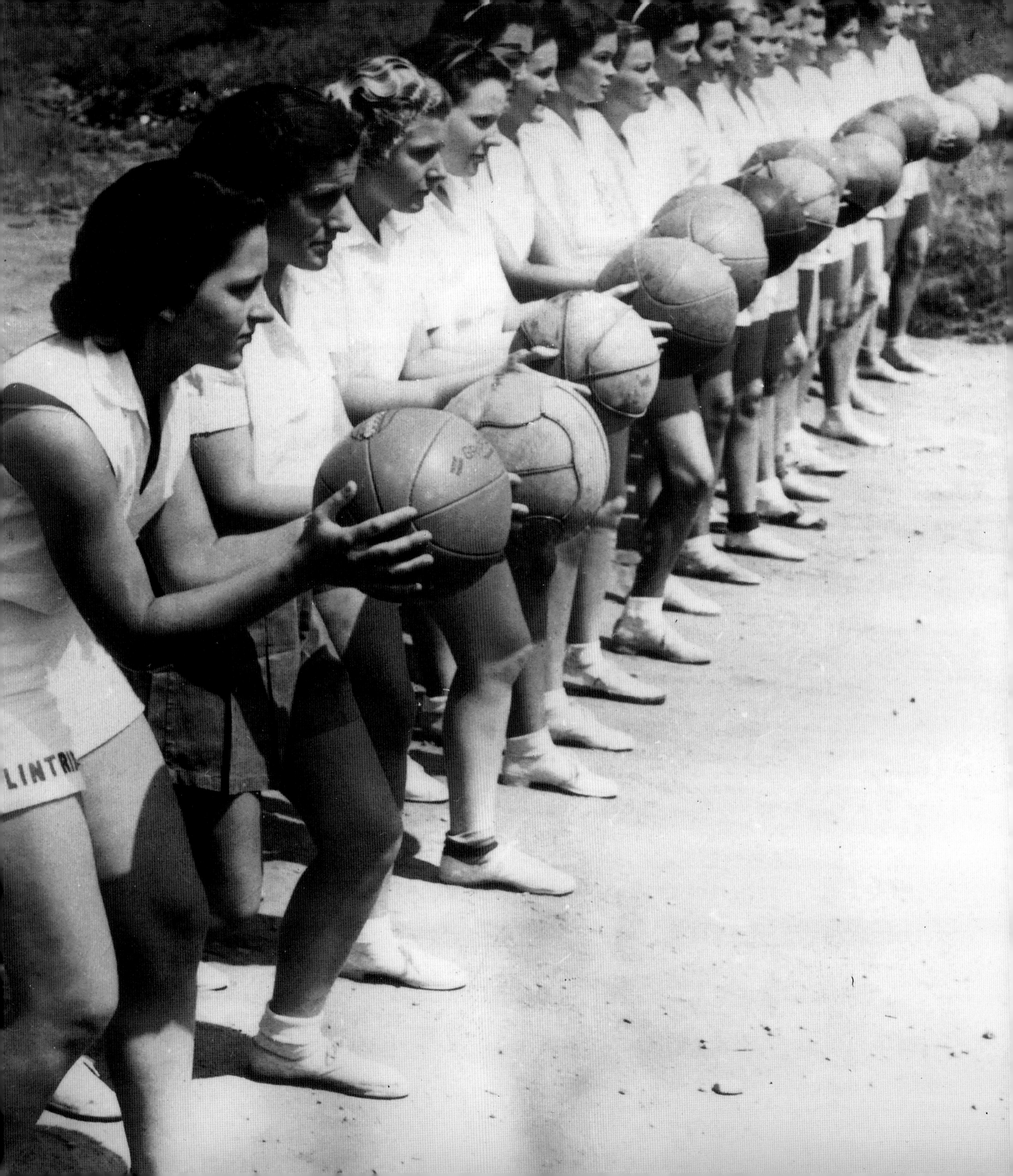
LINTRI

08 (PREVIOUS PAGE)
Schoolboys giving a wrestling display, *c.* 1932

09
Pasadena schoolgirls taking part in basketball practice, *c.* 1940

10
German housewives demonstrating a 'useful exercise that can be performed while making the bed', 1935

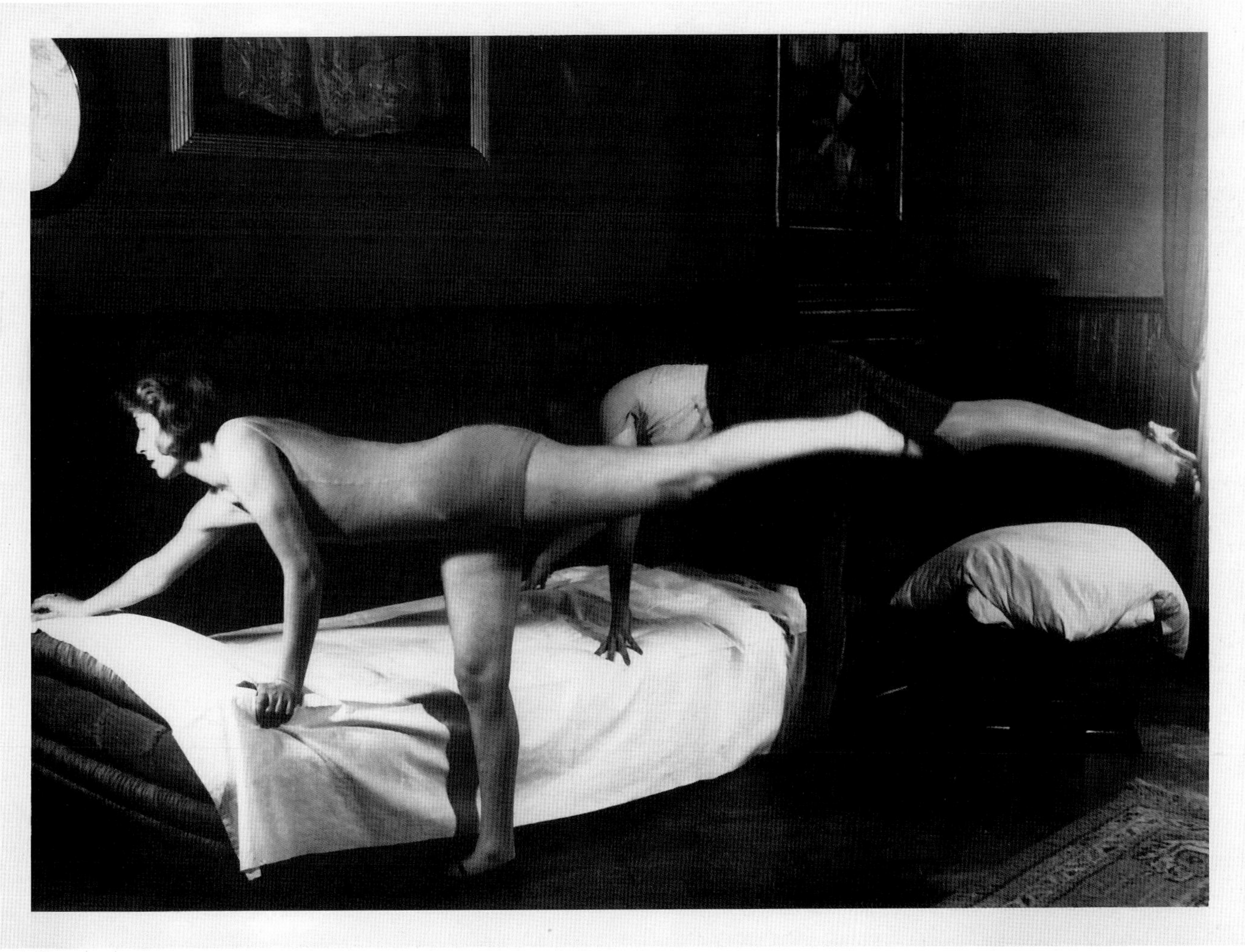

10

01
Arsenal versus Chelsea, London, 1937
A Hudson

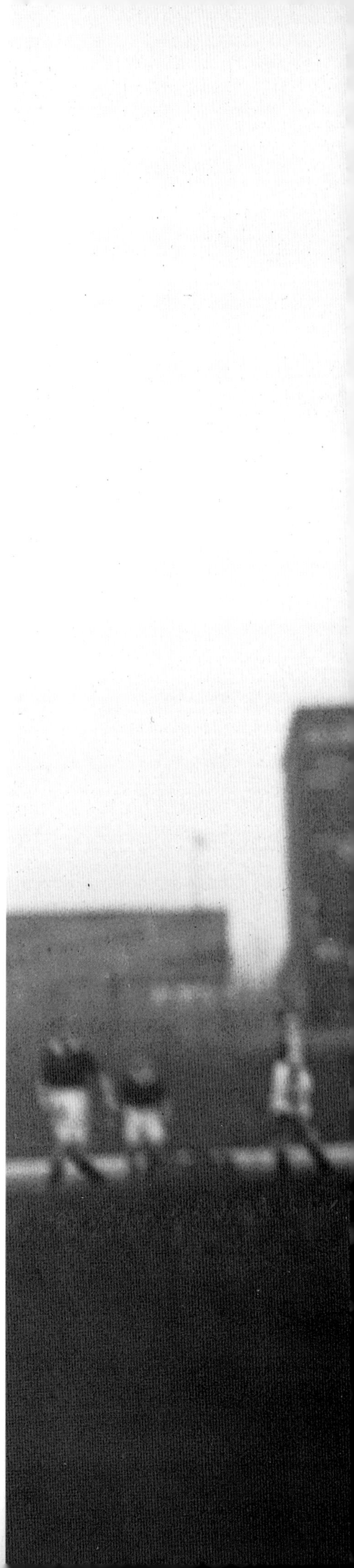

THE EDGE

Because of the limitations of their equipment, photographers had a restricted range of possibilities open to them when responding to action during a game or race. Telephoto lenses not yet being available they could not hope to capture incidents taking place at the centre of the field of play. Instead the photographers found themselves at the edge of the event, waiting for the action to come towards the camera. These limitations created sporting images of extraordinary drama where an incident can be seen as part of a wider view of the stadium and fellow team members. The edge was not just the side of the pitch, it was anywhere the photographer could get close to the action: in horse racing it was the side of the course where the riders and horses were released before making their way towards the start, or adjacent to a fence where experience suggested that there would be some fallers.

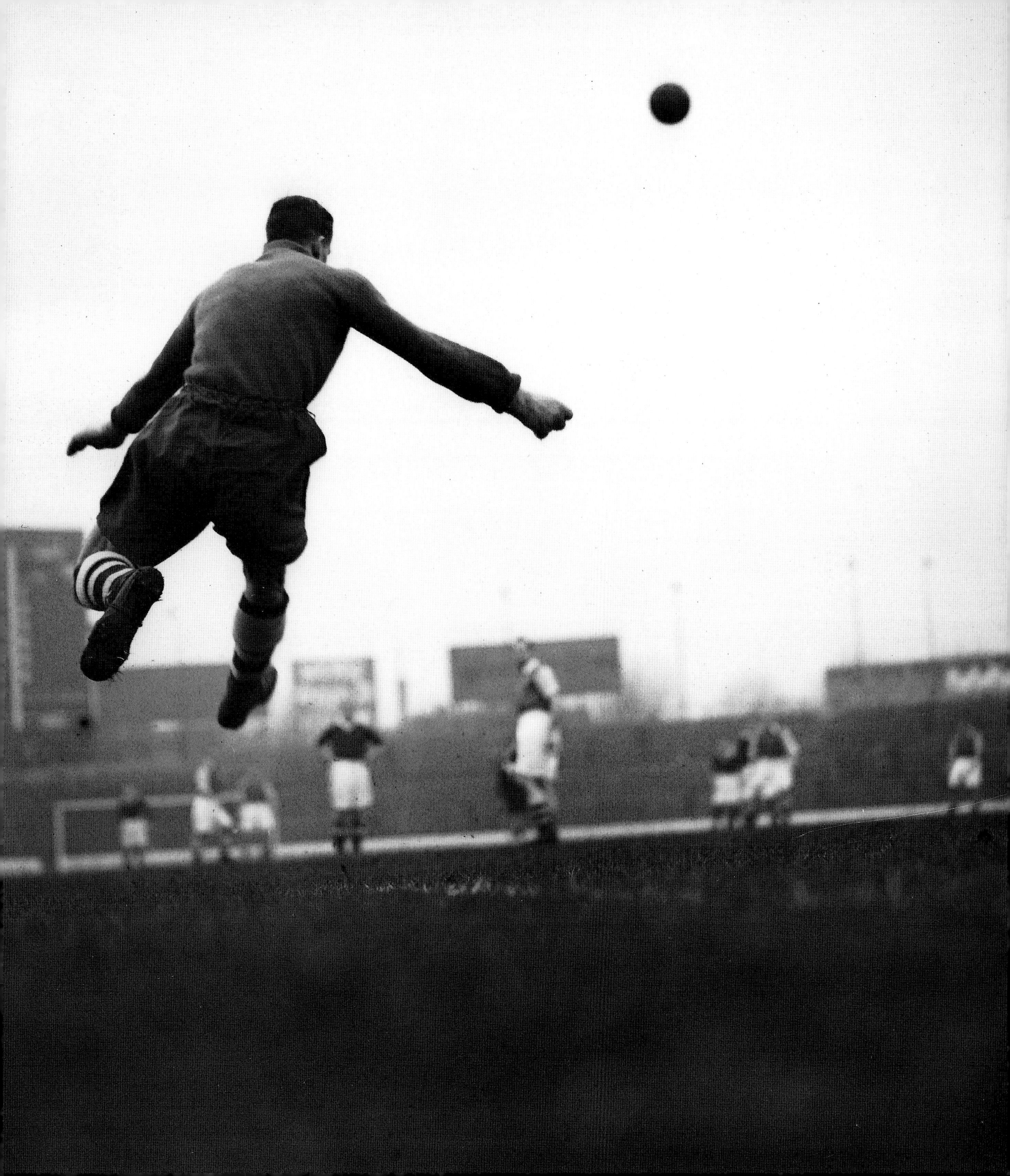

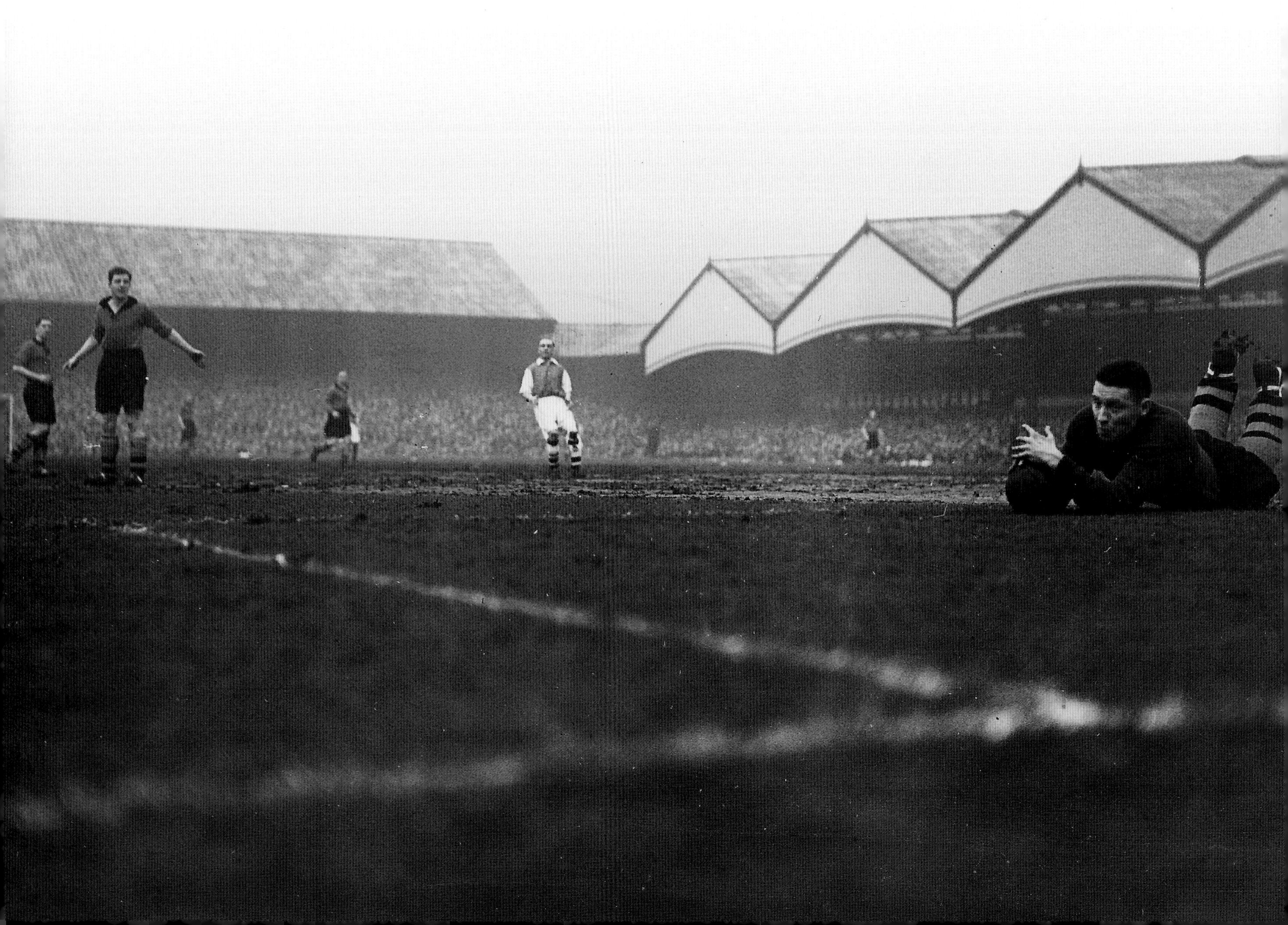

02
Wolverhampton Wanderers versus Arsenal,
Wolverhampton, England, 1938
H F Davis and A Hudson

03
Luton Town score against Scarborough,
Luton, England, 1938
H F Davis

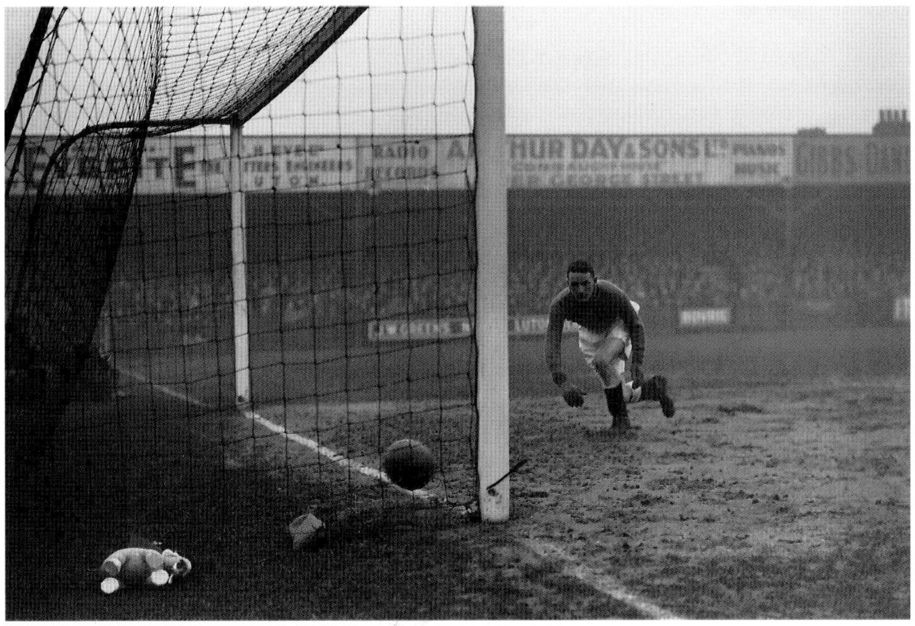

03

04
Rugby match between King's College and Guy's Hospital, London, 1930

05
Tottenham Hotspur versus Newcastle United soccer match, London, 1933
J A Hampton

06
Rugby League game between Leeds and Acton, London, 1936
J A Hampton

07 (OVERLEAF)
Geneva College versus Boston College, Boston, *c.* 1940

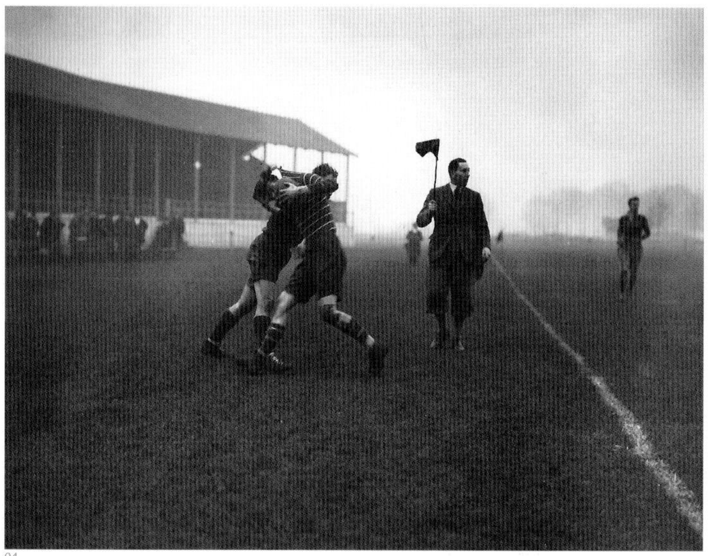

04

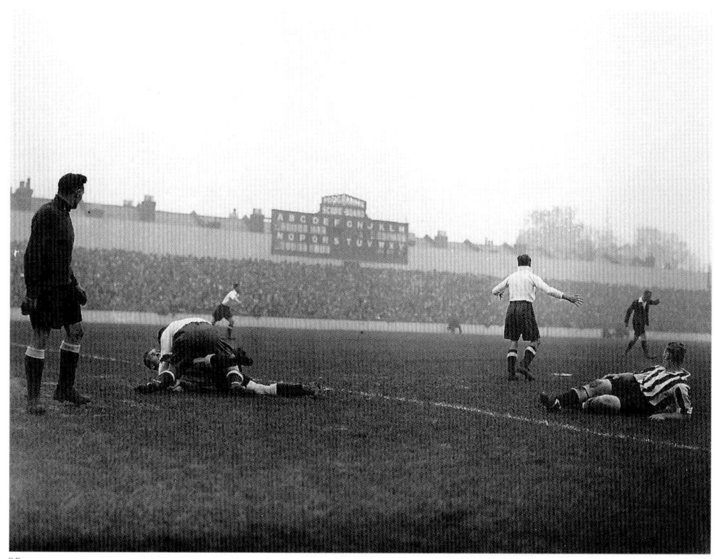

05

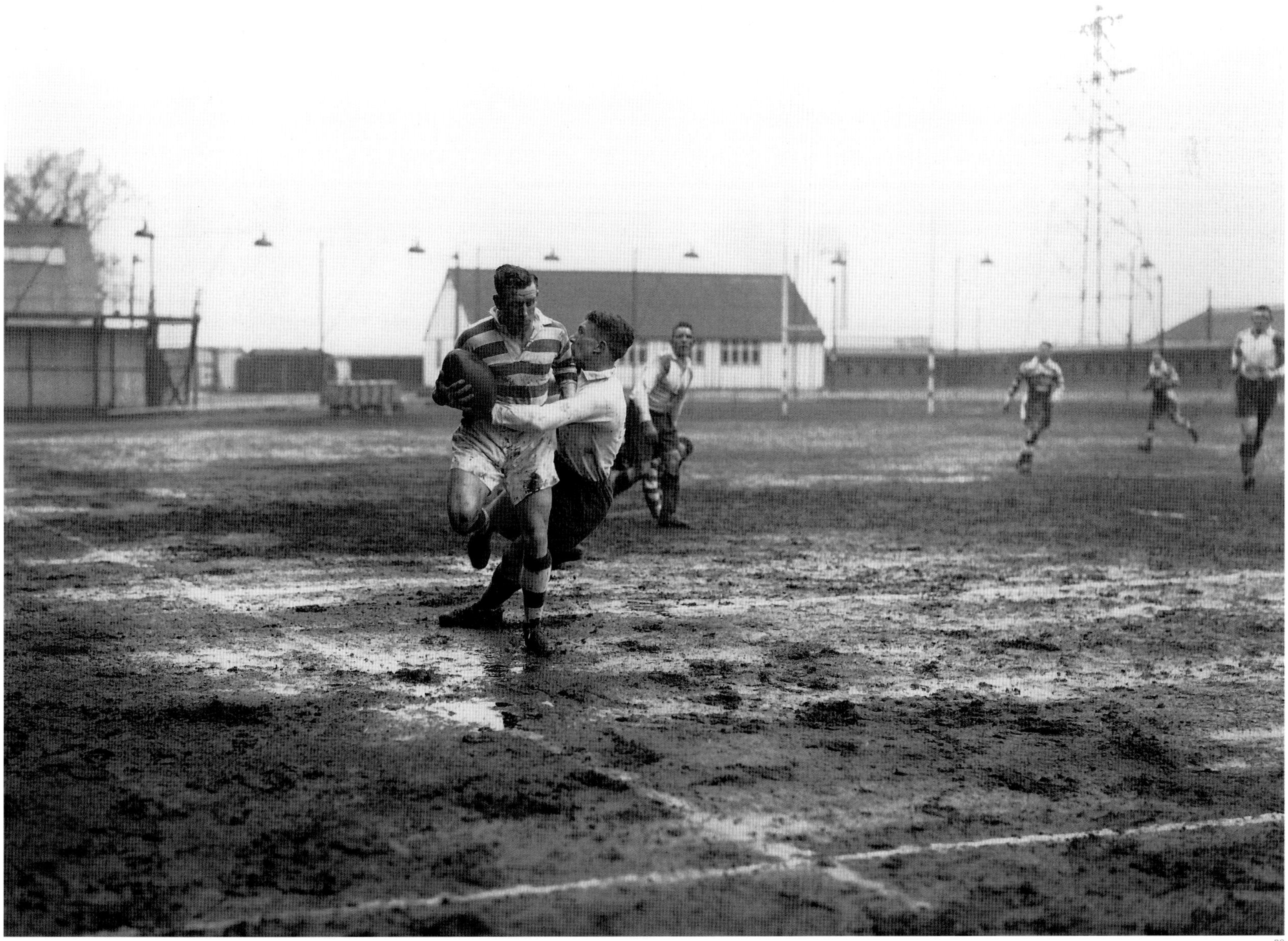

06

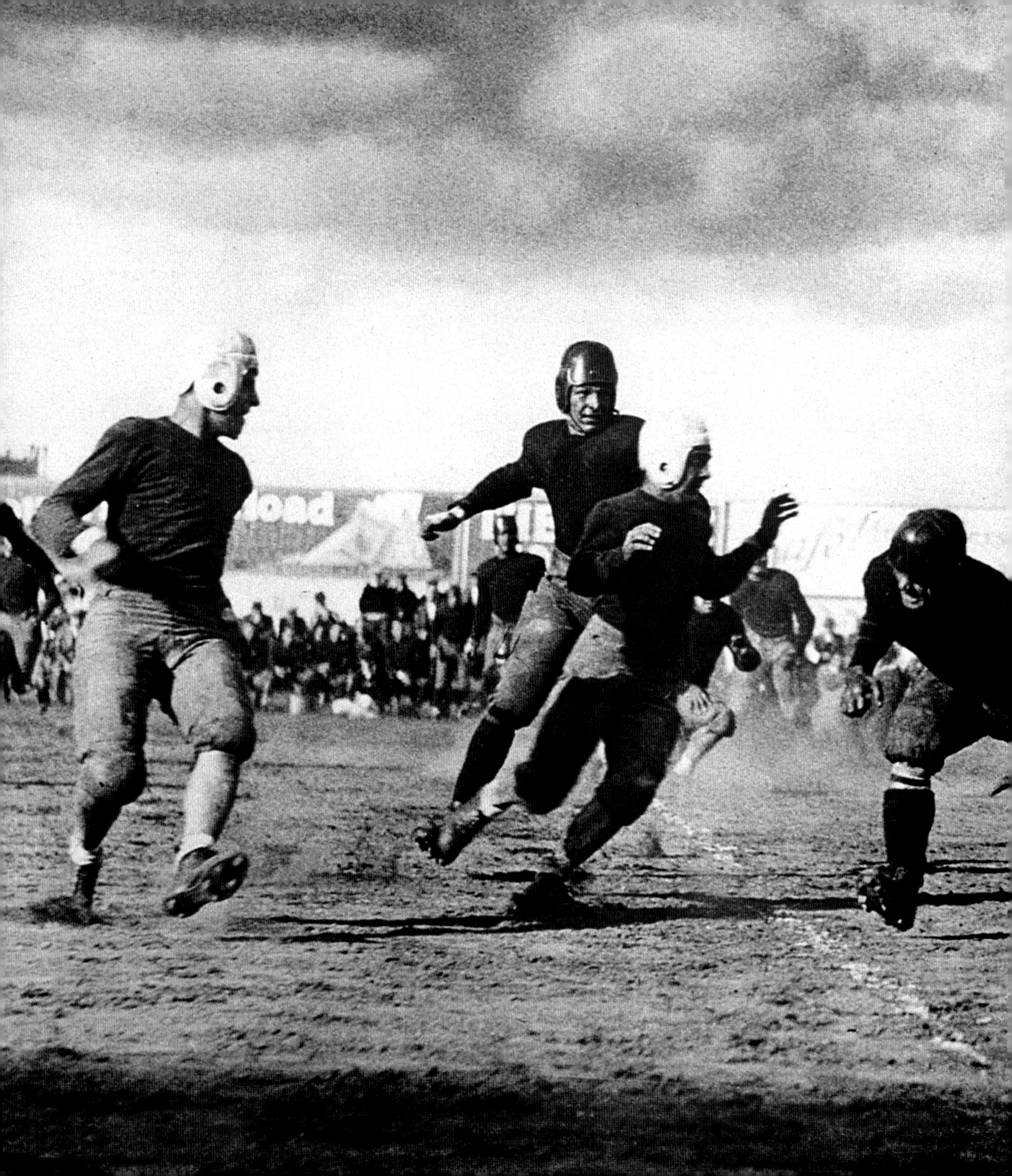

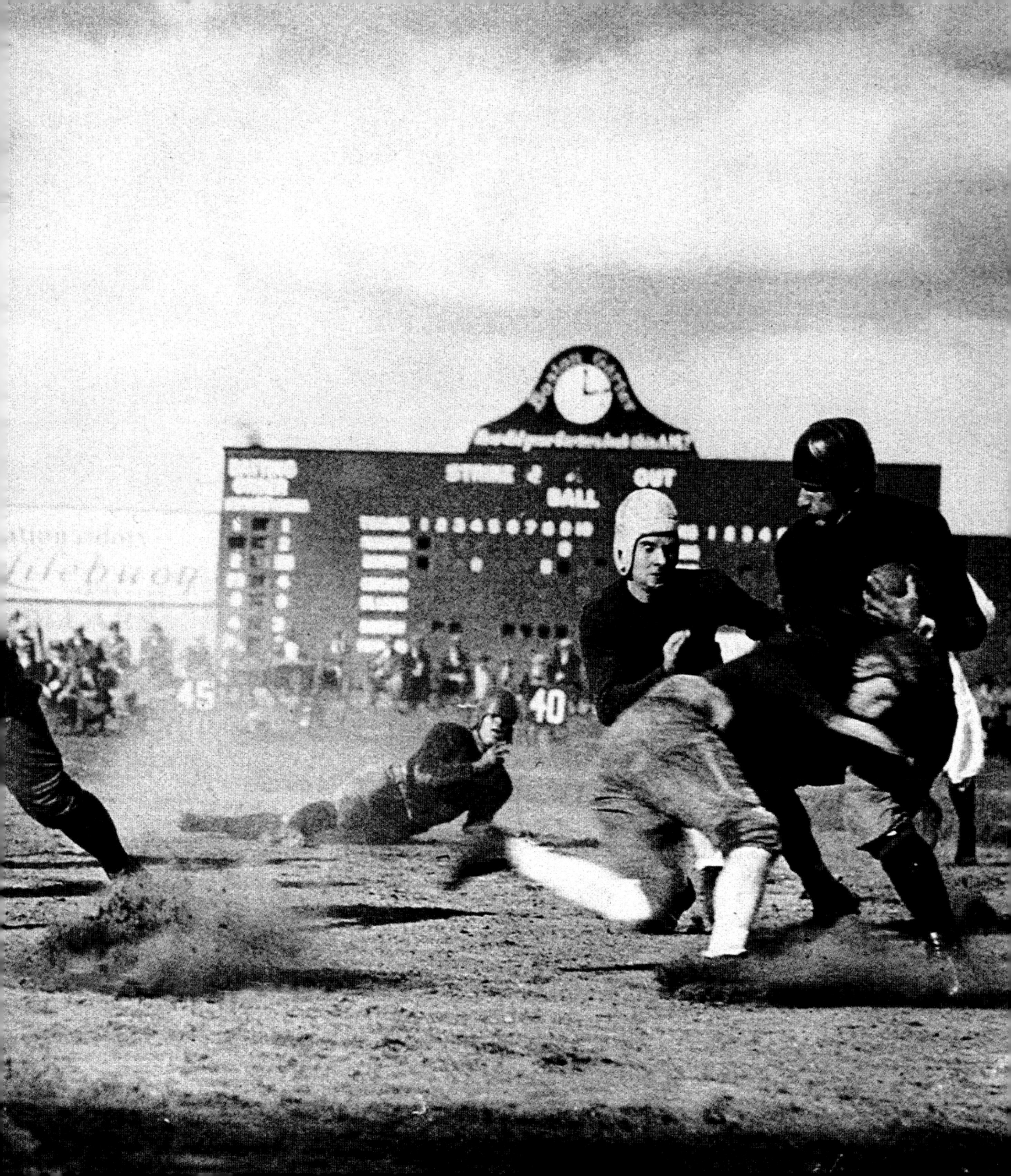
STRIKE
OUT
BALL
45
40

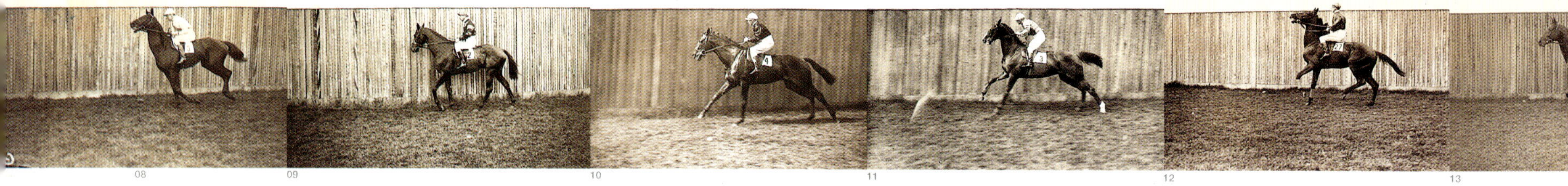

08 09 10 11 12 13

08–18
Racehorses at Epsom, England
From left: Meistersinger, *c.* 1930; Portlaw, 1931; Prester John, *c.* 1927; Money Maker, *c.* 1927; Homer, 1931; His Grace, 1936; Legality, 1923; Monument, 1936; Birthright, *c.* 1927; Powerful Prince, 1935; Haytime, 1934

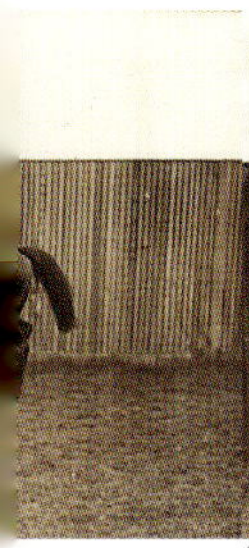

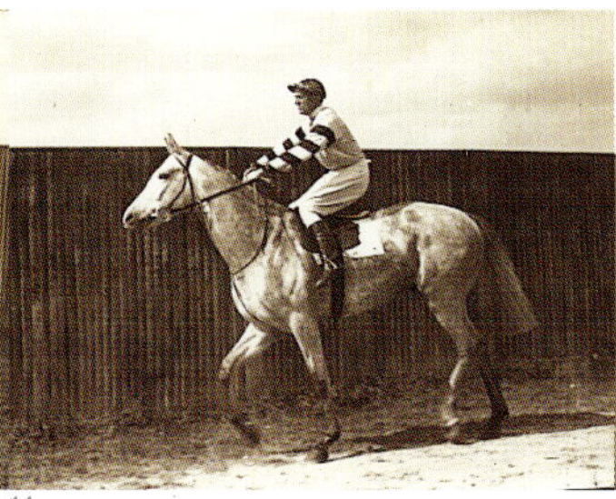

14

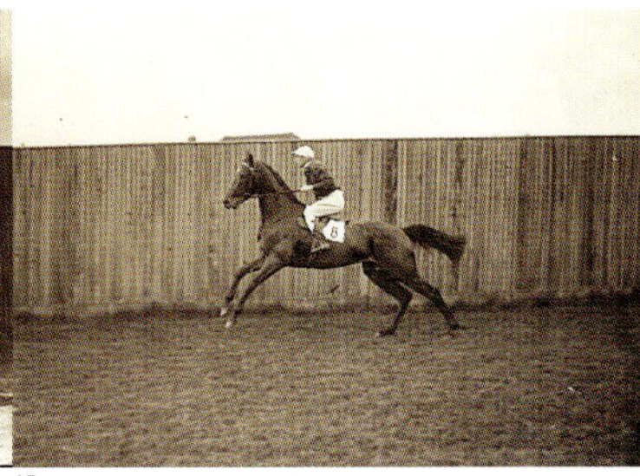

15

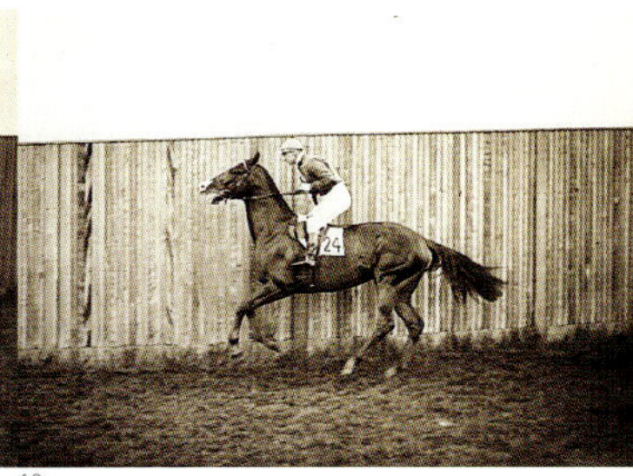

16

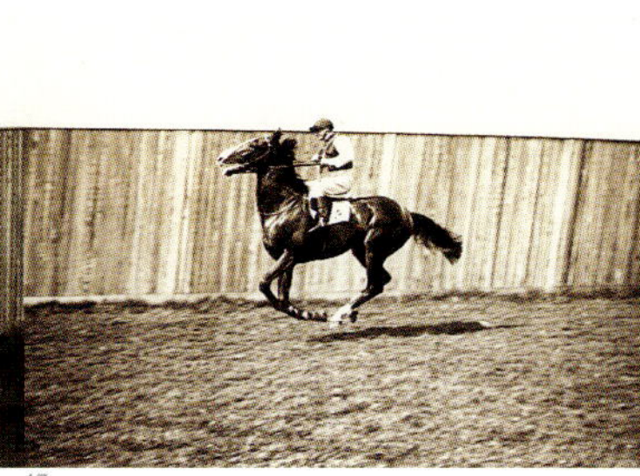

17

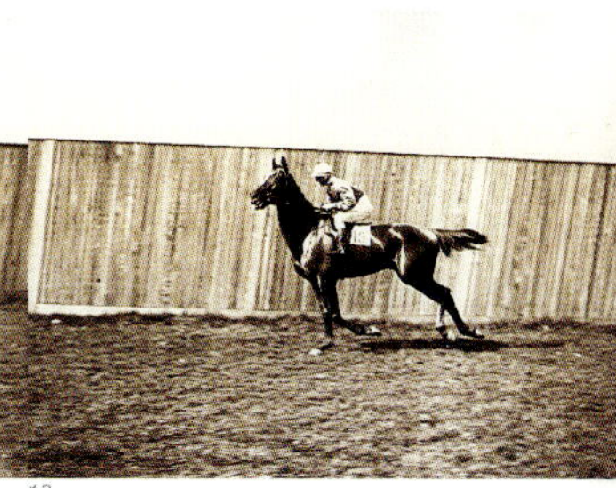

18

19
First fence at the Grand National, Liverpool, 1927

20
Fallers at the Grand National, Liverpool, 1922

21
Beecher's Brook at the Grand National, Liverpool, 1938

19

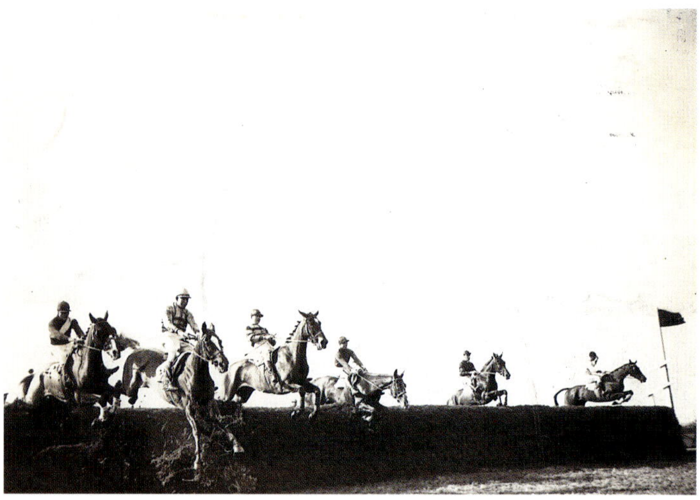

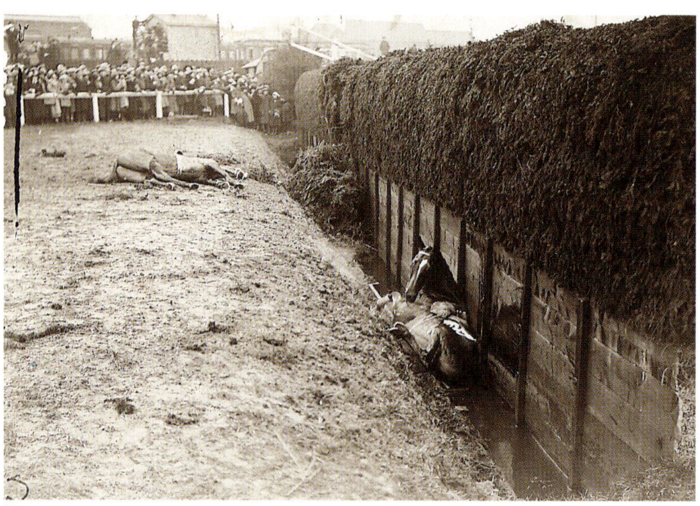

20

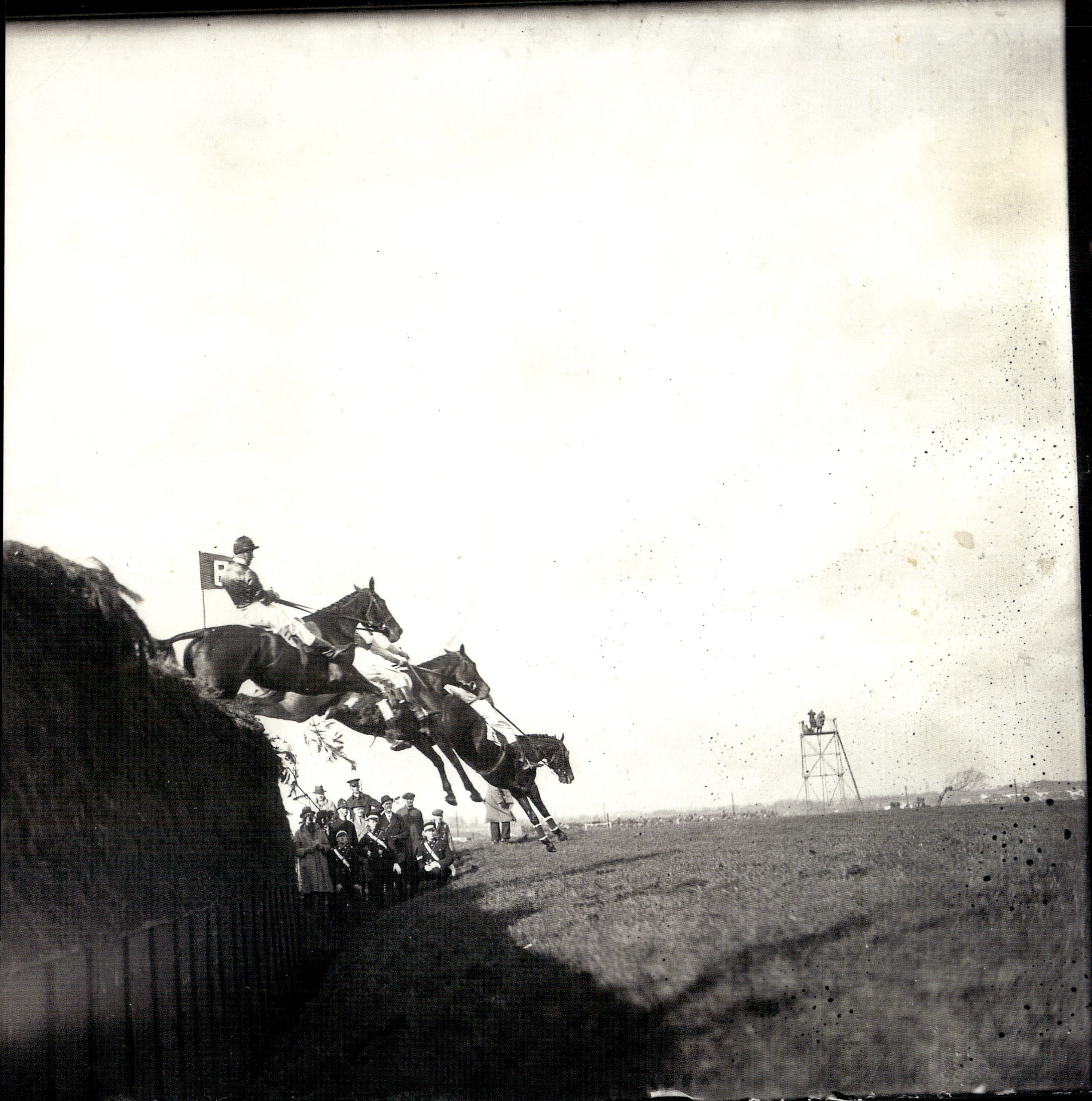

01/02 (OVERLEAF)
Frank Goddard, 1922

WHITE OUT

By isolating the sporting figure against a plain white background portraits could be created that were not associated with a specific time or event and could therefore easily be used to illustrate articles and news stories for many years. If it was not possible to make these portraits in the studio they could be made by painting out the area surrounding the figure, so obliterating the original location where the photograph was taken. This technique was so common that photographers anticipated the whiting-out when taking their photographs by allowing space around the figure so the photographic print could be altered.

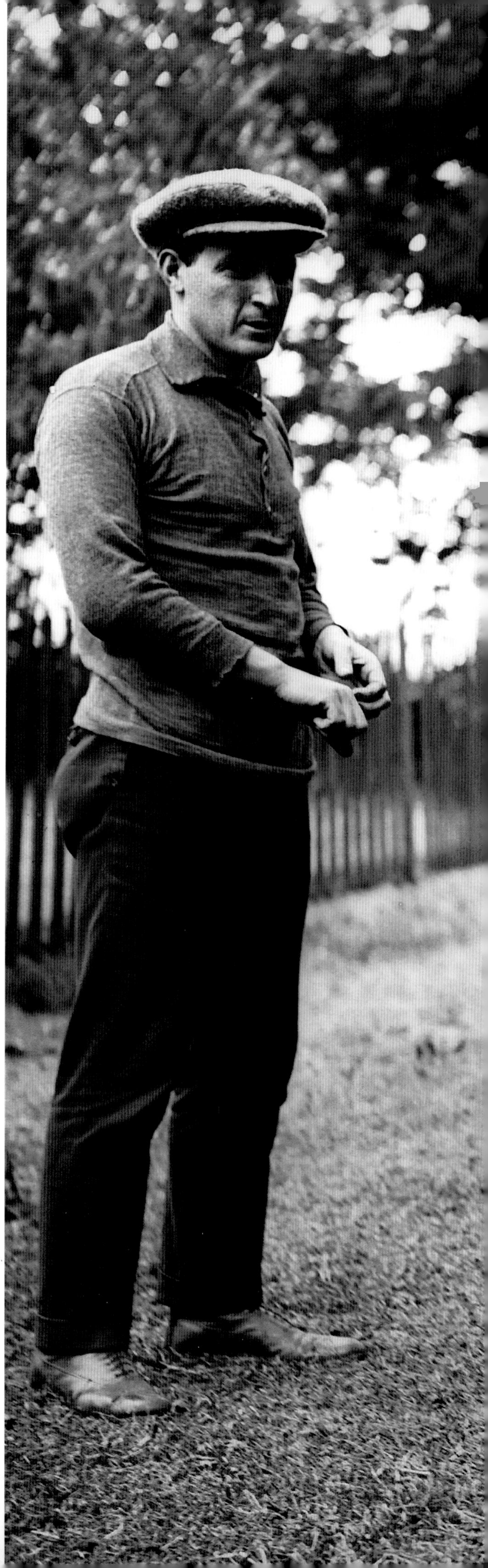

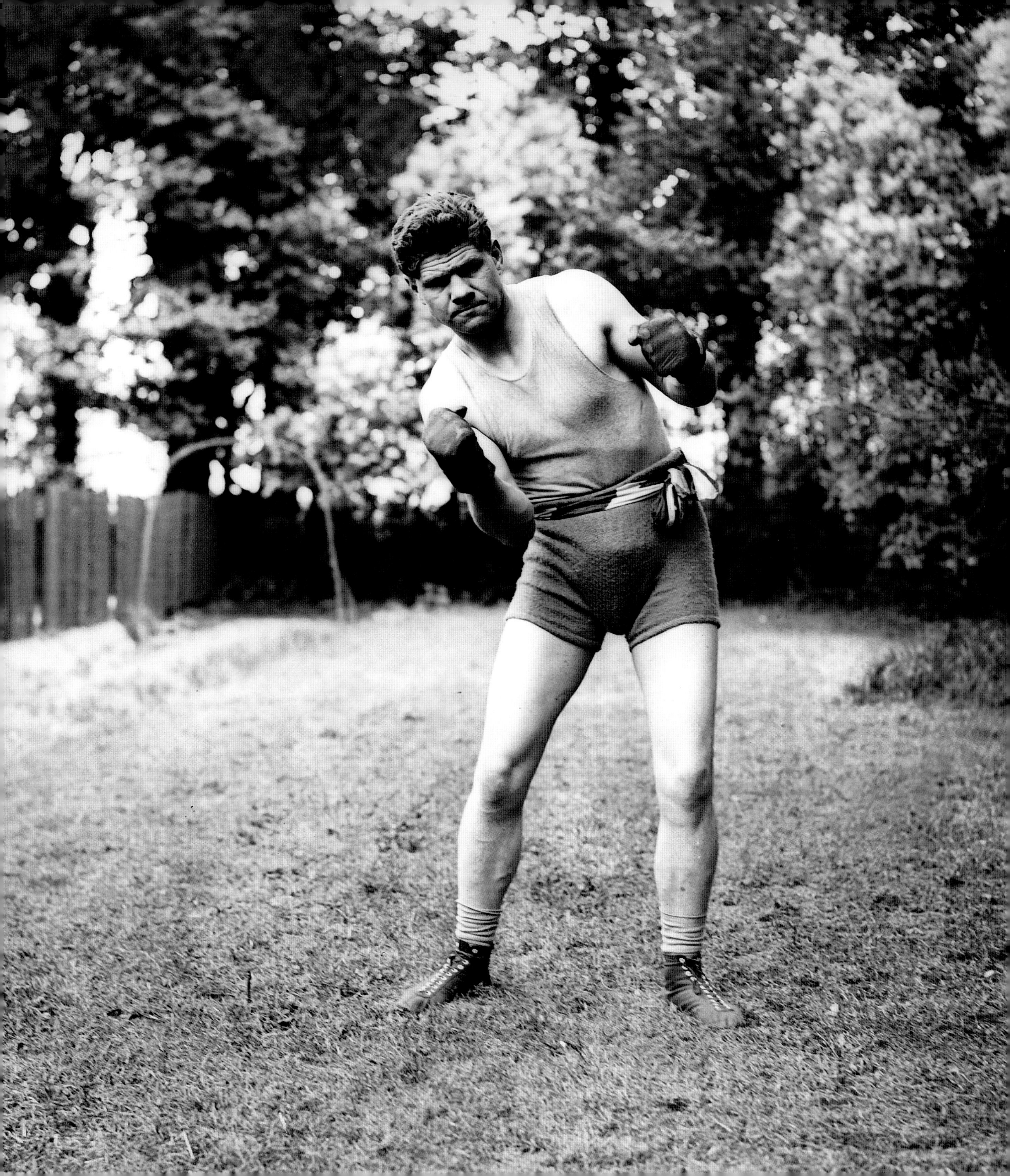

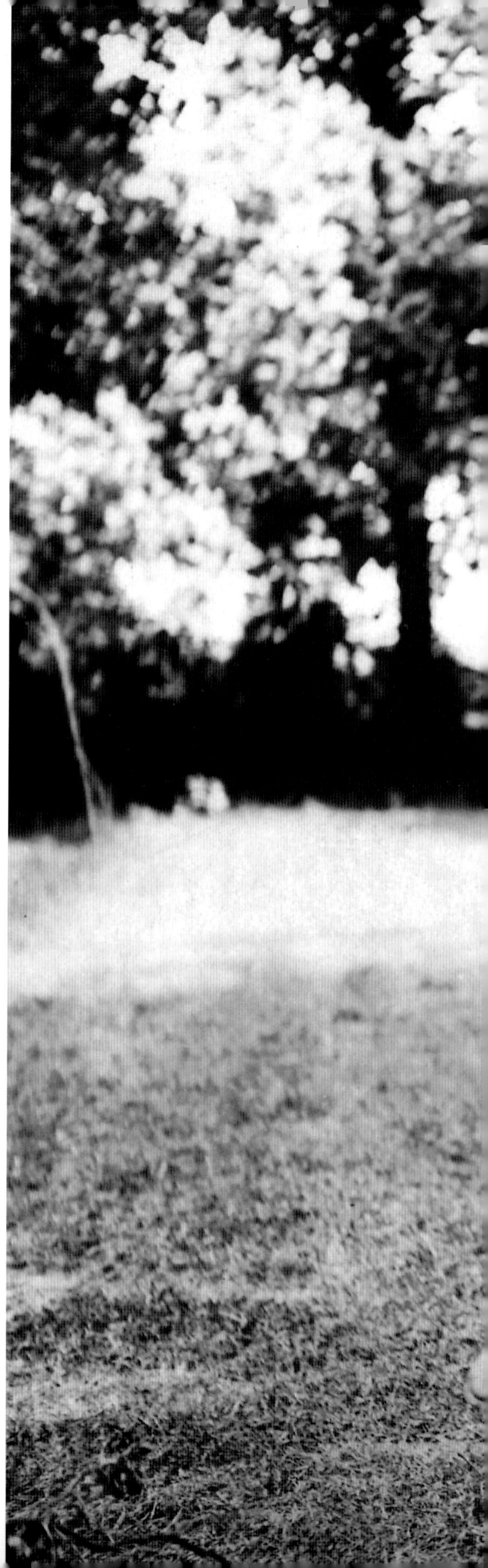

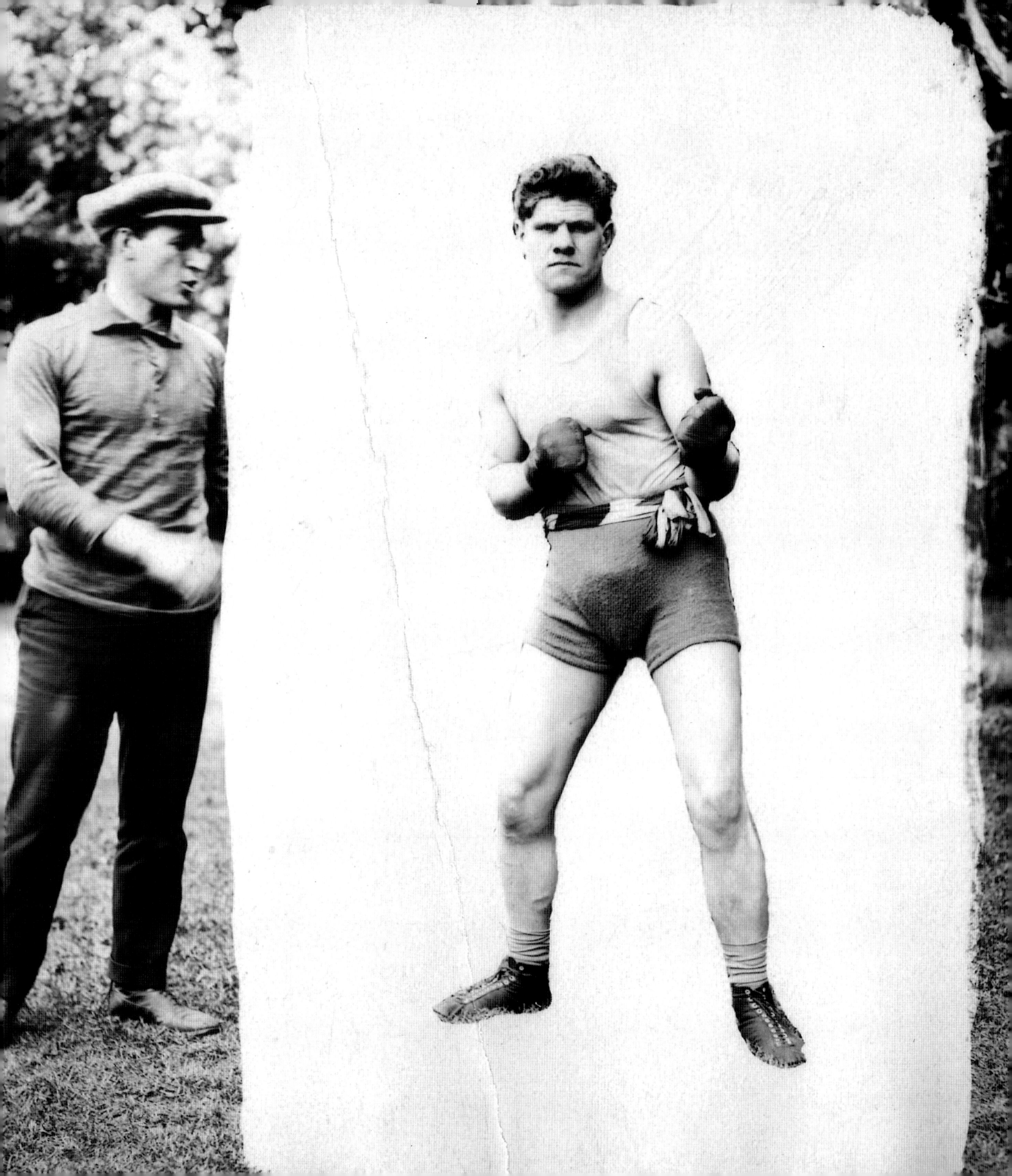

03

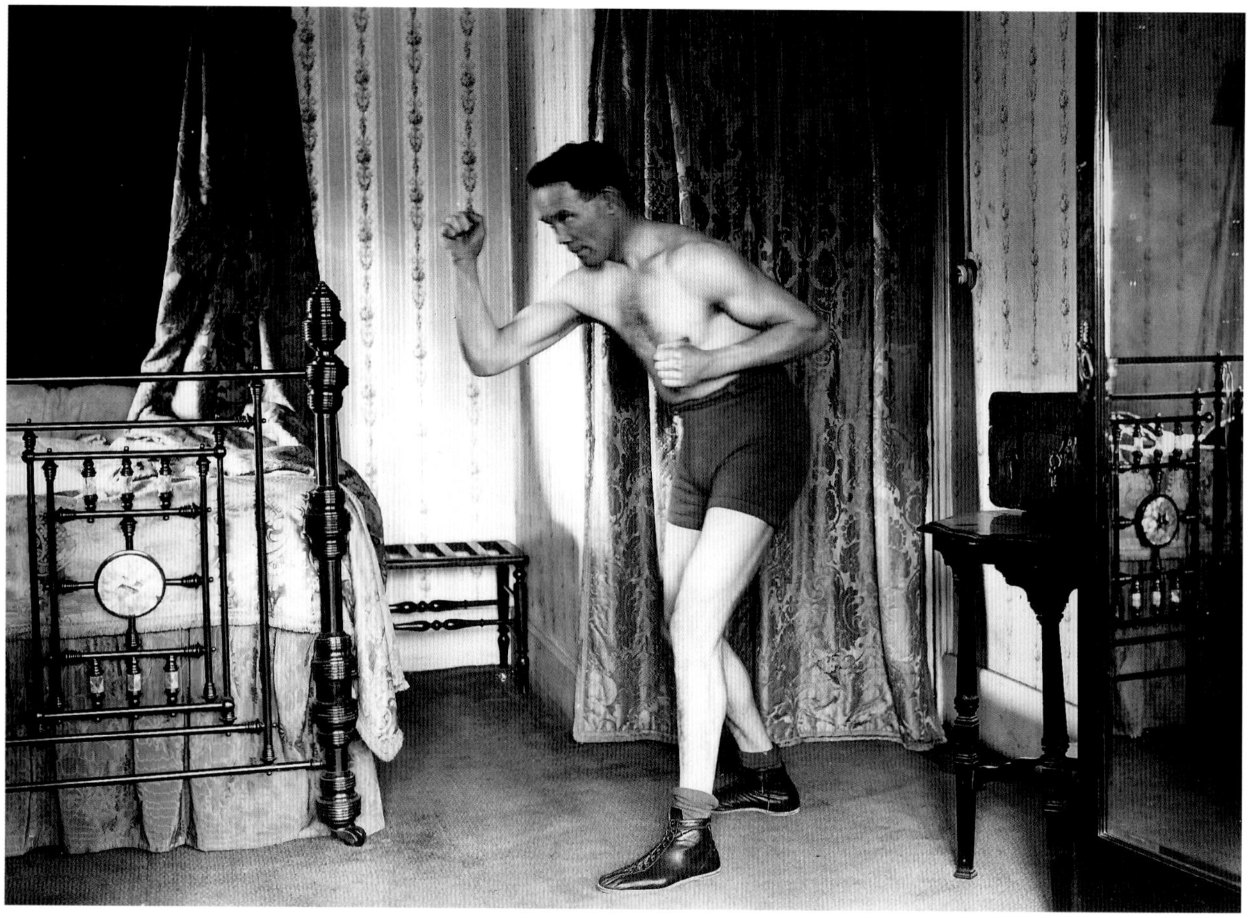

04

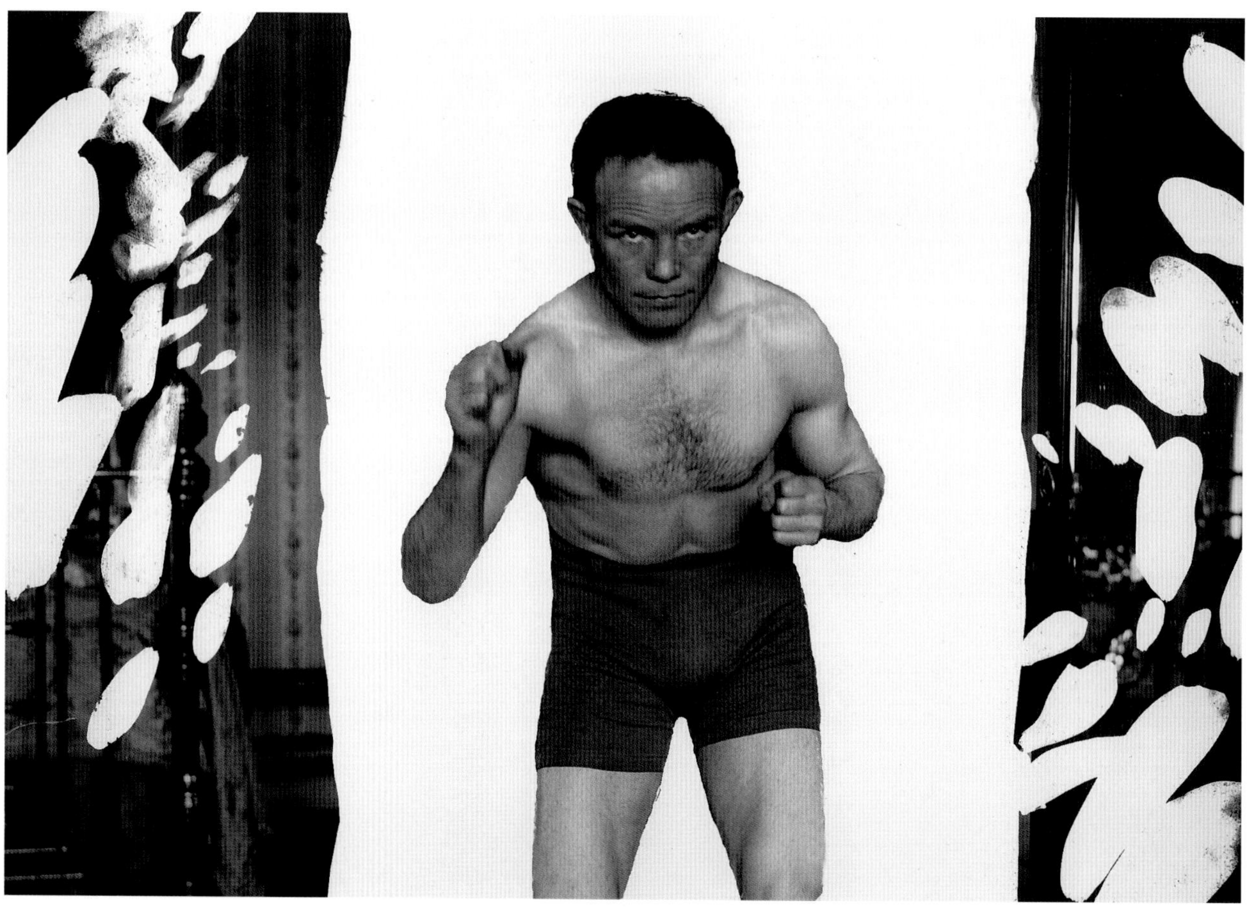

03/04
Mike McTigue, 1923

05
T Wilson, 1922

06
F Moss, 1922

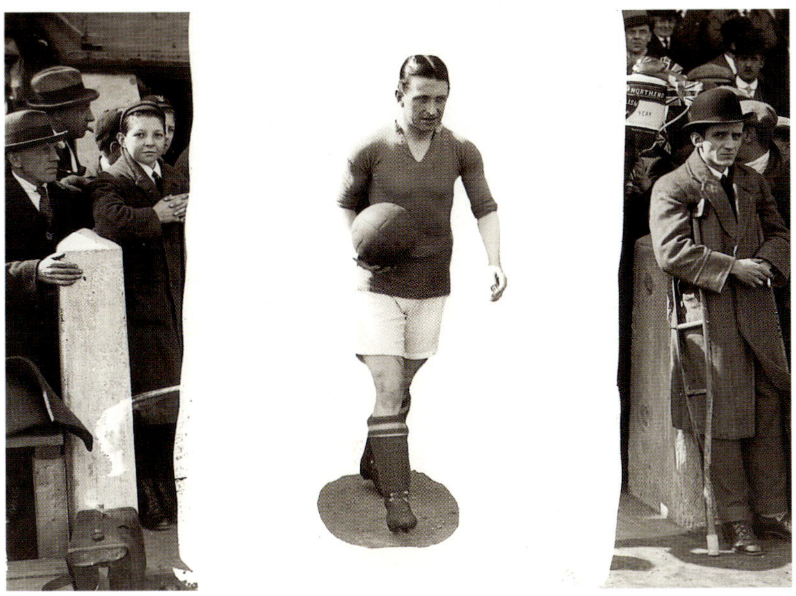

05

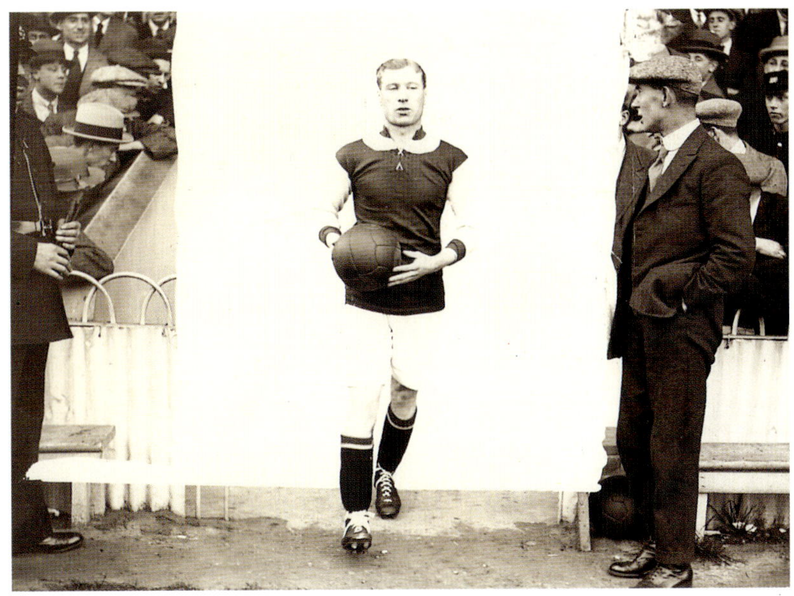

06

01
Jean Gilbert, 1937

IMPOSSIBLE VIEW

Creating images that give the impression that the photographer was defying gravity, or part of the action on the field of play, are two visual tricks that are central to sports photography. By angling the camera up or down and placing figures against the sky or a distant background, the photographer could give the impression that they were also in the sky tracking the competitor. Action images of individual players on the pitch, 'playing', were only possible during training sessions where the photographer could control the situation by arranging for the action to take place to suit the camera.

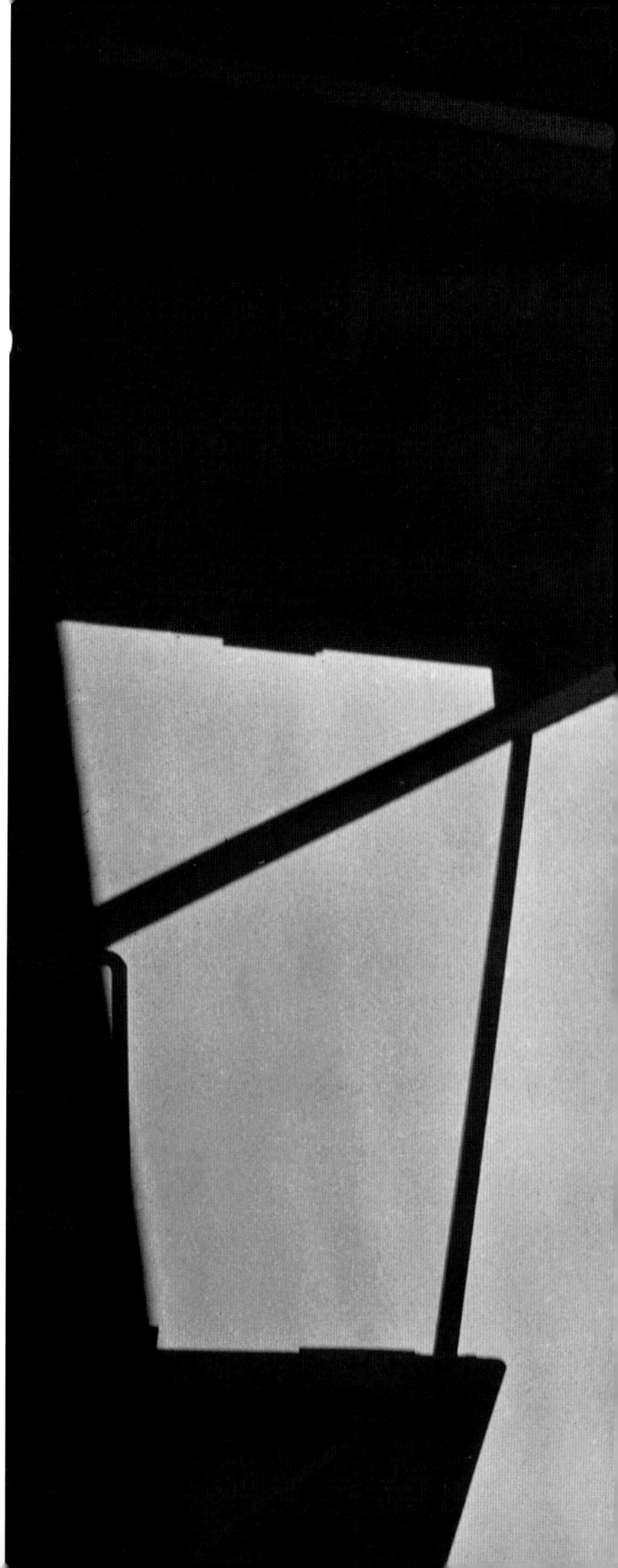

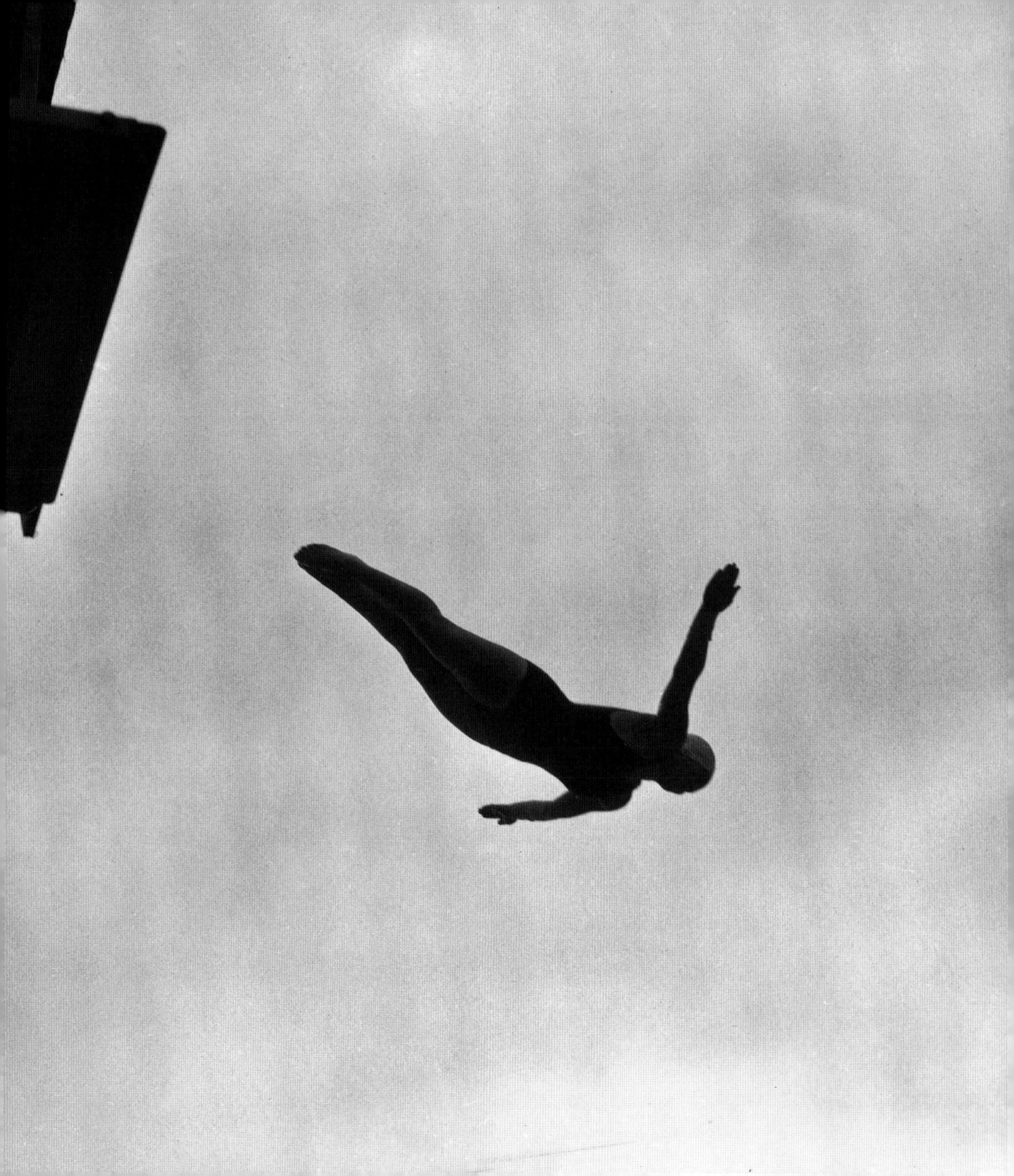

02
Pete Desjardins, 1930s

03
Albert Dicken at the National High Diving Championships, Plymouth, England, 1930s

04
Acta Aggerholt, 1939

05 (OVERLEAF)
Accola René at the Swiss Ski Championships, Grindlewald, Switzerland, 1923

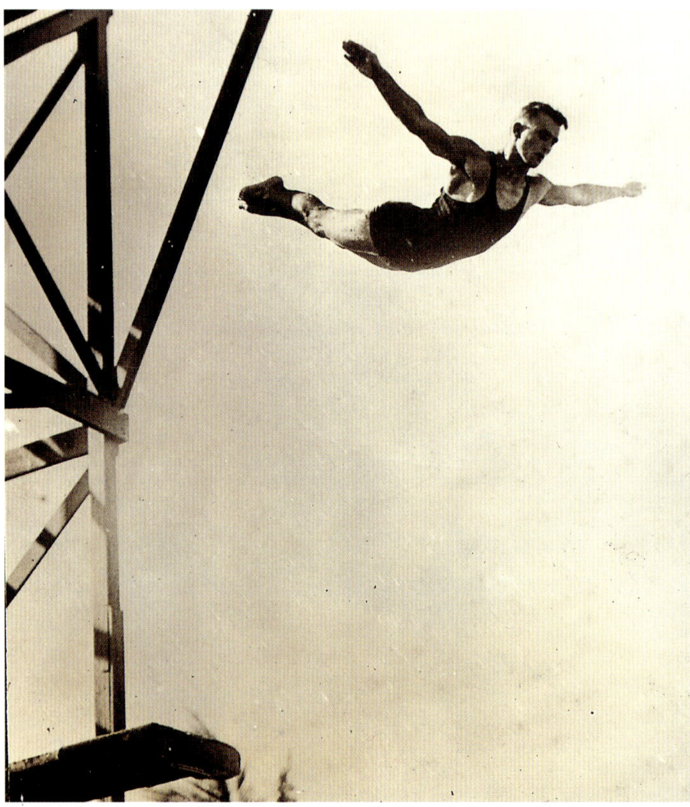
02

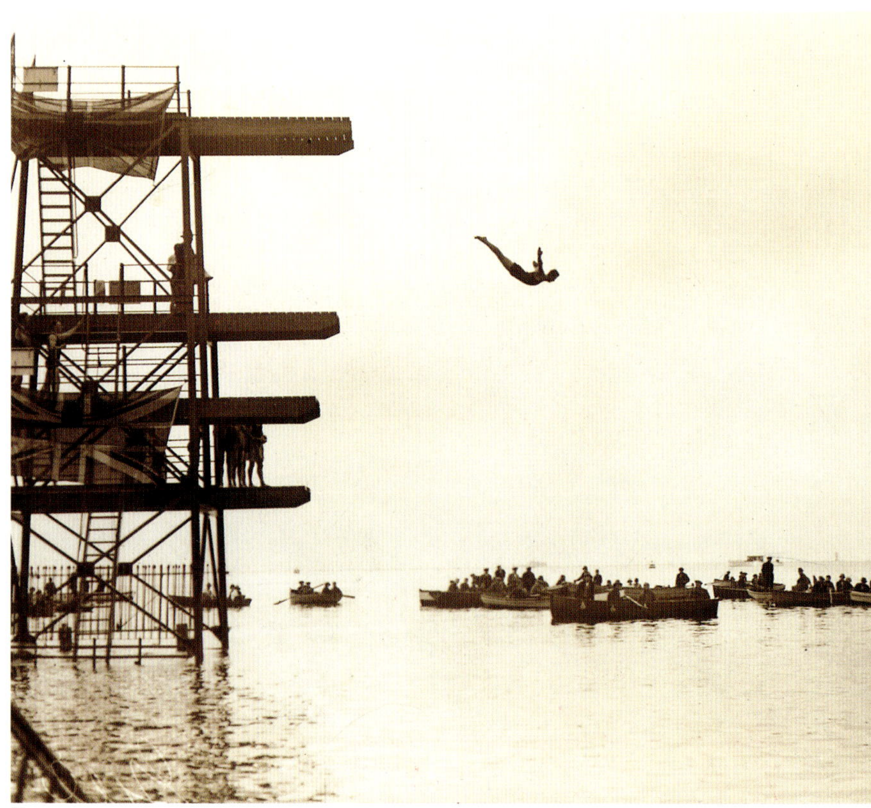
03

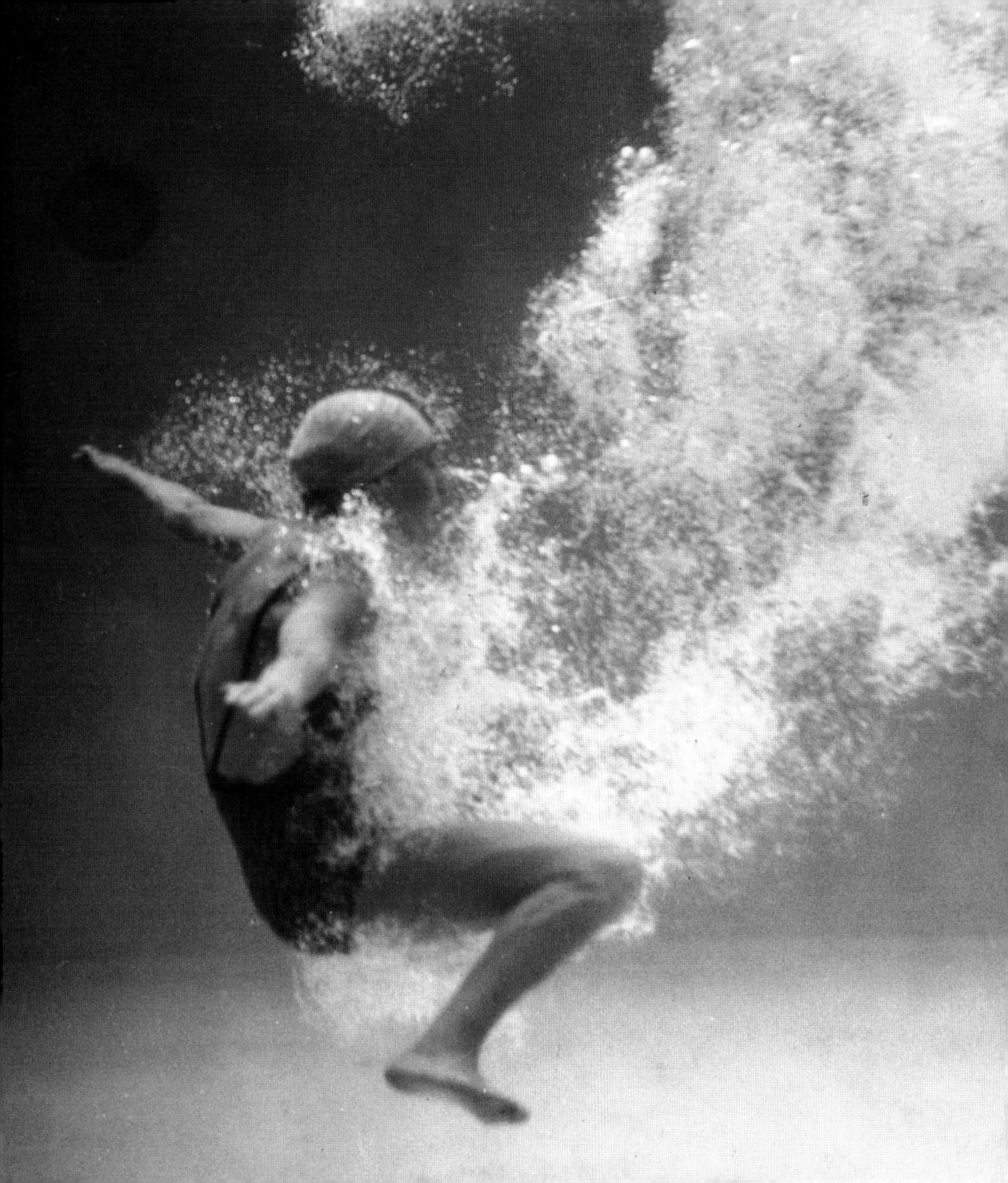

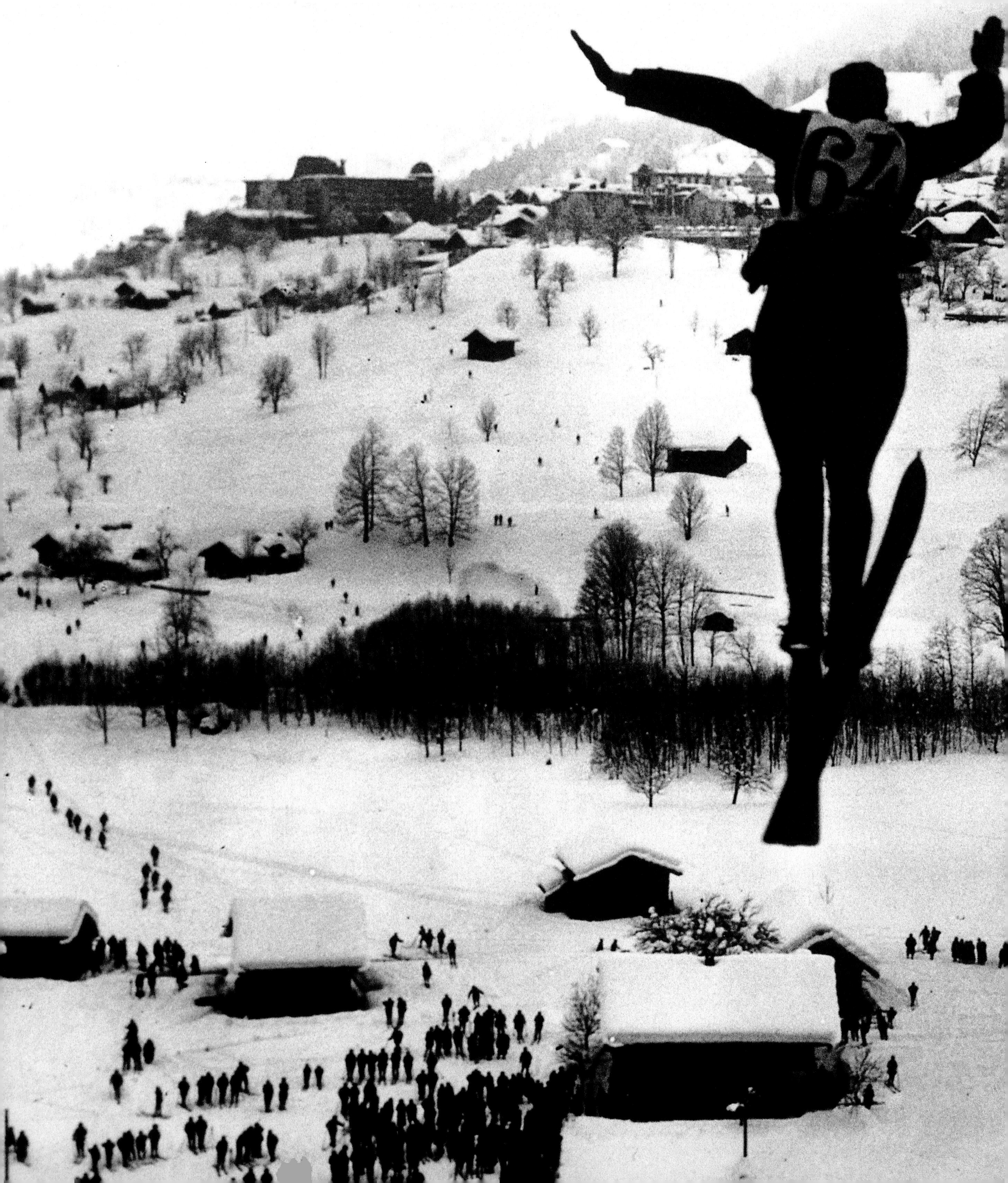

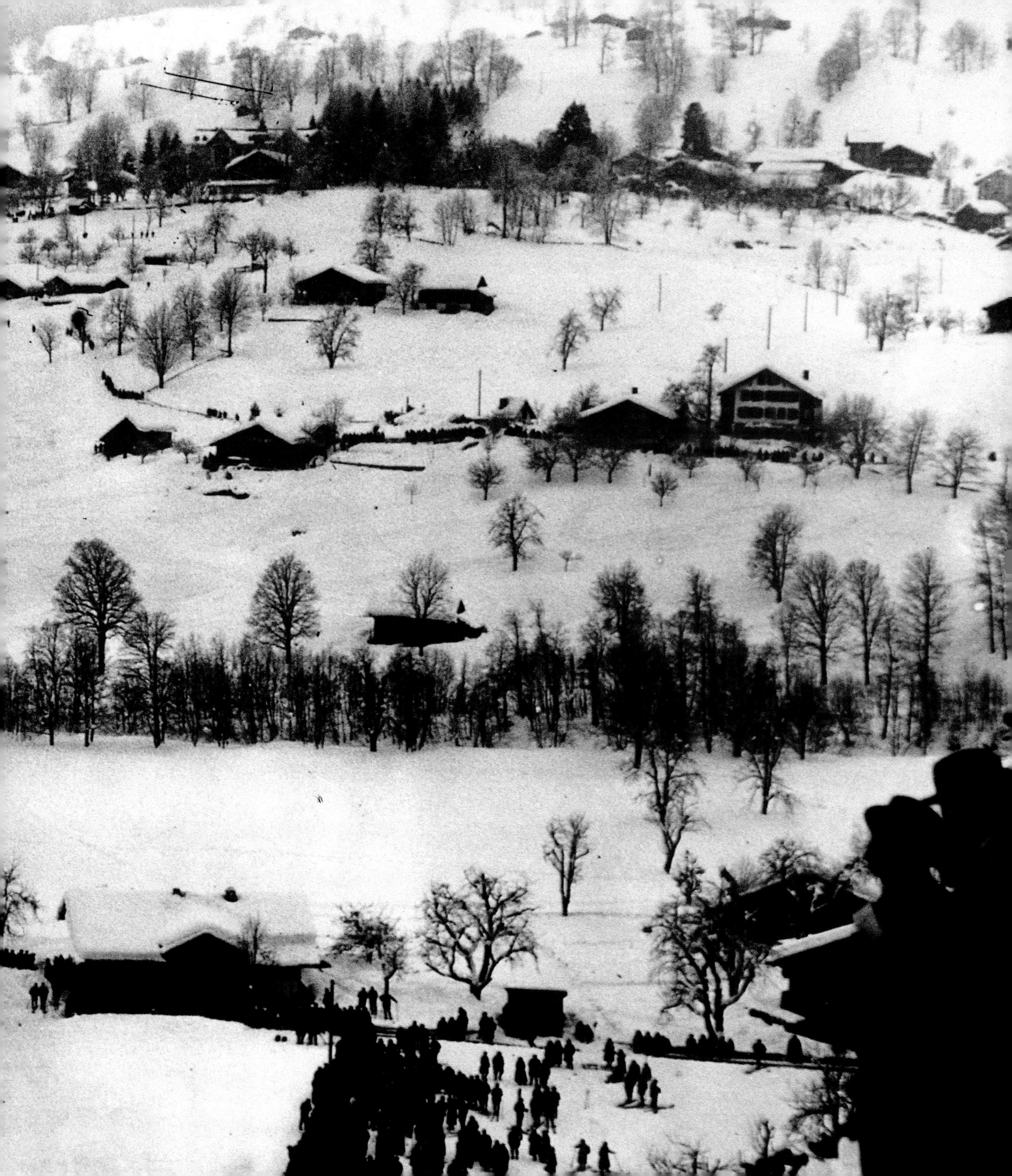

06/08
Tom Whittaker, 1922

07
Harry Nuttall, 1923

09
Albert Barnett, 1921

10
Gerald Matier, 1936

11 (OVERLEAF LEFT)
Bobby Jones, 1930

12 (OVERLEAF RIGHT)
London Americans baseball players, 1935

06

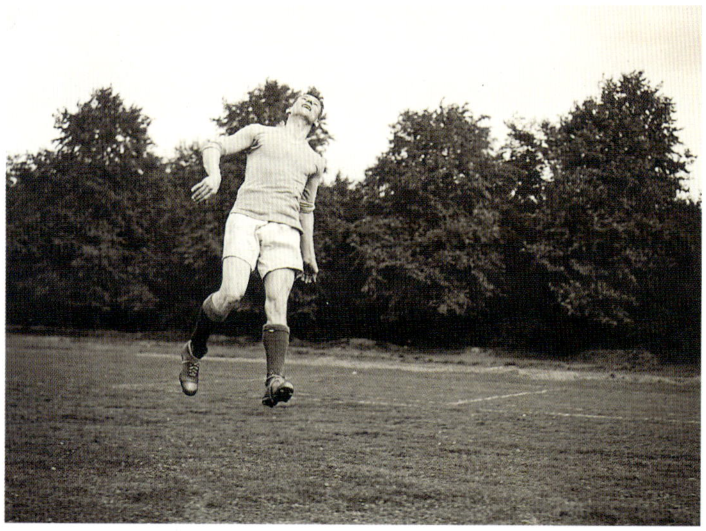

07

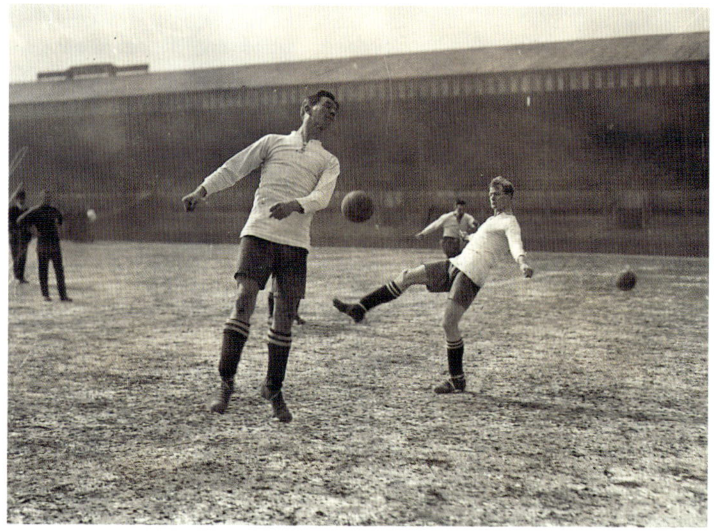

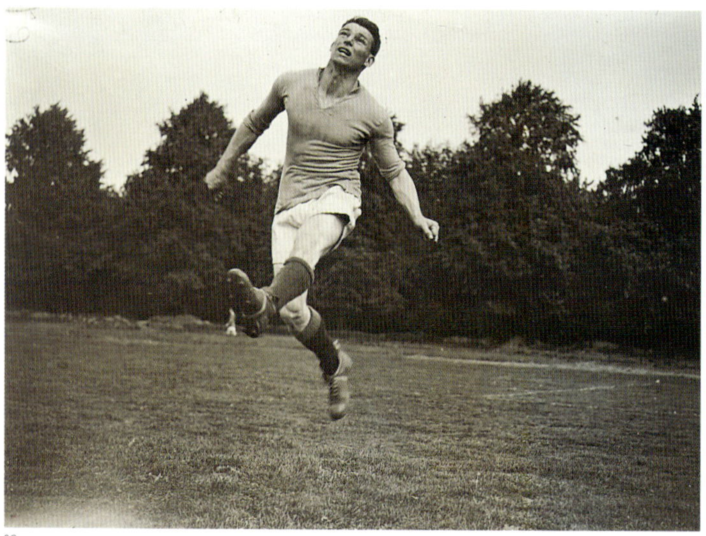

08

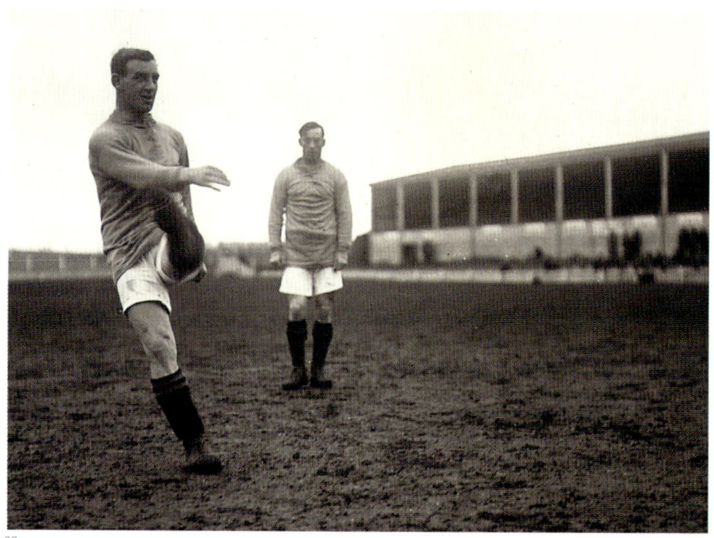

09

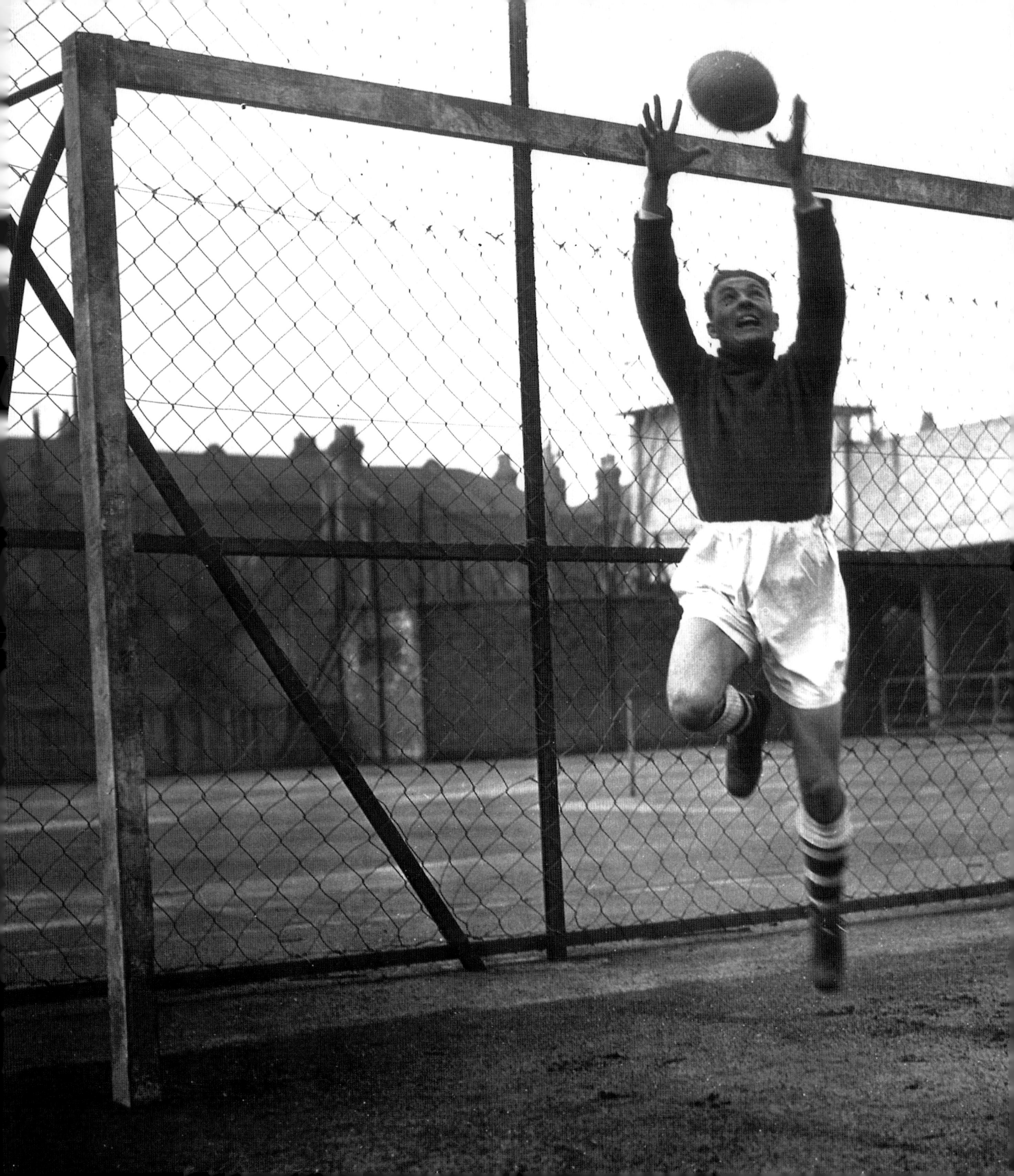

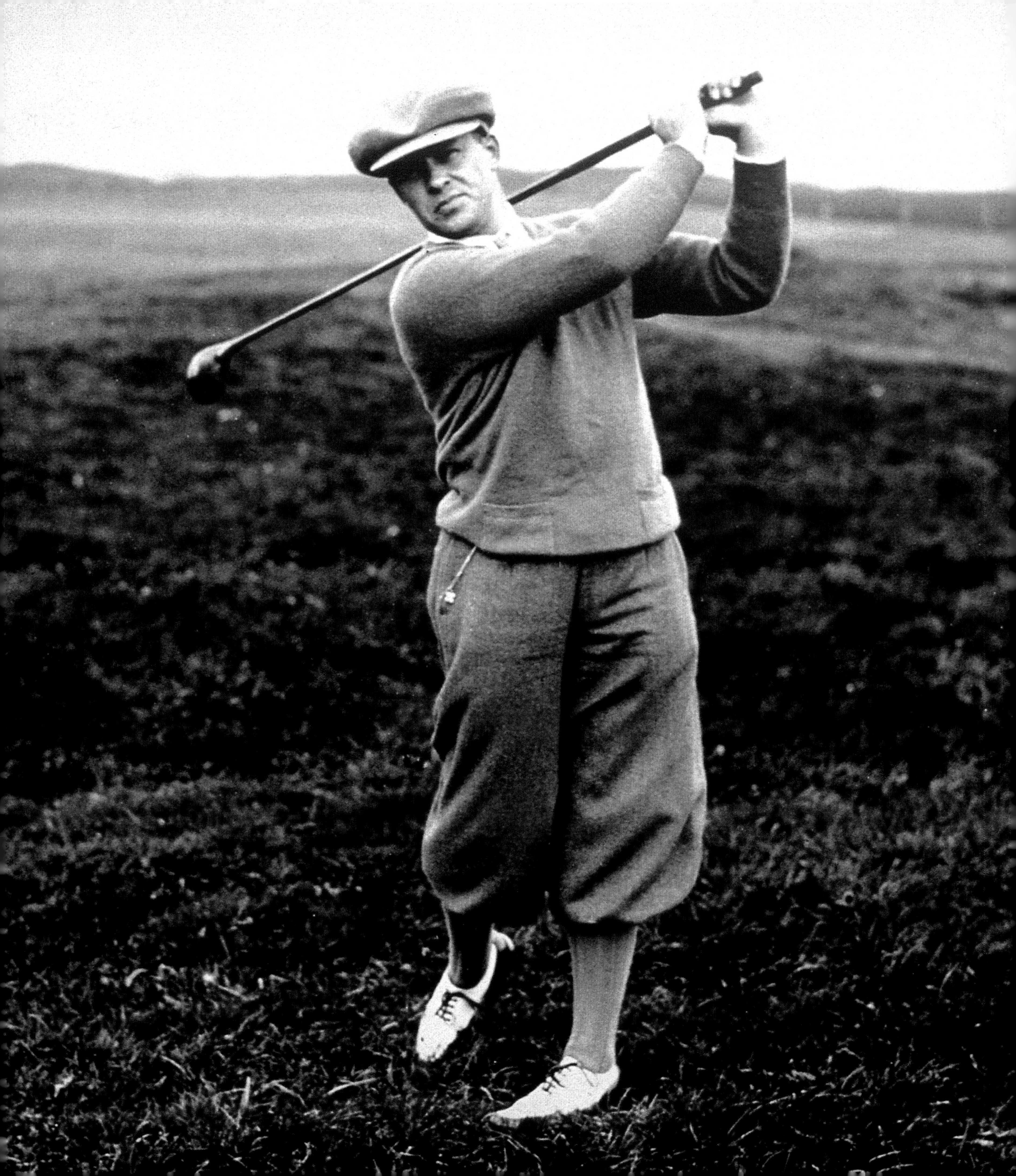

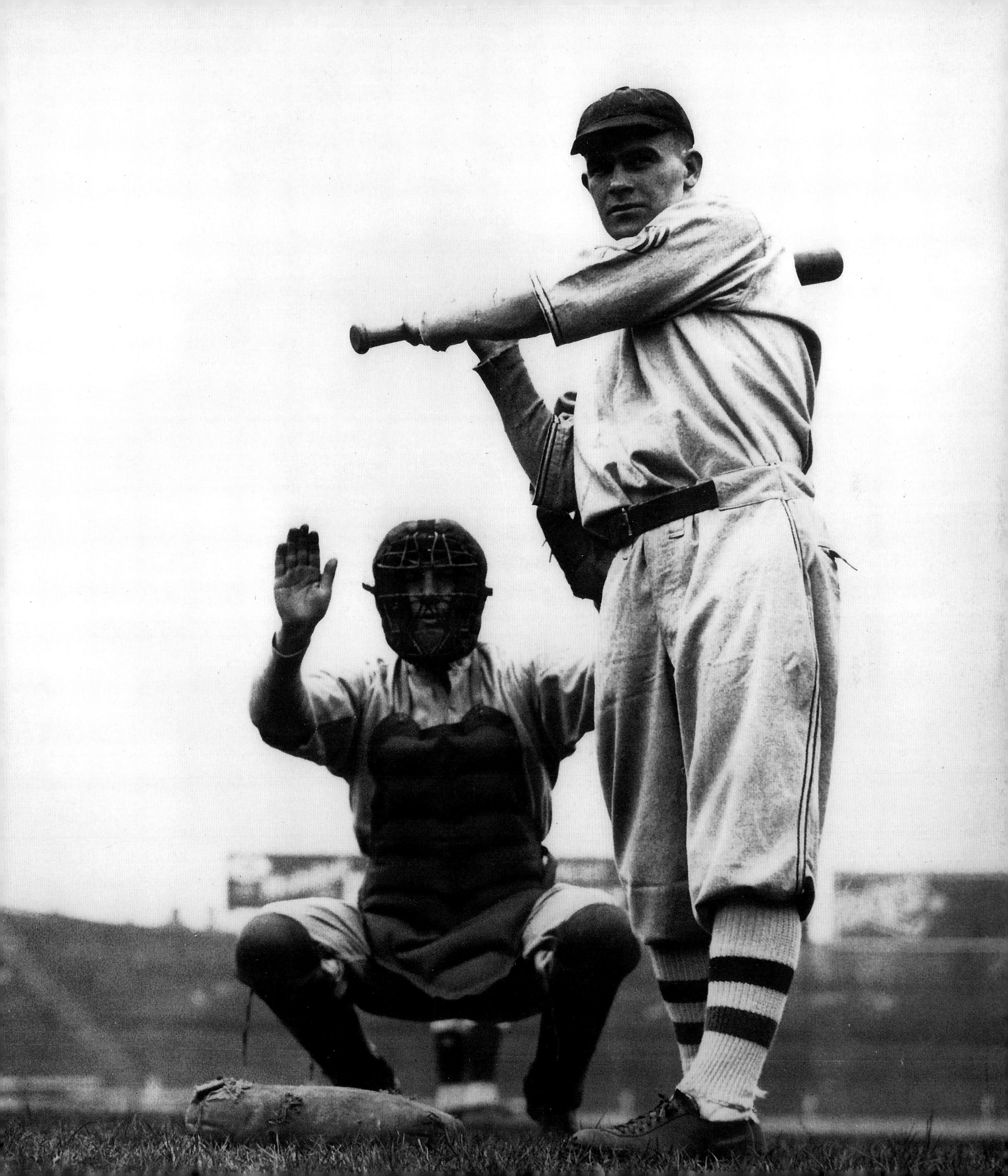

13
Walter Hagen on the roof of the Savoy hotel in London, 1922

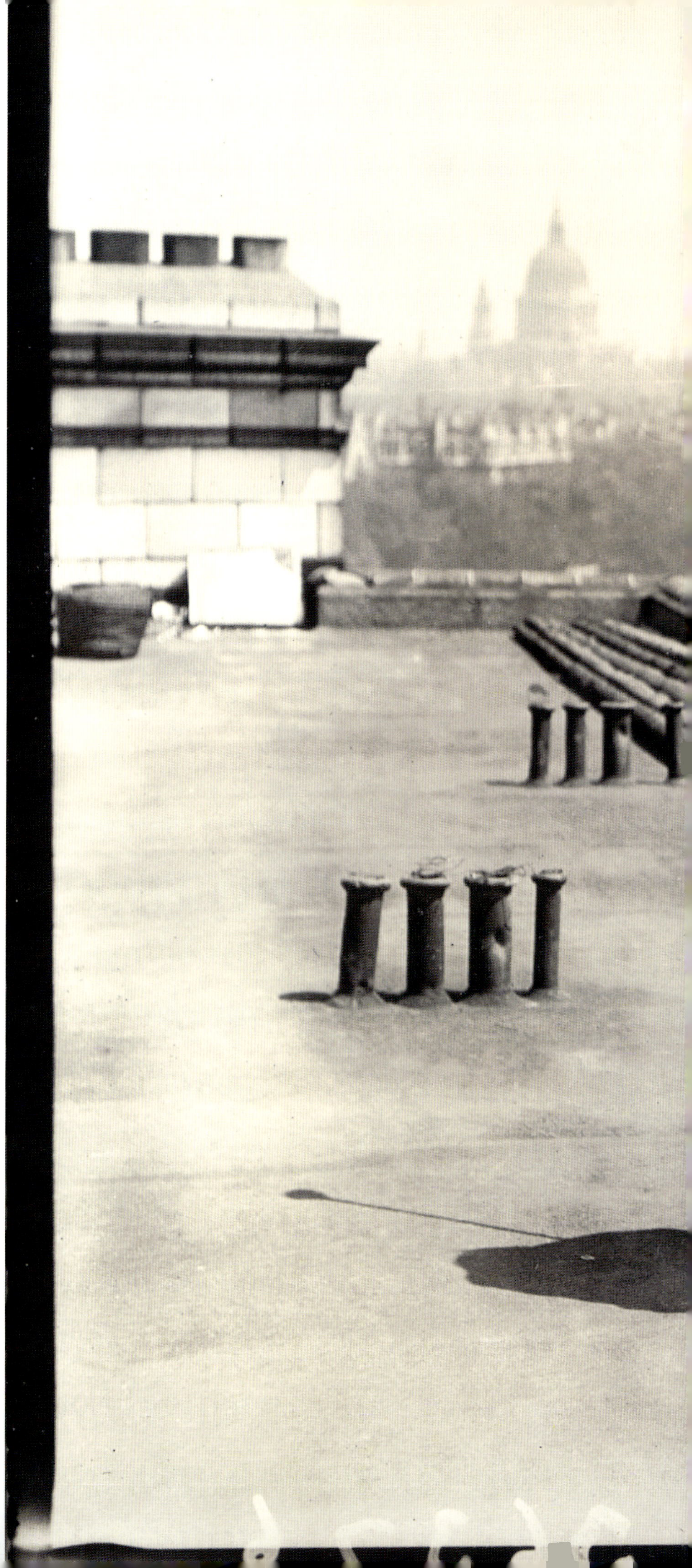

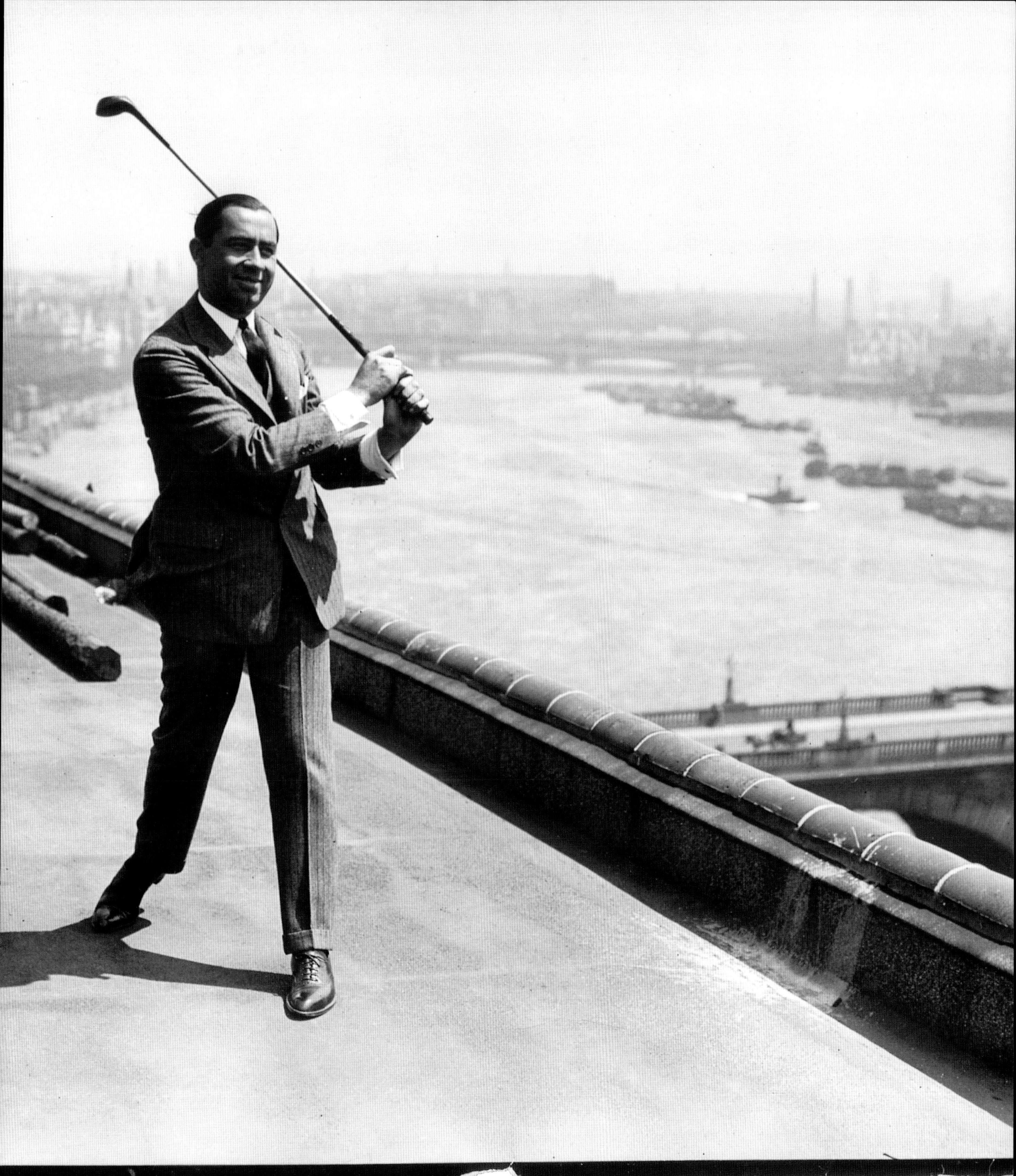

01
Jesse Owens (right) on his way to gold in the 100m

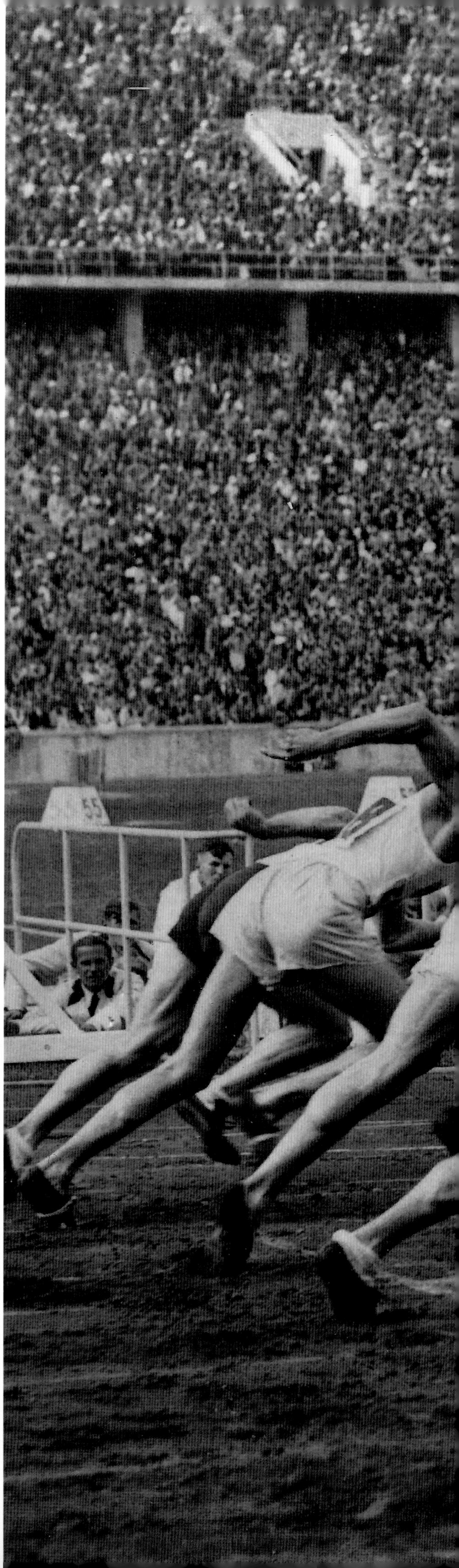

RACE

The Berlin Olympics of 1936 was the first to be systematically recorded by film and photography. It was the intention of the German government to promote visually their view of the Aryan race as superior to all others. Leni Riefenstahl's epic film *Olympia* is well known, but photography also played an important role in promoting this vision of Aryan supremacy. Thousands of photographs were taken of the Games and distributed around the world by the German government, presenting a positive view of the new social order under Nazi leadership.

There had been a call to boycott the Games because Germany was openly discriminating against the Jews and the German government called for black athletes to be barred because it was degrading and disgraceful to have to compete with 'negroes' for trophies. Jesse Owens was the star of the Games, winning four gold medals for the USA. Even the German photographers could not ignore his achievement.

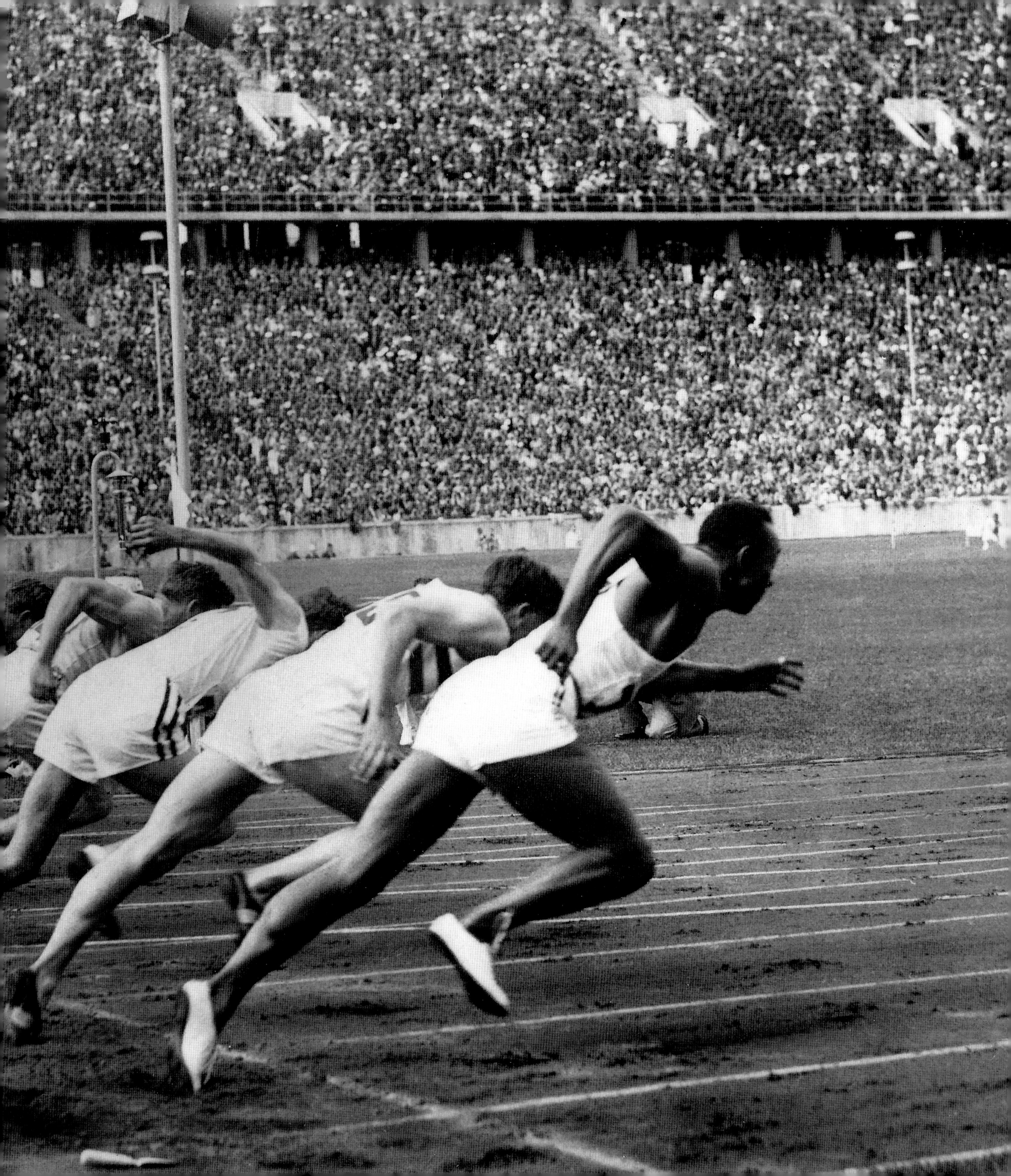

ILLUMI

NATION

1940–1960

The cancellation of the 1940 Olympic Games, when hostilities broke out in Europe in 1939, was the beginning of a general suspension of major international sporting events for the duration of the war. The decade was nearly out before the Olympic Games were held again, in London in 1948, and the soccer World Cup competition didn't resume after the break for war until 1950. By the time sport had finally settled down a new era was well underway: the baseball World Series was televised for the first time in 1947 and over the next decade and beyond this new medium was to have a dramatic effect on sport, bringing international events into people's living rooms, increasing popularity in existing sports, encouraging interest in new television-friendly ones, but also drawing away live spectators from their local teams, particularly outside the main urban areas.

Much of the photography of sport after the war has the appearance of a scientific investigation into time and motion. Taking advantage of technological advances in the speed of film, techniques in flash photography and colour, the sports photographer was revealing movement that was invisible to the naked eye. The camera was used as a microscope to magnify detail, and the photographer's studio became like a laboratory where specimens were exposed under artificial lighting for the camera lens. This scientific vision of sport echoes a wider change taking place in the 1950s where the power of science and technology was being harnessed for the greater benefit of society. In the workplace, in the home and in sport, everyone looked to technology to solve their problems and fell under the spell of this scientific view of the world.

It was on the pages of weekly picture magazines that the new vision of sport found its expression. In these popular journals more space was afforded to the photographic content, giving photographers greater flexibility, the opportunity to tell more complex photo-stories, and to experiment with a more diverse visual language. Able to improve and increase their coverage, photographers could record the background to events and look in depth at sporting personalities. They could point their cameras into previously neglected corners and from unusual angles and look for new ways of illuminating sport.

Great changes were taking place in the world of professional sport. Desegregation in the American armed forces during the war had paved the way for the eventual integration of black players into American major league sport, and Jackie Robinson made history in 1947 – a phenomenal success as major league baseball's first black player. The outstanding athlete of the period was Fanny Blankers-Koen of Holland, winning four gold medals at the London Olympics of 1948. American boxers Rocky Marciano and Sugar Ray Robinson both have legitimate claims to be remembered as the greatest fighter of the century, such was their dominance during the period, and likewise Argentinian racing driver Juan Manuel Fangio's five consecutive Drivers' World Championships is a record that may never be equalled. But the most symbolic sporting achievement came at the Oxford University running track in 1954 when Englishman Roger Bannister became the first man to break through the famous four-minute-mile barrier, with a time of 3 minutes 59.4 seconds.

01
John Unitas, 1950s

FABRICATED ACTION

By the 1950s, with improvements in newspaper and magazine printing, colour photography was being used more frequently in the popular press. Colour film at this time required excellent lighting conditions to achieve good results and so it was extremely difficult to take action photographs outside. One way round the problem was to get sports personalities into the photographer's studio, creating a strange world of stiff portraits and posed action shots inside small rooms. If the photographer wanted to move outside, all the studio lighting had to follow, creating an equally surreal world of bright colour, clean kit and large empty stadiums.

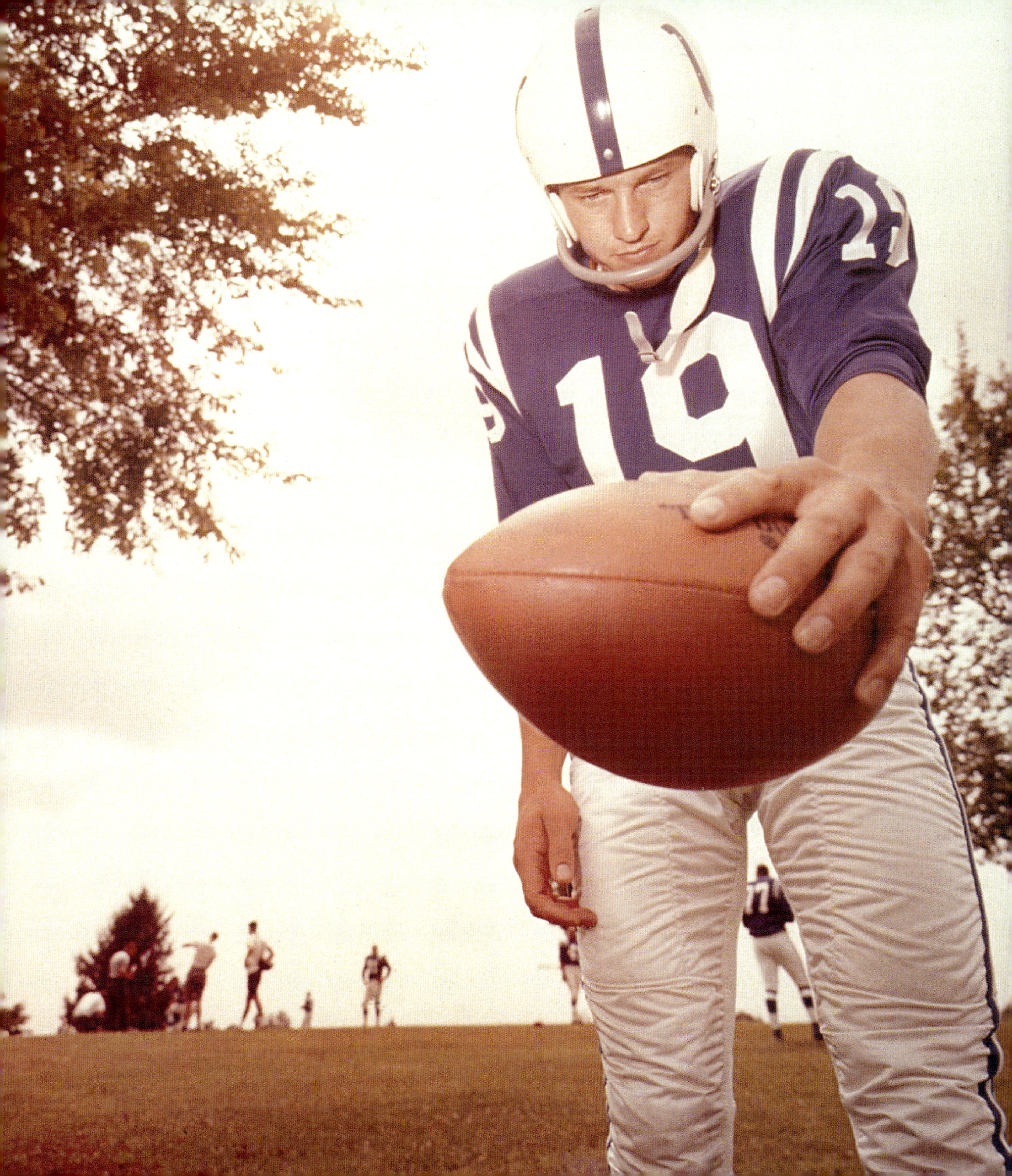
19

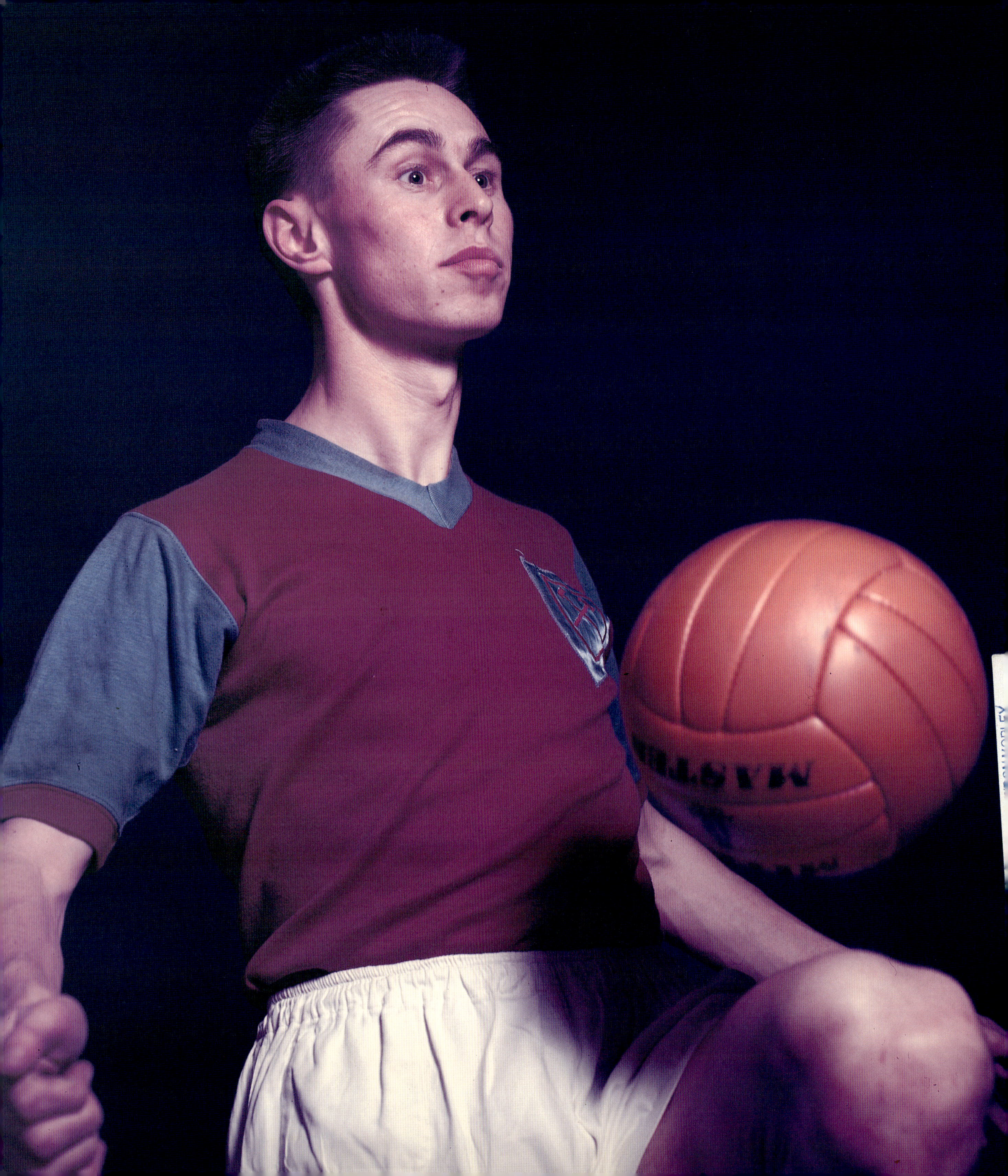

02
Phil Woosnam, 1950s
John Piercy

03
Ron Springett, 1960
Don Morley

04
Jimmy Greaves, 1957
Don Morley

05
Ronnie Clayton, 1959
Don Morley

06
Ron Flowers, 1950s
Don Morley

07
Bill Slater, 1960
Don Morley

08
David Herd, 1950s
John Piercy

09 (OVERLEAF LEFT)
Sugar Ray Robinson, *c.* 1950

10 (OVERLEAF RIGHT)
Rocky Marciano, 1950s

04

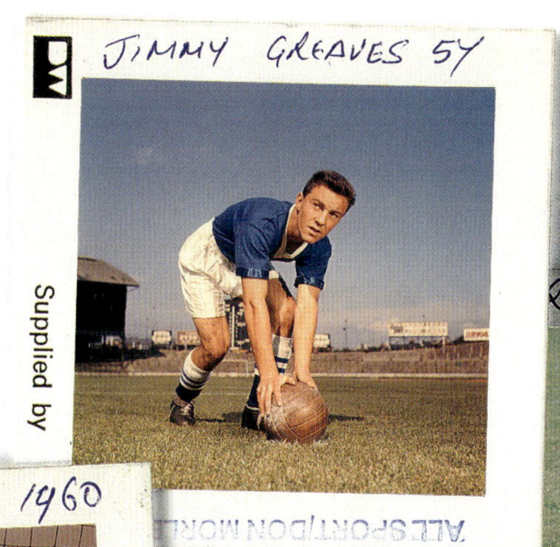

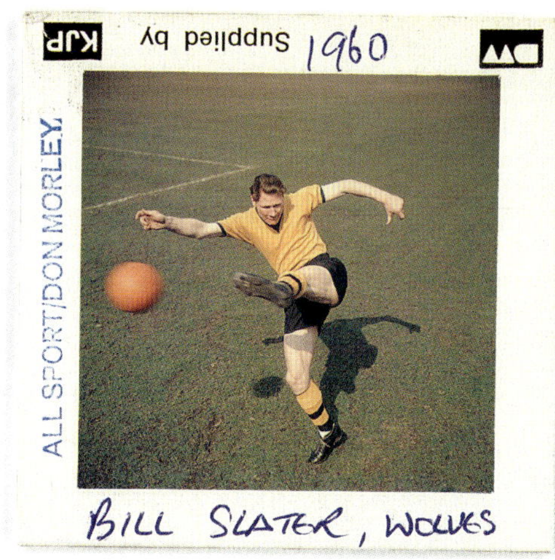

07

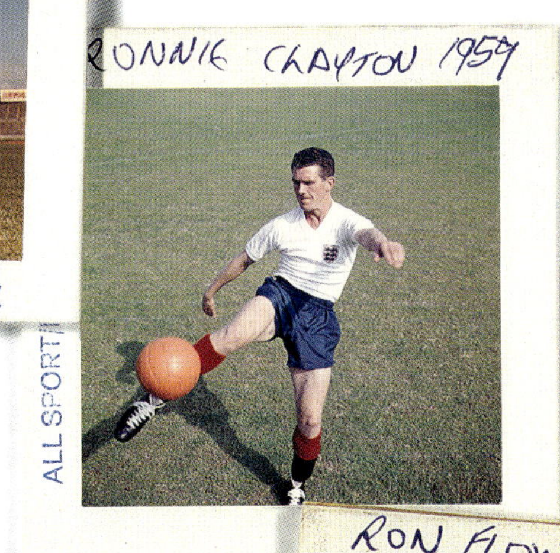

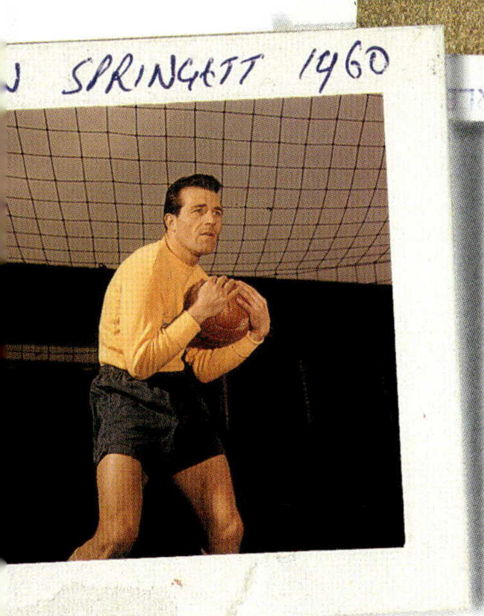

05

03

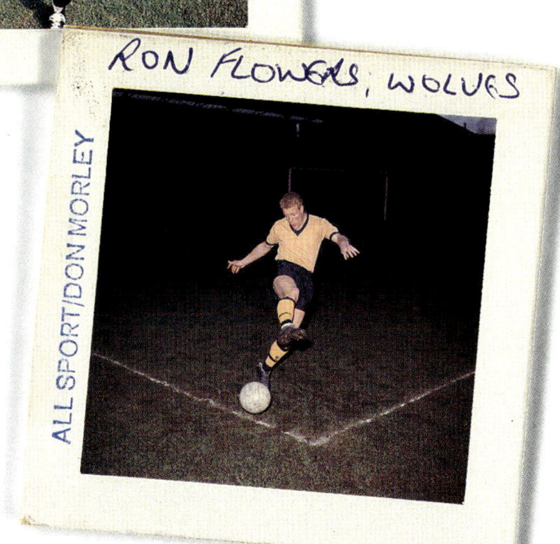

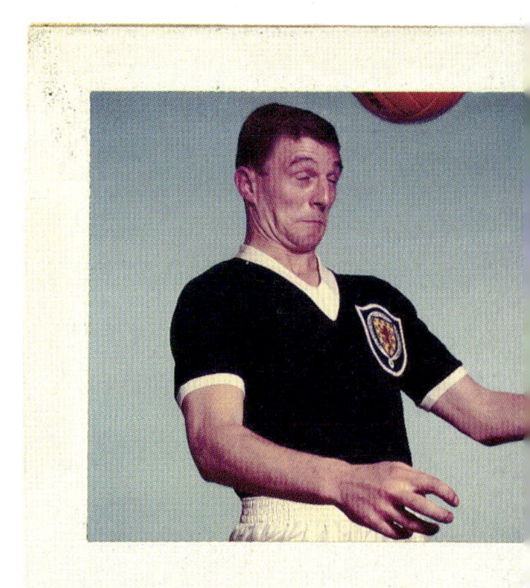

08

06

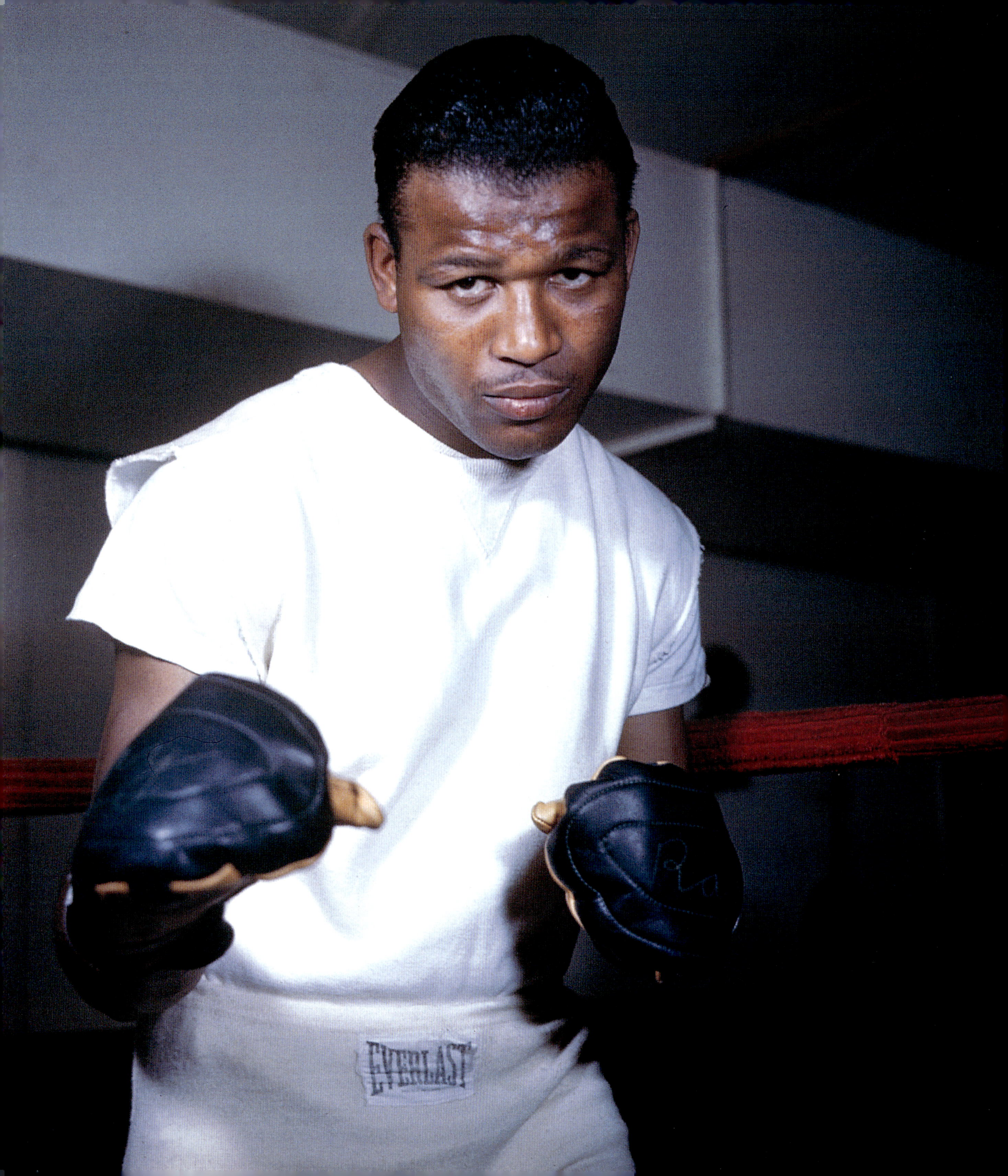
EVERLAST

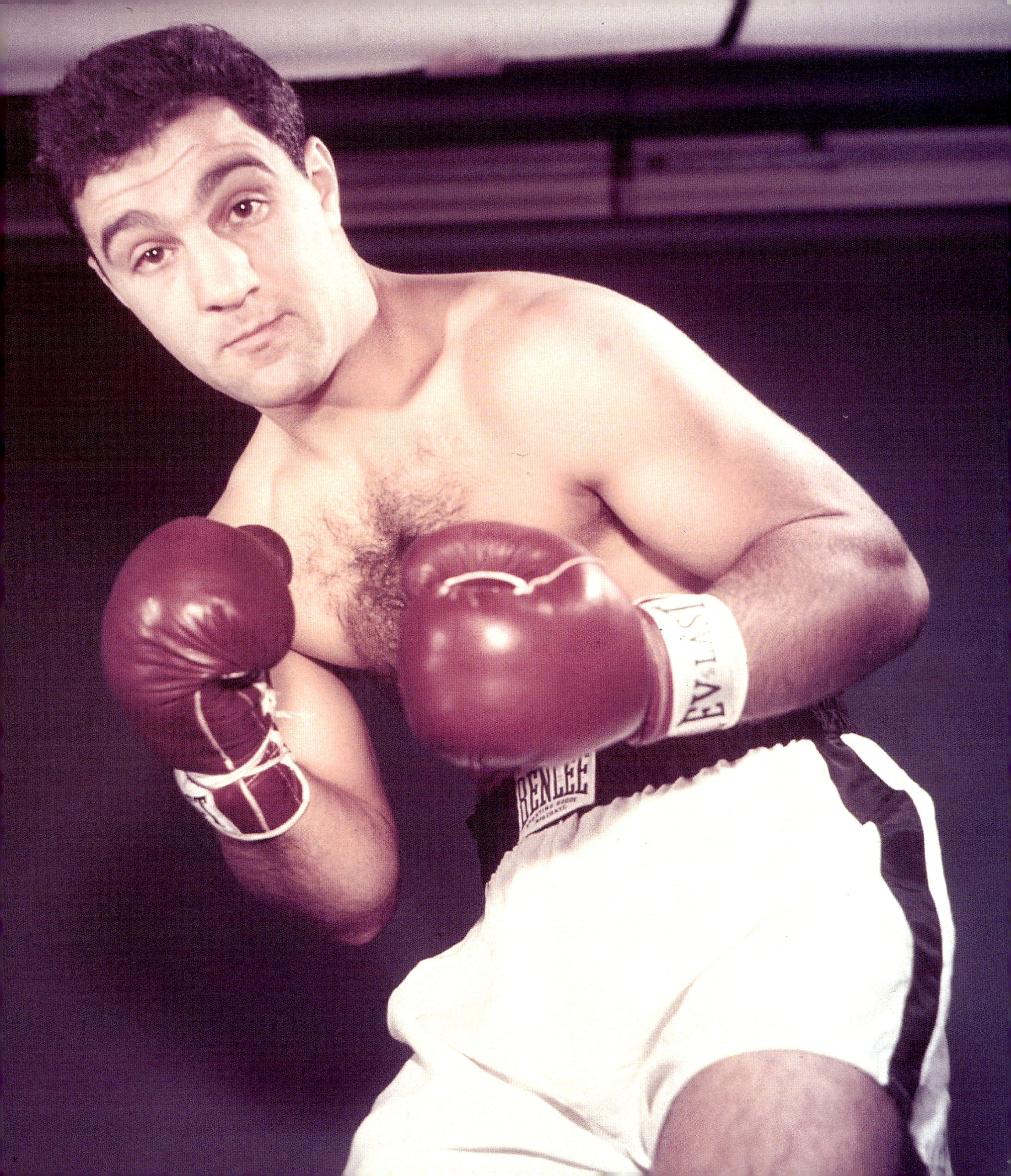
EV LAST
RENLEE

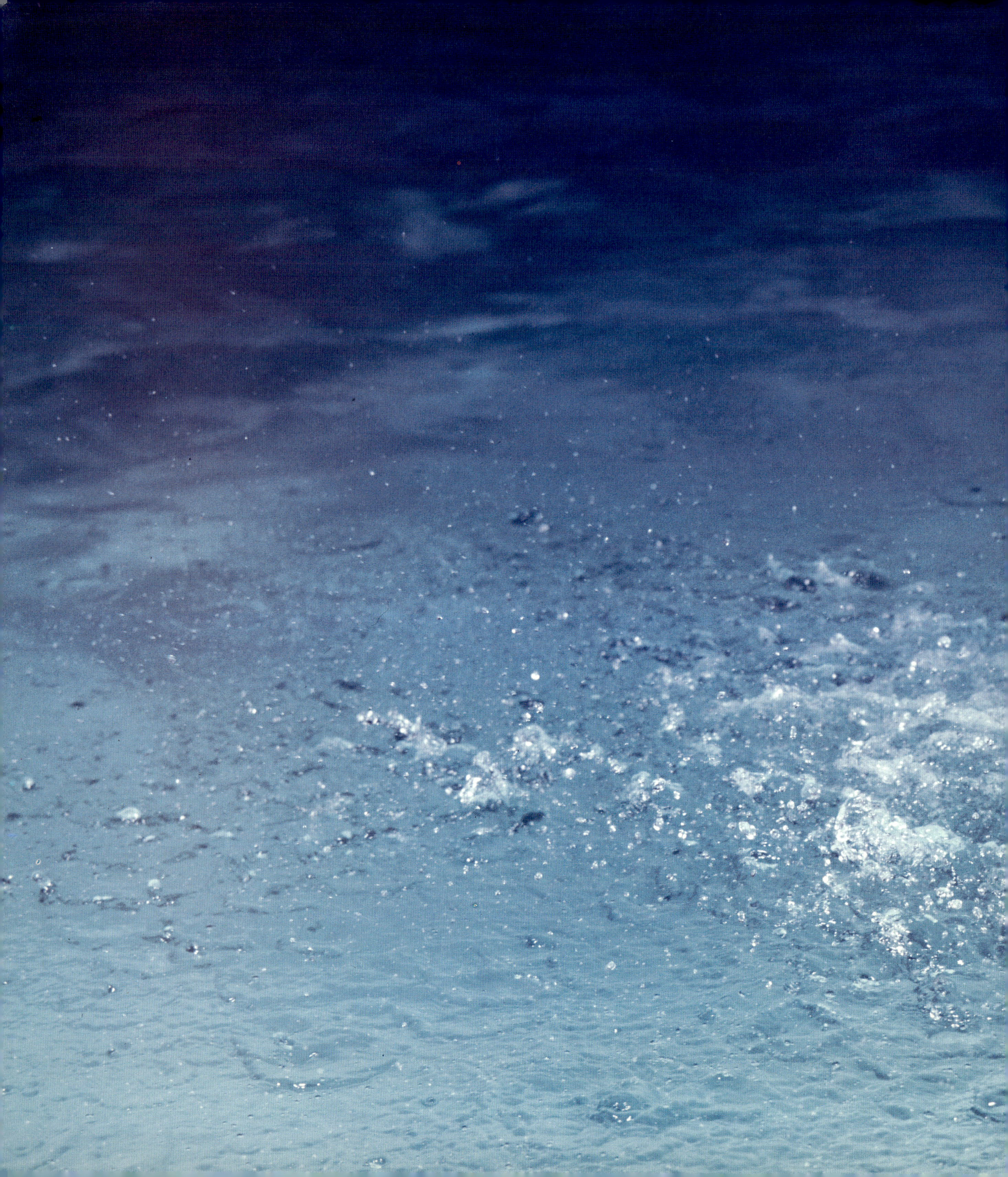

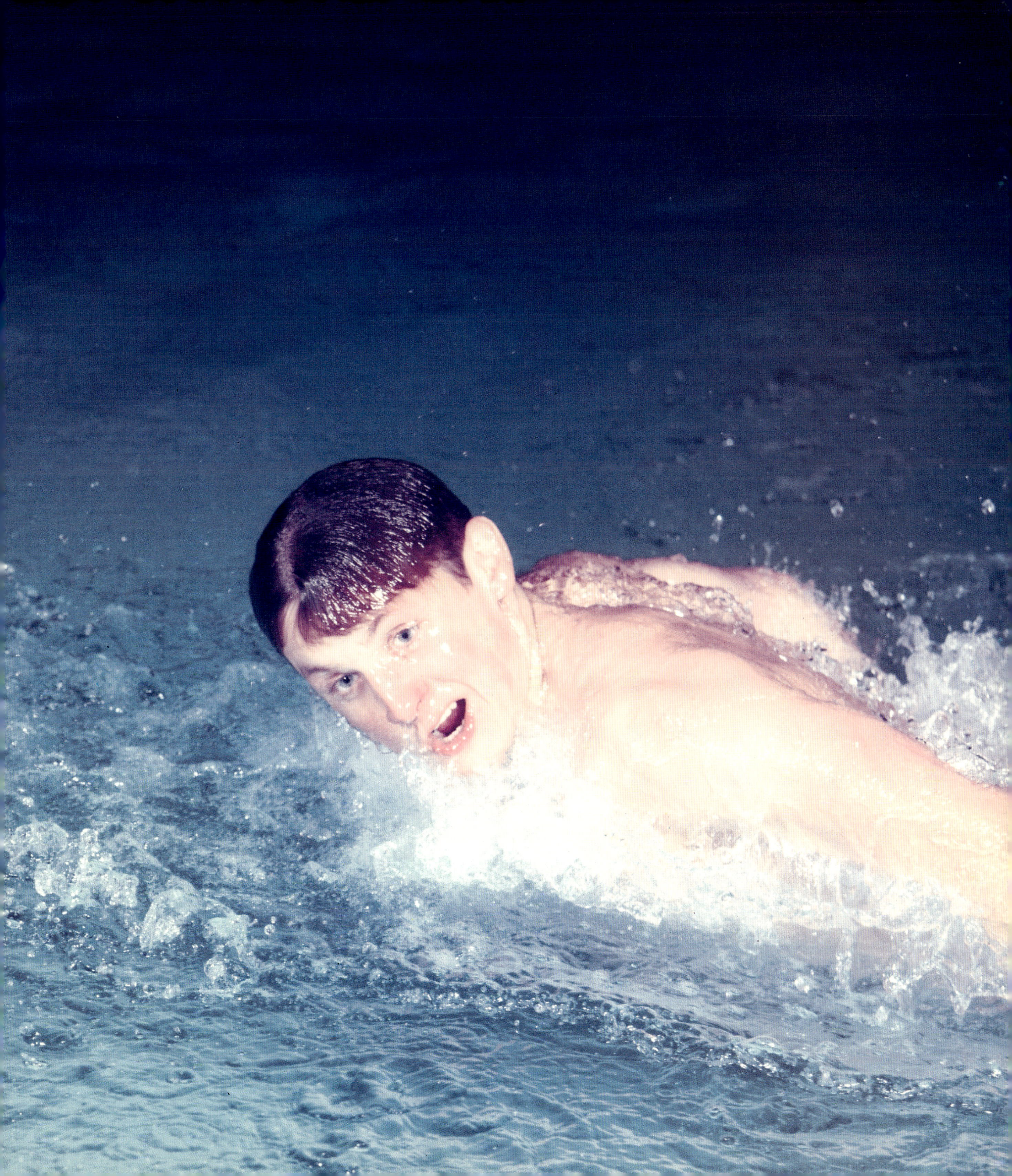

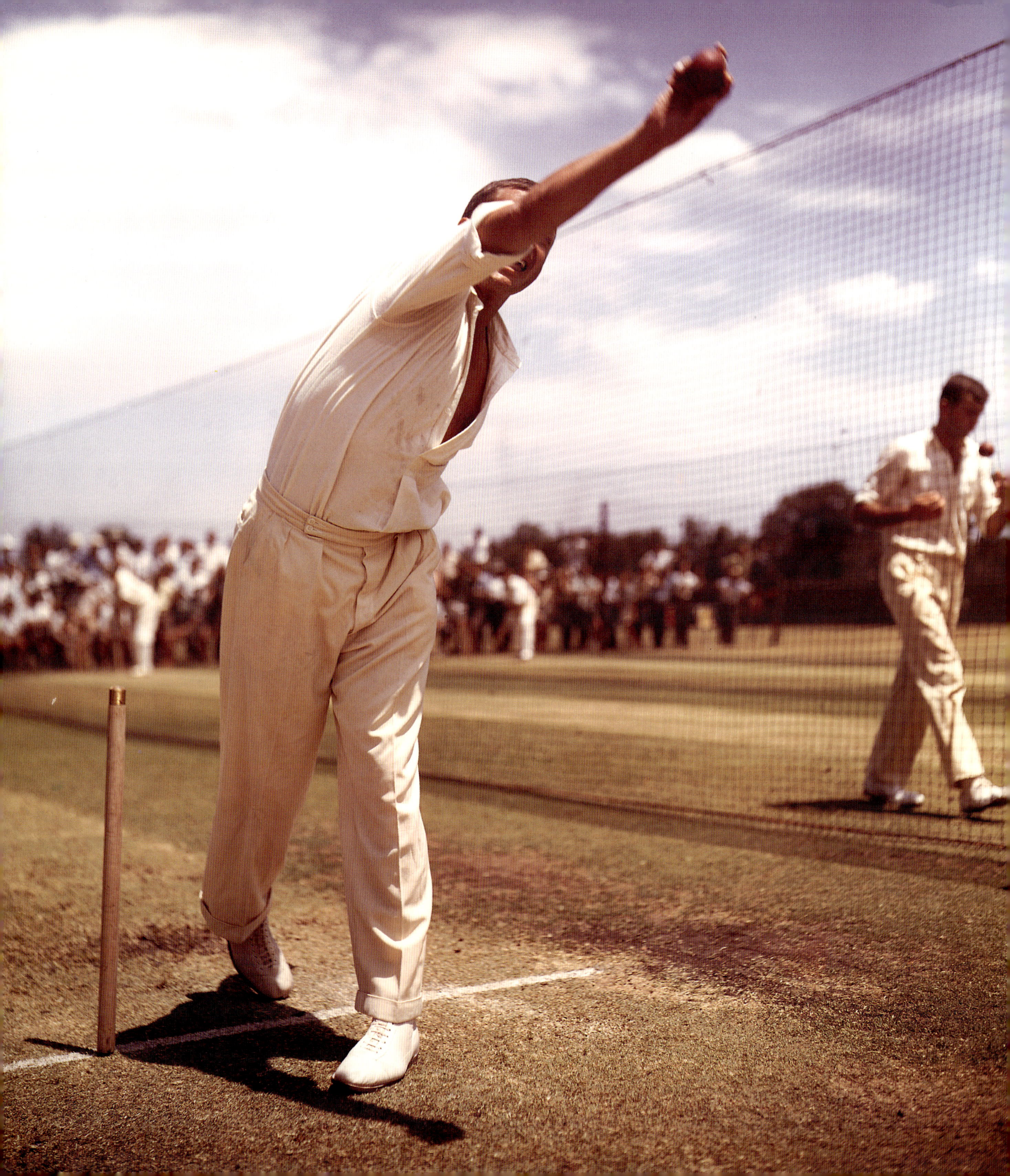

11 (PREVIOUS PAGE)
Ian Black, 1950s
John Piercy

12
Richie Benaud, 1950s

13
Colin Cowdrey, 1950s
John Piercy

14 (OVERLEAF LEFT)
Geoff Duke, 1950s
Howard Byrne

15 (OVERLEAF RIGHT)
Stirling Moss, 1950s

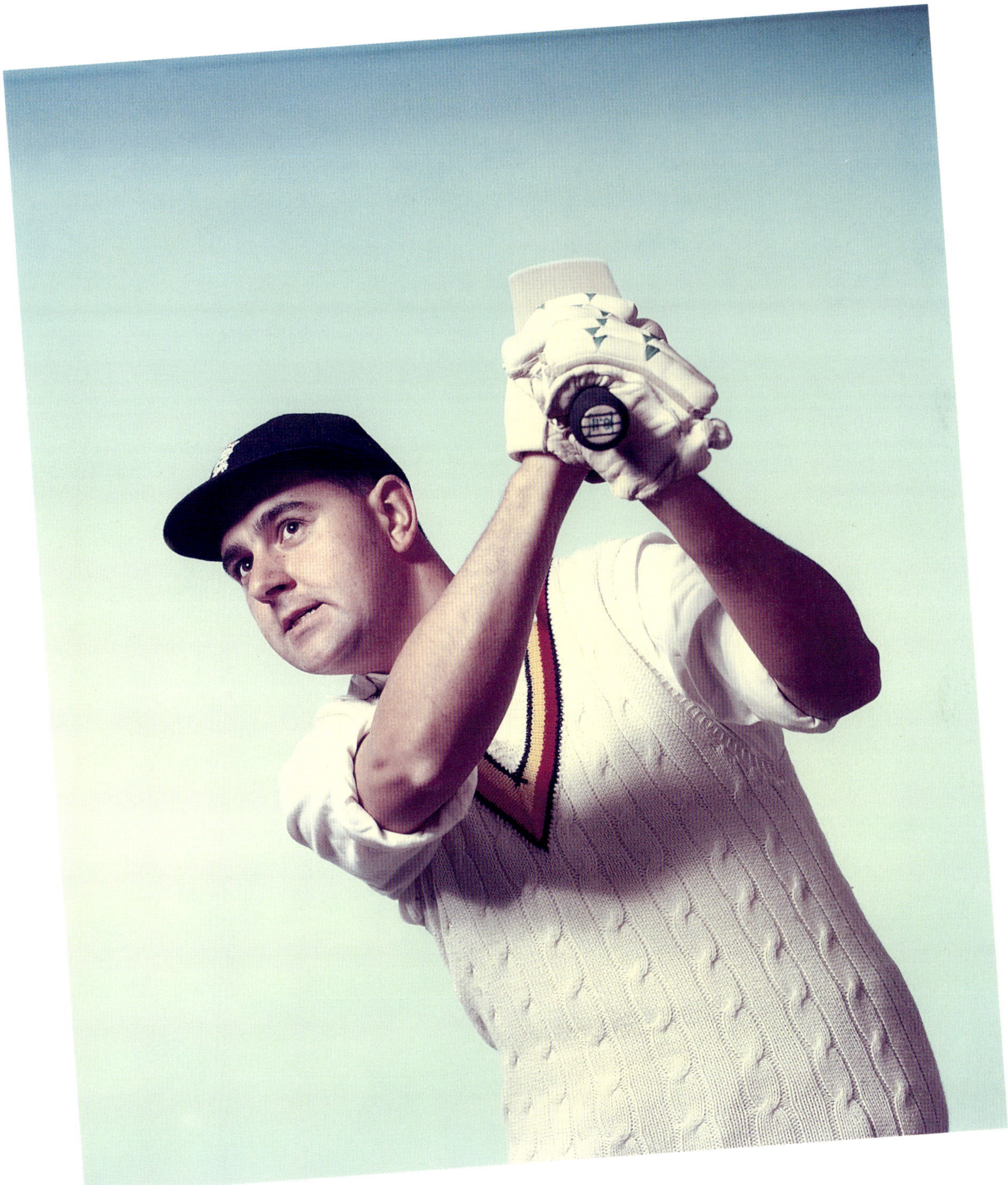

13

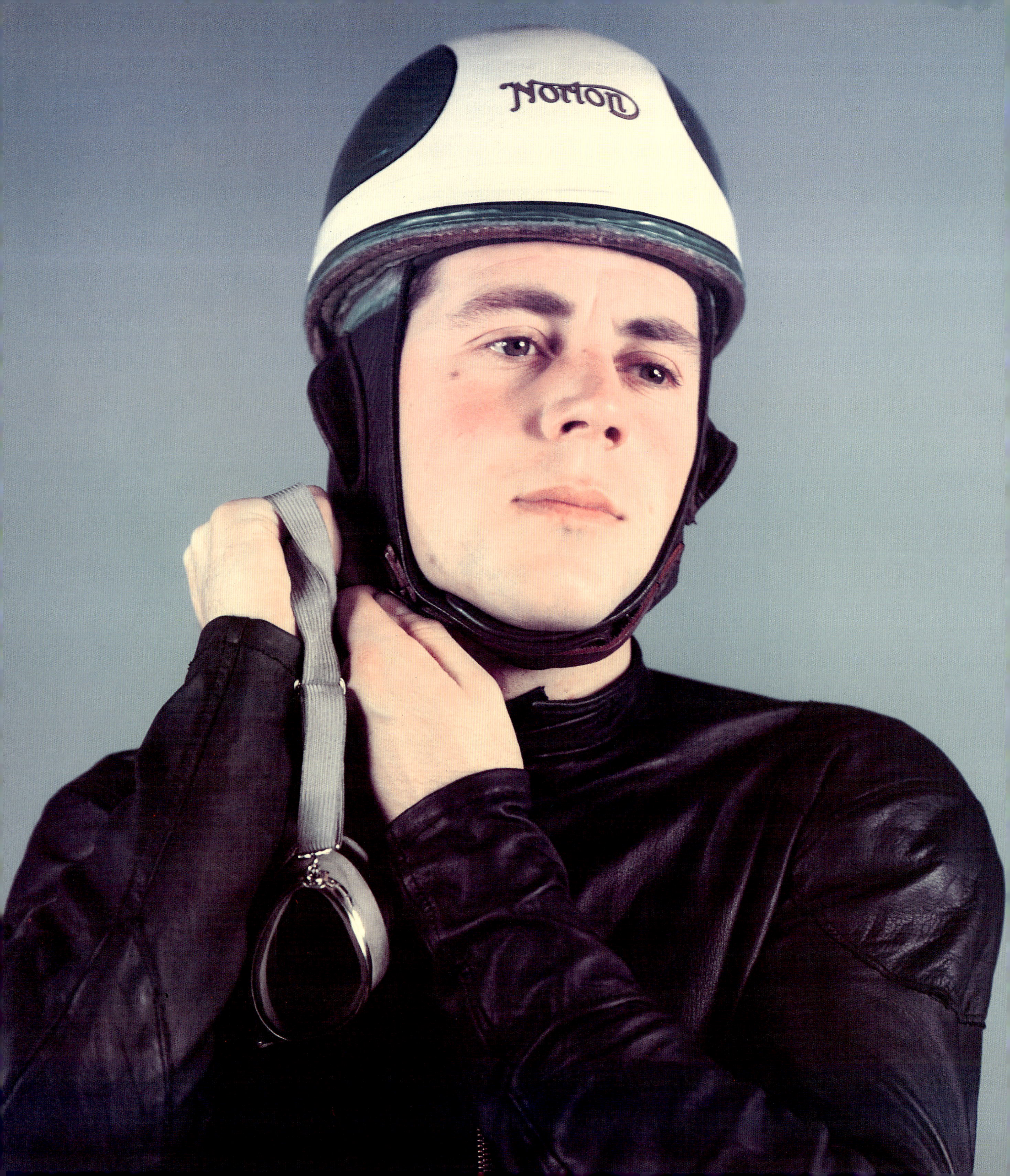
Norton

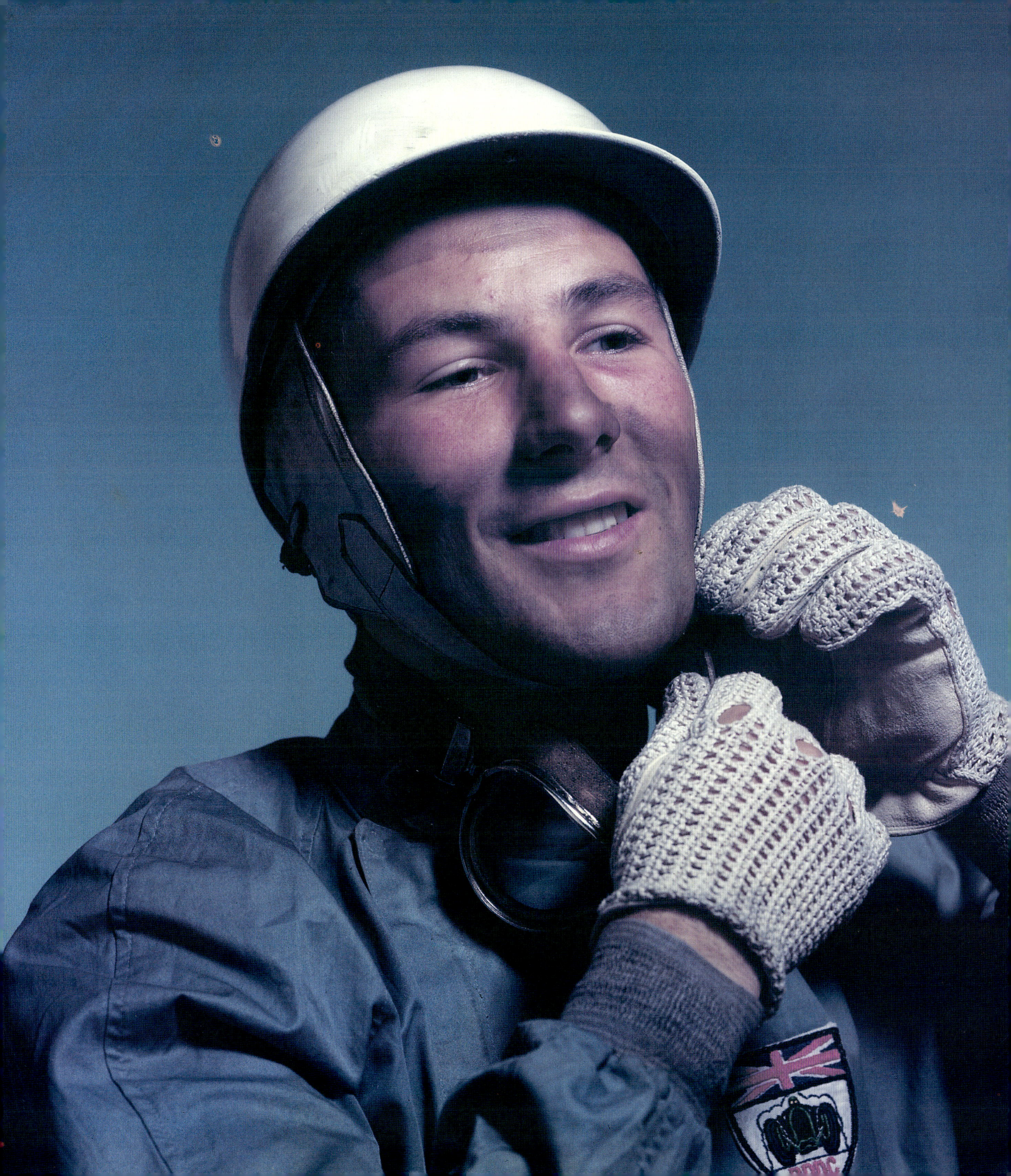

16
Dorothy Tyler, 1950s

17
John Savidge, 1950

18/19 (OVERLEAF)
Joe DiMaggio, 1940s

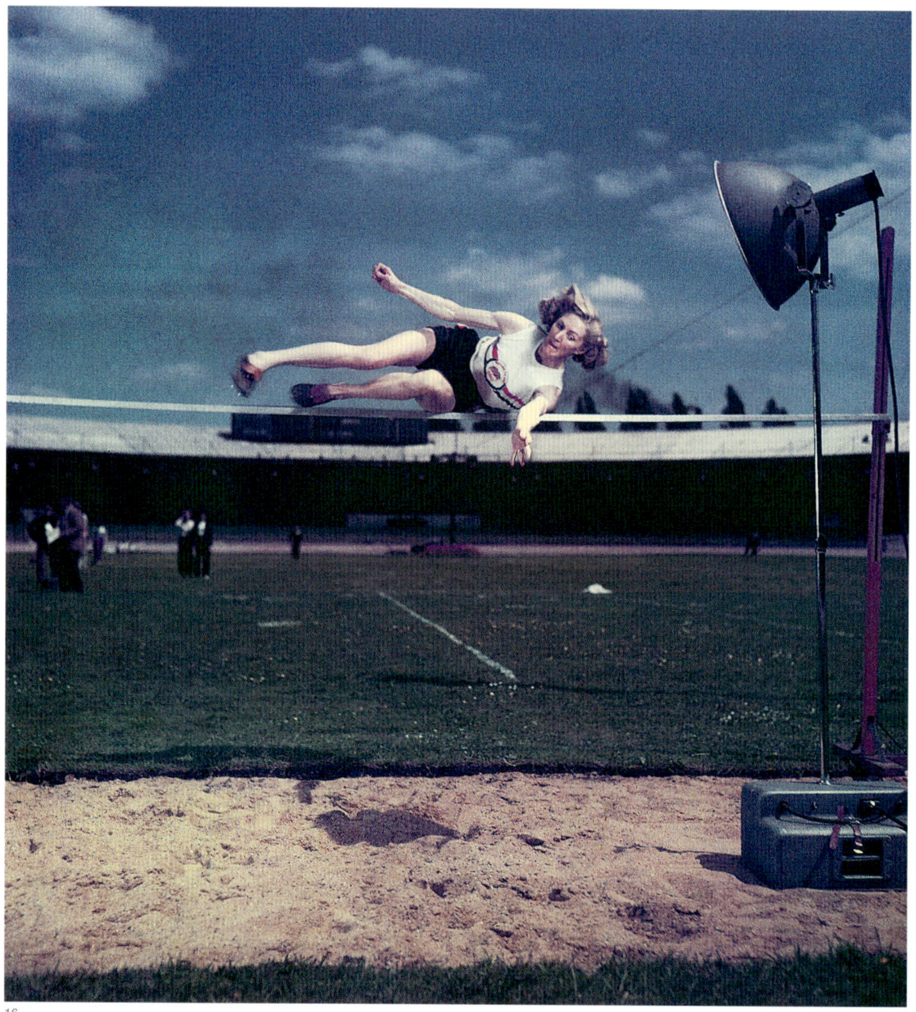

16

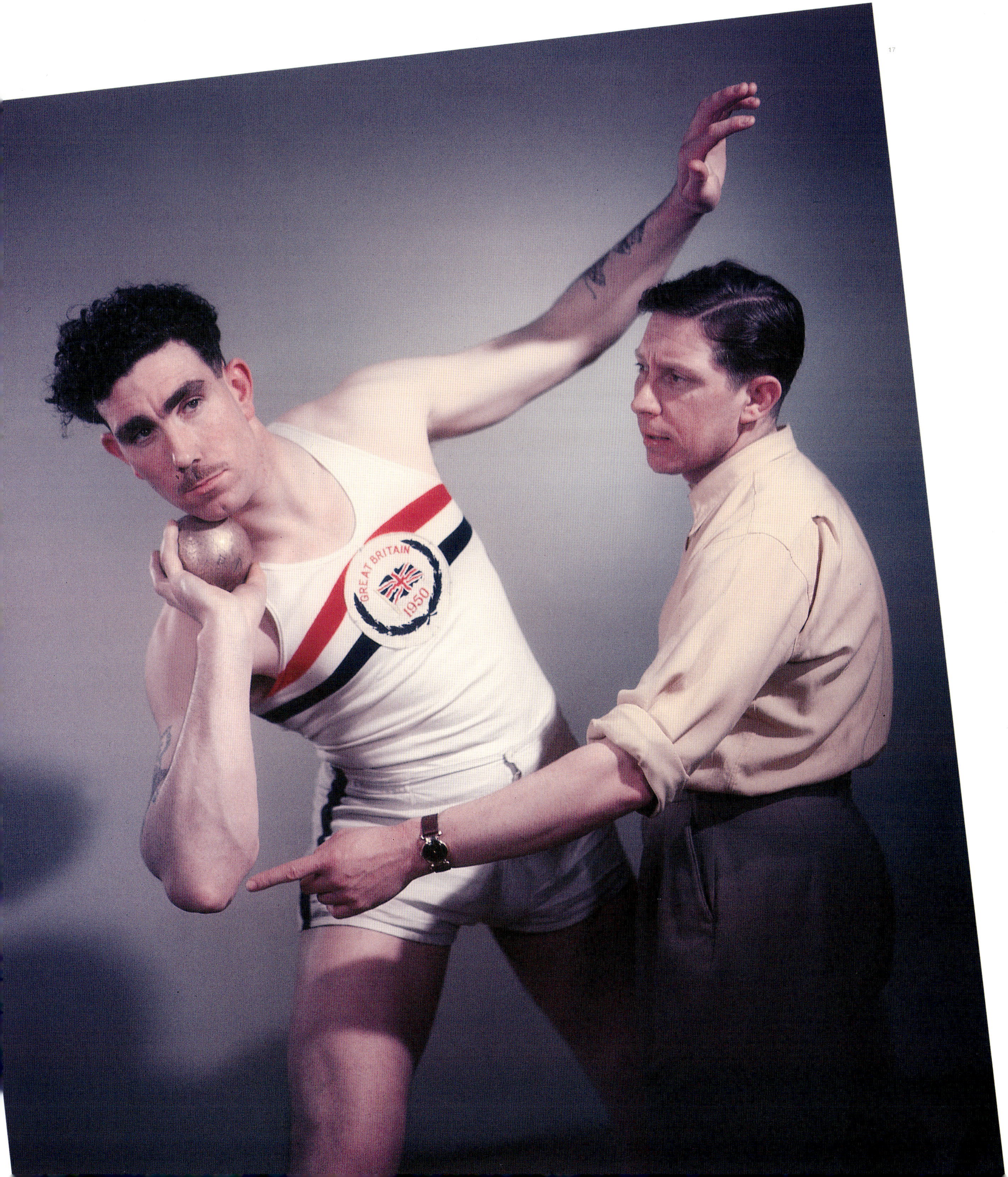
GREAT BRITAIN
1950

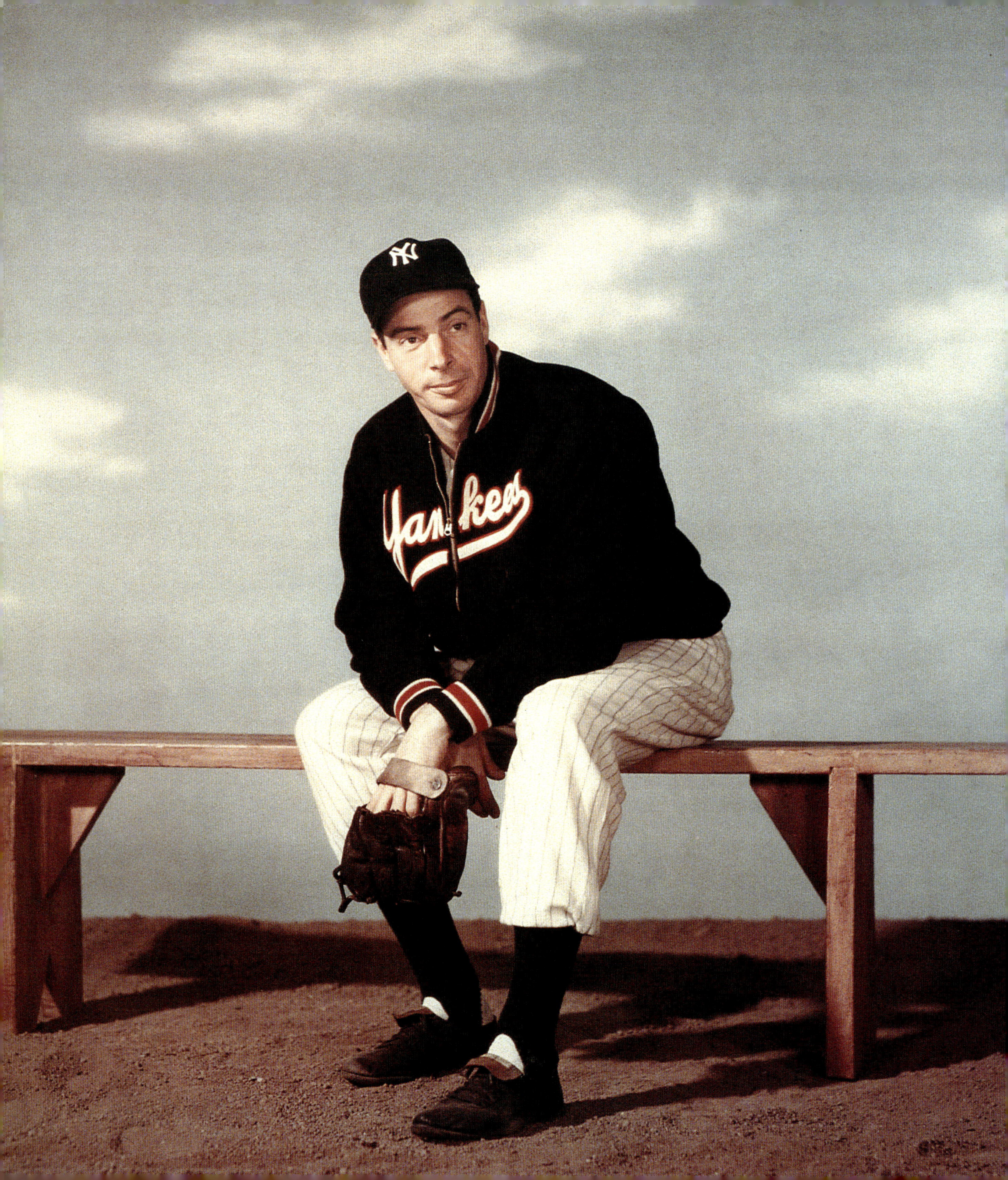
NY
Yankees

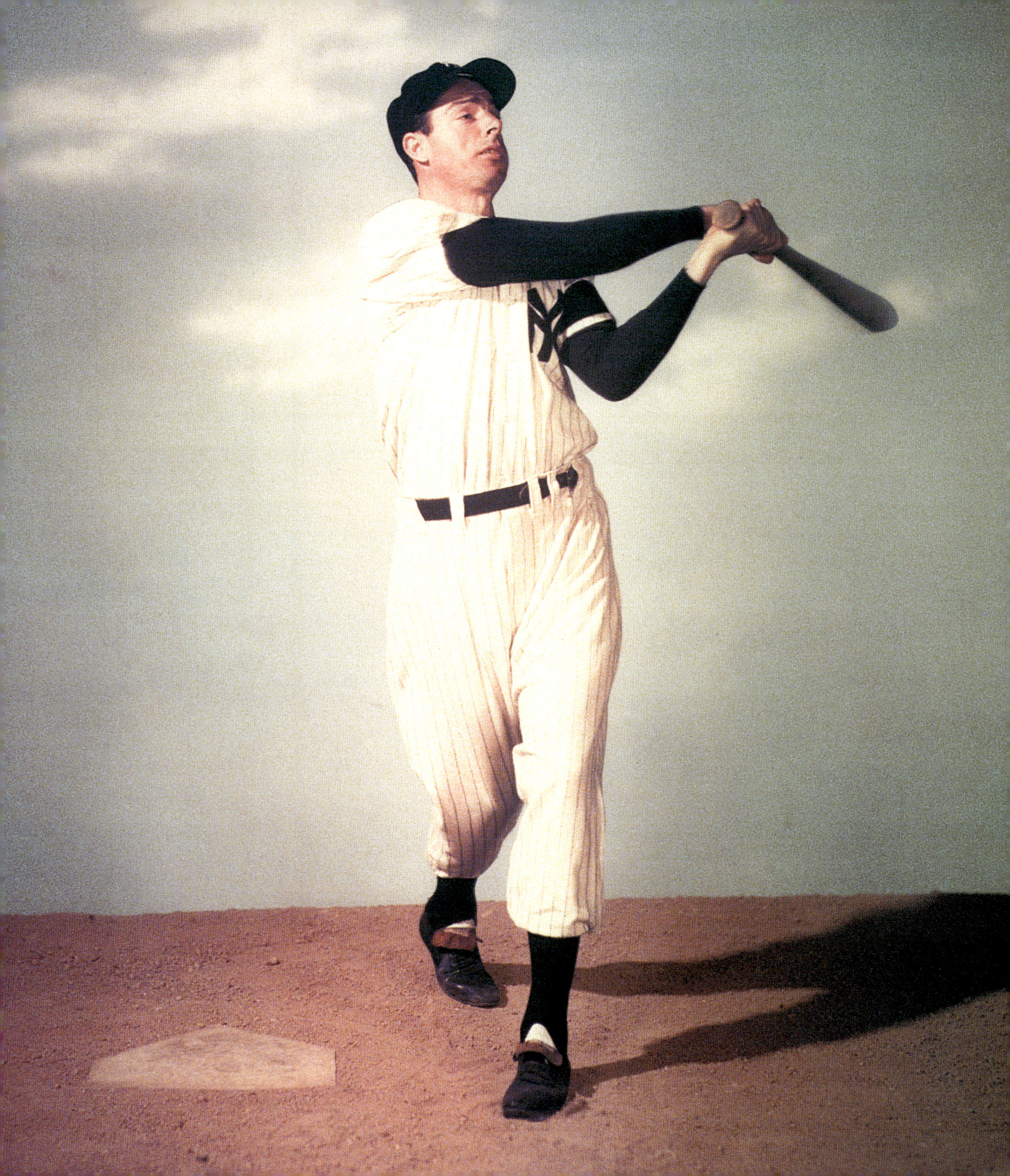

01
Richard Bergmann, 1951
Roger Wood

FLASH

The photographic flash enabled the photographer to create dramatic lighting effects, brightly illuminating the subject and casting everything else into deep shadow. It could also be used to freeze movement: to make visible action otherwise too quick for the eye. This was used extensively in the 1950s, giving an analytical quasi-scientific quality to sports photography. Also, by using strobe lighting movement could be further studied capturing a series of moments of continuous motion that could be viewed in a single picture.

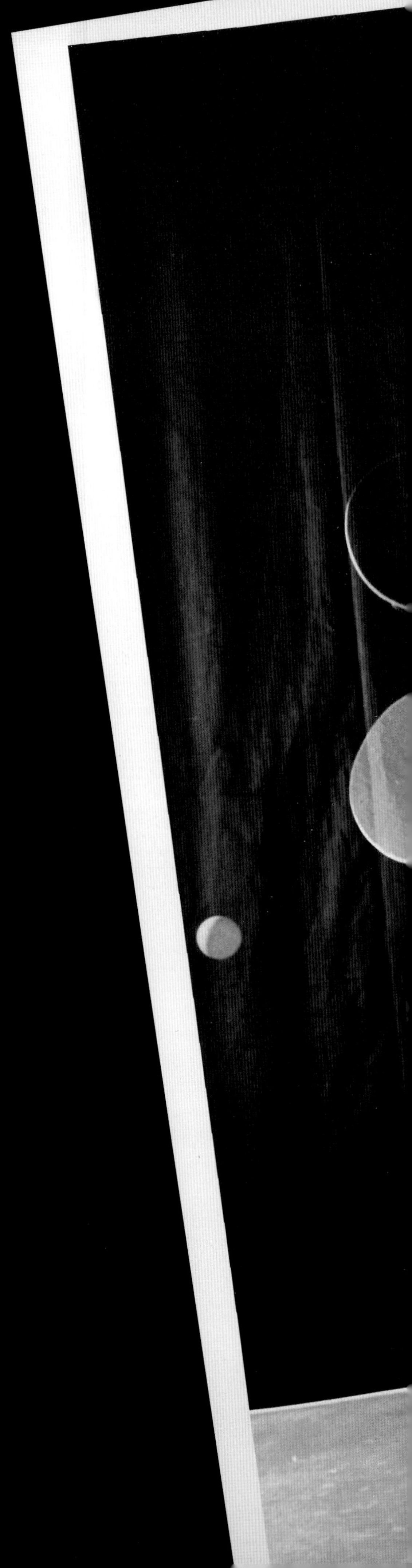

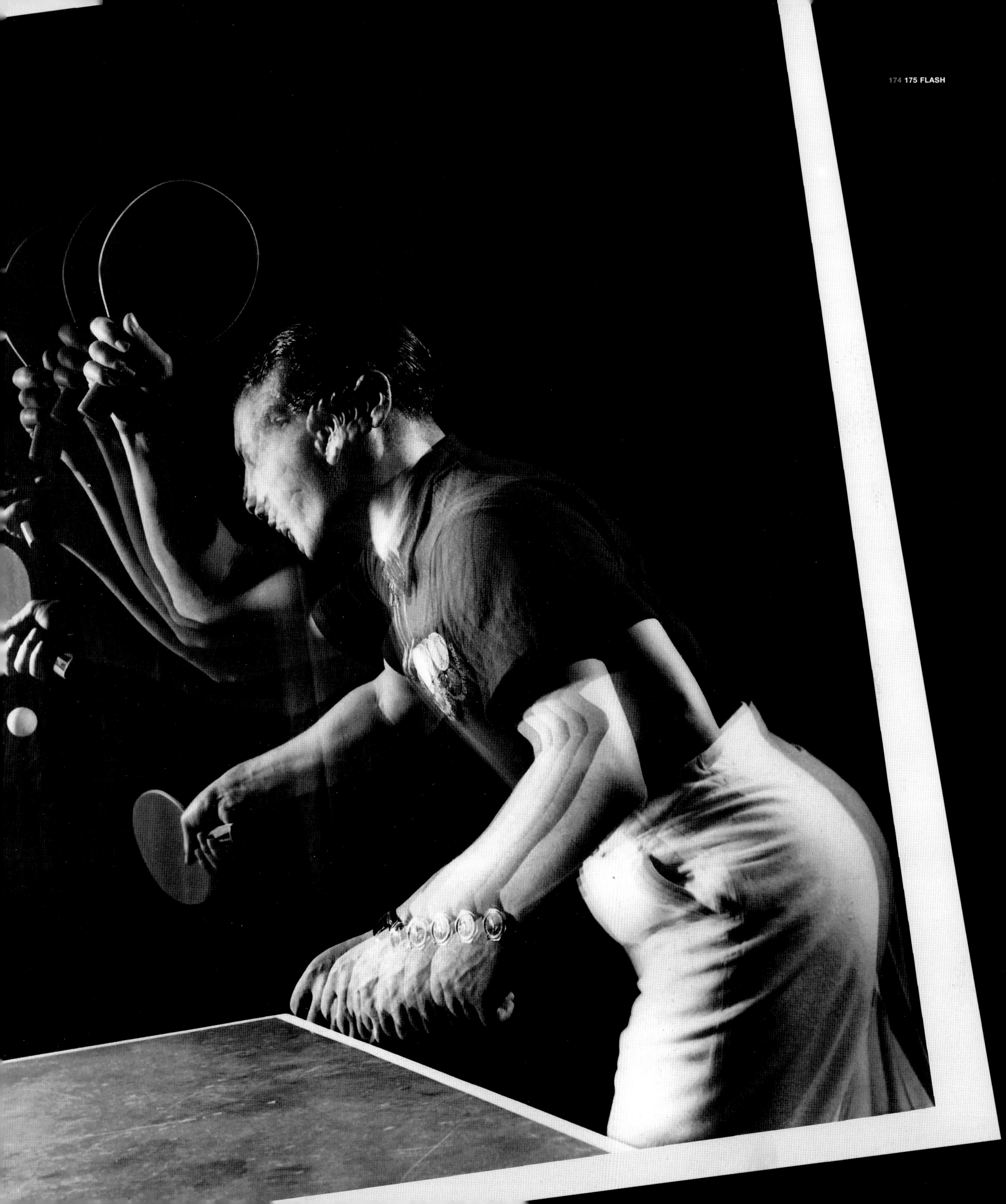

02
Helen Elliot, London, 1950
Bert Hardy

03
Vera Dace Thomas, London, 1950
Bert Hardy

04
Martin Reisman, London, 1950
Bert Hardy

05
G Amouretti, London, 1950
Bert Hardy

06 (OVERLEAF LEFT)
A game of pelota, *c.* 1950

07 (OVERLEAF RIGHT)
The basketball team of Wilbraham Academy in Massachusetts in training, *c.* 1955
Barry

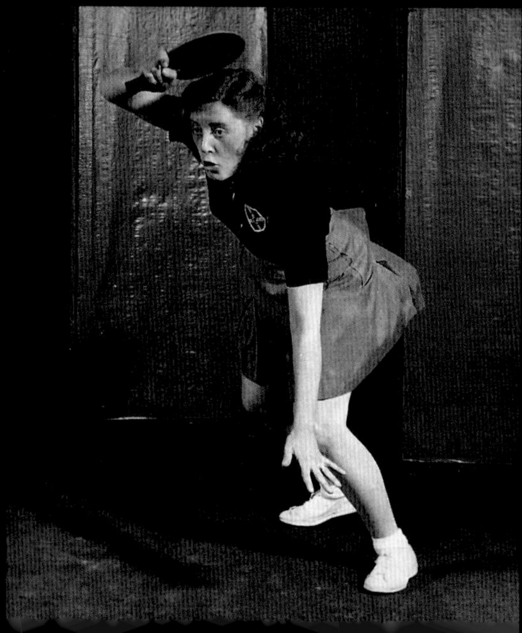

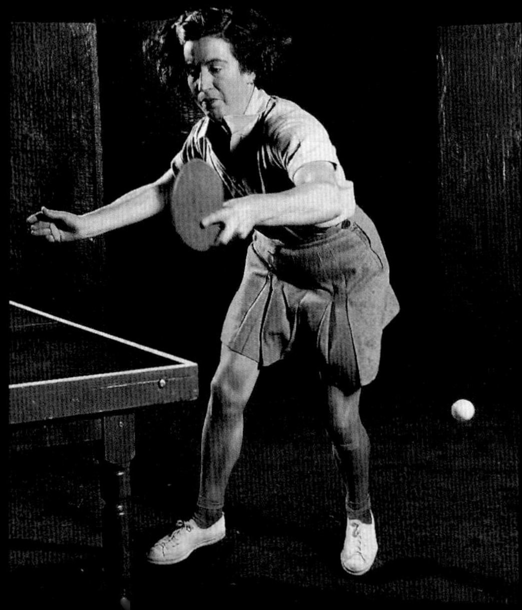

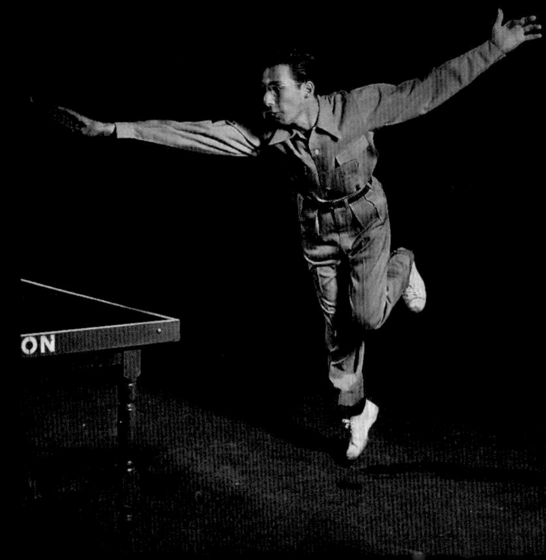

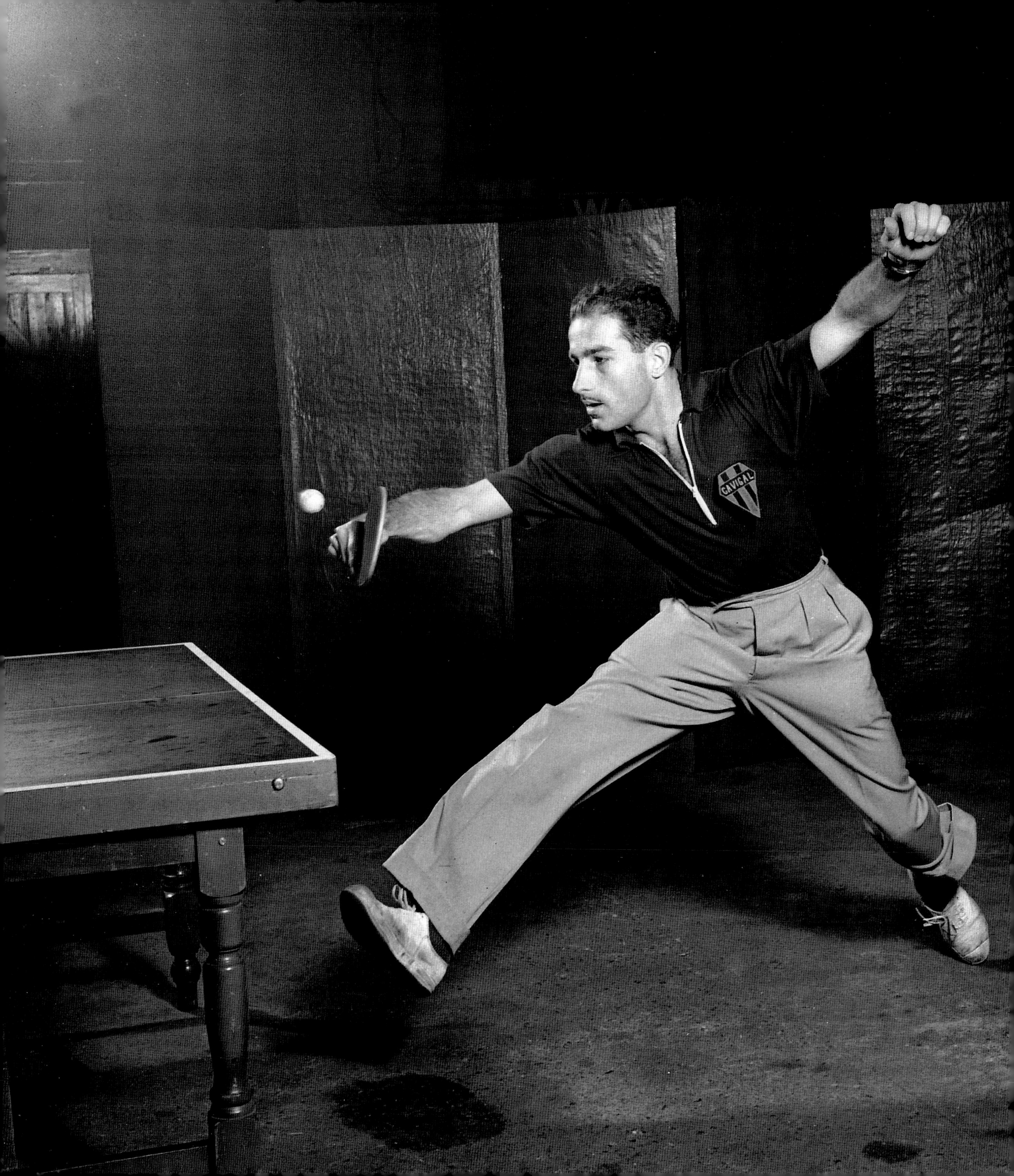
CAVIGAL

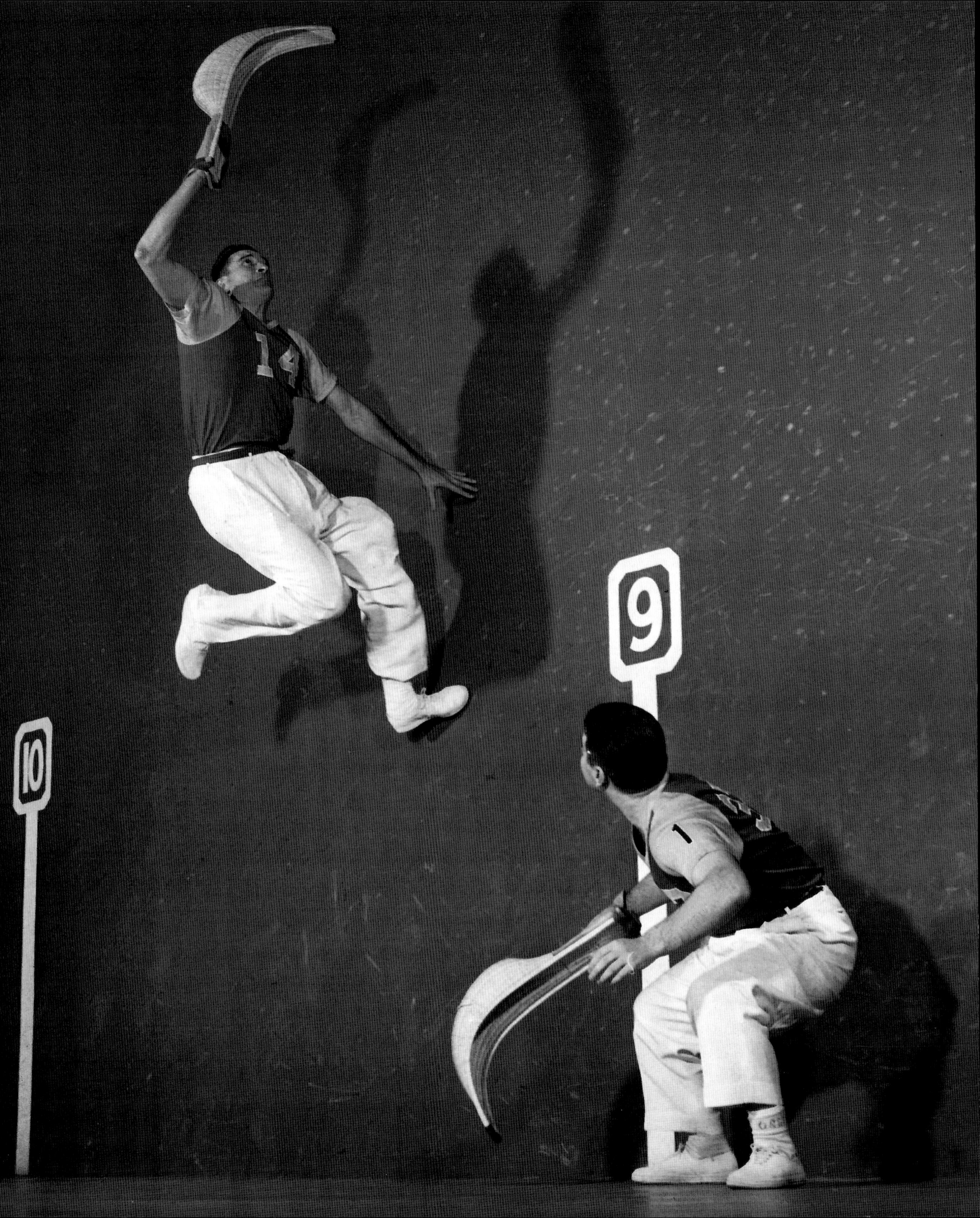
14
9
10

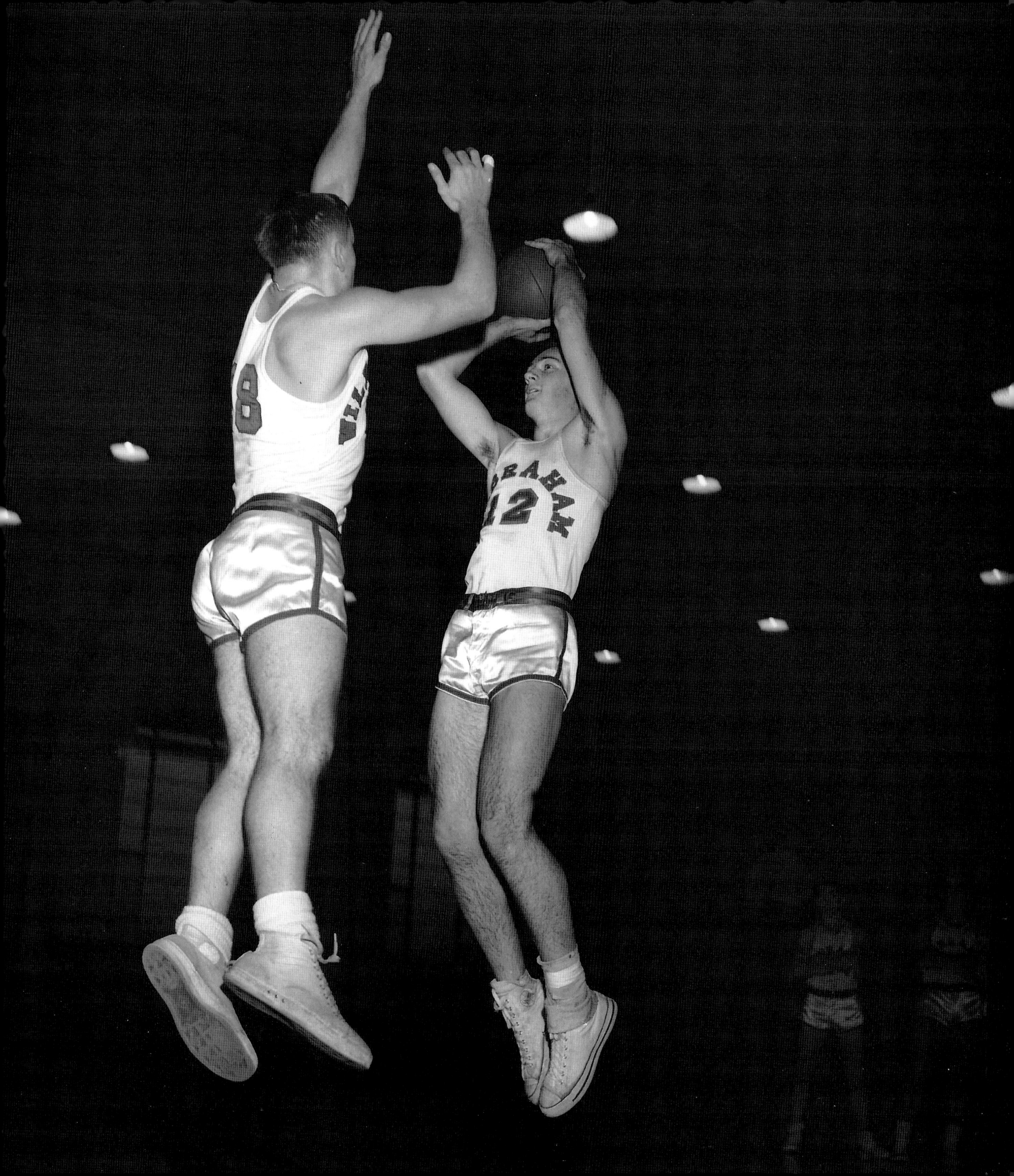

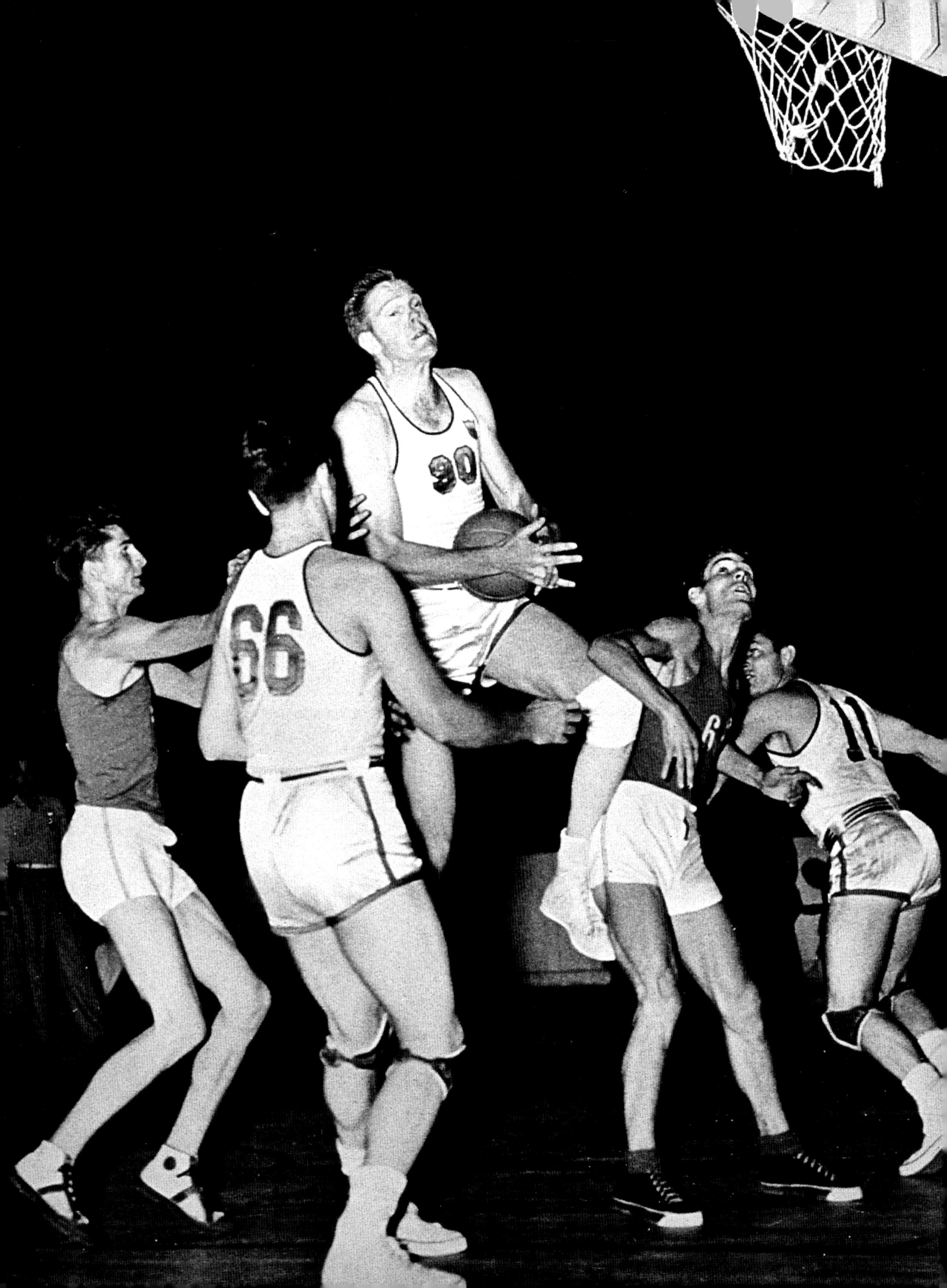

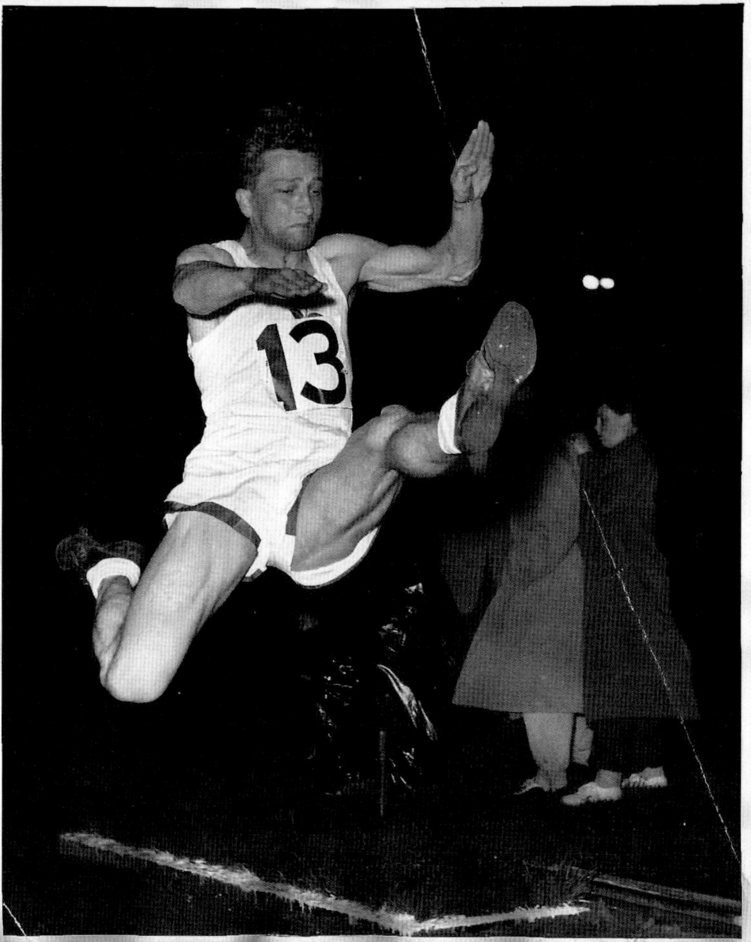

13

01
Ball's-eye view of an underhand shot at the basket, 1950s

CLOSE-UP

During the 1940s and 1950s sports photography started to develop a more versatile repertoire of image-making. Instead of relying on darkroom techniques to create more dramatic pictures, photographers moved in closer, looking for detail to fill the frame. These close-up photographs would generally be one image in a larger picture-story of six or more, but the close-up soon secured its own space on the page as a stand-alone image which could tell sports stories in a new and imaginative way.

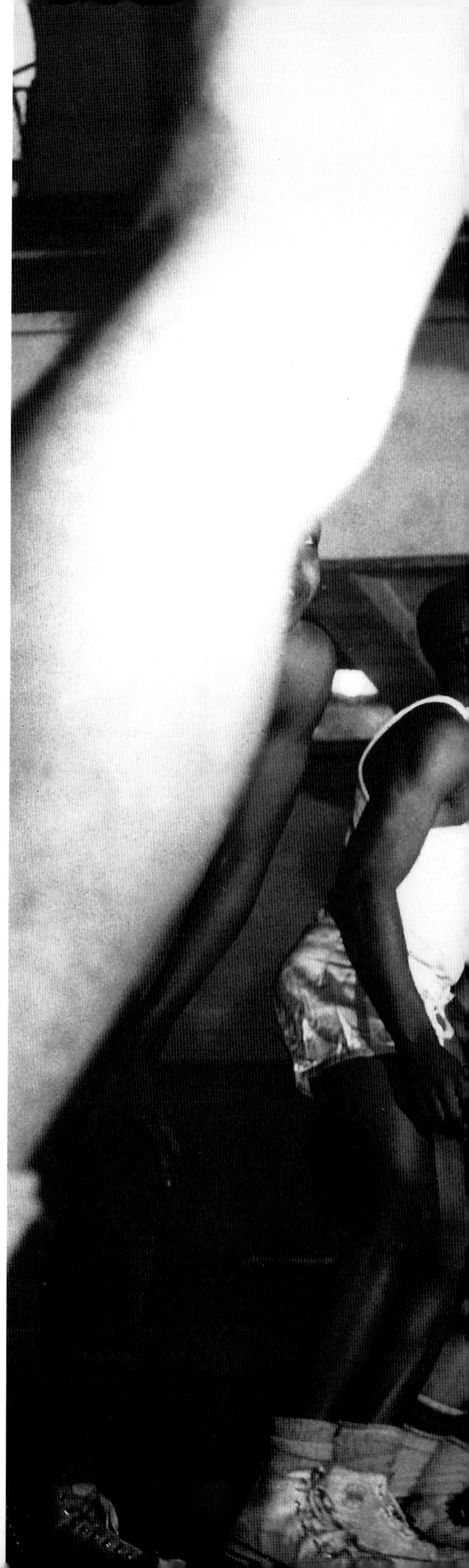

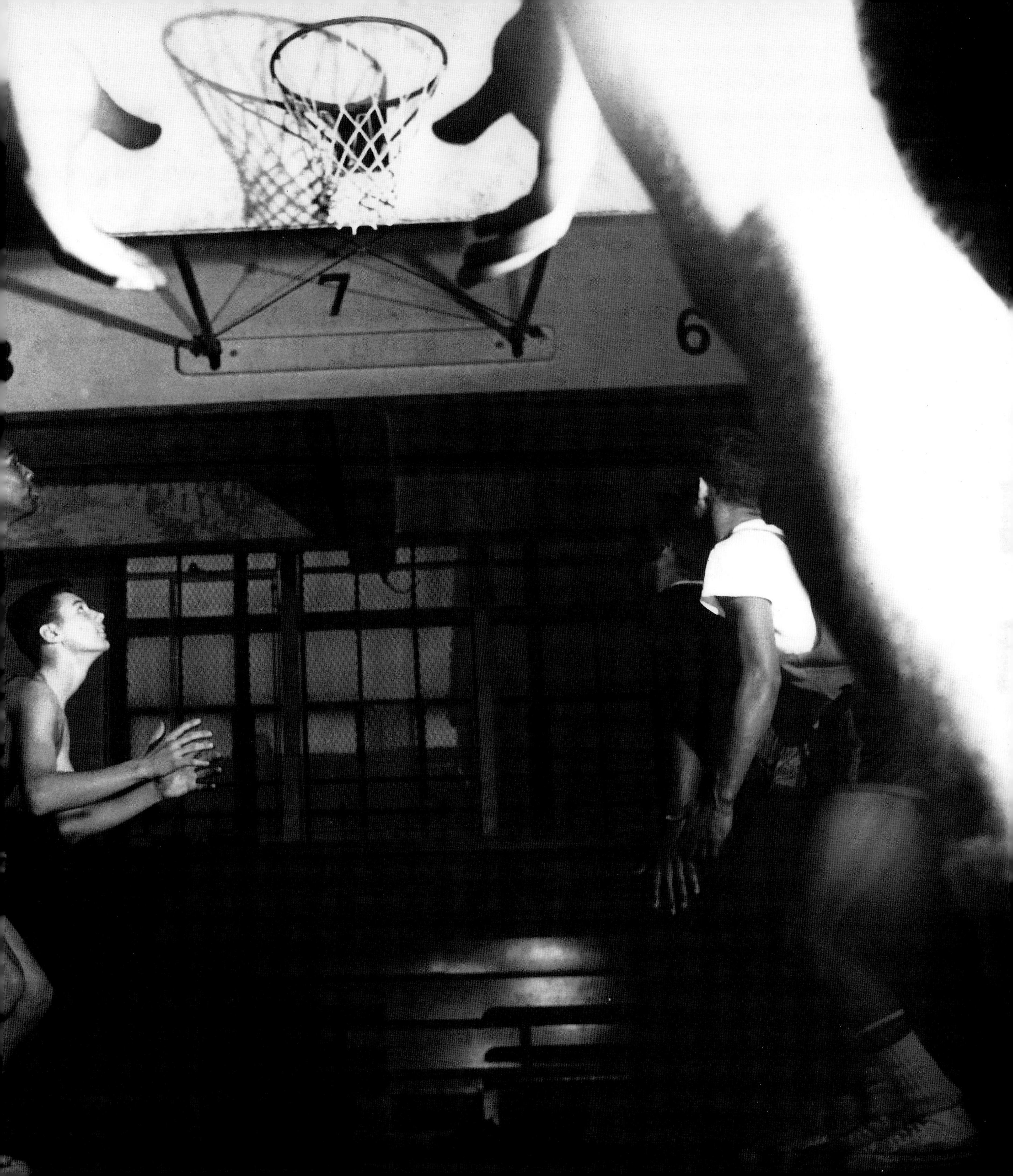
7
6

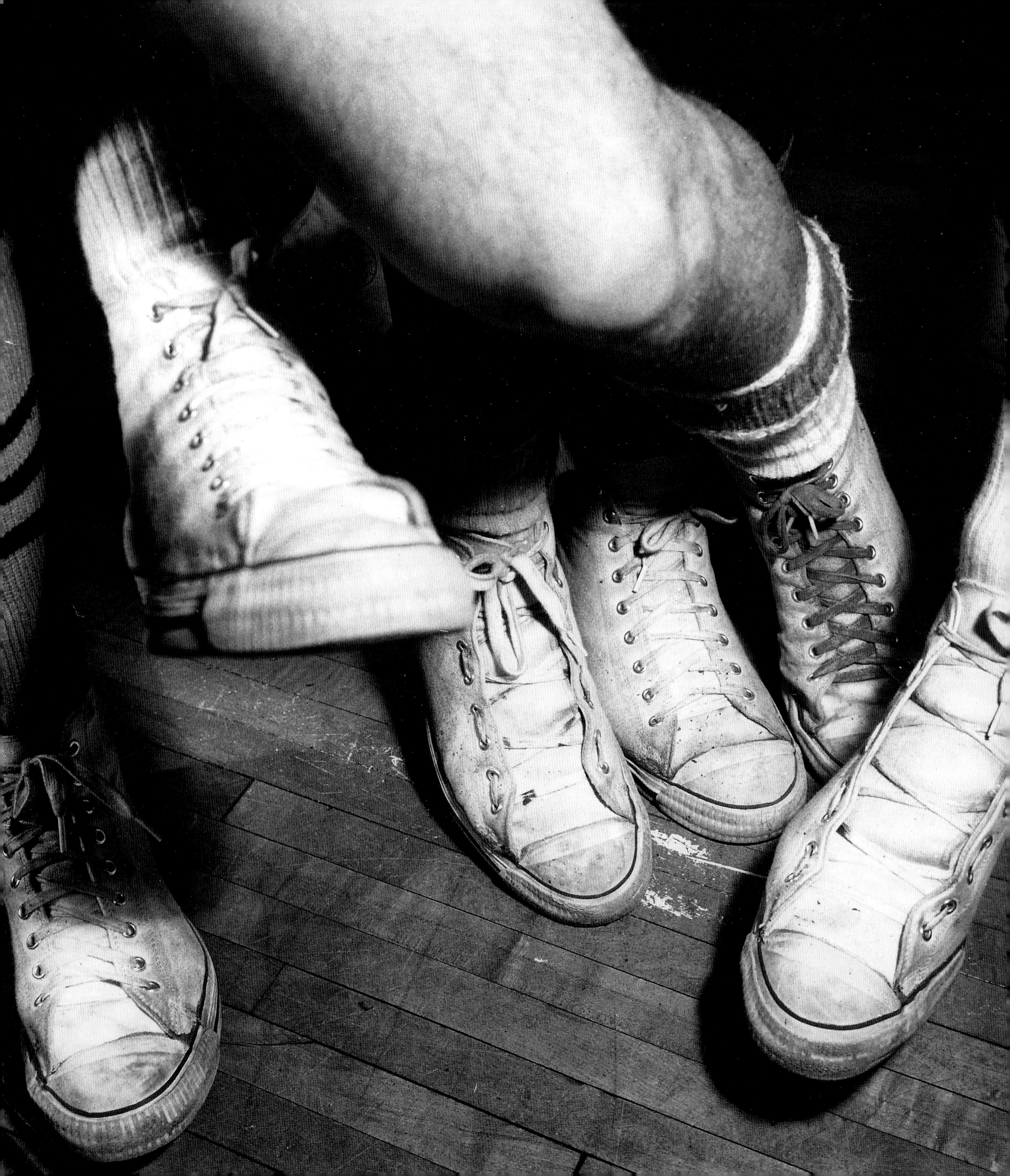

02
Basketball players scrambling for a loose ball, 1950s

03
The feet of members of the Nigerian international soccer team, preferring to play without boots, 1950

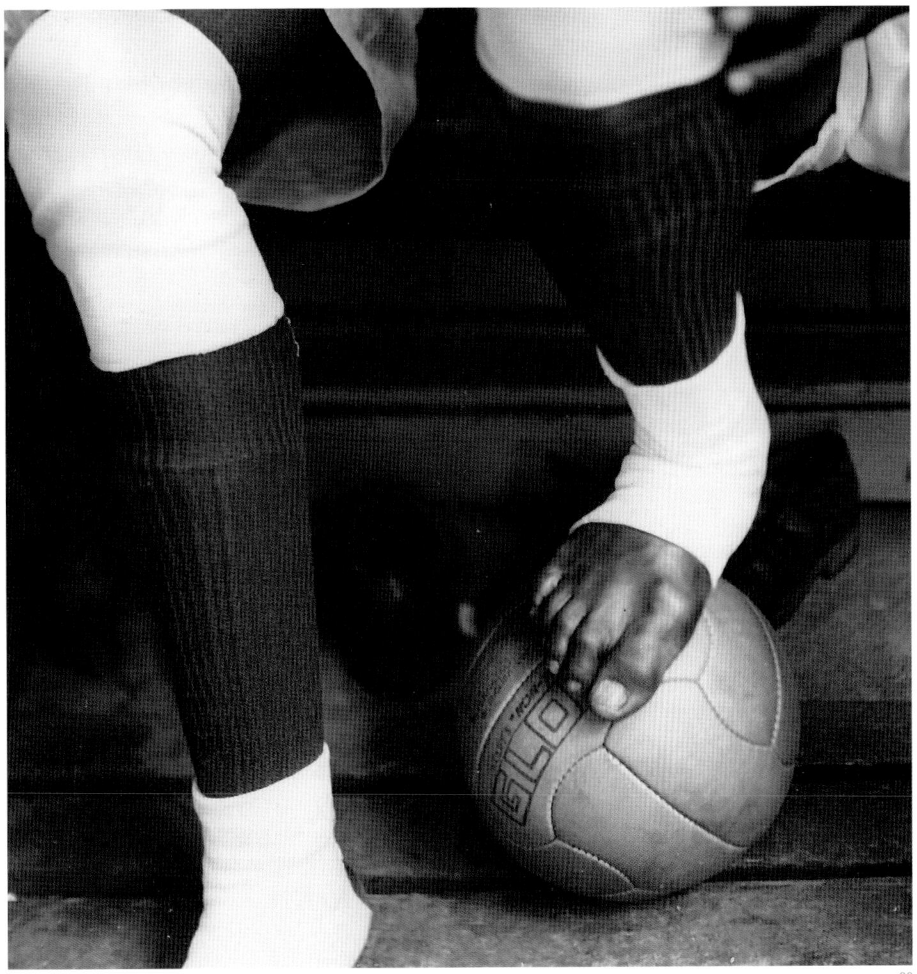

03

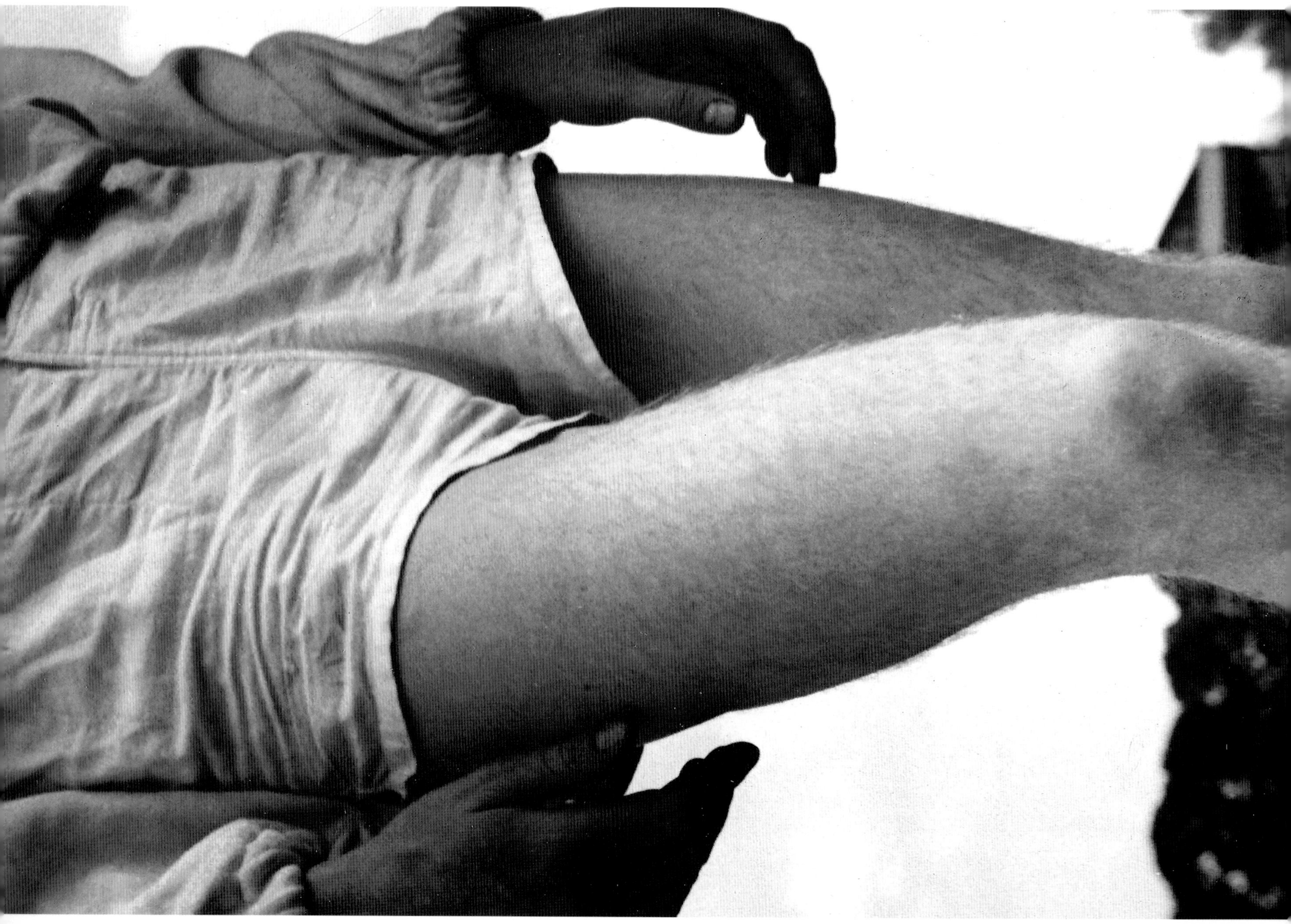

04
The legs of Roger Bannister, 1951
John Chillingworth

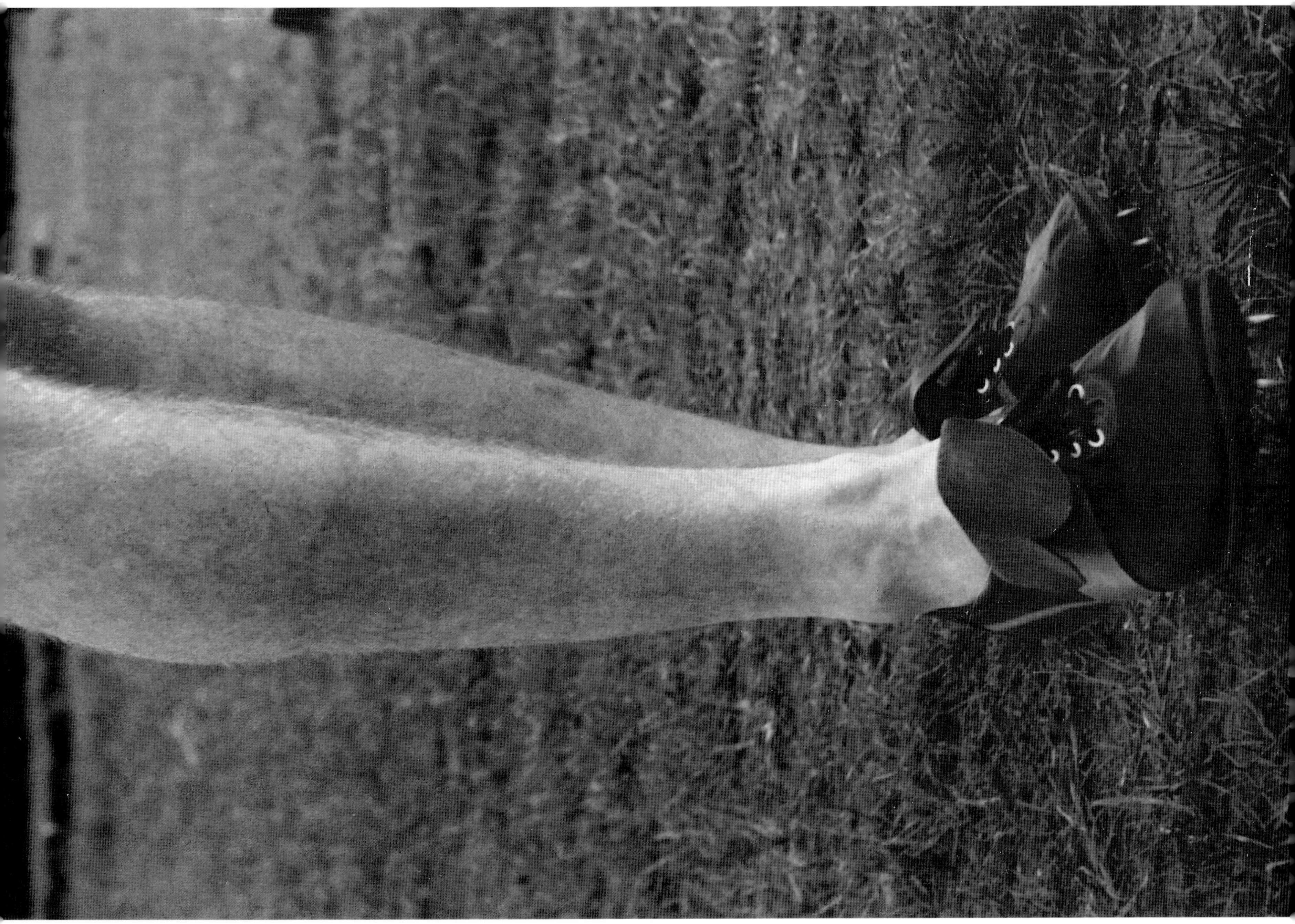

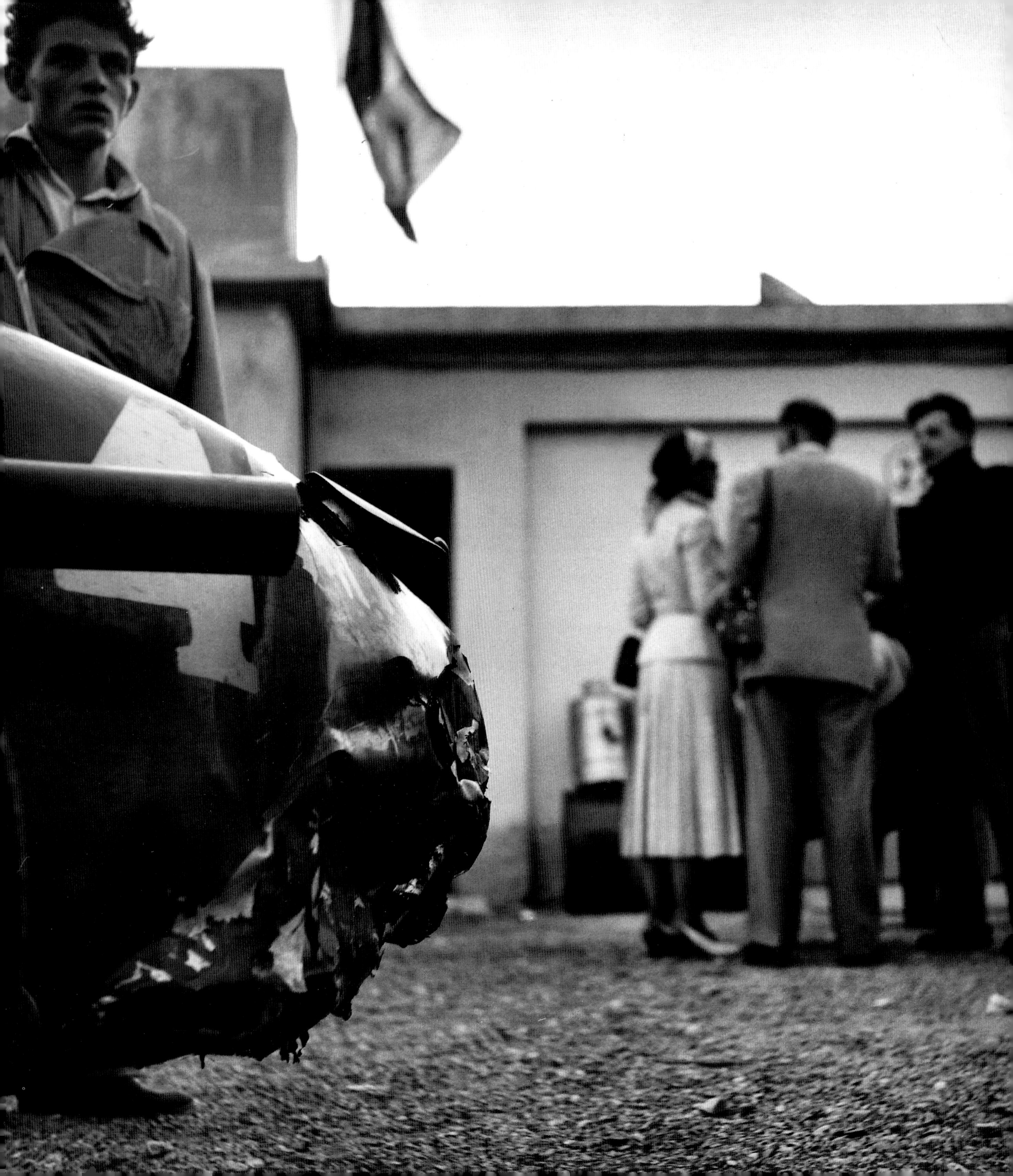

05
The tail of Alberto Ascari's Ferrari following a collision with his team-mate Farina at the Italian Grand Prix, 1953
Ronald Startup

06
Tommy McGovern in training, 1953
Ronald Startup

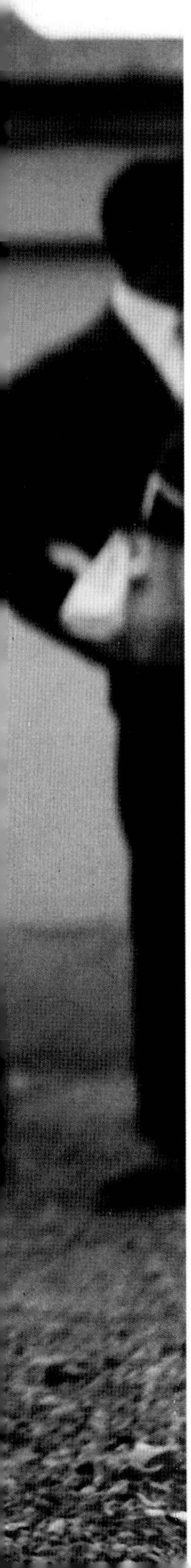

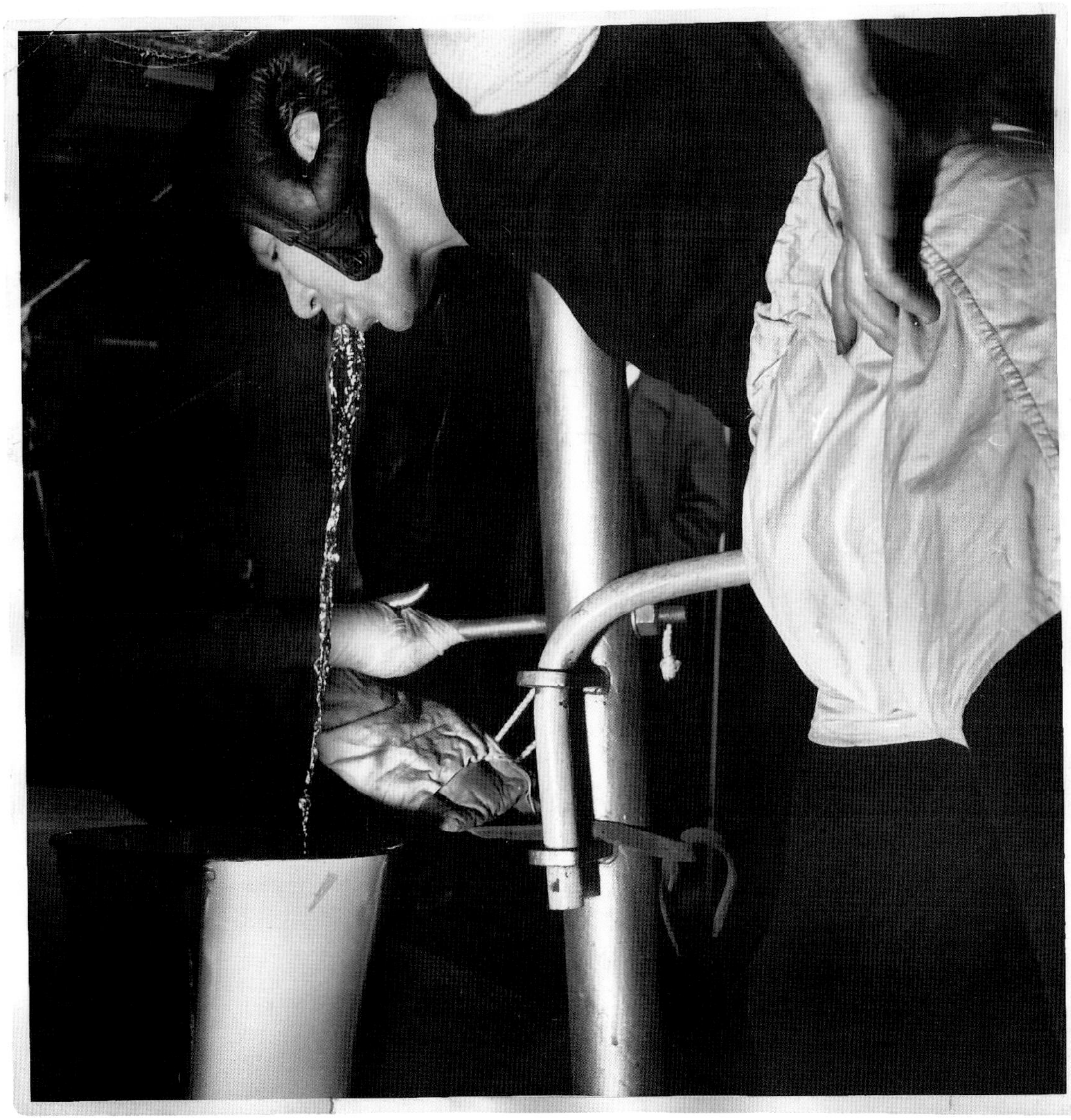

06

01/02 (OVERLEAF)
Aberdeen versus Heart of Midlothian, Aberdeen, 1955
Malcolm Dunbar

BLOW-UP

The technique of cropping out part of the photograph in the darkroom and printing only one section of the negative has been part of the repertoire of sports photography since its beginnings. The impulse during the 1950s to crop the wider view of the game was in response to changing layout styles in newspaper and magazine design, which required a more immediate view of the sporting event. Photographs were now playing a more important role in selling publications and had to focus on the action – the main characters – and so tell the story at a glance. Because of improvements in film stock the blow-up versions had the same print quality as the full-frame prints, as can be seen in these examples.

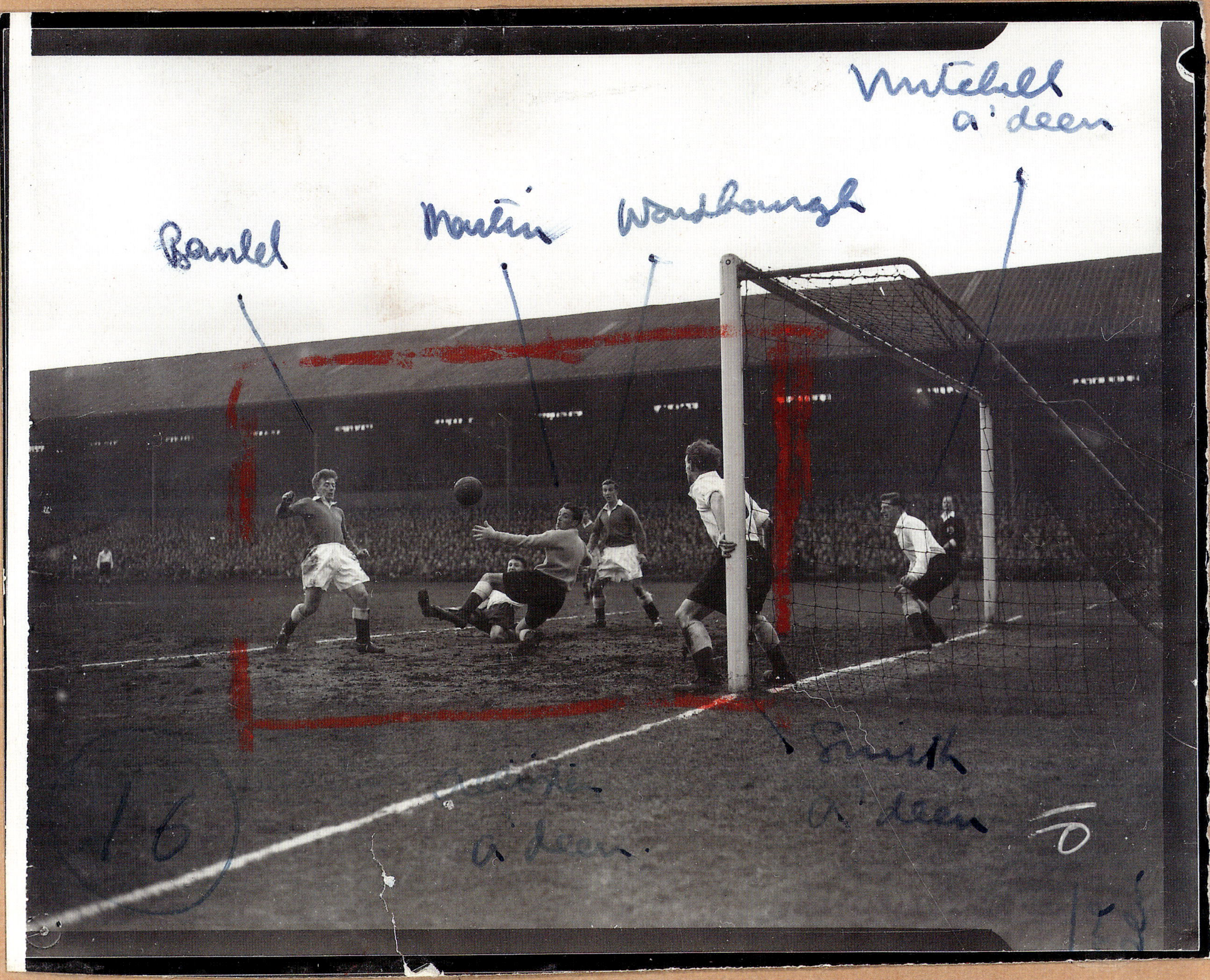

Mitchell a'deen
Bauld
Martin
Wardhaugh
Smith a'deen
16

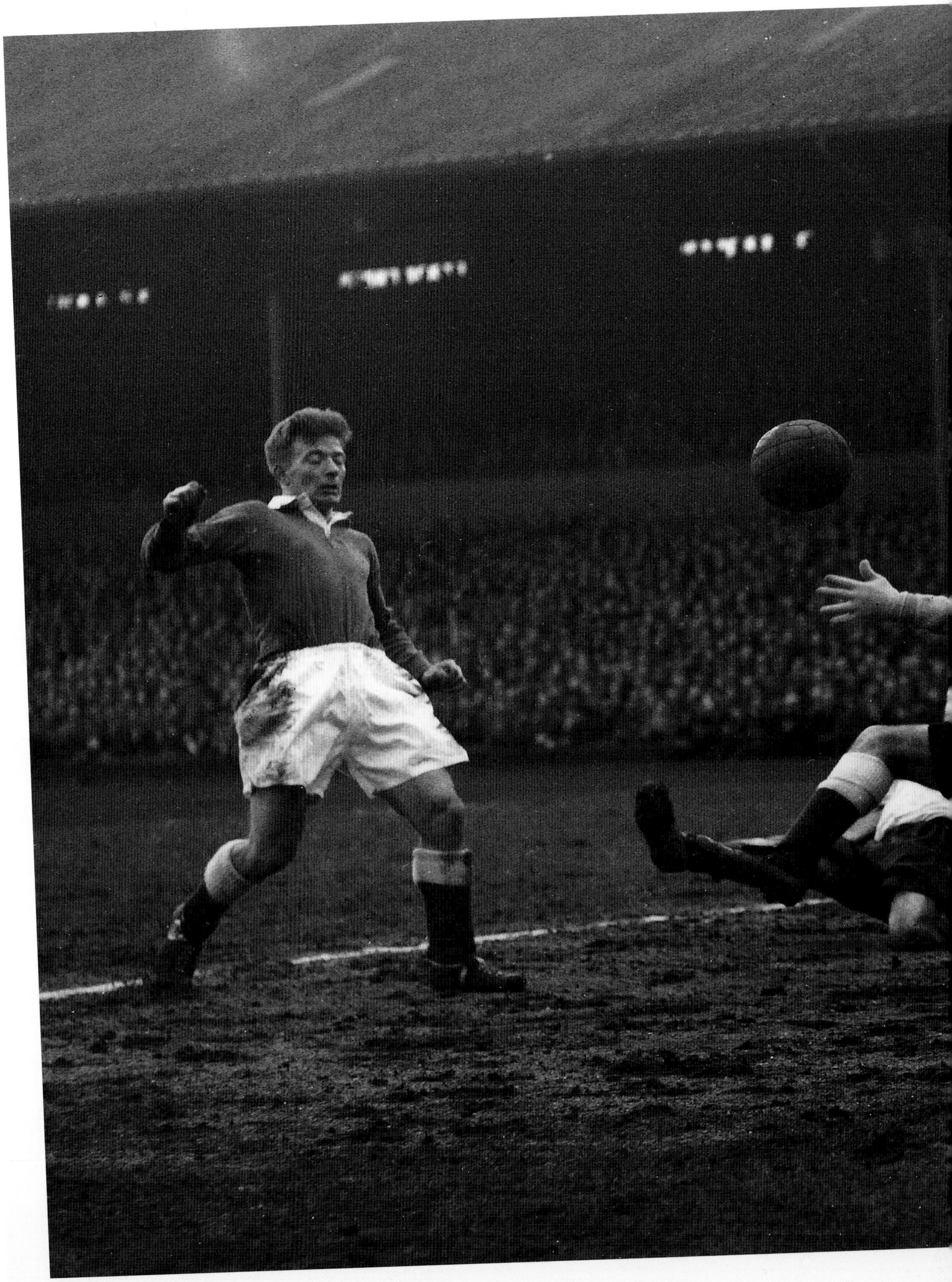

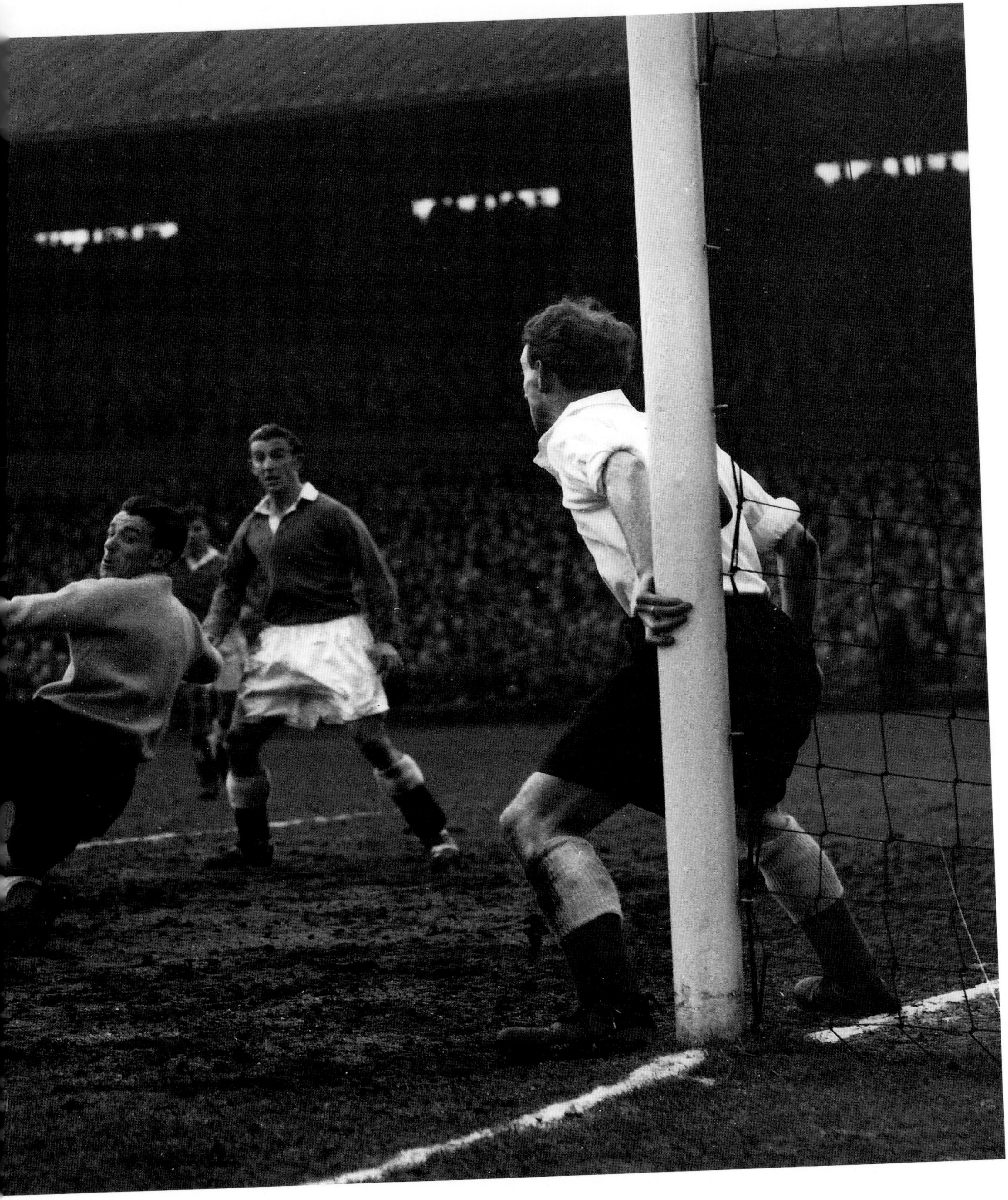

03/04
I Murchison winning the 200m race at the Whitsuntide British Games and CAV Championships, London, 1956
Folb

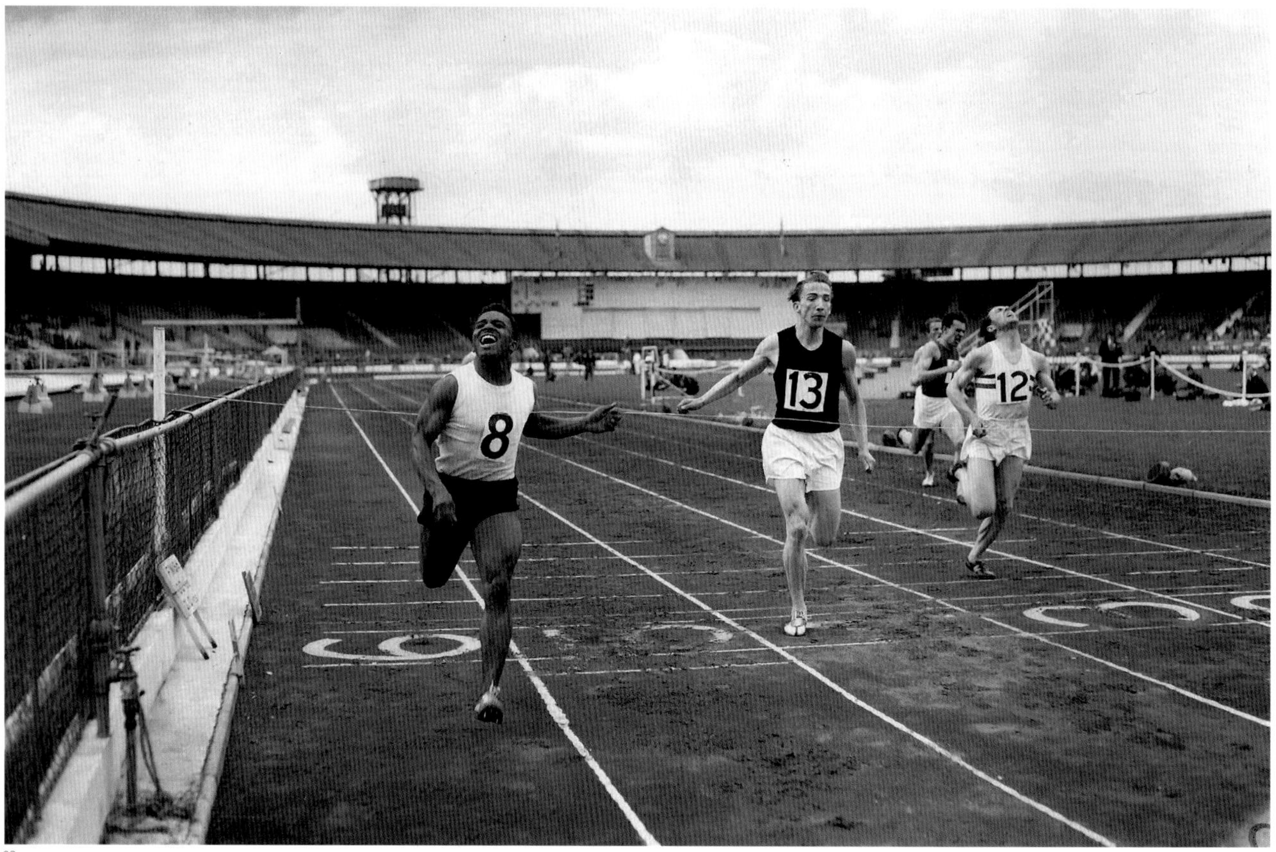

03

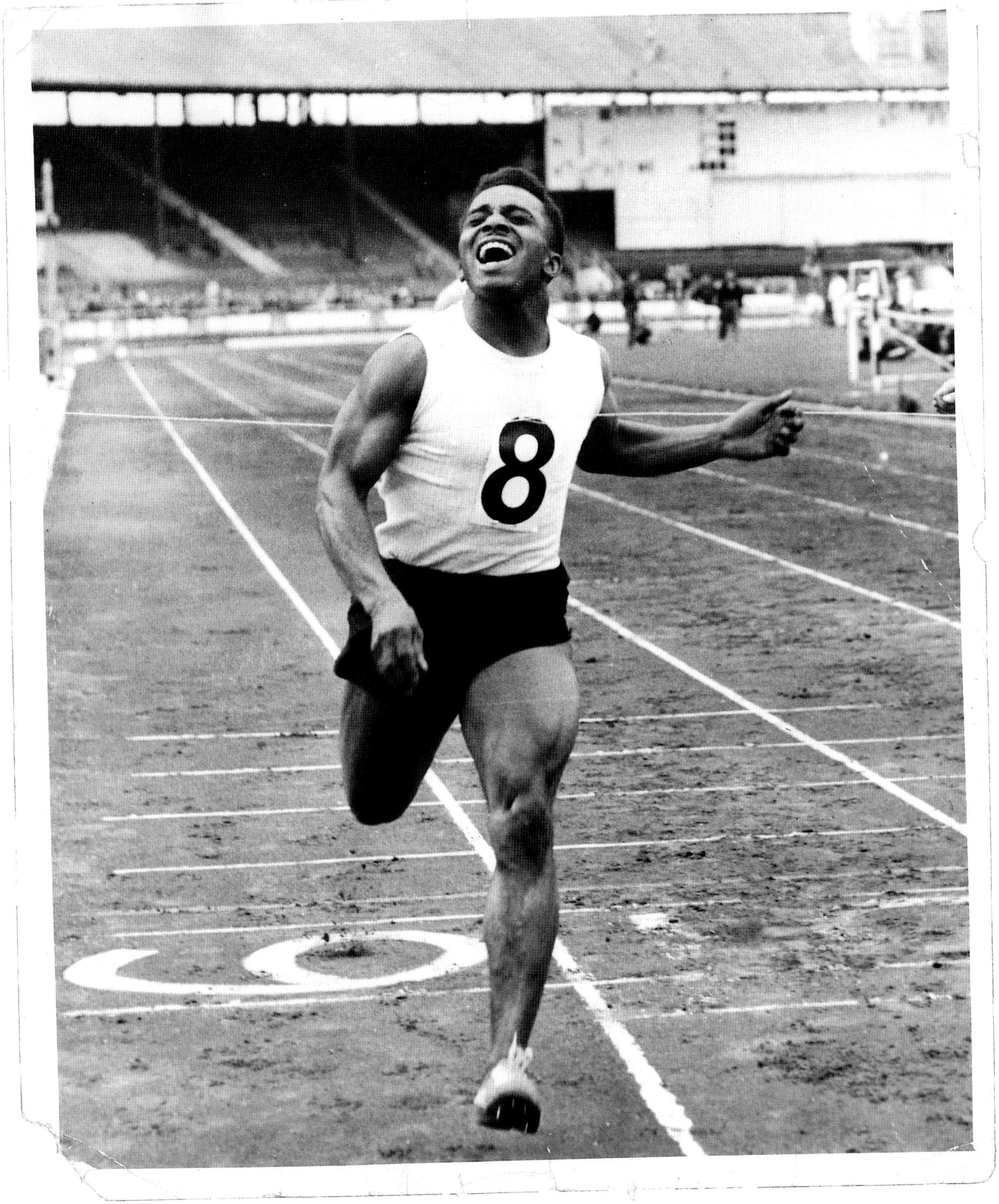
8

05/06
June Paul winning the 100 yards at the Women's Amateur Athletics Association Championships, London, 1956
Monty Fresco Jnr

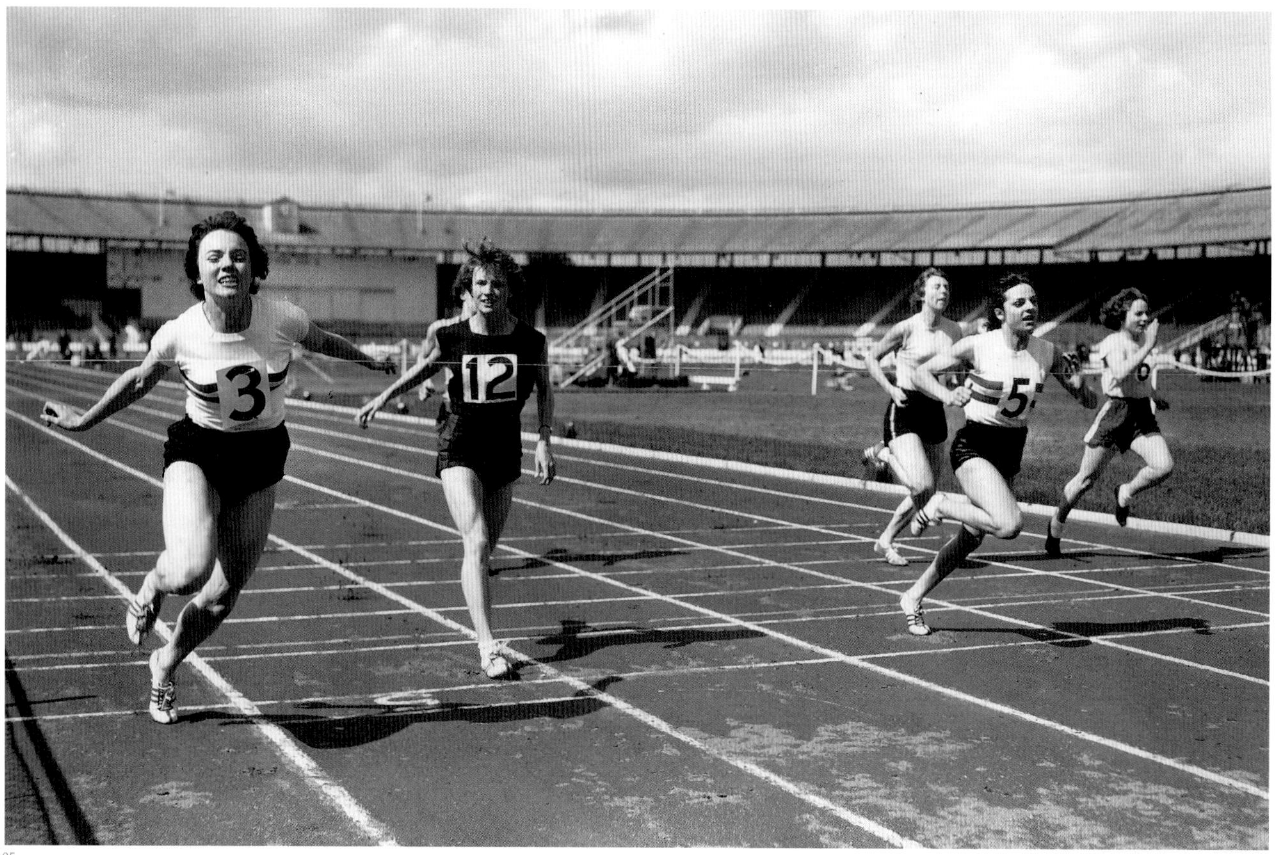

05

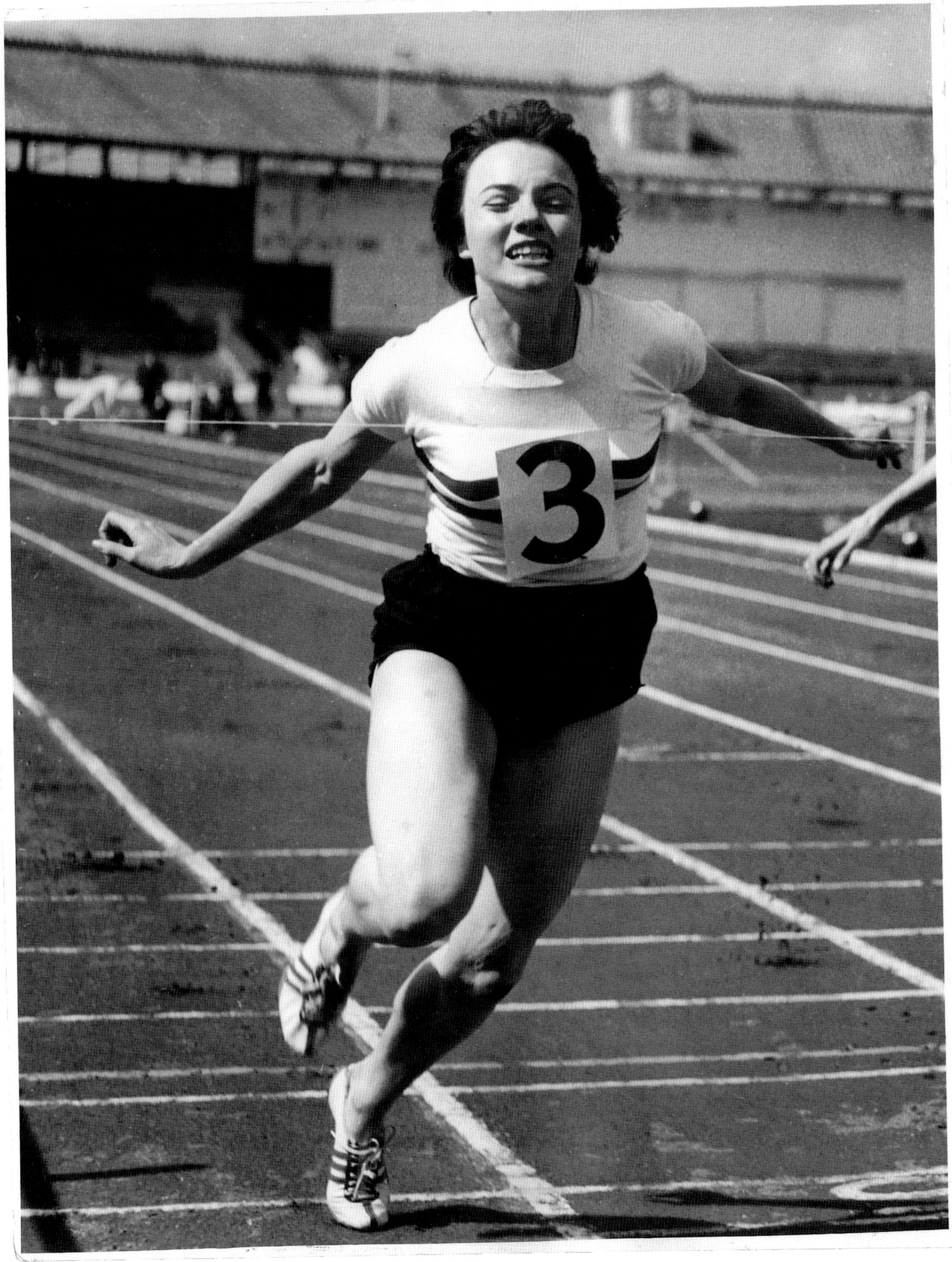
3

RECORDS

Time and photography are inextricably interwoven. Making a photographic image requires a precise mechanism that can control tiny amounts of time as light is allowed to pass through a lens onto light-sensitive film. Recording accurate times for track events is equally crucial; accuracy to fractions of a second is also necessary. It seems inevitable that the photographer would join the timekeeper at the finishing line to record the moment when new records are set.

01
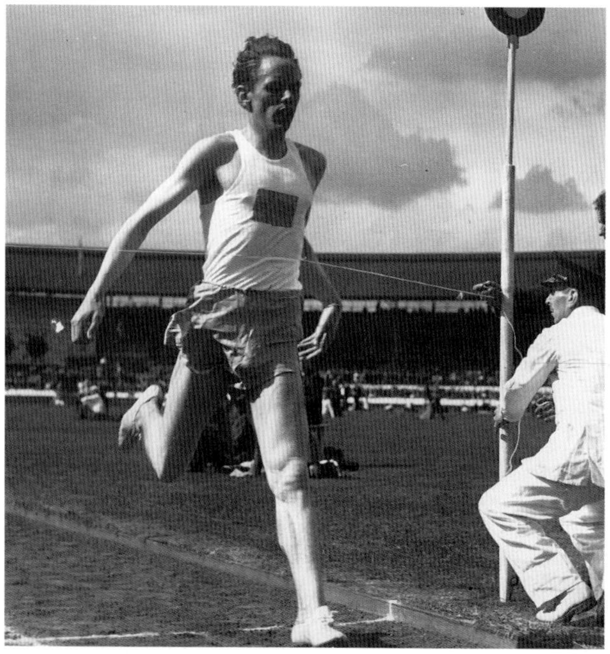

02
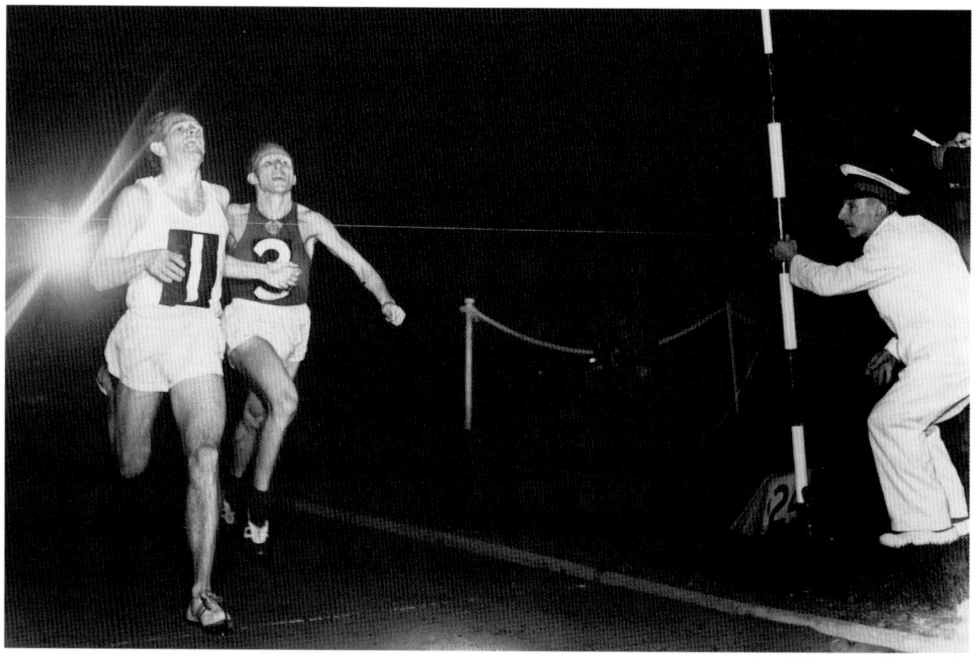

01
Gundar Haegg setting a new British all-comers 2 mile record, London, 1945

02
Chris Chataway breaking the world 5000m record, London, 1954

03
Sándor Iharos breaking the world 2 mile record, London, 1955

04 (OVERLEAF)
Roger Bannister setting a new world mile record of under four minutes, Oxford, 1954

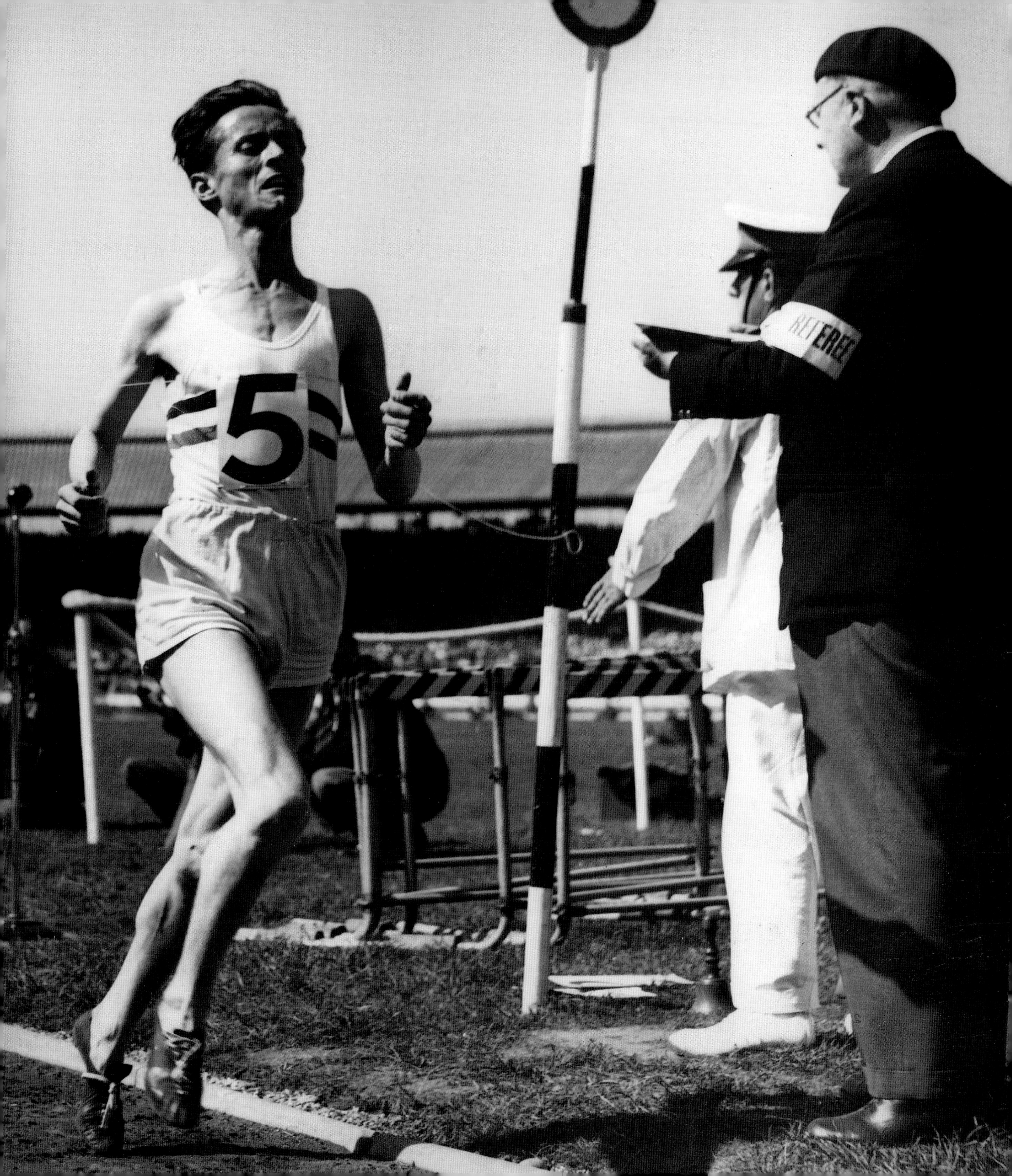
5

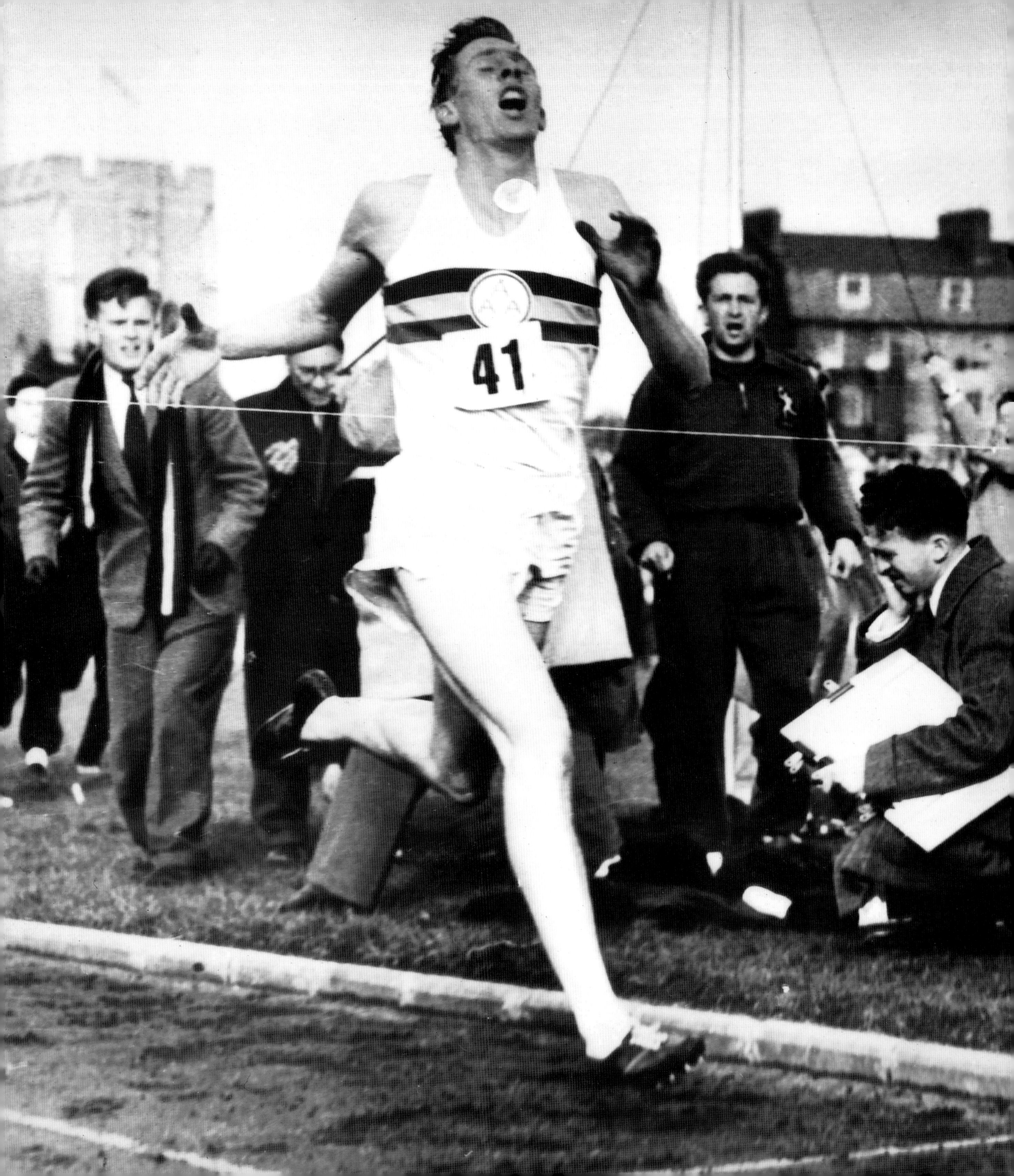
41

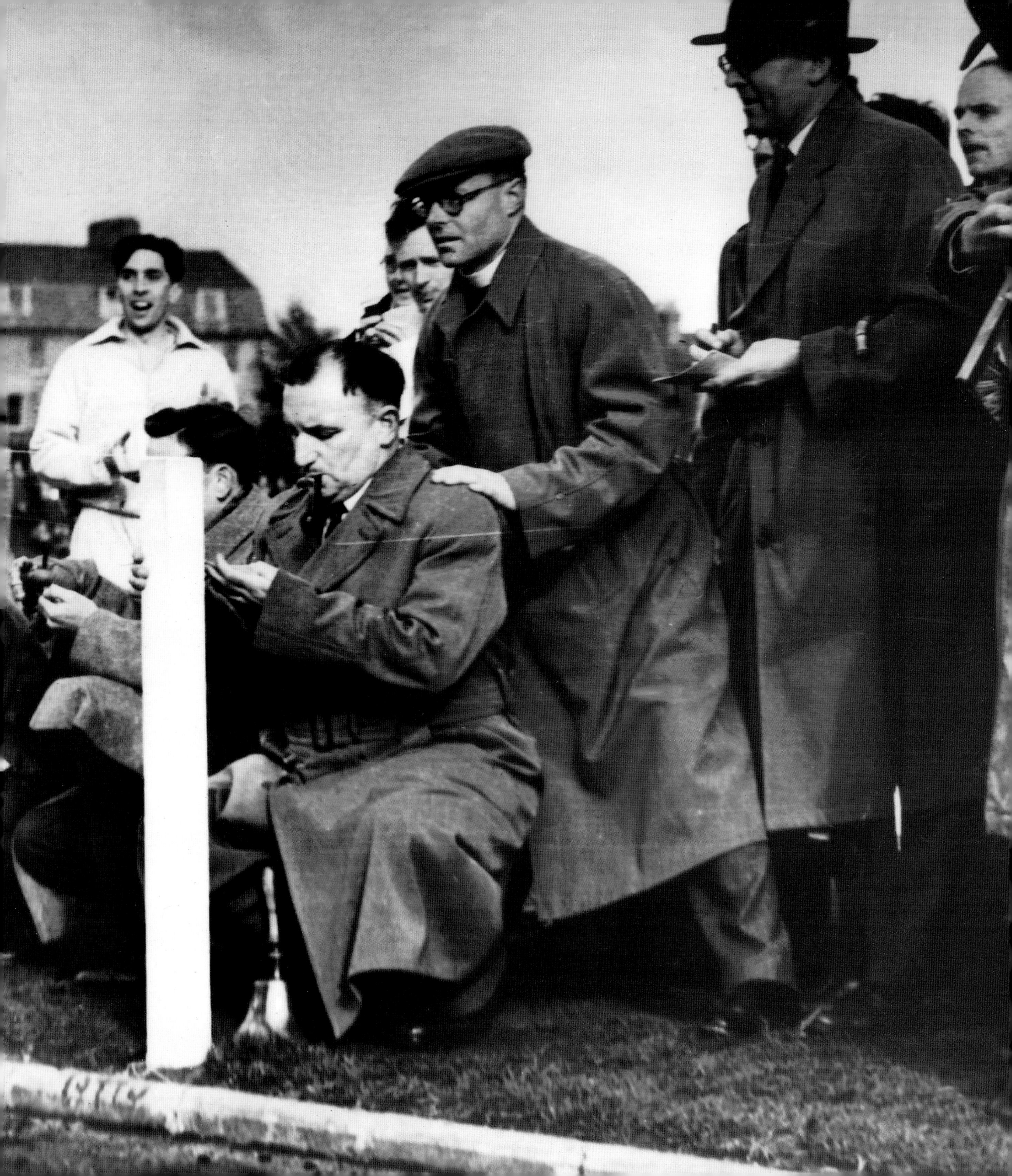

01
Frank Johnson versus Joe Lucy, London, 1953
Monty Fresco

RINGSIDE

Under the bright lights the elevated platform of the boxing ring seems more like a theatre stage upon which men act out an age-old drama or engage in some strange ritual dance. Photographers at ringside required extensive knowledge of the choreography of boxing: they had to know when one of the boxers was planning that punch to the jaw and how to be ready, with split-second timing, to catch the moment when the punch hit and the glove made contact with the face. The confined area of the ring, bright lighting conditions and the ability of the photographer to get to ringside, within a few feet of the fighters, made boxing a perfect subject for the photographer and give us some of the most dramatic and compelling images in sports photography. No other sporting activity allowed photographers so close that there was no need for a telephoto lens or extensive cropping of the picture. The drama was played out right in front of the camera.

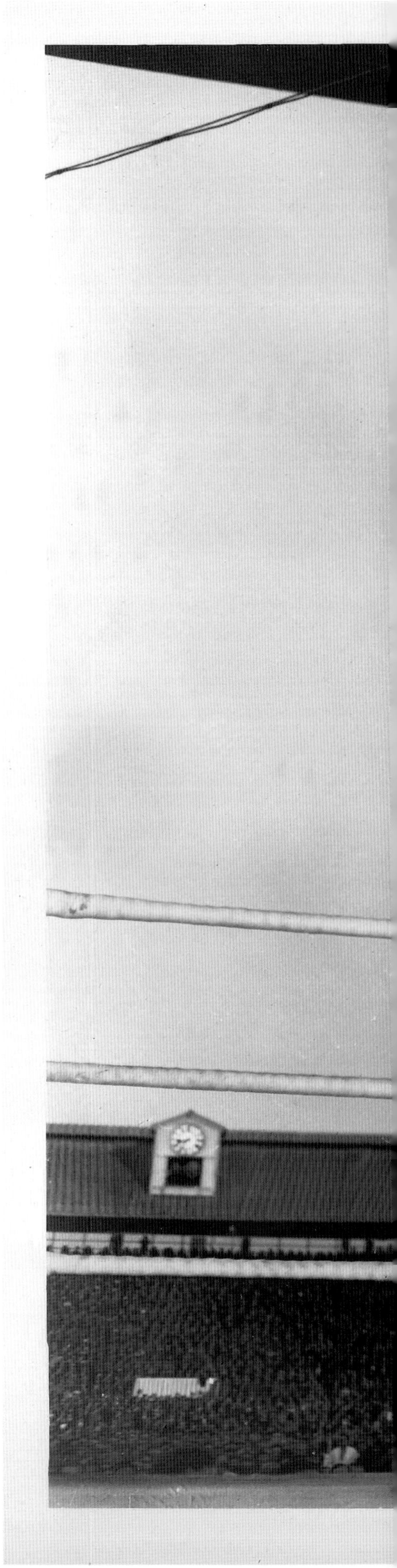

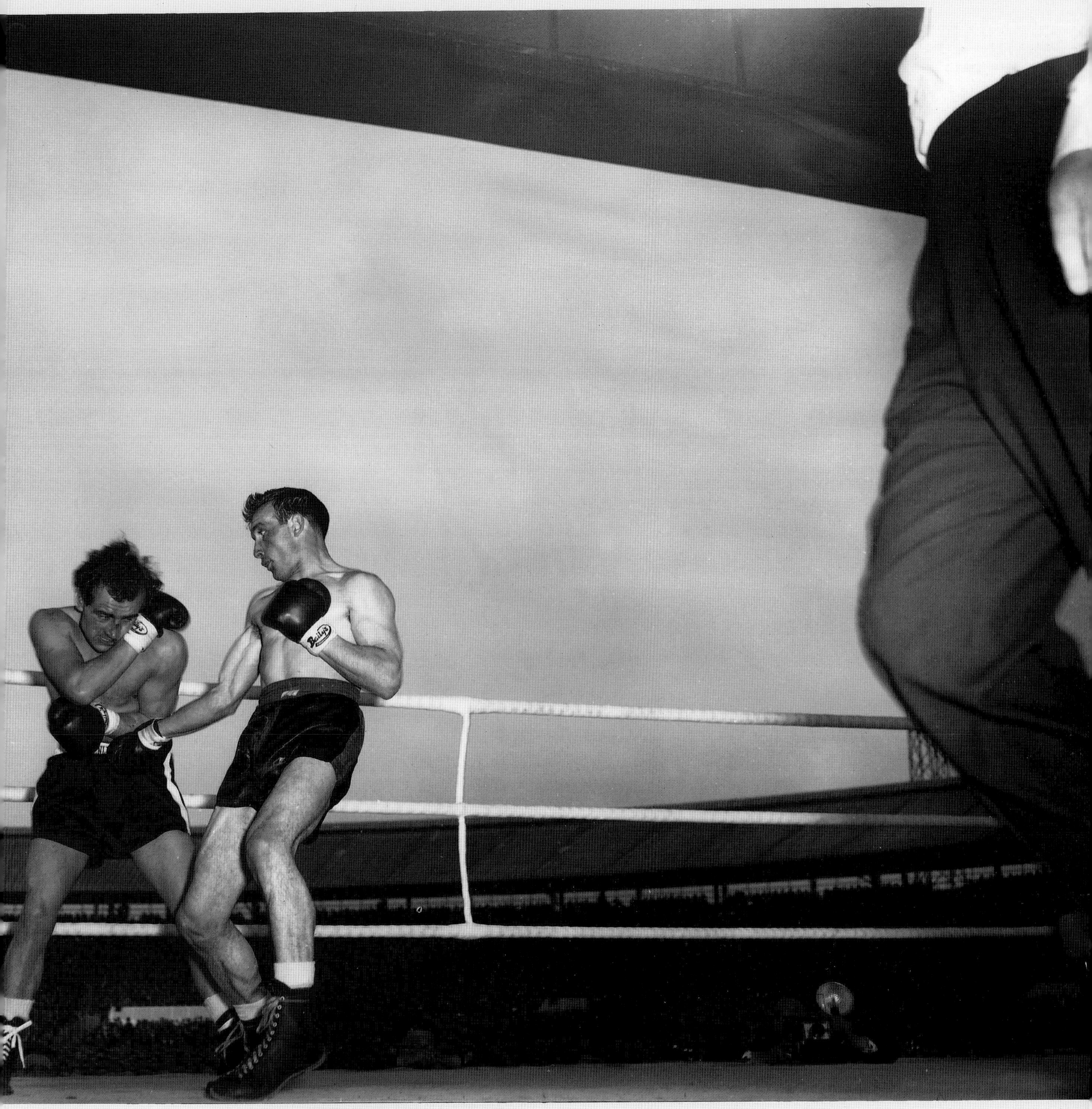

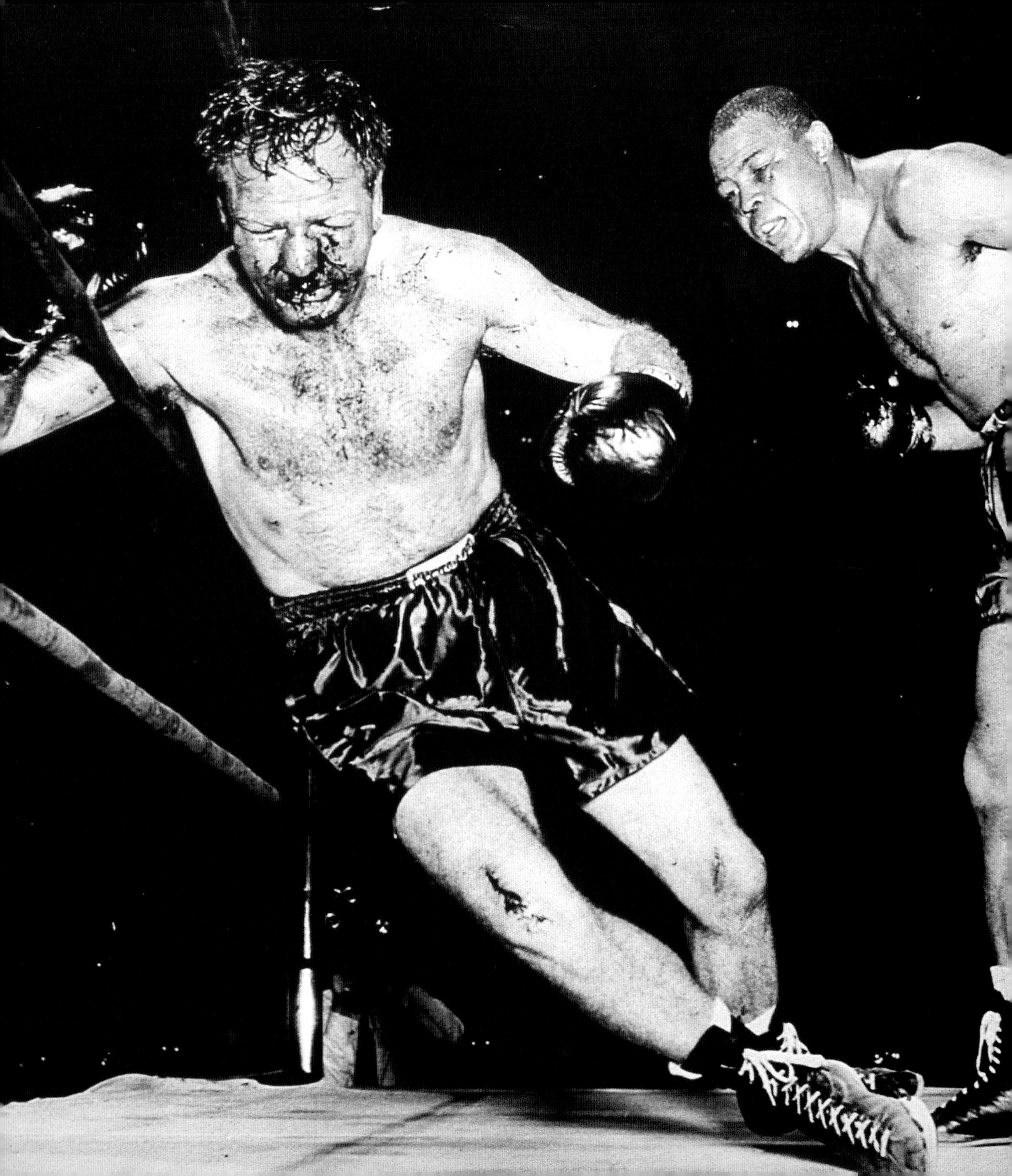

02
Joe Louis knocks out Lee Savold, New York, 1951

03
Terry Allen (right) and Eric Marsden, London, 1952

04
The referee shows Eric Marsden to his corner after a low blow to Terry Allen, London, 1952
Monty Fresco

05
Ray Barnes and Yolande Pompee (standing), London, 1953

06
Ray Barnes following a knock-out punch from Yolande Pompee, London, 1953

07 (OVERLEAF)
Albert Finch watches Ron Barton on the ropes, London, 1956
Monty Fresco

03
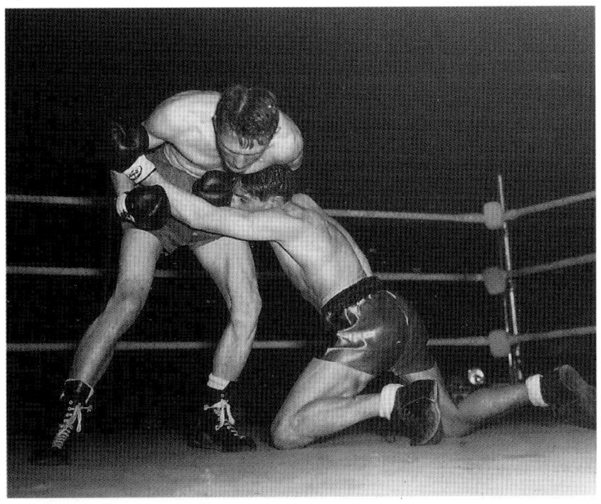

04
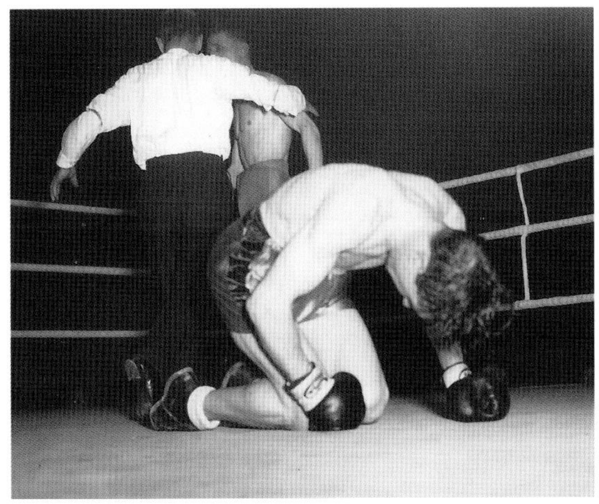

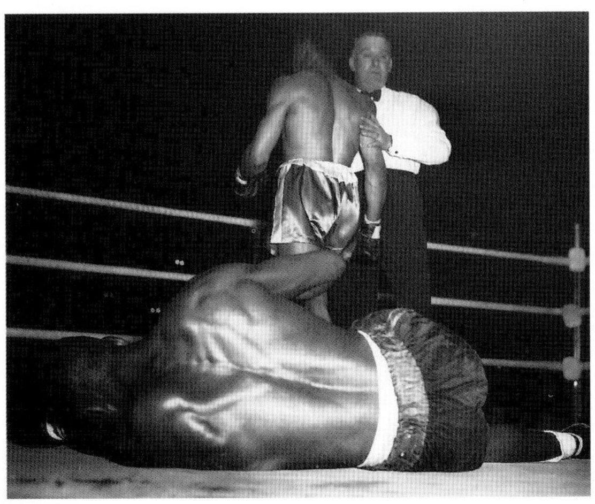
05

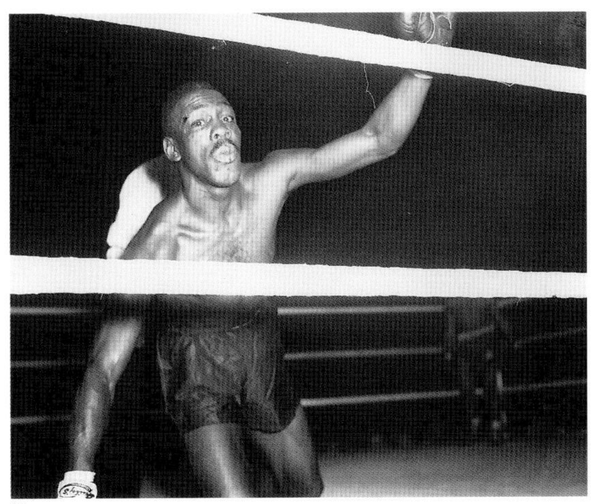
06

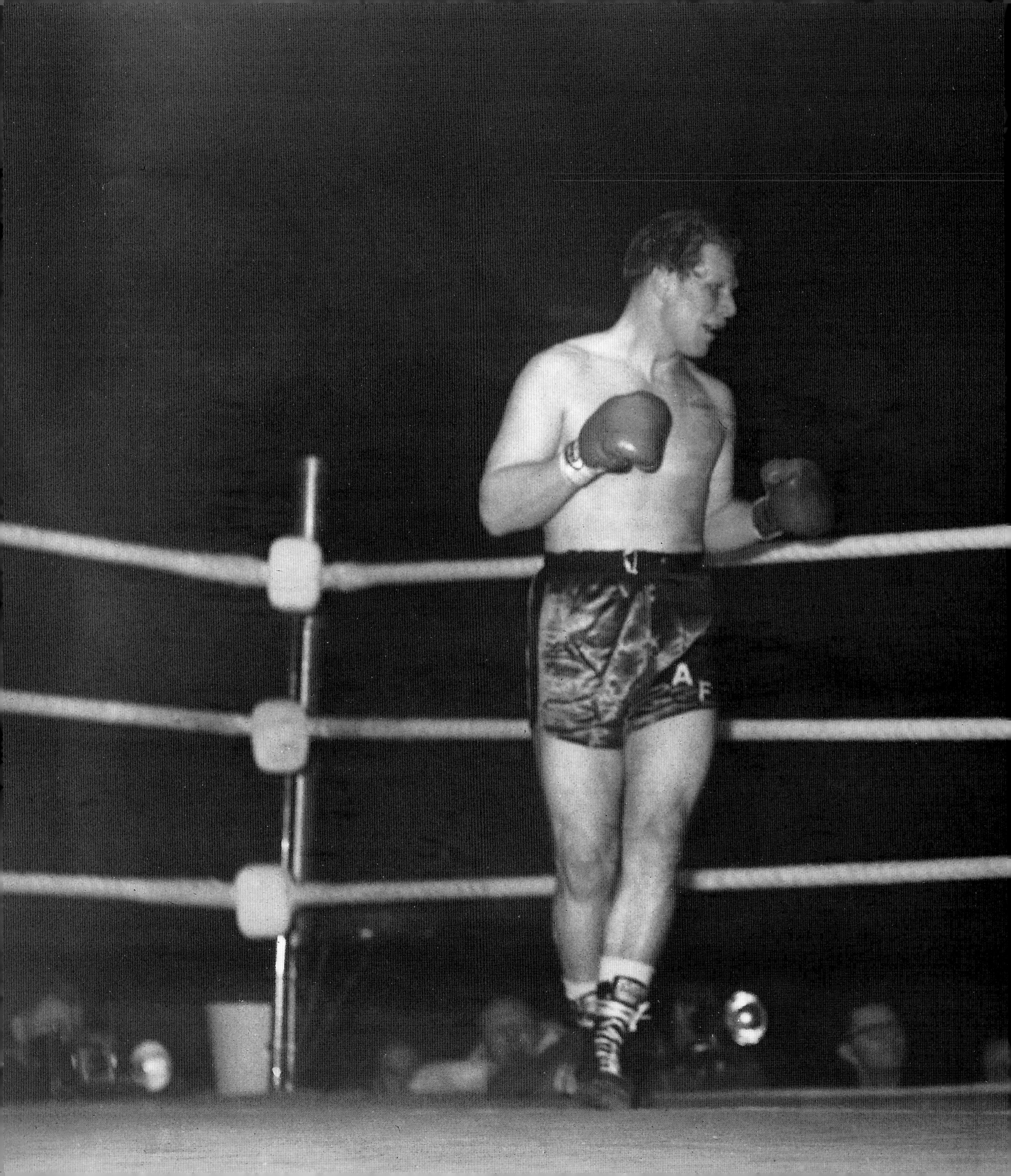
A F

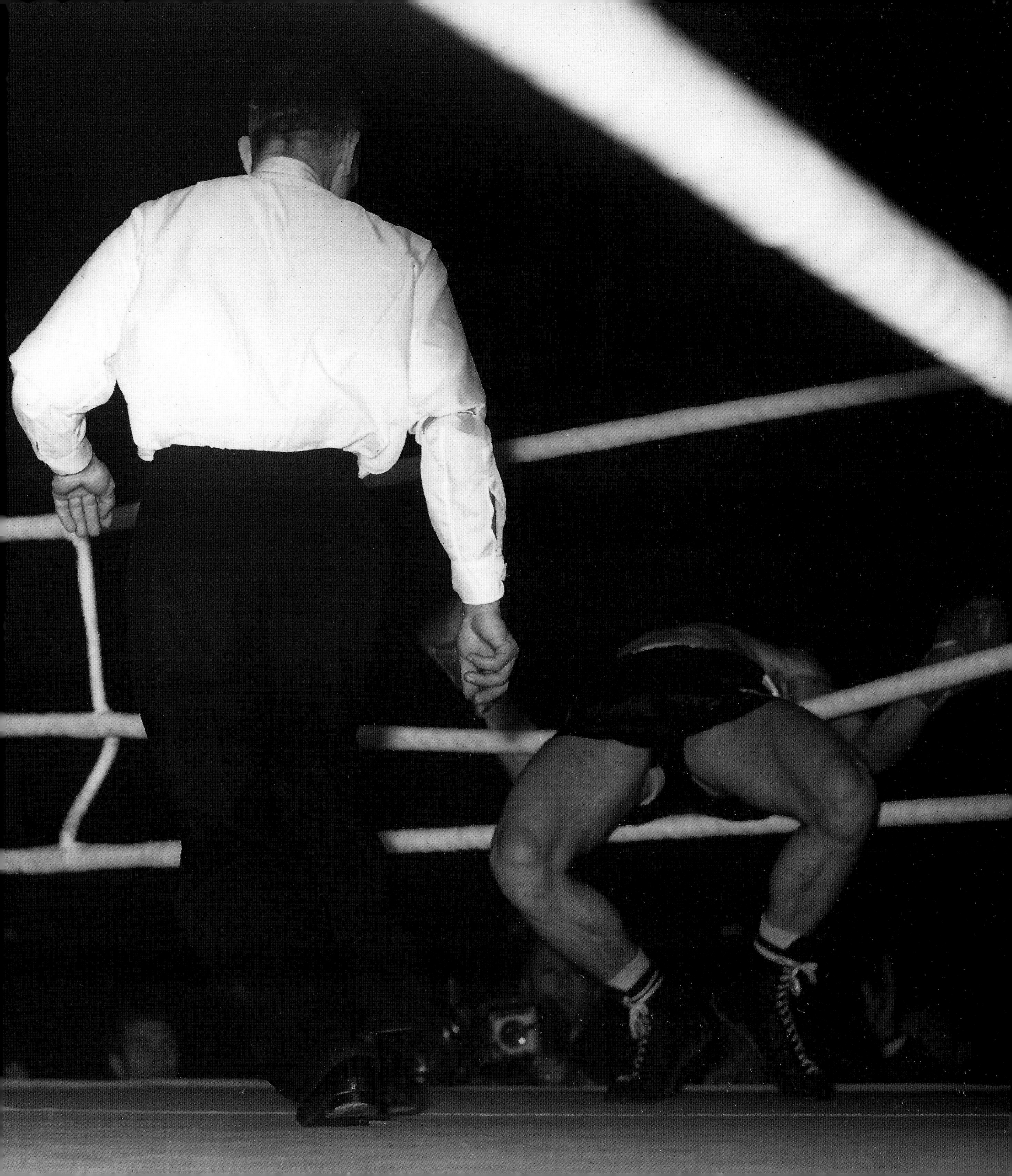

08/09
Sammy McCarthy and Jean Sneyers before and during their fight, London, 1954
Monty Fresco

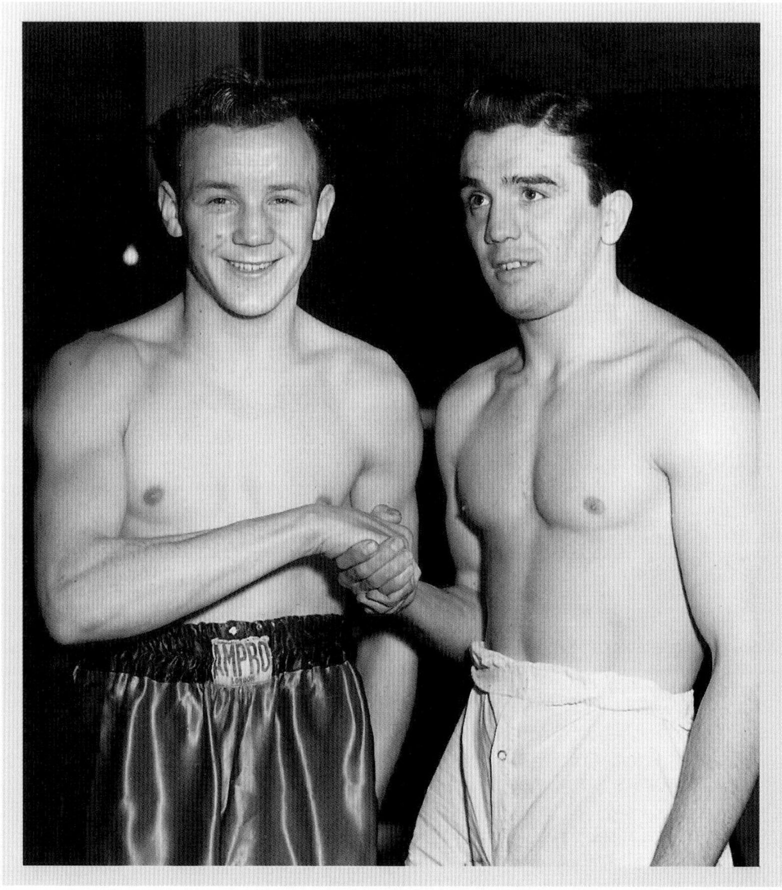

08

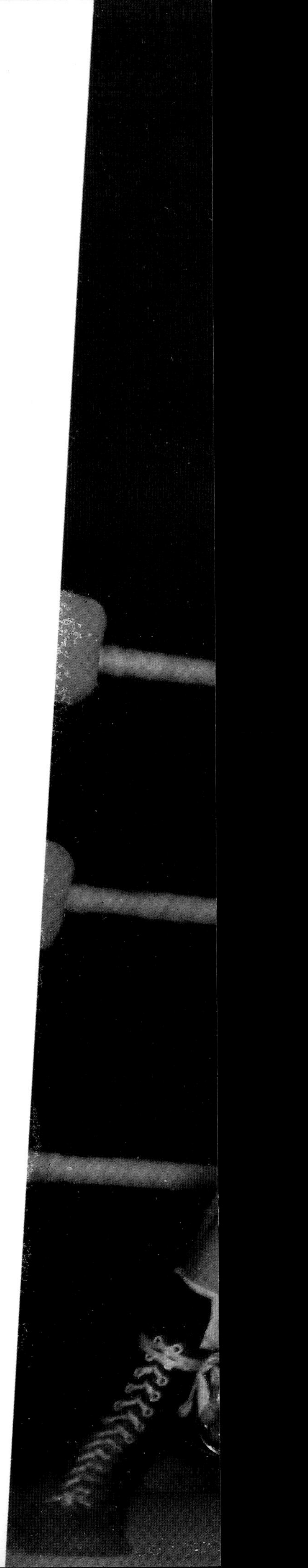

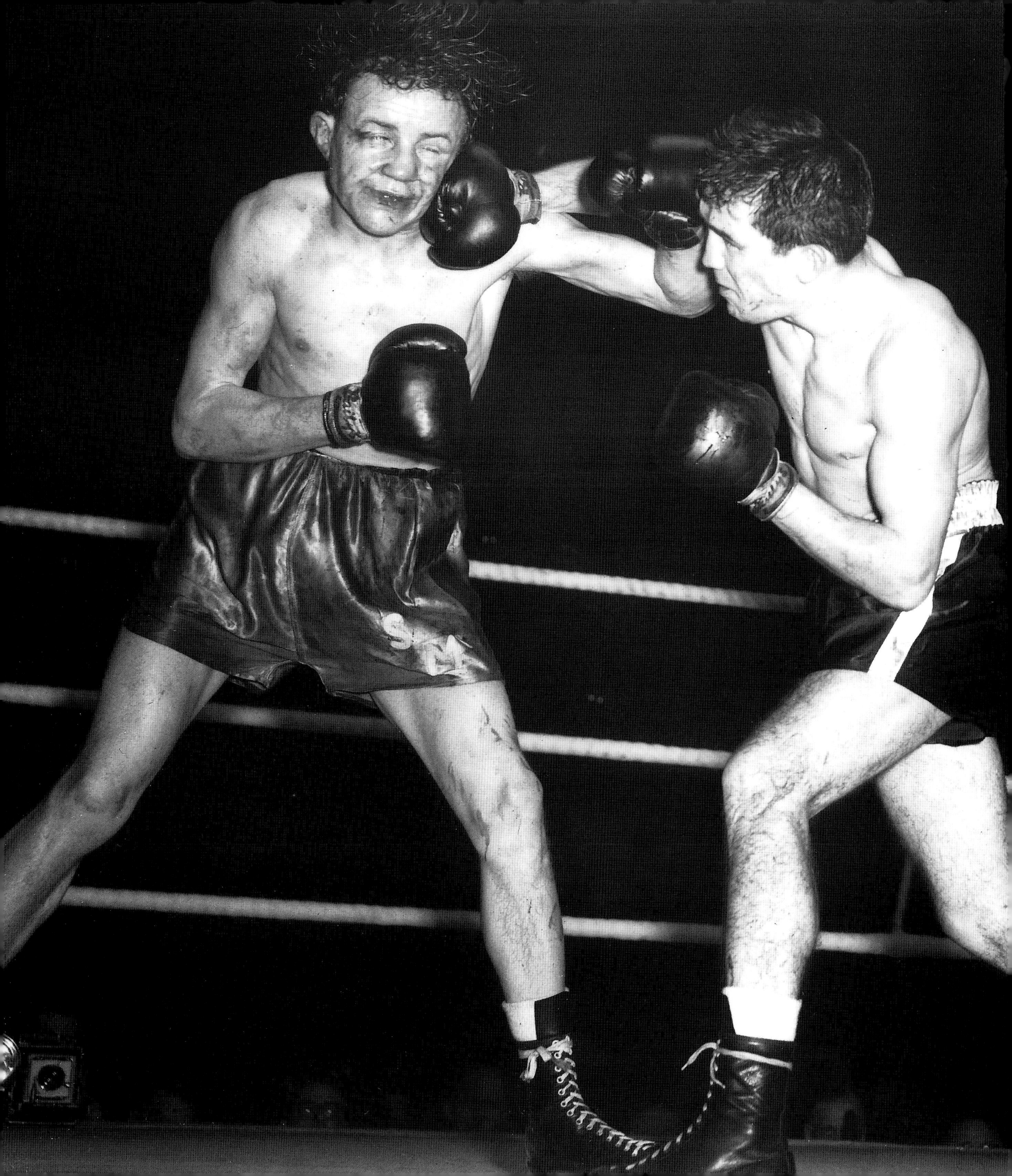

10
Rocky Marciano walks away from Joe Walcott, Philadelphia, 1952

11
Rocky Marciano about to land a punch on Roland La Starza, New York, 1953

12
Rocky Marciano versus Joe Walcott, New York, 1953

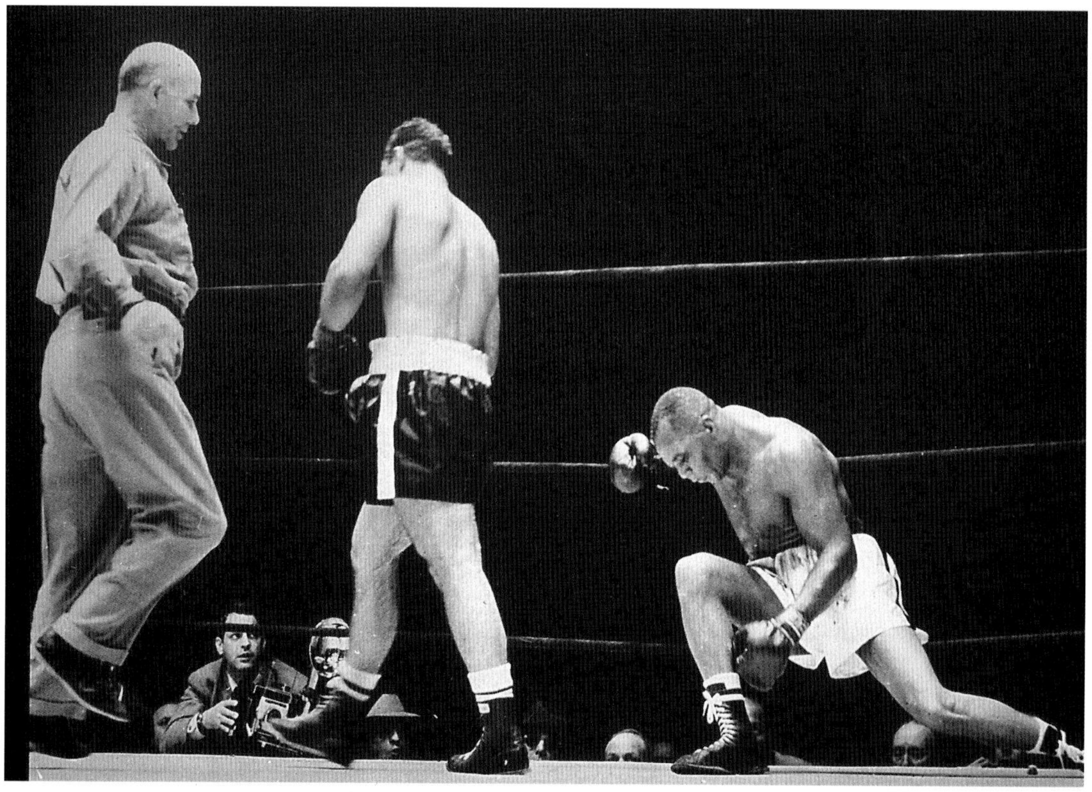

10

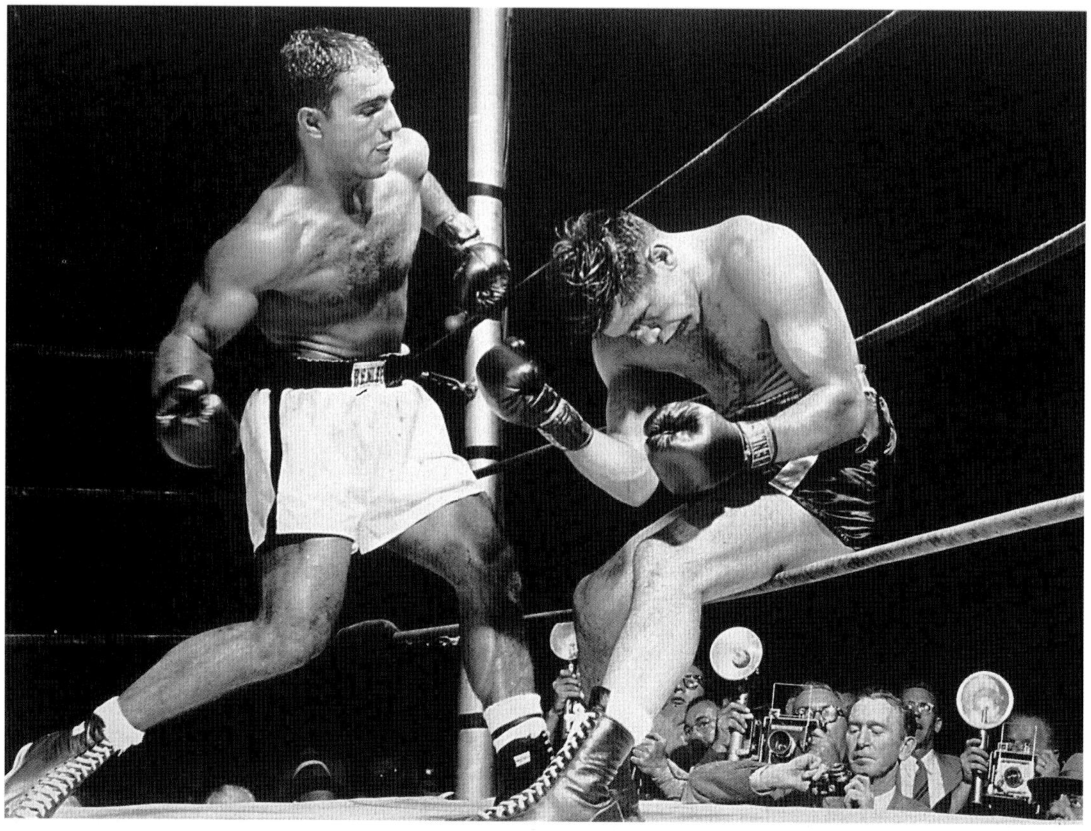

11

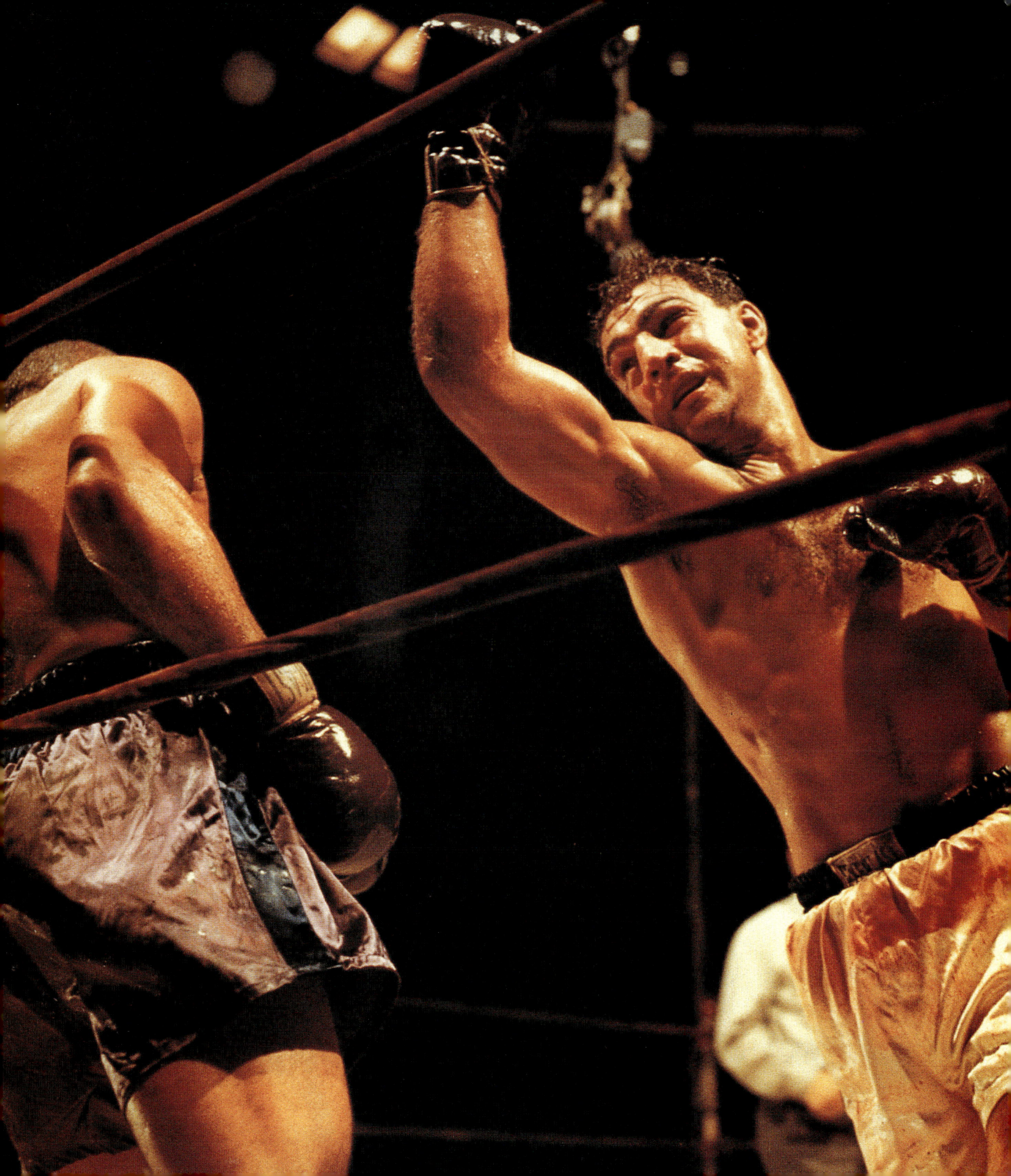

01
The bedroom of sixteen-year-old jockey Lester Piggott, 1952
Ronald Startup

SPORTING PRINT

Because of its ease of reproduction, photography played an important role in the popularization of sport. By the post-war period photography had secured its place in printed publications and had therefore become available to almost everyone. Where once paintings and prints had illustrated sporting subjects, photography now provided a much more plentiful and easily accessible means of representation. Sports photography had replaced the traditional framed sporting print on people's walls and become the medium through which the majority of people, public and sports stars alike, would visualize sport.

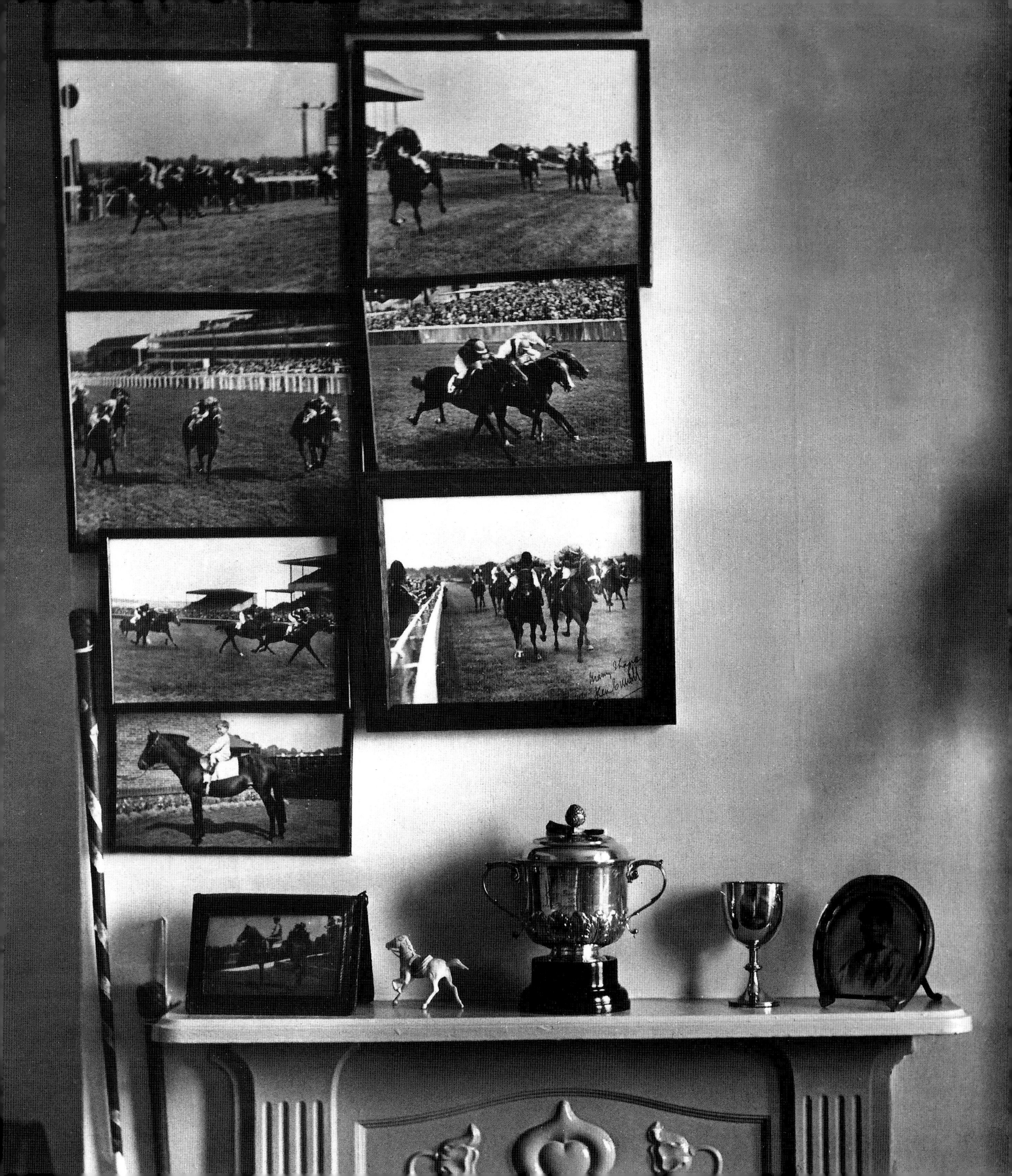

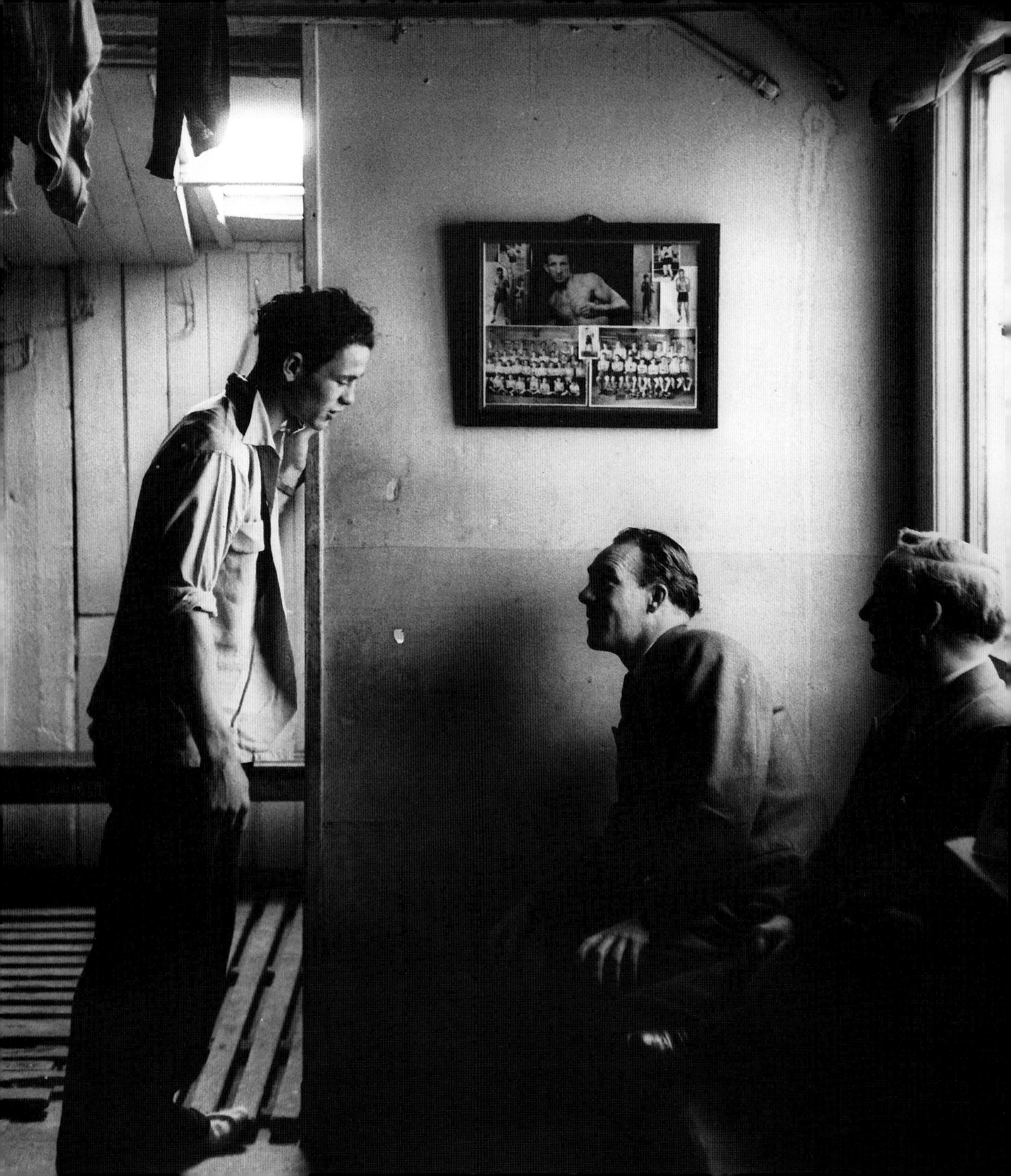

02
Boxer Pat McAteer (left) in the changing room at Johnny Campbell's gym, 1954
Bert Hardy

03
Boxer Brian London at home with his mother, 1955
Bert Hardy

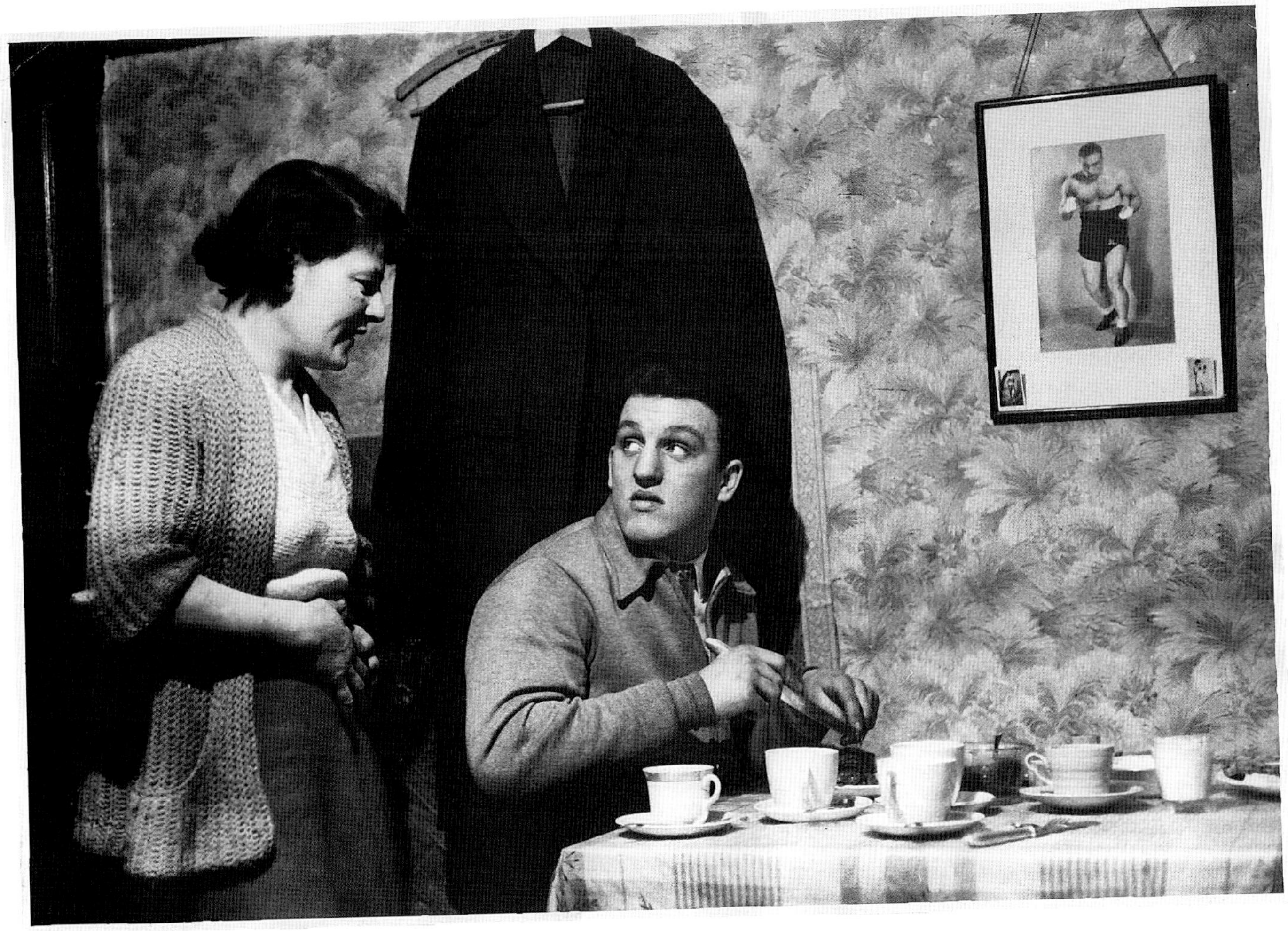

03

01/02
Competitors feel the strain of the Tour de France's mountain stages, 1951
Bert Hardy

03
Riders in the Tour de France, 1951
Bert Hardy

04 (OVERLEAF)
Approaching the snow-line in the Alps, 1951
Bert Hardy

TRAVEL

After World War II, photographers working for the British picture magazine *Picture Post* were given the opportunity to travel abroad to cover news stories. This was the first time that sporting events like the Tour de France had been covered in such an extensive way by a British publication. Previously, if magazines featured international sporting events the photographs would have come from foreign picture libraries using local photographers. The British photographers took advantage of the opportunity to tell a more complete story, photographing many different aspects of the event and exploring the background of the sport and its personalities.

The two sequences in this selection show the riders of the Tour de France, and follow Rae Johnstone, a jockey based at Auteuil in France, in the days leading up to the St Leger, run at Doncaster in England.

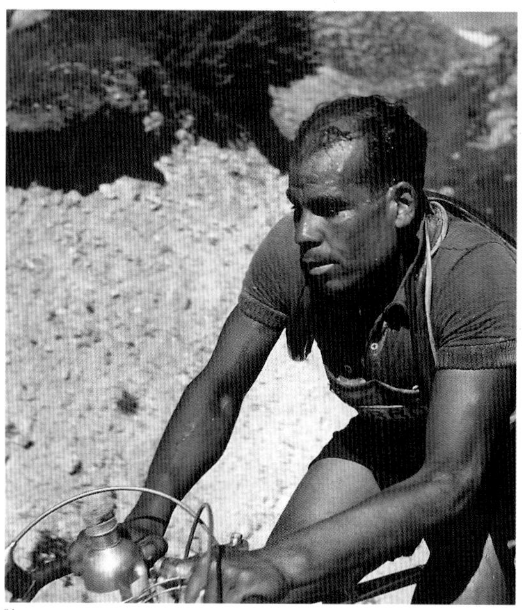
01

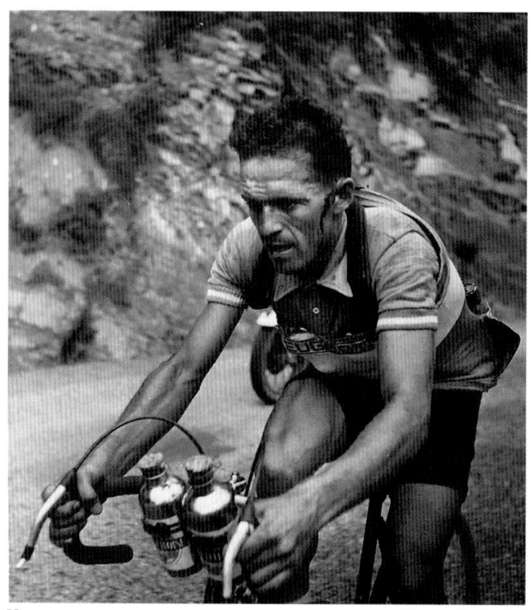
02

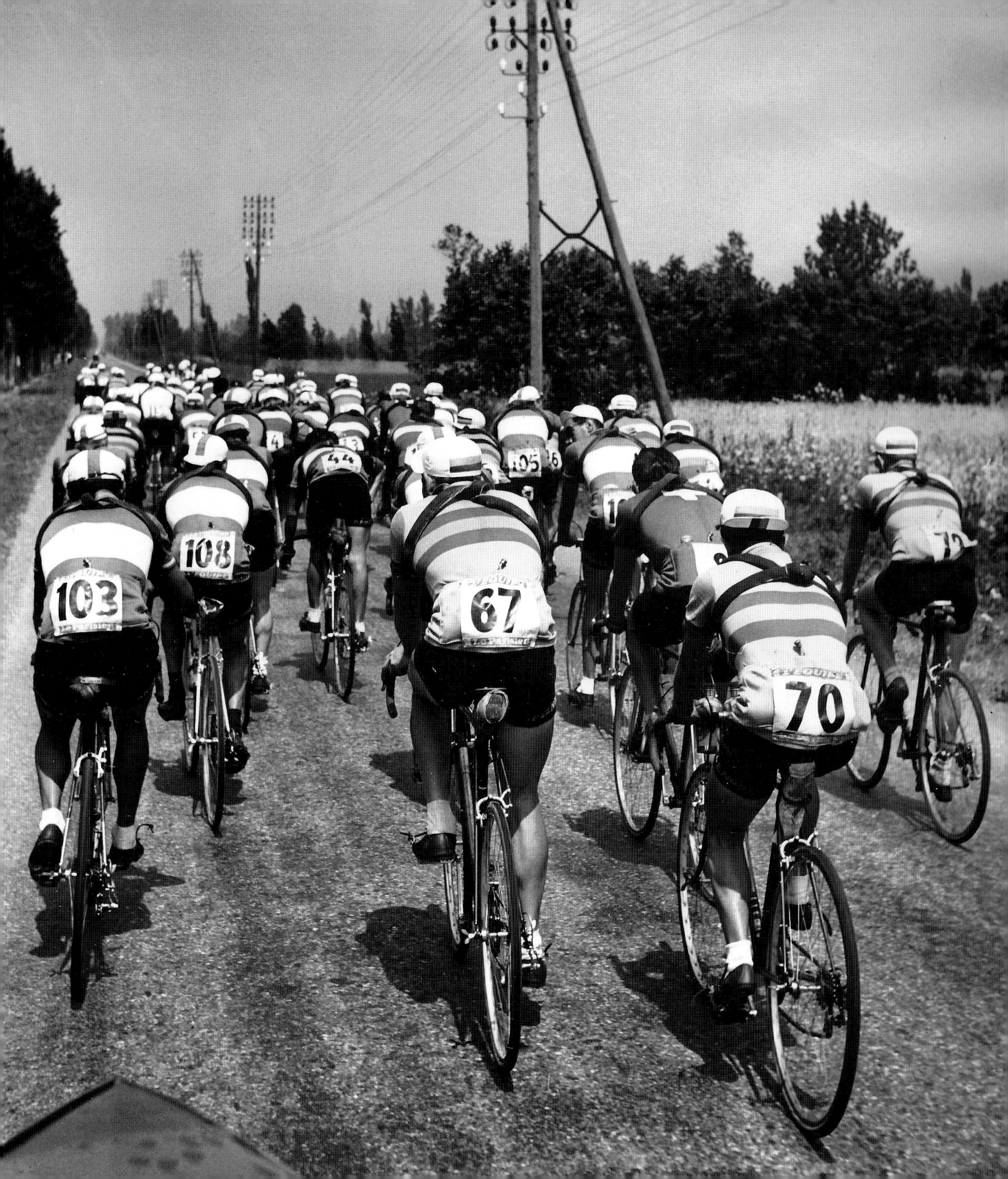
103
108
67
70
105
44

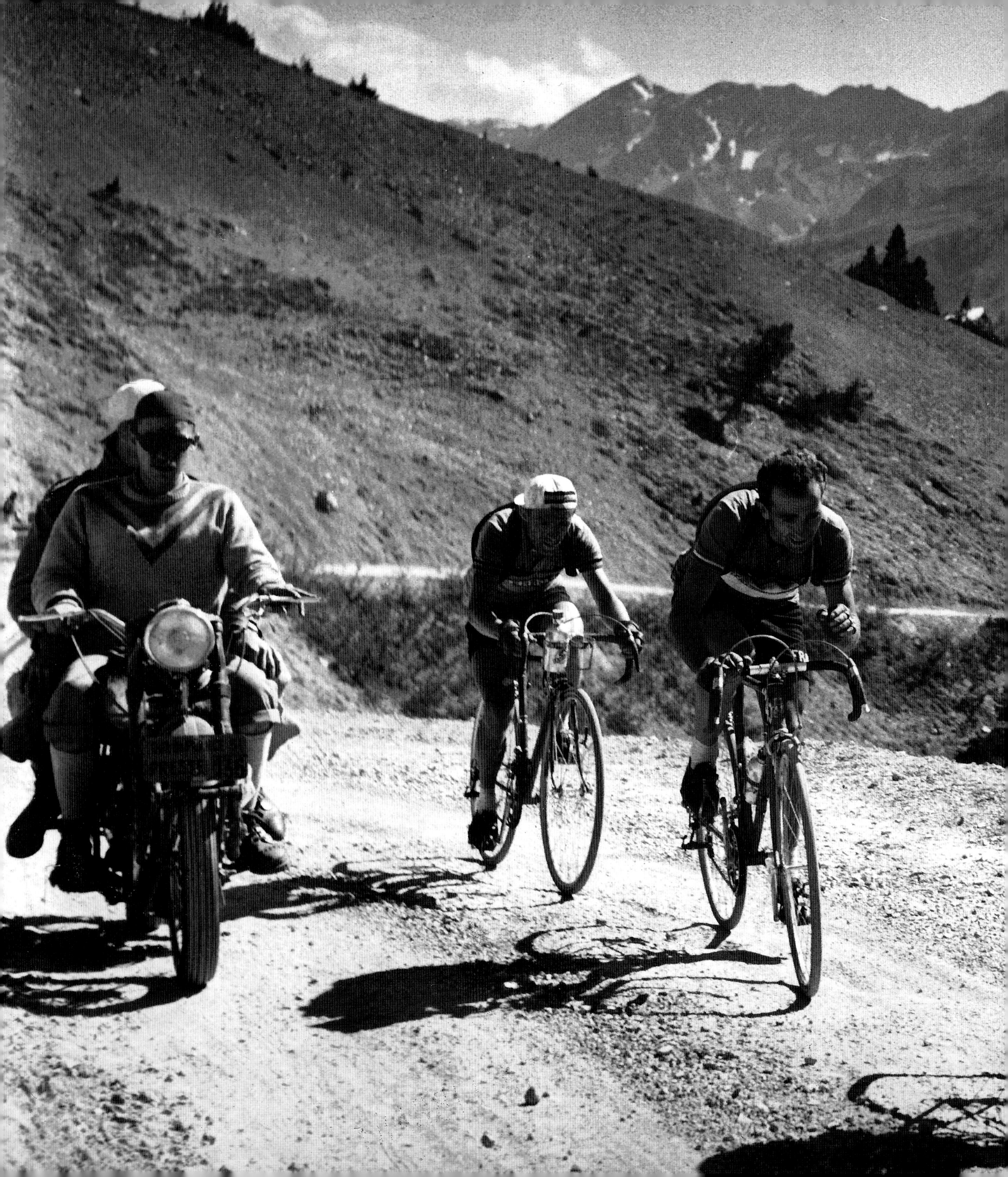

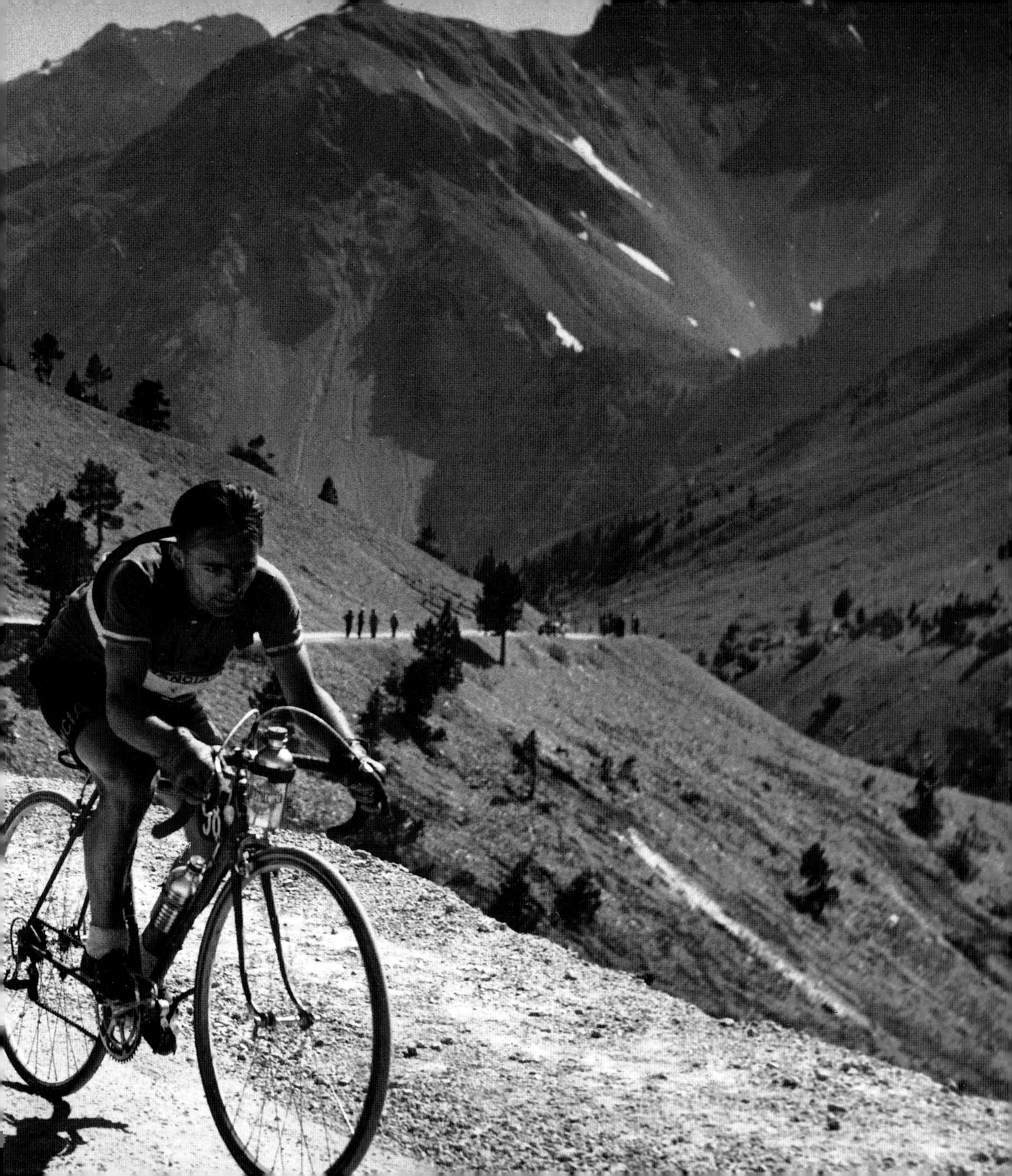

05
Rae Johnstone with his wife, at his flat in Auteuil, 1950
Bert Hardy

06
Johnstone chatting to a journalist before the St Leger, 1950
Bert Hardy

07
Johnstone says goodbye to his wife as he leaves for Chantilly racecourse, 1950
Bert Hardy

08
Johnstone on his way to Chantilly racecourse for exercise, talking to trainer, M Semblat and French jockey, Bertiglia, 1950
Bert Hardy

05

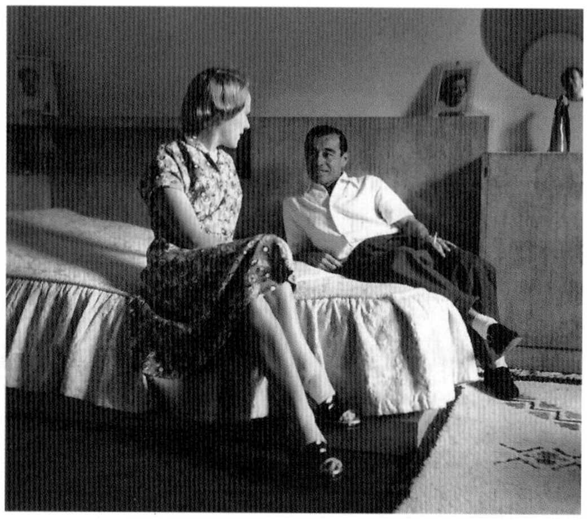

06

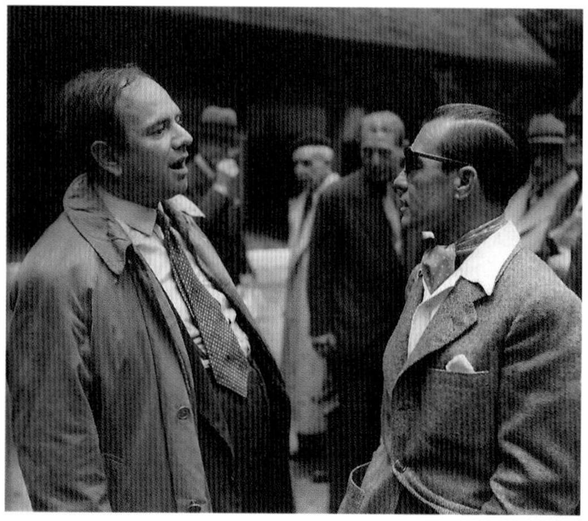

07

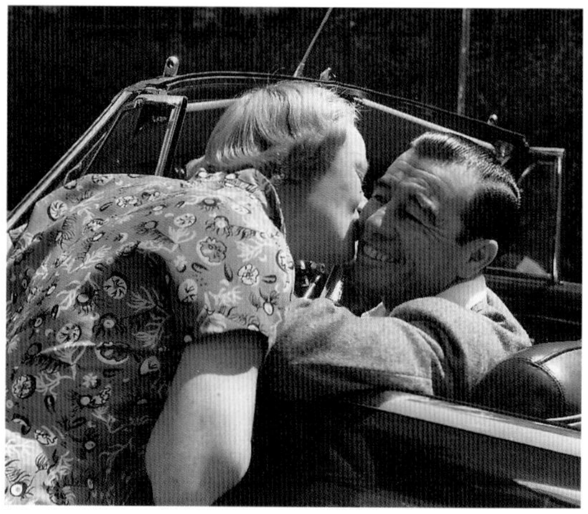

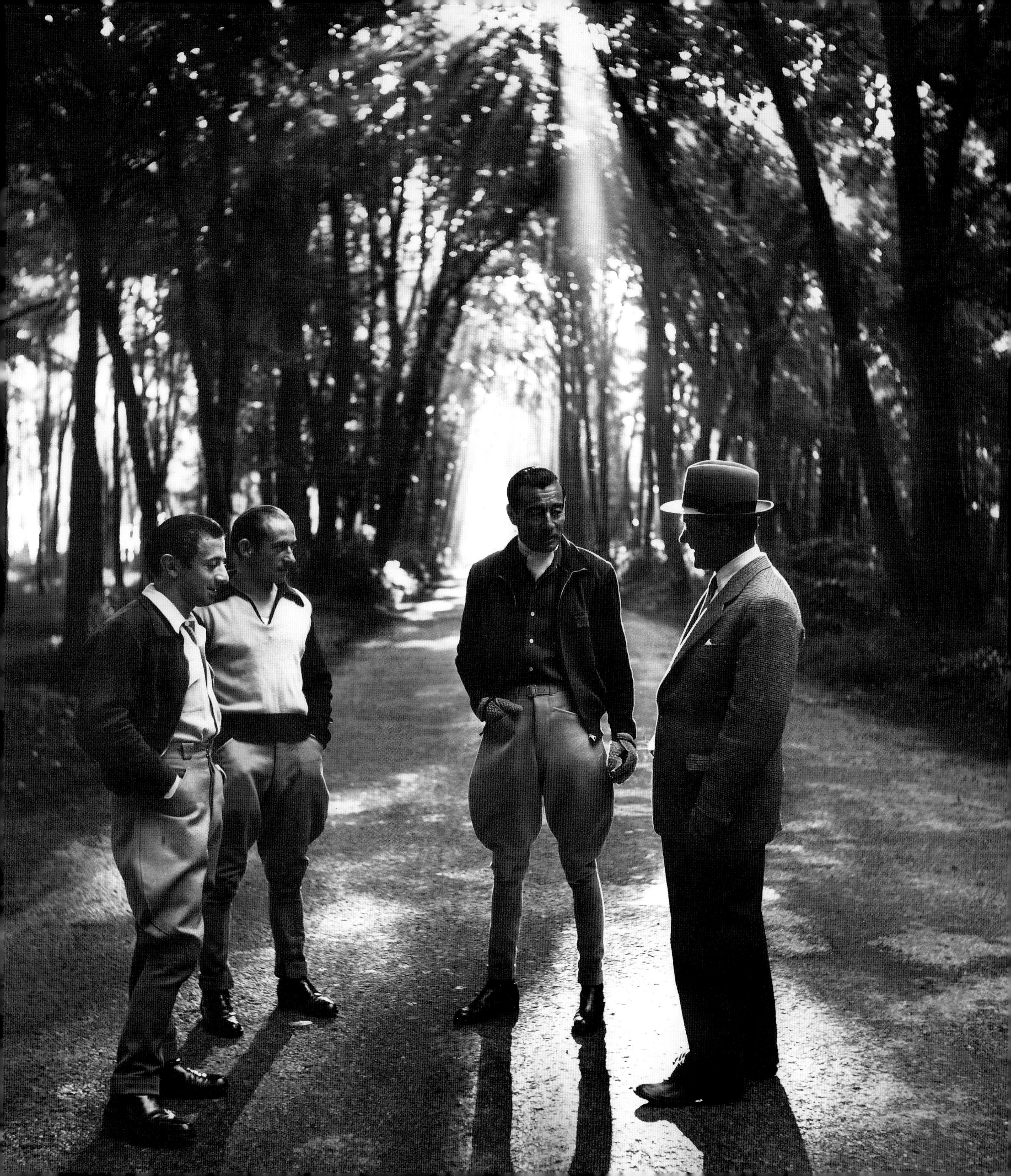

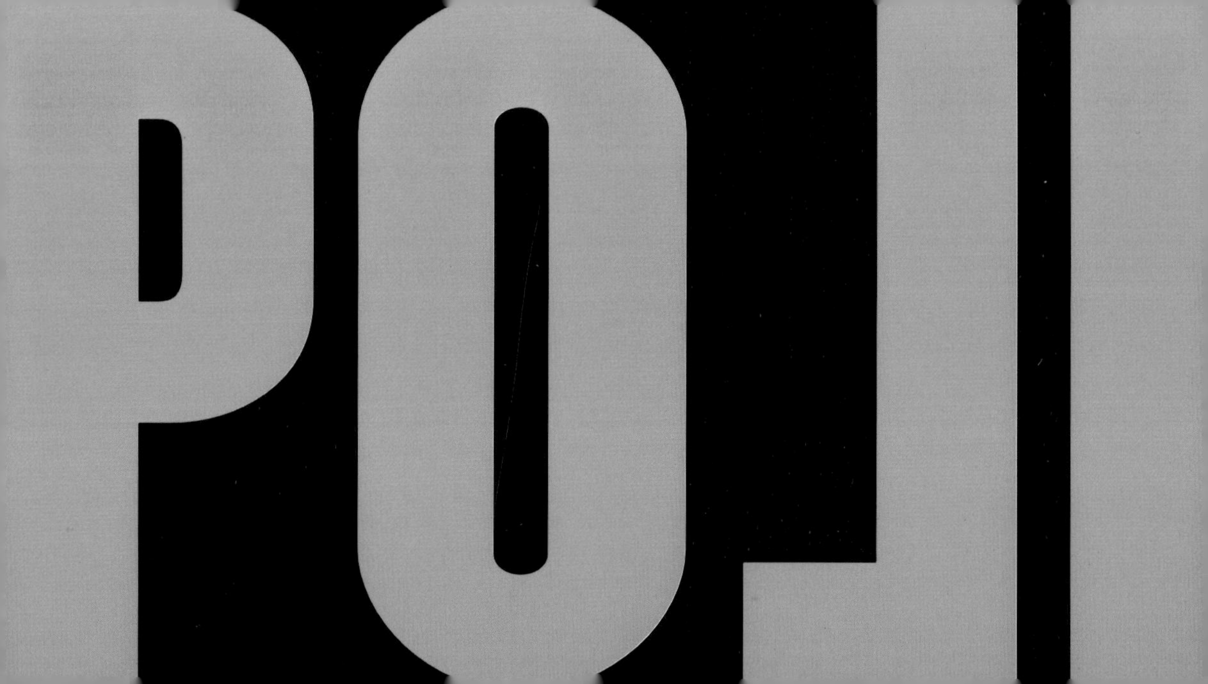
PO

TICS

05

1960–1980

If many of the pictures in this chapter are not of sport actually taking place, it is, of course, not because less sport was happening. The contrary is true: sport was beginning to occupy a greater part of people's lives as growing affluence allowed them to give more of their time and money over to leisure. But sport was becoming infinitely more complex; there was much more to it than the game itself. Television provided a previously unimagined access to sport all over the world, and sport became increasingly professional, learning to hype itself, promoting its stars and selling its product better. Sport's top stars were now world names, uniquely appealing to advertisers and politicians as possessing the desirable qualities of a high public profile, a positive image and an international reputation.

In this period of political uncertainty and international tension sport reflected the times and was sometimes overshadowed by politics. Television coverage meant that millions of people around the world could watch live sport, and major events like the Olympic Games became huge global spectaculars. Politicians and terrorists alike were not slow to see the propaganda potential of this: it was an opportunity to demonstrate the superiority of a social system, the perfect stage for the grand political gesture, or an opportunity to play out an act of terrorism and hold the world to ransom.

Television was changing the way people consumed news, entertainment and sport, and the photo agencies and picture libraries found themselves having to react to an altered market. The weekly publications covering all aspects of daily life that had been popular in the 1950s were giving way to new supplement sections to existing newpapers, and specialist magazines covering single subjects like gardening, music, cars or sport. Not only did the picture libraries respond by creating collections that specifically catered for the new magazines, but the photographers themselves were at last able to specialize: the idea of sports photography as a separate discipline was born. Versatile 35mm cameras and equipment like the telephoto lens and special filters allowed photographers to create dramatic, dynamic images; they were able to zoom in close to their subjects and control their photographs as never before, at last bringing sports photography right to the heart of the action.

Among the most remarkable sporting achievements of the 1960s and 1970s, Australian tennis player Rod Laver won the Grand Slam of the sport's four major championships on two occasions, American Mark Spitz won an unprecedented seven gold medals at the 1972 Olympic Games in Munich, and Bob Beamon's legendary jump at the 1968 Mexico Games broke the long jump world record by nearly two feet, a record that was to stand for twenty-three years. But in a period when the top sports stars became more famous and celebrated than ever before, the 1960s established the reputations of two of the century's truly great sporting figures: Pelé, perhaps the greatest soccer player of all time, who helped his country Brazil win the World Cup on three occasions, and Muhammad Ali, who achieved a status far beyond that of a sporting hero, such was his talent and charisma.

01
The Aztec Stadium, Mexico, 1966
02
River Plate Stadium, Buenos Aries, 1970s
03
Shea Stadium, New York, 1965
04
The National Stadium, Tokyo, 1964
05 (OVERLEAF)
The Sports Palace, Mexico, 1968

STRANGE BUILDINGS

The new sporting arenas planned and built from the 1960s onwards were stars in their own right. Innovations in design and engineering paved the way for bold and futuristic new stadiums built for a more affluent spectator who demanded comfortable seating, excellent transport links, good views of the game, catering etc. These buildings were part of a larger game plan where sport and architecture could create new identities for cities, demonstrating affluence, confidence and forward-thinking. Even if they were not eventually built, press photographs of the plans show the ambitions of the local mayor.

01
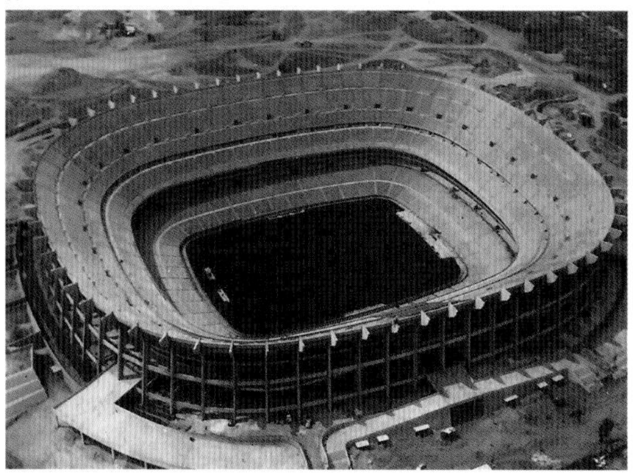

02
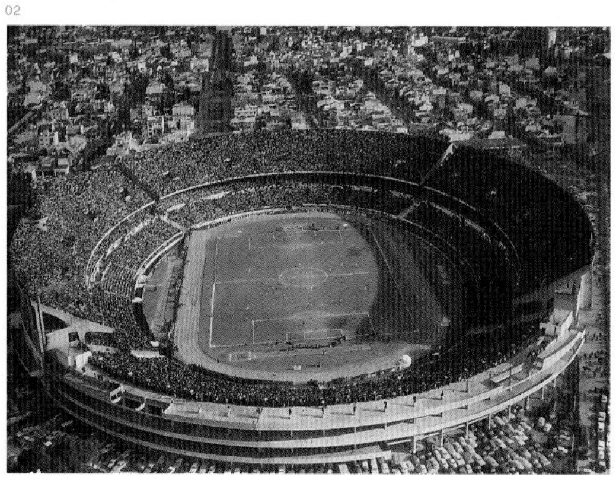

03
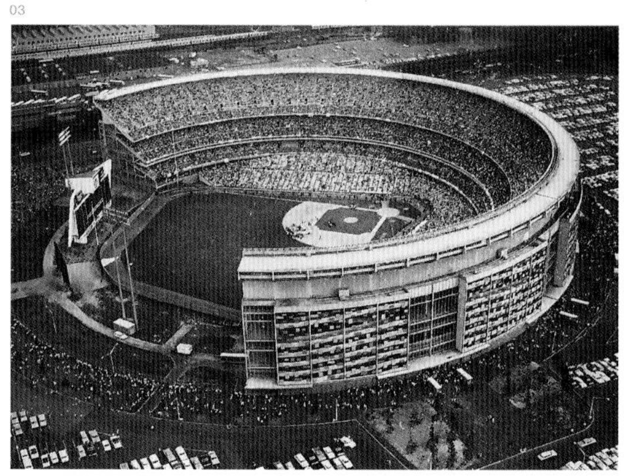

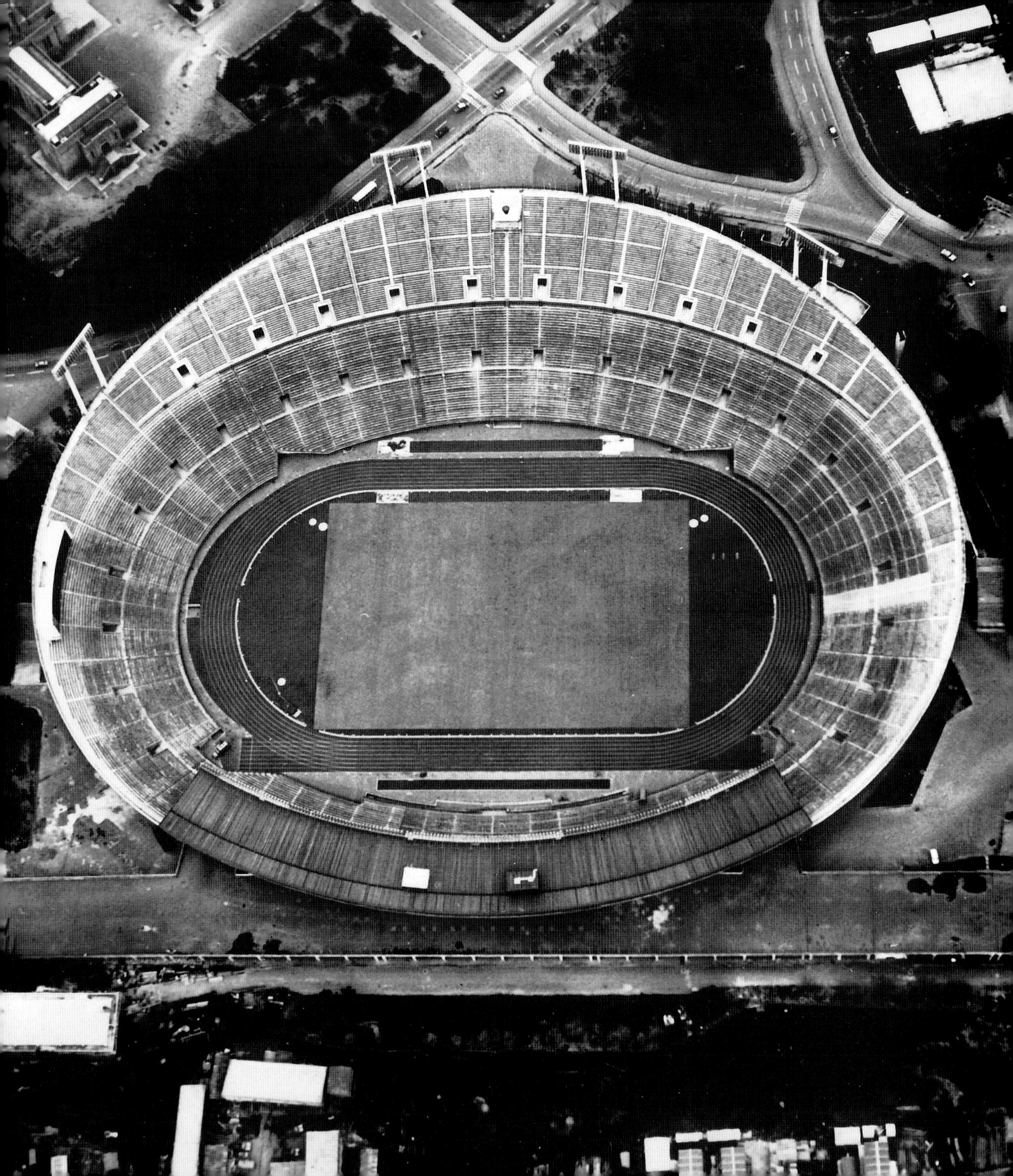

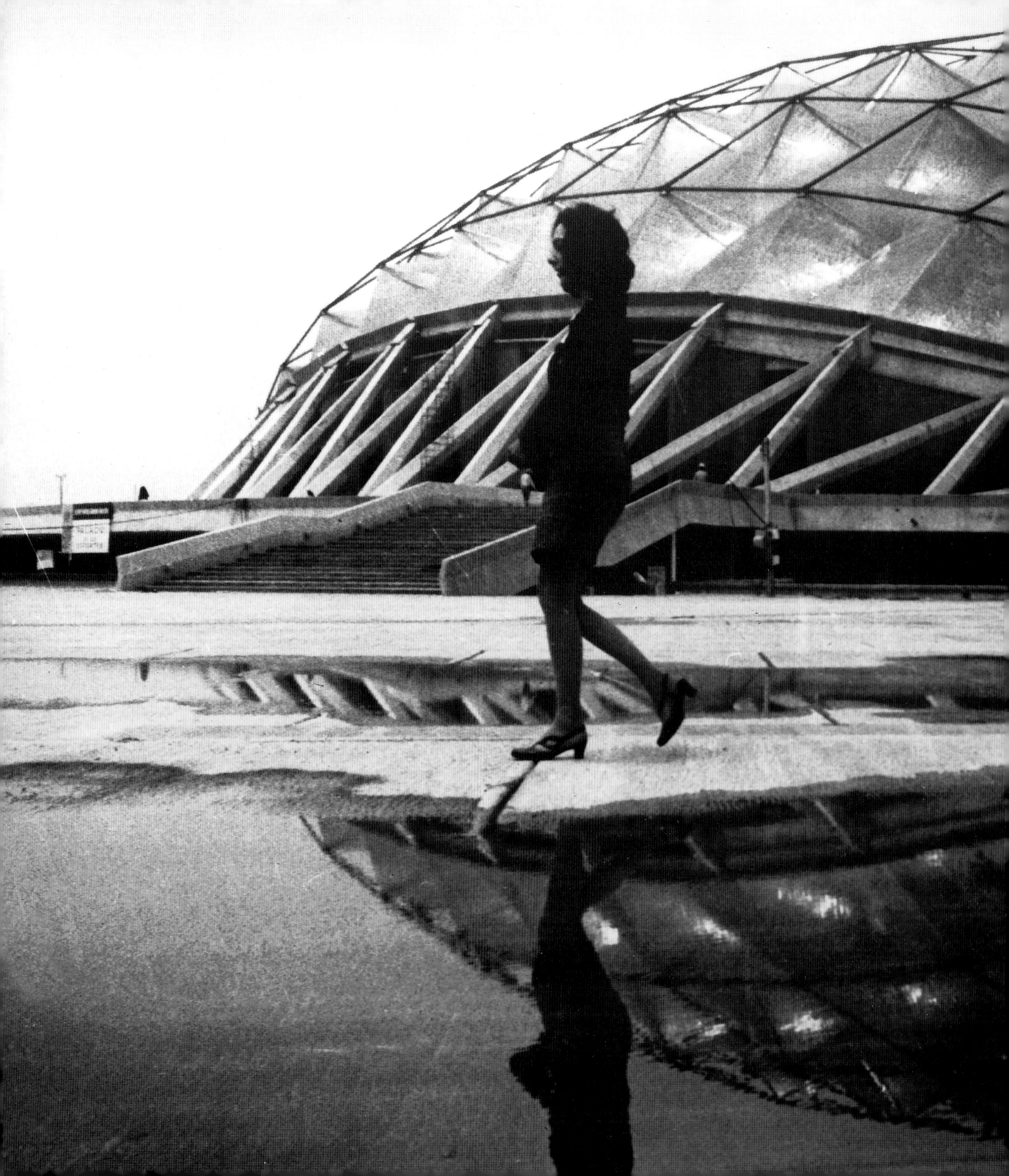

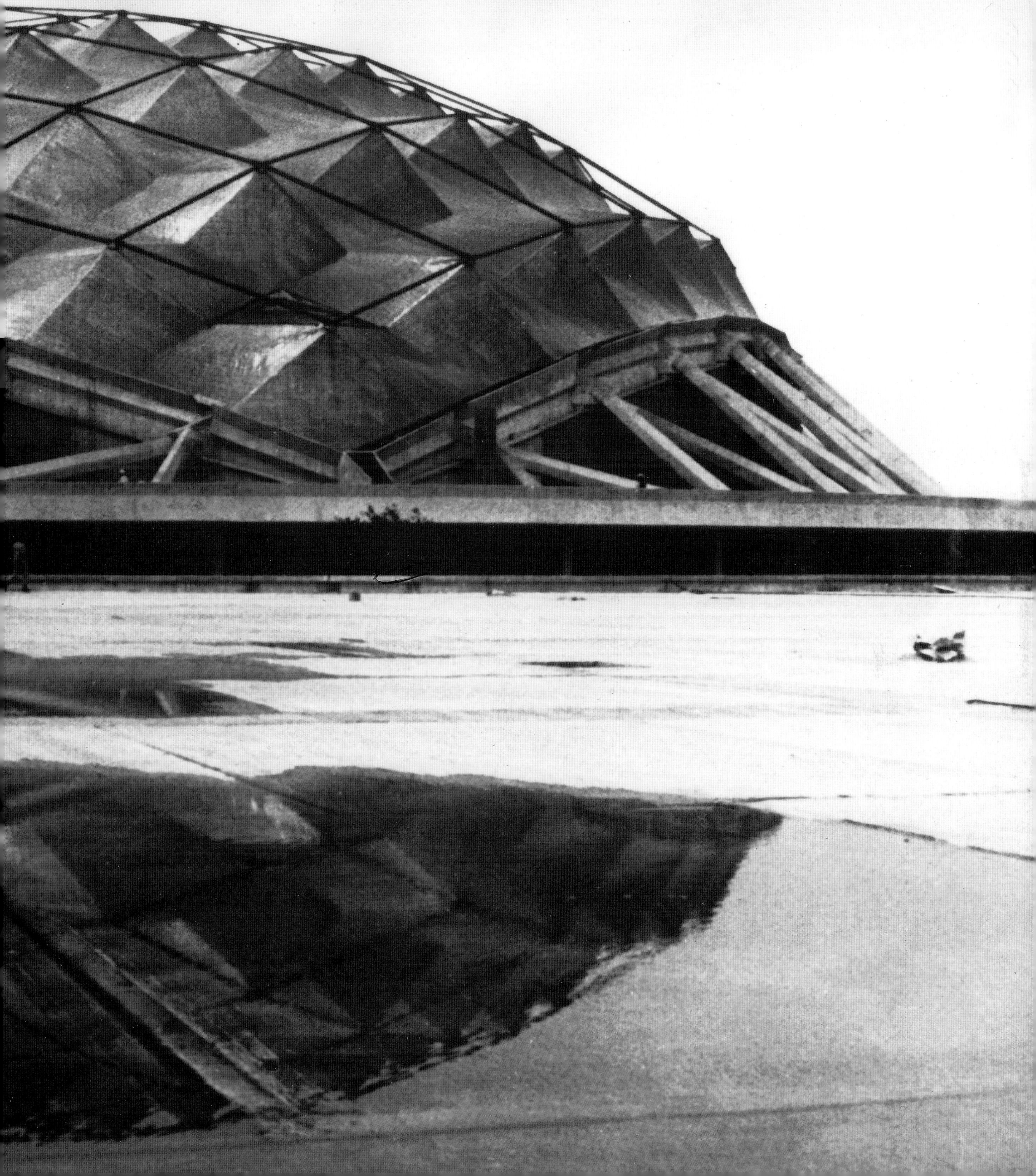

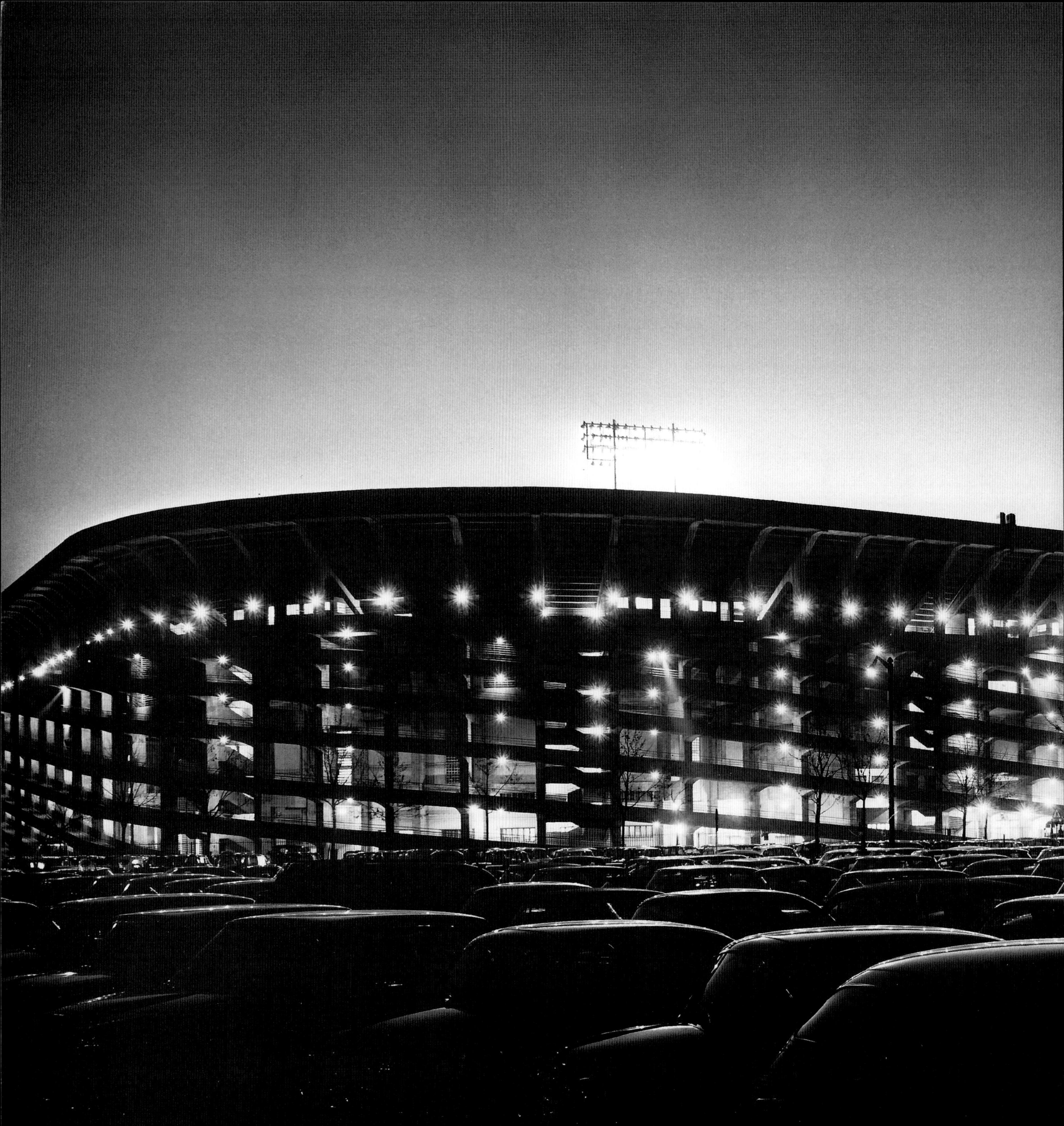

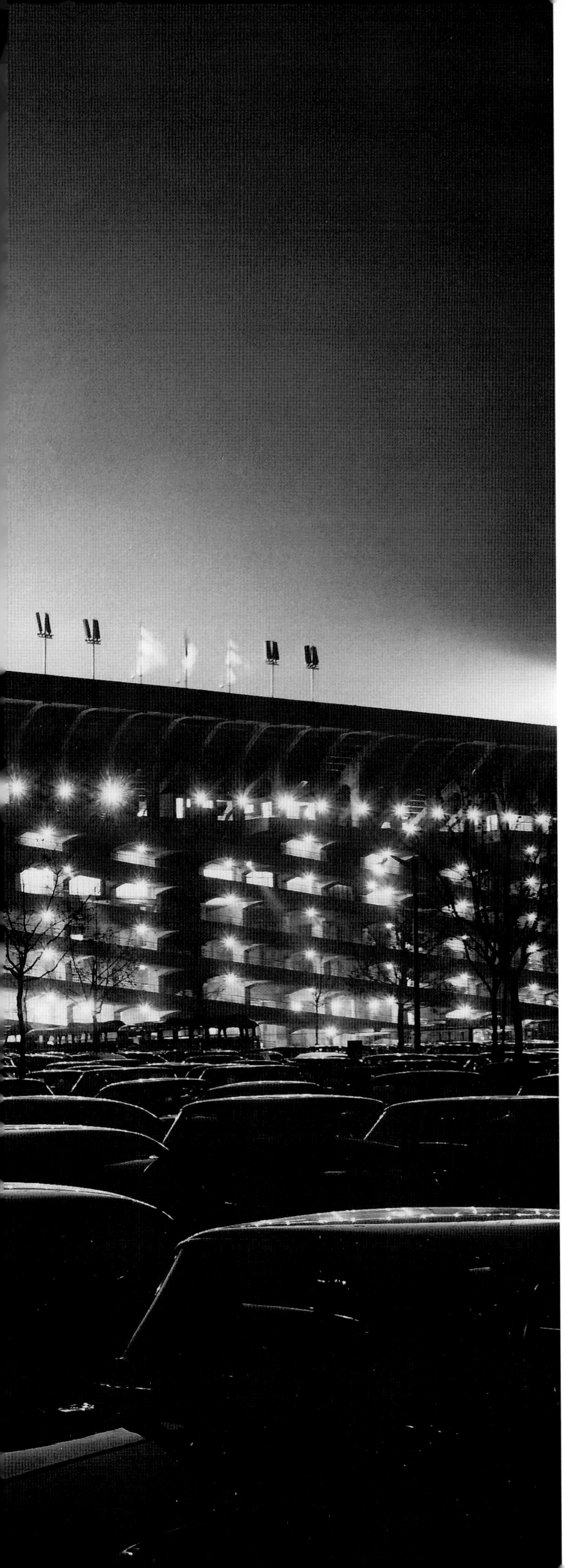

06
The San Siro Stadium, Milan, 1960s

07
Model of planned sports arena in Los Angeles, 1966

07

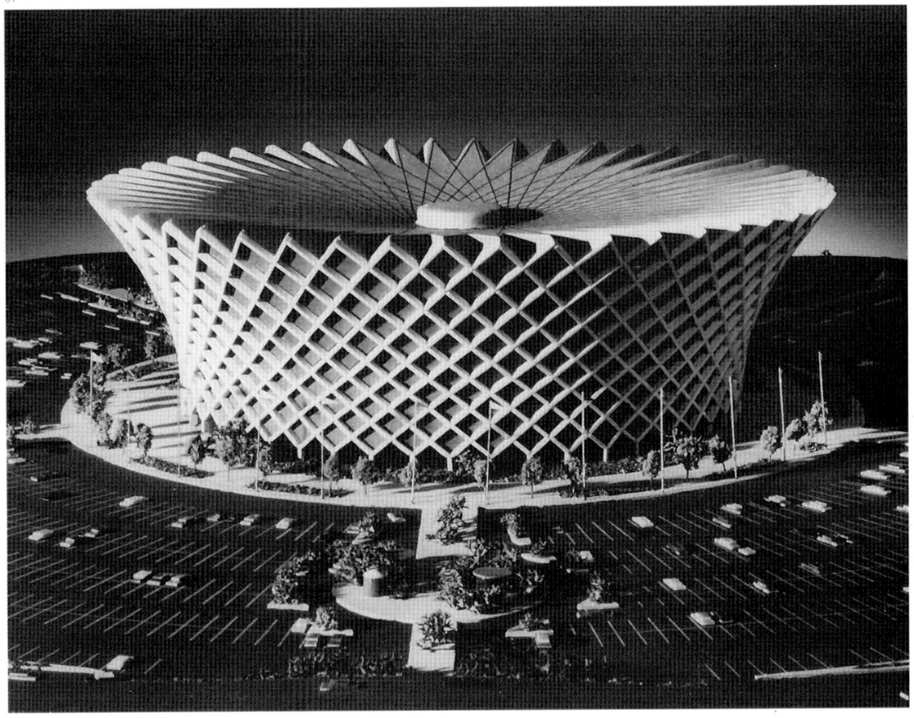

01
The Strahov stadium for the Czechoslovak Spartakiad, Prague, 1975

02 (OVERLEAF)
Members of the crew of the US aircraft carrier *Kearsage* saluting the Tokyo Olympic Games, 1964

FORMATION

During the Cold War sporting events became another part of the battleground between capitalism and communism. Success at sport was interpreted as a product of the more successful political order, therefore to achieve the top spot in the Olympic medal table was something to be fought for. Another way to demonstrate the success of a social system was through the complexity of the opening ceremony: the marshalling of thousands of people into precise patterns was the unofficial sport of the Olympics. Demonstrations of the power to organize people, these formations make powerful visual statements, designed principally for the benefit of photographers and TV cameramen whose images of the event were carried around the world.

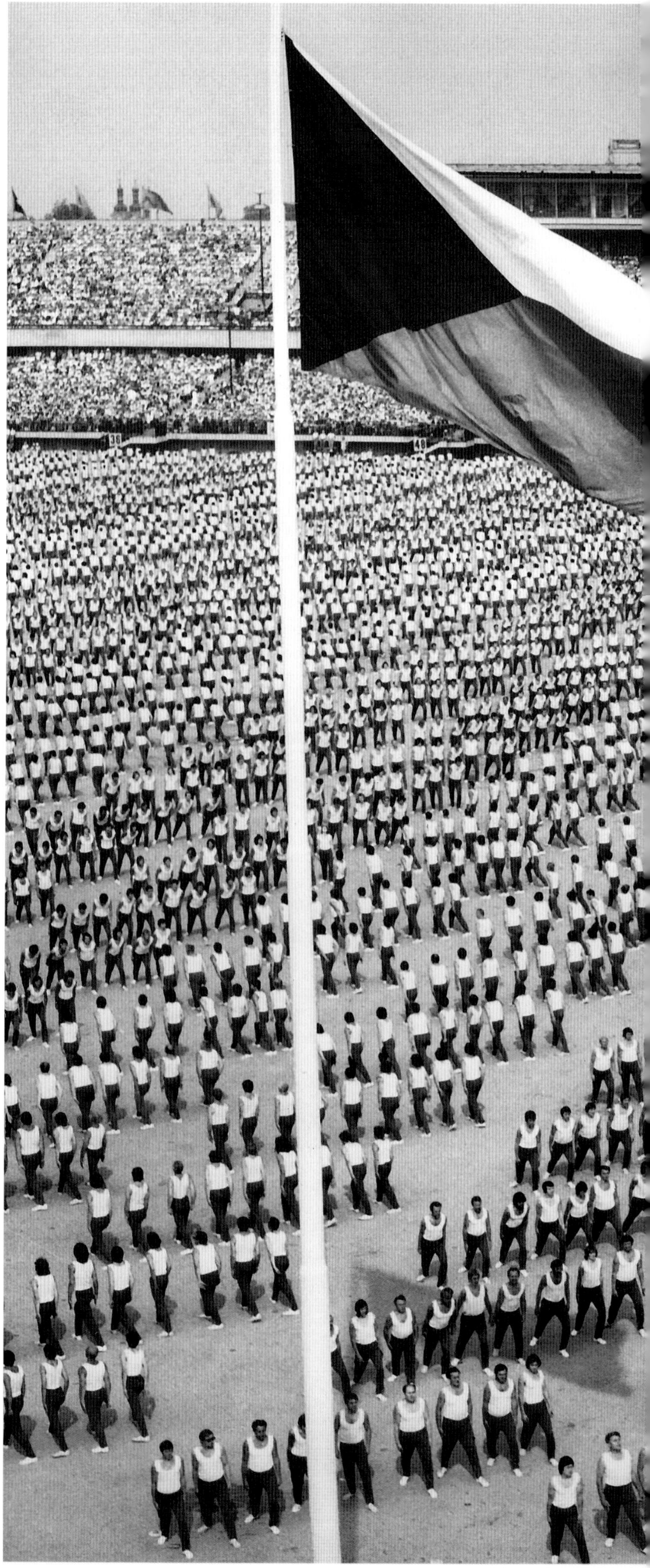

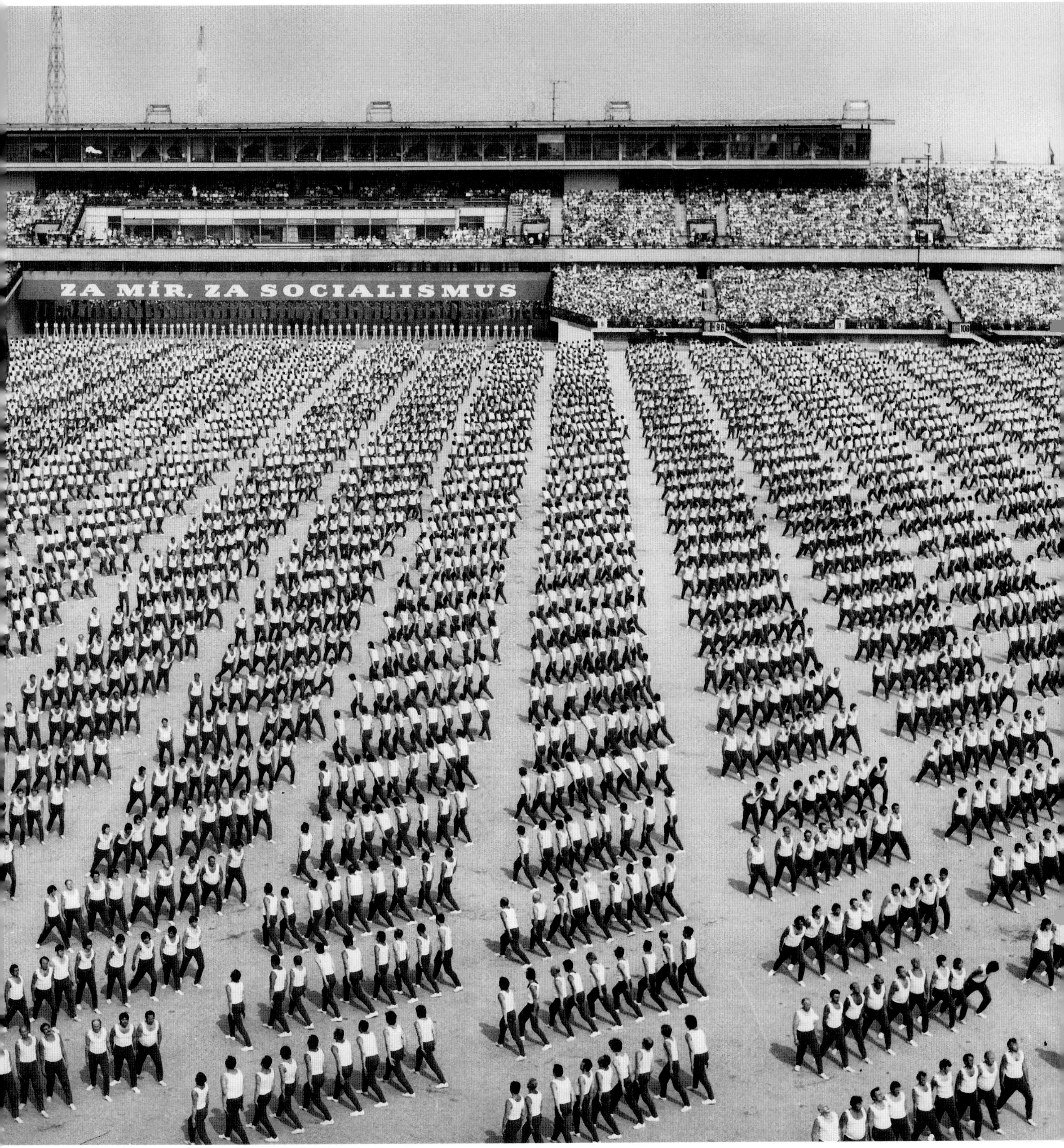

ZA MÍR, ZA SOCIALISMUS

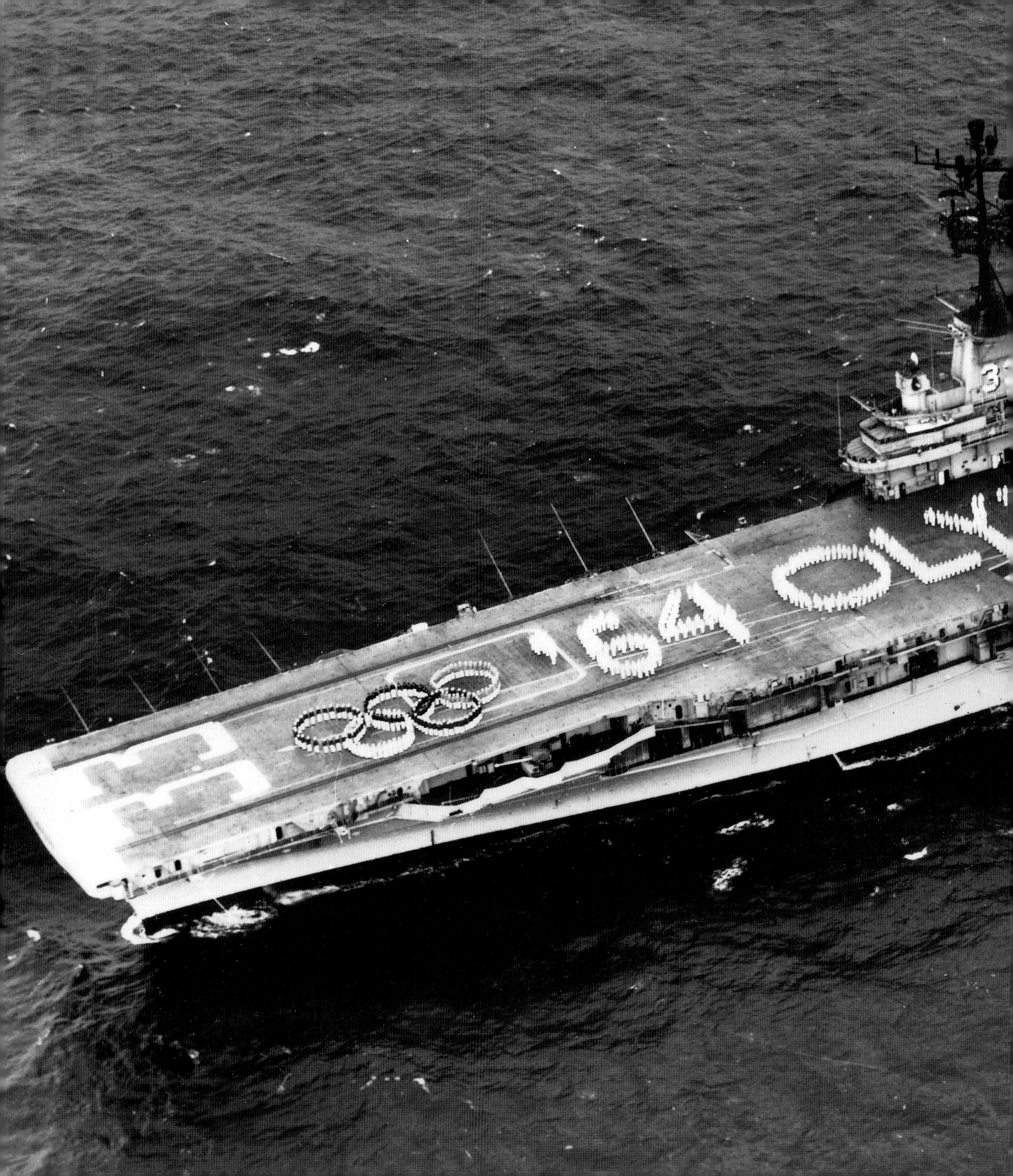
'64 OLY

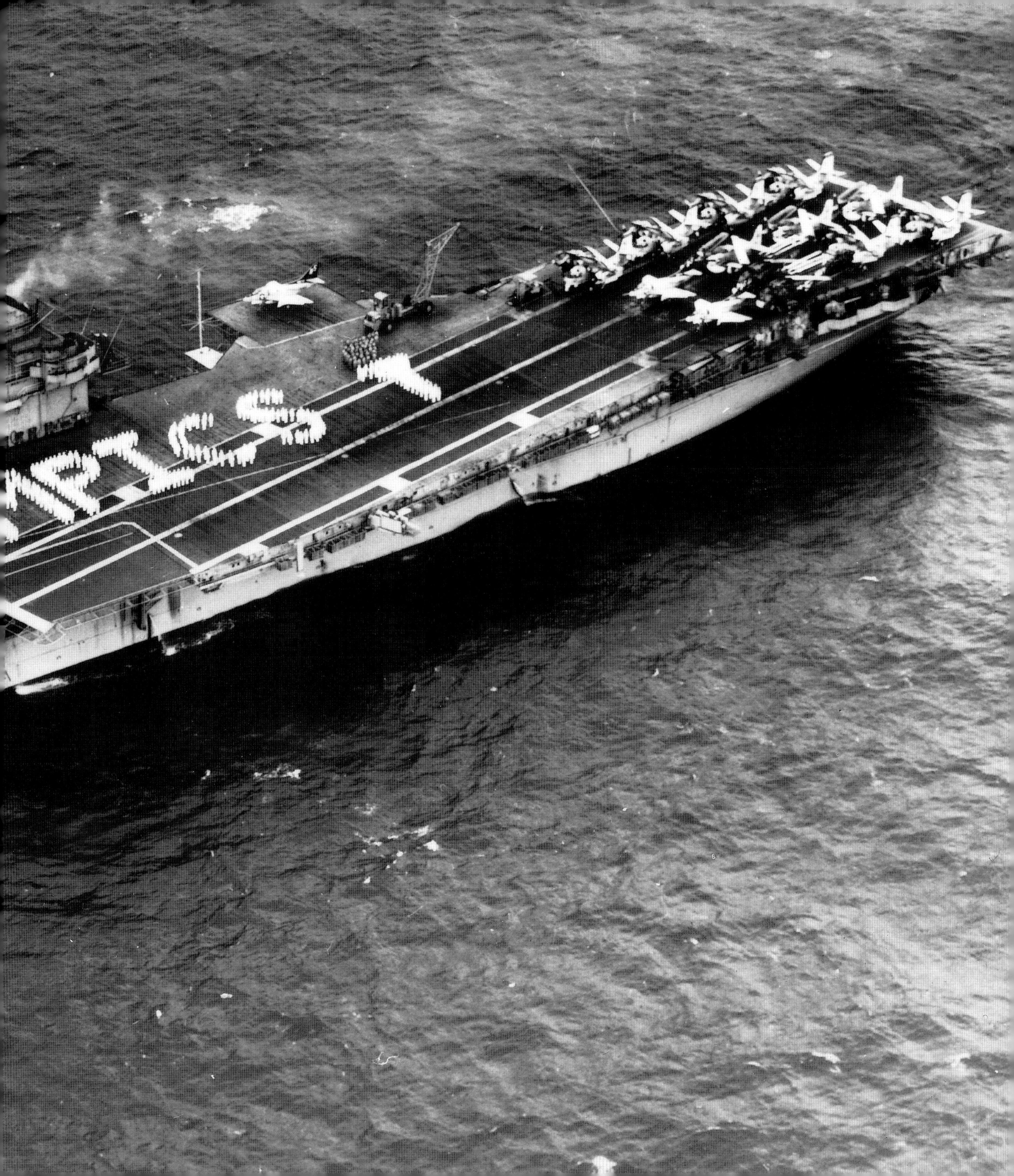

03

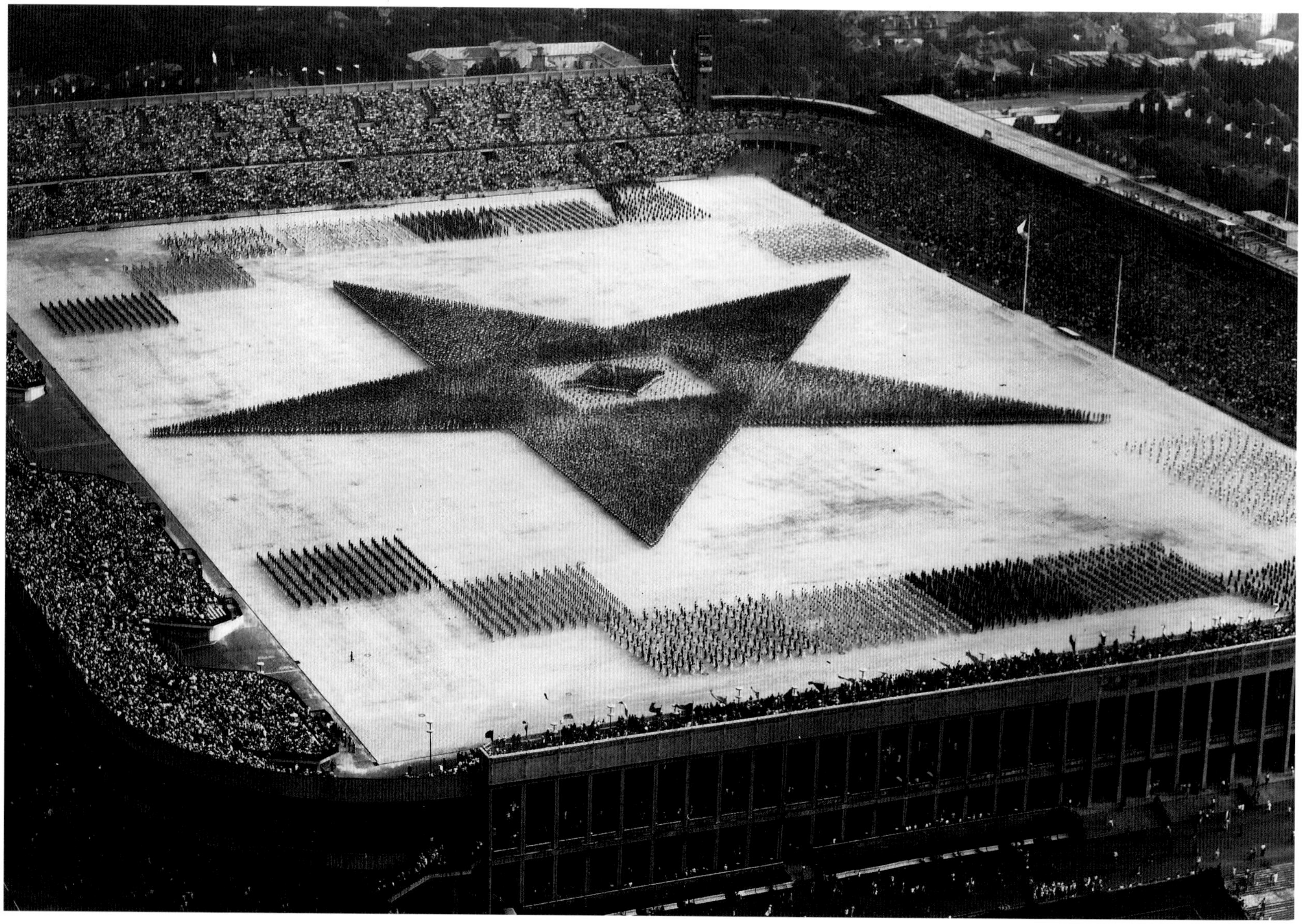

03
Closing ceremony of the Czechoslovak Spartakiad, Prague, 1975

04
Opening ceremony of the Olympic Games, Moscow, 1980
Tony Duffy

05/06 (OVERLEAF)
Opening ceremony of the Olympic Games, Moscow, 1980

04

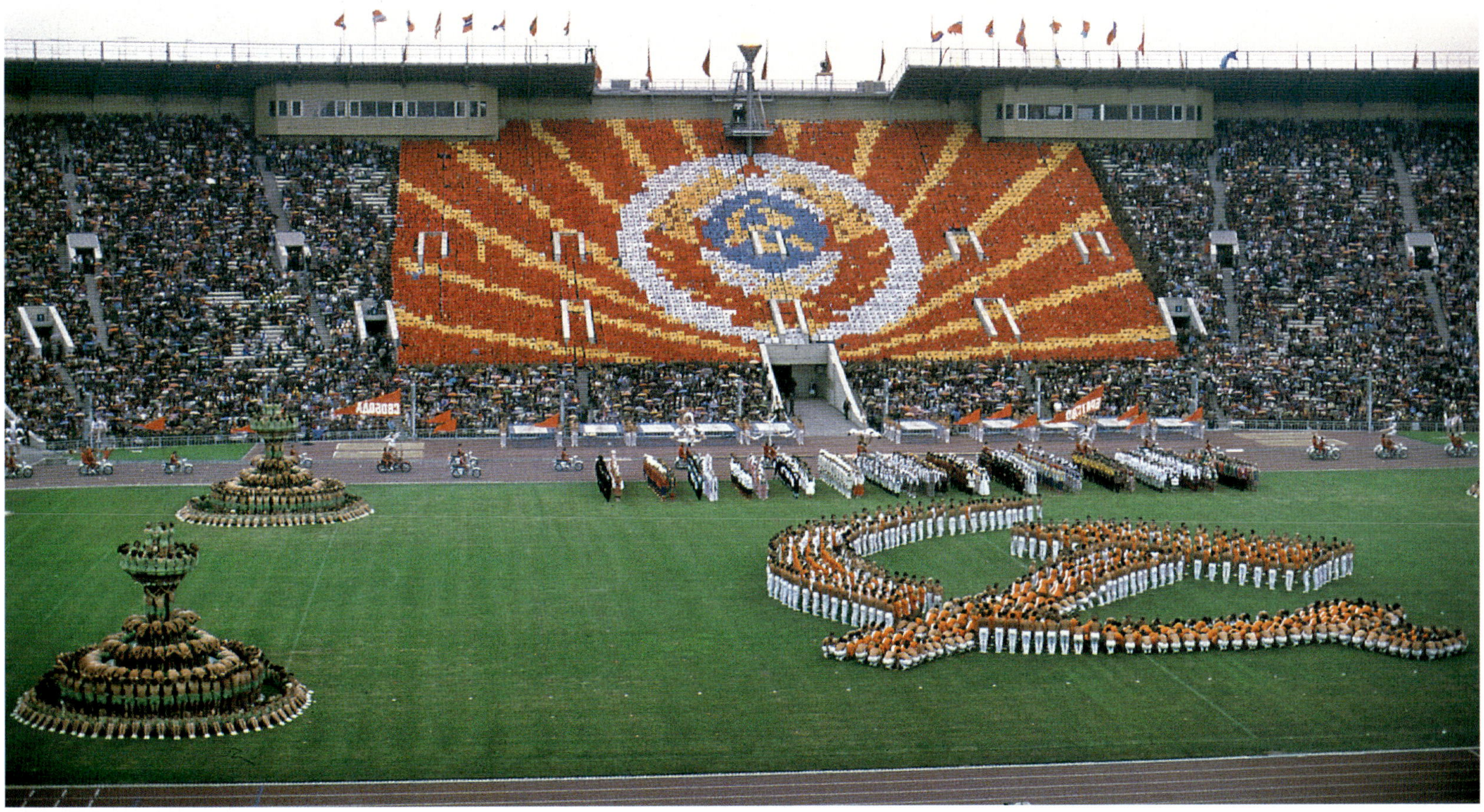

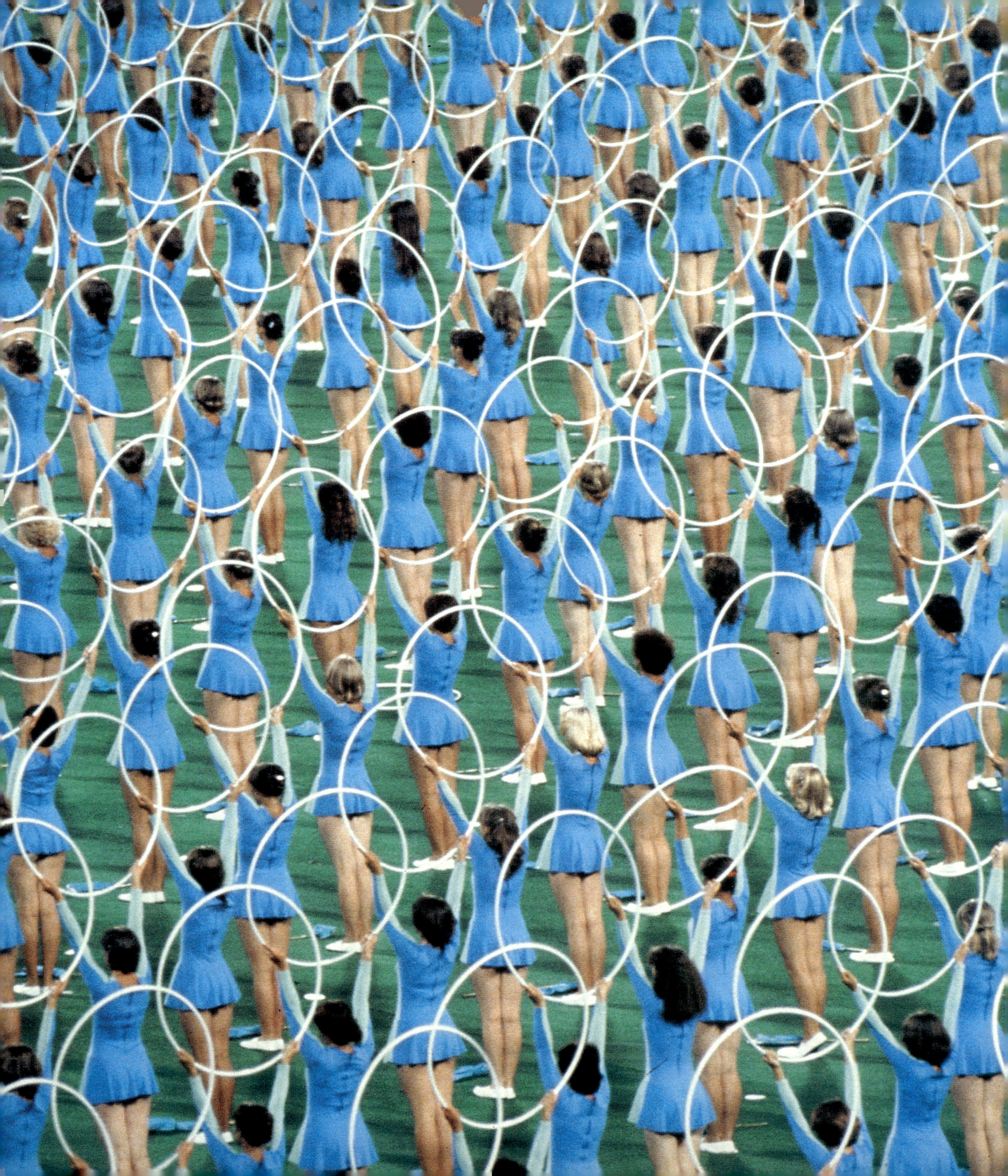

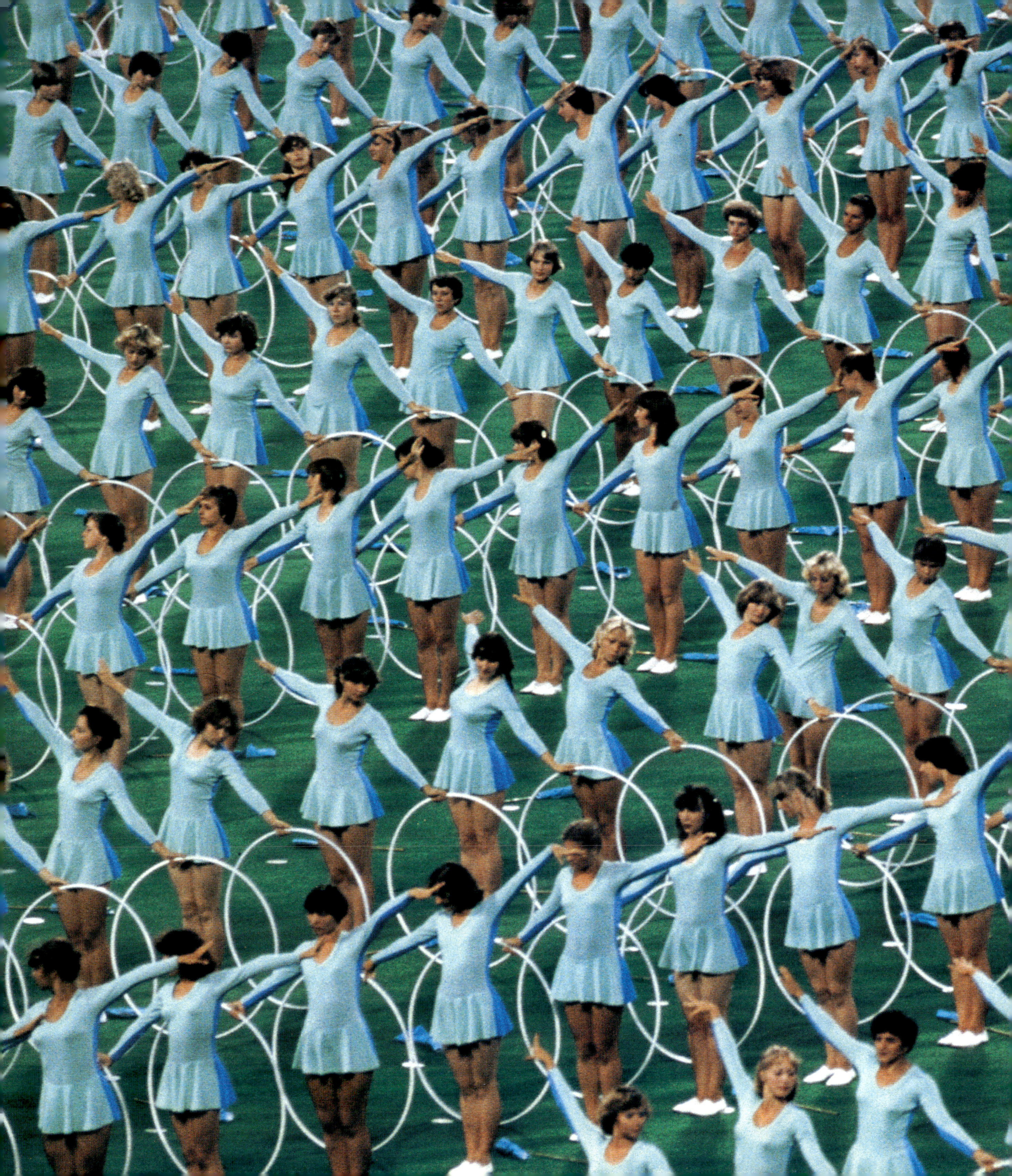

01
Valeri Borzov, Munich, 1972

02 (OVERLEAF)
John Thomas, Munich, 1972

TELEPHOTO

Throughout the century sports photographers had been striving to find ways of getting right to the heart of the action. Hampered by the equipment at their disposal it had been very difficult to get close enough to photograph sport in the heat of competition. The telephoto lens allowed them to overcome this problem. Enabling the photographer to focus in very tightly from great distances is one of the hallmarks of the modern sports image.
The great distances involved also ensure that nothing but the subject can be in focus, further isolating the sports figure from their surroundings. Special filters can further enhance this effect, manipulating the blurry distance into even backdrops, such as the distinctive 'donut effect' created by a mirror lens, which can be seen in the adjacent photograph. As a new breed of sports stars was emerging, photography found a way of accentuating their individuality, isolating them within their own space bubble. A new arena of sport had been created by the photographer.

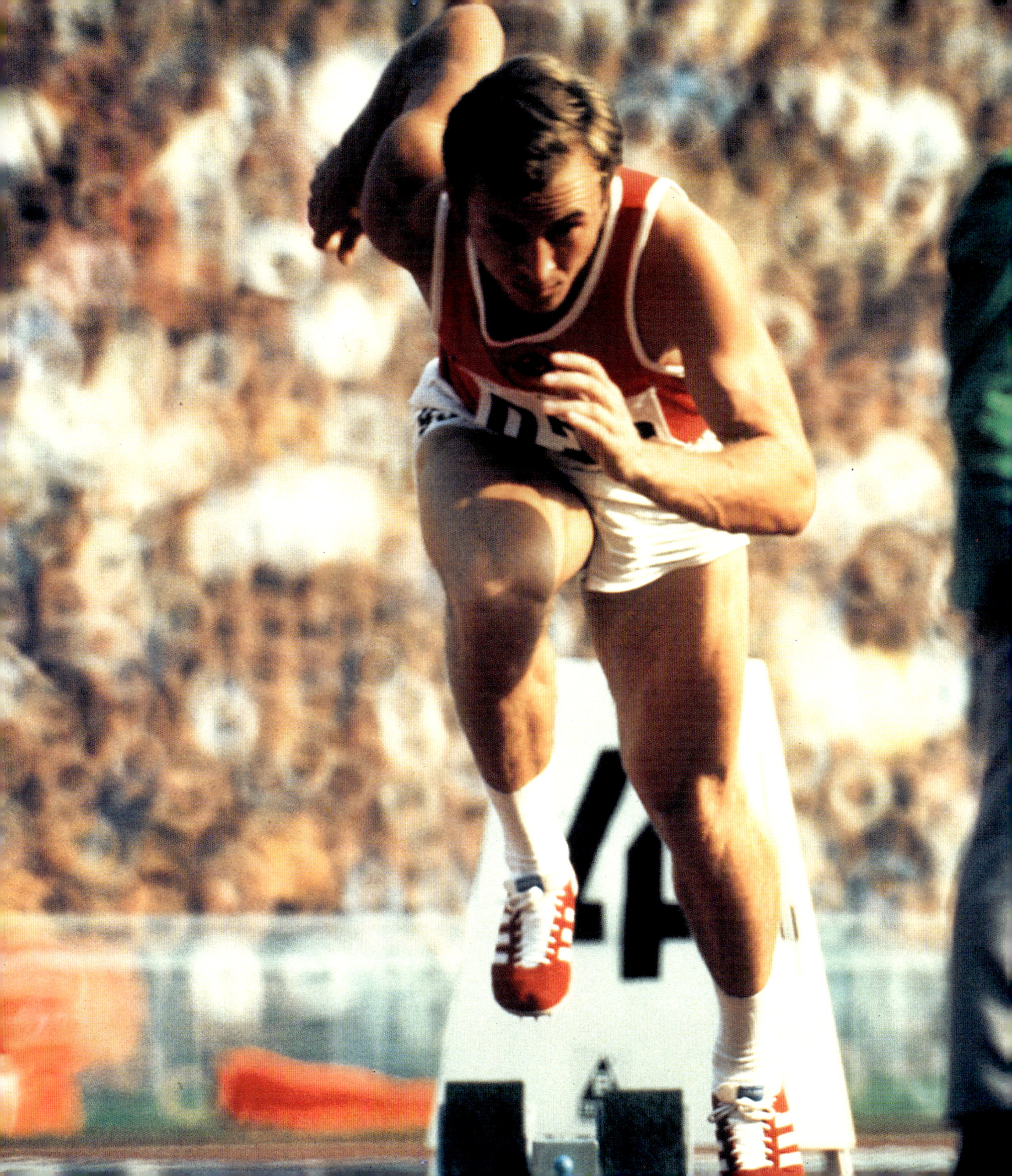
4

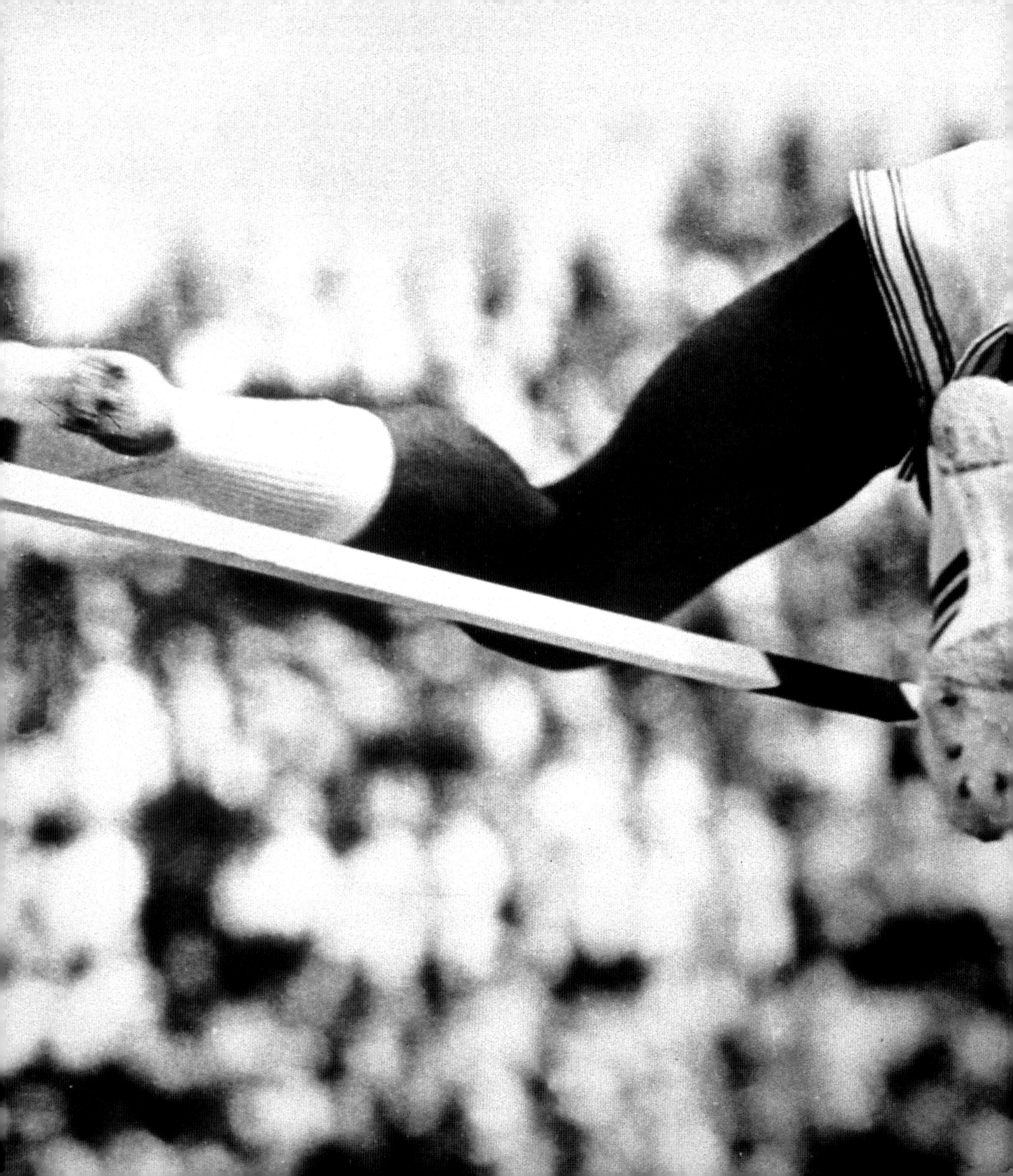

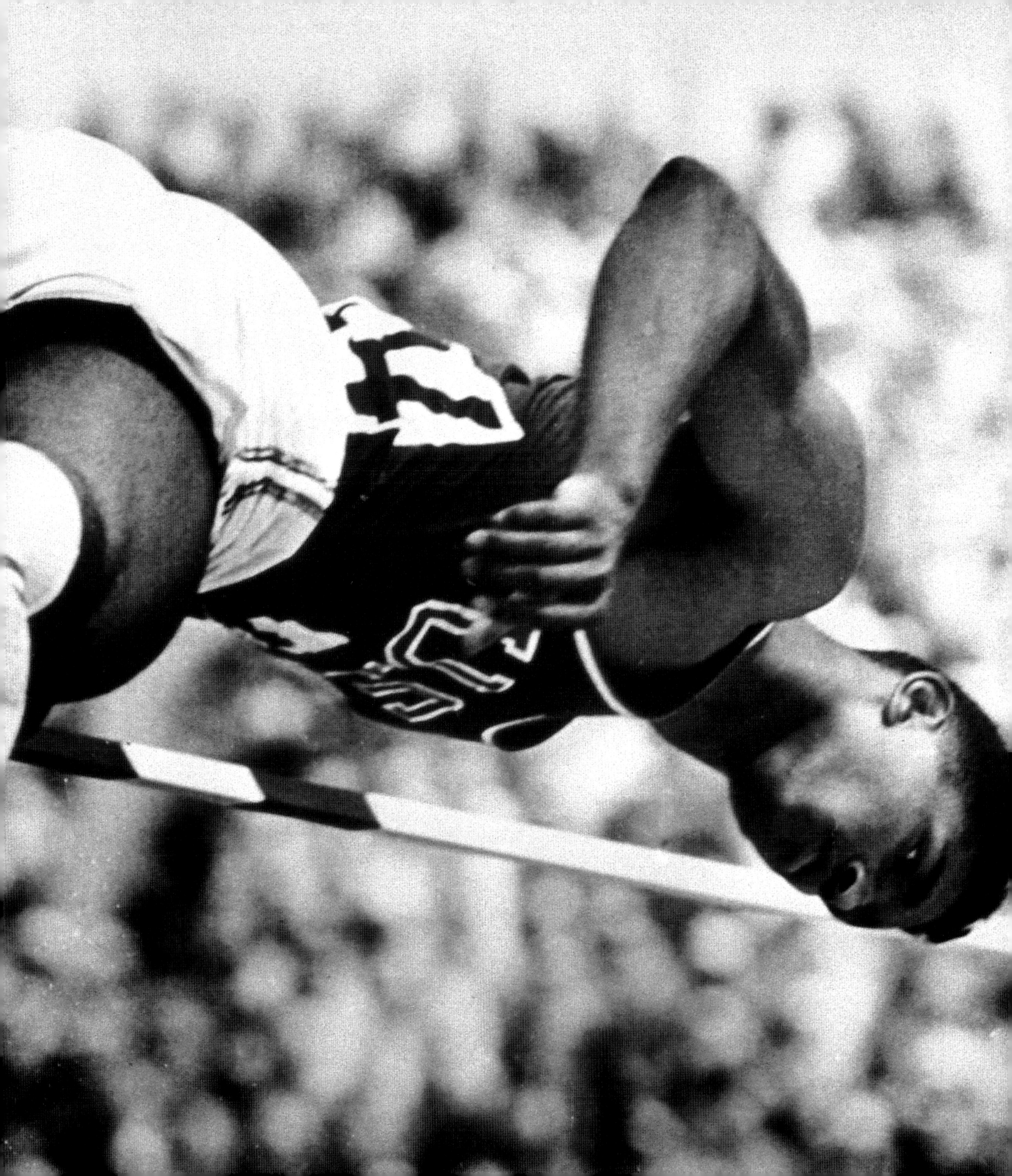

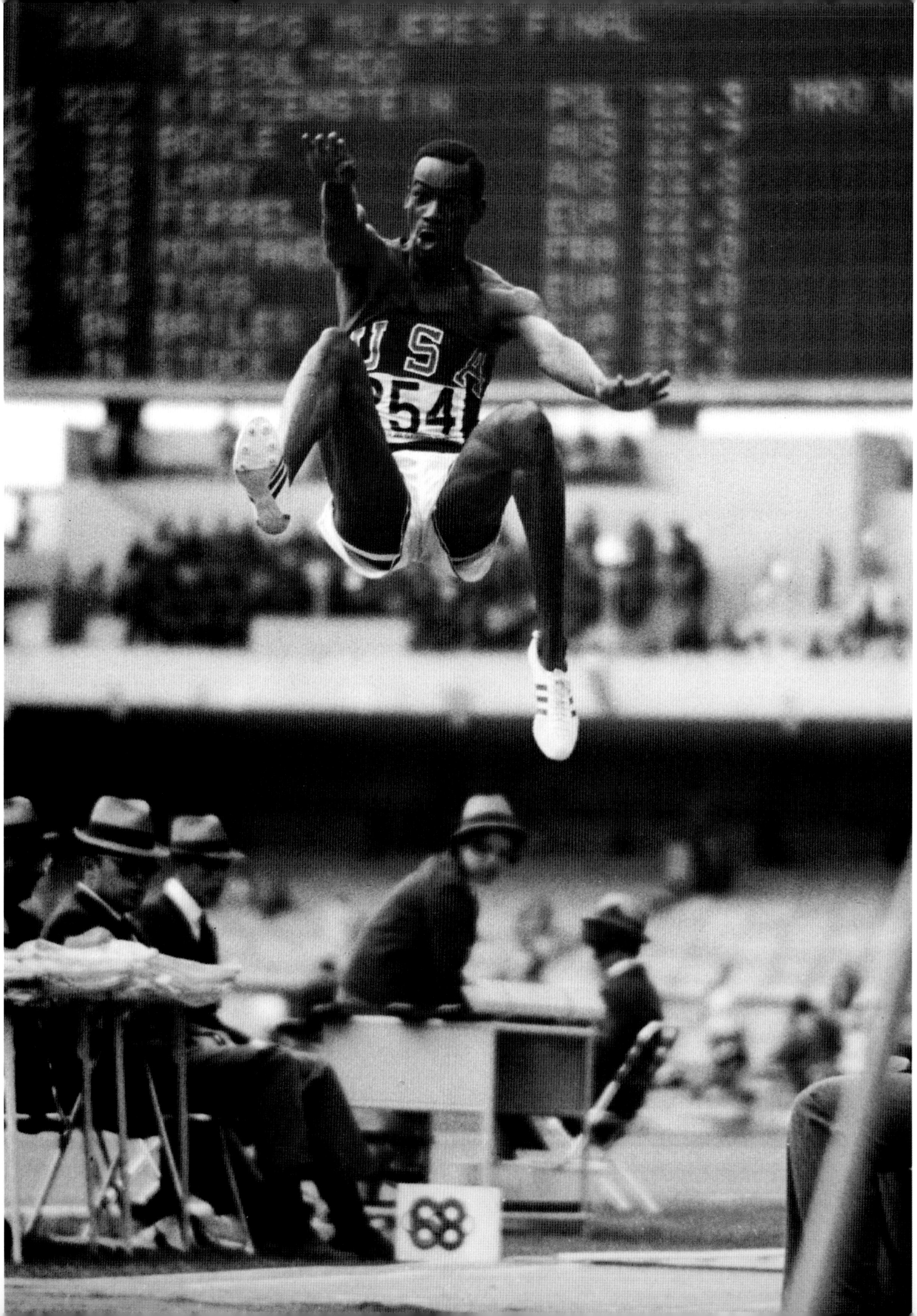
USA

03
Bob Beamon, Mexico, 1968
Tony Duffy

04
Viktor Sanyeyev, Munich, 1972
Tony Duffy

04

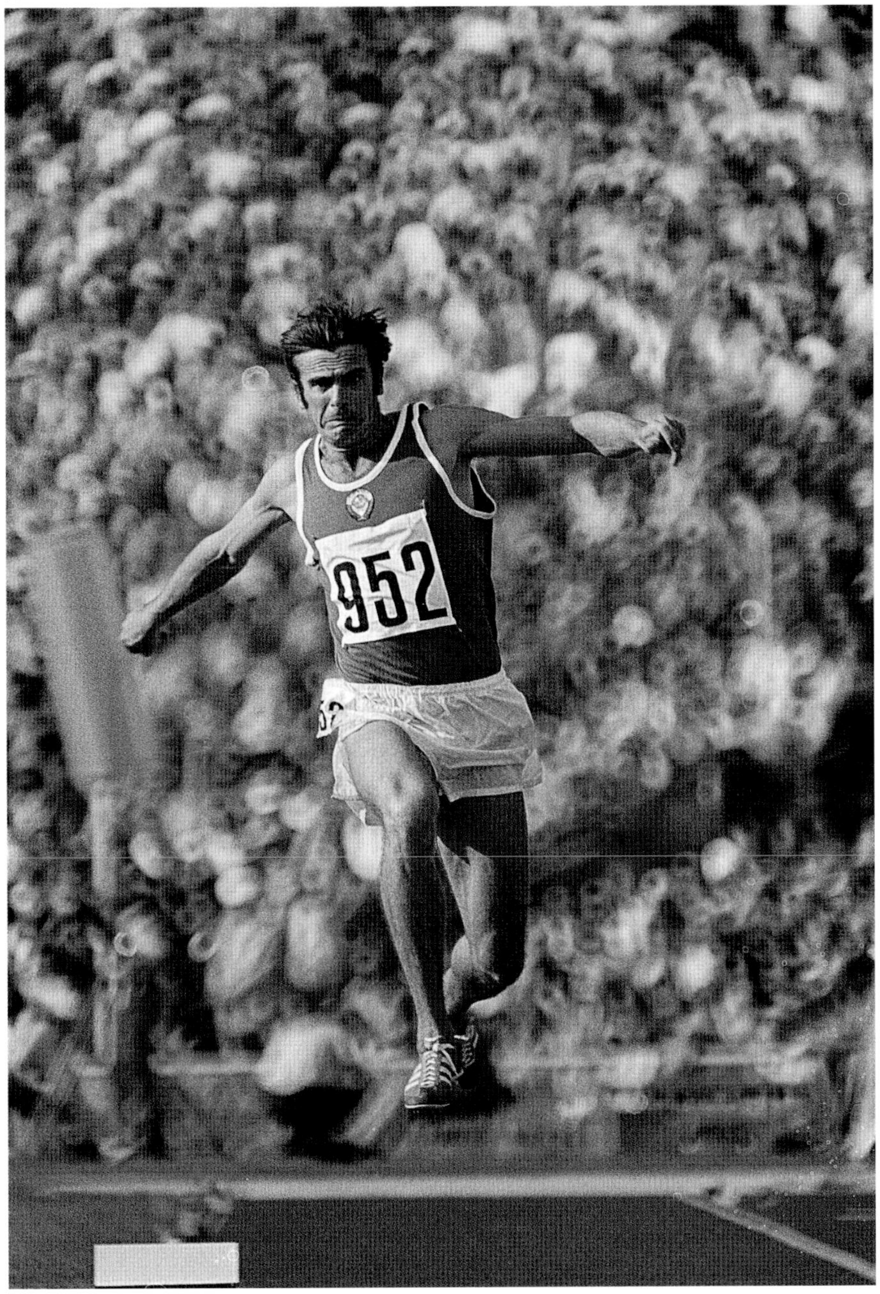

01
Terrorist in the Olympic Village, Munich, 1972

TERRORISM

Sporting stars were learning that a high public profile could substantially increase their earning potential, and the way to achieve it was through the growing media. Working on the same principle, terrorists sought the maximum media coverage possible to promote their cause. Taking advantage of the world's single biggest sporting event, sport and terrorism unfortunately came together at the Munich Olympic Games of 1972. Palestinian terrorists broke into the Israeli compound at the Olympic Village, killed two members of the team and took a further nine hostage. The rescue operation undertaken by the German police was spectacularly unsuccessful and in total eleven athletes, one policeman and five terrorists died. With the same equipment used in the stadium, sports photographers turned their cameras towards the terrorists who had hijacked the Olympics.

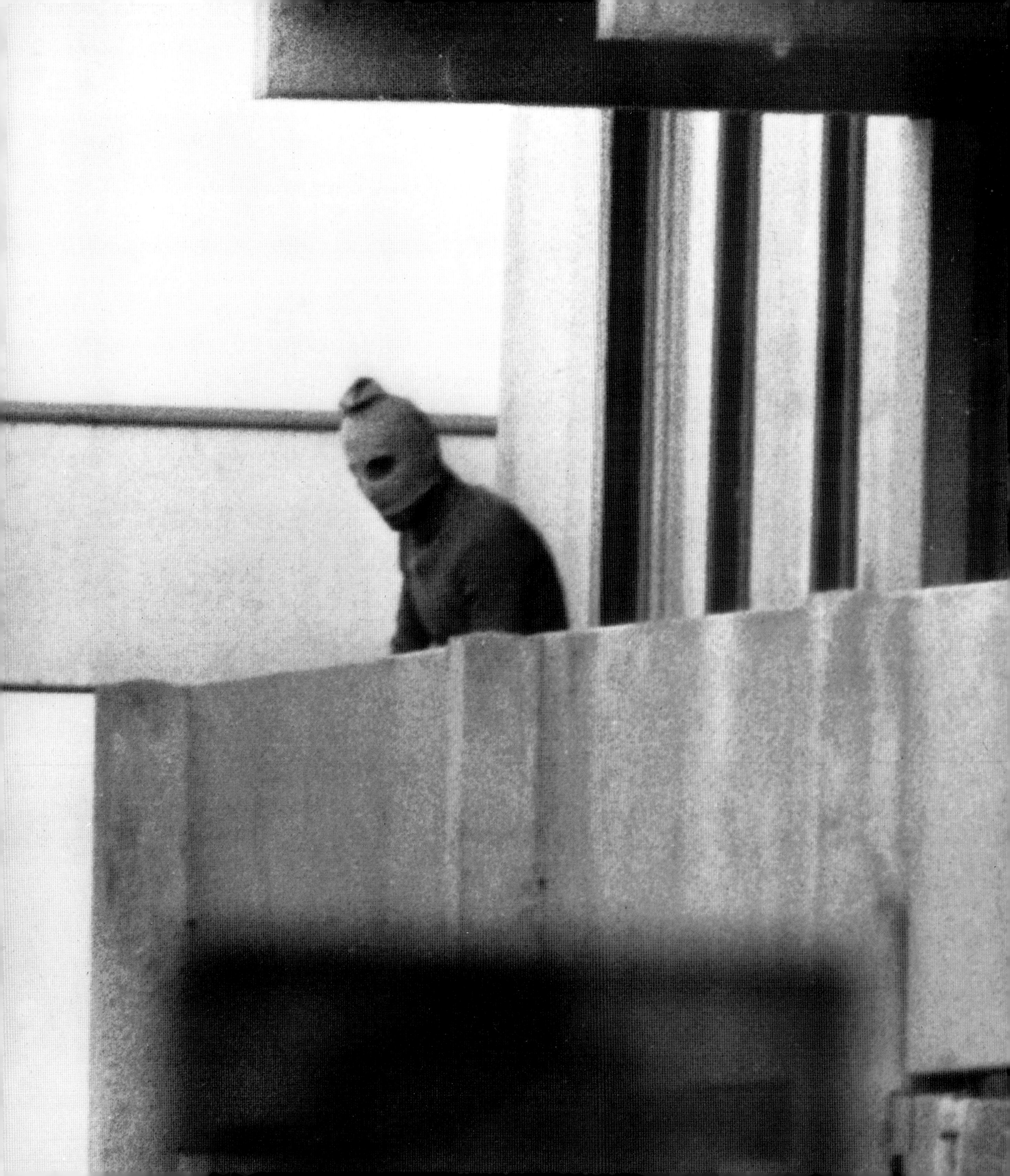

UNIFORM

Competitors in the Olympics had always worn the colours of their country and competed as part of their national team, but these photographs of the outfits of national teams, both casual and sporting, show a different emphasis emerging: the uniforms are designed to show the nation off in front of the world's media as fashionable, modern and stylish. By using recognized fashion designers the clothes could promote the design and manufacturing skills of the nation, and modern tracksuits using new fabrics show the beginnings of a fashion revolution that would see sports clothing become many people's choice for everyday wear. Press and public were increasingly interested in the peripheral aspects of sport, building up the drama or the hype of the events themselves. And to do this sport invited the photographers not to a sporting event, but to a press call, to promote the excitement ahead.

01

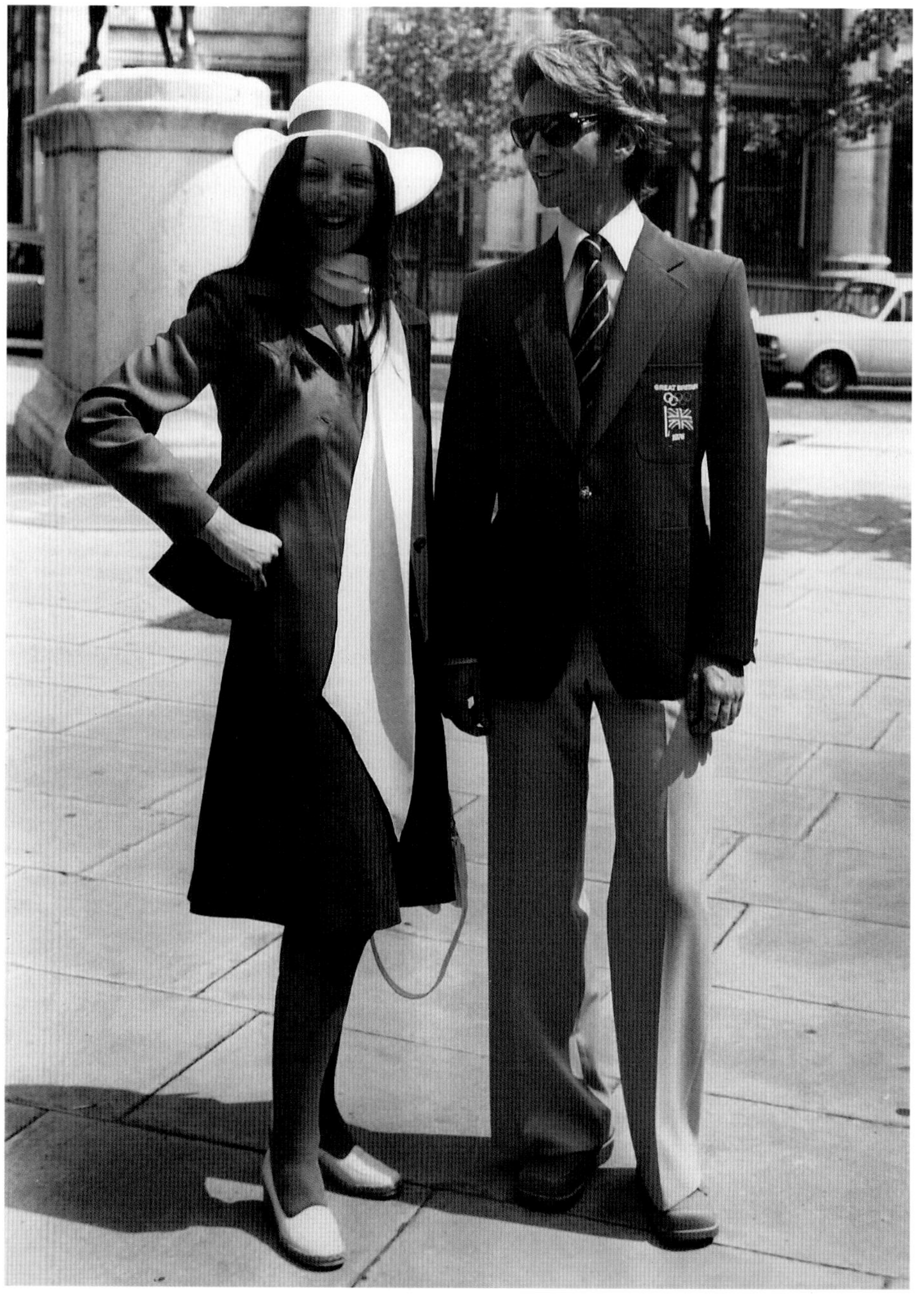

01
Models showing the clothing to be worn by the British Olympic team in Montreal, 1976

02
Outfits by Jacques Esterel for French athletes going to the Olympic Games in Tokyo, 1964

03
Modelling the uniforms that Japanese athletes will wear at the Rome Olympics, 1960

04
Javelin thrower Gergely Kulcsár and gymnast Anikó Ducza wearing the Hungarian Olympic uniform for the Tokyo Games, 1964
S Bojar

05
Fashion models presenting the uniforms of the Hungarian Olympic team for the Moscow Olympics, 1980
László Petrovits

02
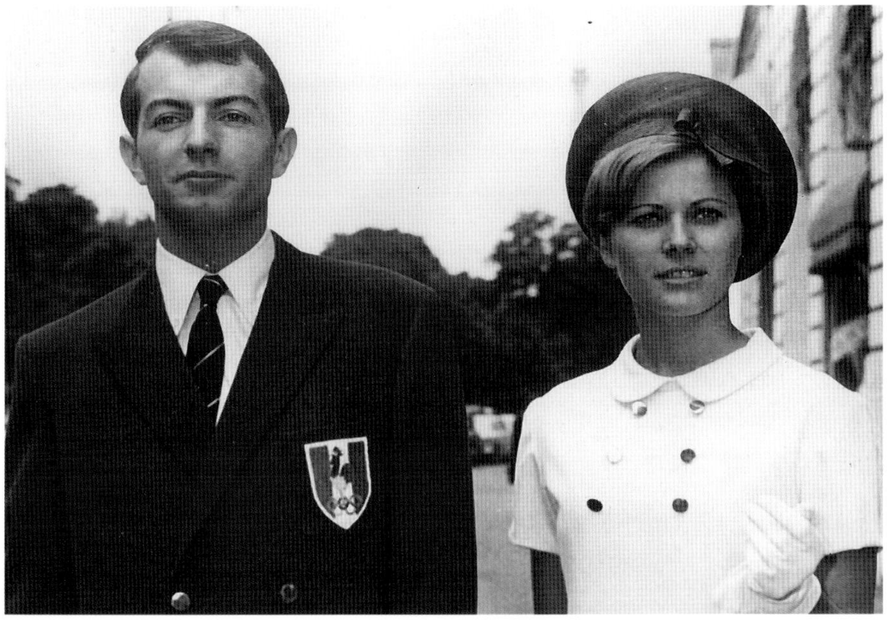

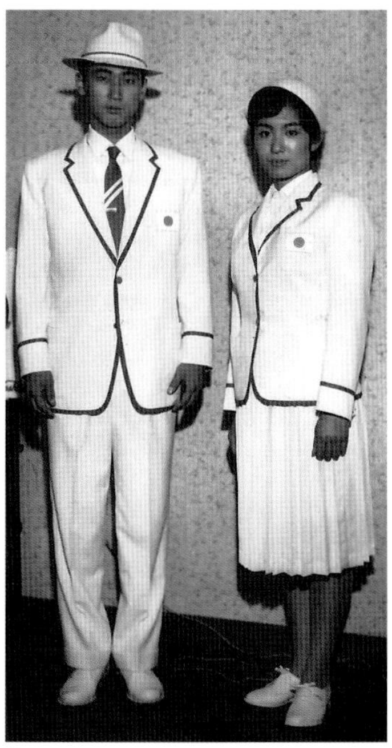
03

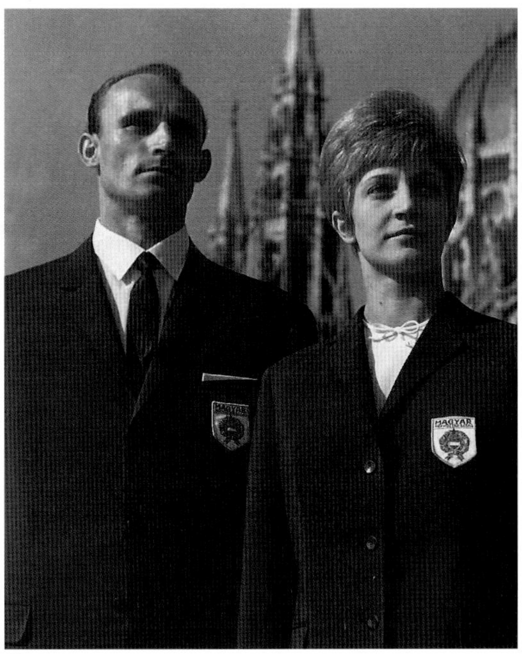

04

05
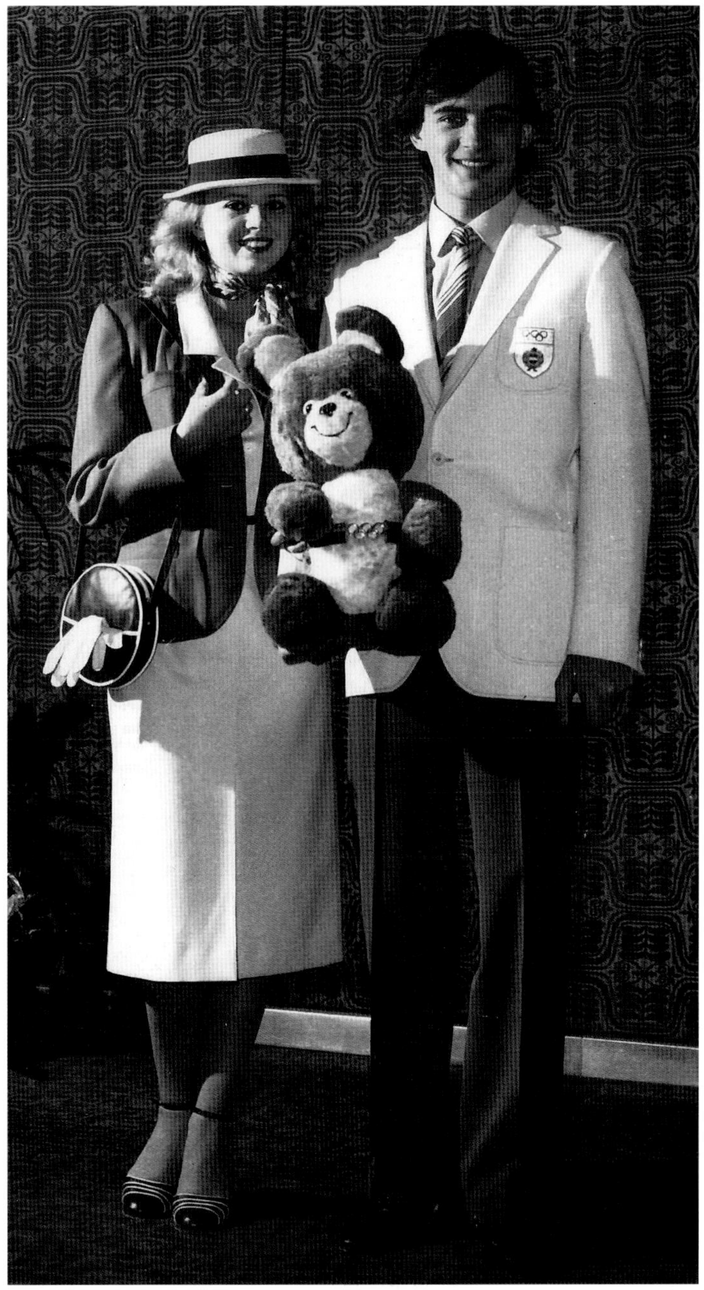

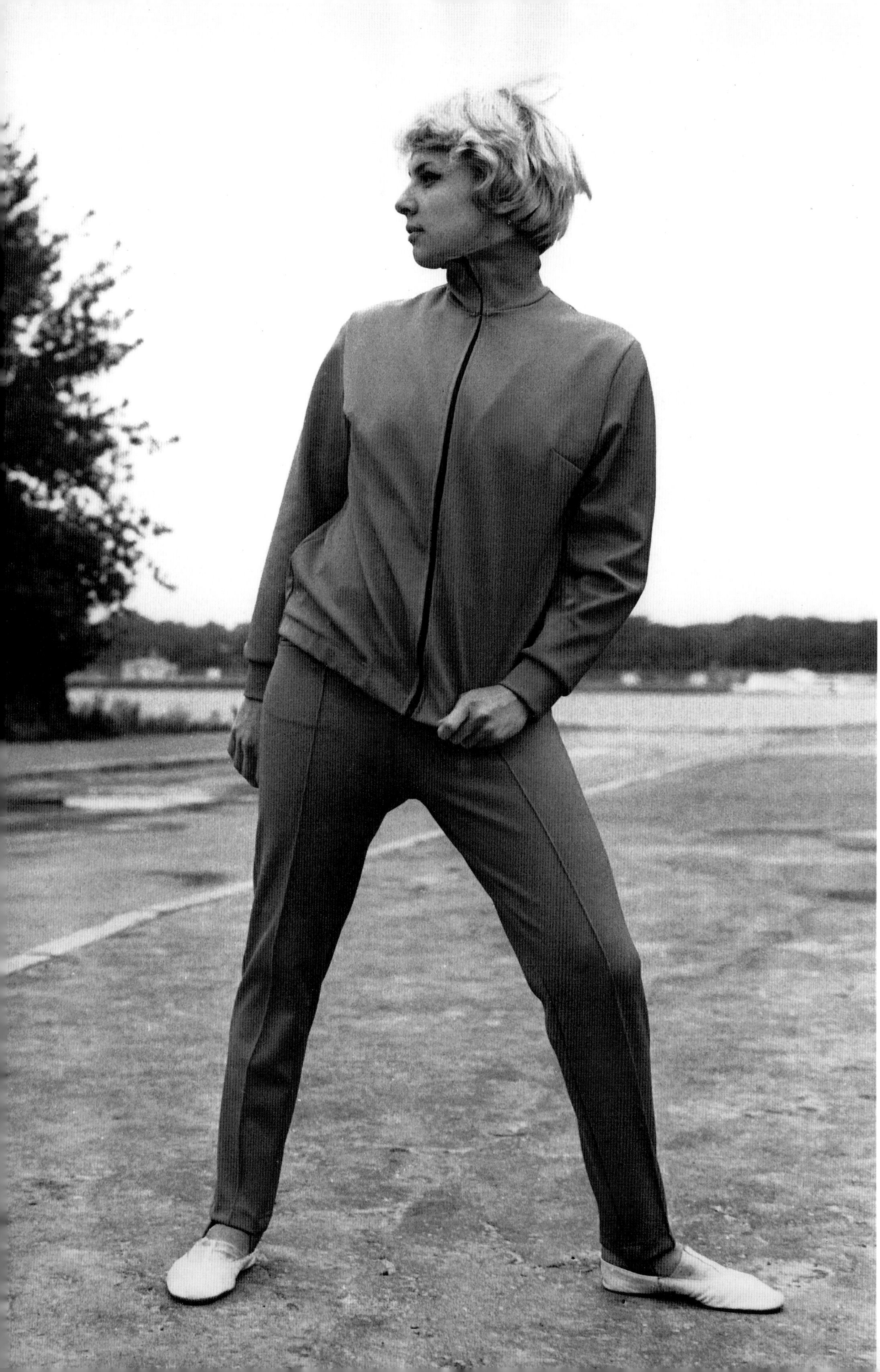

06/07
Training suits designed for Soviet competitors taking part in the Mexico Olympics, 1968
V Un Da-sin

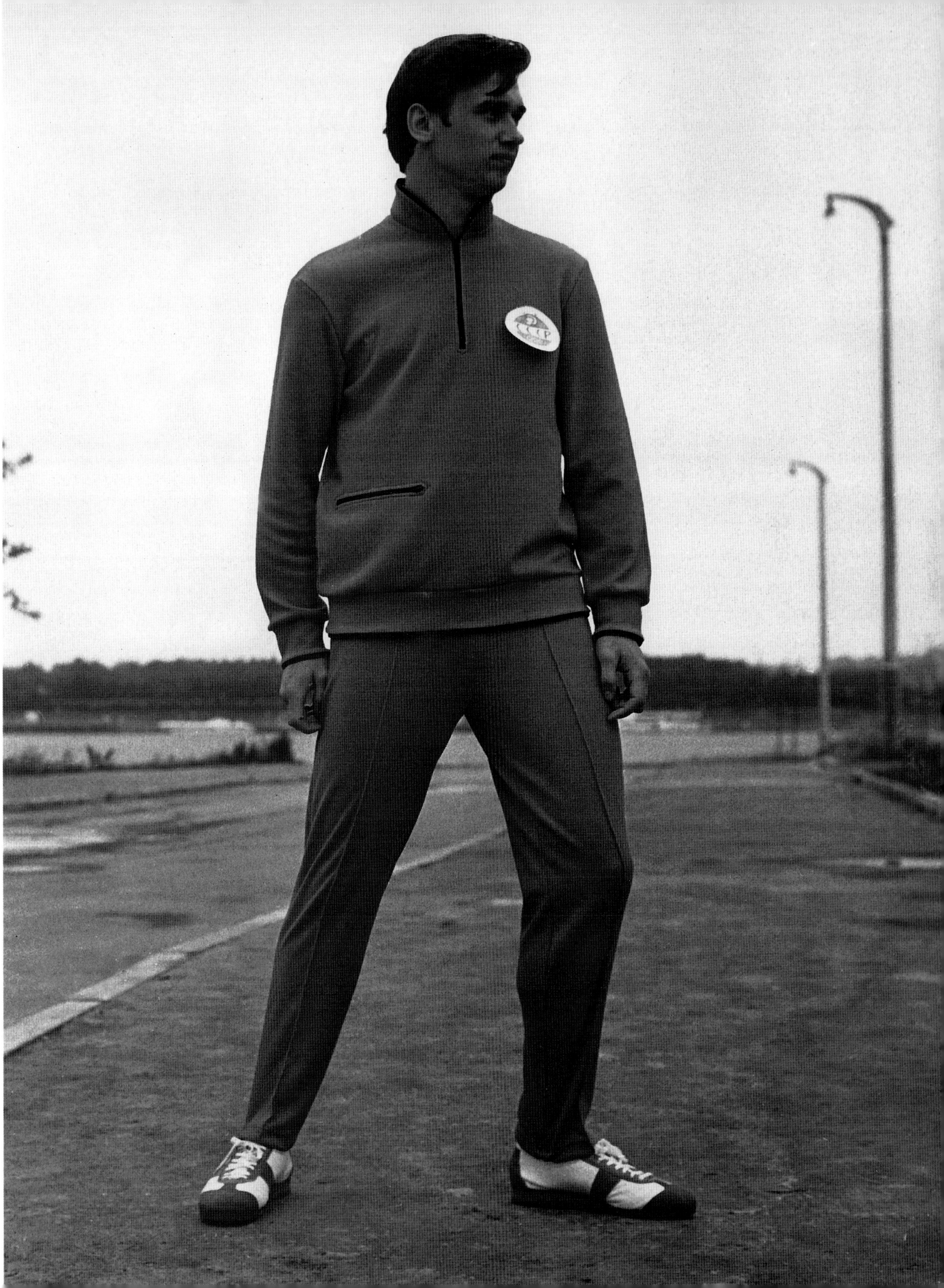
СССР

01/02
Lee Evans, Larry James and Ron Freeman on the podium following the medal ceremony, Mexico, 1968

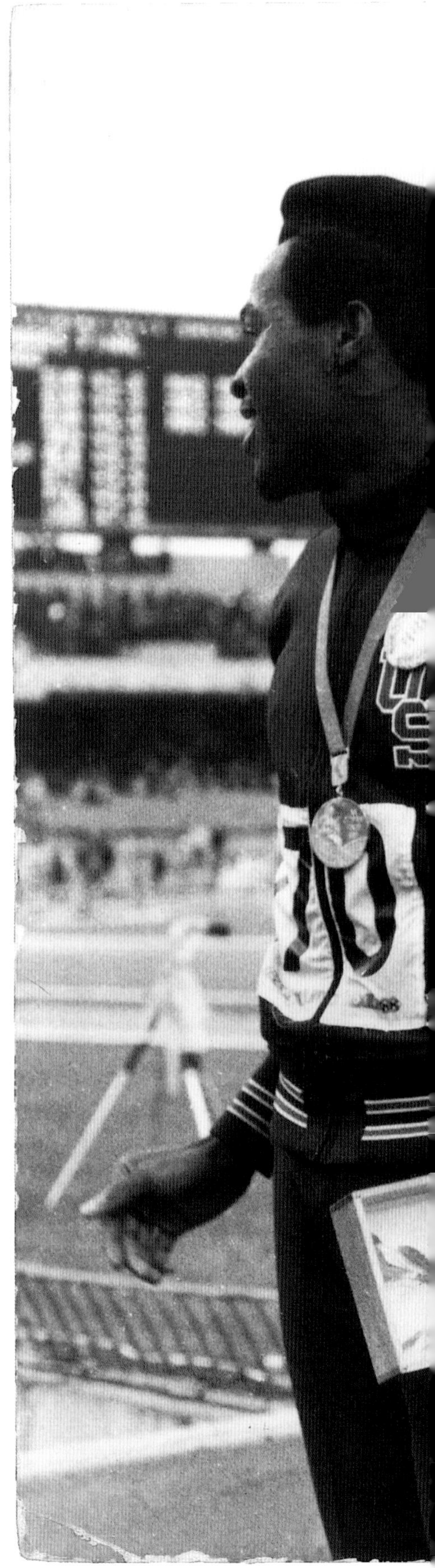

BLACK POWER

Although the racial barriers in sport had started to come down, segregation in training and in university teams was still rife in the USA during the 1960s. A plan for black athletes to boycott the 1968 Mexico Olympics did not receive universal approval, instead it was thought more positive to take part and win, not for the USA, but for the wider international black community. Sport had given black athletes the stage to protest about racial inequality. That statement was made most powerfully during the 1968 Olympics when Tommie Smith – who won the 200m race – and John Carlos – who came third – raised their fists in the gesture of the Black Power movement while the national anthem played. Less well known are these images of Lee Evans, Larry James and Ron Freeman wearing black berets – also a sign of the Black Power movement – when receiving their medals for coming first, second and third in the 400m.

Muhammad Ali was a potent symbol of the civil rights struggle in the USA during the 1960s, infuriating the establishment by embracing the Nation of Islam and with his refusal to fight in the Vietnam War. Ali's fight with Floyd Patterson in 1965 represented a significant change in racial politics. Patterson stated that it was his duty to reclaim the title for America, because a Black Muslim as champion disgraced the sport and the nation. Ali convincingly won and taunted Patterson with 'Come on America! Come on white America!' throughout the fight. Ali's fights had become political statements about equality for the black community.

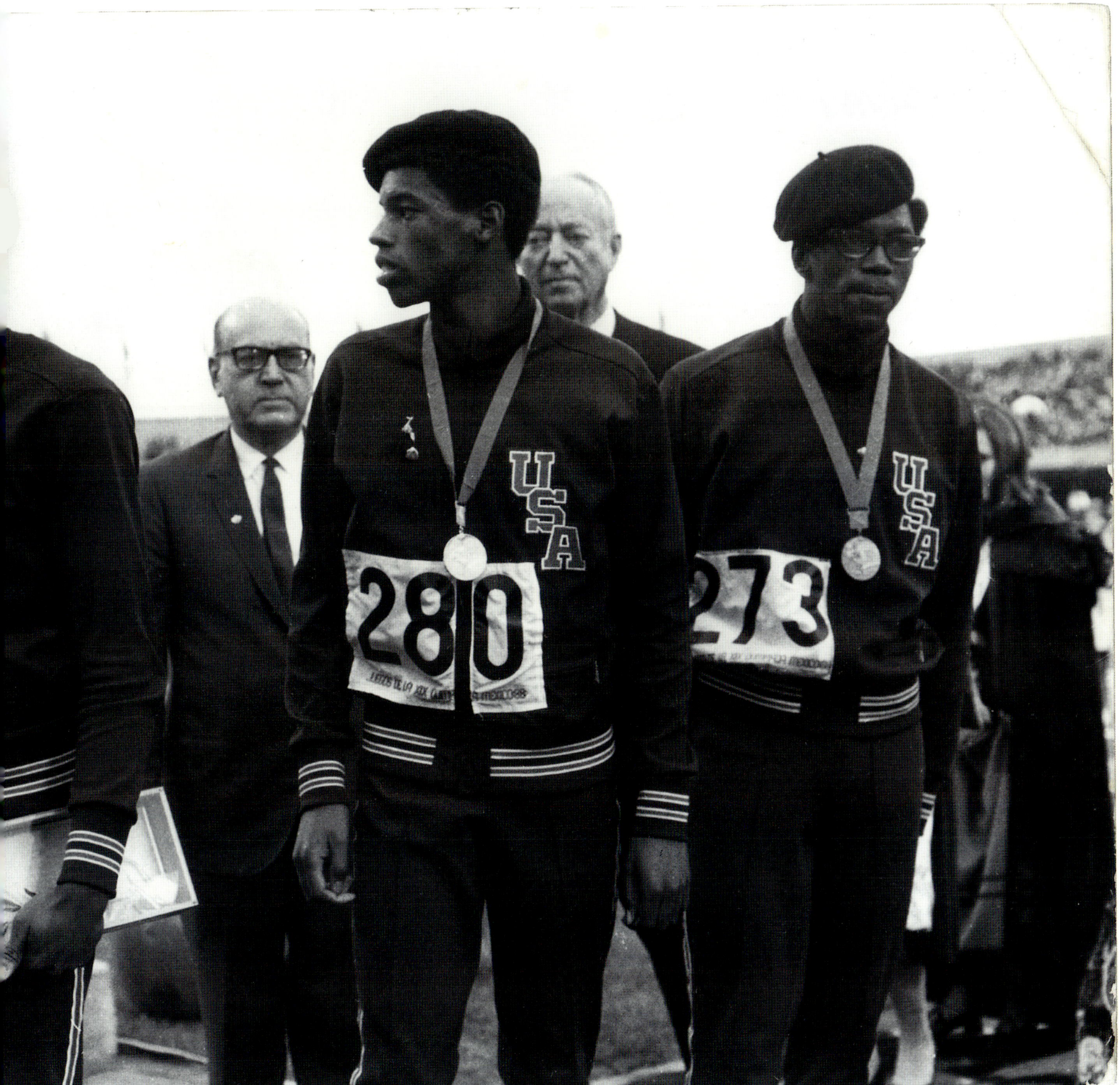
USA
280
USA
273

02/03
Muhammad Ali versus Floyd Patterson, Las Vegas, 1965

04
Muhammad Ali stands over a defeated Sonny Liston, Maine, 1965

02

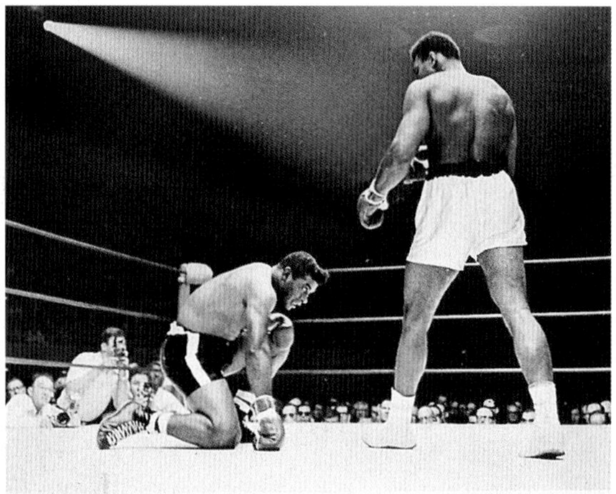

03

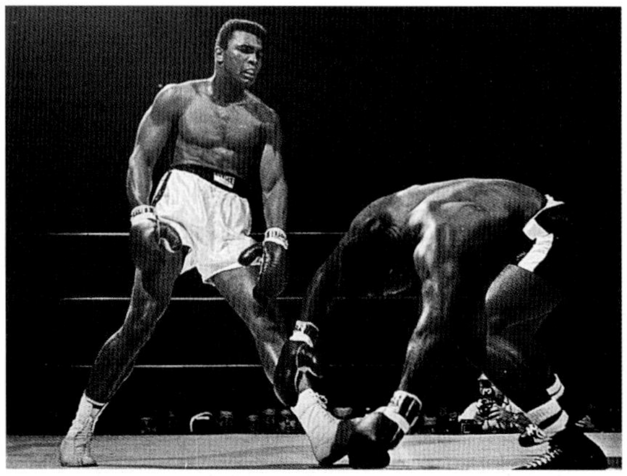

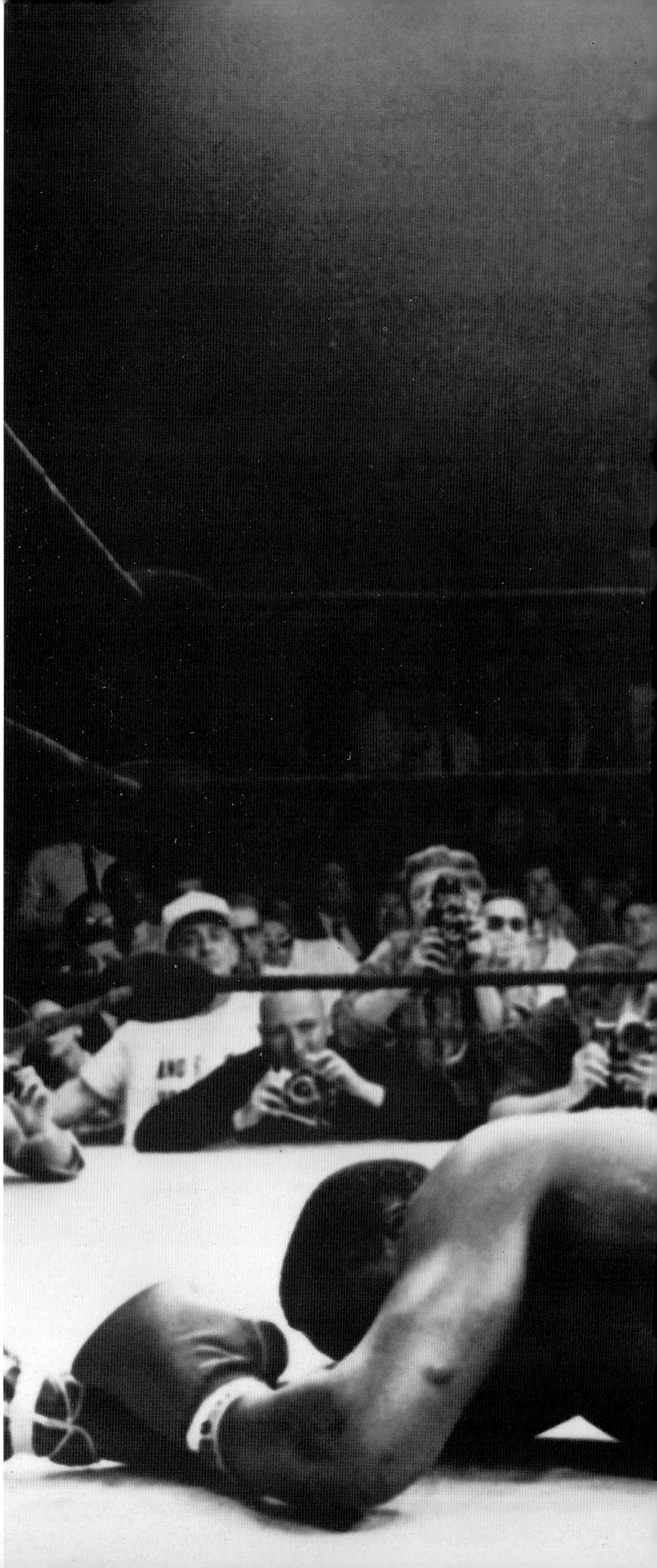

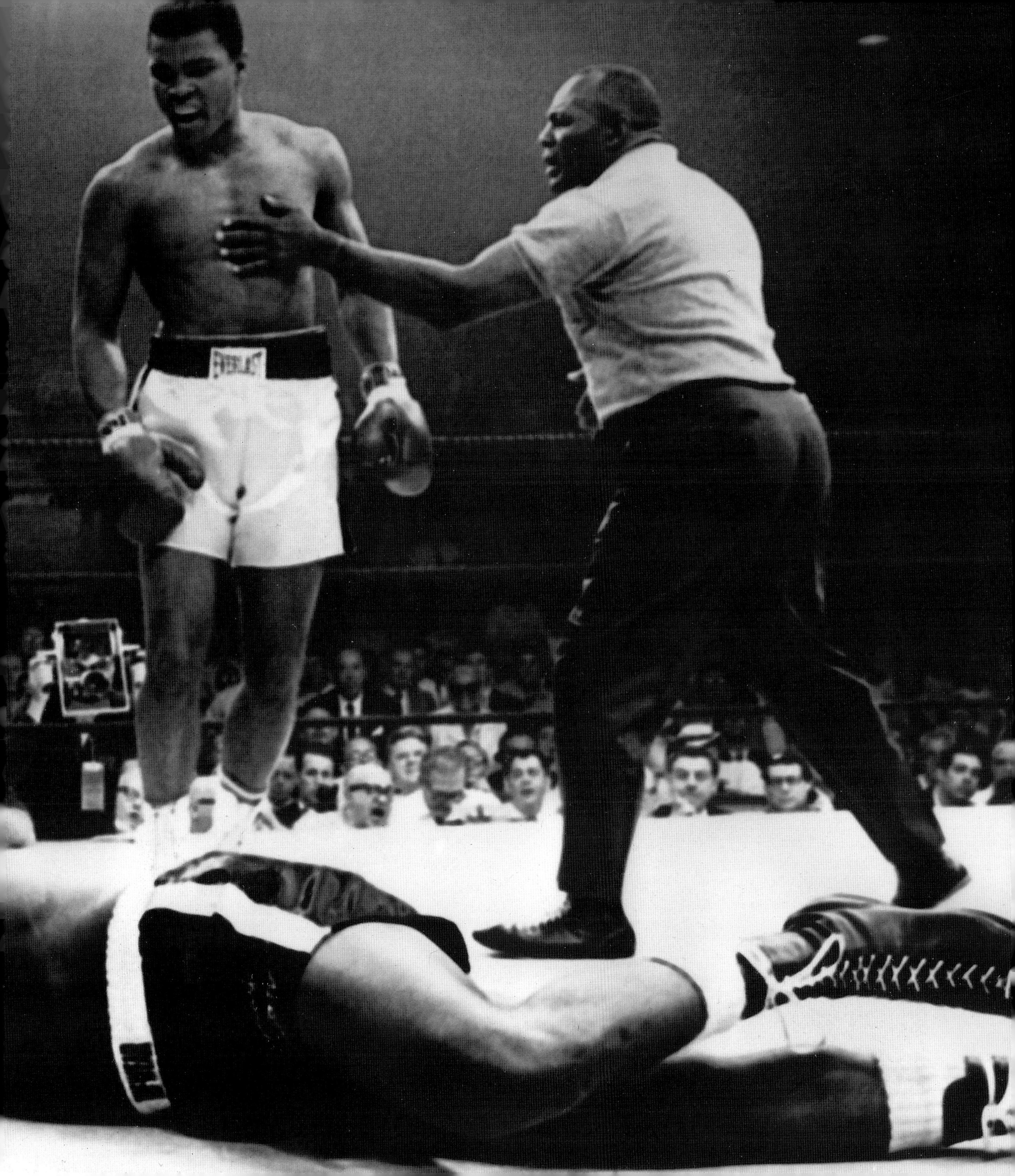
EVERLAST

01
George Best relaxes at his Cheshire home, 1972

THE MODERN SPORTS STAR

As the fame and celebrity of sport's top performers increasingly rivalled that of film stars and politicians, the public was naturally interested in their lives beyond the sporting arena. Photographs of sports stars started to move from the sports sections at the back of newspapers to the news pages and lifestyle sections in magazines. The uniquely positive profile of a famous sporting personality – popular, young, wealthy, successful – made them prime targets for figures from the world of entertainment and politics whose own popularity could be enhanced by association. The modern sports star was moving beyond sport into the world of news and entertainment, and could expect the cameras to follow them far beyond sport into their private lives. Sports stars had joined the world of media celebrity.

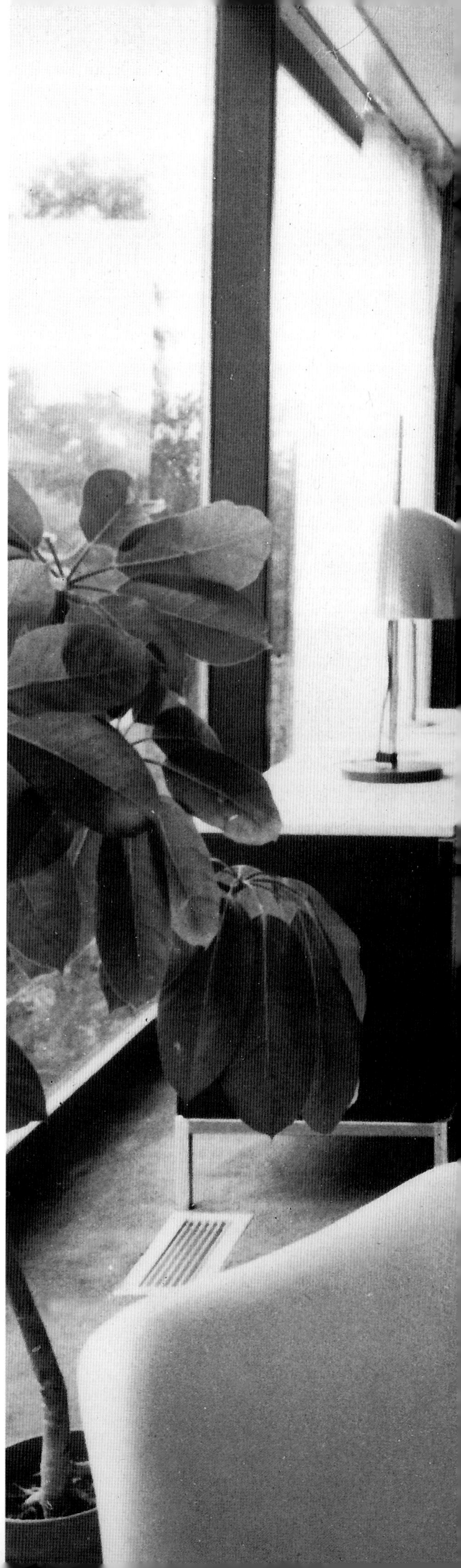

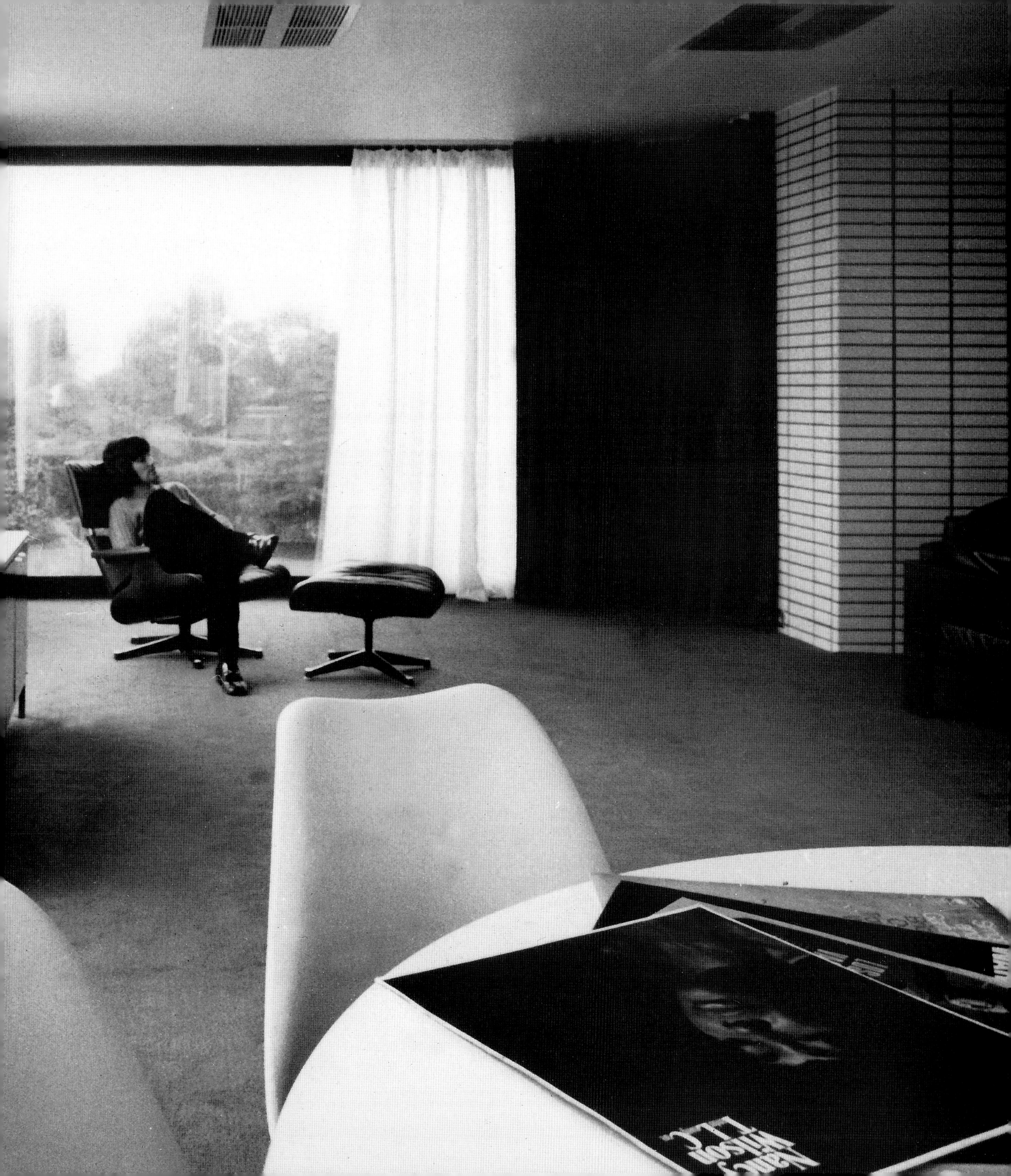

02

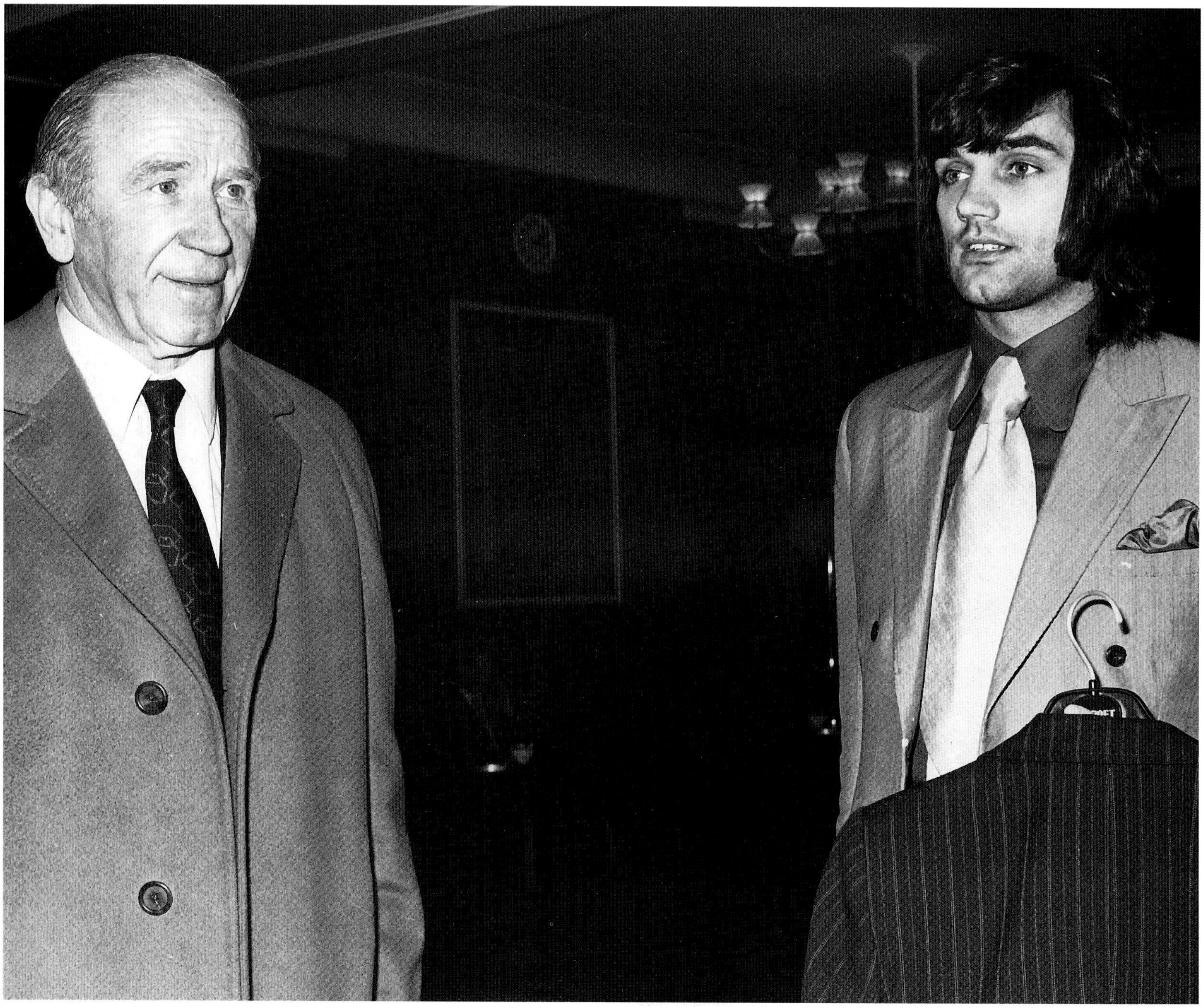

02
George Best with Manchester United manager Matt Busby at a disciplinary hearing, 1972

03
George Best with actress Sue Whitman at the opening of his boutique, 1968

04
George Best with British prime minister, Harold Wilson, 1970

05
George Best is given a bicycle when he is banned from driving, 1968

06
George Best appearing on a radio show alongside broadcaster Michael Parkinson, 1975

07 (OVERLEAF)
Muhammad Ali on 'The Eamonn Andrews Show' with fellow guests (from right): not known, Dudley Moore, Noel Coward and Lucille Ball, 1966
Les Lee

03
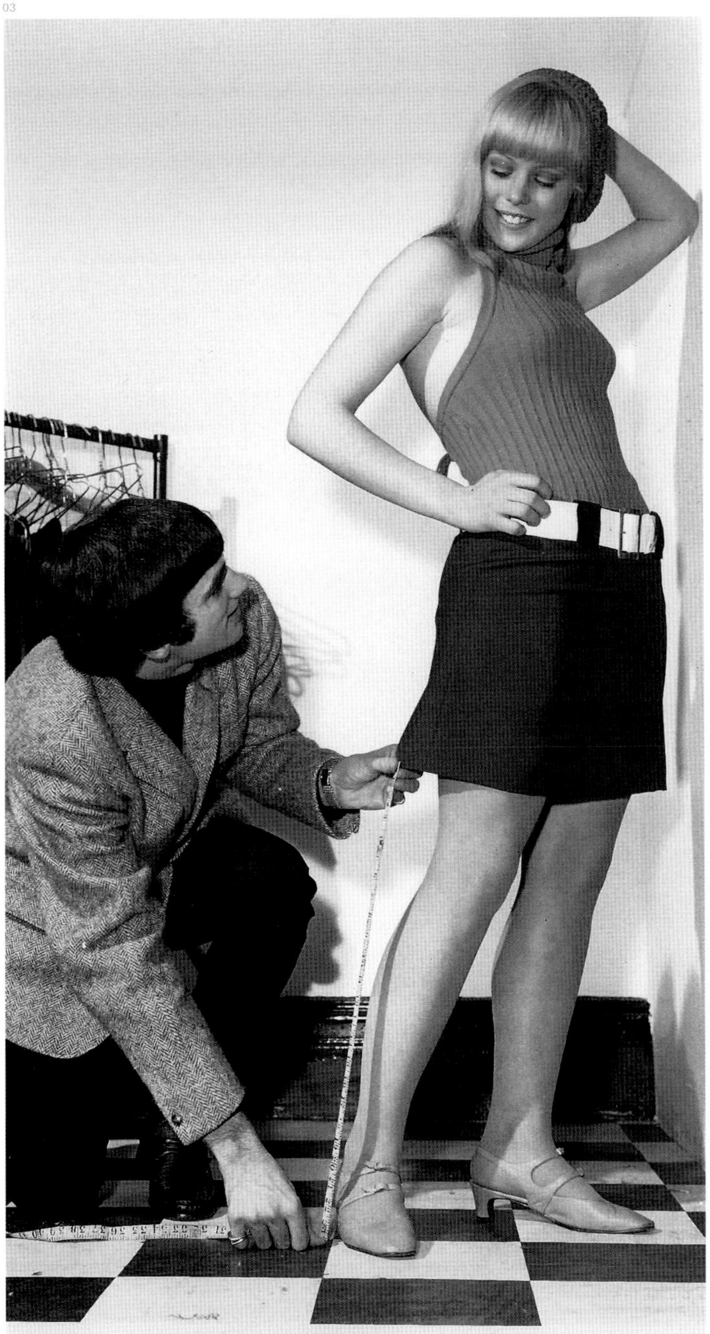

04
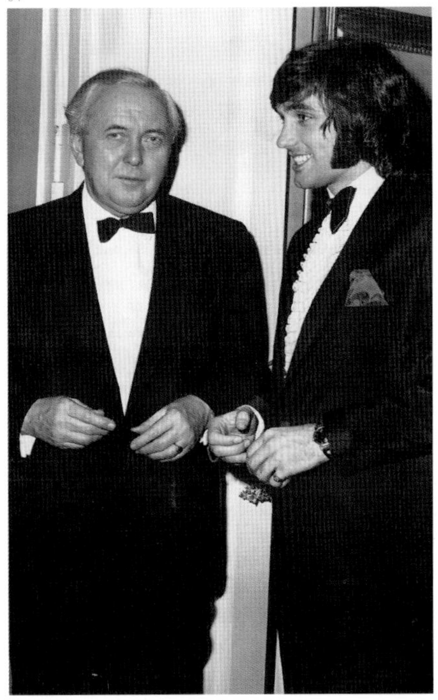

05
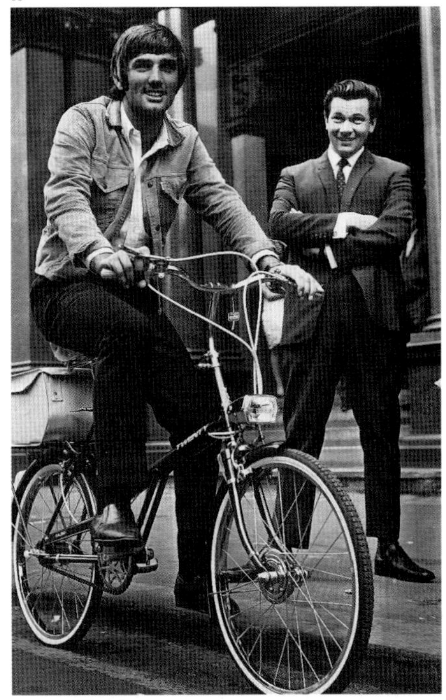

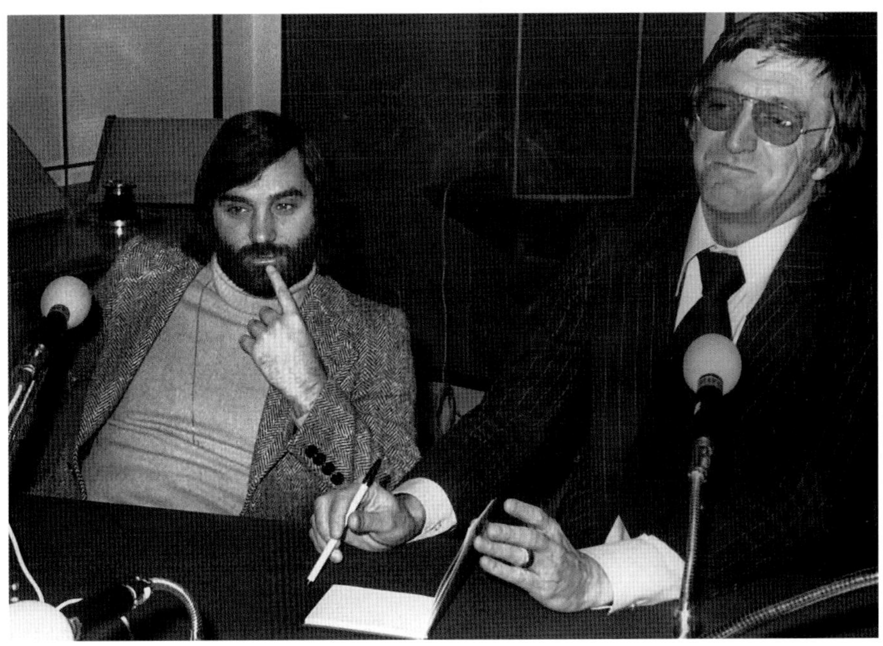
06

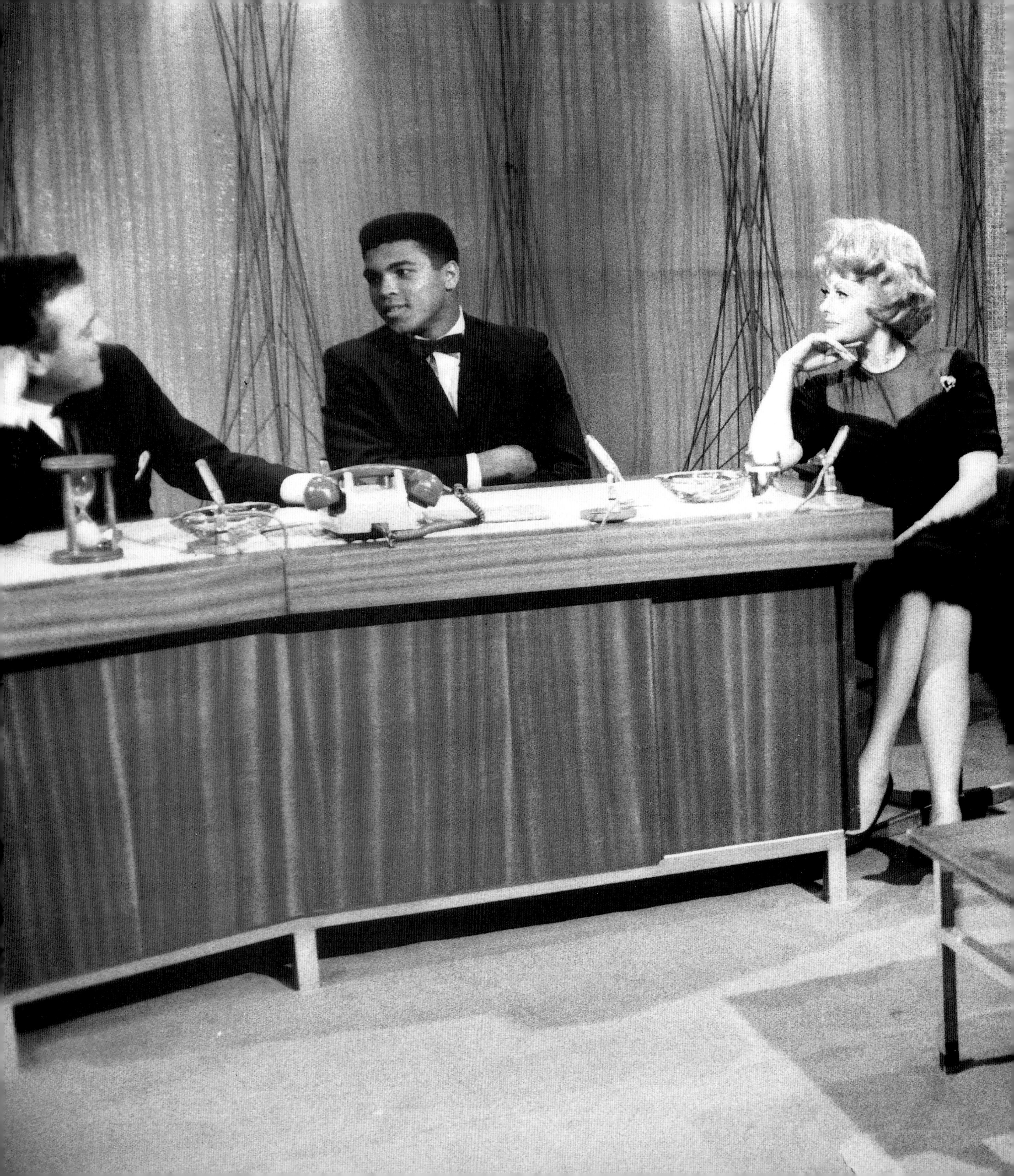

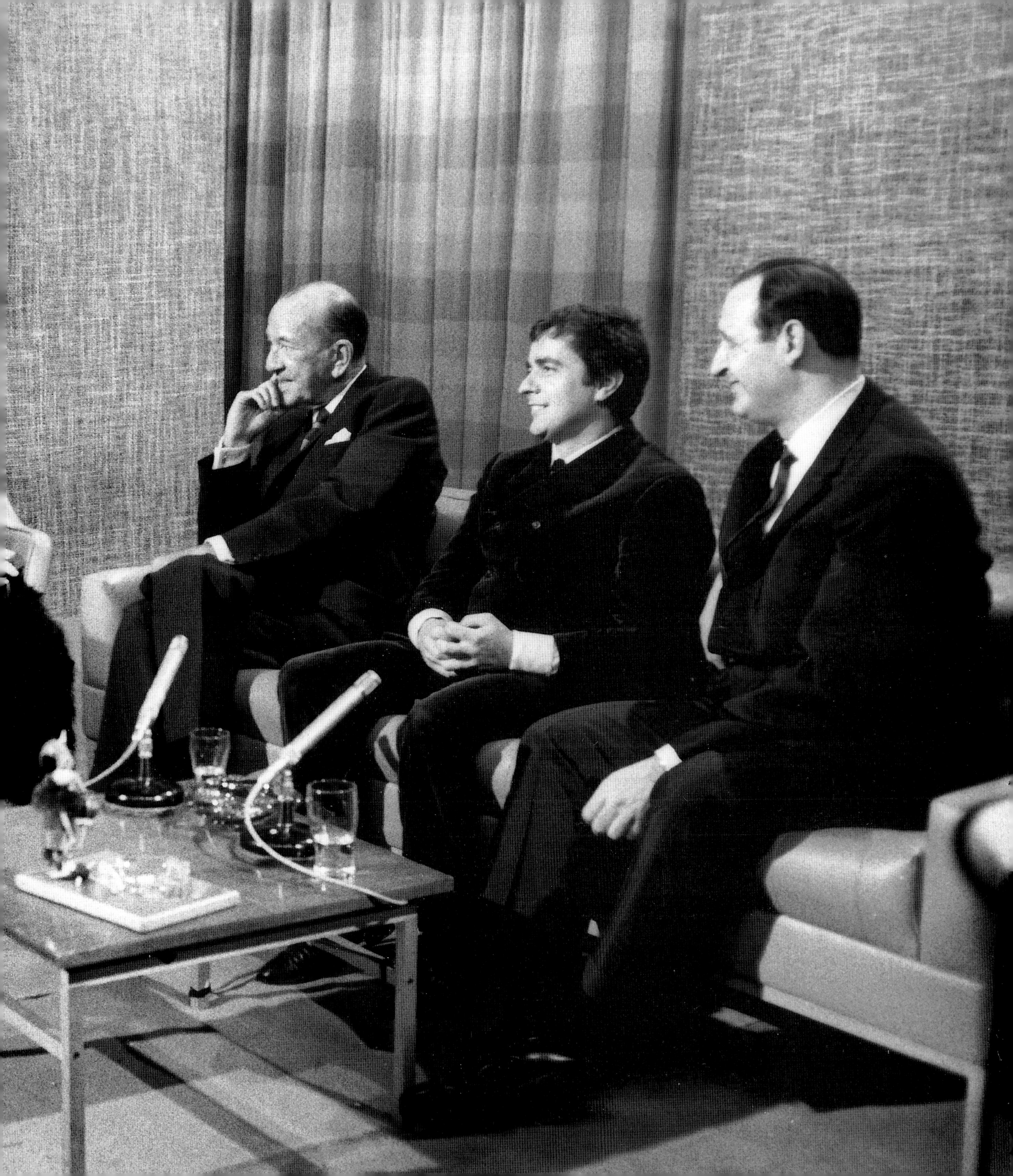

08
Muhammad Ali and his brother Herbert Clay with President Gerald Ford at the White House, 1974

09
Pelé meets Senator Robert Kennedy, 1965

08

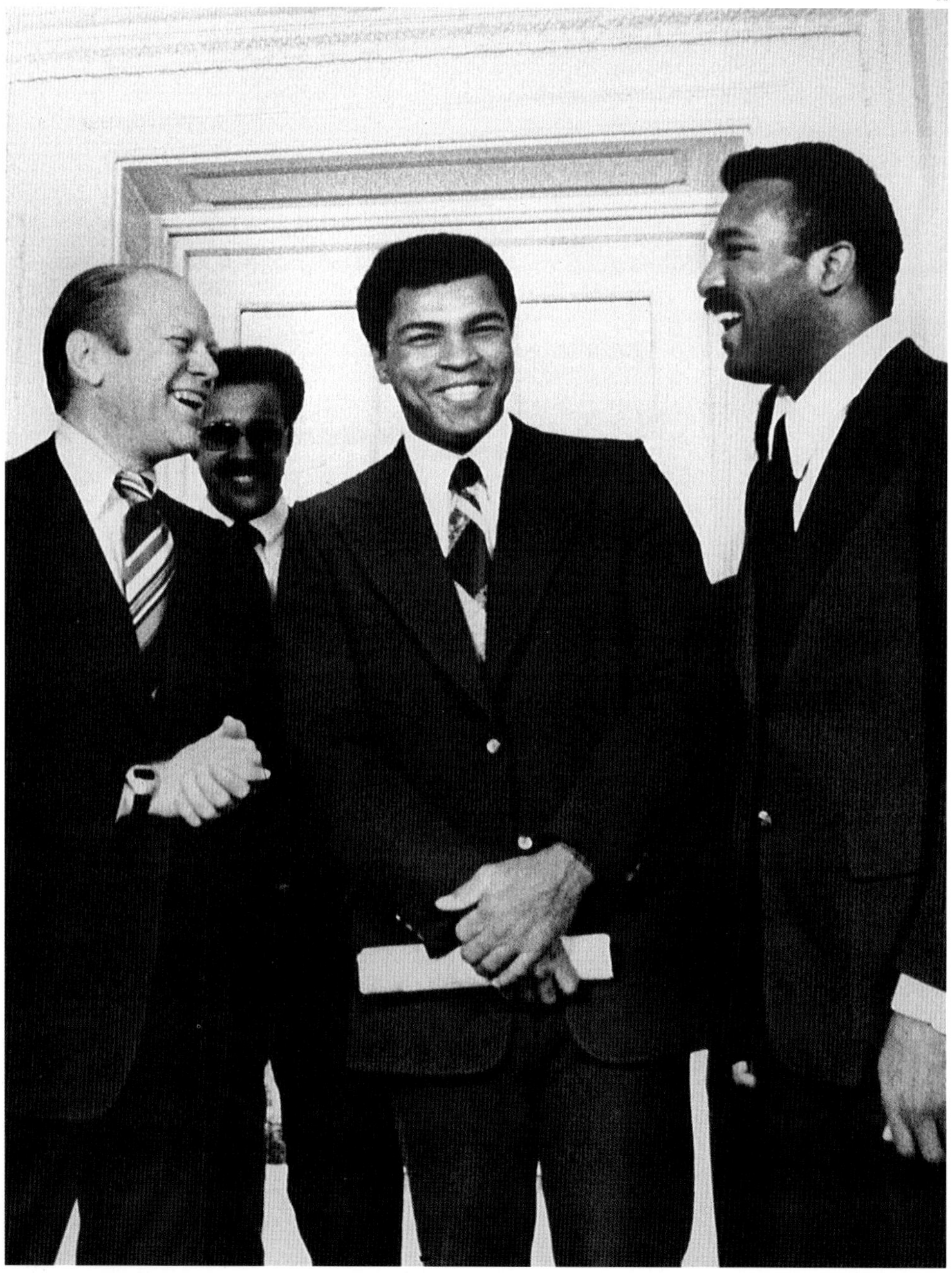

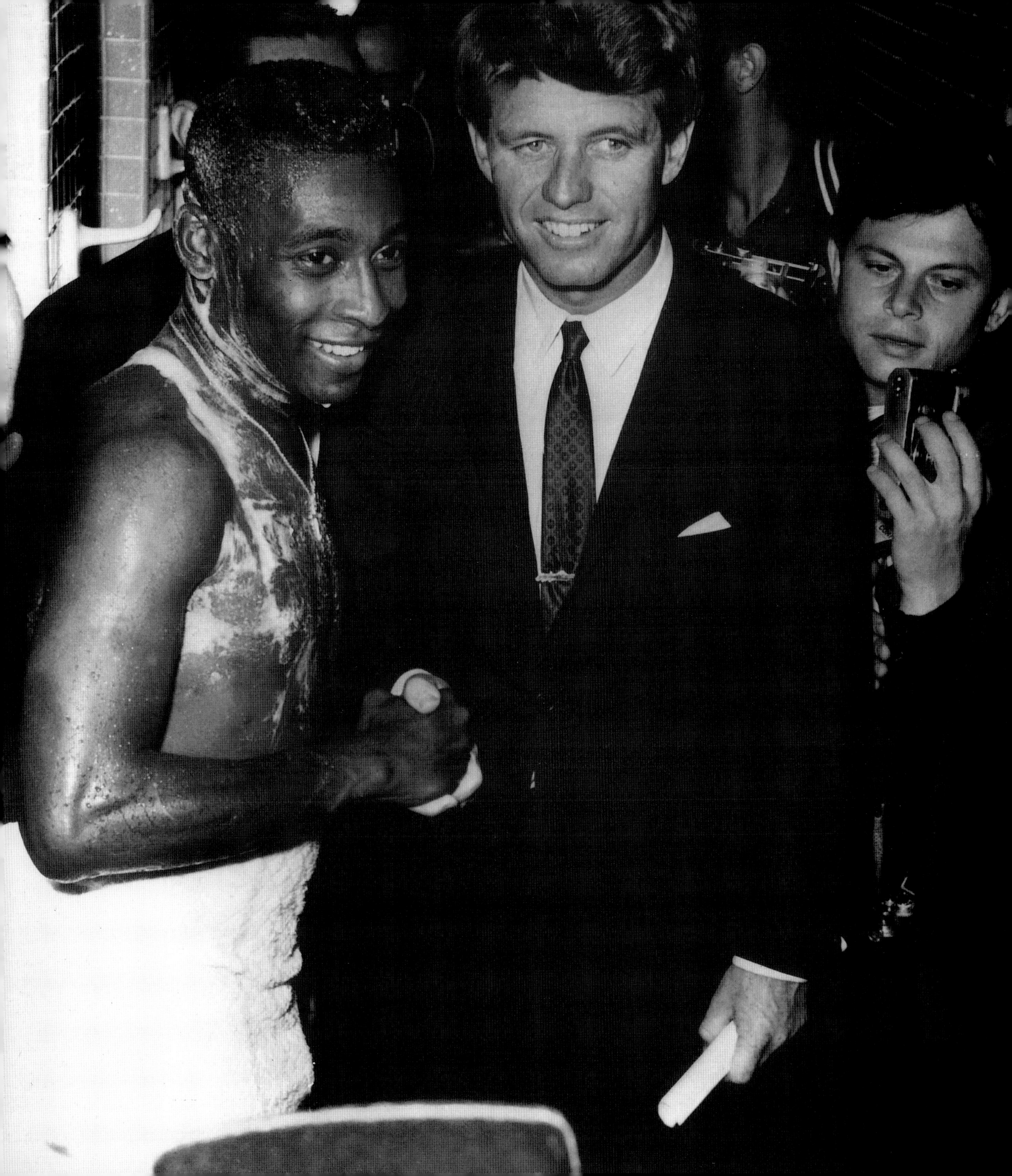

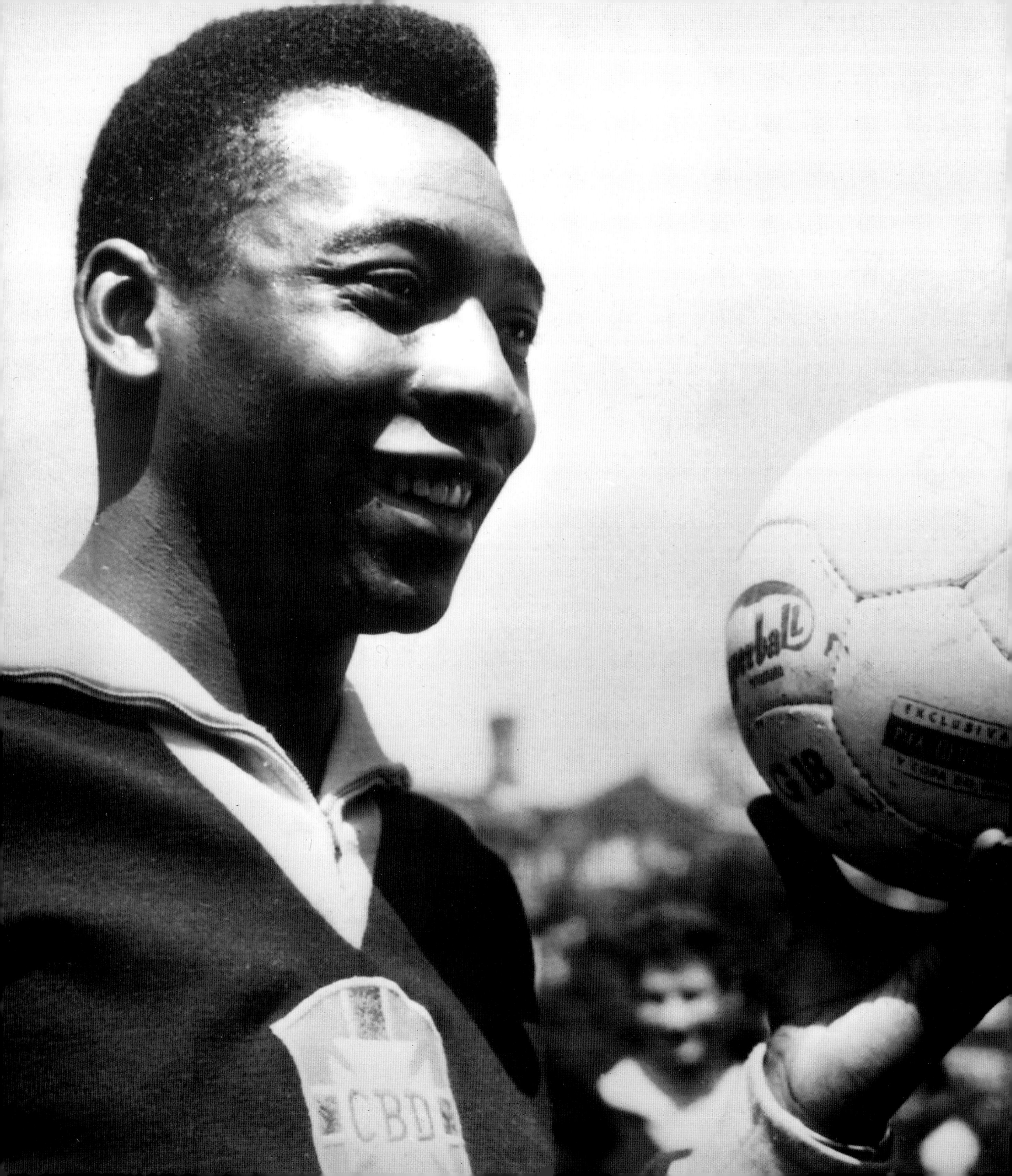
EXCLUSIVA
CBD

10
Pelé, 1963

11
Wax figures of Pelé and Stanley Matthews, 1966

11

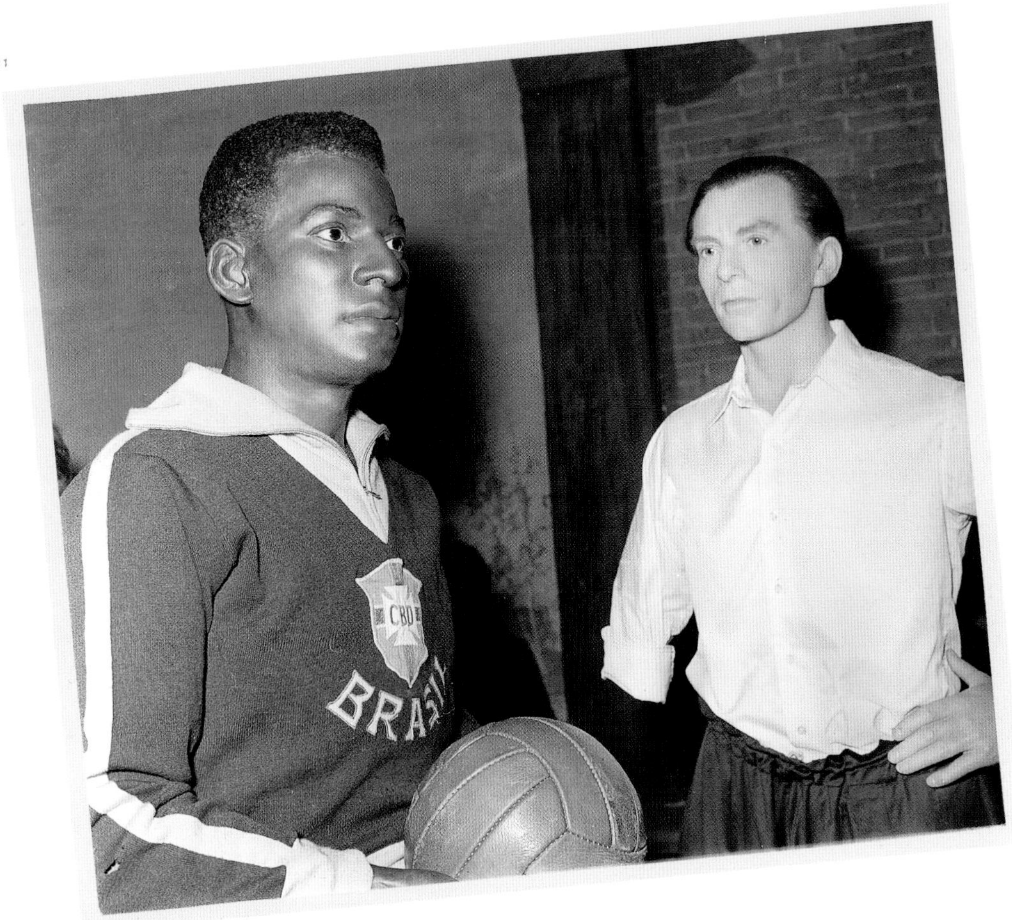

SPEC

TACLE

1980–2000

The triumph of professional sport at the beginning of the twenty-first century is everywhere to be seen. Although mirrored by a decline in amateur participation, spectator sport has never been more popular – television schedules are dominated by it. Global events attract huge television audiences of millions around the world, television channels are dedicated to single sports; sportswear, from tracksuits to ski-wear, from running shoes to soccer shirts has become the dominant street fashion of the day; top stars earn multi-million dollar fees matched by few film stars; pages of sport fill newspapers and magazines. Sport has become a dominant influence in world culture. Inevitably it has also become big business, and commercialism is part and parcel of the modern sports image: all sportswear now carries the manufacturer's name, if not a sponsor's logo, and many top sports stars earn more from endorsement contracts than from prize money.

Where photographic technology had in the past restricted sports photographers in what they could achieve, by the 1980s their equipment had advanced to the point where they were able to capture with ease what their forbears at the turn of the nineteenth century could only dream of. It was now possible to take a picture, apparently from the middle of the pitch, from hundreds of yards away, isolate a subject against a blur of action, freeze a fast-moving object with perfect clarity, trigger a camera remotely so a shot could be taken from inside a racing car or from the back of a hockey goal, or fire off many frames a second with a motorized camera, recording every precious moment of a race. Computer technology can then transmit the images to the four corners of the world in a matter of seconds.

Throughout the 1980s newspapers devoted more and more space to sport, with extensive daily coverage and regular sport-only supplements. The computer revolution in the publishing industry made it possible for hundreds of new magazines on every imaginable subject, not least sport, to emerge and find an eager readership. Photographers could now dedicate themselves to sport alone, and one aspect of this process of specialization has been for sports photography to become more abstract, reporting less directly on the sporting event, and more concerned with creating a feeling of excitement, colour and speed. Unable to compete with television coverage photographers have been forced to find new ways of showing their subject, creating startling photographic visions of sport that television could never achieve. These images make for dramatic spreads in magazines and have also helped the sports photograph to cross into new contexts, beyond sport. Representing aspirational lifestyle values, excitement and success, the sophisticated world of advertising has made extensive use of sporting images and personalities.

The significance of great sporting achievements at the end of the twentieth century will be easier to judge in years to come, but Michael Jordan stands out as perhaps the most famous sportsman of the modern era and Wayne Gretzky has dominated his sport as ice hockey's greatest ever player. Martina Navratilova's record makes her the most successful tennis player of the century, Carl Lewis will be remembered as one of the century's top Olympians, with gold medals in four consecutive Games, and golfer Tiger Woods is already showing signs that he might be a contender for the greatest sportsman of the twenty-first century.

01
Ed Moses, Los Angeles, 1984
Tony Duffy

02
Carl Lewis, Los Angeles, 1984

03 (OVERLEAF)
Carl Lewis, Los Angeles, 1984
David Cannon

SPECTATOR

Just as the early photographers of sport took their subjects into the studio to isolate them against plain backgrounds, or artificially painted around figures to pick them out clearly, the modern sports photographer can achieve the same ends by manipulating his picture so the background becomes a harmonious field against which the action and movement of the athlete is accentuated. Using a bank of spectators as a backdrop, or allowing the stadium to blur into a wash of colour, no longer do the athletes have to visit the studio, nor is painstaking work done in the darkroom; the flexibility of modern cameras allows the skilled photographer to create a backdrop 'in the camera', isolating the figure of the athlete in a perfectly controlled environment.

01

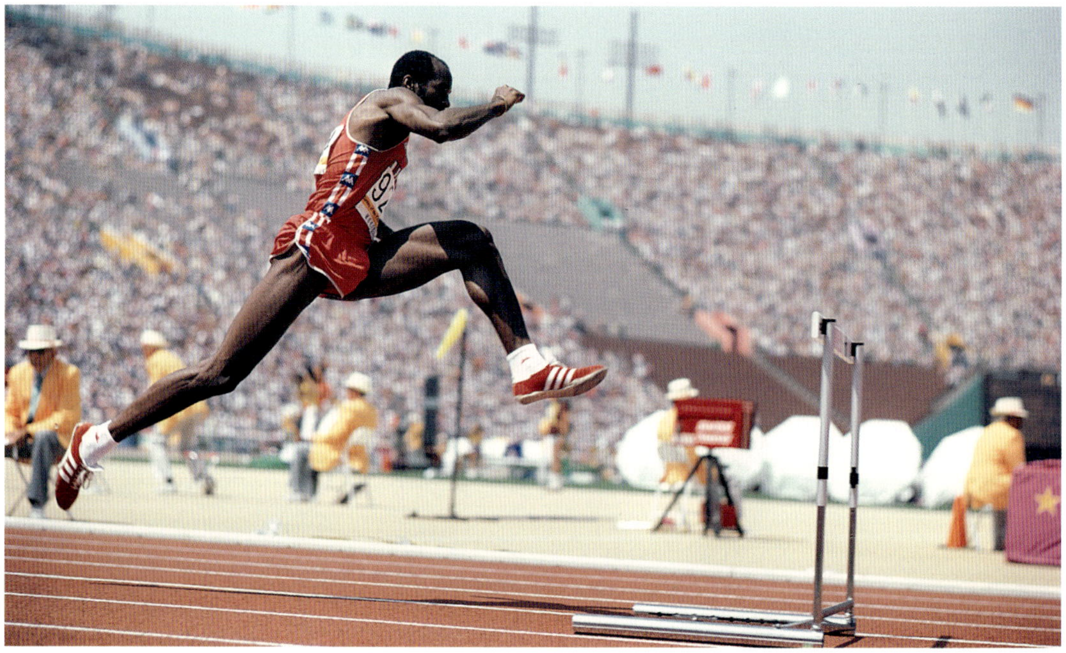

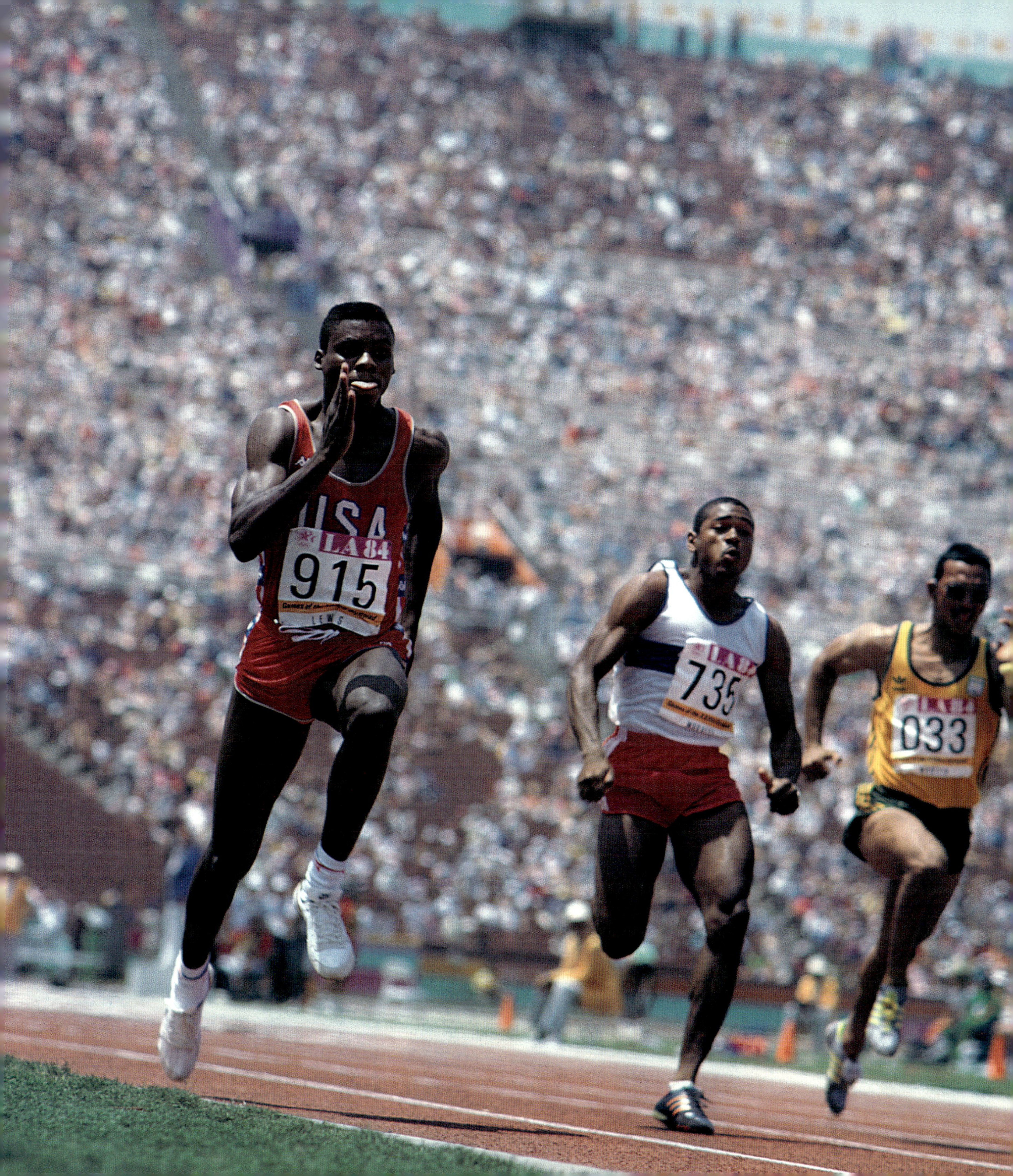
USA
LA 84
915
735
033

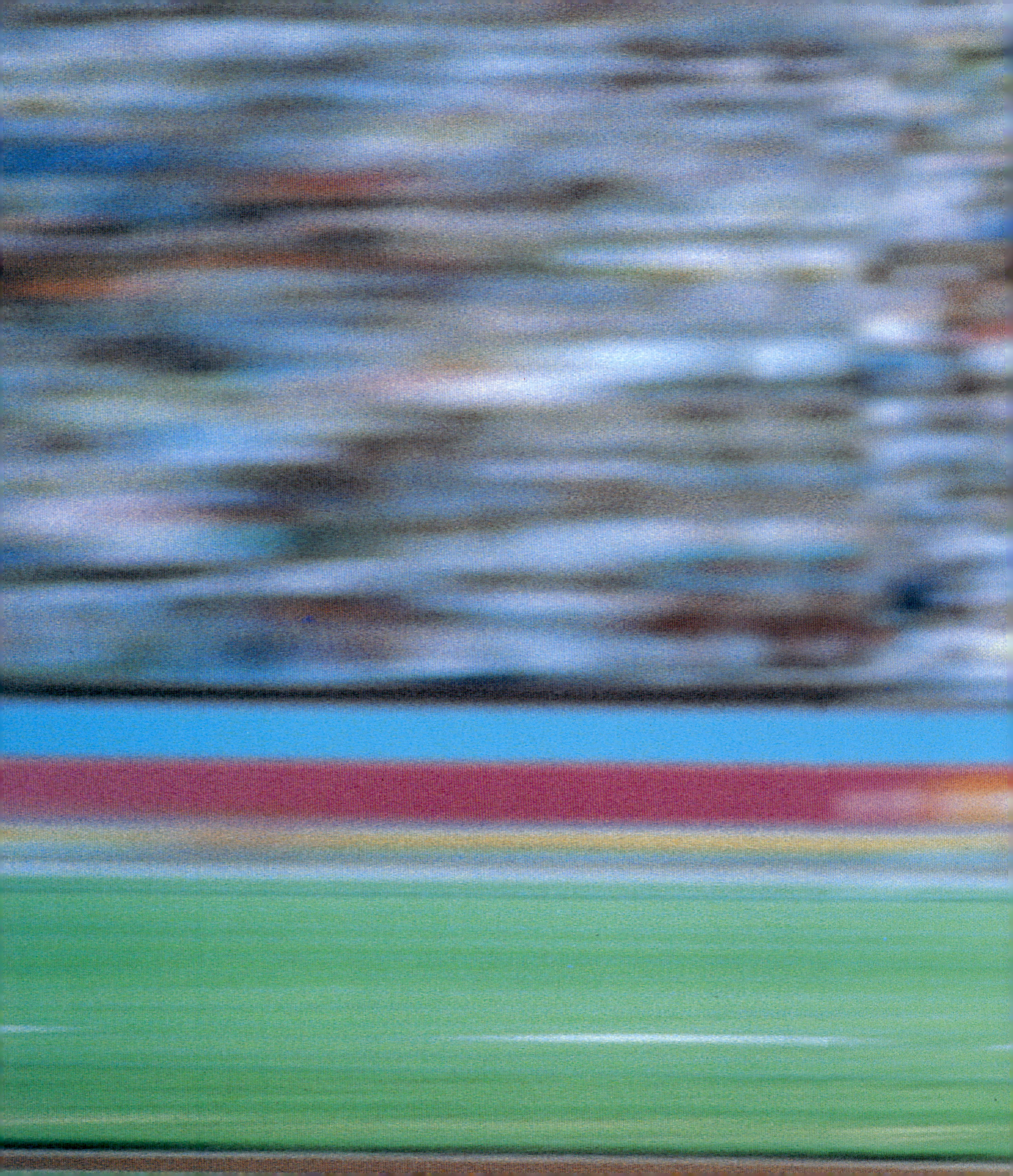

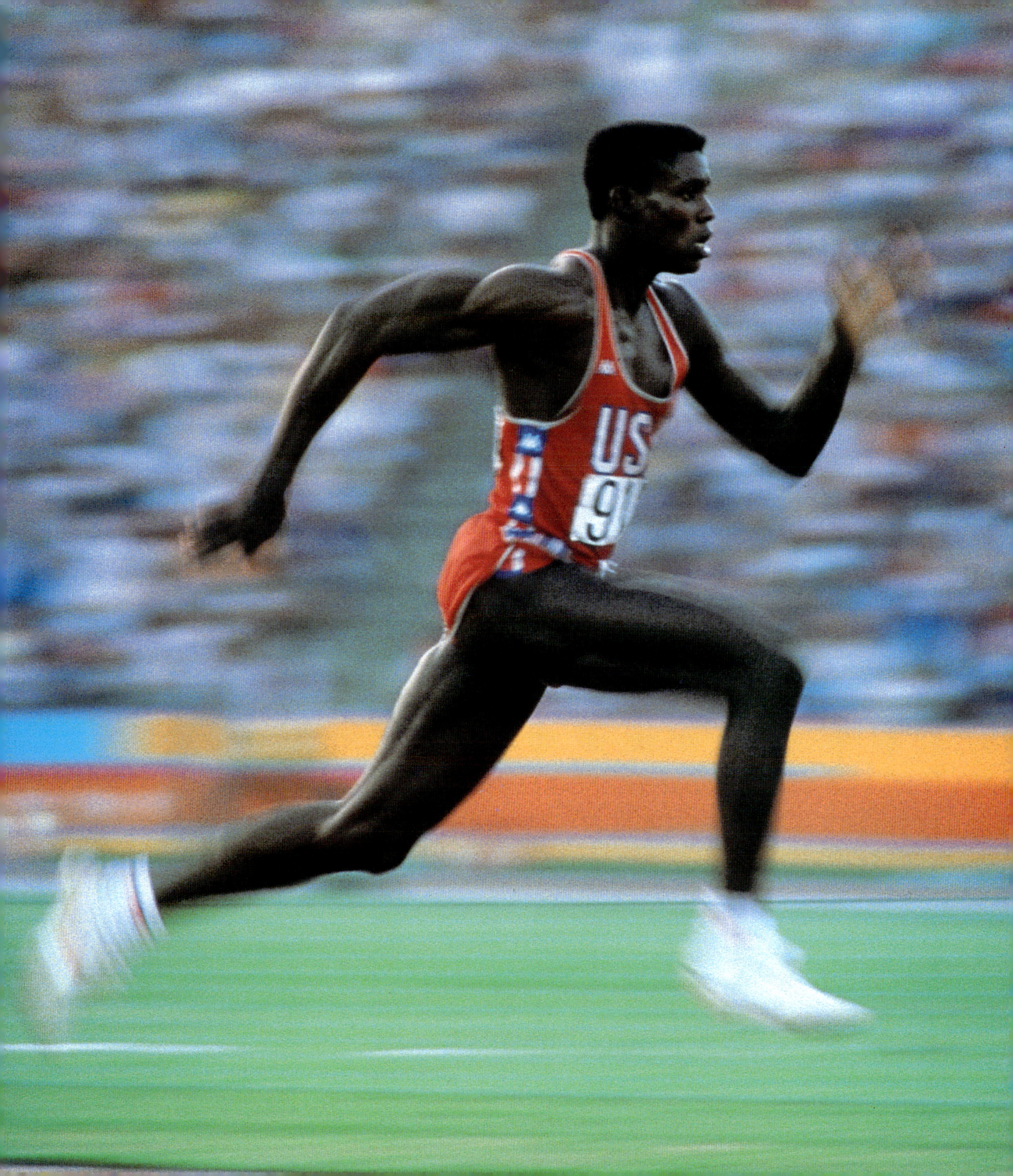
US

01
A camera above the start line shows Ben Johnson take a lead straight from the gun
Yann Guichaoua

02–08, 10–13 (OVERLEAF)
The race unfolds second by second
Bruno Bade

09 (OVERLEAF)
During the race
Billy Stickland

9.79

The 1988 Olympic men's 100m final in Seoul, Korea, was one of the most eagerly anticipated races of the century. The fastest men in the world lined up: Da Silva, Stewart, Lewis, Christie, Smith, Johnson, Williams and Mitchell, with Canadian Ben Johnson and American Carl Lewis expected to be in contention for the gold medal. Using the motor-driven camera, every moment of the race was recorded. Frame by frame we can see the story of the race unfold, with Johnson winning in a new world record time of 9.79 seconds.

The race had lived up to all the hype; the world had witnessed an historic sporting event in which Johnson had proved himself the fastest man on earth. But what we saw was not the real story, because that had not taken place in front of the cameras. Three days after his victory, officials announced that Johnson had tested positive for performance enhancing drugs. He was stripped of the world record and gold medal and Lewis was awarded the title.

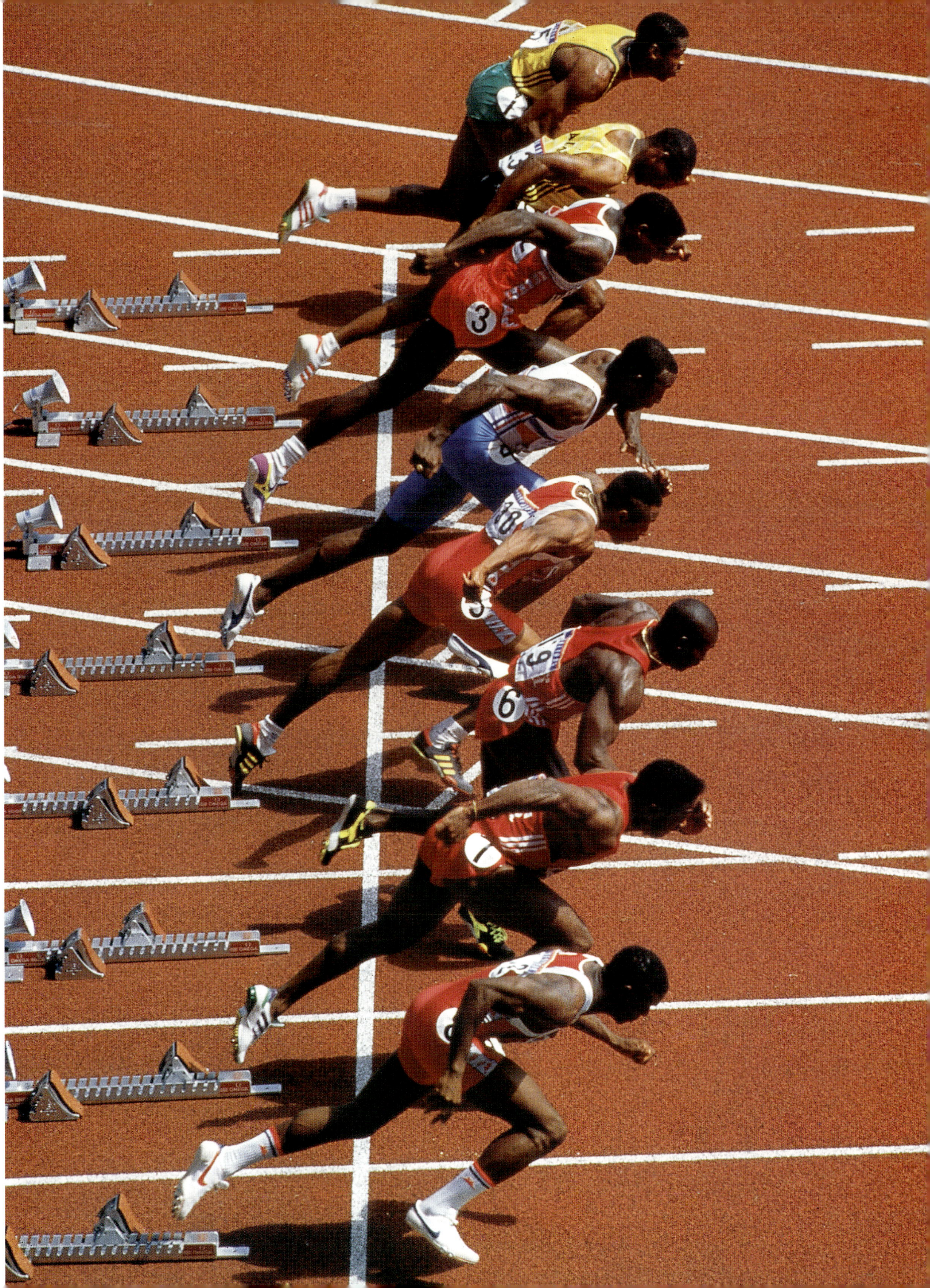

02

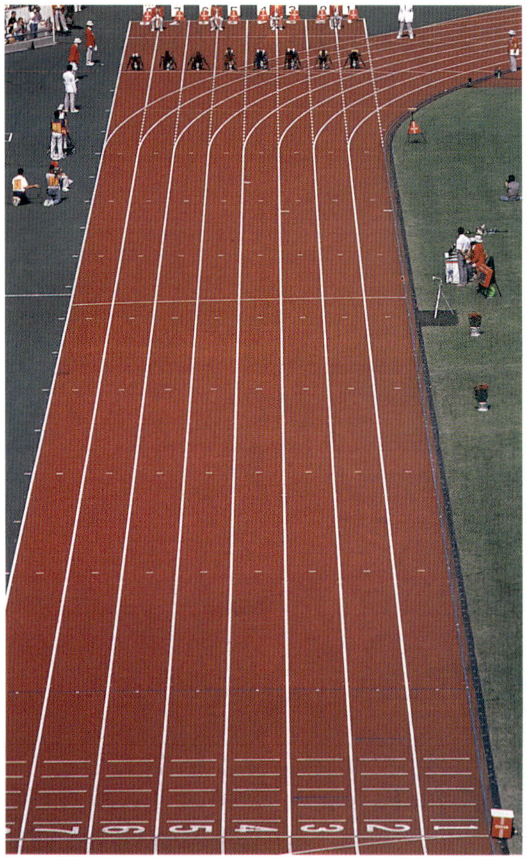

03

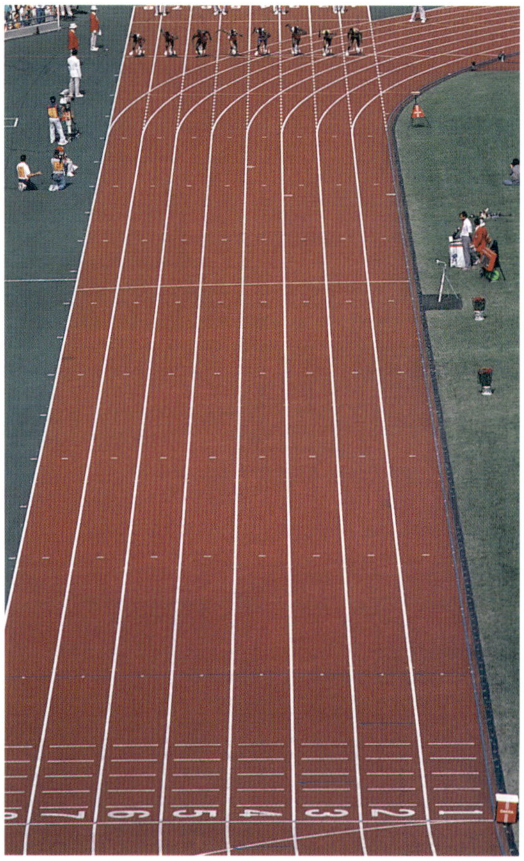

04

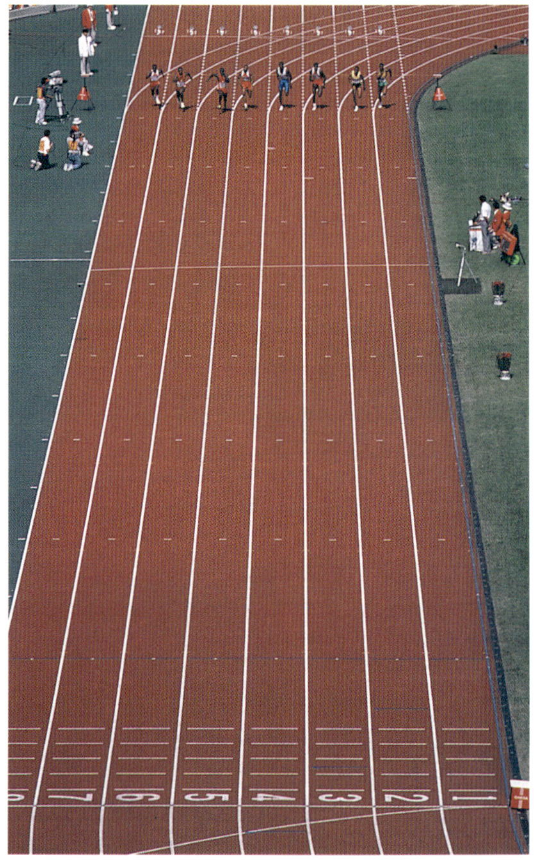

08

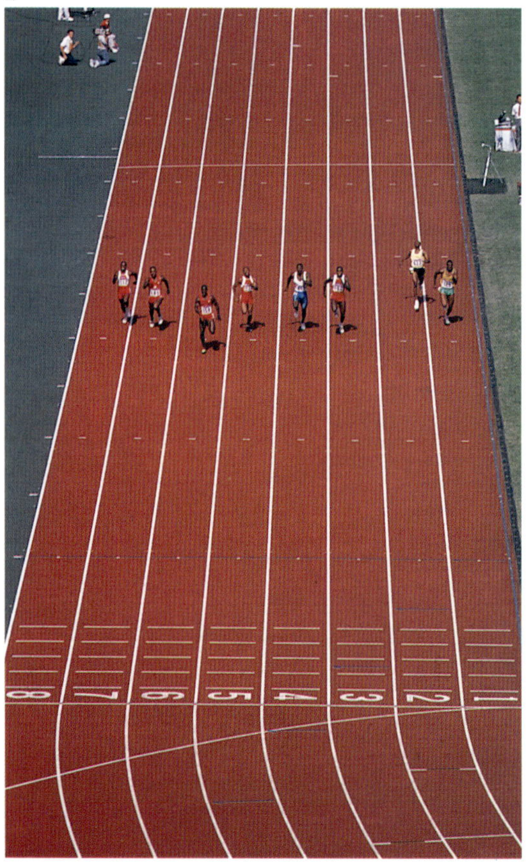

09

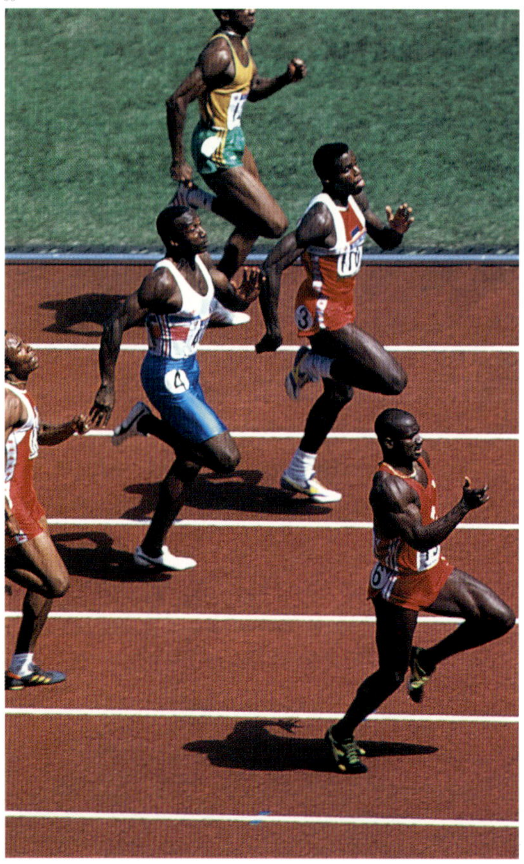

10

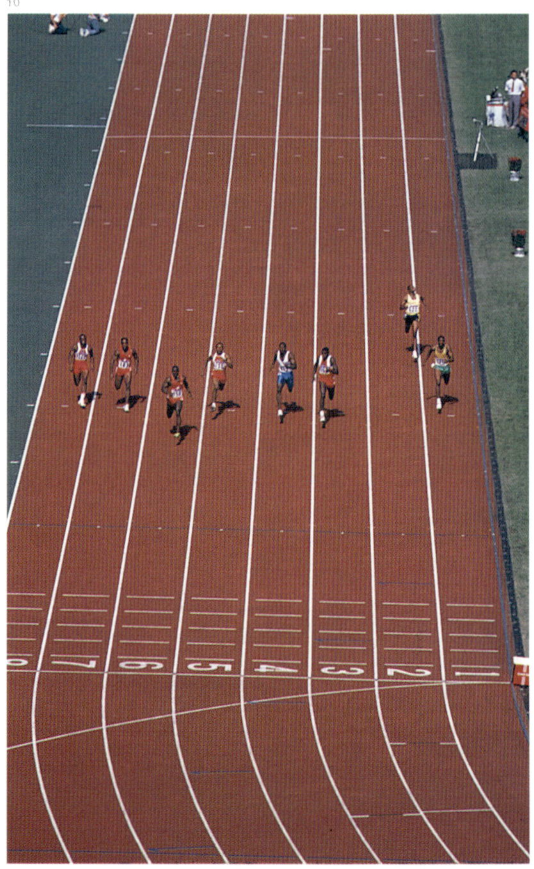

05

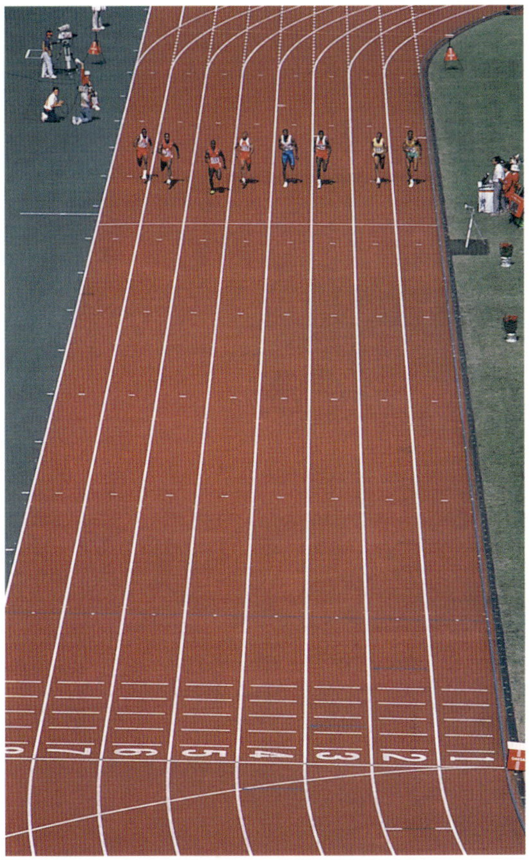

06

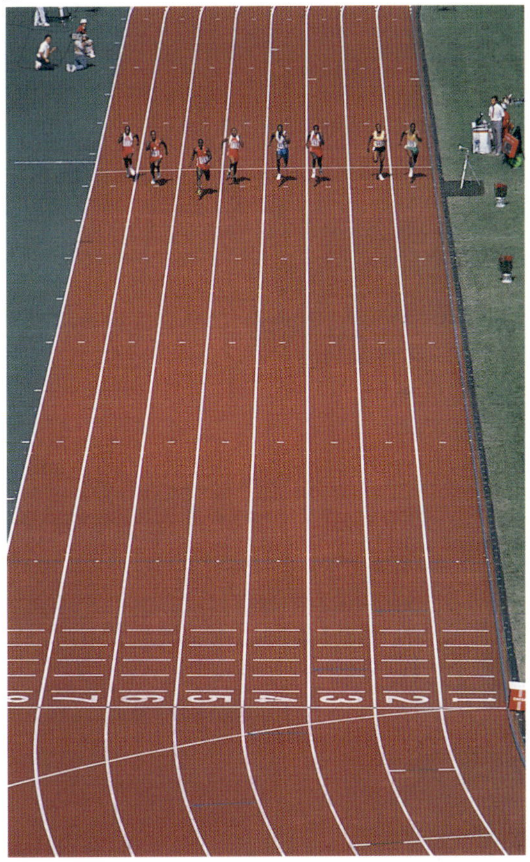

07

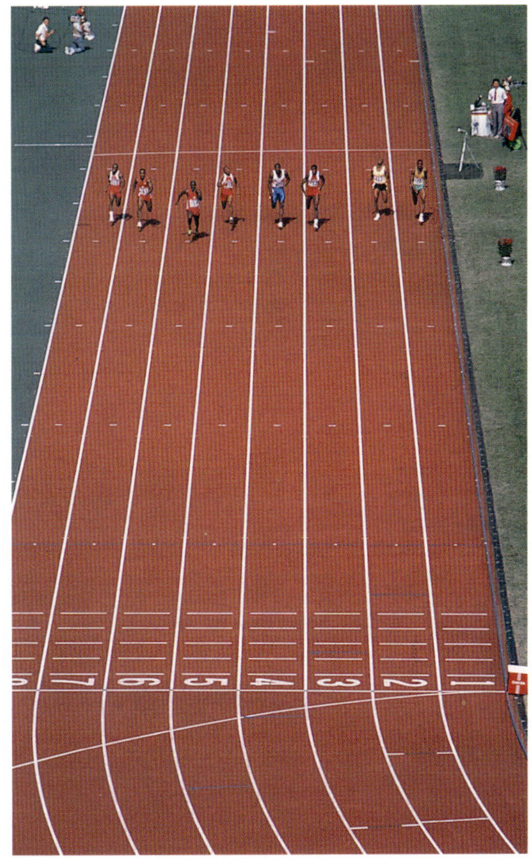

11

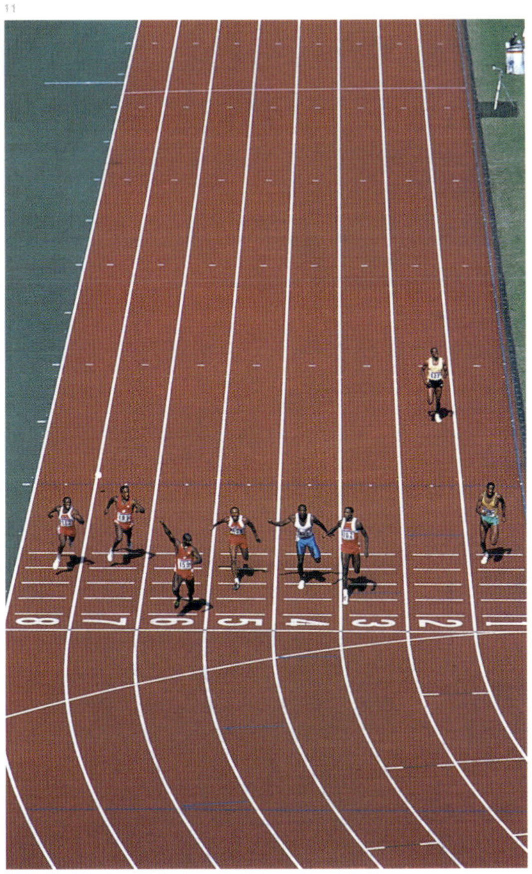

12

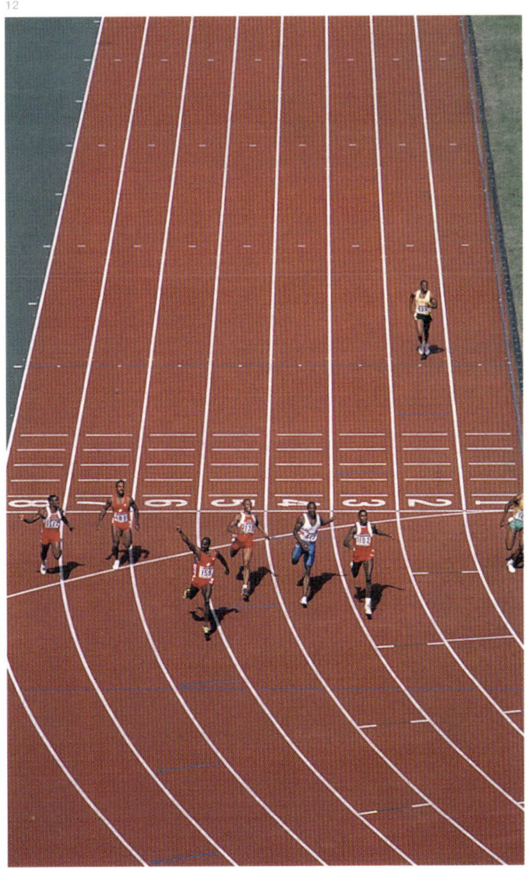

13

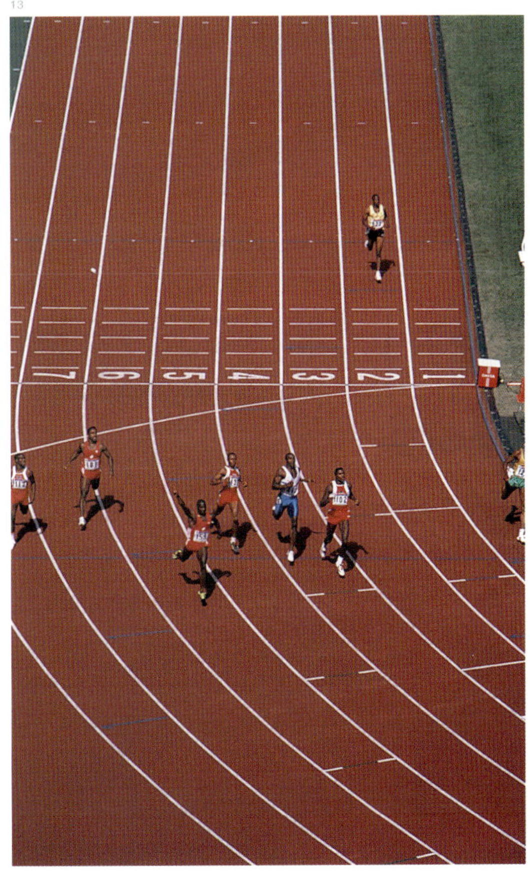

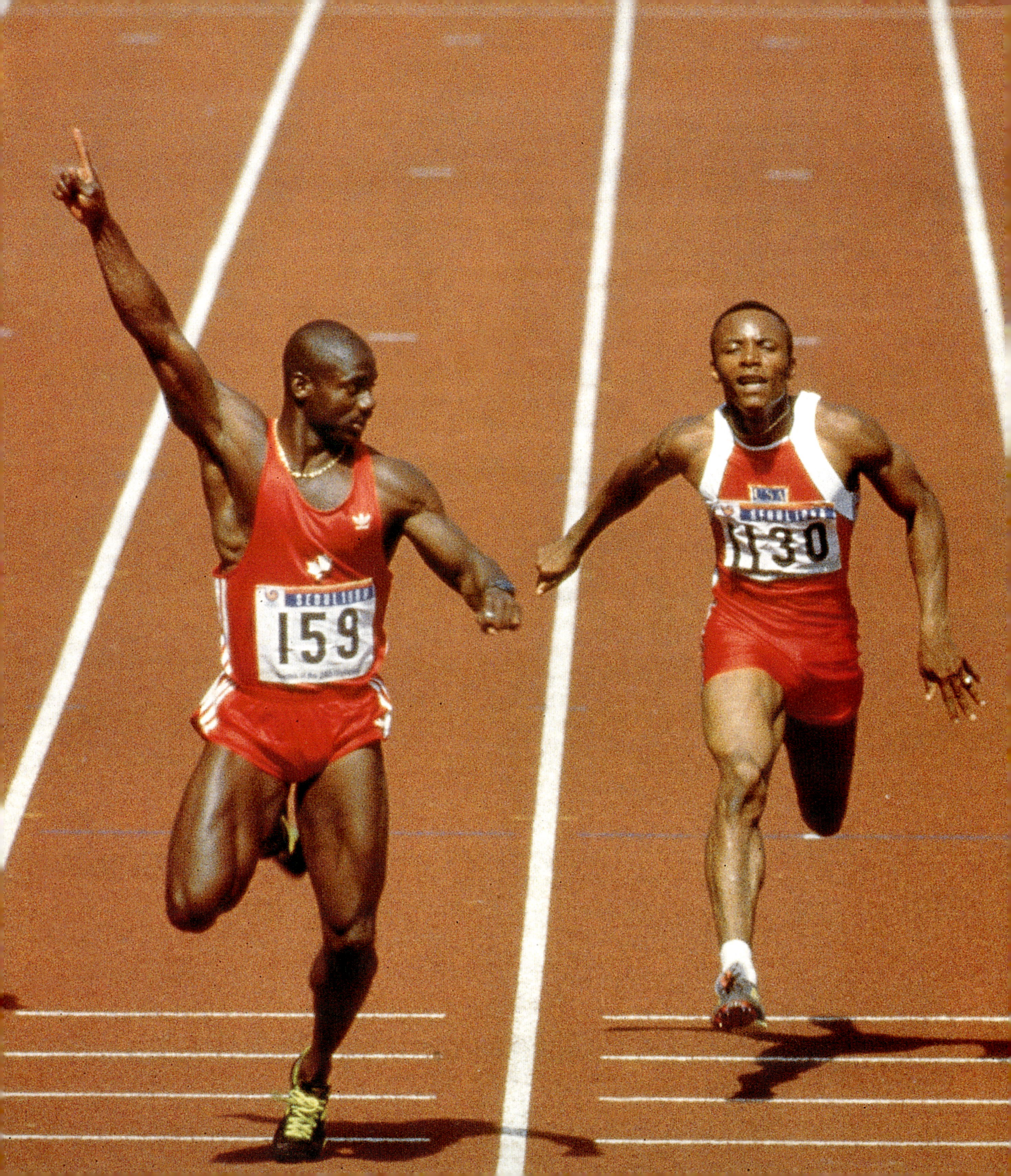

USA
159

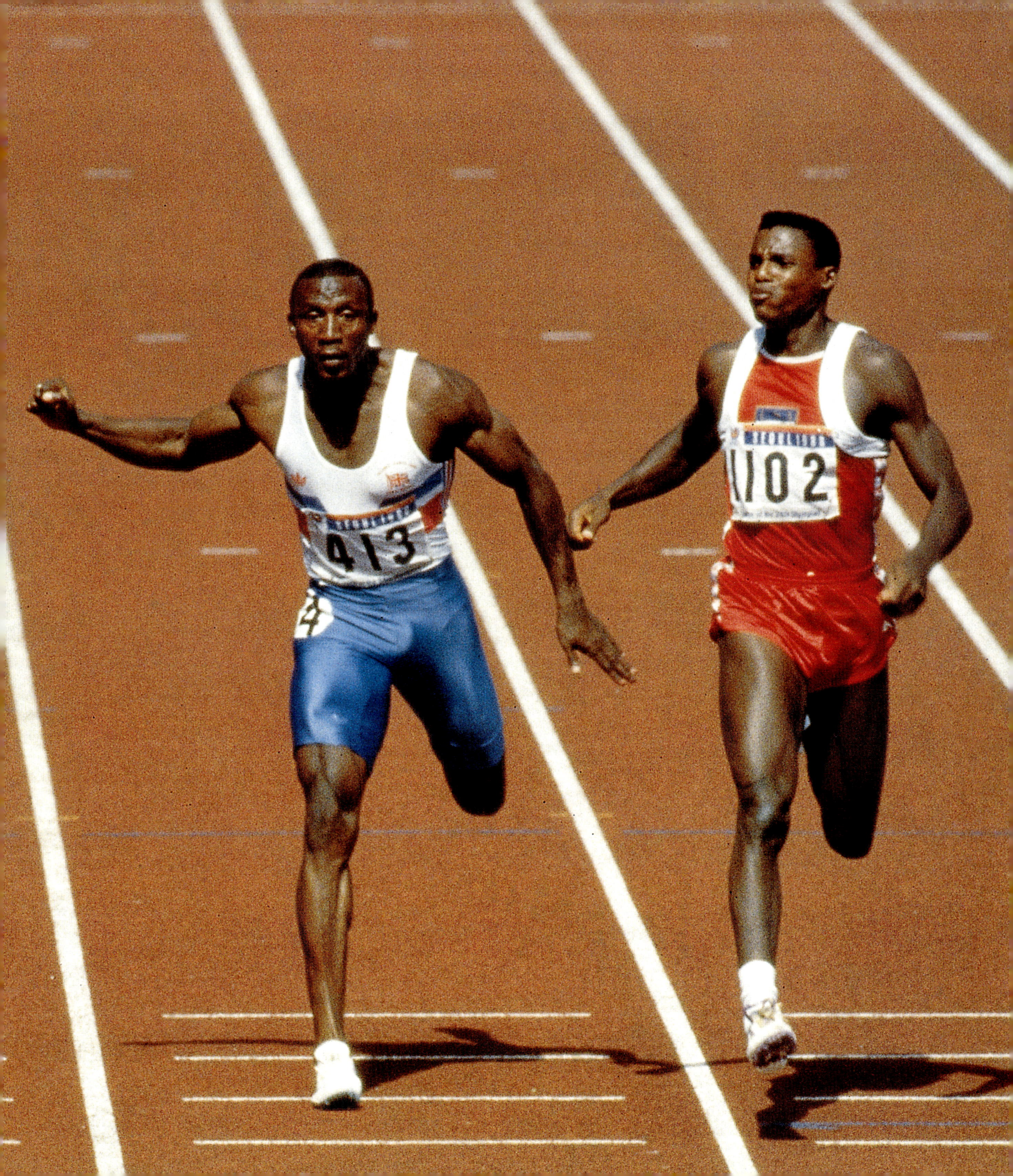
413
4
1102

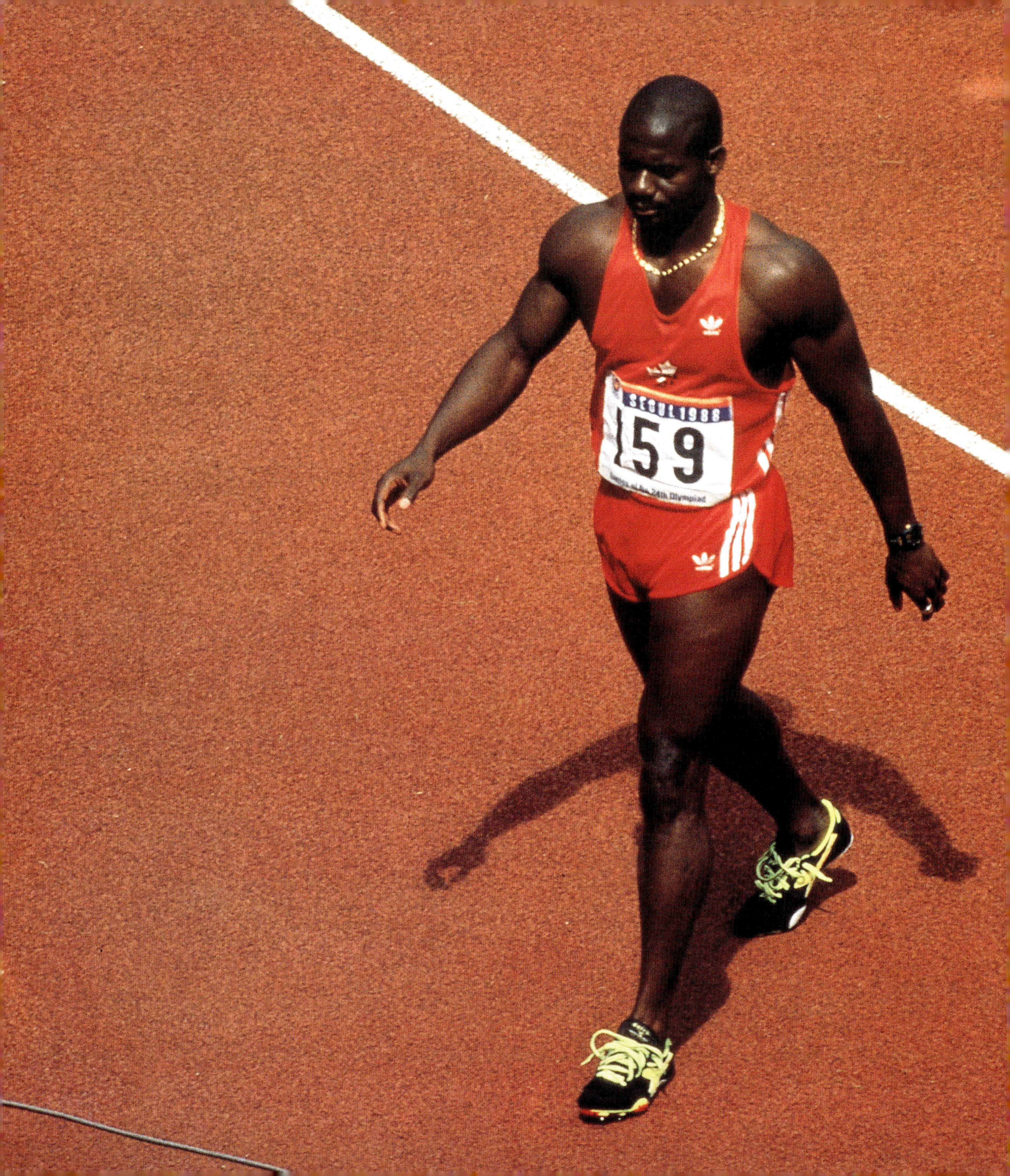
SEOUL 1988
159

14 (PREVIOUS PAGE)
Ben Johnson looks over to see Carl Lewis (far right) finish behind him
Jean-Marc Loubat

15
The victorious Ben Johnson walks away

FLAGS

In a world where the logos of clothing manufacturers are more visible than national flags, nationhood still plays a significant role in sport. Participating and winning medals at major sporting events like the Olympics is seen by all nations as an important opportunity to show off the sporting prowess of its citizens. This is more important for developing countries who are using sport to create a modern international identity for their country, equal to the more established and more powerful nations of the world. These photographs of athletes celebrating, dressed in their national flag, are intended both for domestic and international consumption. With the knowledge that the cameras will follow the winner, the athletes give their home fans a chance to celebrate the nation's victory, while at the same time taking the opportunity to put the national colours in front of the world's media and to promote their country as equal competitors on the international stage.

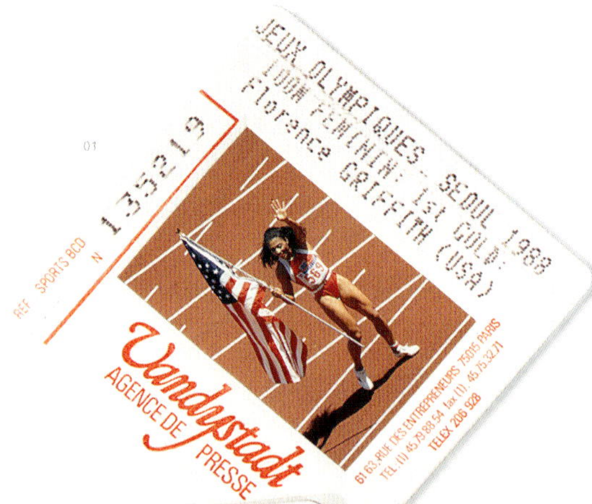

01

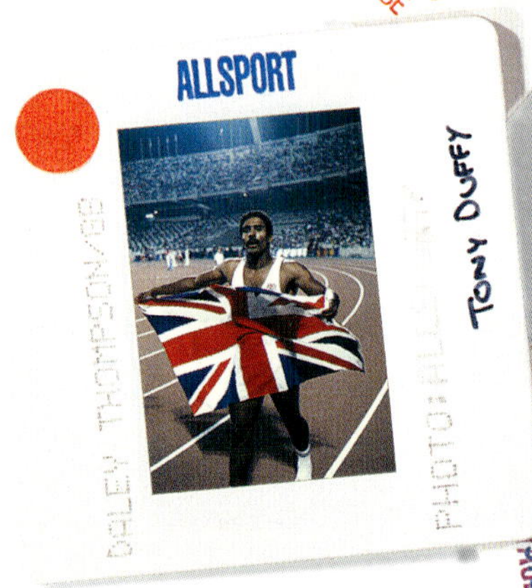

02

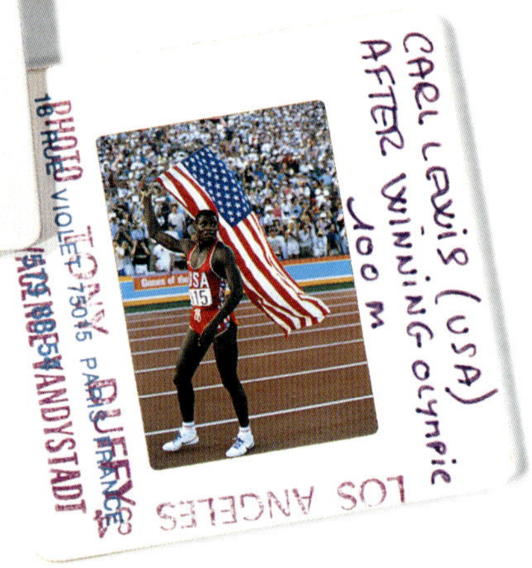

03

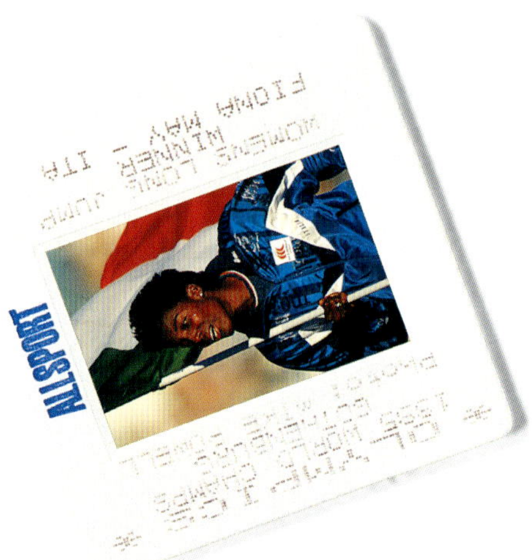

04

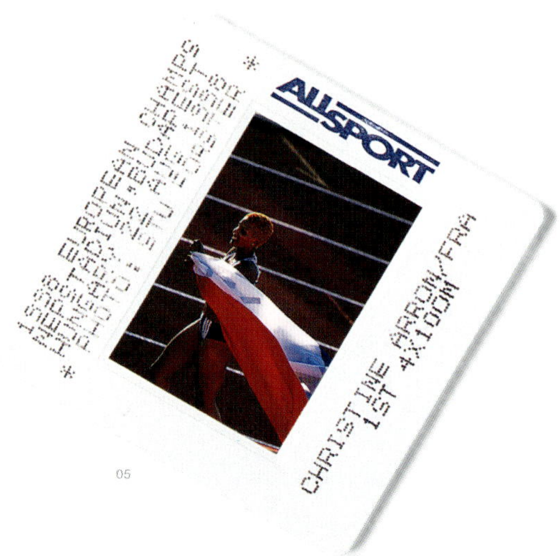

05

01
Florence Griffith-Joyner, Seoul, 1988
Gerard Vandystadt

02
Daley Thompson, Athens, 1982
Tony Duffy

03
Carl Lewis, Los Angeles, 1984
Tony Duffy

04
Fiona May, Gothenburg, 1995
Mike Powell

05
Christine Arron, Budapest, 1998
Stu Forster

06
Sam Matete, Victoria, Canada, 1994
Mike Powell

07
Hicham El Guerrouj, Seville, 1999
Shaun Botterill

08
Christine Arron, Budapest, 1998
Mark Thompson

09
Michael Johnson, Atlanta, 1996
Mike Hewitt

10
Florin Ionescu, Gothenburg, 1996
Mike Powell

11
Gillian Russell, Plovdiv, Bulgaria, 1990
Gray Mortimore

12
Scottie Pippen, Michael Jordan and Clide Drexler, Barcelona, 1992
Mike Powell

13
Olabisi Afolabi, Atlanta, 1996
Stu Forster

14
Deon Hemmings, Atlanta, 1996
Mike Hewitt

06
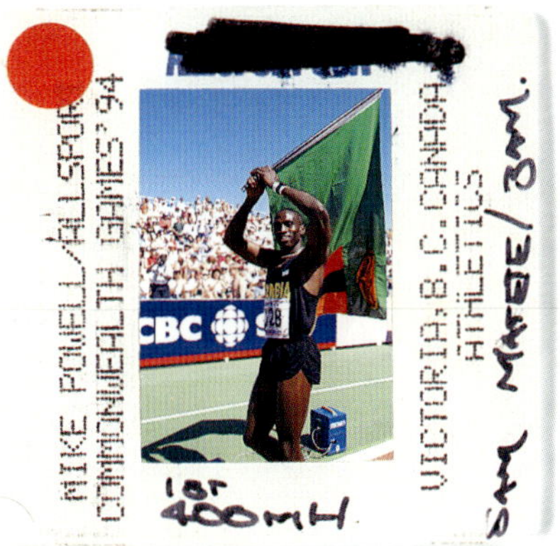

07
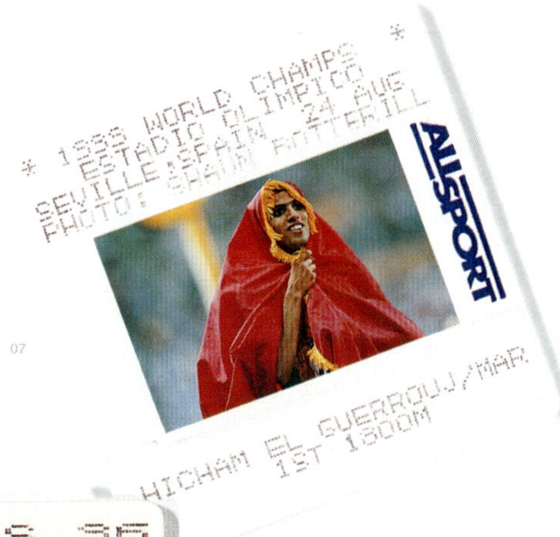

08
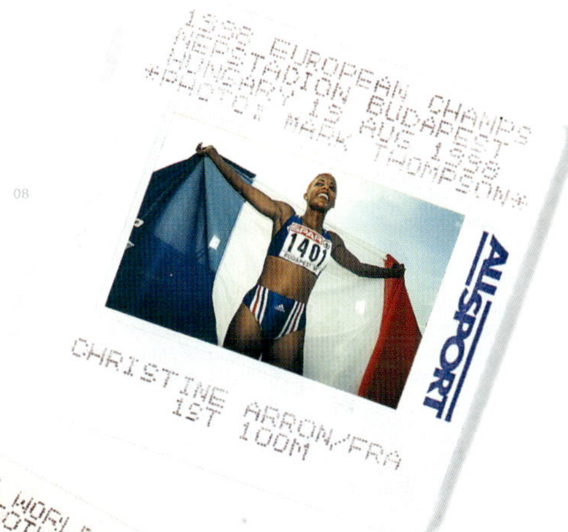

09
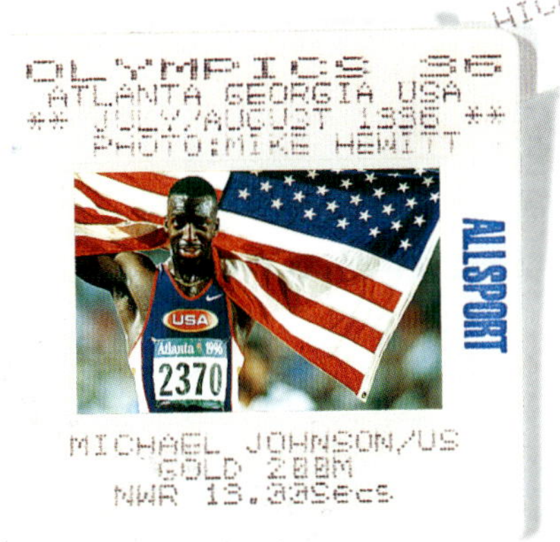

10

11
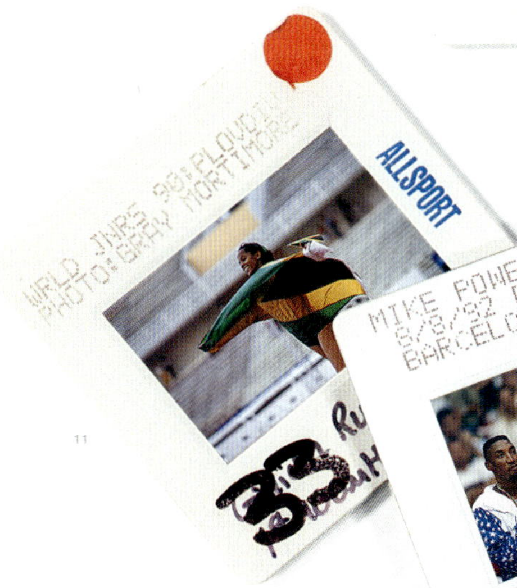

12

13
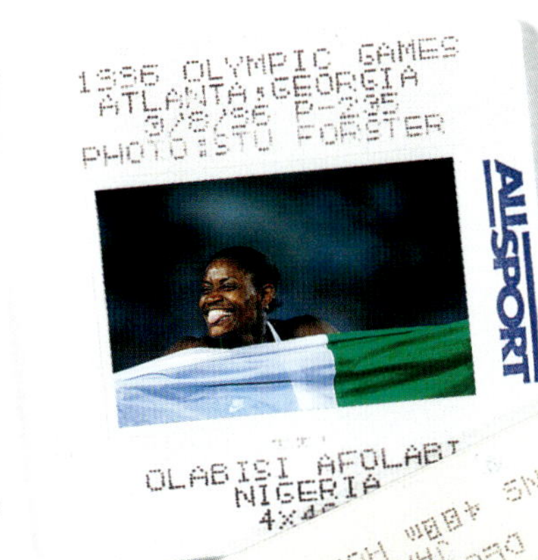

14
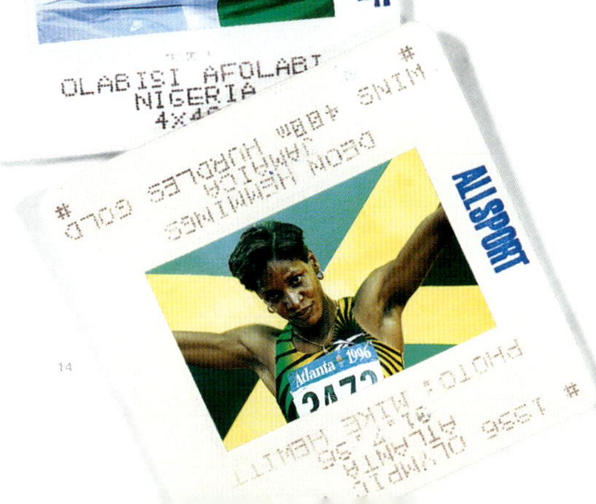

01
Practice session for Alain Prost in his Renault, 1982
Bernard Asset

02 (OVERLEAF)
Junior World Championship wrestling, Sydney, 1999
Adam Pretty

REMOTE CONTROL

Use of the remote control camera, that can automatically release the shutter without the presence of the photographer, continues the tradition of the 'impossible shot'. By placing the camera in unusual or dangerous positions and using long shutter releases or electronic signals to expose the film, photographers have created images that place the spectator in impossible positions to view sporting events. Sometimes this gives the impression of a surveillance camera viewing from above or total spectator involvement right from the heart of the action.

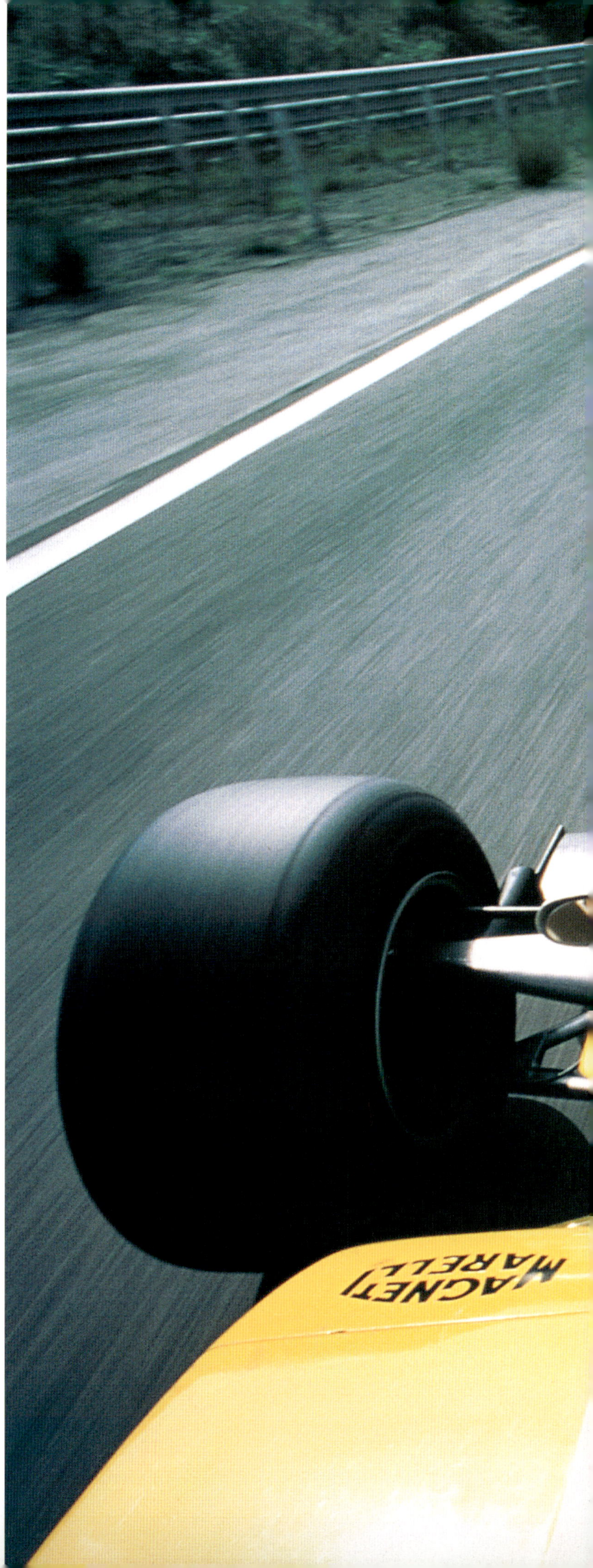

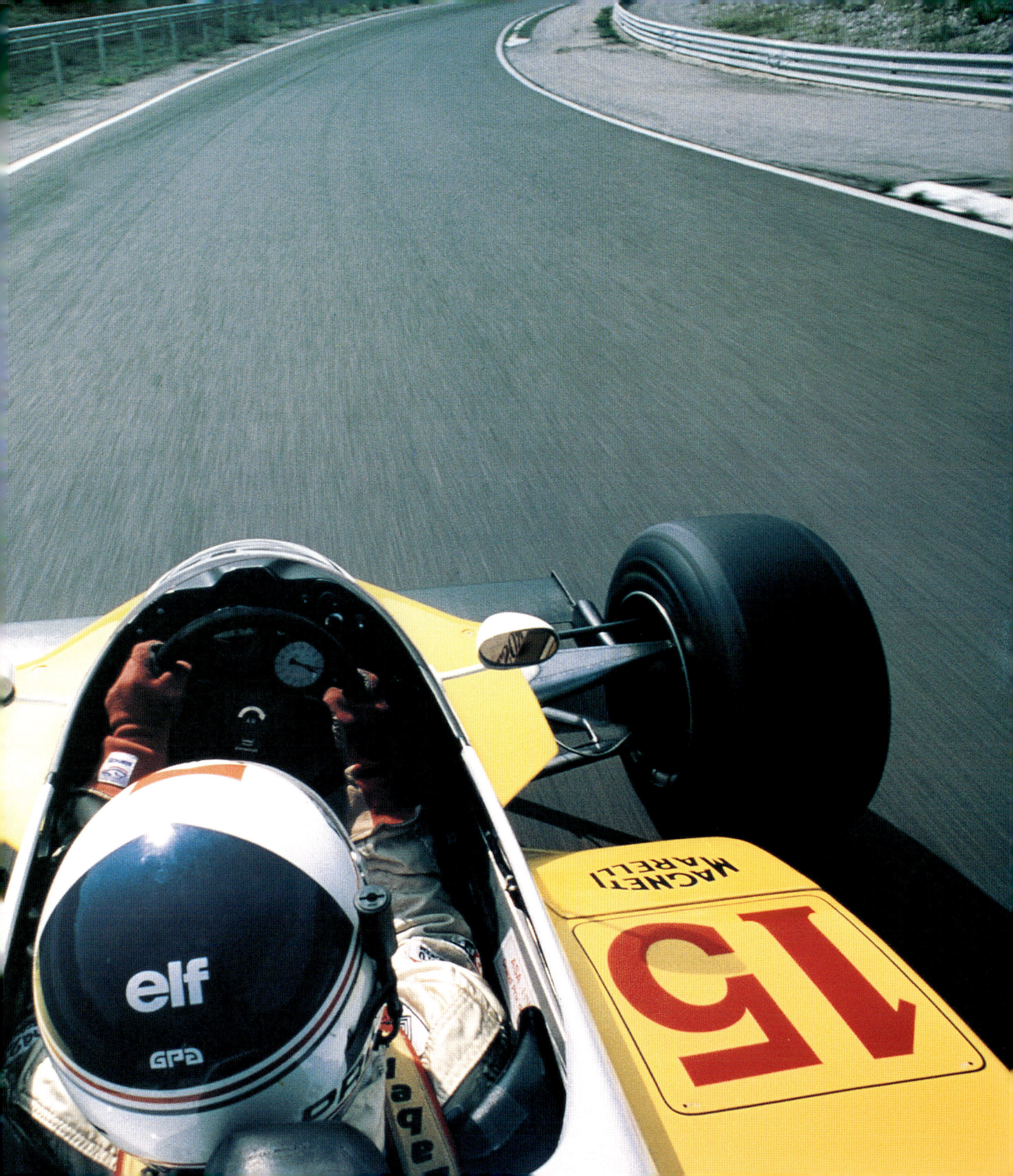
elf
GPA
MAGNETI MARELLI
15

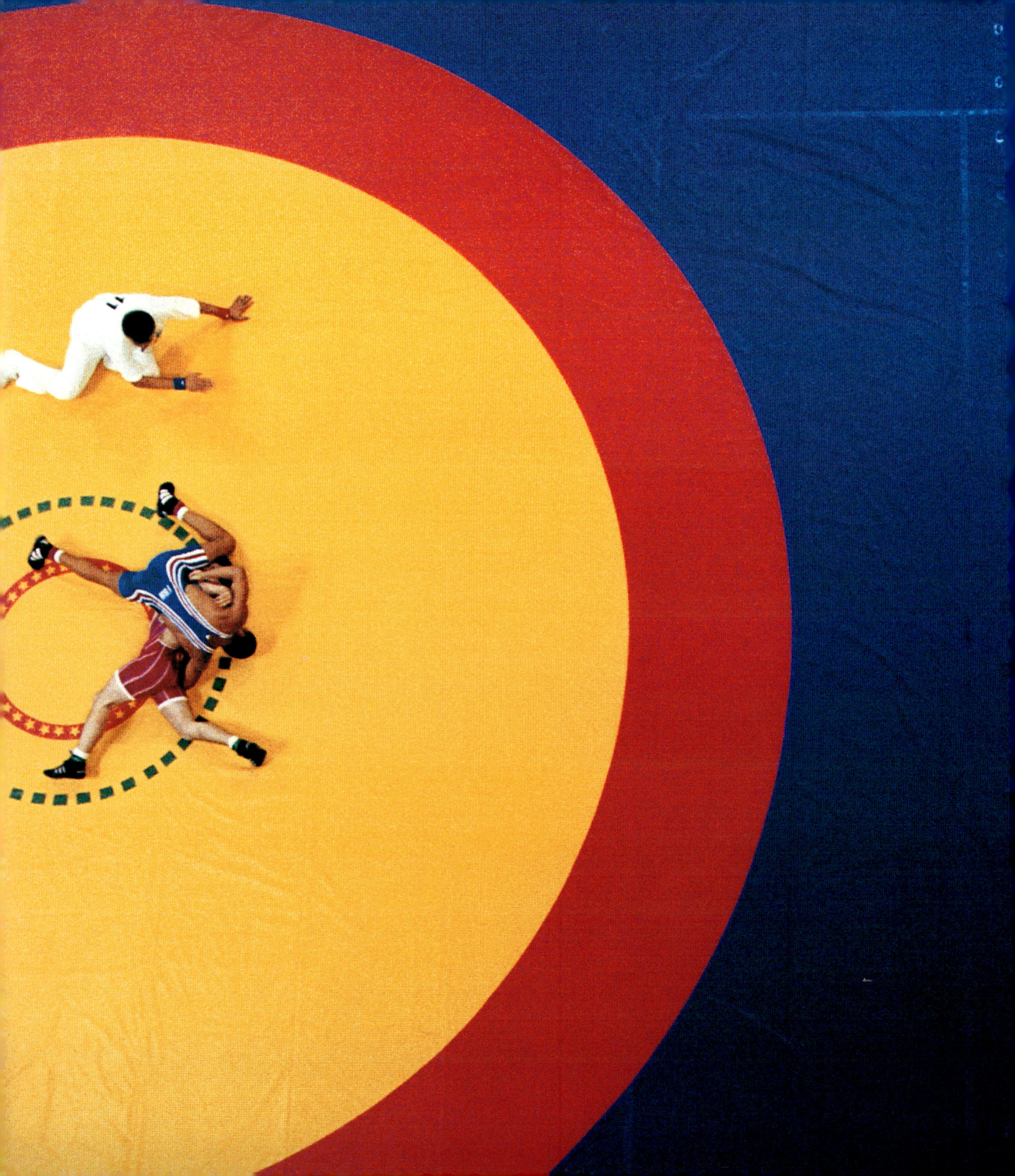

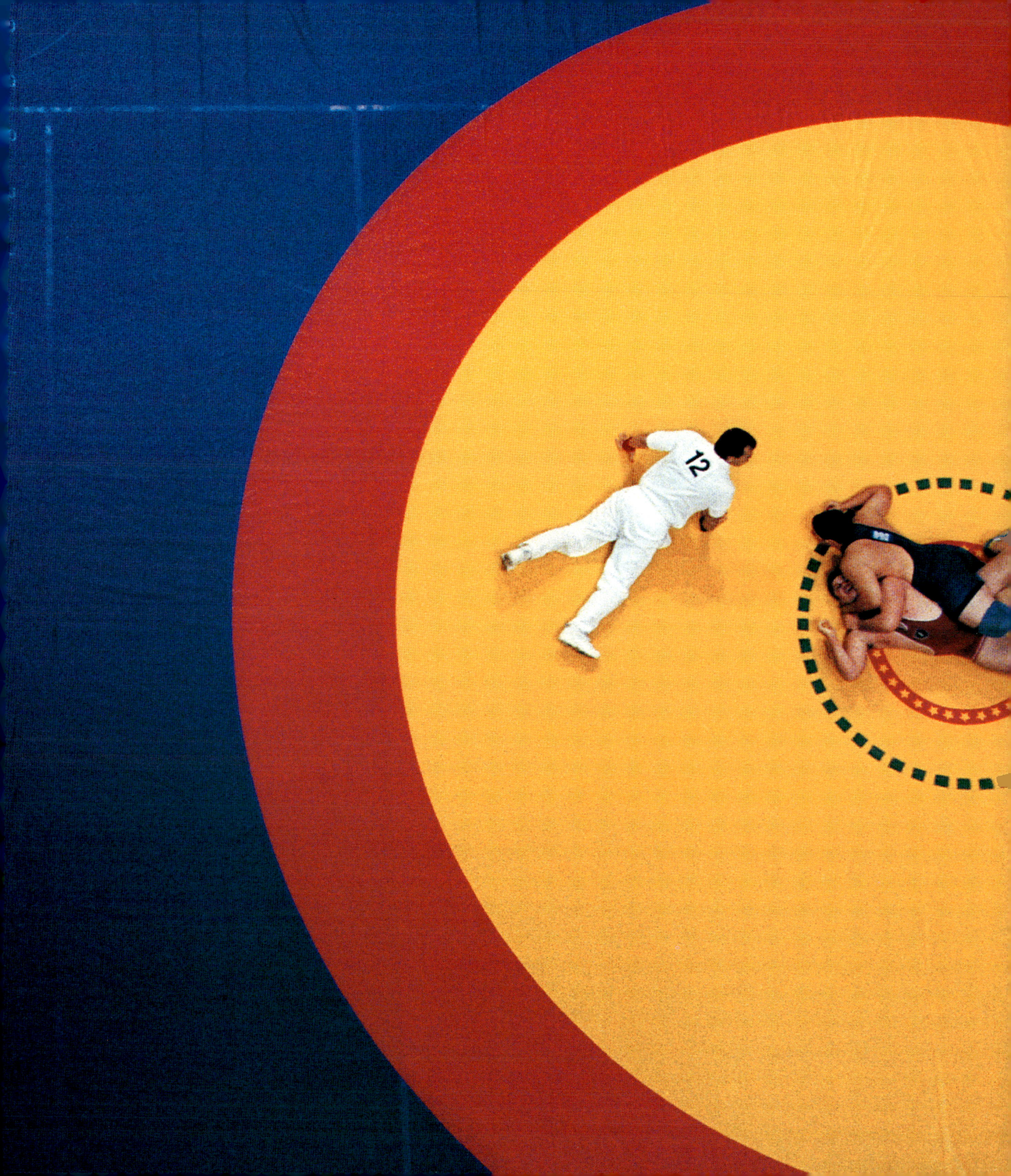
12

03
Washington Capitals versus Detroit Red Wings
Stanley Cup Finals, Michigan, 1998
Robert Laberge

04
Curtis Joseph of the Edmonton Oilers, Denver, 1997
Brian Bahr

05 (OVERLEAF)
Hakeem Olajuwon of the Houston Rockets and Shaquille O'Neal of Orlando Magic, Houston, 1995

03

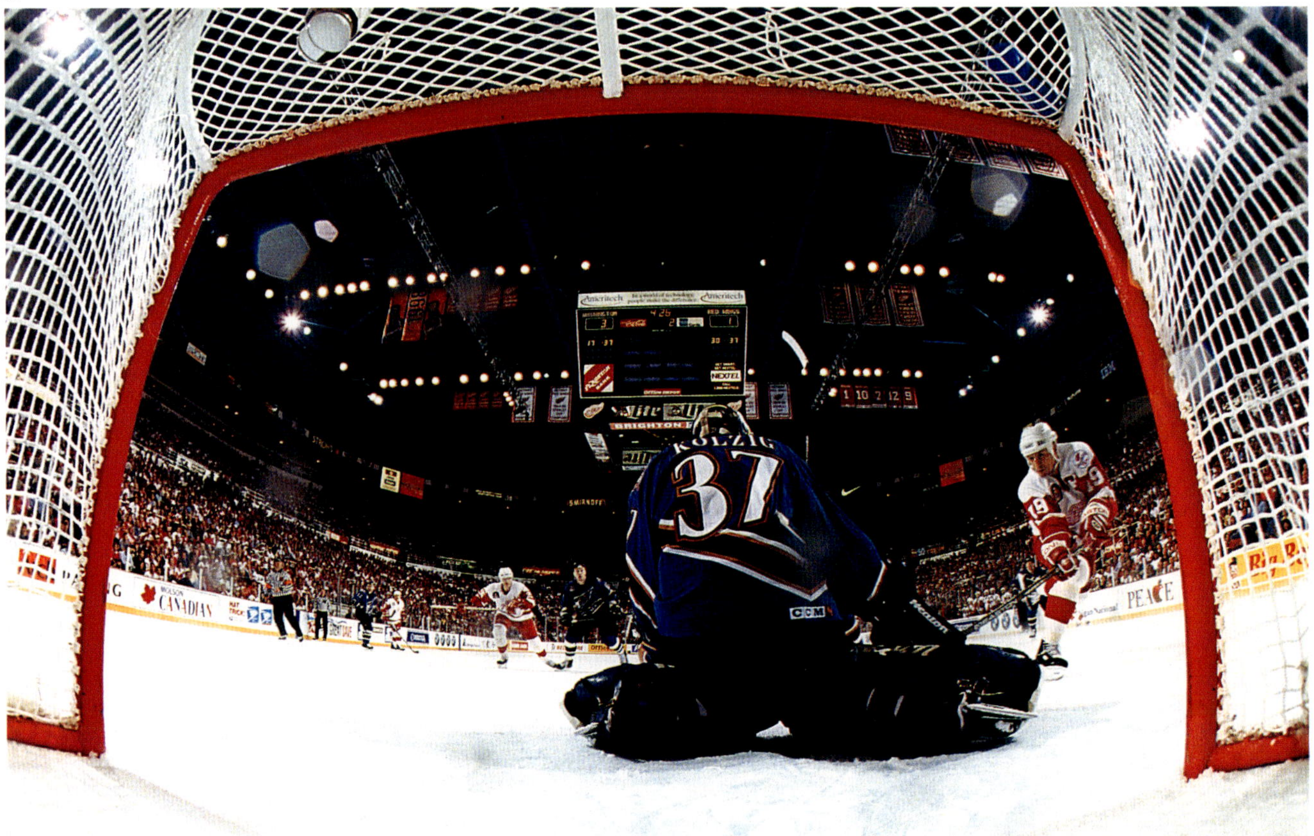

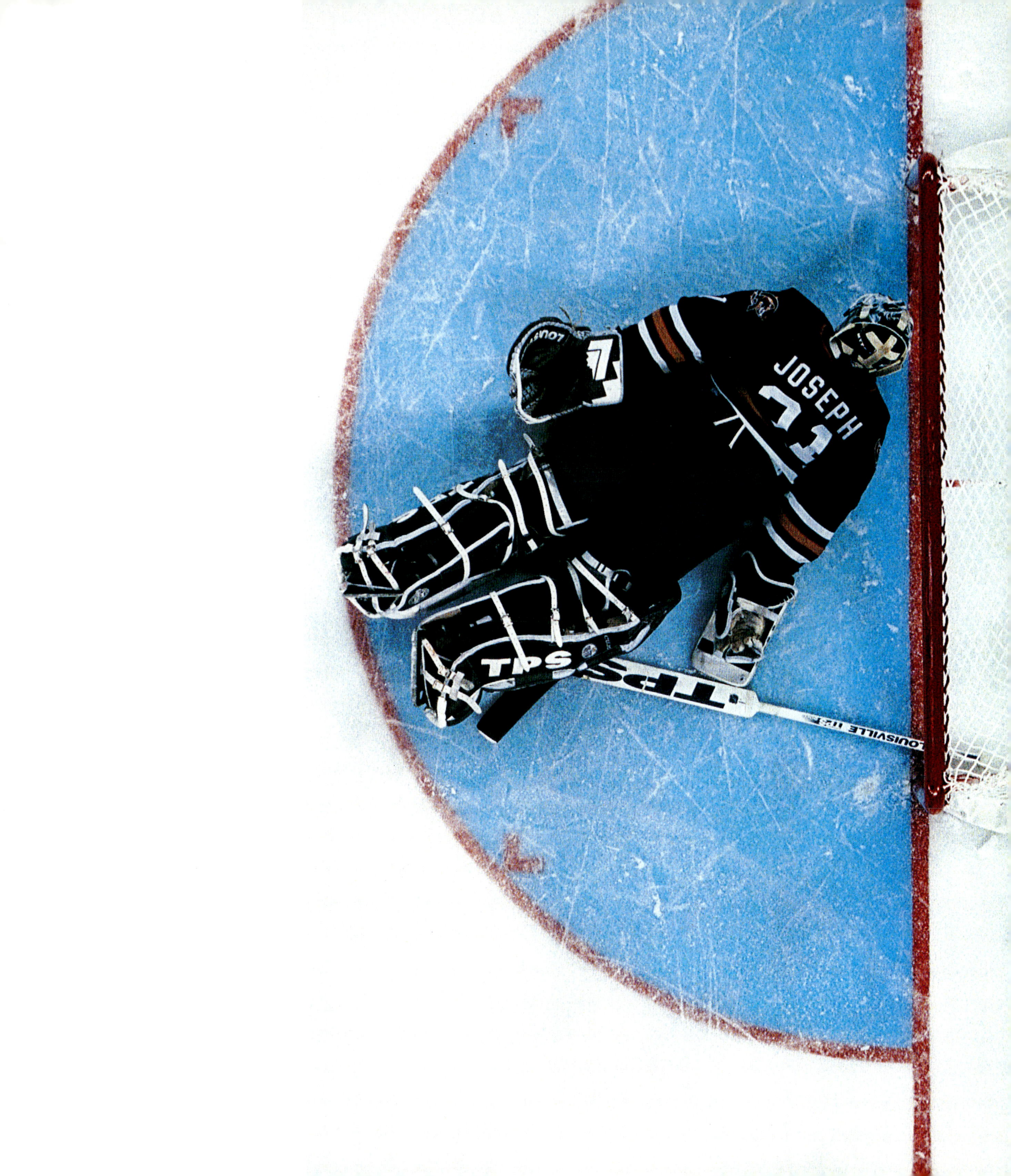
JOSEPH
TPS
TPS
LOUISVILLE

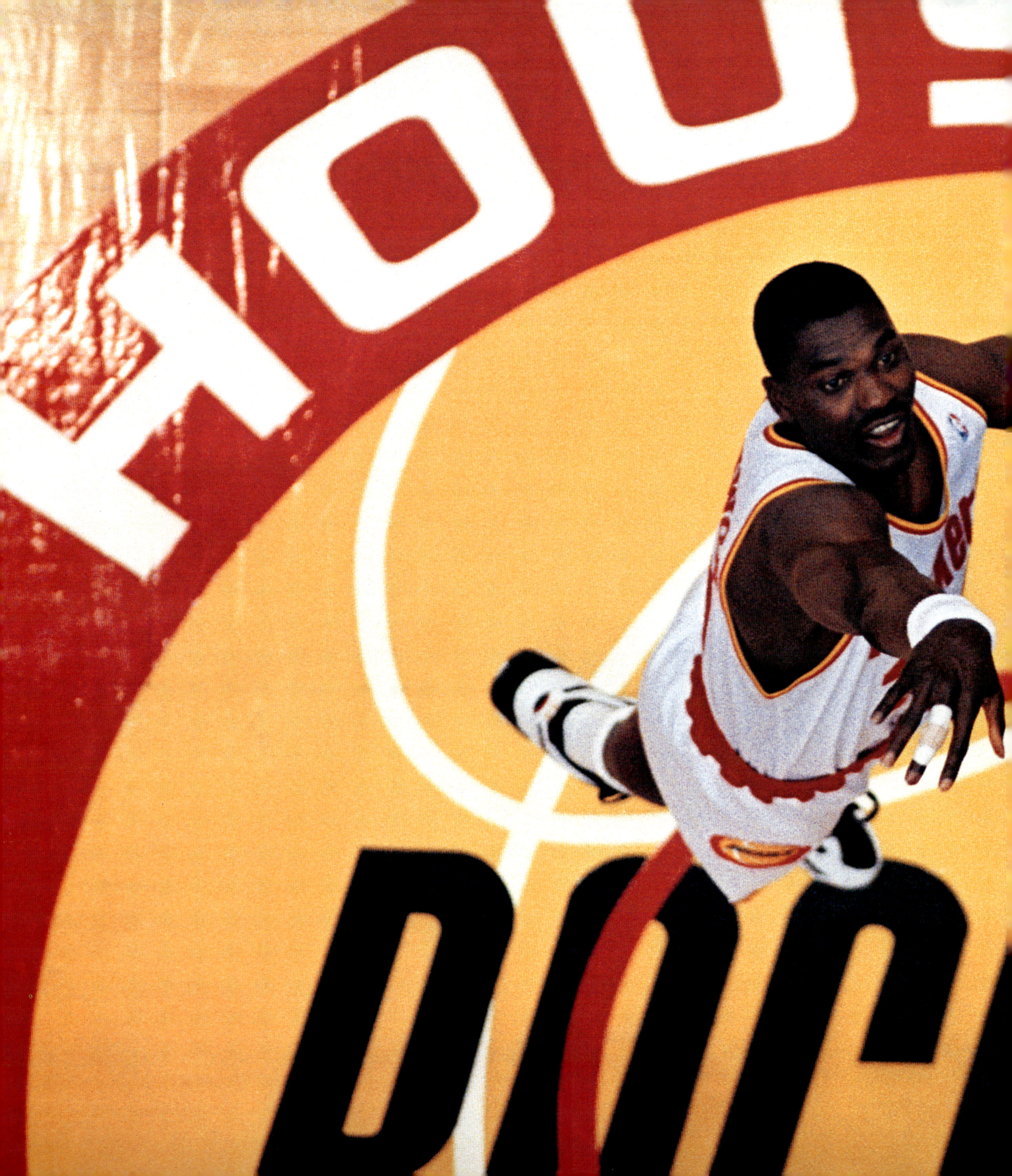

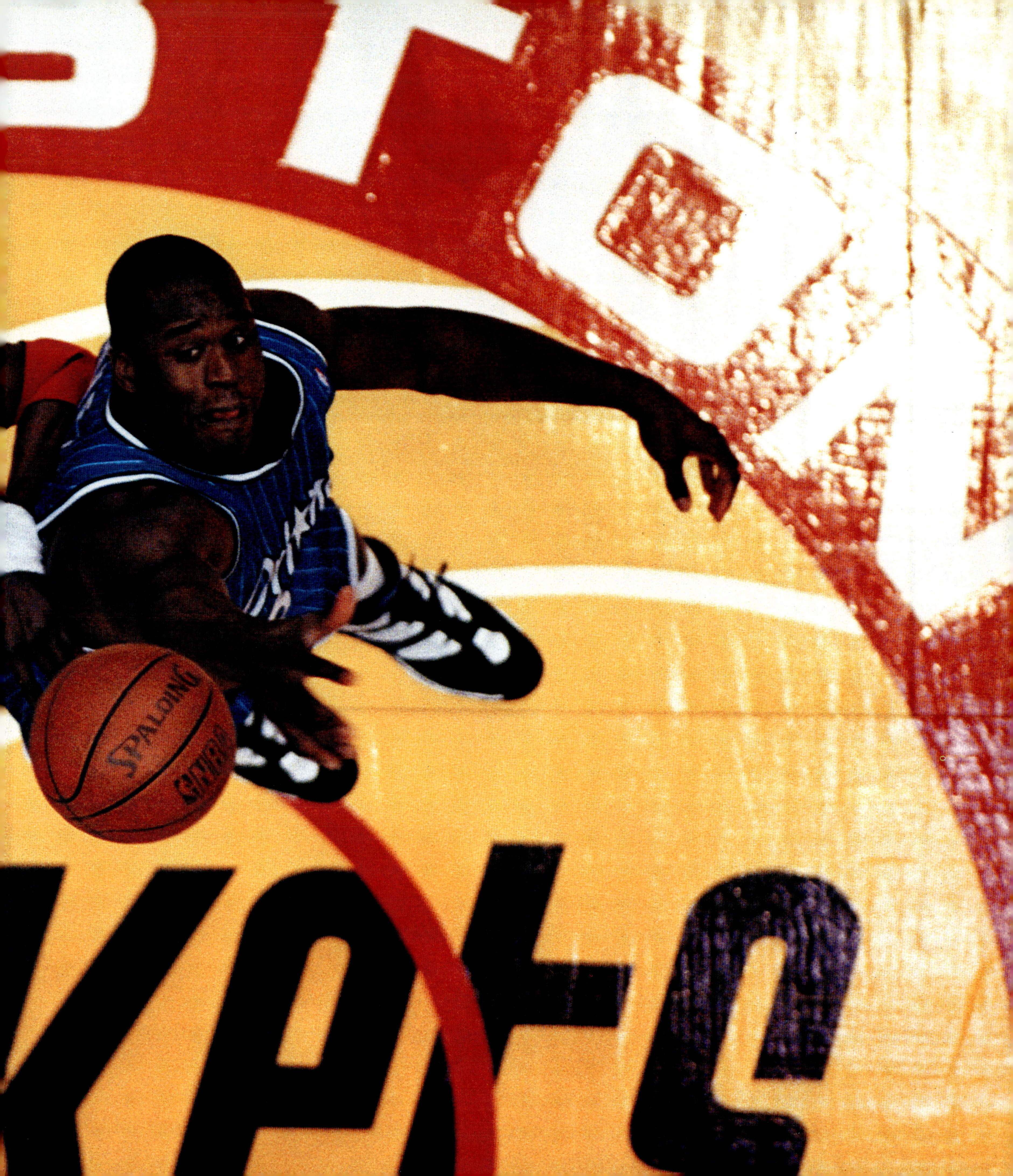
SPALDING

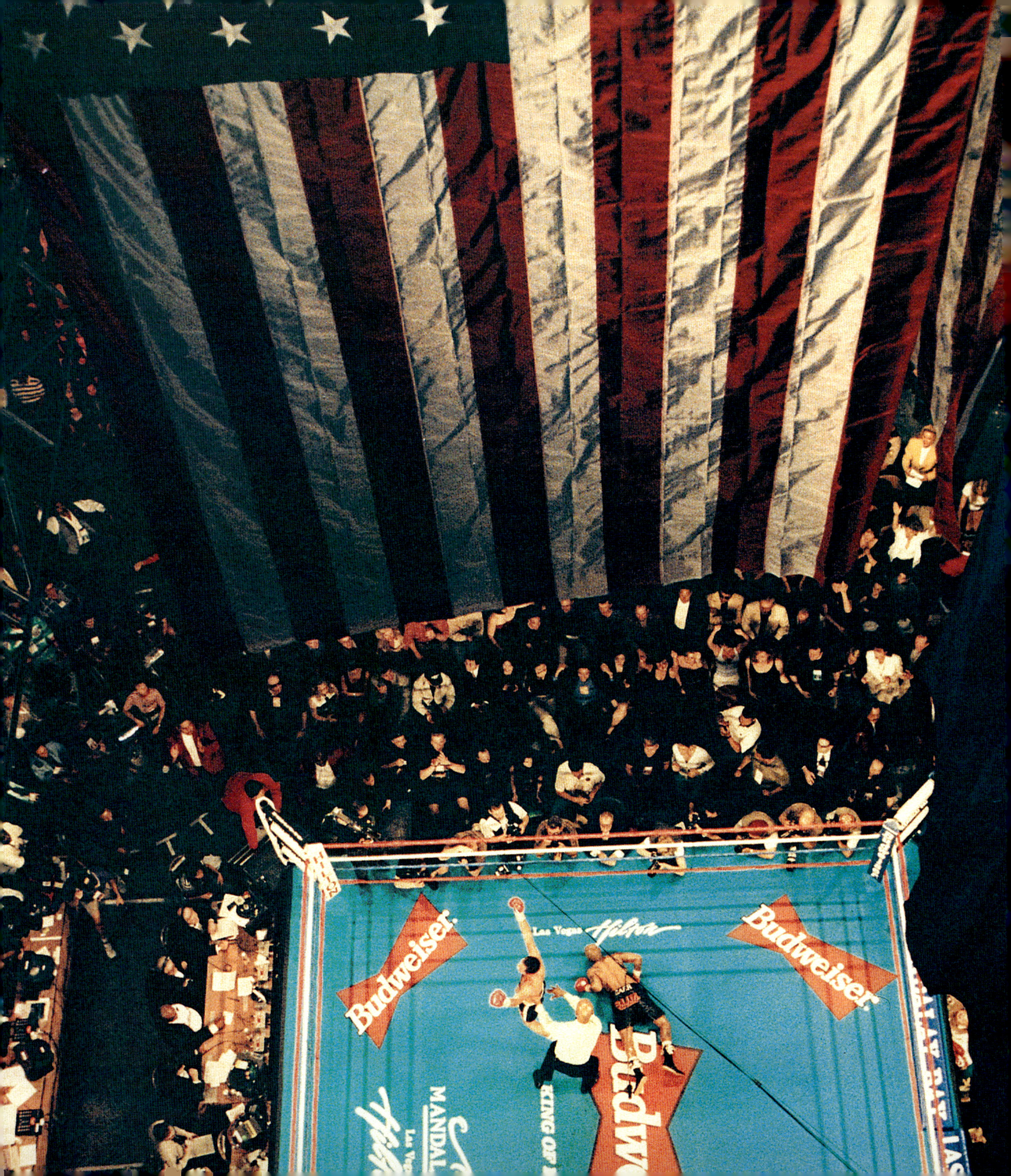
Budweiser
Las Vegas Hilton
Budweiser

06
Oscar De La Hoya versus Oba Carr, Las Vegas, 1993
Jed Jacobsohn

07
Liverpool versus Wimbledon FA Cup Final, London, 1988
David Cannon

07

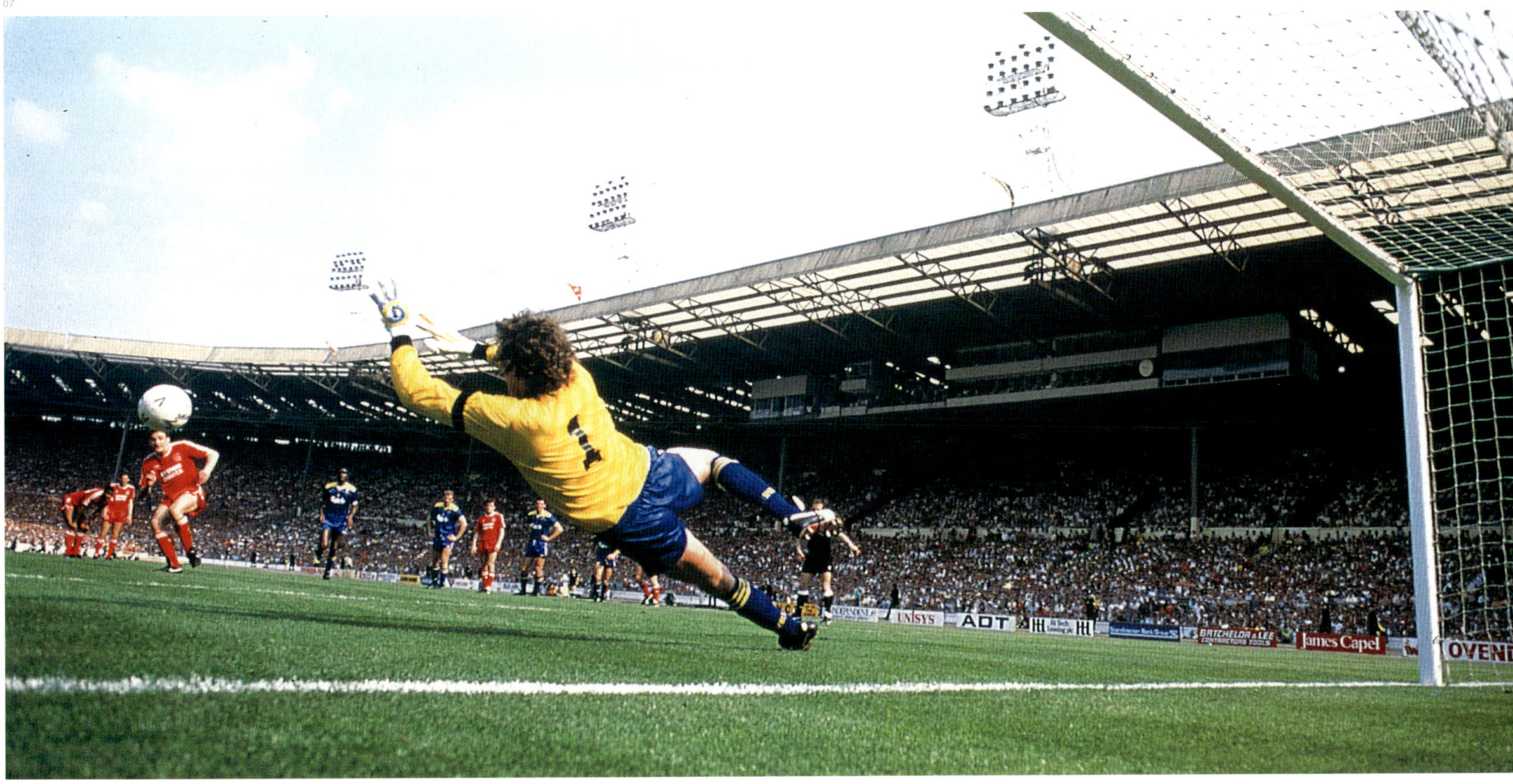

01
Ronaldo of Barcelona, Florence, 1997
Shaun Botterill

02
Ronaldo of Barcelona, Barcelona, 1997
Shaun Botterill

03
Ronaldo of Inter Milan, Graz, Austria, 1998
Alex Livesey

04
Ronaldo of Inter Milan, Milan, 1998
Claudio Villa

05
Ronaldo of Inter Milan, Lyon, France, 1997
Frederic Nebinger

06
Ronaldo of Brazil, Lyon, France, 1997
Ben Radford

07
Ronaldo of Brazil, Lyon, France, 1997
Shaun Botterill

08
Ronaldo of Brazil, Lyon, France, 1997
Ben Radford

09
Ronaldo of Brazil, Riad, Saudi Arabia, 1997

10
Ronaldo of Brazil, St Denis, France, 1998
Clive Brunskill

11
Ronaldo of Brazil, Nantes, France, 1998
Ross Kinnaird

PRIME SITE

The refinement in photographic technology – faster film, the telephoto lens, power driven cameras – has resulted in the photograph of the isolated moment of the sports star in action. Always in control, always in their own space, dictating events around them. This also makes the sports star a prime advertising space, the tight focus on them a perfect billboard for advertising. Ronaldo the Brazilian soccer player is a world superstar; the myriad images of him playing for various different clubs or for his country advertise not only the kits but the manufacturer's brand name, not to mention the team sponsor's logo across his chest. Likewise, the flamboyant Italian skier Alberto Tomba parades an ever-changing kaleidoscope of clothing designs and colours, adding a new role to his job as a leading sporting star – that of model. And perhaps the highest priced site of all is the Grand Prix racing driver's helmet: impossible for the photographer to capture a driver in action without taking a picture of his helmet, the classic sporting picture of the racing driver is the most lucrative site available to the racing team's marketing departments.

01
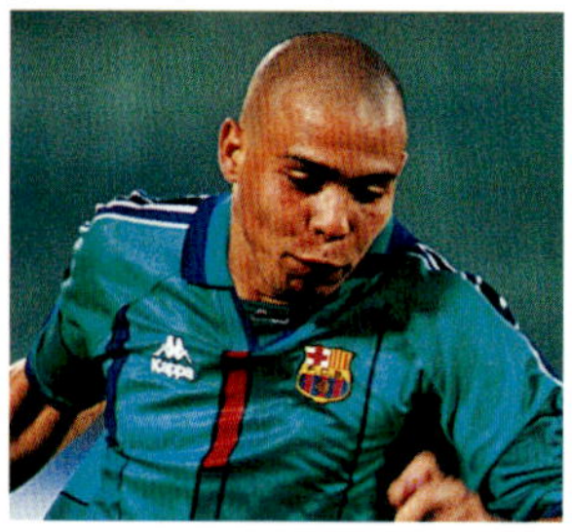

02
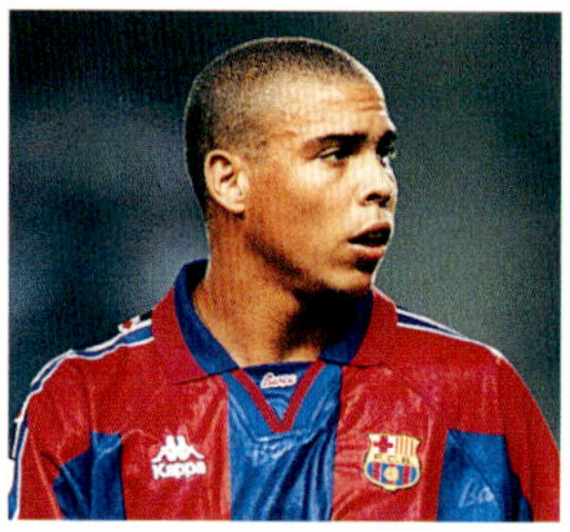

03
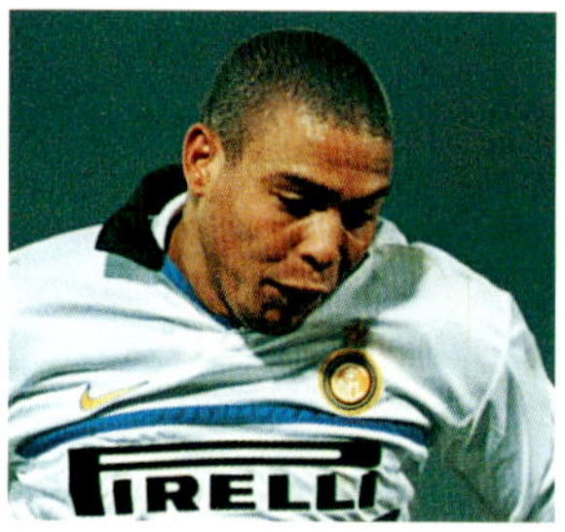

04
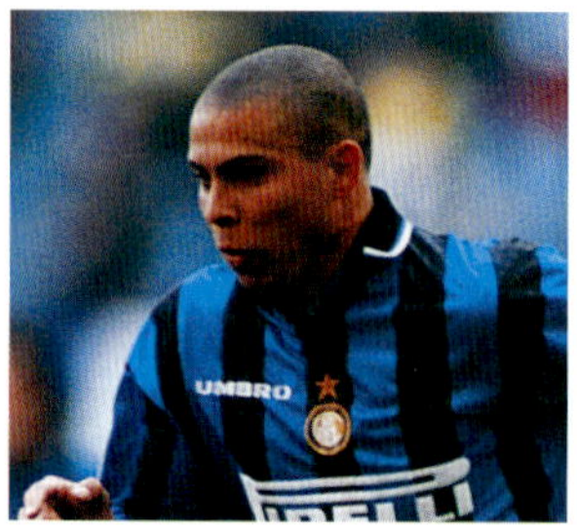

05
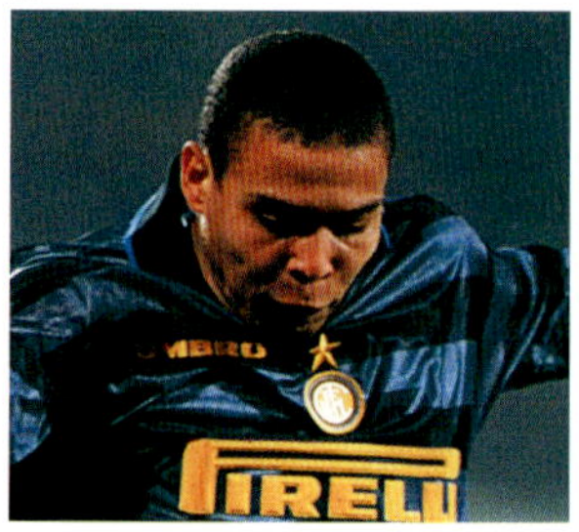

06
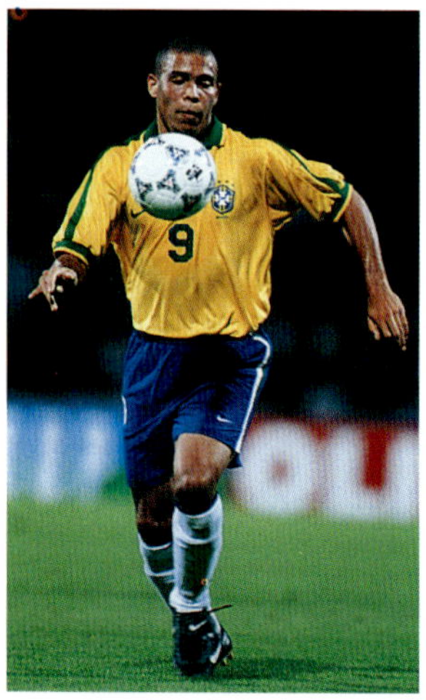

07
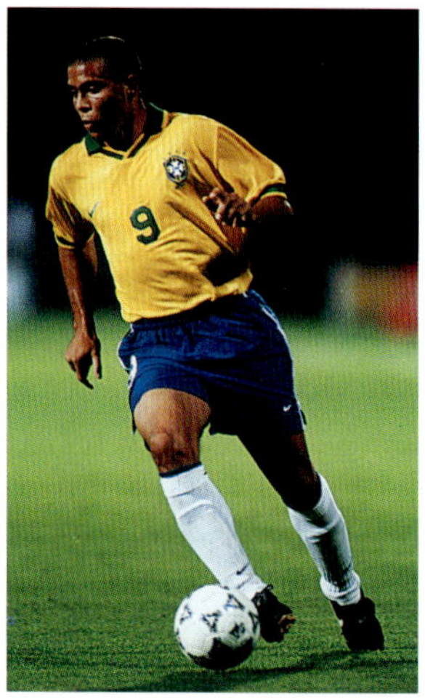

08
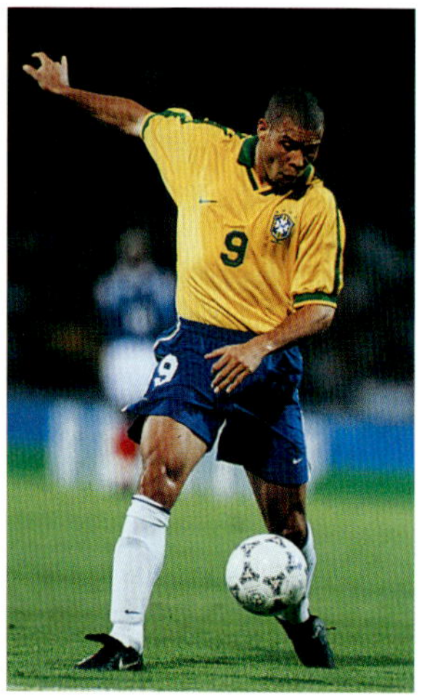

09
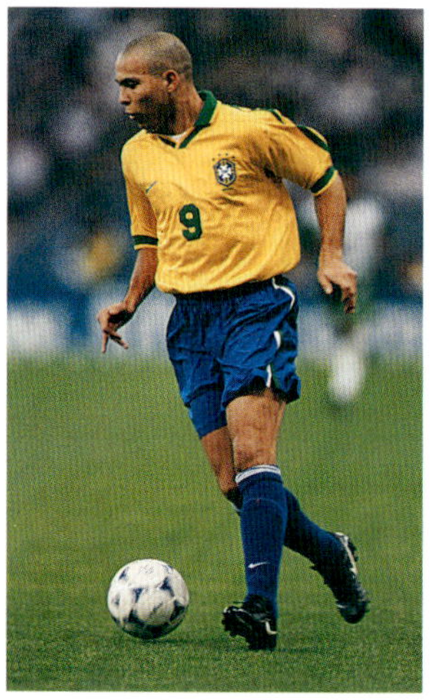

10
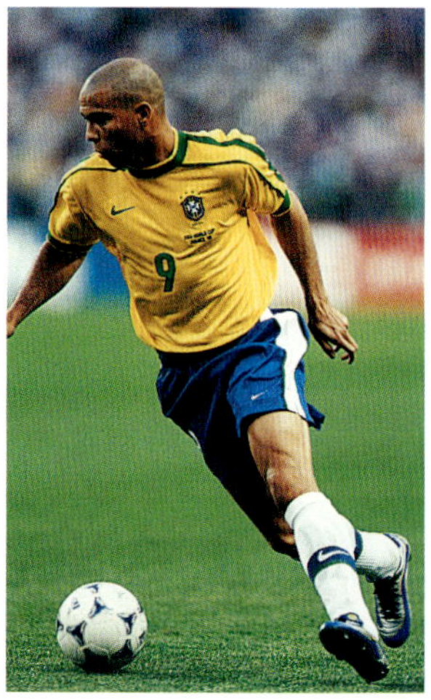

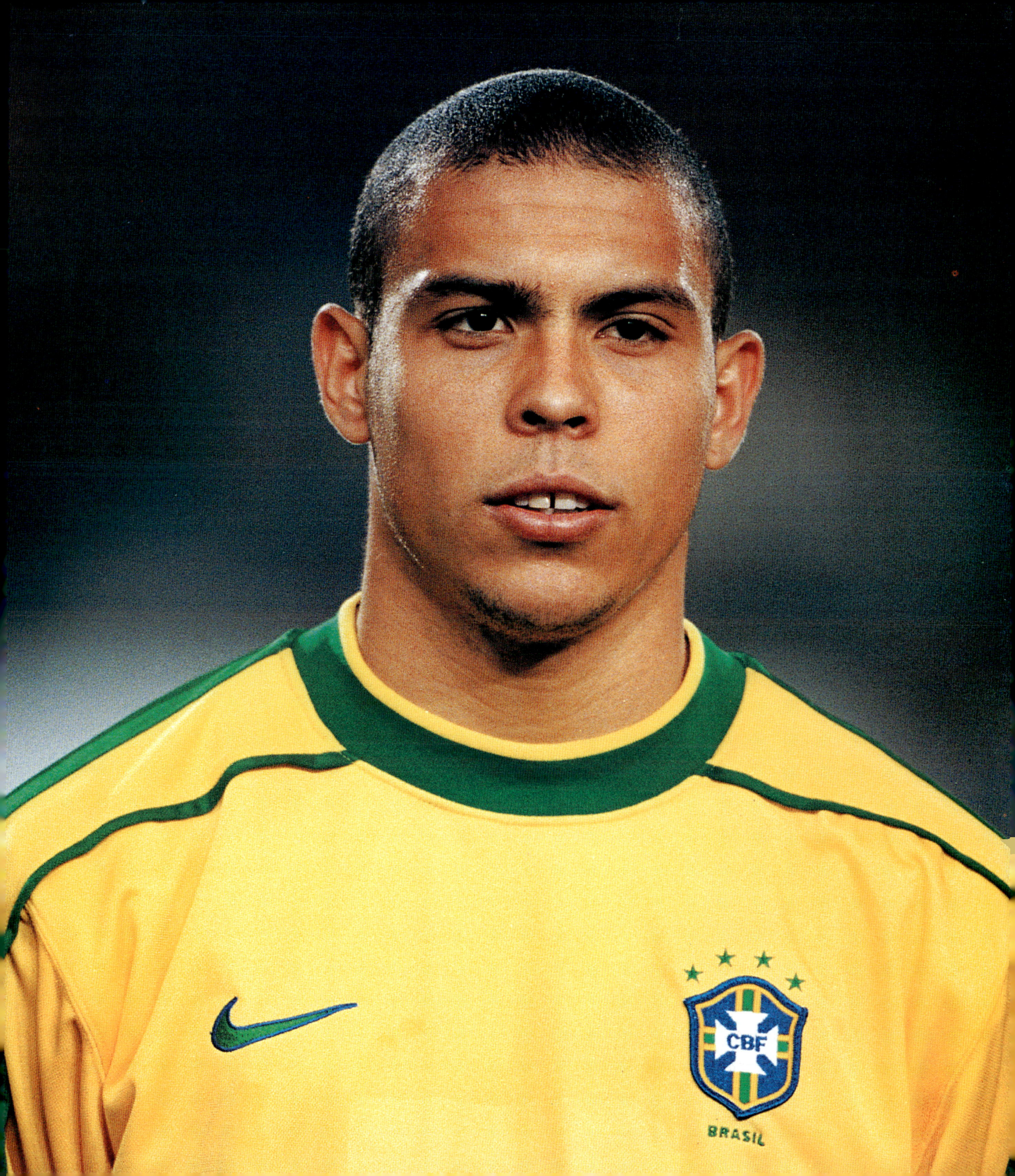
CBF
BRASIL

12

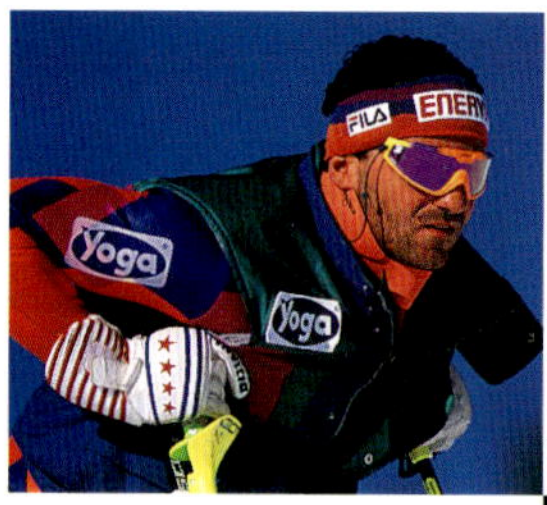

13

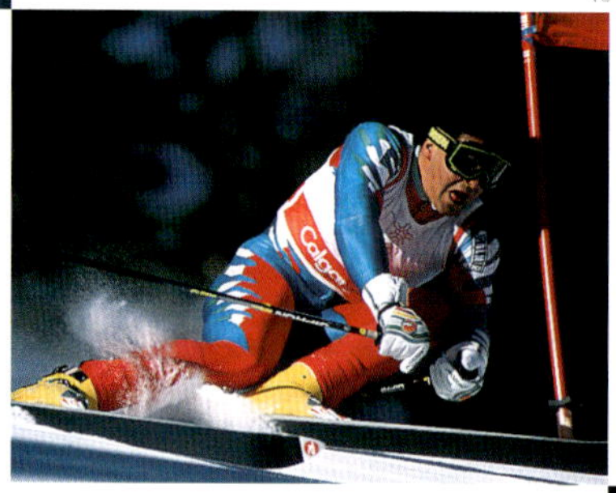

14

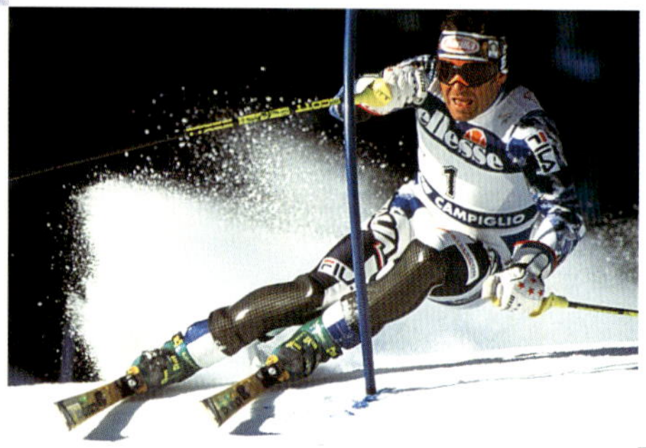

15

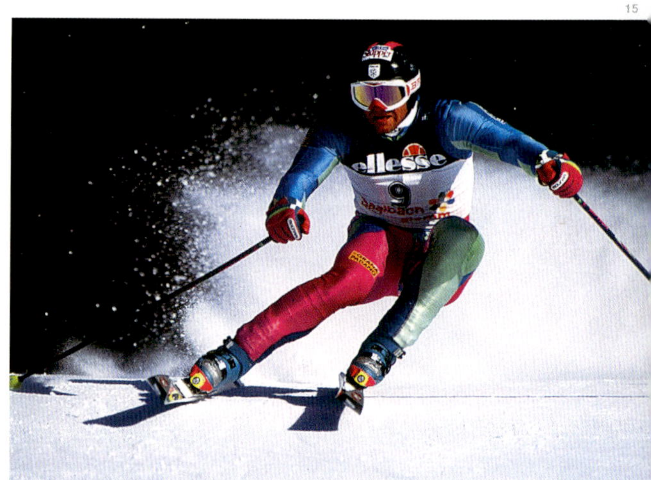

12
Alberto Tomba, c.1991
Shaun Botterill

13
Alberto Tomba, Calgary, 1988
Mike Powell

14
Alberto Tomba, Madonna di Campiglio, Italy, 1997

15
Alberto Tomba, Saalbach, Austria, 1991
Bob Martin

16
Alberto Tomba, Crans Montana, Switzerland, 1994

17
Alberto Tomba, Park City, USA, 1995

18 (OVERLEAF)
Natalie Coughlin, California, 1999
Vincent Laforet

16

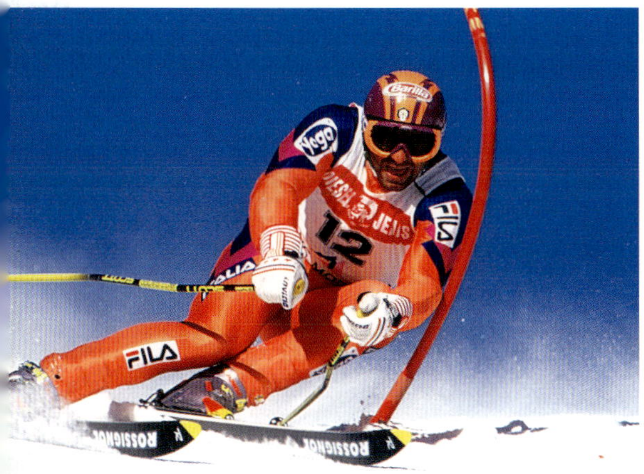

17

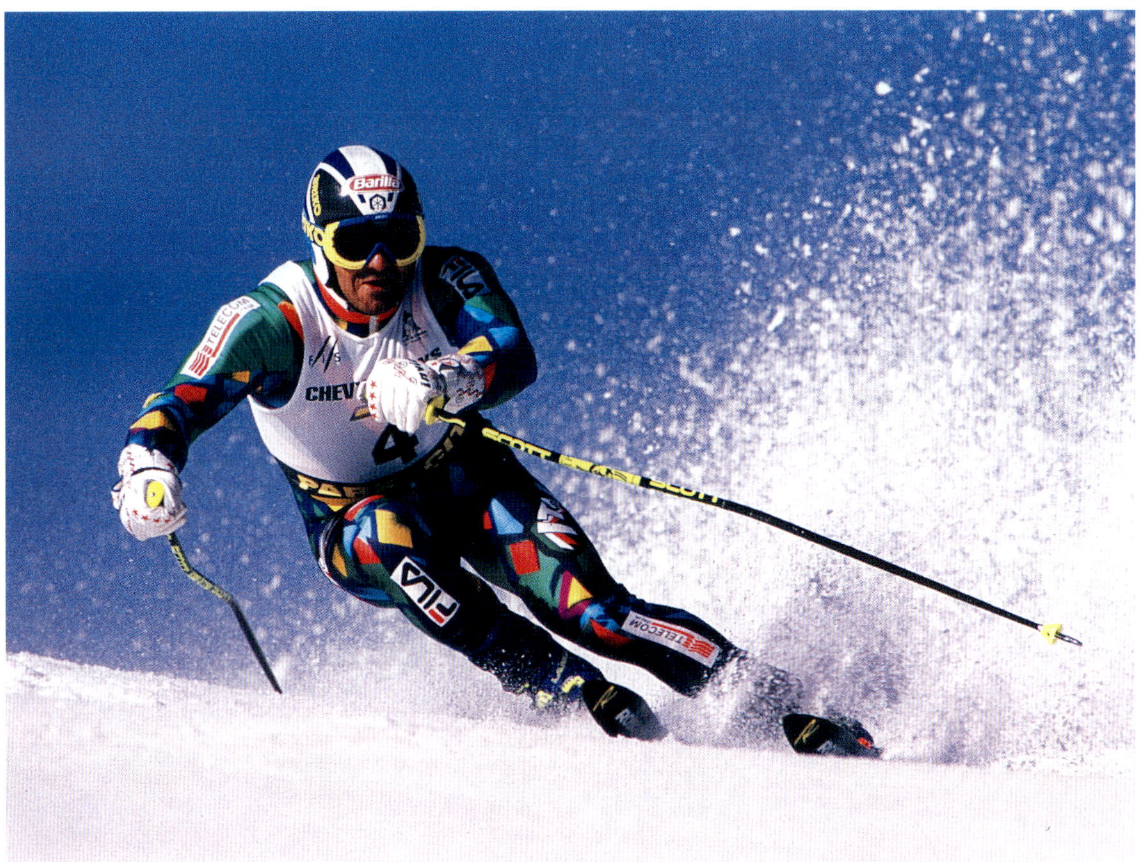

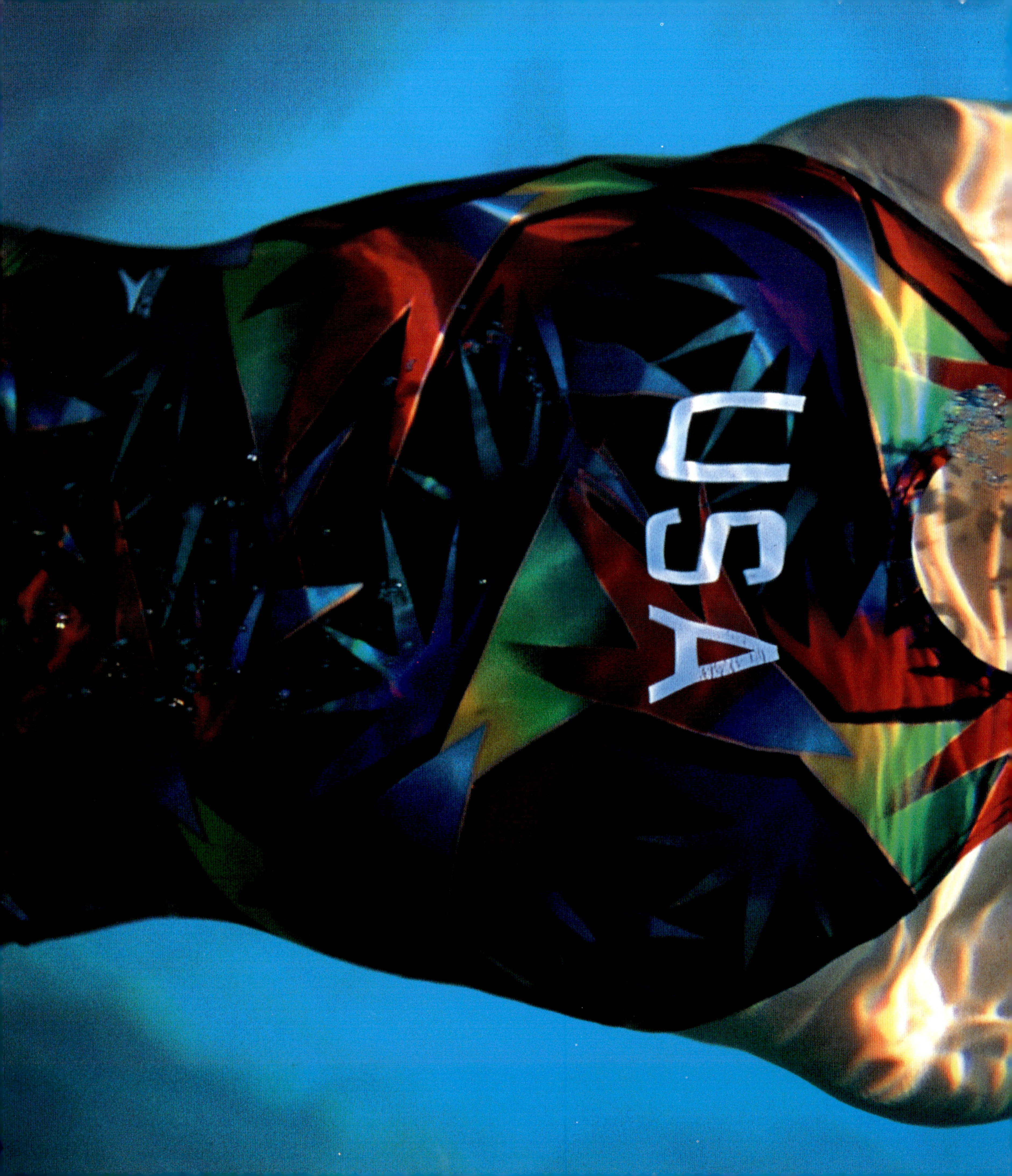
USA

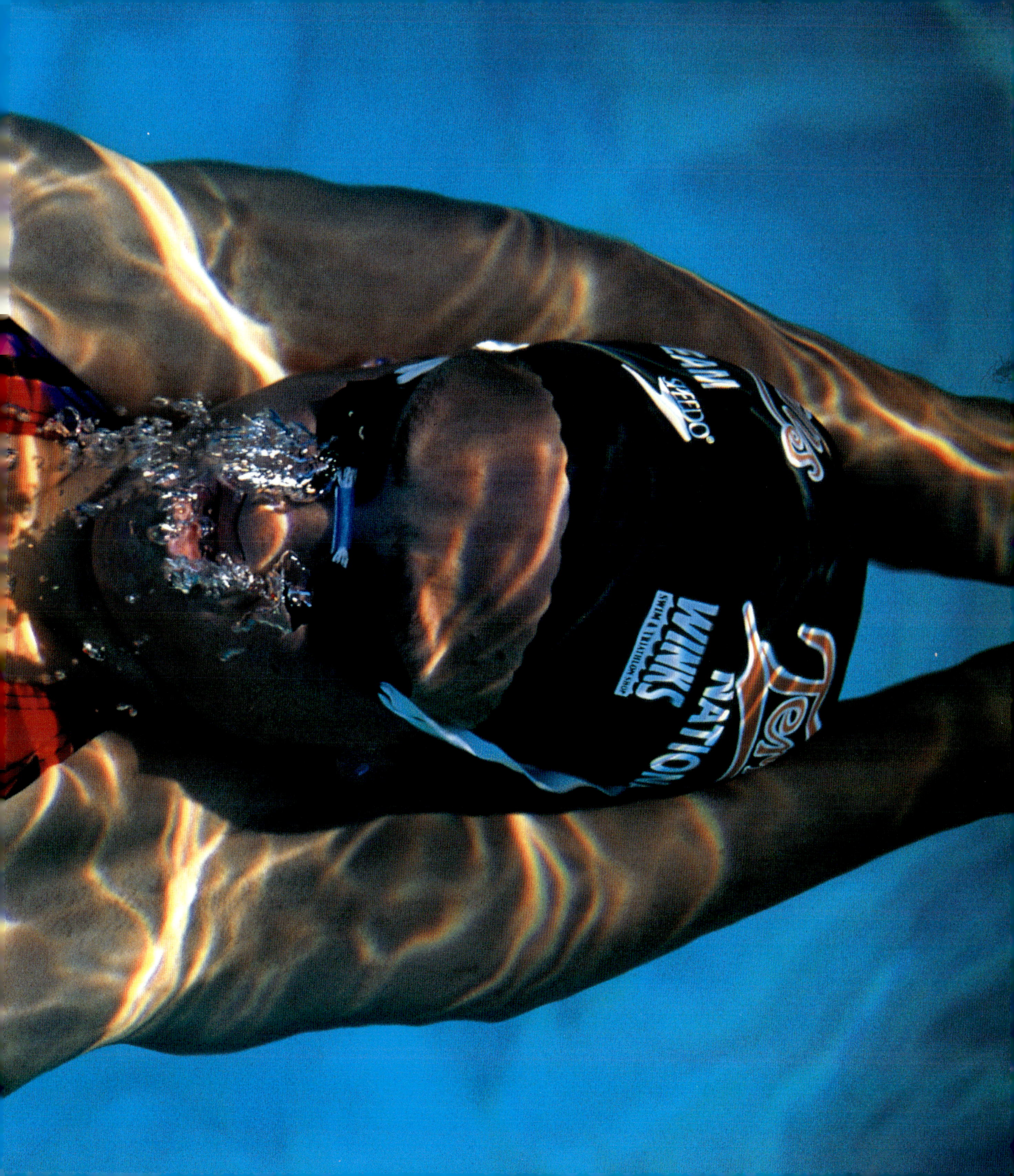
SPEEDO
WINKS

19
Mika Hakkinen, Melbourne, 1998
Michael Cooper

20
Ayrton Senna, Monza, Italy, 1992
Alain Patrice

21
Michael Andretti, Le Castellet, France, 1993
Simon Bruty

22
Jacques Laffite, São Paulo, Brazil, 1986
Bernard Asset

23
Damon Hill, Magny Cours, France, 1999
Michael Cooper

24
Alain Prost, Spa, Belgium, 1993
Vincent Kalut

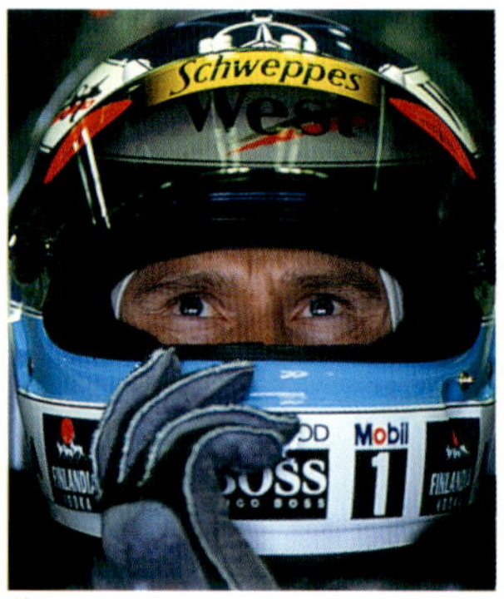

19

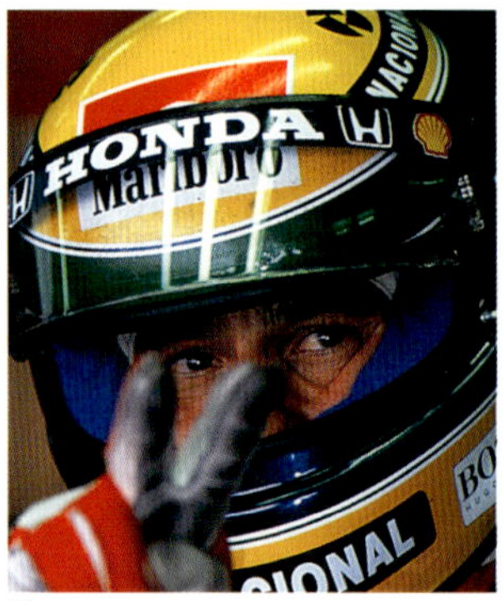

20

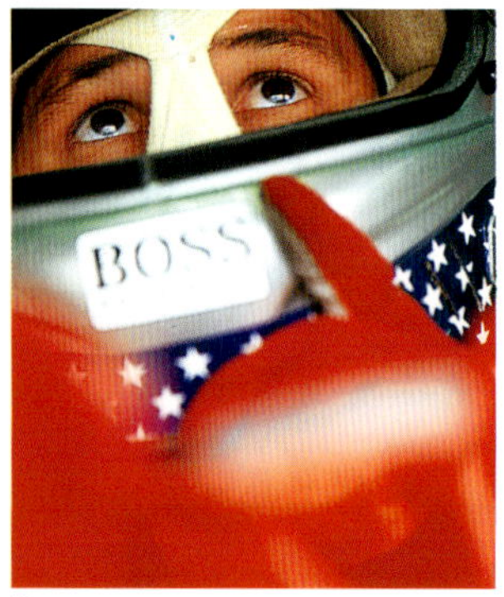

21

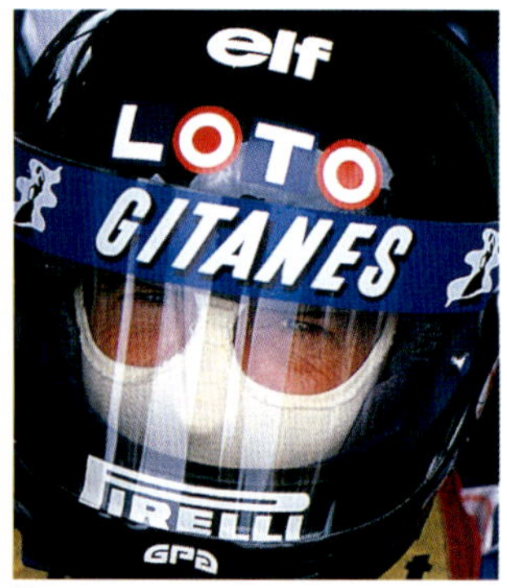

22

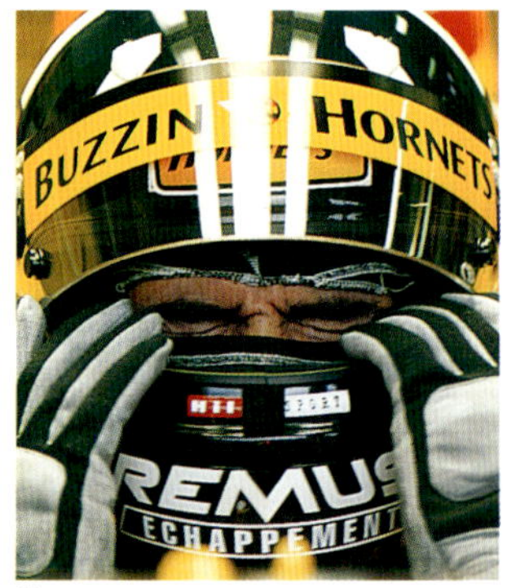

23

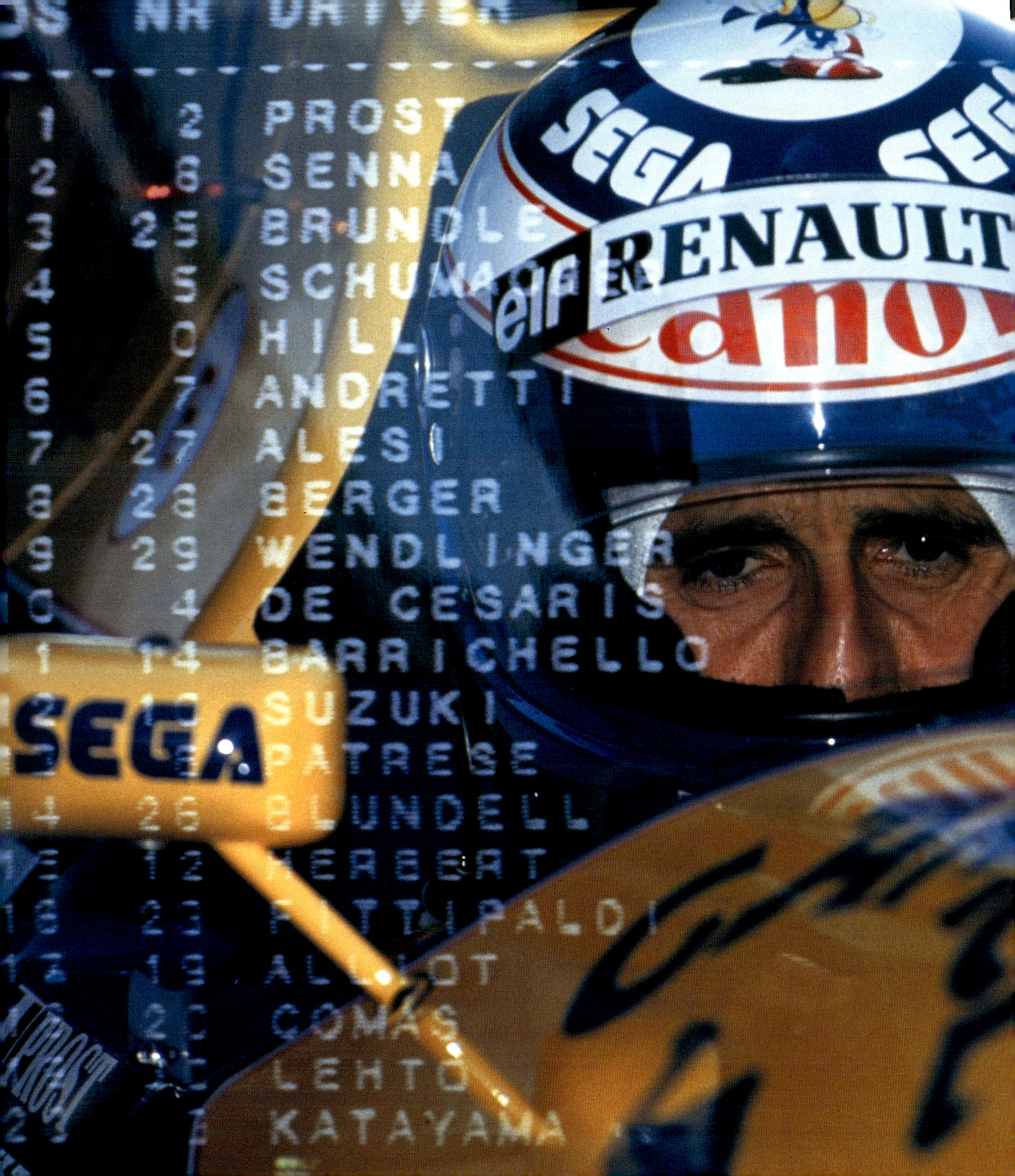
PROST
SENNA
BRUNDLE
SCHUMACHER
HILL
ANDRETTI
ALESI
BERGER
WENDLINGER
DE CESARIS
BARRICHELLO
SUZUKI
PATRESE
BLUNDELL
HERBERT
FITTIPALDI
ALLIOT
COMAS
LEHTO
KATAYAMA
SEGA
SEGA
elf
RENAULT
SEGA

10–OUT

When a boxer hits the canvas he has ten seconds to get back to his feet, or the fight is over. During the countdown conducted by the referee time enters a twilight zone: action is suspended, but the fight is not over. The boxer will either rise to continue fighting and so time will begin again, or will be defeated and the clock stops. The photographer has only the power to stop time, recording one moment and freezing it for ever in the limbo between ten and out.

01
Patrick Charpentier knocked down by Oscar De La Hoya, Texas, 1993
Jed Jacobsohn

02
Crawford Ashley knocked down by Michael Nunn, Tennessee, 1993
Chris Cole

03
Lucien Rodriguez knocked down by Frank Bruno, London, 1985
Michael King

04
Calvin Jones knocked down by Lennox Lewis, Gateshead, England, 1990
Russell Cheyne

05
Narcisco Valenzuela knocked down by Shane Mosley, California, 1994
Stephen Dunn

06
Buster Mathis Jr knocked down by Mike Tyson, Philadelphia, 1995
Simon Bruty

07
Chris Eubank knocked down by Carl Thompson, Manchester, 1998
John Gichigi

08
Jorge Paez knocked down by Martin Felix, Las Vegas, 1993
Chris Cole

09
Wayne Powell attended by Mills Lane, 1991
Ken Levine

10 (OVERLEAF)
Dave Dixon knocked down by Mike White, Los Angeles, 1992
Holly Stein

01
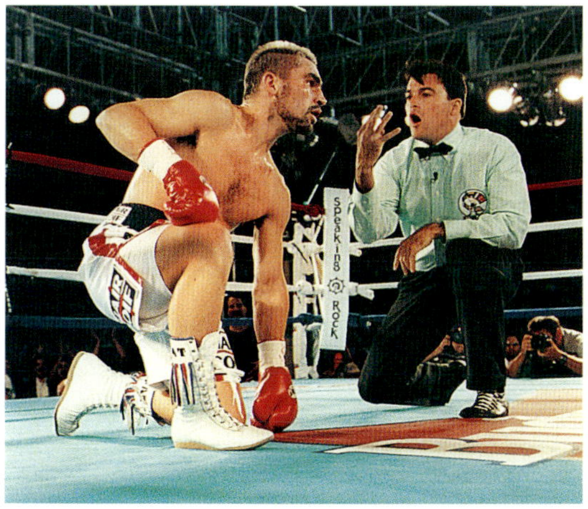

02
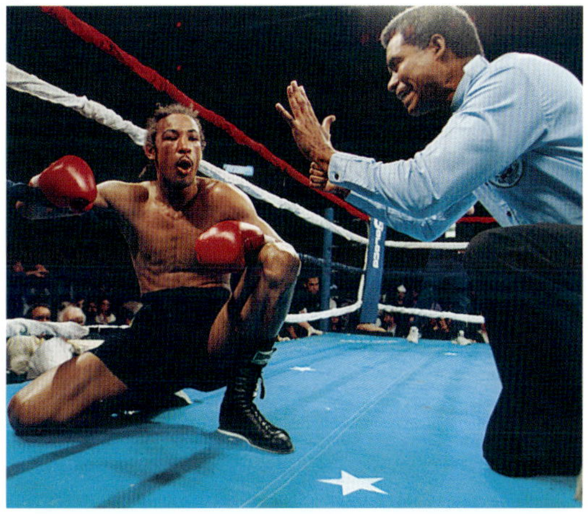

03
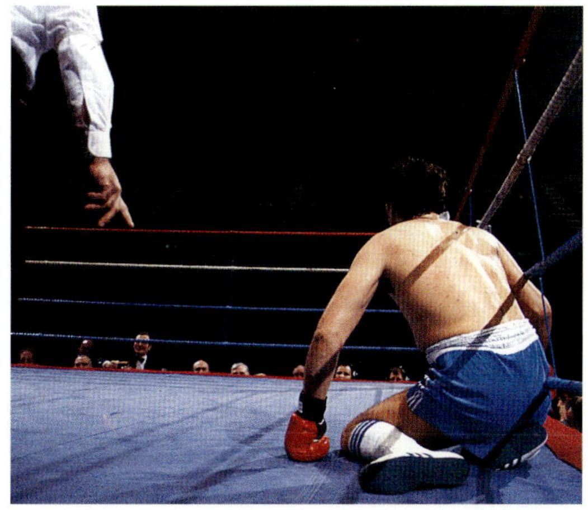

04
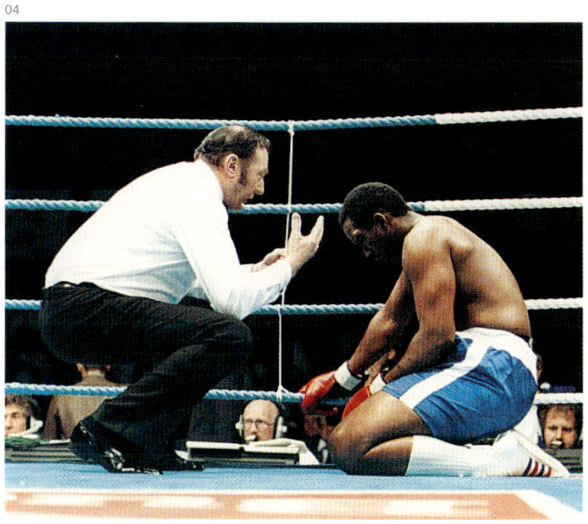

05
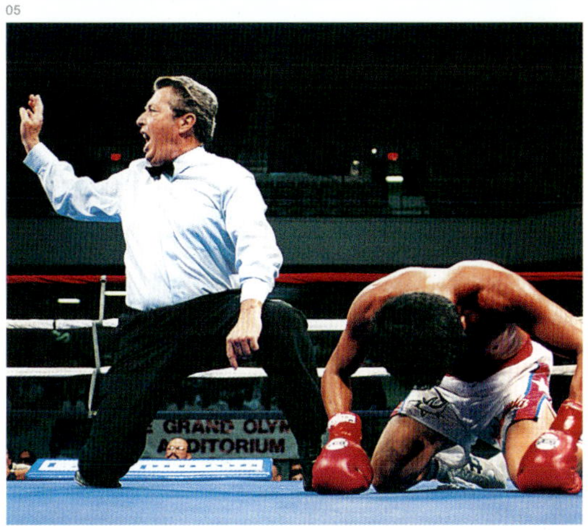

06
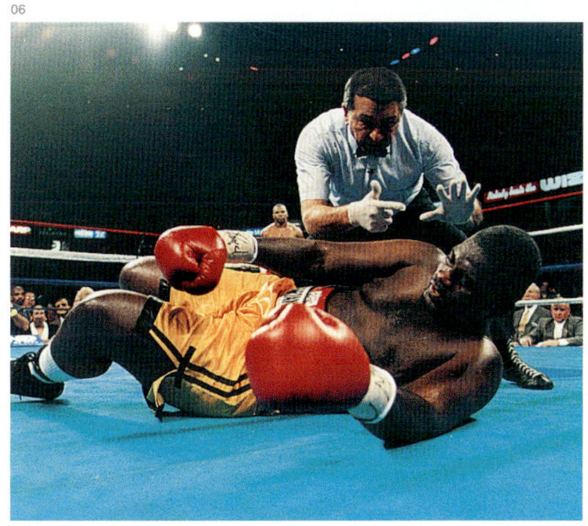

07
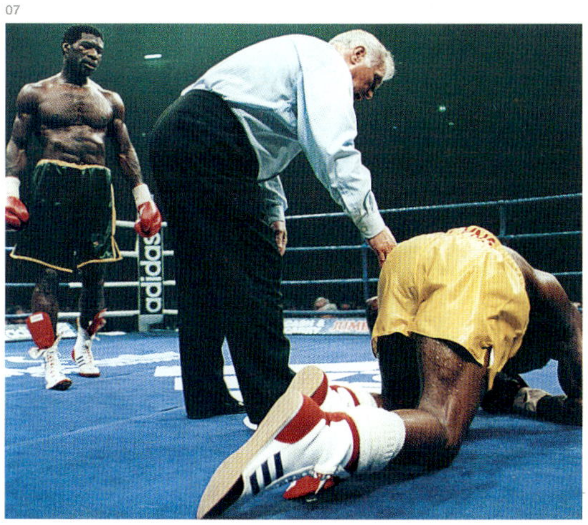

08
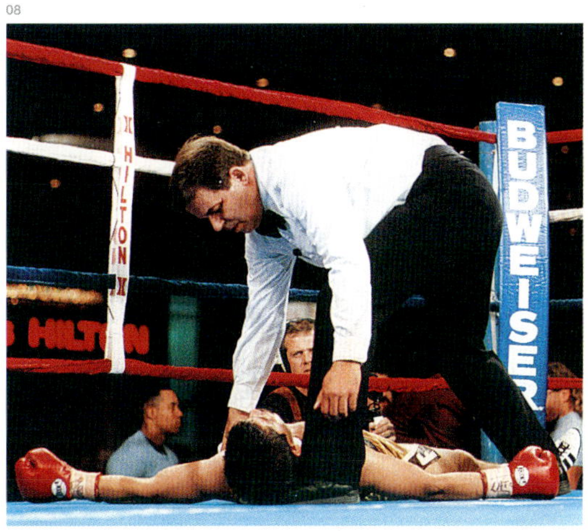

09
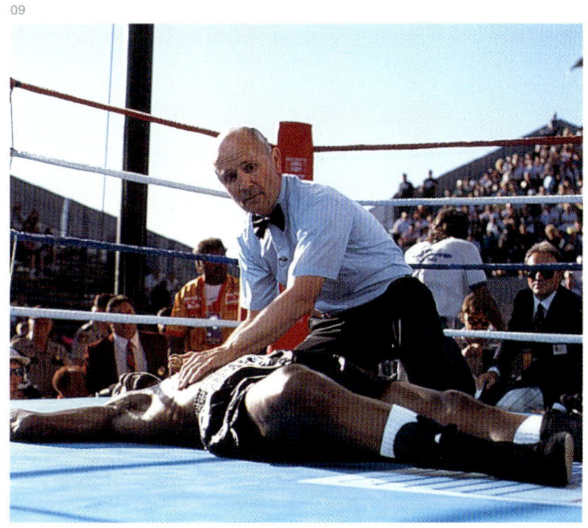

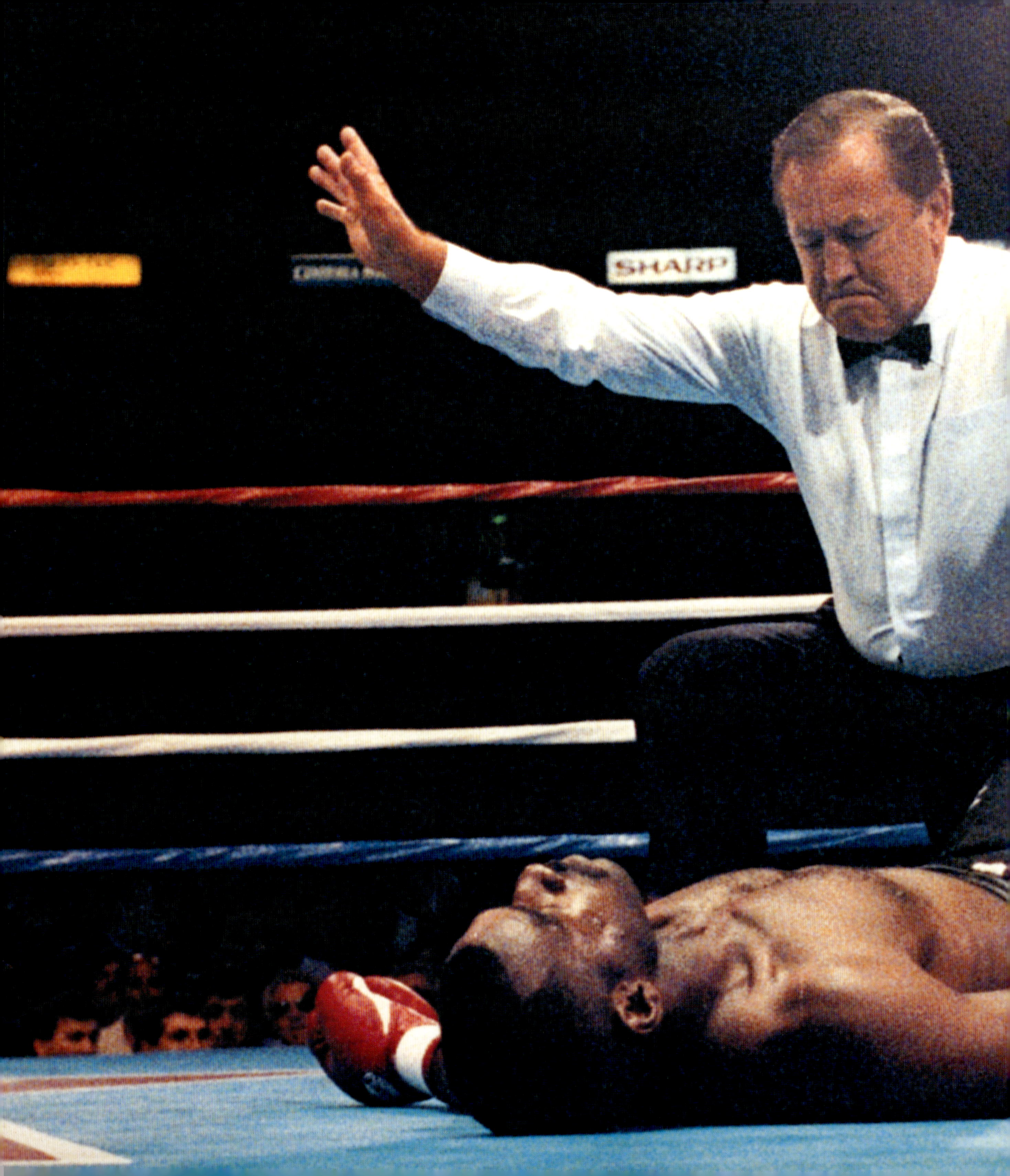
SHARP

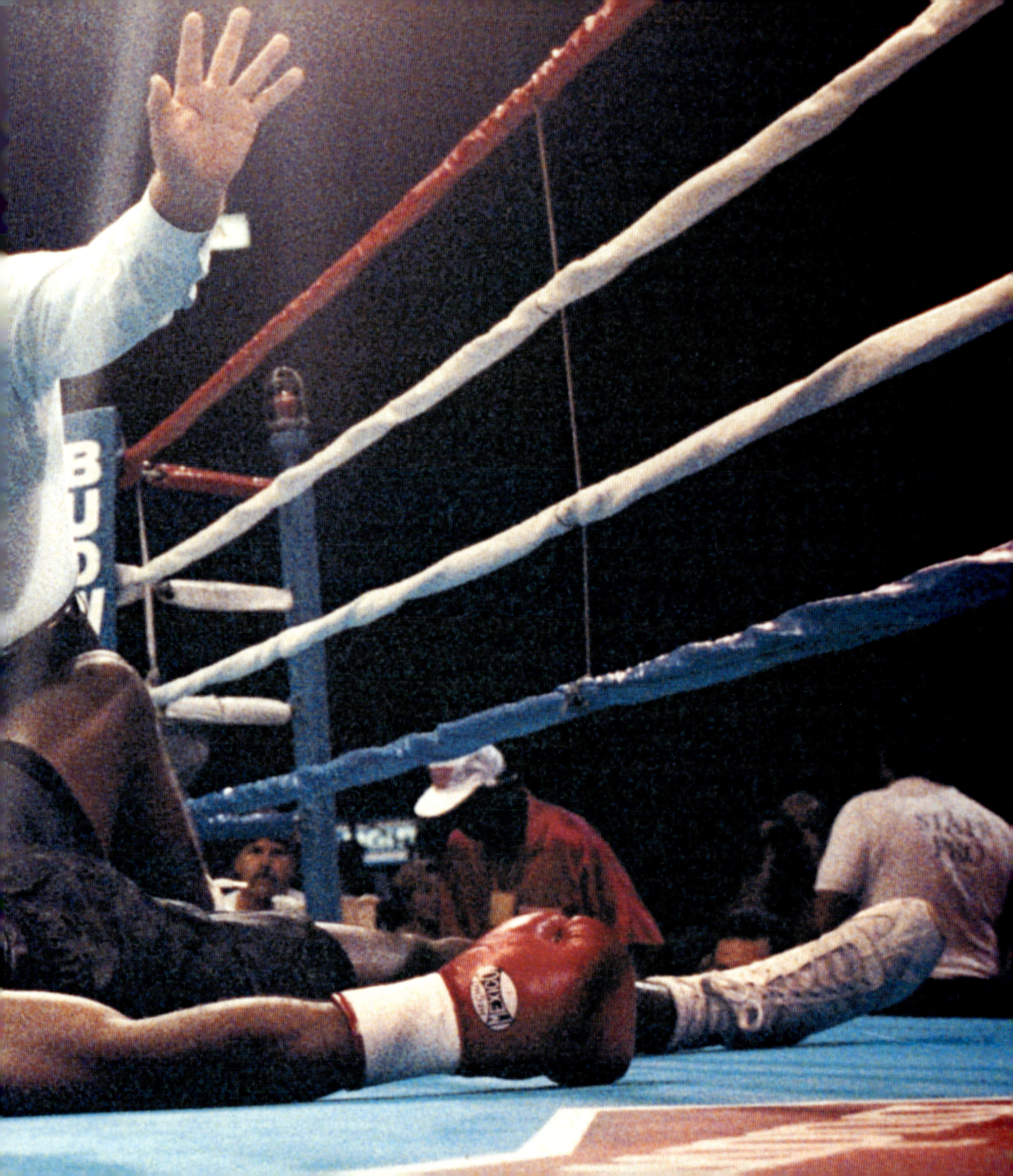
BUD

01
Boxing, 1997
Mike Powell

02 (OVERLEAF)
Hockey, 1997
Mike Powell

CONCEPT

Acting has always played a significant role in sport, with the specific elements of drama and tension being the key moments which the sports photographer aims to record. As sport becomes ever more popular, sporting images are increasingly used outside the context of sports journalism, particularly in advertising. The positive image of sport and its personalities make it perfect for product endorsement, but today's top stars can command high prices for the use of their image. Thus the need has been created for readily available images embodying the positive values of sport, but free for commercial use without the payment of a fee to a well-known star. Known as 'model released' images, photographers can pose these shots exactly as they want, the players entirely at their beck and call.

Under these controlled circumstances, photographers have seized the opportunity to create 'perfect' shots not possible in the photography of live sport, sometimes sacrificing realism to achieve the higher quality of the finished image. The photographer can work more like a movie director to create these key moments from a fictional game. This form of image-making is, in effect, the distillation of thousands of sports photographs into one that represents the archetypal image of sport.

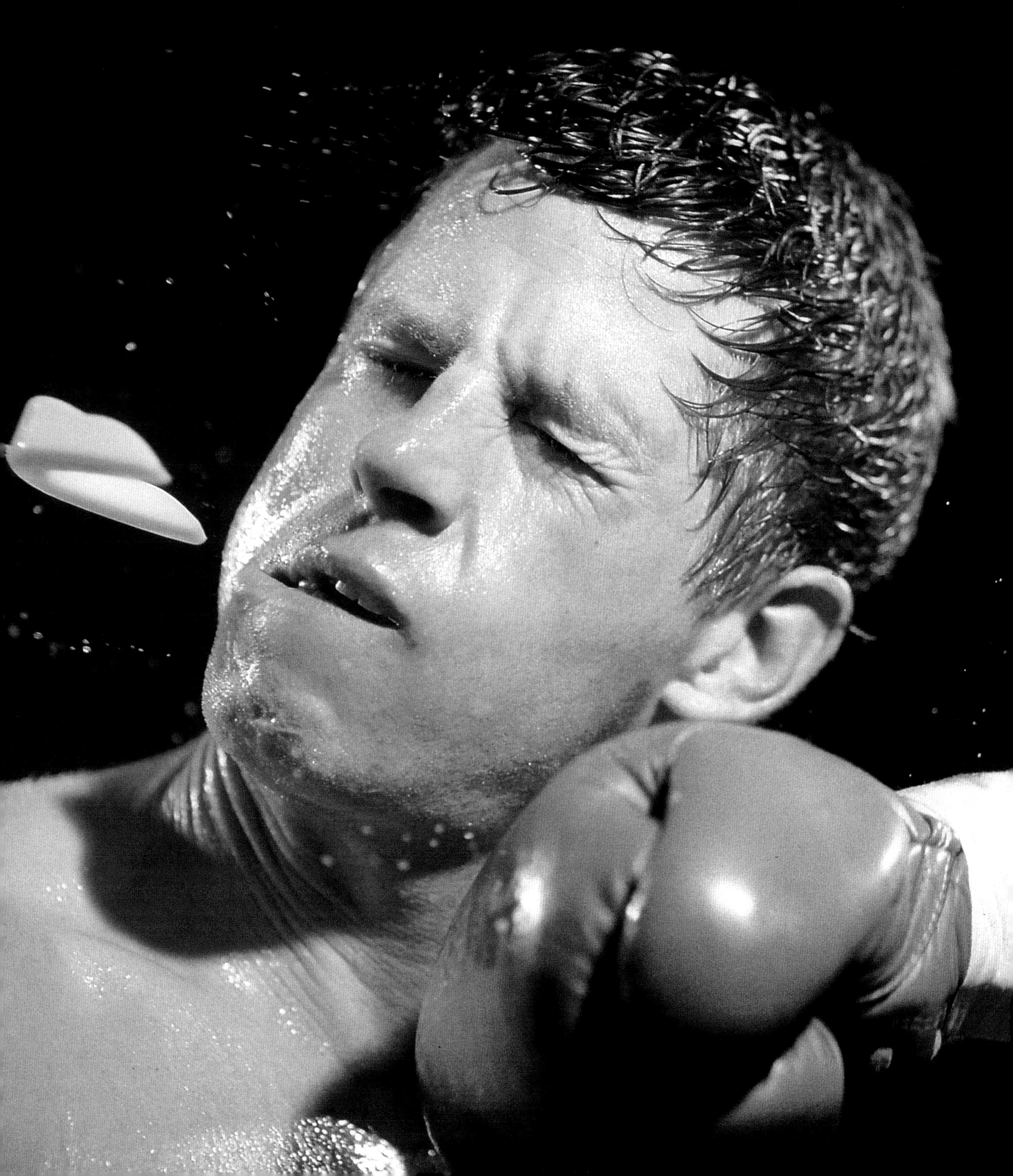

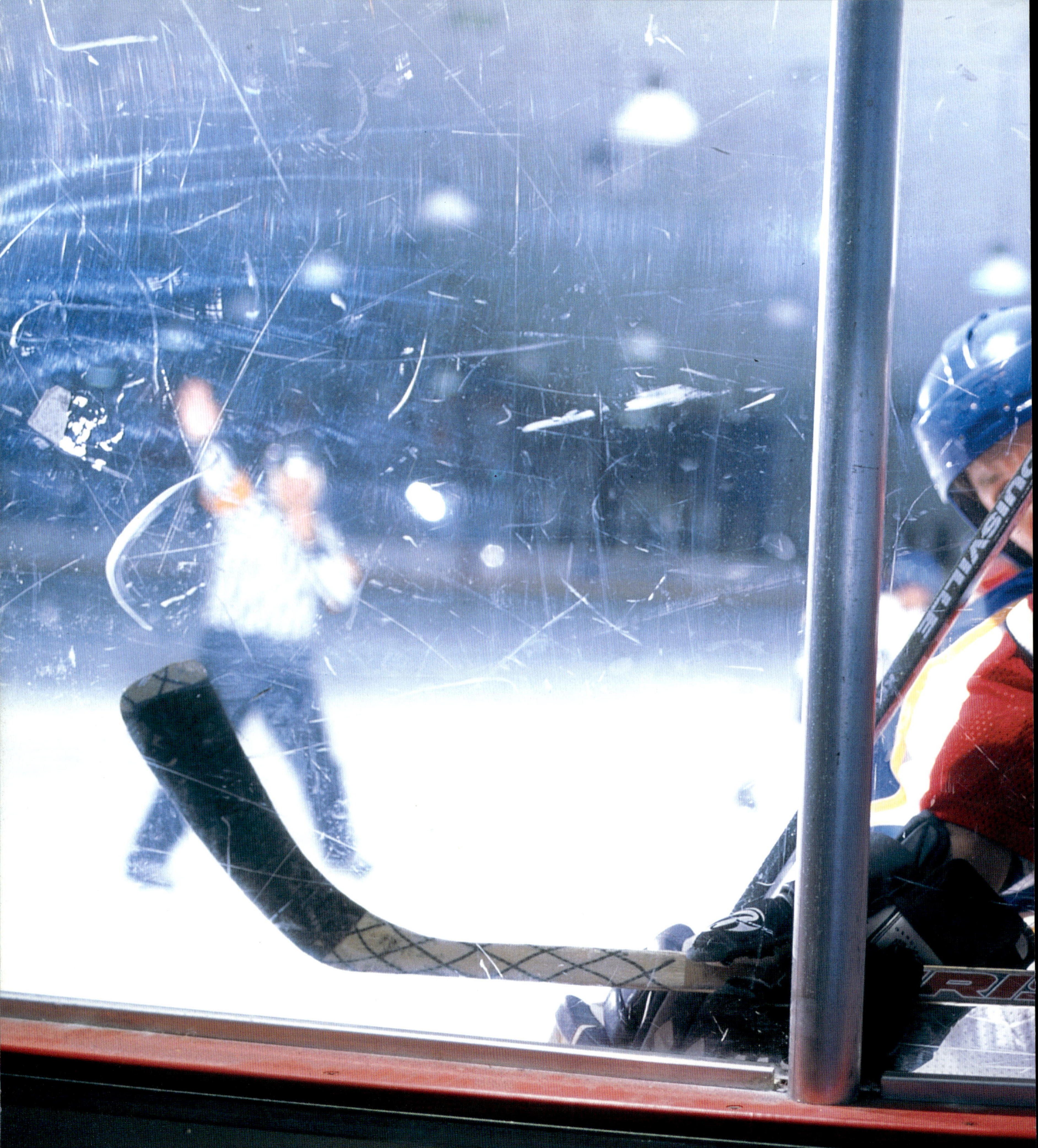

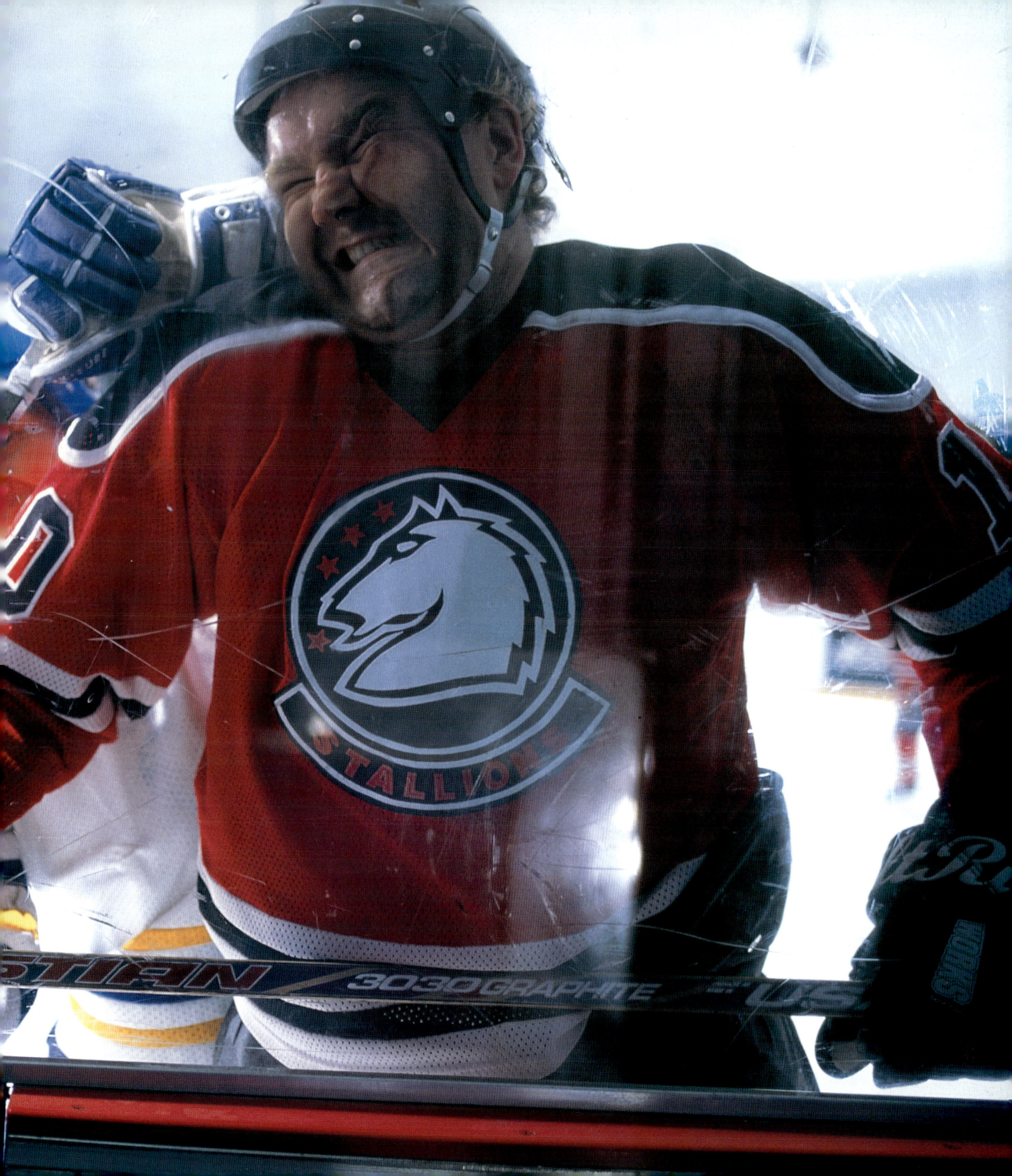
STALLIONS
3030 GRAPHITE

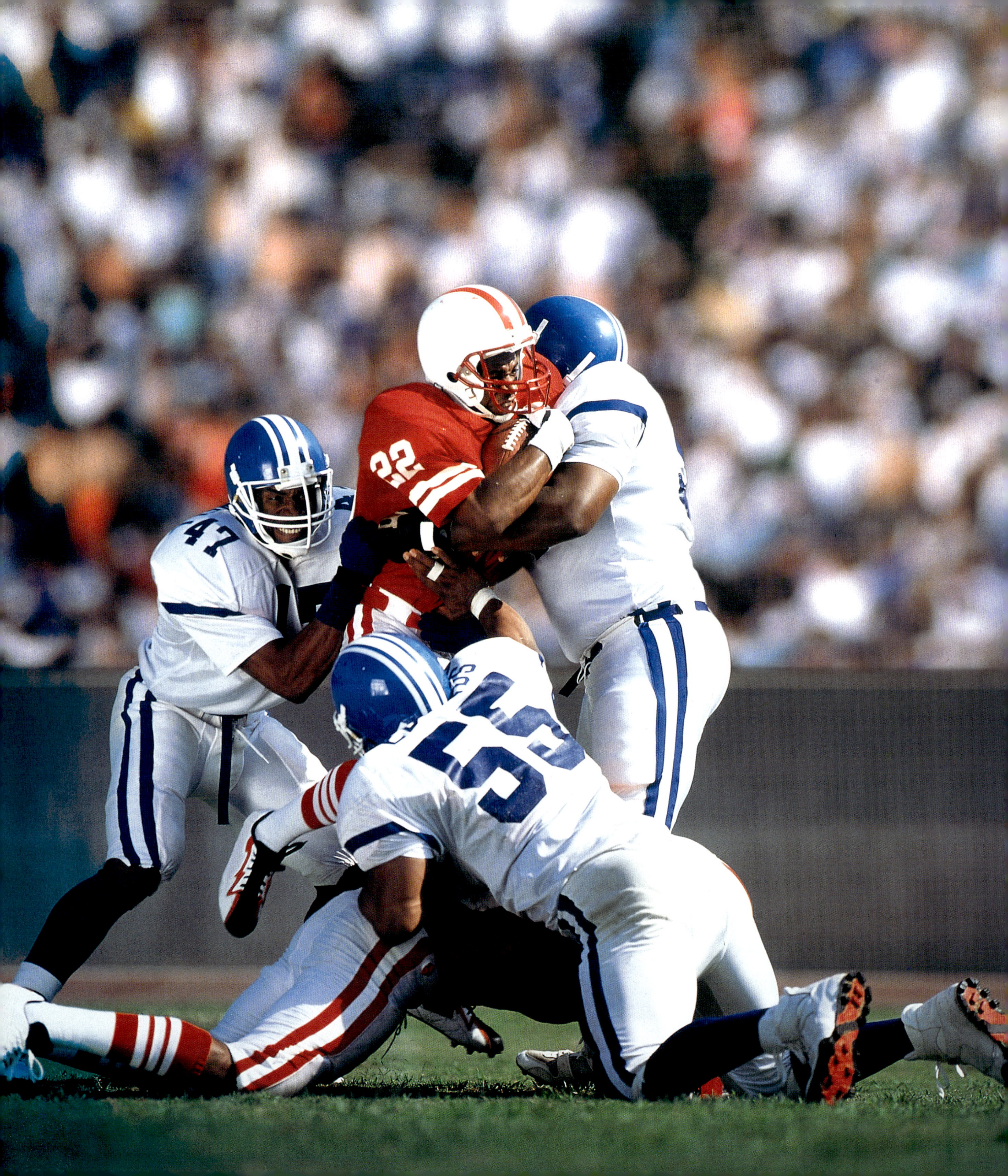
22
47

03
Football, 1997
Mike Powell

04
Soccer, 1997
Mike Powell

05
Soccer, 1997
Mike Powell

04

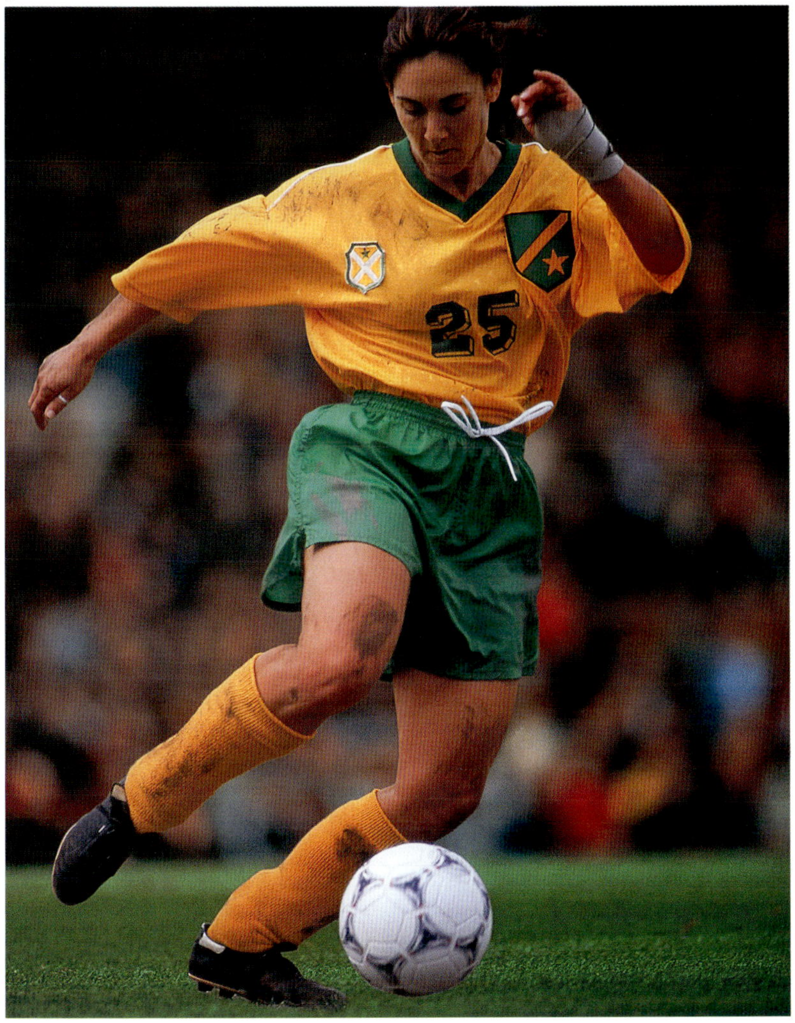

05

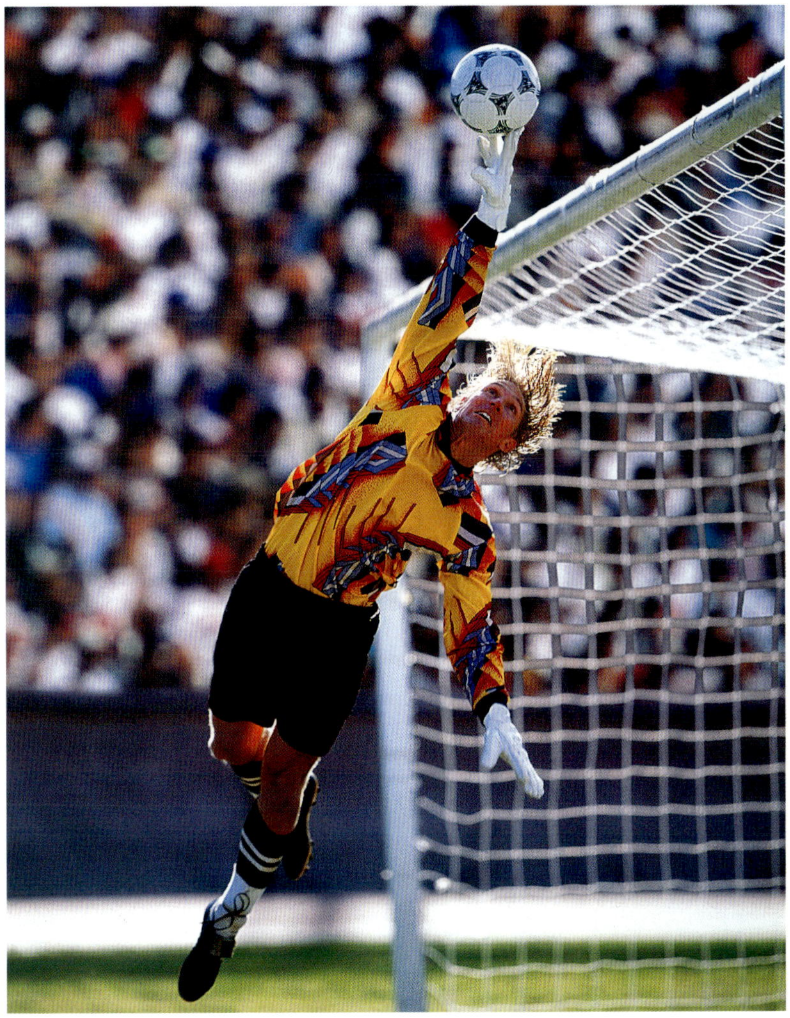

01
Evander Holyfield's chewed ear following Mike Tyson's disqualification for biting, Las Vegas, 1998
Jed Jacobsohn

02 (OVERLEAF)
Wyoming versus Colorado State, Fort Collins, Colorado, 1998
Brian Bahr

THEATRE

As sport changed in response to the demands of television, striving to become more entertaining and camera-friendly, sports photography also adapted to the increasing dominance of the small screen. Photography cannot replay and analyse segments of the game in the way that television does, nor can it follow the entire action of a game as it ebbs and flows, so a more stylized image of sport has developed, attempting to encapsulate the essence of sport in a single startling image. Vibrant colour and strong graphic design are the ingredients that have made this new photographic vision of sport, each picture is a dramatic visual statement demanding space on the page without recourse to a written text. These photographs are moments of pure entertainment and high emotion that leave the spectator in wonderment as they watch the theatre of sport.

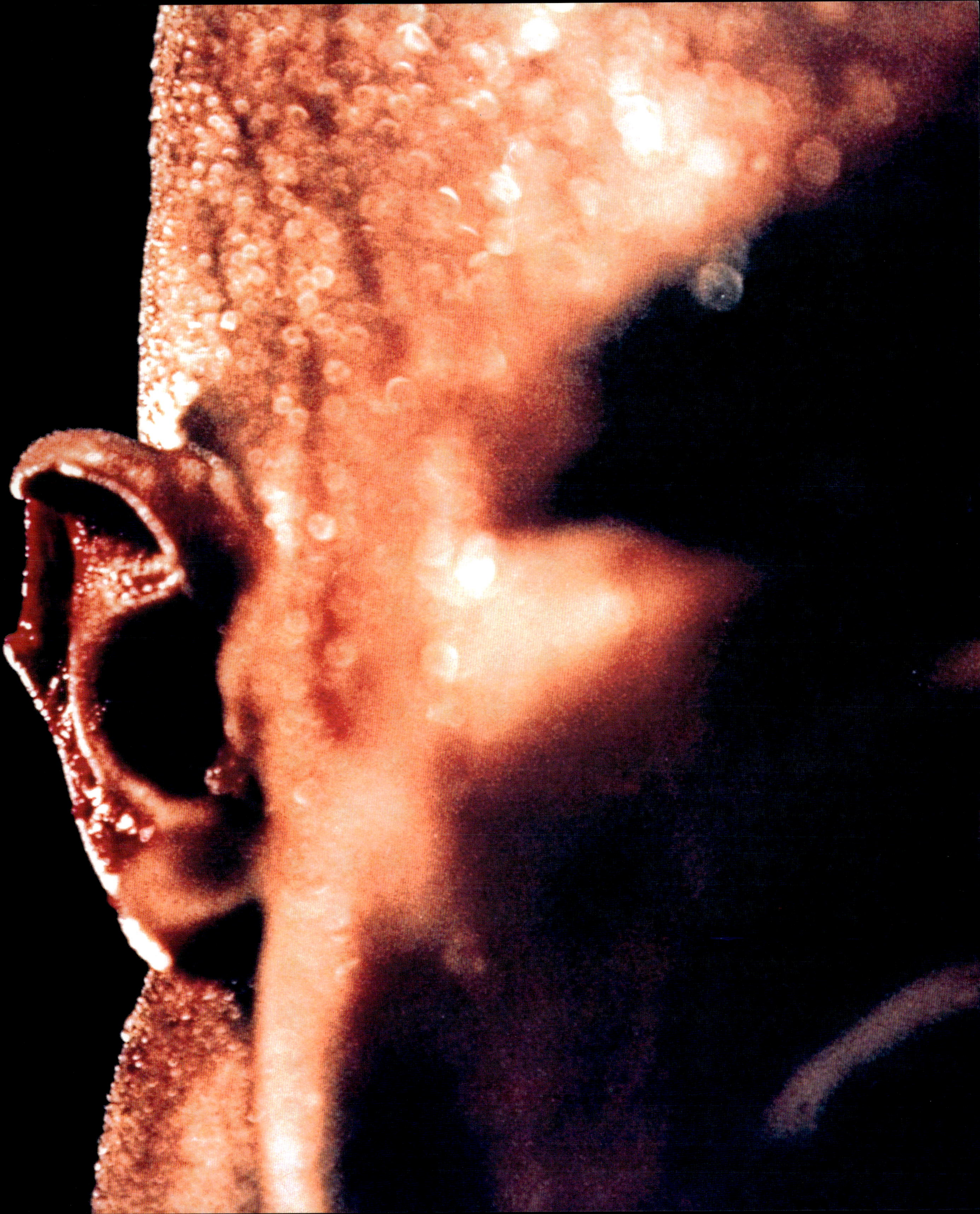

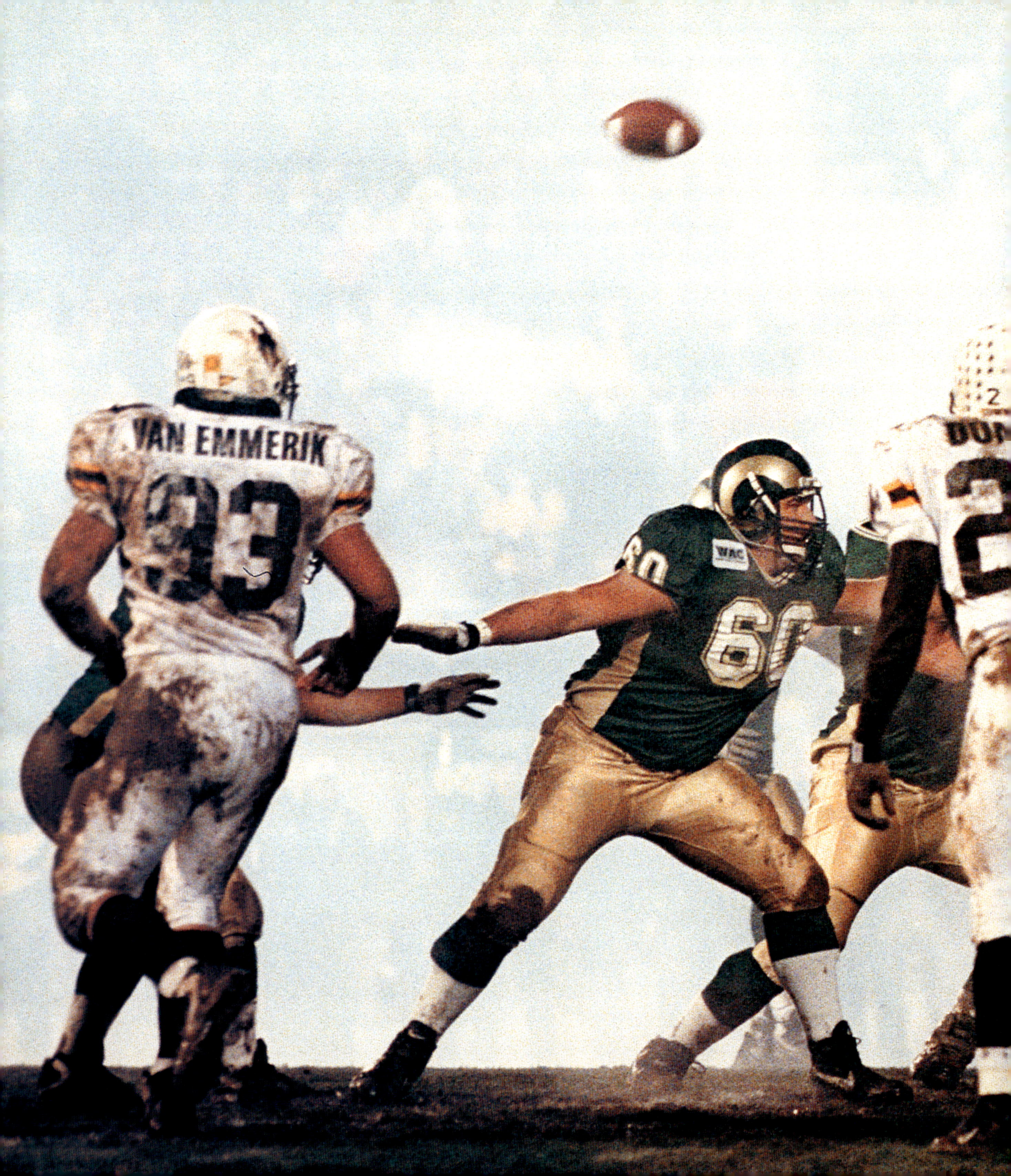
VAN EMMERIK
93
60
WAC

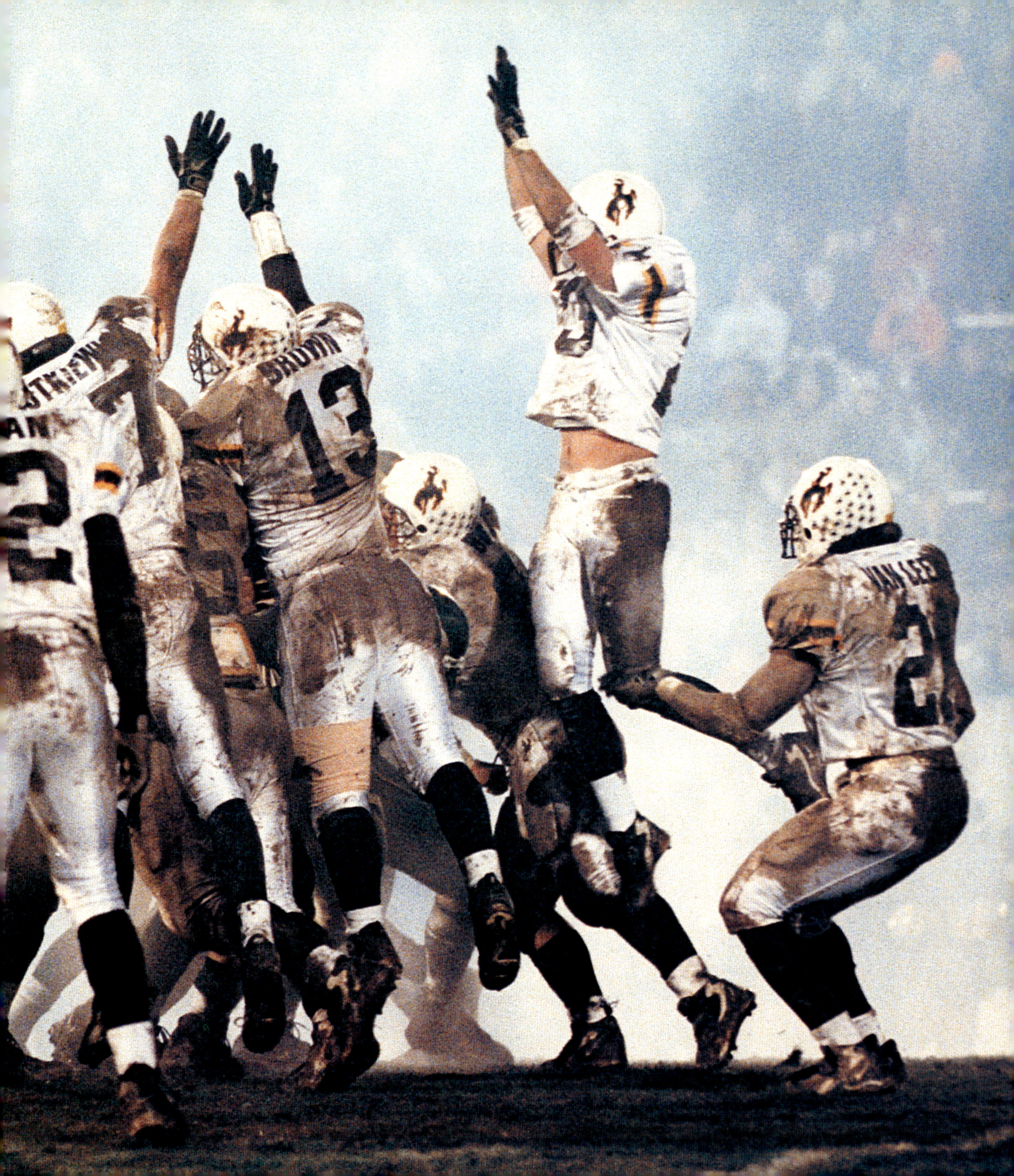
BROWN
13

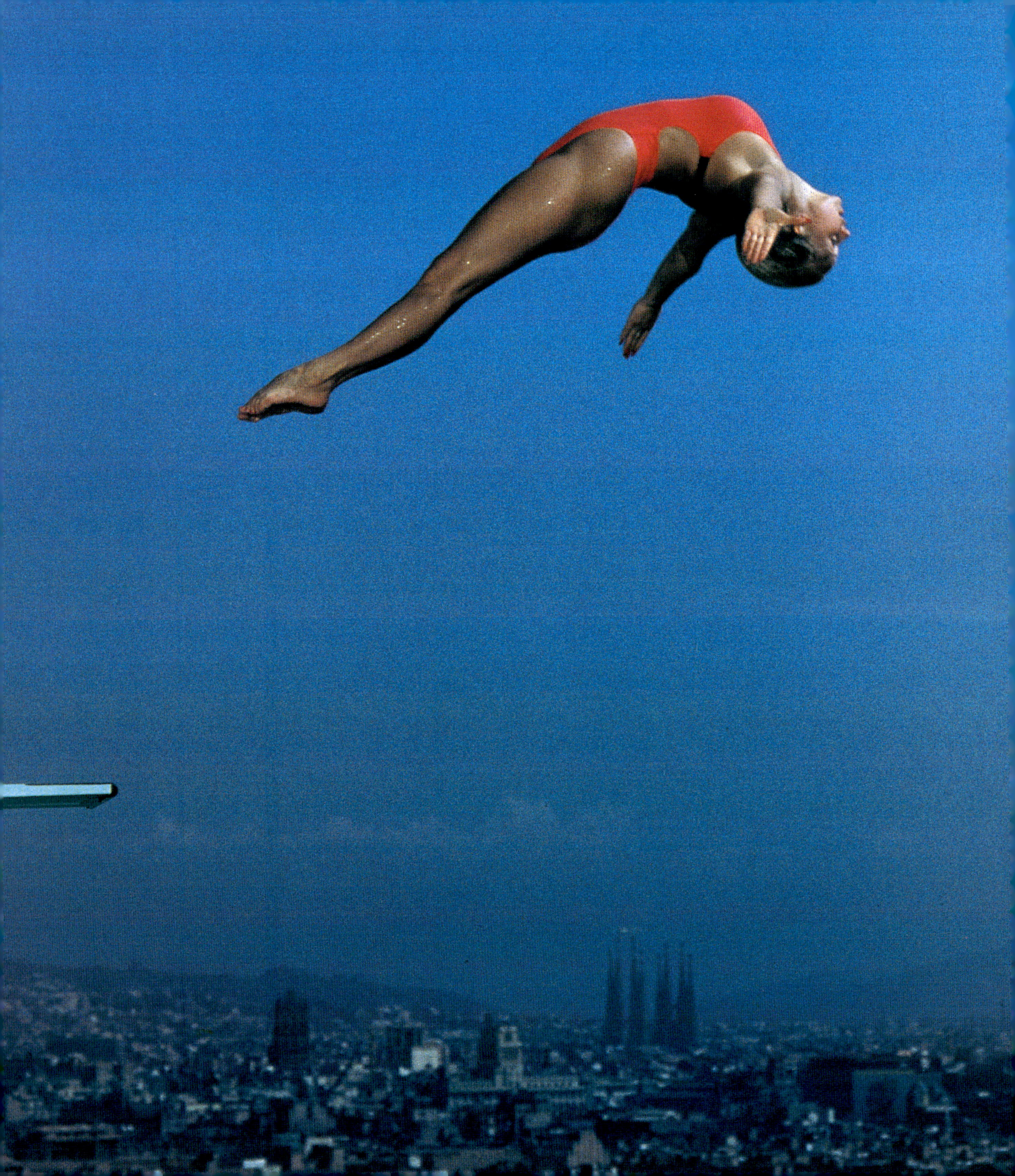

03
Tracey Miles, Barcelona, 1992
Bob Martin

04
The New York Yankees' Paul O'Neil, New York, 1998
Ezra O Shaw

05 (OVERLEAF)
Alexander Wurz crashes, Montreal, 1998
David Taylor

04

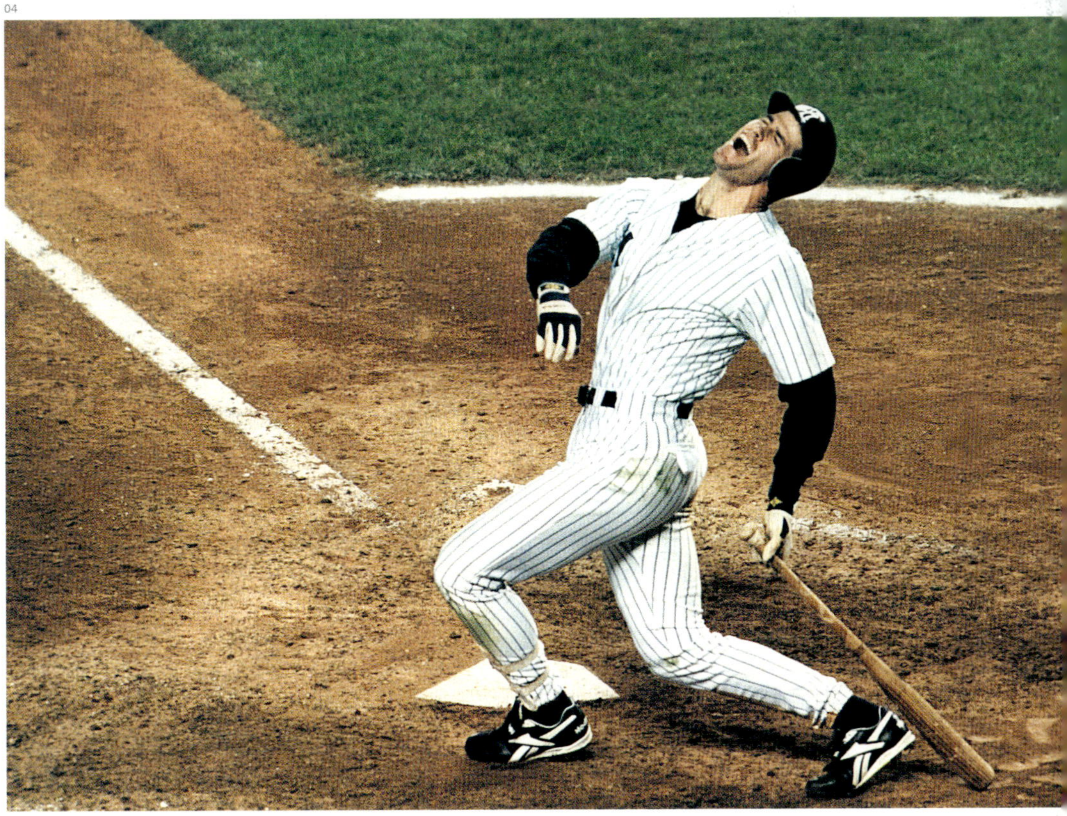

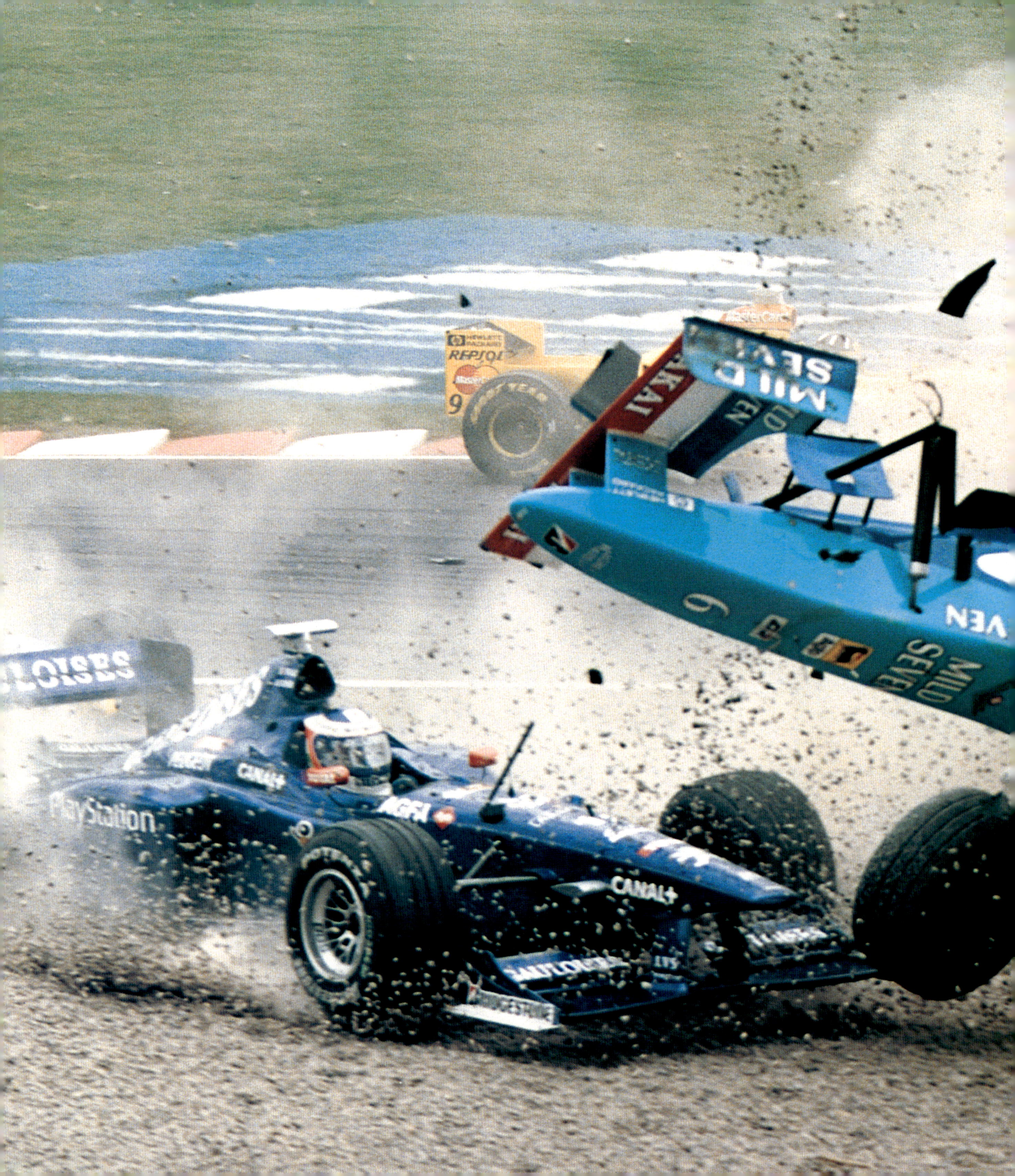
REPSOL
PlayStation
CANAL+
AGFA
CANAL+

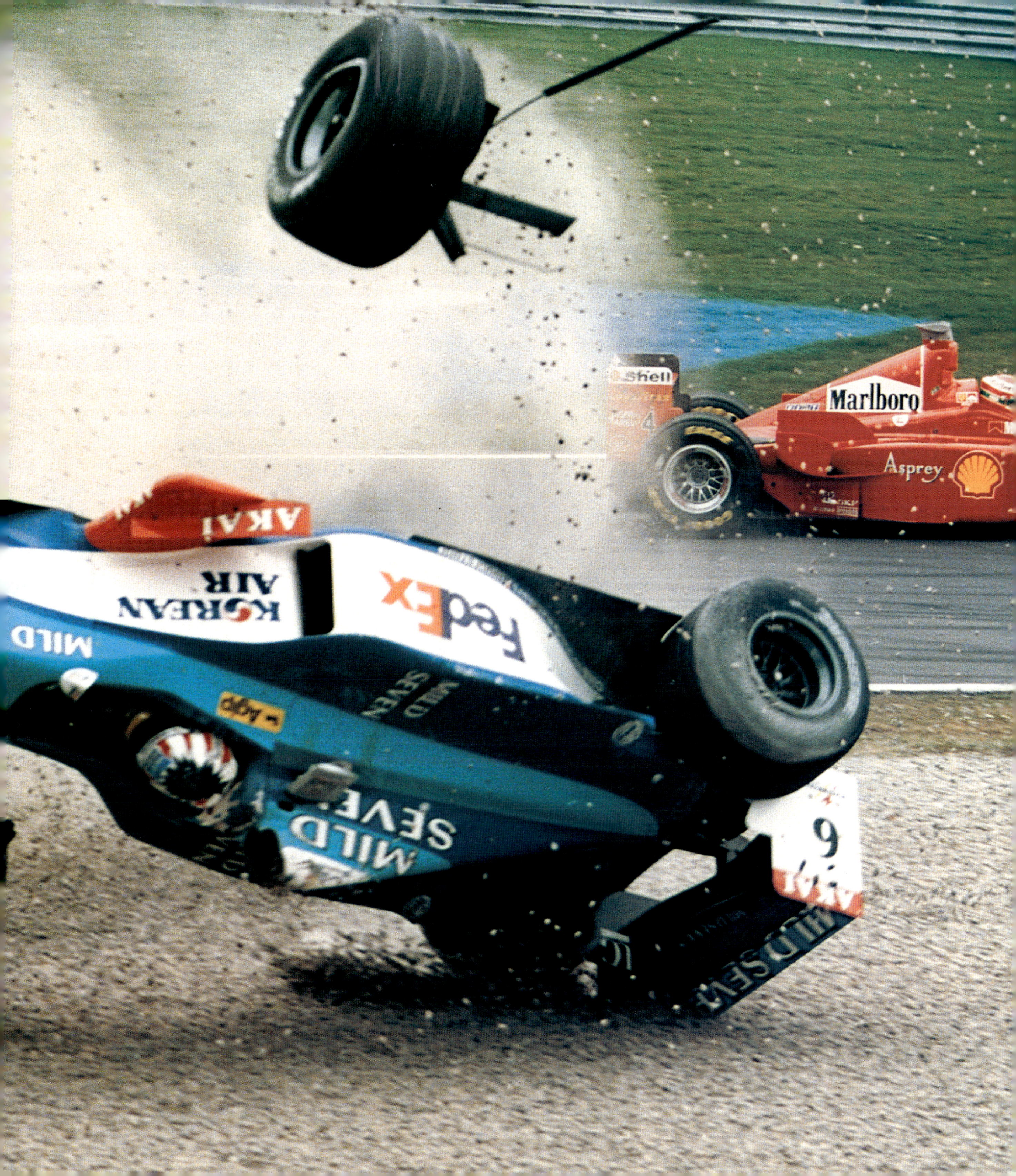
Shell
Marlboro
Asprey
AKAI
KOREAN AIR
FedEx
MILD
MILD SEVEN
9

06
Gail Devers celebrates victory, Merlene Ottey (foreground) reflects on second place, Atlanta, 1996
Gerard Vandystadt

07
Diego Maradona of Argentina, against Belgium, Barcelona, 1982
Steve Powell

08 (OVERLEAF)
Mike Powell, Atlanta, 1996
Gary M Prior

06

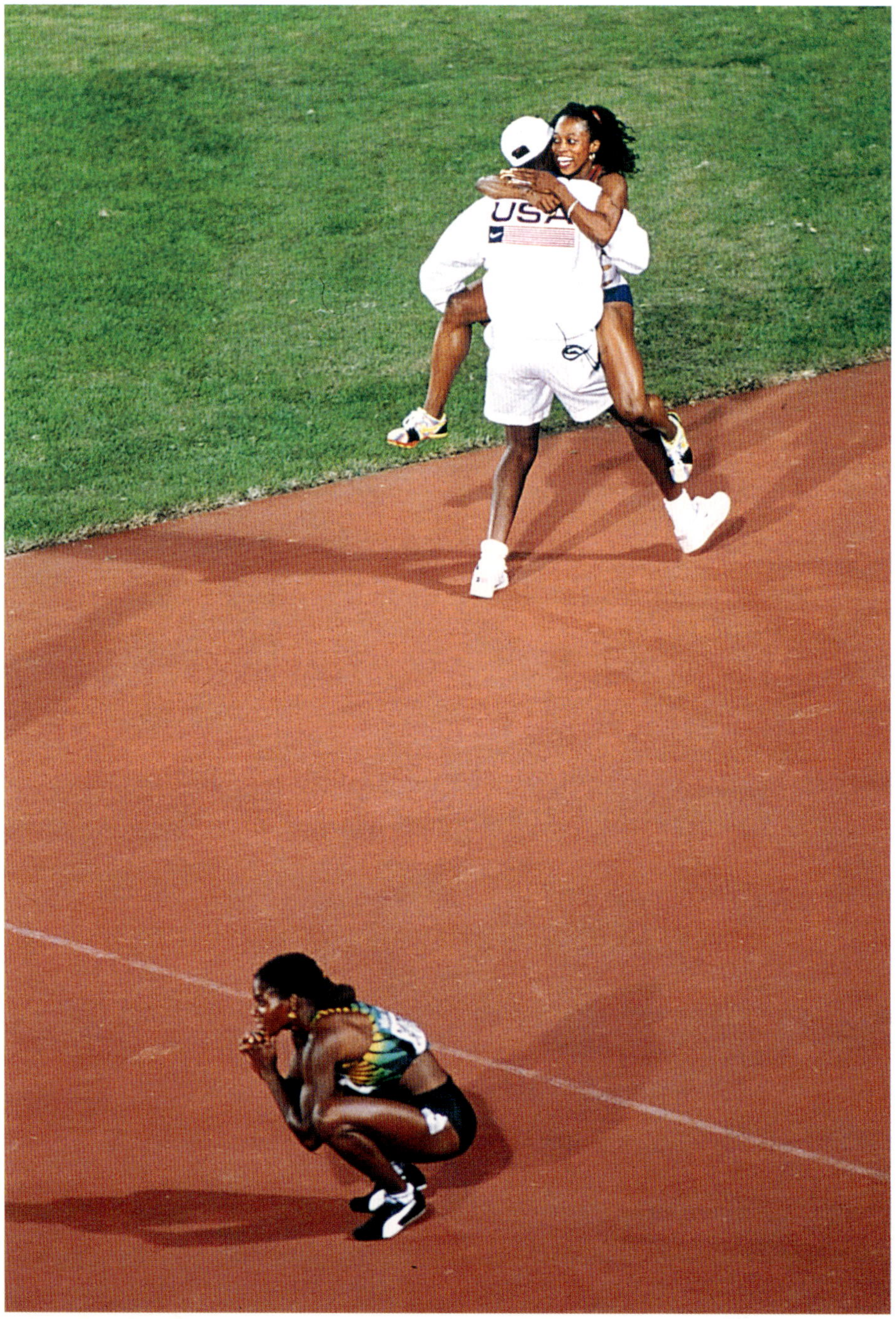

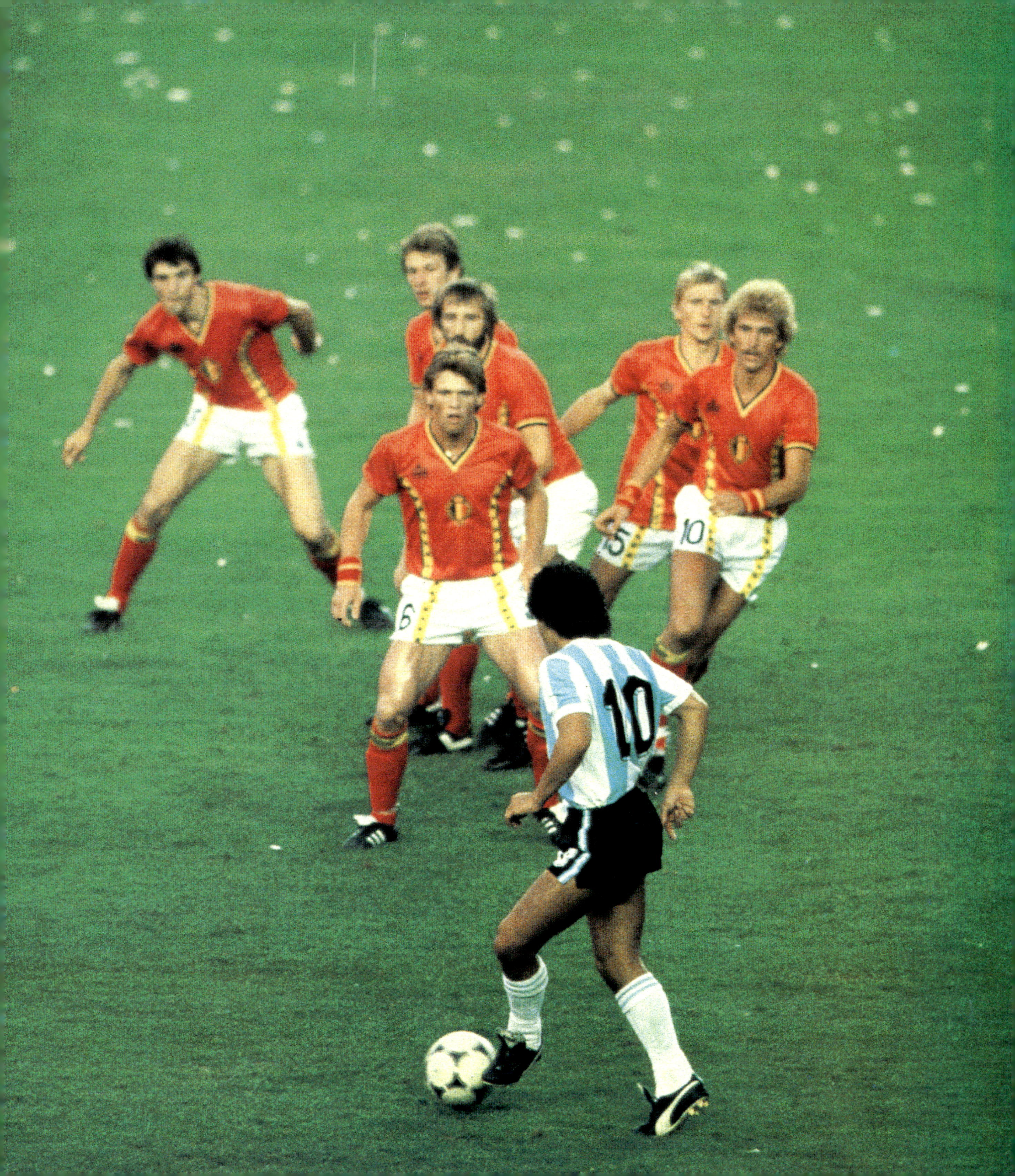

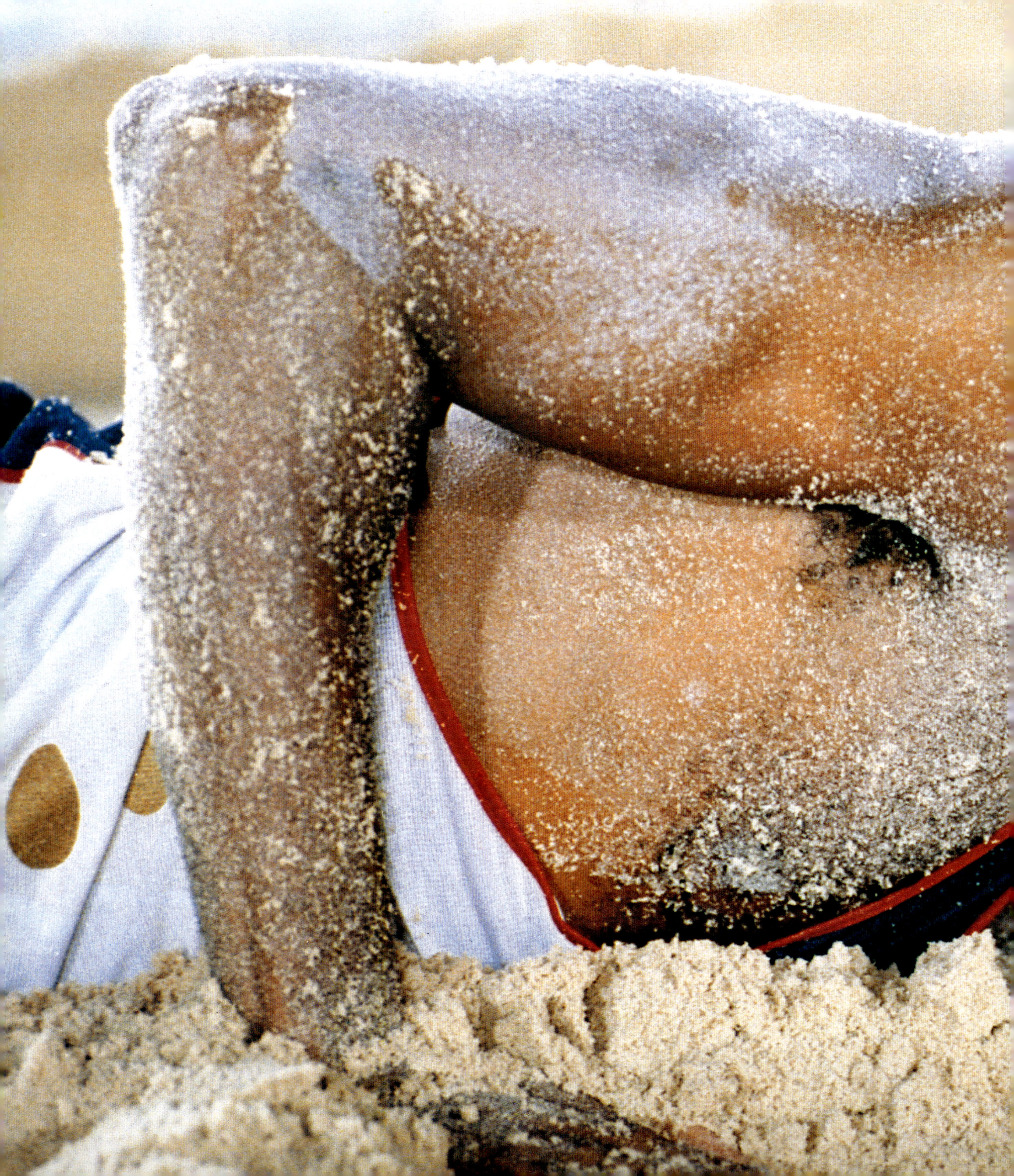

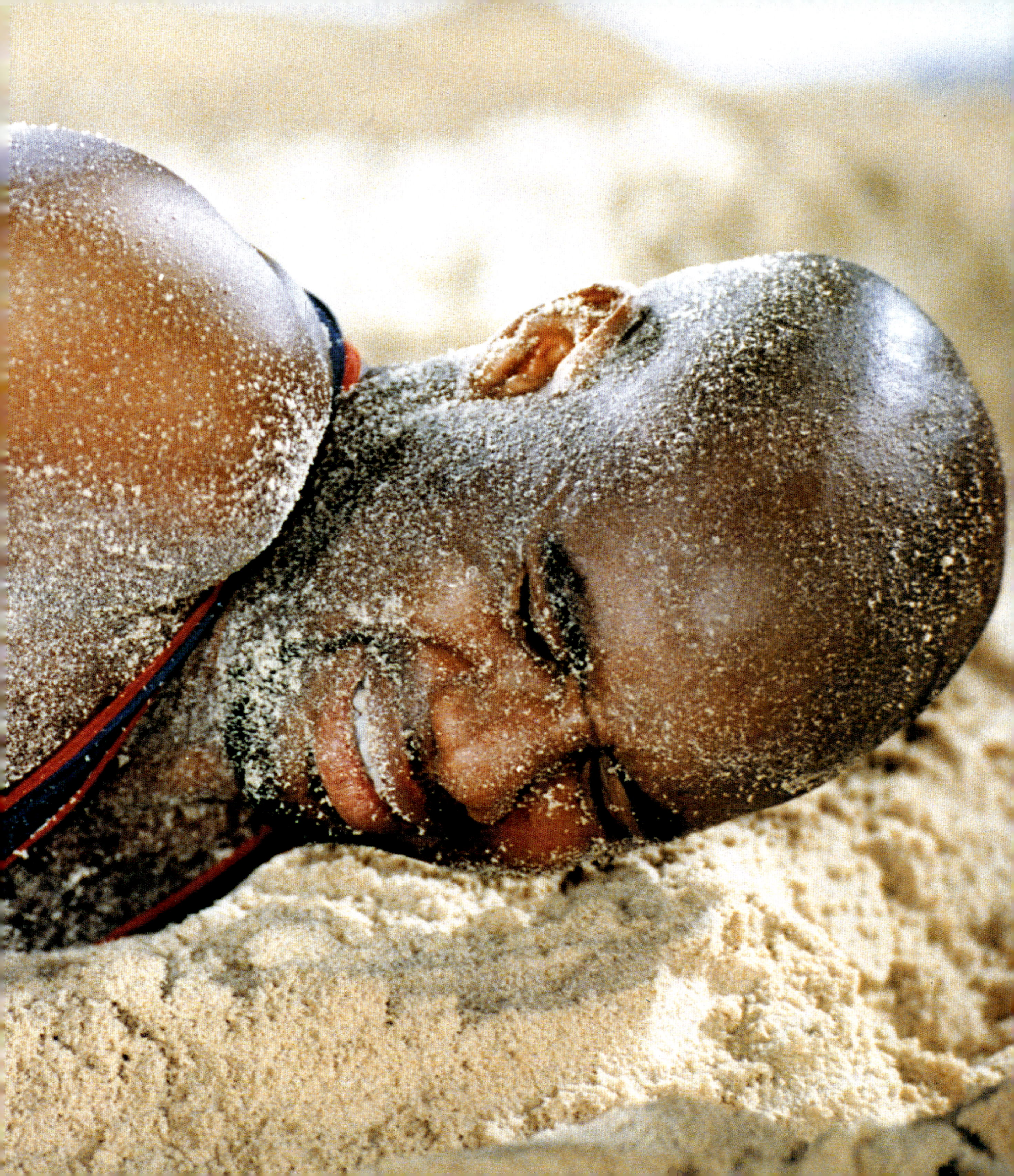

01
Michael Johnson's golden running shoe, 1996
Gary M Prior

02 (OVERLEAF)
Michael Jordan's 'Air Jordans', 1995
Jonathan Daniel

IDENTITY

The requirements of marketing and corporate sponsorship in contemporary sport have resulted in sporting personalities having to go further than just being dedicated to their sport, possessing excellent skills and having the will to win. To be a successful contemporary sports star means to be different and highly visible. Body adornments like jewellery, make-up and tattoos create new sporting identities which the media are eager to consume. With a degree of flare and flamboyance a sports star can create an image that stands out from their fellow competitors, bringing notoriety, popularity and extra sponsorship endorsements.

For a smaller group of élite athletes, corporate sponsorship has helped make them world superstars. Companies that manufacture sportswear have invested vast amounts of money in global marketing, associating their logos with the pinnacle of excellence in sport.

The one product that has defined this relationship between sport and commerce most clearly is the shoe. That it is possible to recognize someone by only seeing the shoes they are wearing, and that photographers consider them a subject worth portraying, illustrates the power of marketing and corporate sponsorship. Sports shoes have come to embody the aspirations of ordinary people as well, representing the cutting edge in design and technology. Fashion, advertising and sport have all come together in the photography of the sports shoe.

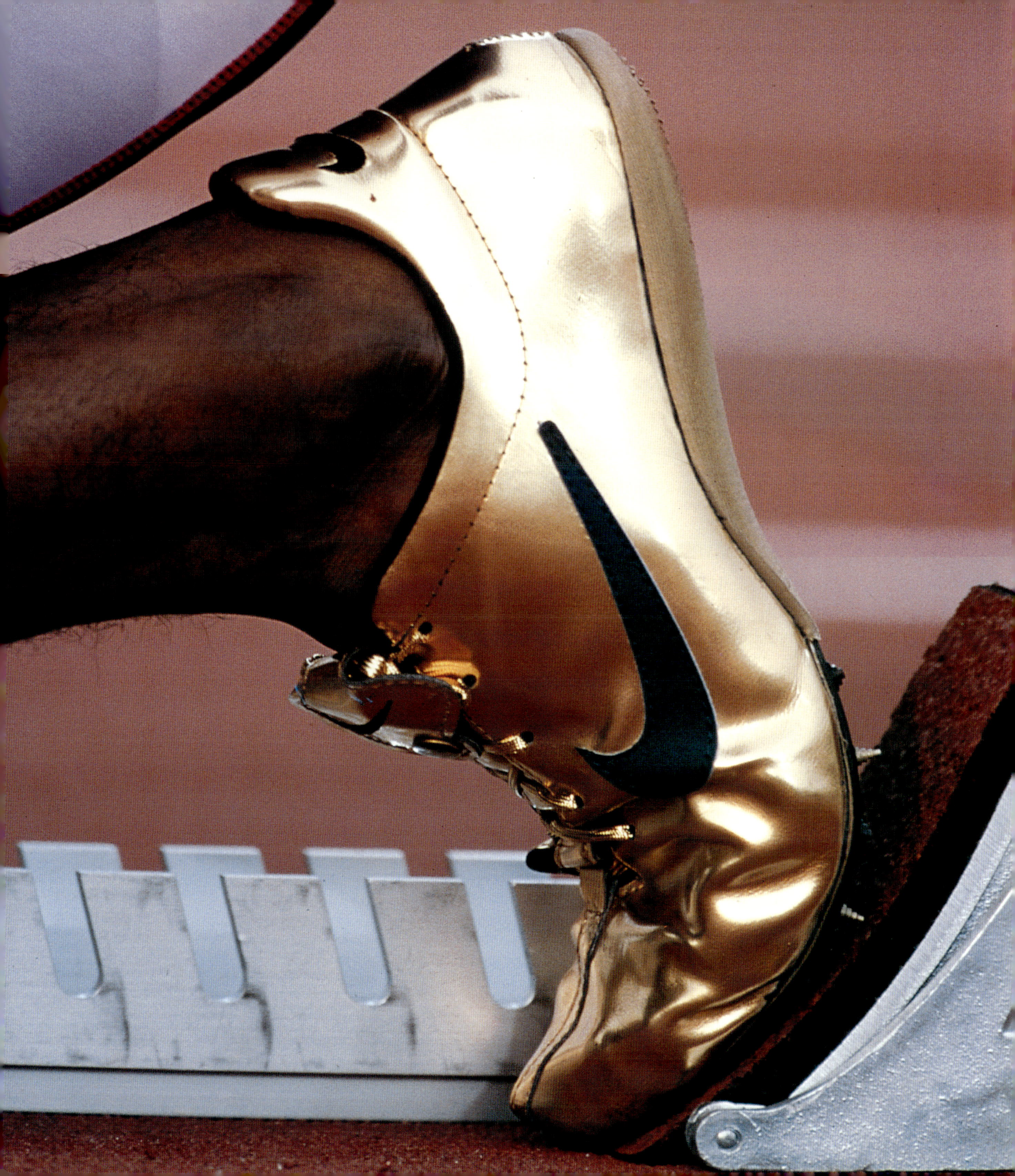

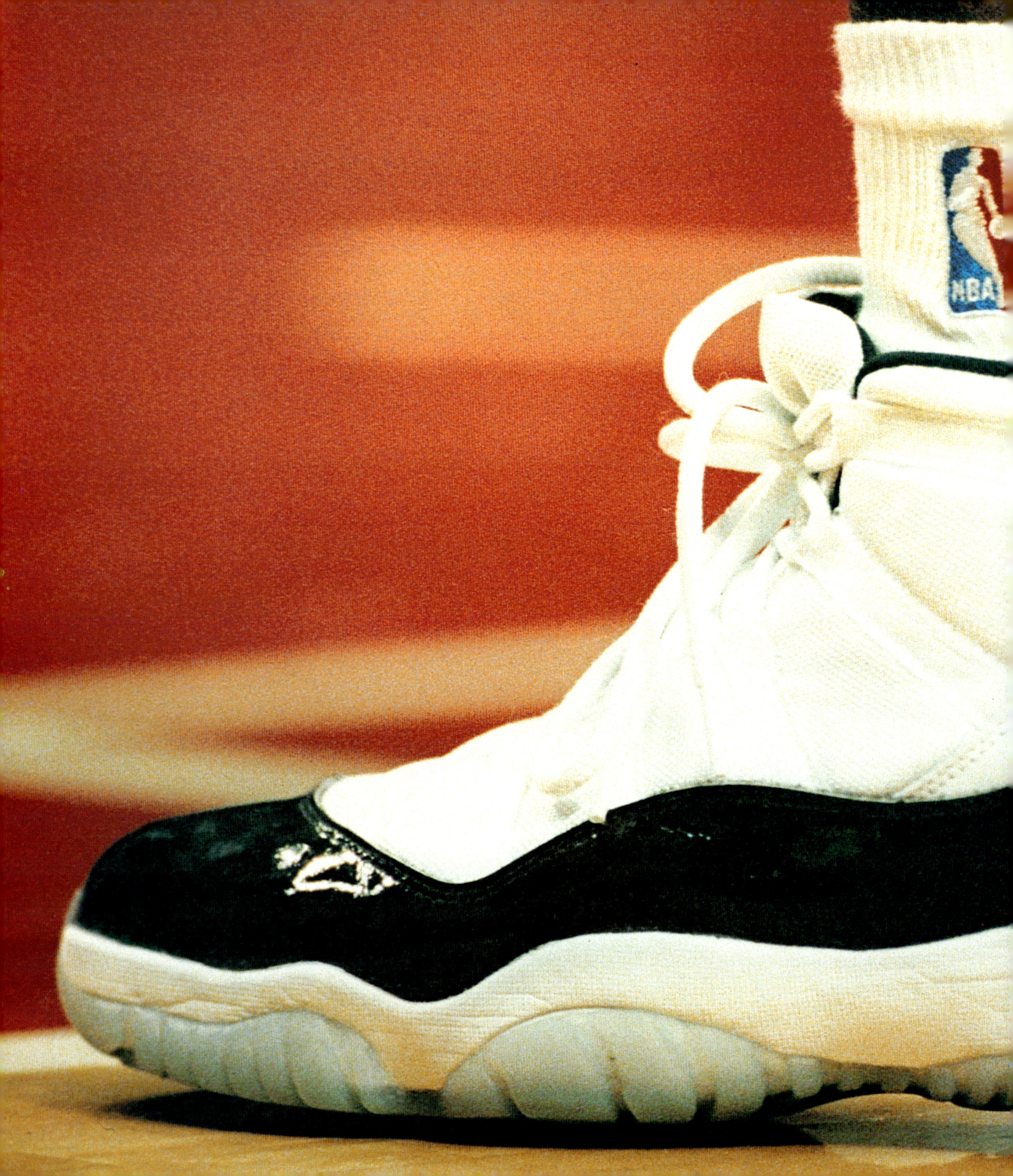
NBA

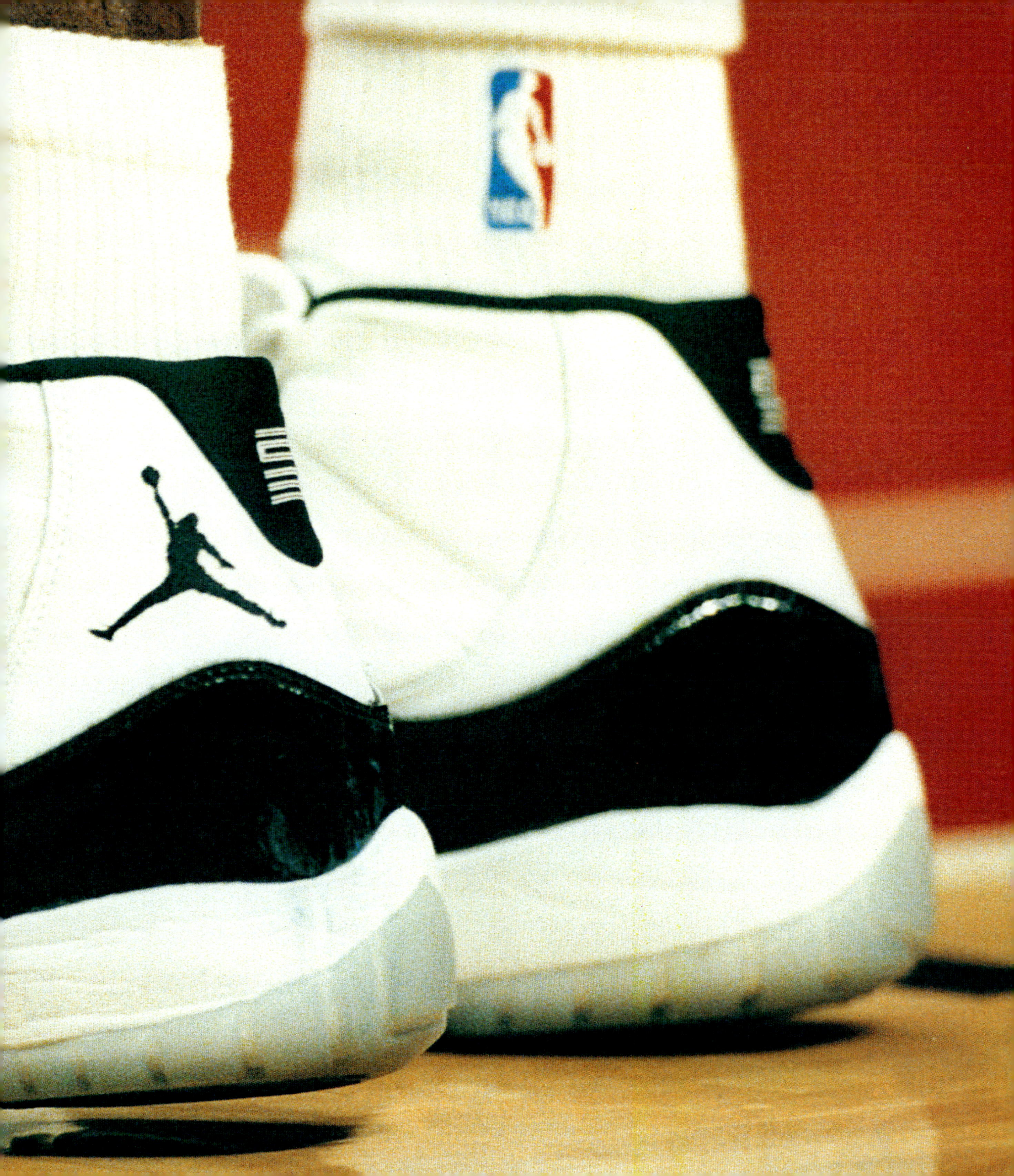

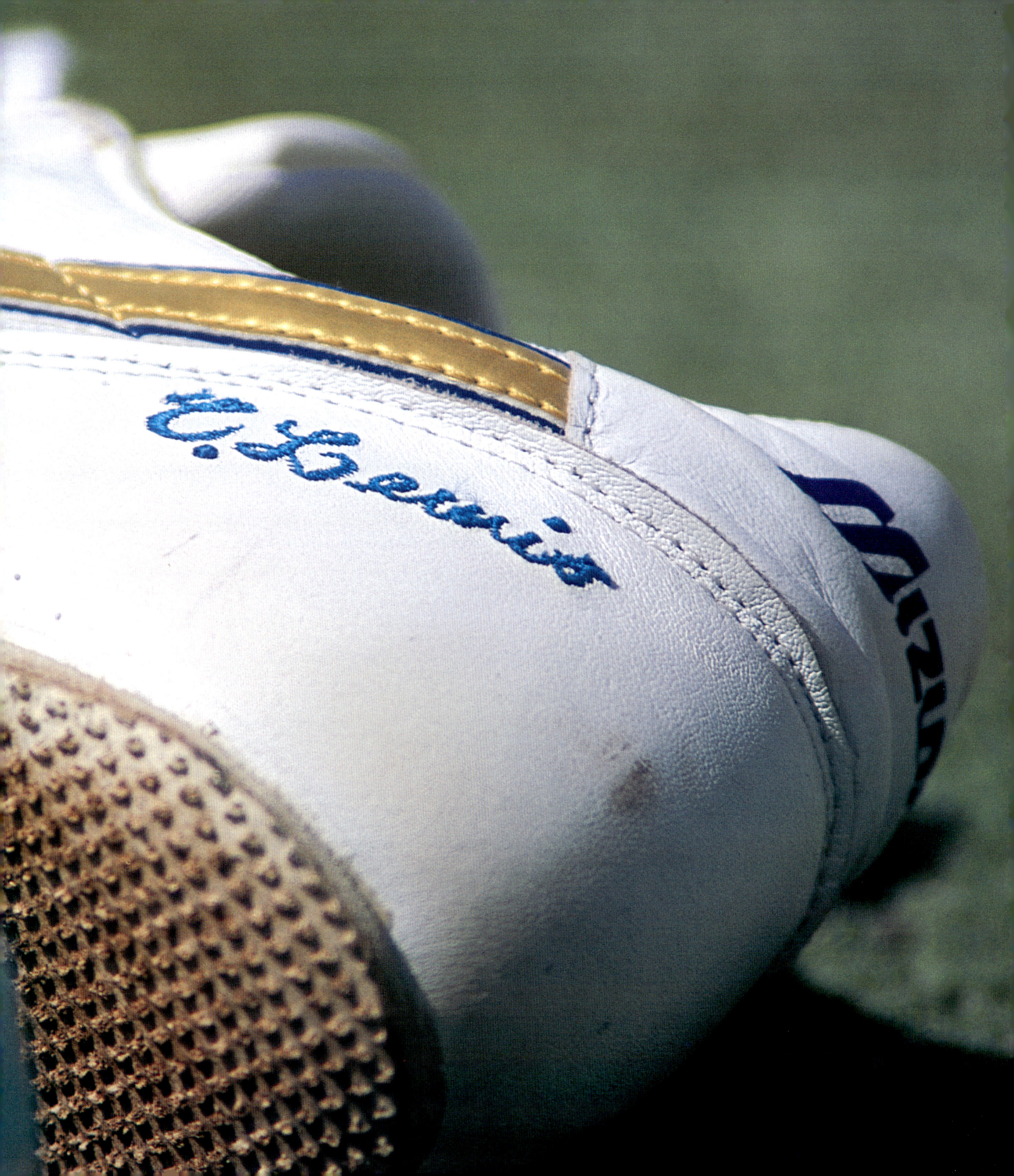
C.Lewis

03
Carl Lewis's running spikes, 1991
Gray Mortimore

04
Betty Lise, 1999
Stephane Kempinaire

05 (OVERLEAF)
Colin Jackson, 1997
Clive Brunskill

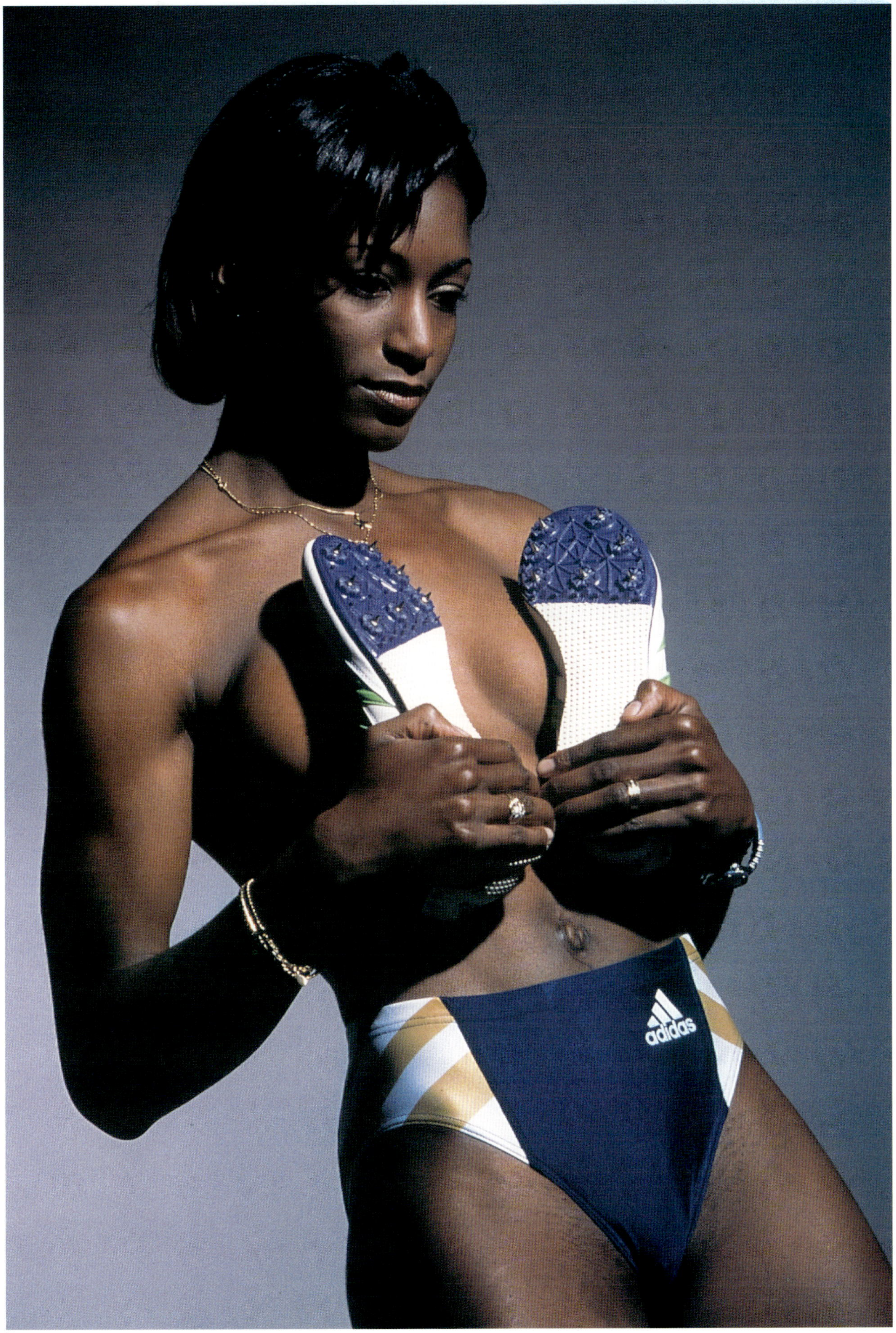

04

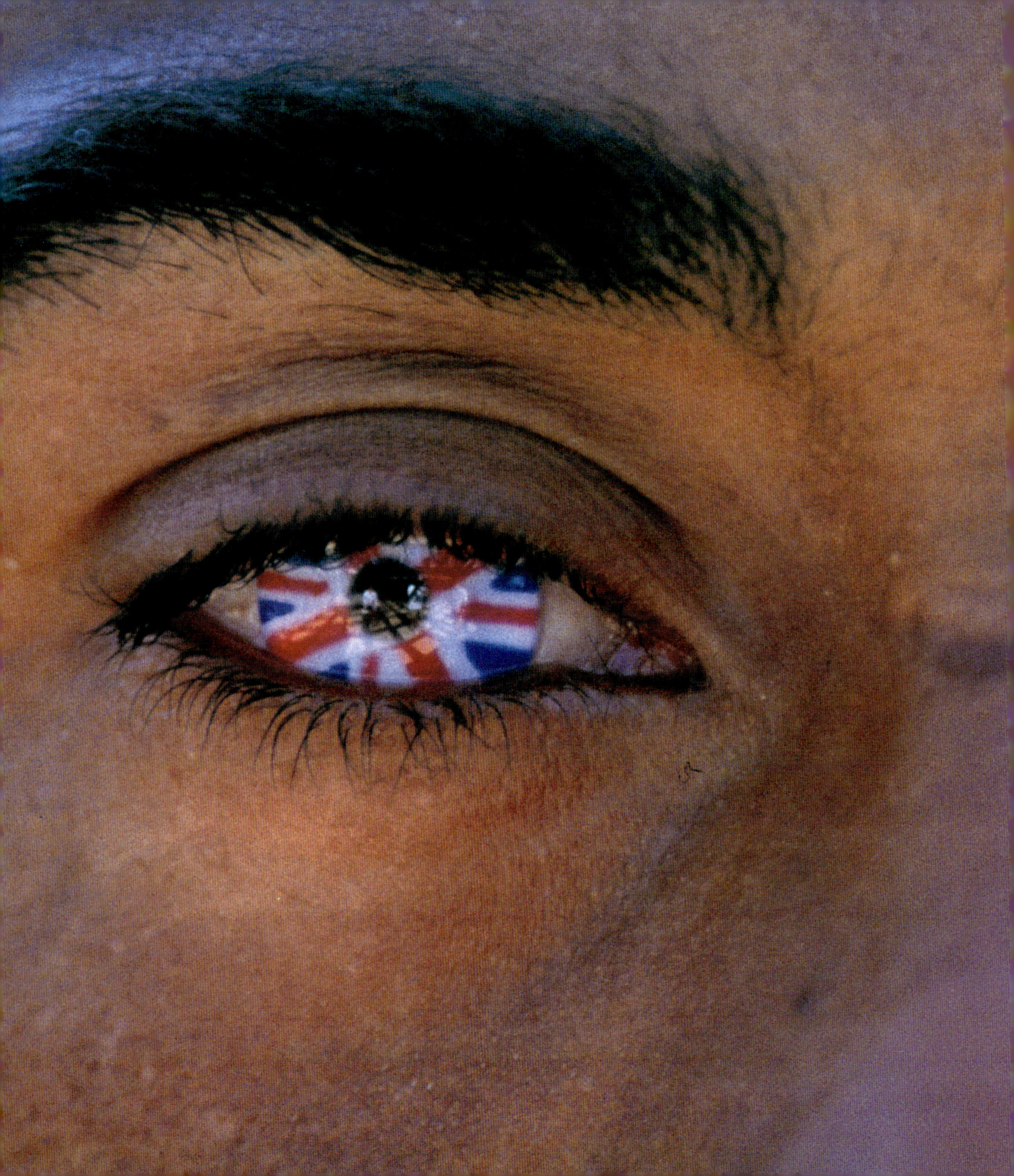

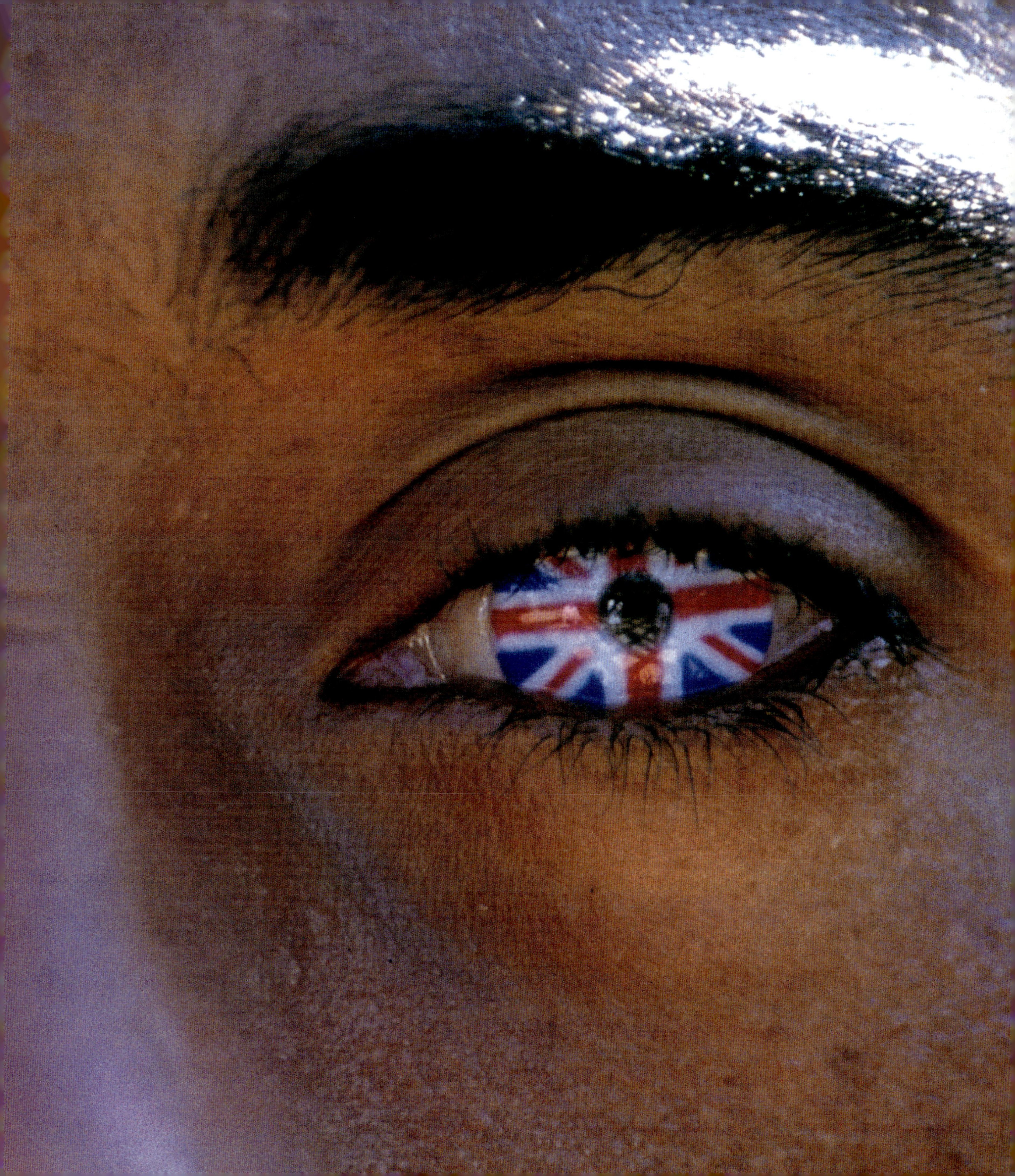

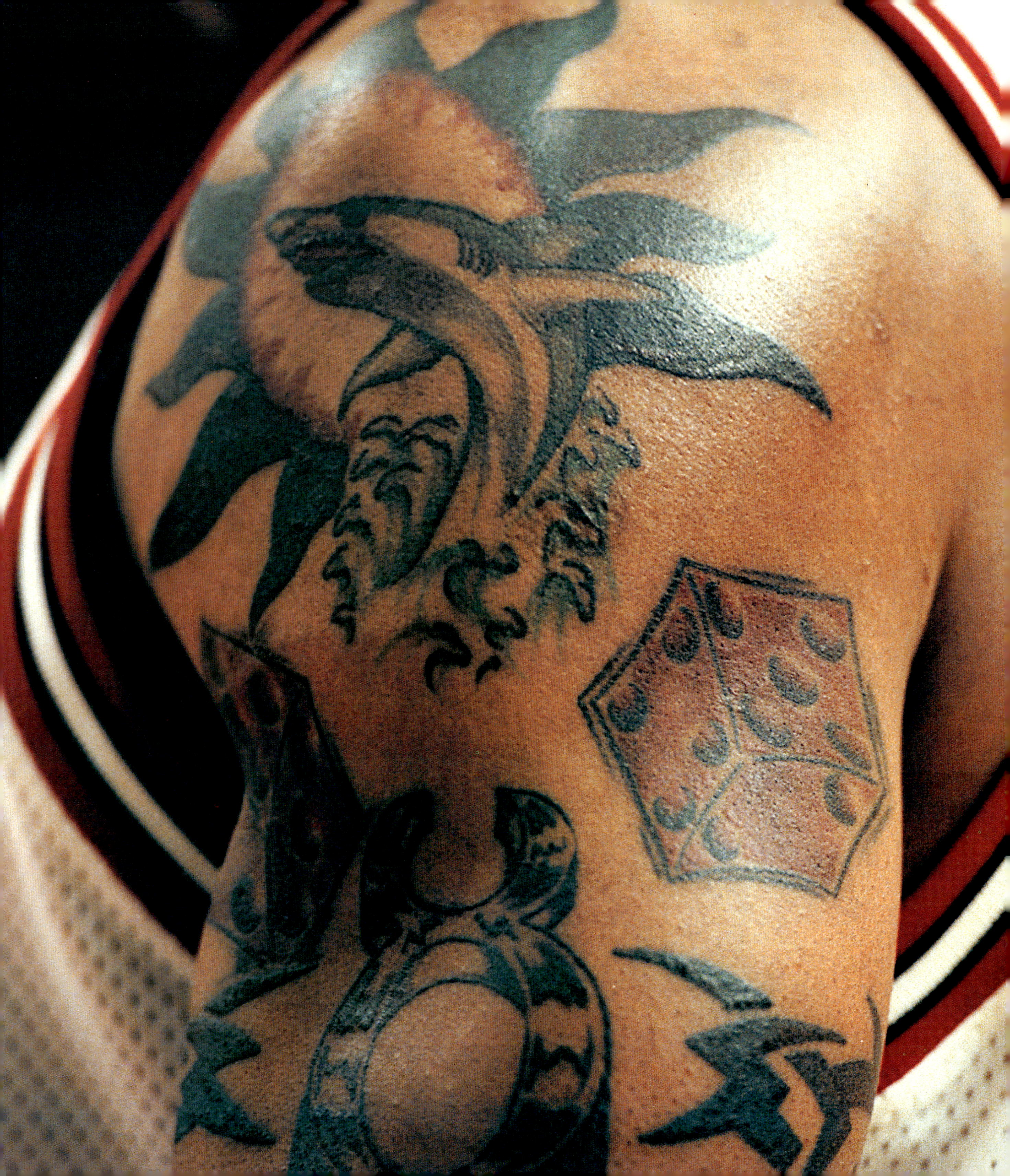

06
Dennis Rodman, 1996
Jonathan Daniel

07
Gail Devers, 1997
Stephane Kempinaire

07

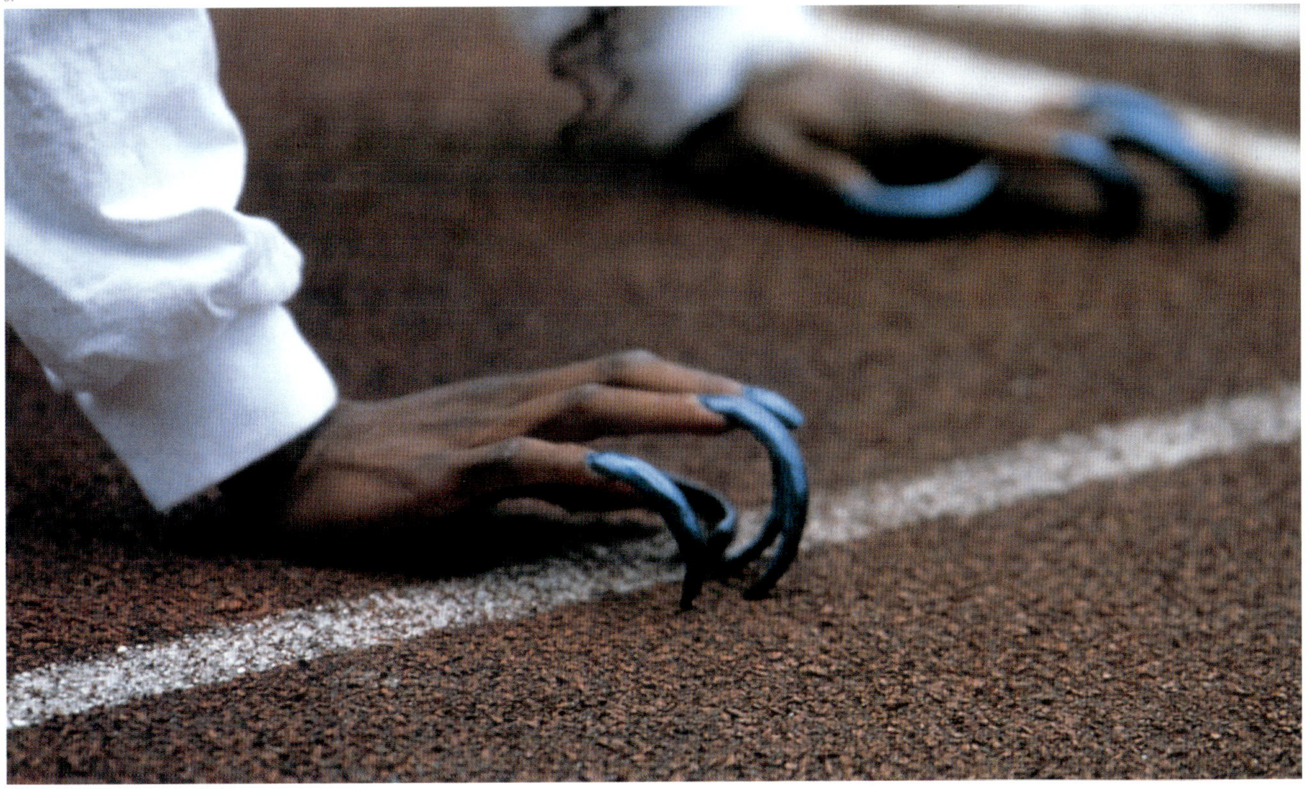

01
Jonty Rhodes of South Africa, Birmingham, 1998
Adrian Murrell

02 (OVERLEAF)
Adrian Ilie, Paris, 1999
Clive Brunskill

THE MOMENT

At important sporting events hundreds of photographers wait with their cameras, poised ready to get the crucial shot. Though a photographer may spend long days sitting on the sidelines and shoot many rolls of film, very few of the frames will ever be reproduced; capturing the one defining moment of an event is what counts. Helped by motor-driven cameras, capable of taking multiple frames a second, and a great deal of skill and experience, the modern sports photographer is often able to capture the instant of heroic action or the defining moment of an event – the very fraction of a second, from many hours or even days, that matters most. Also captured are those moments of chance when the usual chaotic patterns of running and jumping may fall for a fleeting second into apparently choreographed harmony, and the ballet of sport is displayed for all to see. This is unique to photography and part of the arsenal sports photography uses to compete with television.

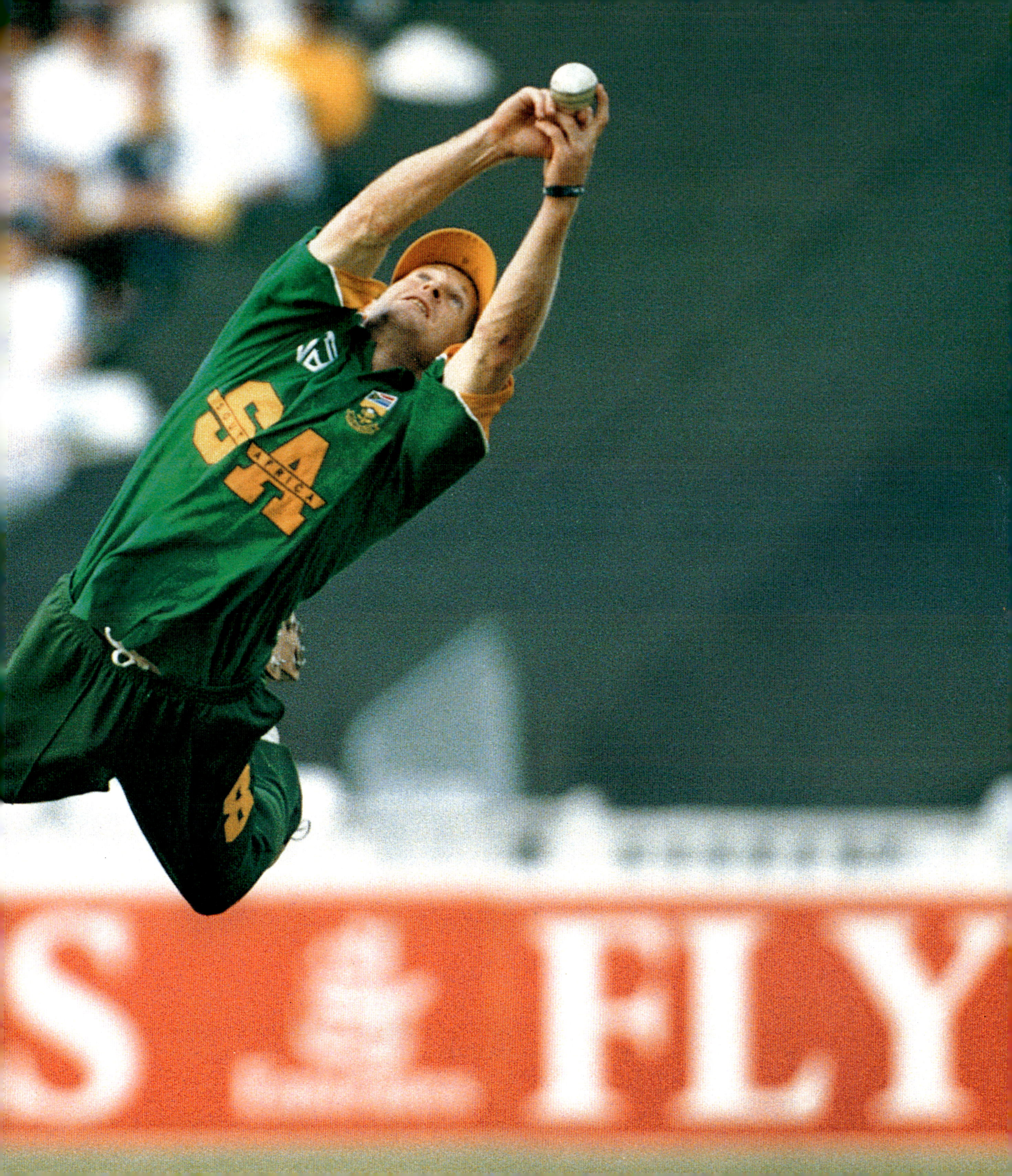
SA
FLY

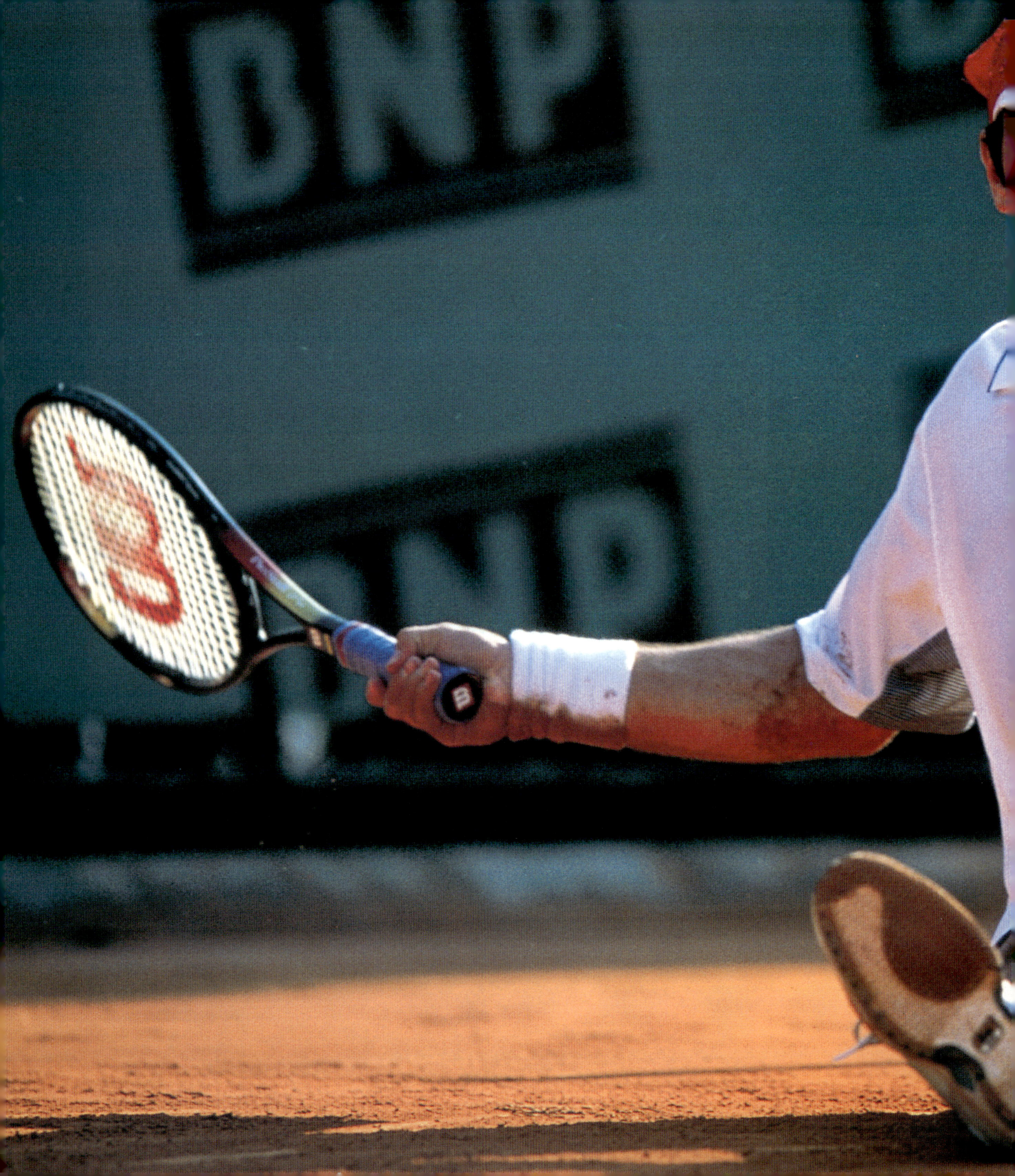
BNP

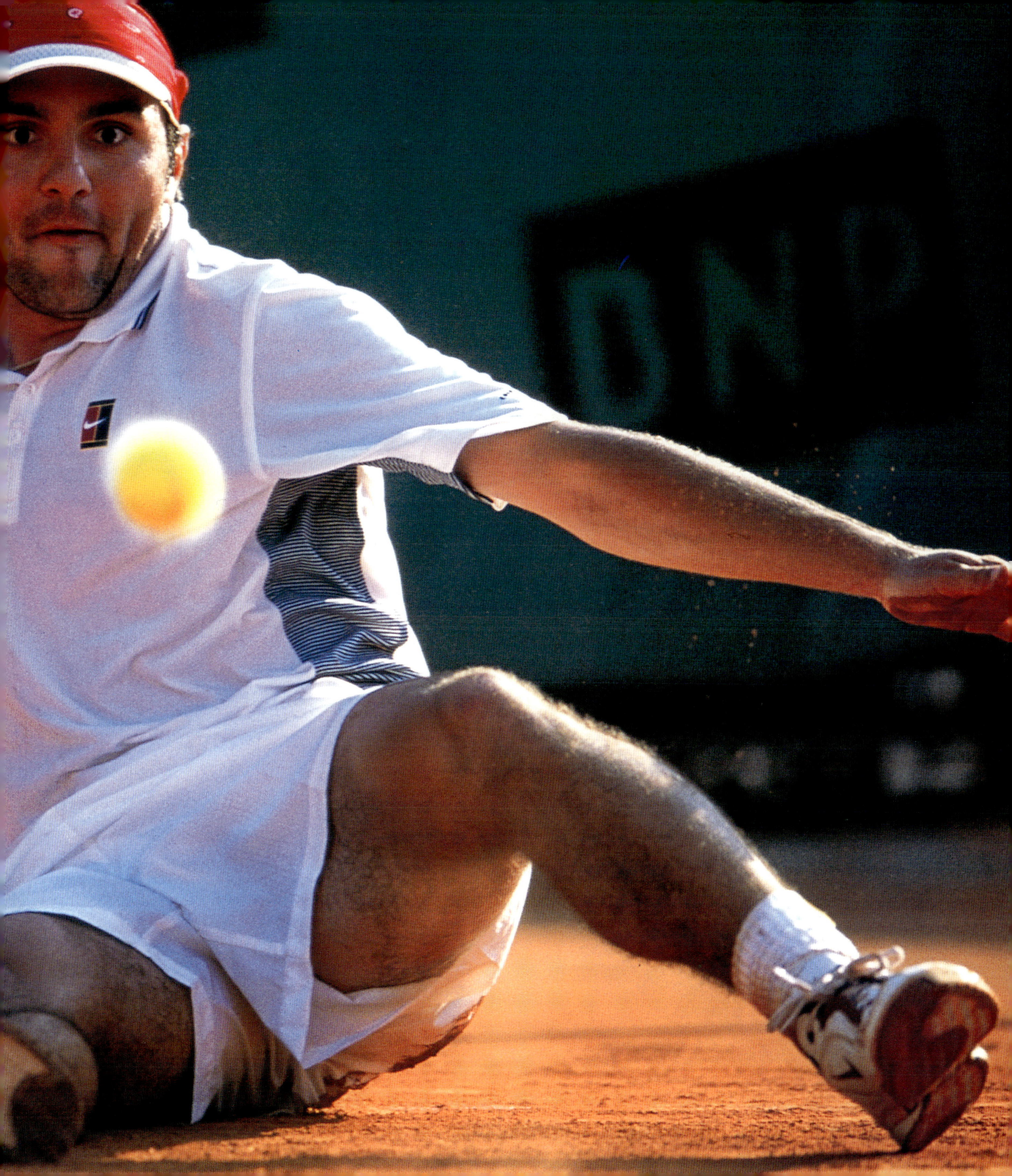

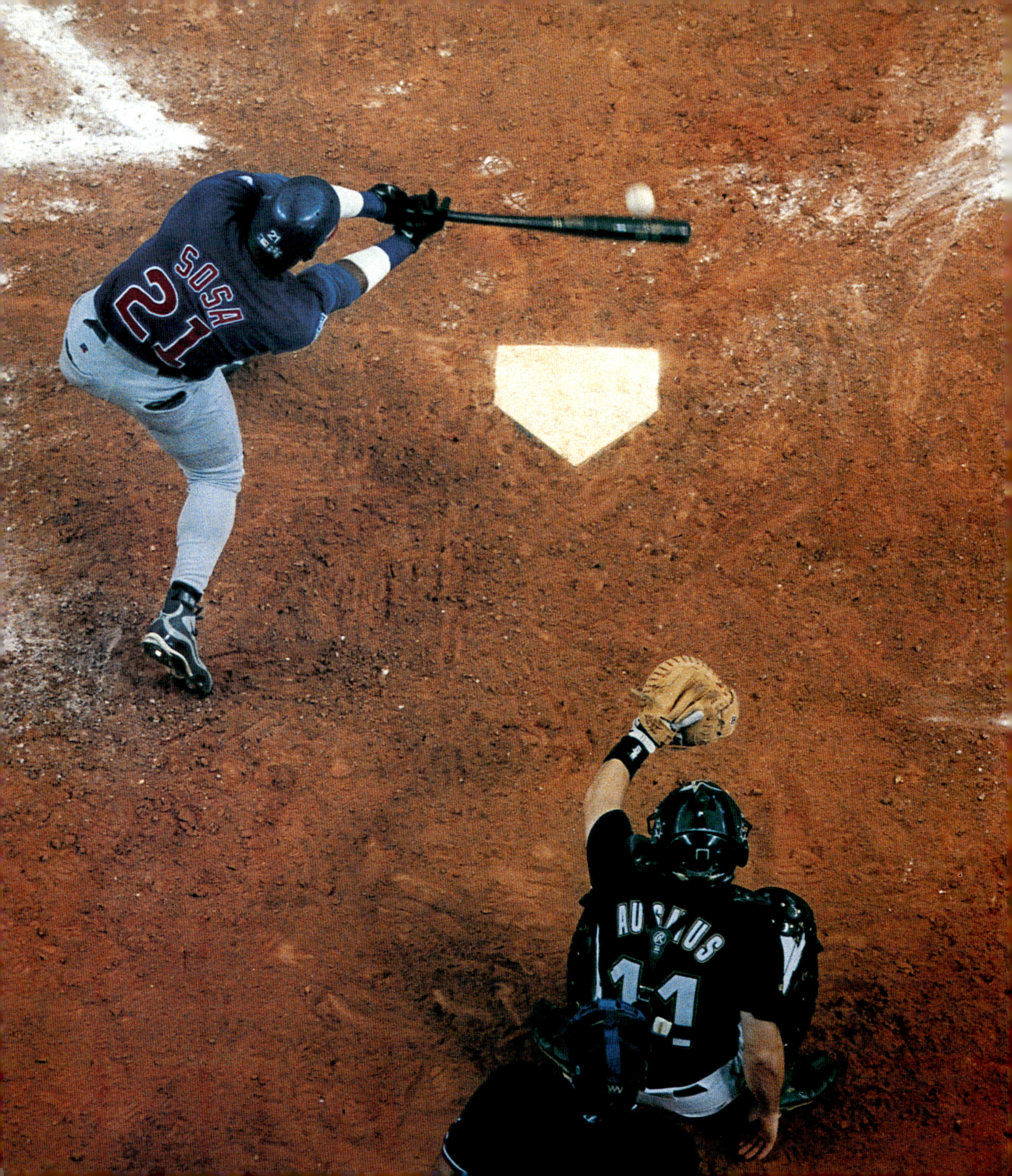
SOSA
21

03
Sammy Sosa of the Chicago Cubs, Houston, 1998
Vincent Laforet

04
Marie-José Pérec, Atlanta, 1996
Mike Hewitt

05 (OVERLEAF)
Seattle Seahawks' Joey Galloway and New York Jets' Aaron Glenn, New York, 1998
Al Bello

04

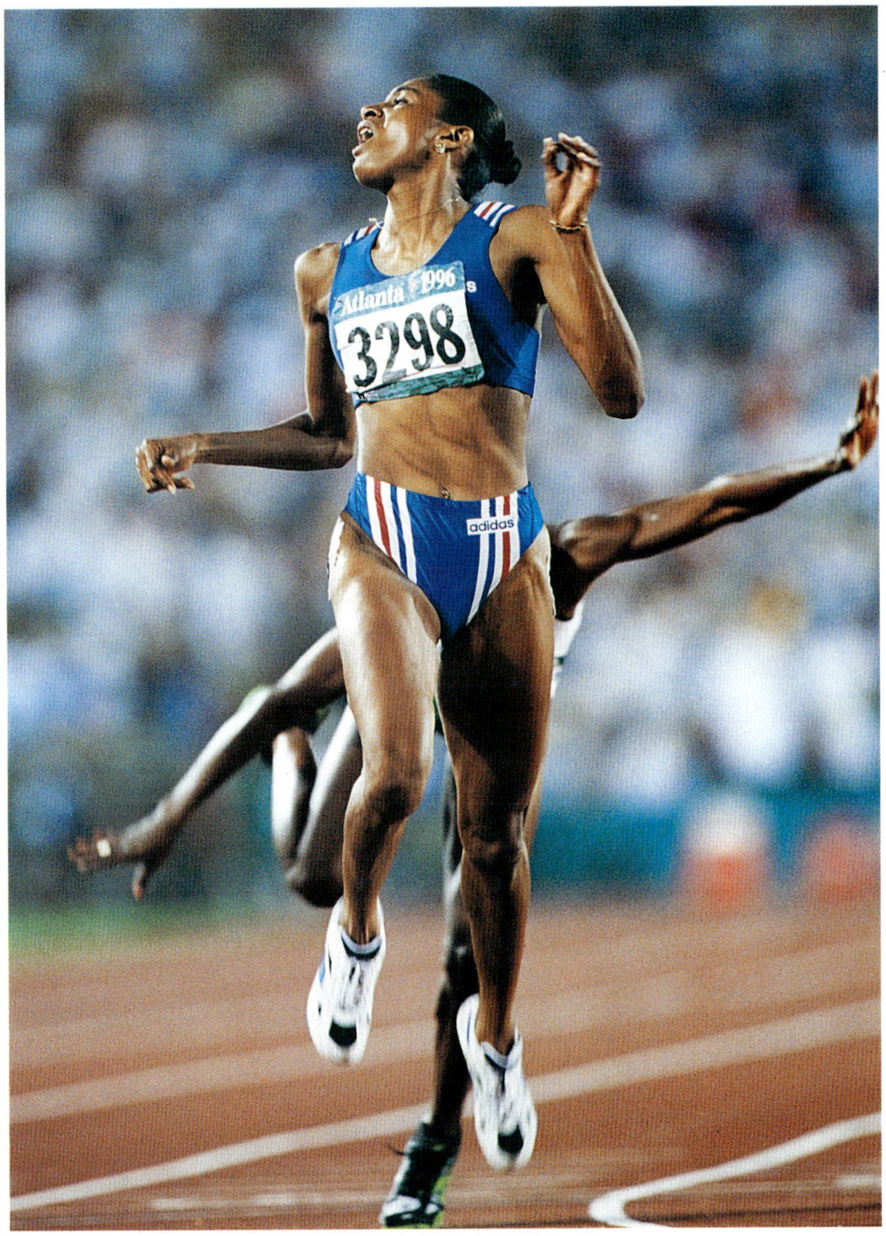

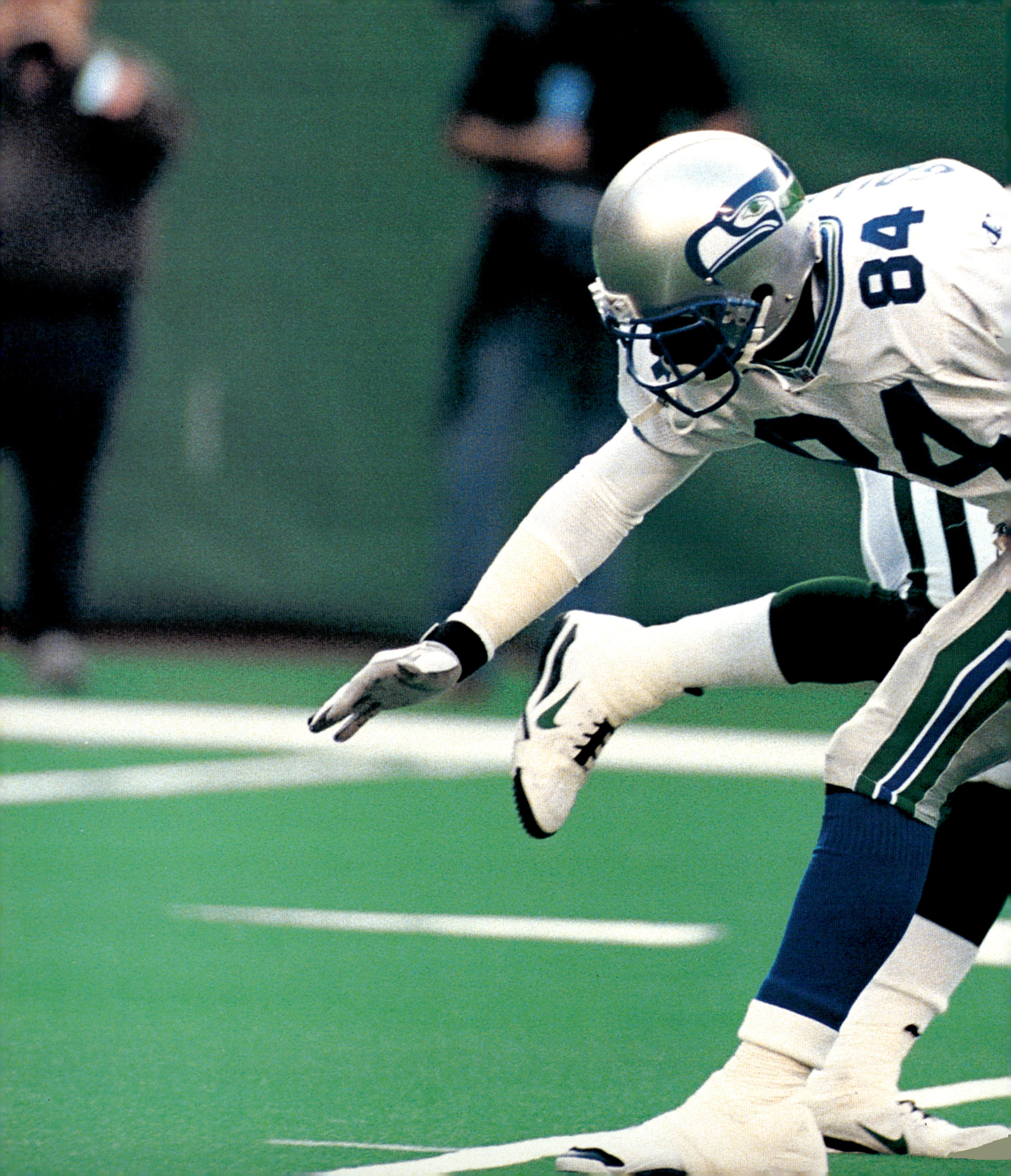
84

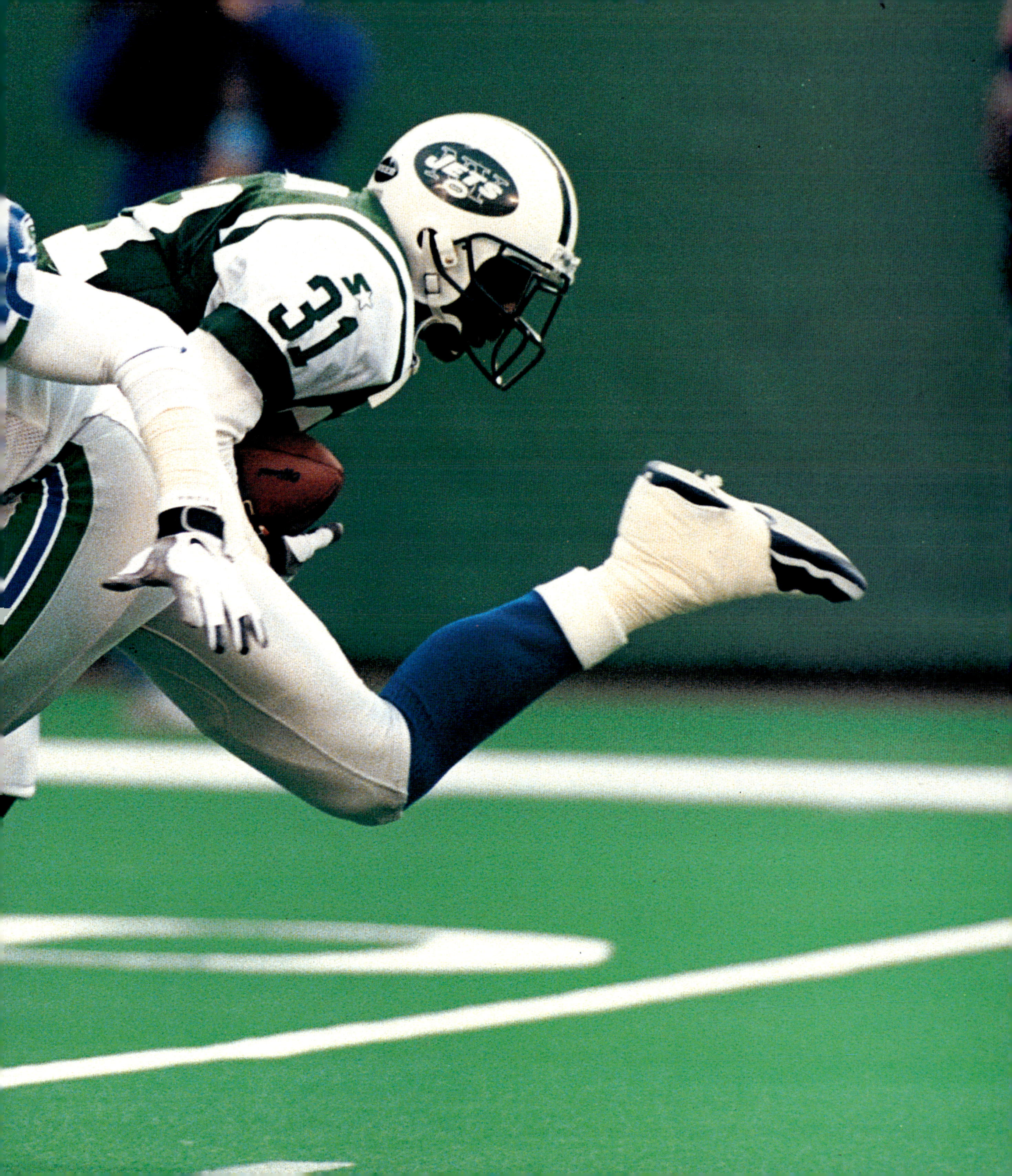
JETS
31

ARENA

The modern stadium is more than just the backdrop for sporting events; it is the stage where audience, media, marketing and corporate sponsorship come together as one. The stadium integrates all these activities to make the spectacle of contemporary sport. Stadiums have become more than buildings, they have their own identities that transcend their locations and become sites in the virtual space of the broadcasters' time schedules. Spectacular architectural designs and the glamour of the associated events have made the stadiums themselves emotional subjects for the photographer, embodying in their structure the glamour of sport, the memory of great moments of the past and the anticipation of future glory.

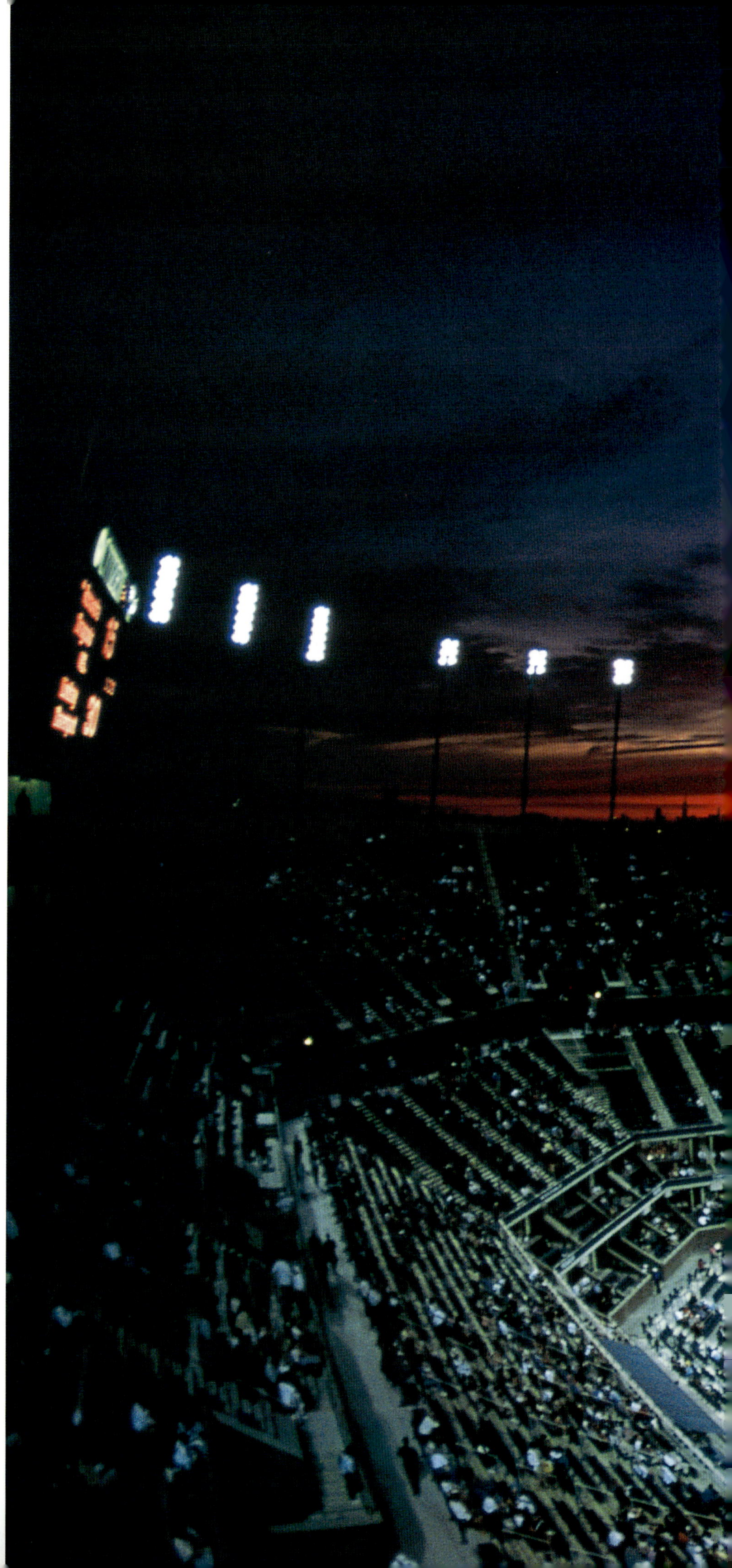

01
US Open at the Arthur Ashe Stadium, Flushing Meadows, New York, 1999
Al Bello

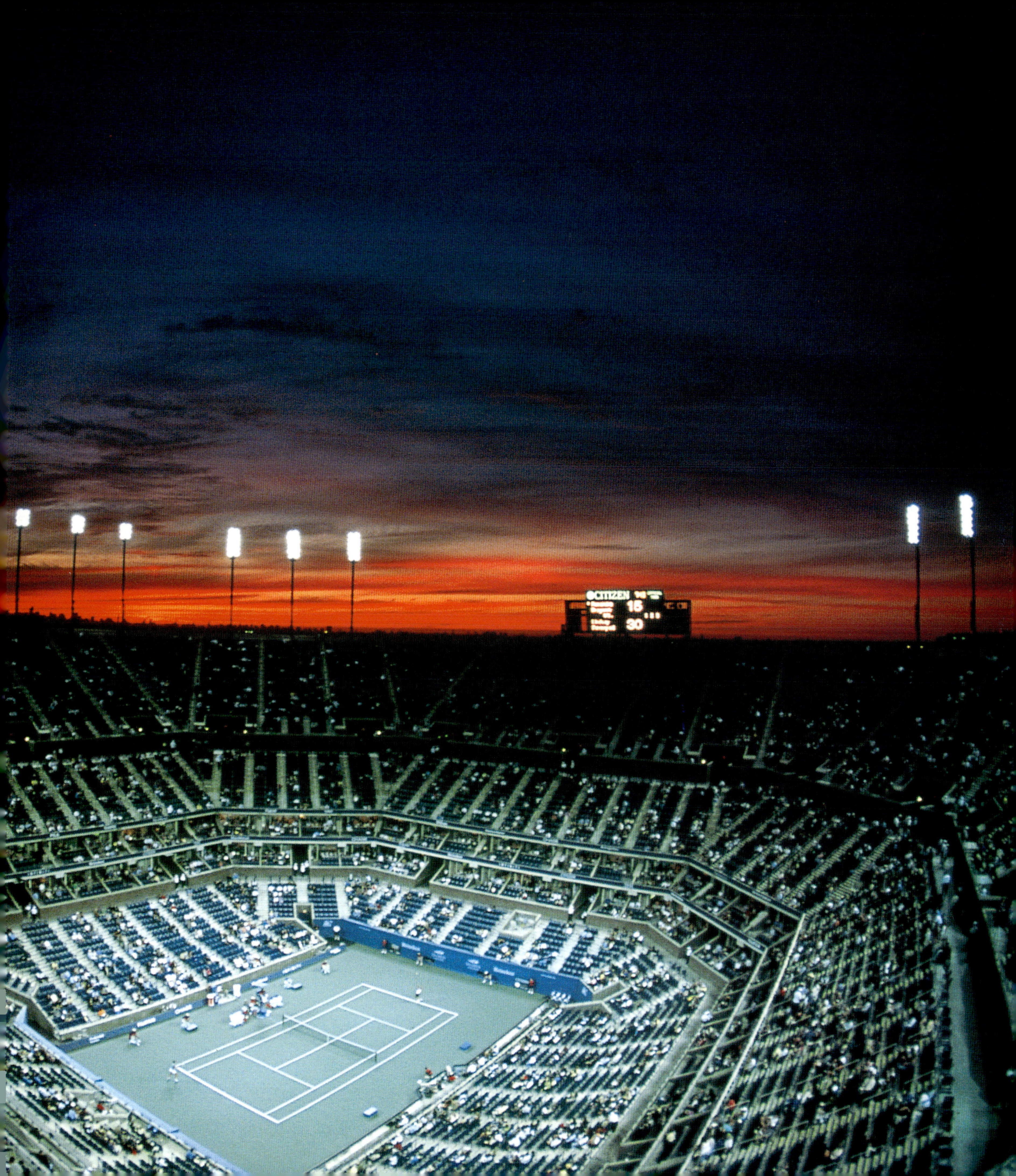
CITIZEN
15
30

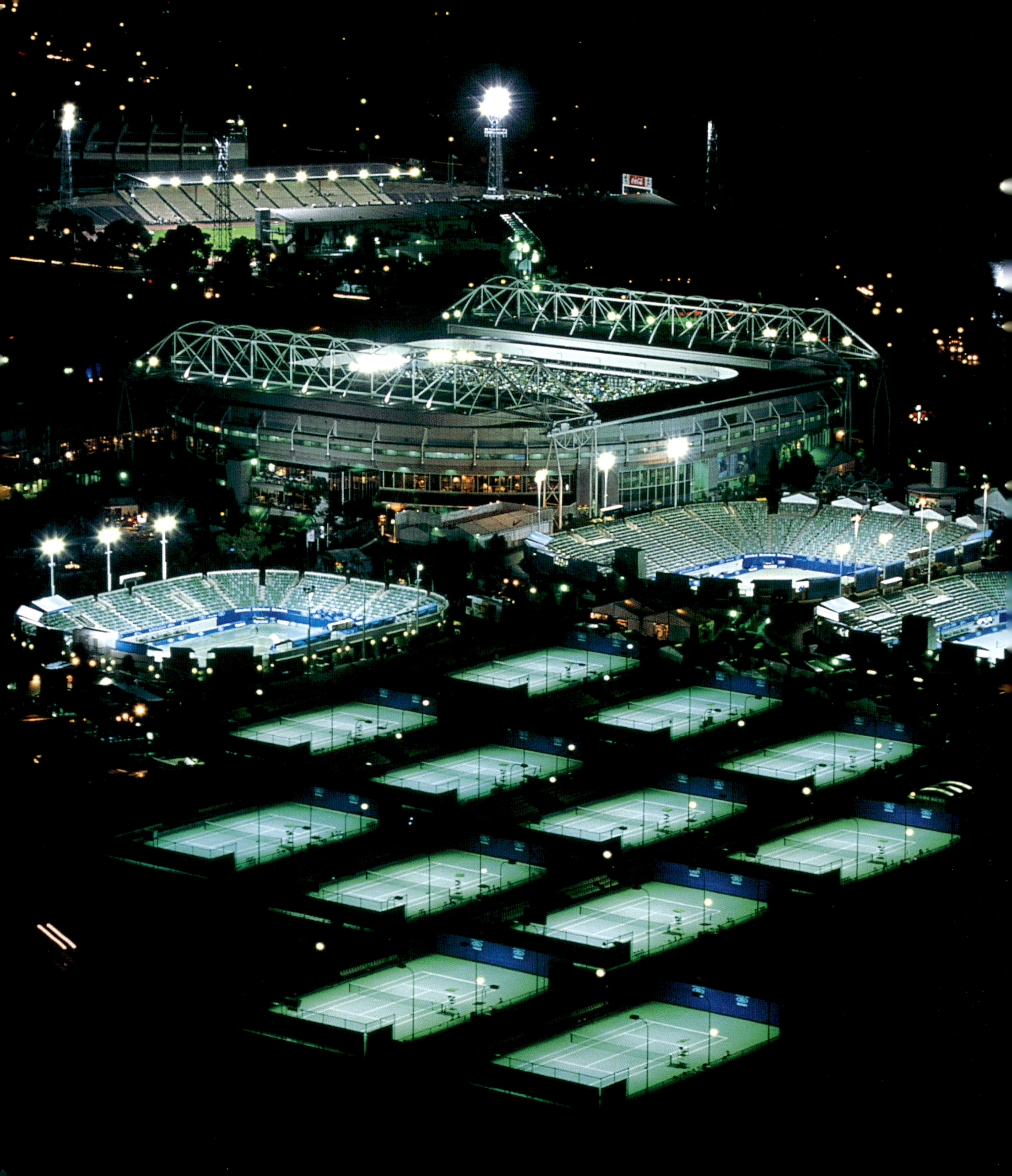

02
Melbourne Park Tennis Centre, Melbourne, 1999
Stuart Milligan

03
Mingxia Fu at the Diving World Cup, Atlanta, 1995
Jamie Squire

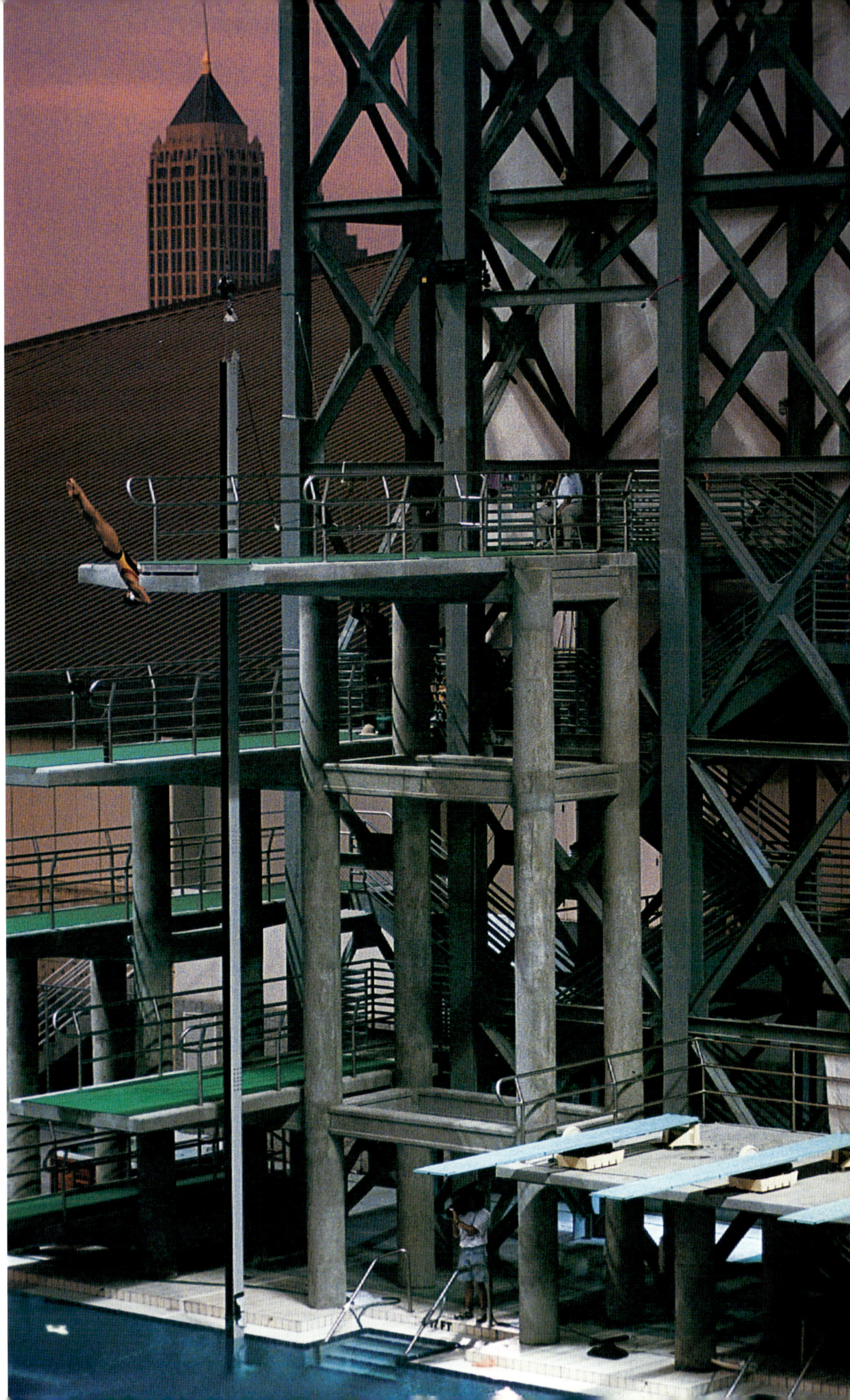

04
FNB Stadium during the African Cup of Nations, Johannesburg, 1996
Gary M Prior

05
Oscar De La Hoya versus Julio Cesar Chavez, Thomas and Mack Center, Las Vegas, 1998
Elsa Hasch

06 (OVERLEAF)
Denver Broncos versus Seattle Seahawks, Mile High Stadium, Denver, 1995
Al Bello

04

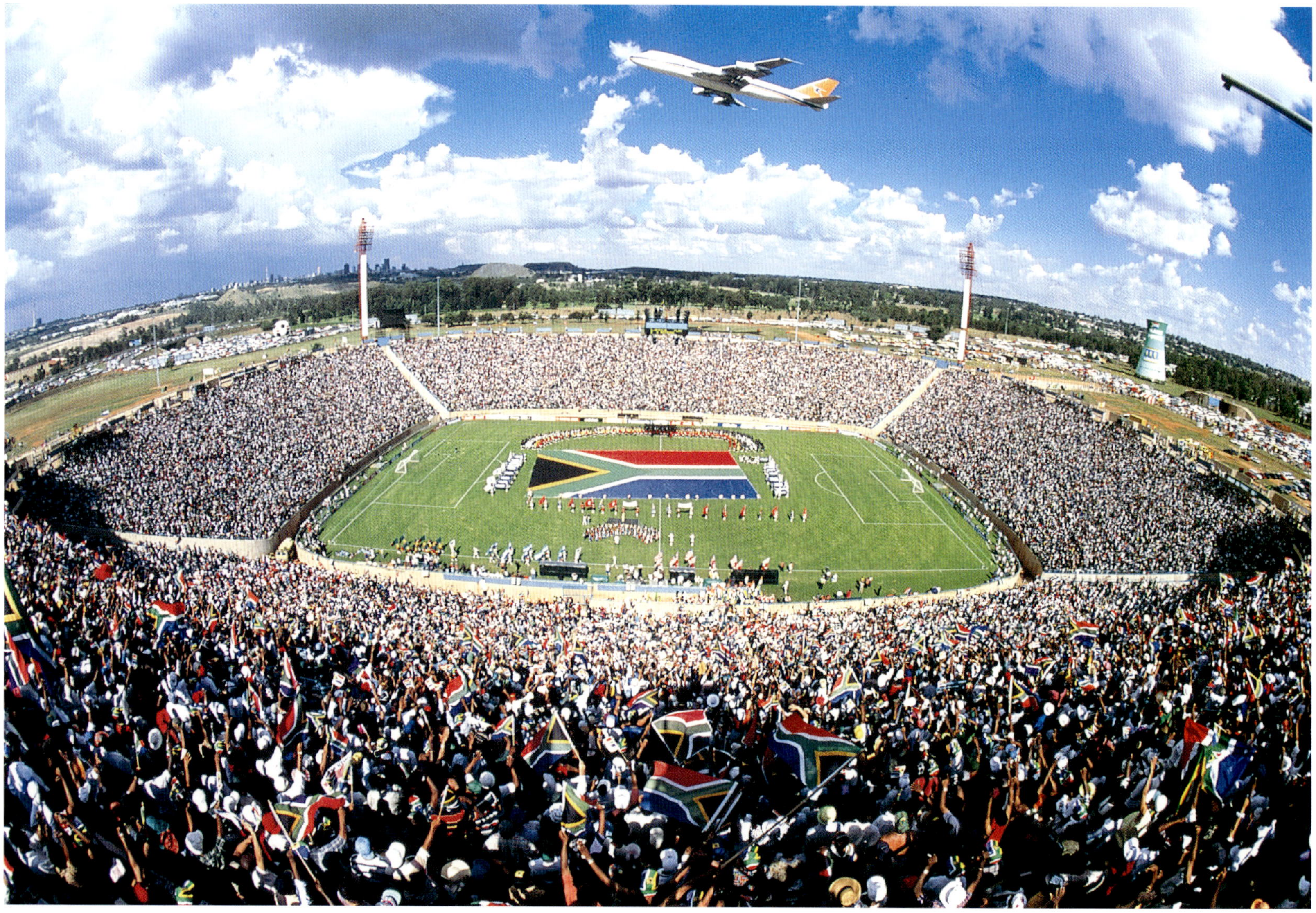

05

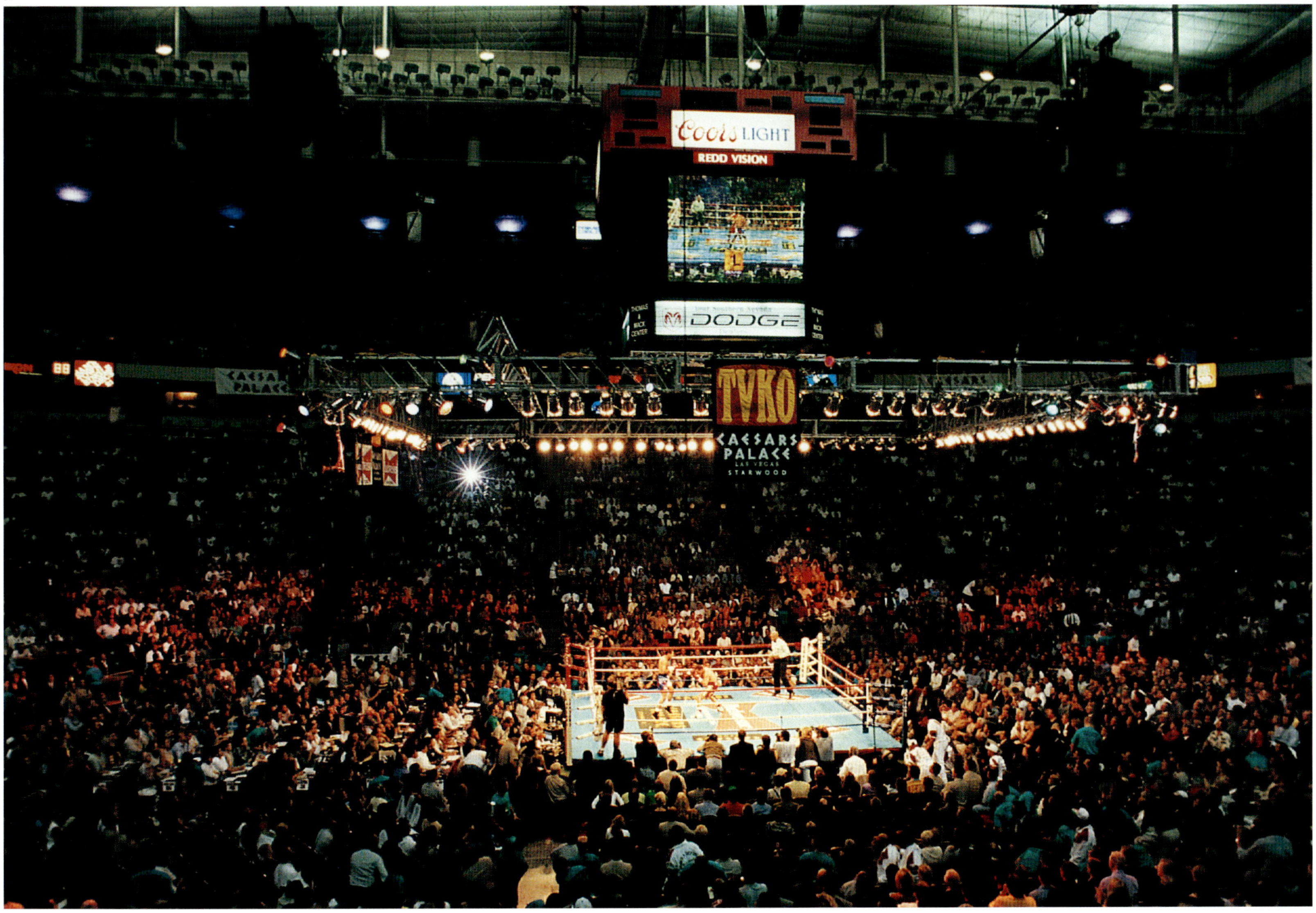
Coors LIGHT
REDD VISION
DODGE
TYKO
CAESARS PALACE
LAS VEGAS
STARWOOD

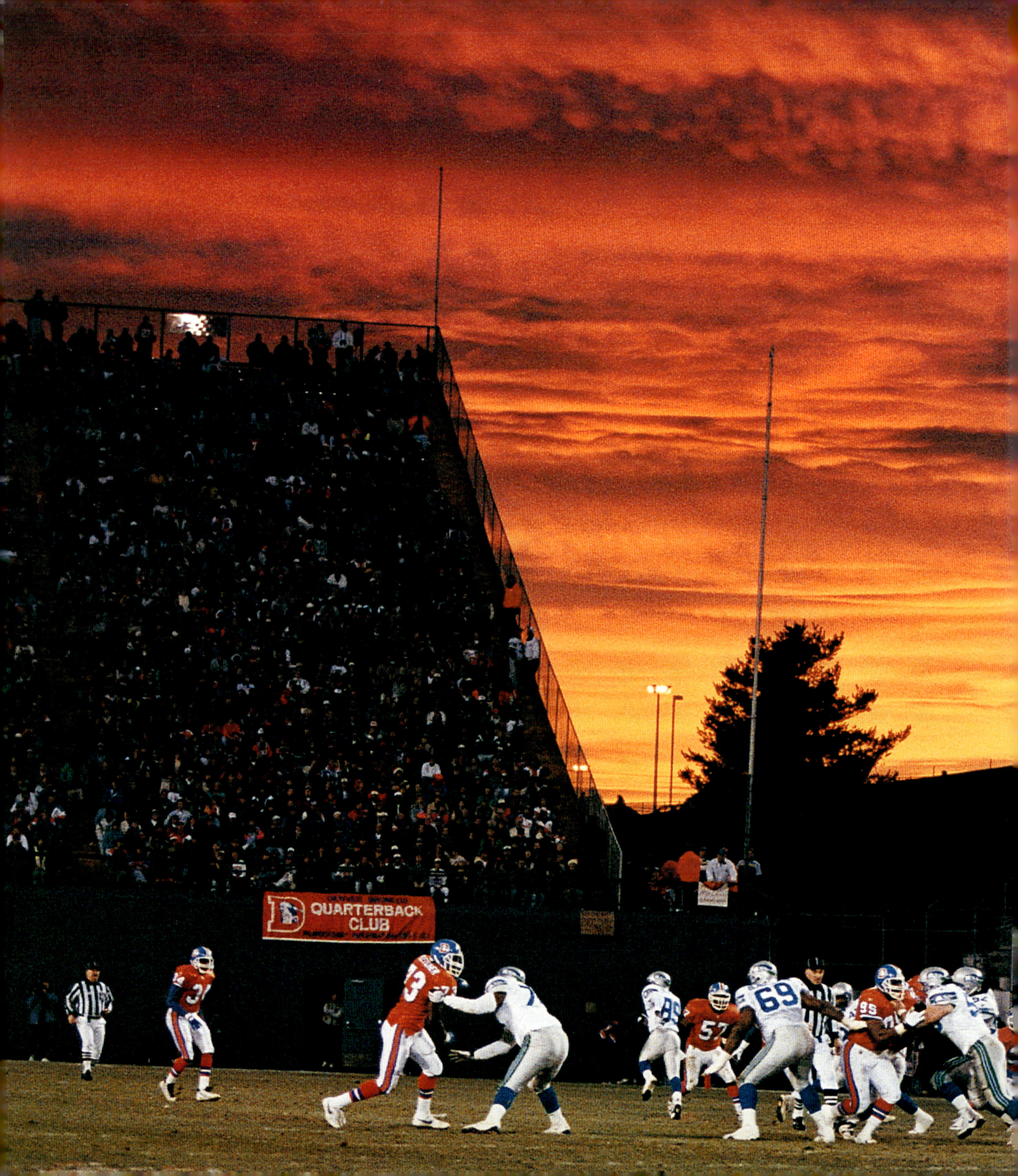
QUARTERBACK
CLUB

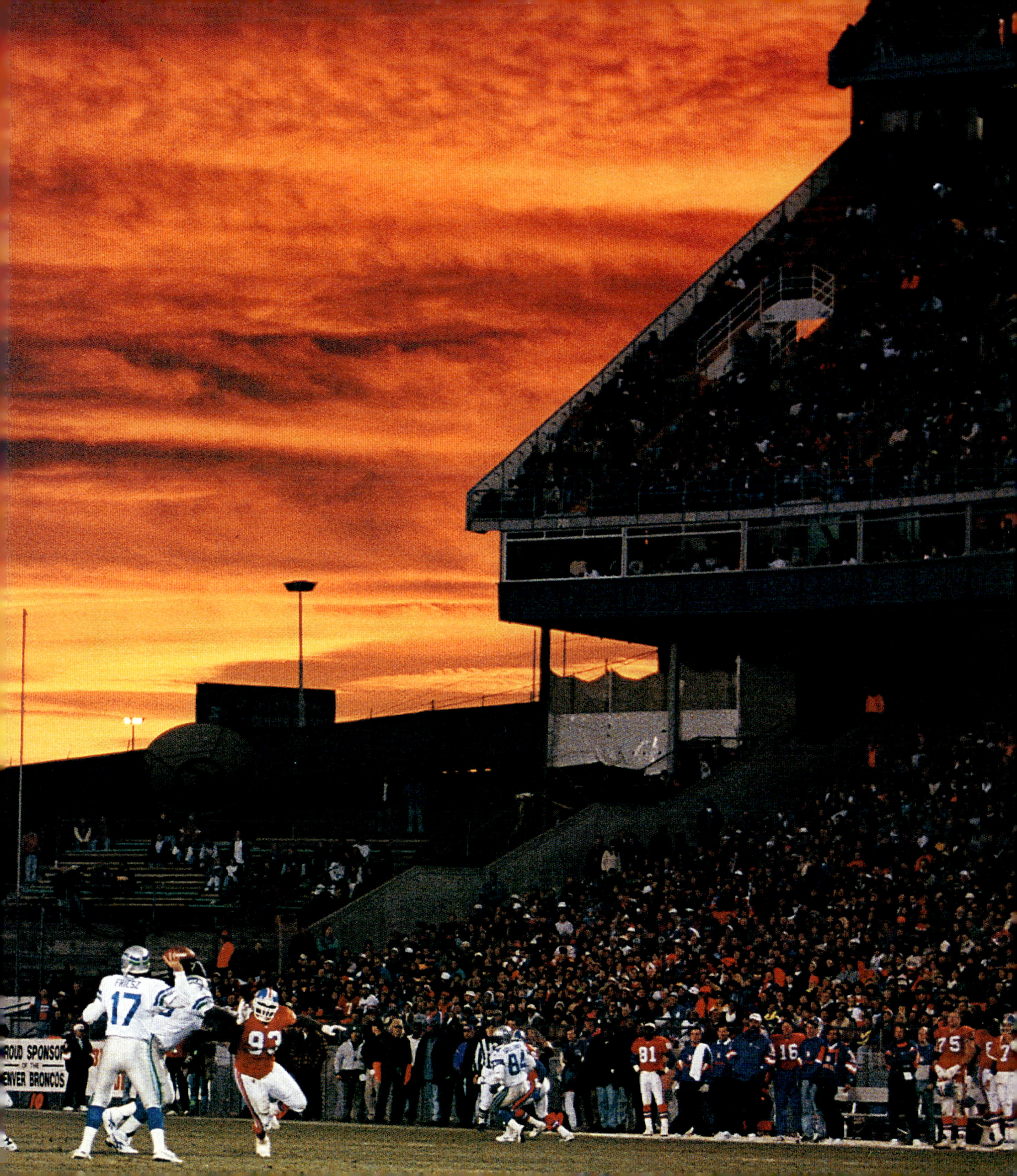
ROUD SPONSOR
OF THE
ENVER BRONCOS

INDEX TO PHOTOGRAPHS

PHOTO FINISH